Successful Project Management

Successful Project Management

SIXTH EDITION

JACK GIDO

Penn State University

JAMES P. CLEMENTS

Clemson University

CENGAGE
Learning®

Andover • Melbourne • Mexico City • Stamford, CT • Toronto • Hong Kong • New Delhi • Seoul • Singapore • Tokyo

Successful Project Management, 6e
Jack Gido and James P. Clements

© 2015 Cengage Learning

ISBN-13: 978-81-315-3169-3
ISBN-10: 81-315-3169-4

Cengage Learning India Private Limited
418, F.I.E., Patparganj
Delhi 110092
India

Tel: 91-11-43641111
Fax: 91-11-43641100
Email: asia.infoindia@cengage.com

Cengage Learning is a leading provider of customized learning solutions with office locations around the globe, including Andover, Melbourne, Mexico City, Stamford (CT), Toronto, Hong Kong, New Delhi, Seoul, Singapore, and Tokyo. Locate your local office at: www.cengage.com/global

Cengage Learning Products are represented in Canada by Nelson Education, Ltd.

For product information, visit our website at **www.cengage.co.in**

Printed in India
Second Indian Reprint 2017

Disclaimer:
This book contains link to resources which are a part of the US edition. The same may not be available with the Indian edition. The buyer needs to purchase a copy of the US edition to have full access to those resources. In no event the publisher shall be liable for any limitation or performance due to unavailability of these resources.

*To my wonderful family: my wife, Rosemary; our sons, Steve and Jeff;
our "daughters," Teresa and Wendy; and our marvelous grandchildren,
Matthew, Alex, Allison, Meghan, and Sophie.*

J.G.

*To my mother and father for all their love and support throughout my life;
and to Beth, the love of my life, and our four incredible children—Tyler, Hannah,
Maggie, and Grace. I love you all very much.*

J.P.C.

Brief Contents

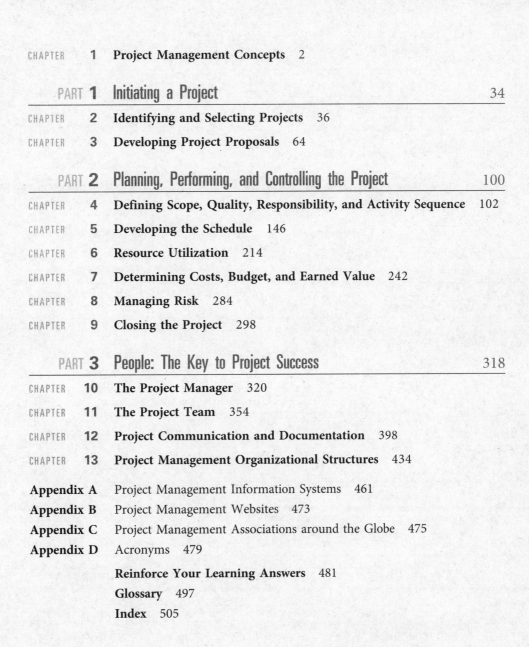

Contents

PART **3** People: The Key to Project Success

Preface

There are those who make things happen,
those who let things happen, and
those who wonder what happened.

We hope that *Successful Project Management* will help you have an enjoyable, exciting, and successful experience as you grow through future project endeavors, and that it will be the catalyst for enabling you to **make things happen**!

Best wishes for enjoyment, satisfaction, and success in all that you do.

Jack Gido
James P. Clements

Our Approach

Project management is more than merely parceling out work assignments to individuals and hoping that they will somehow accomplish a desired result. In fact, projects that could have been successful often fail because of such take-it-for-granted approaches. Individuals need hard information and real skills to work successfully in a project environment and to accomplish project objectives. *Successful Project Management* is written to equip its users with both—by explaining concepts and techniques and by using numerous examples to show how they can be skillfully applied.

Although the focus of the book is squarely on the practical things readers absolutely need to know to thrive in project environments, the book does not forsake objective learning; it simply challenges readers to think critically about project management principles and to apply them within the context of the real world. We capture lessons learned from years of managing projects, teaching project management, and writing extensively about it.

Successful Project Management is intended for students as well as for working professionals and volunteers. The book is designed to present the essential skills readers need to make effective contributions and to have an immediate impact on the accomplishment of projects in which they are involved. It prepares students with marketable and transferable skills and sends them into the workforce ready to apply project management knowledge and skills. The book also supports employer talent development and lifelong learning programs to develop and train employees to work effectively in multifunctional teams and apply project management tools and techniques to successfully accomplish project objectives.

Successful Project Management is written for everyone involved in projects, not just project managers. Projects with good or even great project managers still may not succeed, as the best efforts of all involved are essential. All the people on the

project team must have the knowledge and skills to work effectively together in a project environment. People do not become project managers by reading books; they become project managers by first being effective project team members. This book provides the foundation individuals need to be effective members of project teams and thereby boosts everyone's potential to rise to the challenge of managing teams and projects.

The book is written in an easy-to-understand, straightforward style with a minimum of technical terms. Readers acquire project management terminology gradually as they read the text. The mathematics is purposely kept simple. The text does not use complex mathematical theories or algorithms to describe scheduling techniques, nor does it include highly technical projects as examples. An overtly technical approach can create a barrier to learning for individuals who lack deep understanding of advanced mathematics or technical backgrounds. Separate appendixes are provided for those readers who want more in-depth coverage of probability considerations and time-cost trade-offs. Our book includes a broad range of easily understood examples based on projects encountered in everyday situations. For example, real-world applications include conducting a market survey, building an information system, and organizing a community festival.

Enhancements to the Sixth Edition

Based on the excellent and supportive comments we received from our reviewers, we are pleased to incorporate the following enhancements in the sixth edition of *Successful Project Management*:

- Revised the chapter concepts and contents to support the Project Management Knowledge Areas of the Project Management Institute's *A Guide to the Project Management Body of Knowledge (PMBOK® Guide)* Fifth Edition as shown in the table on the following page.

- Added the following **new sections:**
 - Stakeholder Engagement (in Chapter 1)
 - Agile Project Management (in Chapter 5)
 - Stakeholder Communication (in Chapter 12)

- Replaced all Real World Project Management vignettes (two in each chapter) with more up-to-date vignettes that discuss a variety of applications and industry sectors, both North American and International.

- Enhanced and updated the Microsoft Project Appendixes in Chapters 4 through 7 based on Microsoft® Project 2013, including all new figures of screen captures

- Made minor edits in the chapters to support the Project Management Knowledge Areas of *A Guide to the Project Management Body of Knowledge (PMBOK® Guide)* Fifth Edition and to provide consistency of concepts and terminology among the chapters

- Updated Appendix B, Project Management Websites

	PMBOK® Project Management Knowledge Areas									
Chapter	Integration	Scope	Time	Cost	Quality	Human Resource	Communications	Risk	Procurement	Stakeholder
1. Project Management Concepts	✓									✓
2. Identifying and Selecting Projects	✓								✓	
3. Developing Project Proposals									✓	
4. Defining Scope, Quality, Responsibility, and Activity Sequence	✓	✓	✓		✓					
5. Developing the Schedule	✓		✓							
6. Resource Utilization			✓			✓				
7. Determining Costs, Budget, and Earned Value	✓			✓						
8. Managing Risk								✓		
9. Closing the Project	✓									
10. The Project Manager	✓						✓			✓
11. The Project Team							✓			
12. Project Communication and Documentation	✓						✓	✓		✓
13. Project Management Organizational Structures	✓						✓			

- Updated and reformatted Appendix C, Project Management Associations around the Globe, to list the associations alphabetically by country

- Integrated definitions of additional terms in the glossary into the appropriate chapter text

Distinctive Features

Successful Project Management has many distinctive features to enhance learning and build skills.

Supports *PMBOK® Guide*—Concepts in the chapters support the project management knowledge areas of the Project Management Institute's *A Guide to the Project Management Body of Knowledge (PMBOK® Guide).*

Learning Outcomes—The beginning of each chapter identifies specific outcomes the learner should be able to accomplish after studying the material.

Real-World Vignettes—Each chapter contains two real-world vignettes that illustrate the topics in the chapter. These vignettes not only reinforce chapter concepts but also draw readers into the discussion and pique their interest in applications of project management.

Examples and Applications—Specific relevant real-world examples and applications are incorporated throughout this text to reinforce the concepts presented.

Reinforce Your Learning Questions—Brief questions appear alongside the text to ensure that learners retain key concepts and that the fundamentals are not ignored. These in-the-margin questions "pop up" throughout the text to provide positive reinforcement and to help learners to gauge their comprehension of the material.

Critical Success Factors—Each chapter contains a concise list of the important factors that project managers and team members need to know to help make their projects successful.

Chapter Outlines—Each chapter opens with an outline of the key topics that will be covered. These outlines clarify expectations and allow readers to see the flow of information at a glance.

Graphics and Templates—Numerous exhibits and templates appear in the text to illustrate the application of important concepts and project management tools.

Chapter Summaries—At the end of each chapter is a concise summary of the material presented in the chapter—a final distillation of core concepts.

Review Questions and Problems—Each chapter has a set of questions and problems that test and apply chapter concepts, support the learning outcomes, and reinforce understanding and retention.

Internet Exercises—Each chapter has a set of exercises to invite learners to research and review information about real-world applications of various project management topics and summarize their findings.

Case Studies—End-of-chapter case studies provide critical-thinking scenarios for either individual or group analysis. Variety in case format ensures that all learners can relate to the scenarios presented. The cases are fun and are intended to spark interesting debates. By fostering discussion of various viewpoints, the cases provide opportunities for participants to expand their thinking about how to operate successfully when differing views arise in the work environment. Thus students gain valuable insight into what teamwork is all about.

Microsoft® Project 2013—Examples of how to use and apply Microsoft® Project 2013 are included in appendixes in Chapters 4–7. Detailed instructions and a number of sample screen displays are included.

Project Management Information Systems—A comprehensive appendix discusses the use of project management information systems as a tool to plan, track, and manage projects. Common features of project management information systems are discussed, along with selection criteria.

Project Management Websites—An appendix of project management websites is provided as a good resource for additional information, applications, tools, and research about project management. The book's companion website includes links to each of the project management websites listed.

Project Management Associations—A list of project management associations around the globe is provided in an appendix for individuals who want to contact these organizations about professional development, access to periodicals and other publications, or career opportunities. The book's companion website includes links to each of the project management associations listed.

Organization and Content

Successful Project Management comprises 13 chapters plus appendixes with an opening foundation chapter on project management concepts and the remaining 12 chapters divided into three parts:

- Part 1, Initiating a Project, discusses identifying and selecting projects, and developing project proposals.

- Part 2, Planning, Performing, and Controlling the Project, covers defining scope, quality, responsibility, and activity sequence; developing the schedule; resource utilization; determining costs, budget, and earned value; managing risk; and closing the project.

- Part 3, People: The Key to Project Success, discusses the project manager; the project team; project communication and documentation; and project management organizational structures.

Chapter 1, Project Management Concepts, is a foundation chapter that discusses the definition of a project and its attributes; managing a project within the constraints of scope, quality, schedule, budget, resources, risks, and customer satisfaction; the project life cycle of initiating, planning, performing, and closing a project, as well as monitoring and controlling the project and managing changes; the definition of project management and the steps of the project management process; stakeholder engagement; implications of global project management; project management associations; and the benefits of project management. The concepts in this chapter support two *PMBOK® Guide* project management knowledge areas: project integration and stakeholder management.

Part 1, Initiating a Project, discusses identifying and selecting projects, and developing project proposals. It includes two chapters:

- Chapter 2, Identifying and Selecting Projects, covers how projects are identified, selected, authorized, and outsourced. The project charter is also discussed. The concepts in this chapter support two *PMBOK® Guide* project management knowledge areas: project integration and procurement management.

- Chapter 3, Developing Project Proposals, deals with building effective relationships with customers and partners; proposal marketing strategies; decision making to go forward with a proposal; creating winning proposals; proposal preparation and contents, including simplified project proposals;

pricing considerations; customer evaluation of proposals; types of contracts; and measuring success of proposal efforts. The concepts in this chapter support the *PMBOK® Guide* project management knowledge area of project procurement management.

Part 2, Planning, Performing, and Controlling the Project, covers project management techniques and tools. It includes six chapters:

- Chapter 4, Defining Scope, Quality, Responsibility, and Activity Sequence, discusses clearly defining the project objective; preparing a project scope document; the importance of planning for quality; creating a work breakdown structure; assigning responsibilities for work elements; and defining specific activities and creating a network diagram. The concepts in this chapter support four *PMBOK® Guide* project management knowledge areas: project integration, scope, quality, and time management.

- Chapter 5, Developing the Schedule, deals with estimating the resources and durations for activities; developing a schedule that indicates the earliest and latest start and finish times for each activity; and determining slack and identifying the critical path of activities. It also explains the project control process, including monitoring and controlling progress; the effects of actual performance; updating the schedule; approaches to controlling the schedule; and agile project management. This chapter also includes an appendix on using probabilistic activity durations. The concepts in this chapter support two *PMBOK® Guide* project management knowledge areas: project integration and time management.

- Chapter 6, Resource Utilization, addresses taking resource constraints into account when developing a network plan and project schedule; preparing a resource requirements plan; leveling the use of resources within the required time frame for a project; and determining the shortest project schedule when the number of available resources is limited. The concepts in this chapter support two *PMBOK® Guide* project management knowledge areas: project time and human resource management.

- Chapter 7, Determining Costs, Budget, and Earned Value, covers estimating the costs of activities; creating a time-phased budget; cumulating actual costs; determining the earned value of work actually performed; analyzing cost performance; estimating project cost at completion; approaches to controlling costs; and managing cash flow. This chapter also includes an appendix on time–cost trade-off. The concepts in this chapter support two *PMBOK® Guide* project management knowledge areas: project integration and cost management.

- Chapter 8, Managing Risk, includes identifying and categorizing risks and their potential impact; assessing the likelihood of occurrence and degree of impact; prioritizing risks; preparing risk response plans; creating a risk assessment matrix; and controlling and monitoring risks. The concepts in this chapter support the *PMBOK® Guide* project management knowledge area of project risk management.

- Chapters 4–8 include several continuing multi-chapter integrated examples and case studies that apply the concepts and tools discussed in the chapters.

The examples and case studies are introduced in Chapter 4 and continue and build through Chapters 5, 6, 7, and 8. Chapters 4 through 7 also include appendixes on Microsoft Project that illustrate how to use and apply Microsoft Project to one of the multi-chapter integrated examples.

- The last chapter in Part 2 is Chapter 9, Closing the Project. It discusses what actions should be taken when closing a project; conducting a postproject evaluation; the importance of documenting and communicating lessons learned; organizing and archiving project documents; obtaining feedback from customers; and early termination of projects. The concepts in this chapter support the *PMBOK® Guide* project management knowledge area of project integration management.

Part 3, People: The Key to Project Success, focuses on the importance of the people involved in a project. It includes four chapters:

- Chapter 10, The Project Manager, discusses the responsibilities of the project manager; the skills needed to manage projects successfully; ways to develop project manager competence; approaches to effective delegation; and how the project manager can manage and control changes to the project. The concepts in this chapter support three *PMBOK® Guide* project management knowledge areas: project integration, human resource, and stakeholder management.

- Chapter 11, The Project Team, covers the development and growth of teams; the project kickoff meeting; effective teams including characteristics of effective project teams, barriers to team effectiveness, effective team members, team building, and valuing team diversity; ethical behavior; sources of conflict during the project and approaches to handling conflict; problem solving, including brainstorming; and effective time management. The concepts in this chapter support the *PMBOK® Guide* project management knowledge area of project human resource management.

- Chapter 12, Project Communication and Documentation, addresses the importance of effective verbal and written communication, including suggestions for enhancing personal communication; effective listening; types of project meetings and suggestions for productive meetings; project presentations and suggestions for effective presentations; project reports and suggestions for preparing useful reports; controlling changes to project documents; creating a project communication plan; and collaborative communication tools. The concepts in this chapter support four *PMBOK® Guide* project management knowledge areas: project communications, integration, human resource, and stakeholder management.

- Chapter 13, Project Management Organizational Structures, explains the characteristics, advantages, and disadvantages of the functional, autonomous project and matrix organizational structures and discusses the role of the project management office. The concepts in this chapter support two *PMBOK® Guide* project management knowledge areas: project integration and human resource management.

Appendix A, Project Management Information Systems, discusses the common features of project management information systems; criteria for selecting

a project management information system; and advantages of and concerns about using such systems. Appendix B provides a list of websites that are good resources for additional information, applications, tools, and research about project management. Appendix C is a list of project management associations around the globe. Appendix D is a list of common project management acronyms. The book also includes answers to the Reinforce Your Learning questions for each chapter, and a Glossary of project management terms used in the book.

Support Materials

This edition of *Successful Project Management* provides a support package that will encourage student success.

Microsoft® Project 2013. A trial version of the software is packaged with every textbook.

Student Companion Site. The Student Companion Site includes Internet exercises from the text, website links, Microsoft® Project tutorial videos, and a glossary. The companion site can be found at http://www.cengagebrain.com. On the home page, students can use the search box to insert the ISBN of the title 9781285068374. This will take them to the product page, where free companion resources can be found.

Acknowledgments

We are very grateful to the individuals who helped with the publication of this book. We would especially like to thank Dr. Rose Baker, PMP, of Penn State University, who made significant contributions. Most of all, we appreciate her meticulous reviews and edits, responsiveness, and enthusiasm. She developed the real-world vignettes for each chapter; updated and enhanced the Microsoft® Project appendixes, including all new screen shots; created tutorial videos for using Microsoft® Project 2013; updated references for each chapter; and updated and enhanced instructor resources, including outlines, Power-Point® slides, and the Test Bank. We also offer special appreciation to Wes Donahue and Beth McLaughlin of Penn State University for providing support materials and suggestions. Jason Oakman did a meticulous job in preparing the original graphics. We want to thank all the members of the project team at Cengage Learning/South-Western who helped turn our vision into reality and contributed to the successful completion of this project. Special recognition goes to Clara Goosman, Product Manager, Mike Guendelsberger, Senior Content Developer, and Jerusha Govindakrishnan, Senior Project Manager at PreMediaGlobal.

We would like to acknowledge the contributions of the Project Management Institute to advancing the project management profession and, in particular, the multitude of volunteers and staff for their diligent work on the current and previous editions of *A Guide to the Project Management Body of Knowledge (PMBOK® Guide).*

We would like to recognize the important contributions of the following reviewers for providing constructive and supportive comments for enhancing this sixth edition:

Dennis Agboh
Morgan State University

Dr. Stephen O. Agyei-Mensah
Clarion University of North Pennsylvania

Basil Al-Hashimi
Mesa Community College

Michael Anderson
Simpson College

Ervin H. Baumeyer, PE
Lone Star College–North Harris

Catherine Beise
Salisbury University

Blaine Boxwell
University of Bridgeport

James Browning
Brunswick Community College

Okiechi Geoffrey Egekwu
James Madison University

Adrienne Gould-Choquette
State College of Florida

Richard Gram
Worcester Polytechnic Institute

Joseph Griffin
Northeastern University

Ken Gyure
University of Arizona

Michael Hashek
Gateway Technical College

Vish Hedge
California State University–East Bay

Andrew Henderson
Barstow Community College

O'Brien Hughes
Lone Star College

Francis Kubicek
Kalamazoo Valley Community College

Ram Kumar
University of North Carolina–Charlotte

Changyue Luo
Governor's State University

Kathryn J. Moland, Ph.D., PMP
Livingstone College

Janet C. Moore
Penn State University

Rakesh Narayan
Mid-State Technical College

Robert Niewoehner
US Naval Academy

William Ramshaw, PMP
Whitworth University

Steven Segerstrom
College of Lake County

We are also grateful to the following reviewers of the first five editions for their valuable comments that continually enriched and advanced the text:

Kwasi Amoako-Gyampah
University of North Carolina at Greensboro

Ed Arnheiter
Rensselaer Polytechnic Institute–Hartford

Fred K. Augustine, Jr.
Stetson University

Mehmet Barut
Wichita State University

Comfort Cover
Adams State College

Craig Cowles
Bridgewater State College

Sam DeWald
Penn State University

Charlene A. Dykman, Ph.D.
University of St. Thomas–Houston

Bari Dzomba
Penn State University

Charles Bilbrey
James Madison University

Vicki Blanchard
Gibbs College of Boston

Daniel Brandon
Christian Brothers University

Dr. Dorothy Brandt
Brazosport College

Daketima Briggs
Saint Mary's University of Minnesota

Tyson Browning
Texas Christian University

Victoria Buenger
Texas A&M University

Thomas Bute
Humboldt State University

Tim Butler
Wayne State University

John H. Cable
University of Maryland

David T. Cadden
Quinnipiac University

Michael Cathey
George Washington University

Paul Chase
Becker College

David E. Clapp
Florida Institute of Technology

Robert Cohn
Long Island University–C.W. Post

Barbara Kelley
St Joseph's University

Laurie J. Kirsch
University of Pittsburgh

Brian M. Kleiner
Virginia Tech

Shawn Krest
Genesee Community College

Richard E. Kust
California State University, Fullerton

Chung-Shing Lee
Pacific Lutheran University

Geoffrey Egekwu
James Madison University

Ike Ehie
Southeast Missouri State University

Mike Ensby
Clarkson University

Lynn Fish
Canisius College

James Ford
Ford Consulting Associates

Philip Gisi
DePaul University

Valarie Griep
Metropolitan State University–Minneapolis

Ronald Grossman
Central Connecticut State University

Darryl S. Habeck
Milwaukee Area Technical College

Mamoon M. Hammad
The George Washington University

William Hayden
State University of New York-Buffalo

Joan E. Hoopes, Ph.D
Marist College

Kimberly Hurns
Washtenaw Community College

Margaret Huron
Lone Star College–North Harris

Bhushan L. Kapoor
California State University, Fullerton

Carl Nelson
Polytechnic University

Hameed G. Nezhad, Ph.D.
Metropolitan State University

Tony B. Noble
Mohave Community College

Michael Okrent
University of Bridgeport

John Olson
DePaul University

Shrikant S. Panwalkar
Purdue University

Lois M. Lemke
Northeast Wisconsin Technical College

Ardeshir Lohrasbi
University of Illinois–Springfield

Larry Maes
Davenport University–Warren

Mary Jo Maffei
MQ Associates

Nicoleta Maghear
Hampton University

Reza Maleki
North Dakota State University

David M. Marion
Ferris State University

James Marlatt, PMP
University of Colorado

Kirsten Mast
Albertson College of Idaho

William Milz
Northeast Wisconsin Technical College

David Moore
Colorado School of Mines

Herbert Moskowitz
Purdue University–West Lafayette

William A. Moylan
Eastern Michigan University

Jim Murrow
Drury University

Dr. Philip F. Musa
The University of Alabama at Birmingham

P.K. Shukla
Chapman University

Al Skudzinskas
Towson University

Anne Marie Smith
La Salle University

Taverekere Srikantaiah
Dominican University

Jimmy C. Stallings
Webster University

Fariborz Y. Partovi
Drexel University

Reed E. Pendleton
DeVry University–Fremont

Joseph A. Phillips
DeVry University

George Radu
Chancellor University

Tim Ralston
Bellevue Community College

H. Dan Reid
University of New Hampshire

Pedro M. Reyes
Baylor University

Sandra Robertson
Thomas Nelson Community College

Eltgad Roces
Penn State University

Carl R. Schultz
University of New Mexico

Sophia Scott
Southeast Missouri State University

Wade H. Shaw
Florida Institute of Technology

Kevin P. Shea
Baker University

Dr. Yosef S. Sherif
California State University, Fullerton

William R. Sherrard
San Diego State University

Anthony P. Trippe
Rochester Institute of Technology

Sudhi Upadhyaya
Bemidji State University

Henri Van Bemmelen
University of Bridgeport

Linda Volonino
Canisius College

Agnieszka K. Waronska
Colorado State University–Pueblo

Christy Strbiak
New Mexico State University

Cindy Wessel
Washington University

Fredrick A. Tribble
California State University, Long Beach

We would like to acknowledge all the individuals with whom we worked on projects and all the people who participated in our many project management courses and workshops. They provided a learning environment for testing the practical lessons included in this book.

About the Authors

Jack Gido was most recently Director of Economic & Workforce Development and Director of PennTAP, the Pennsylvania Technical Assistance Program at Penn State University. In this position, he directed the program, obtained funding, and provided leadership for a statewide staff who provide technology assistance and workforce development to Pennsylvania business and industry to improve their global competitiveness. Jack has 20 years of industrial management experience, including the management of productivity improvement and technology development projects. He has an M.B.A. from the University of Pittsburgh and a B.S. in Electrical Engineering from Penn State University. Jack is a member of the Project Management Institute and former President of the Upstate New York Chapter, and teaches courses on project management.

James P. Clements currently serves as the 15th President of Clemson University. Prior to becoming President at Clemson University, Jim served as President of West Virginia University. Previously he was Provost and Vice President for Academic Affairs, Vice President for Economic and Community Outreach, Chair of the Computer and Information Sciences Department, and the Robert W. Deutsch Distinguished Professor of Information Technology at Towson University. He holds a Ph.D. in Operations Analysis from the University of Maryland, Baltimore County, an M.S. in Computer Science from the Johns Hopkins University, and a B.S. and M.S. in Computer Science from the University of Maryland, Baltimore County. He is the author of more than 50 research publications. During the past 25 years, Dr. Clements has served as a consultant for a number of public and private organizations. He is also a four-time winner of the Faculty Member of the Year Award given by students at Towson University.

Successful Project Management

CHAPTER 1

Project Management Concepts

Rob Crandall/Alamy

Concepts in this chapter support the following Project Management Knowledge Areas of *A Guide to the Project Management Body of Knowledge (PMBOK® Guide)*:

Project Integration Management
Project Stakeholder Management

REAL WORLD PROJECT MANAGEMENT

World Bank Success Factors

International development projects are undertaken by the World Bank through partner organizations to prepare, implement, and evaluate complex projects. Strict guidelines are overseen by the World Bank project supervisor and the national Project Management unit national project coordinator. Day-to-day project management of the international development projects is the responsibility of the partner organization. An independent evaluation group completes an assessment two years after a project is completed or aborted to determine the relevance, efficiency, and effectiveness of the terminated project.

How well the project outcomes meet the priorities of the target group indicates the relevance of the project. Efficiency success of a project is measured by assessing the use of the least costly resources to achieve the desired results indicated in the project plan. The project's effectiveness is the extent the project objectives, those proposed and those created through change management of the project during its implementation, are met. Sustainability of the project and its impact for making change for the target group are examined during the evaluation. These measures are in addition to the traditional project success criteria measures of objectives, time, and budget.

Sadly, a number of projects undertaken by the World Bank have not been successful and have failed due to managerial and organizational issues. Problems associated with project design, stakeholder management, implementation delays, cost overruns, lack of coordination, and misunderstanding of the political, cultural, technical, and environmental conditions of the project location have doomed nearly half of the international development projects sponsored through the World Bank.

Research of World Bank projects' factors has revealed five critical success factors that increase the probability of meeting the project's objectives: monitoring, coordination, design, training, and institutional environment. Well-documented project progress and increased communication supported the five critical success factors and improved the level of involvement of the World Bank project supervisors and coordinators. The partner organizations are now required to develop increasingly rigorous project plans to emphasize results-based management.

The complexity of the environment that has impacted the level of success must be addressed during the project design phase to identify the needs, problems, stakeholders, constraints, and risks to assure the project is feasible. Stringent reporting and controlling the project's performance have been found to increase the probability of success of the project to meet the needs of the target group.

These success factors for complex World Bank international development projects are concepts discussed in detail in this book. Success or failure of projects is founded in the critical component–project management. Planning, scheduling, team

building, communicating, and leading are all part of the organization necessary in the life of a project.

Mastery of these concepts will improve your probability of successfully managing projects to complete the objectives on time and on budget.

Based on information from Lavagnon, A. I., D. Amadou, and D. Thuillier (2012). "Critical Success Factors for World Bank Projects: An Empirical Investigation," *International Journal of Project Management, 30*, 105–116.

This chapter presents an overview of project management concepts. You will become familiar with the

- Definition of a project and its attributes
- Key constraints within which a project must be managed
- Life cycle of a project
- Definition of project management
- Elements of the project management process
- Identification and engagement of stakeholders
- Implications of global project management
- Project Management Institute
- Benefits of project management

LEARNING OUTCOMES

After studying this chapter, the learner should be able to:

- Define what a project is
- List and discuss the attributes of a project
- Explain what is meant by project objective
- Define what is meant by project deliverable
- Provide examples of projects
- Discuss project constraints

- Describe the phases of the project life cycle
- Define and apply project management
- Discuss the steps of the planning process
- Identify the three elements of the executing process
- Create a stakeholder register

- Discuss stakeholder engagement
- Discuss some implications of global project management
- Discuss the Project Management Institute
- List benefits of project management techniques

Project Attributes

A **project** is an endeavor to accomplish a specific objective through a unique set of interrelated activities and the effective utilization of resources. The following attributes help define a project:

- A project has a clear **objective** that establishes what is to be accomplished. It is the tangible end product that the project team must produce and deliver. The project objective is usually defined in terms of *end product* or *deliverable*, *schedule*, and *budget*. It requires completing the project work scope and

producing all the deliverables within a certain time and budget. For example, the objective of a project might be to introduce a new portable food preparation appliance in 10 months and within a budget of $2 million.

The project objective may also include a statement of the expected *benefits* or *outcomes* that will be achieved from implementing the project. It is why the project is being done. For example, a project with the objective to develop a new product may have an expected outcome to sell a certain number of units of that new product within a year, or to increase market share by a specific percent. The project objective might be to expand market share by 3 percent by introducing a new portable food preparation appliance within 10 months with a budget of $2 million. In this case, the outcome of increased market share would not be known until some time period has elapsed after the new product development project is completed. Another example is a project with an objective to put on an event to raise funds for a particular cause, such as diabetes research, but the expected benefit of the event is to raise a certain amount of money, such as $20,000. In this case, the completion of the project—holding the fund-raising event—enables the benefit to be achieved.

- A project is carried out through a set of *interdependent activities* (also referred to as *tasks*)—that is, a number of nonrepetitive activities that need to be accomplished in a certain sequence in order to achieve the project objective.
- A project utilizes various *resources* to carry out the activities. Such resources can include different people, organizations, equipment, materials, and facilities. For example, a project to perform a complex series of surgical operations may involve doctors with special expertise, nurses, anesthesiologists, surgical instruments, monitoring equipment, prosthetic devices or transplant organs, and special operating facilities.
- A project has a *specific time frame* or *finite life span*. It has a start time and a date by which the objective must be accomplished. For example, the refurbishing of an elementary school might have to be completed between June 20 and August 20.
- A project may be a *unique* or *one-time* endeavor. Some projects, like designing and building a space station, are unique because they have never been attempted before. Other projects, such as developing a new product, building a house, or planning a wedding, are unique because of the customization they require. For example, a wedding can be a simple, informal occasion, with a few friends in a chapel, or a spectacular event, staged for royalty.
- A project has a **sponsor** or **customer**. The sponsor/customer is the entity that provides the funds necessary to accomplish the project. It can be a person, an organization, or a partnership of two or more people or organizations. When a contractor builds an addition to a house, the homeowner is the customer who is funding or paying for the project. When a company receives funds from a government agency to develop a robotic device for handling radioactive material, the sponsor is the government agency. When a company's board of directors provides funds for a team of its employees to upgrade the firm's management information system, the board is the sponsor of the project. In this last case, the term *customer* may take on a broader definition, including not only the project sponsor (the company's management) but also other *stakeholders*, such as the people who will be the end users of the information system. The person managing the project and the project team must successfully accomplish the project objective to satisfy the project sponsor as well as the users of the project's end product—an upgraded information system.

- Finally, a project involves a *degree of uncertainty*. Before a project is started, a plan is prepared based on certain assumptions and estimates. It is important to document these assumptions because they will influence the development of the project work scope, schedule, and budget. A project is based on a unique set of interdependent activities and estimates of how long each activity should take, various resources and assumptions about the availability and capability of those resources, and estimates of the costs associated with the resources. This combination of assumptions and estimates causes uncertainty that the project objective will be completely accomplished. For example, the project scope may be accomplished by the target completion date, but the final cost may be much higher than anticipated because of low initial estimates for the cost of certain resources. As the project proceeds, some of the assumptions will be refined or replaced with factual or updated information. For example, once the conceptual design of a company's annual report is finalized, the amount of time and costs needed to complete the detailed design and produce the final document can be better estimated.

The following are some examples of projects:

Staging a theatrical production

Developing and introducing a new product

Developing a set of apps for mobile business transactions

Planning a wedding

Modernizing a factory

Designing and implementing a computer system

Converting a basement to a family room

Organizing and hosting a conference

Designing and producing a brochure

Executing an environmental cleanup of a contaminated site

Holding a high school reunion

Building a shopping mall

Performing a series of surgeries on an accident victim

Organizing a community festival

Consolidating two manufacturing plants

Rebuilding a town after a natural disaster

Hosting a dinner for 20 relatives

Designing a business internship program for high school students

Building a tree house

Balancing Project Constraints

The successful accomplishment of the project objective could be constrained by many factors, including *scope, quality, schedule, budget, resources, risks, customer satisfaction*, and *stakeholder support*.

The project **scope** is all the work that must be done in order to produce all the project *deliverables* (the tangible product or items to be provided), satisfy the customer that the deliverables meet the requirements and acceptance criteria, and accomplish the project objective. For example, the project scope might be all of the

work involved in clearing the land, building a house, and landscaping to the specifications agreed upon by the contractor and the buyer. Or a project to install new high-speed specialized automation equipment in a factory might include designing the equipment, building it, installing it, testing it to make sure it meets acceptance criteria, training workers to operate and maintain the equipment, and providing all the technical and operating documentation for the equipment.

Quality expectations must be defined from the onset of the project. The project work scope must be accomplished in a quality manner and meet specifications. For example, in a house-building project, the customer expects the workmanship to be of the highest quality and all materials to meet specifications. Completing the work scope but leaving windows that are difficult to open and close, faucets that leak, or a landscape full of rocks will result in an unsatisfied customer and perhaps a payment or legal dispute. Mechanisms such as standards, inspections, audits, and so forth must be put in place to assure quality expectations are being met throughout the project and not just checked or inspected at the end of the project, when it might be costly to correct. All project deliverables should have quantitative acceptance criteria.

The **schedule** for a project is the timetable that specifies when each activity should start and finish. The project objective usually states the time by which the project scope must be completed in terms of a specific date agreed upon by the sponsor and the organization performing the project. The project schedule indicates the dates when specific activities must be started and finished in order to meet the project completion date (for example, when a new bridge is to be open to traffic or when a new product must be launched at an industry exposition).

The **budget** of a project is the amount the sponsor or customer has agreed to pay for acceptable project deliverables. The project budget is based on estimated costs associated with the quantities of various resources that will be used to perform the project. It might include the salaries of people who will work on the project, materials and supplies, equipment, rental of facilities, and the fees of subcontractors or consultants who will perform some of the project tasks. For example, for a wedding project, the budget might include estimated costs for flowers, gown, tuxedo, caterer, cake, limousine rental, videographer, reception facility, and so on.

Various **resources** are needed to perform the project activities, produce the project deliverables, and accomplish the project objective. Resources include people, materials, equipment, facilities, and so forth. Human resources include people with specific expertise or skills. Certain quantities of each type of resource with specific expertise are required at specific periods of time during the project. Similarly, particular equipment may be required during a certain portion of a project, such as equipment needed to excavate the land before construction can start on a new office building. The resource requirements for a project must be aligned with the types and quantities of resources available at the time periods when they are required.

There could be **risks** that adversely affect accomplishing the project objective. For example, designing an information system using the newest technology may pose a risk that the new technology may not work as expected. Or there may be a risk that a new pharmaceutical product may not receive regulatory approval. A risk management plan must be developed that identifies and assesses potential risks and their likelihood of occurrence and potential impact, and delineates responses for dealing with risks if they do occur.

Ultimately, the responsibility of the project manager is to make sure the **customer is satisfied**. This goes beyond just completing the project scope within budget and on schedule or asking if the customer or sponsor is satisfied at the end of

the project. It means not only meeting the customer's expectations but also developing and maintaining an excellent working relationship throughout the project. It requires ongoing communication with the customer or sponsor to keep the customer informed and to determine whether expectations have changed. Regularly scheduled meetings or progress reports, phone discussions, and e-mail are examples of ways to accomplish such communication. Customer satisfaction requires involving the sponsor as a partner in the successful outcome of the project through active participation during the project. The project manager must continually be aware of the degree of the customer's satisfaction. By maintaining regular communication with the customer or sponsor, the project manager demonstrates genuine concern about the customer's expectations; it also prevents unpleasant surprises later.

The project manager and team need to build relationships with, and engage, the various **stakeholders** who may influence or may be affected by the project, in order to gain their support. See the section on Stakeholder Engagement later in this chapter for further discussion.

Successfully completing the project requires finishing the scope of work within budget and a certain time frame, while managing resource utilization, meeting quality specifications, and managing risks—and this must all be done while assuring customer or sponsor satisfaction and dealing with stakeholders' issues and concerns and gaining their support. During the project, it is sometimes challenging to balance or juggle these factors, which often constrain one another and could jeopardize accomplishing the project objective. See Figure 1.1. To help

FIGURE 1.1 Factors Constraining Project Success

ensure the achievement of the project objective, *it is important to develop a plan before starting the project work*, rather than jumping in and starting without a plan. Lack of a plan decreases the chances of successfully accomplishing the full project scope within budget and on schedule.

Once a project is started, unforeseen circumstances may jeopardize the achievement of the project objective with respect to scope, budget, or schedule. They include:

- The cost of some of the materials is more than originally estimated.
- Inclement weather causes a delay.
- Additional redesign and modifications to a new sophisticated medical instrument are required to get it to meet performance specifications and government testing requirements.
- Delivery of a critical component for an aviation control system is delayed several months.
- Environmental contaminants are discovered when excavating for a new building.
- A key project team member with unique technical knowledge decides to retire, which creates a gap in critical expertise.

Any of the above examples could affect the balance of scope, quality, schedule, budget, resources, risks, customer satisfaction, and stakeholder support (or impact these factors individually), jeopardizing successful accomplishment of the project objective. The challenge for the project manager is to not only continually balance these factors throughout the performance of the project but also prevent, anticipate, or overcome such circumstances if and when they occur. *Good planning and communication* are essential to prevent problems from occurring or to minimize their impact on the achievement of the project objective when they do occur. The project manager needs to be proactive in planning and communicating and provide leadership to the project team to keep these constraining factors in balance and to accomplish the project objective.

Reinforce Your Learning

3. What are eight factors that constrain the achievement of a project objective?

Project Life Cycle

The generic **project life cycle** has four phases: initiating, planning, performing, and closing the project. Figure 1.2 shows the four phases and the relative level of effort and time devoted to each phase. The time span of each phase and the associated level of effort will vary depending on the specific project. Project life cycles vary in length from a few weeks to several years, depending on the content, complexity, and magnitude of the project.

In the **initiating phase**, projects are identified and selected. They are then authorized, using a document referred to as a **project charter**. The **planning phase** includes defining the project scope, identifying resources, developing a schedule and budget, and identifying risks, all of which make up the **baseline plan** for doing the project work. In the **performing phase**, the project plan is executed, and activities are carried out to produce all the **project deliverables** and to accomplish the project objective. During this phase, the project progress is monitored and controlled to assure the work remains on schedule and within budget, the scope is fully completed according to specifications, and all deliverables meet acceptance criteria. Also, any changes need to be documented, approved, and incorporated into an updated baseline plan, if necessary. In the **closing phase**, project evaluations are conducted, lessons learned are identified

FIGURE 1.2 Project Life Cycle Effort

and documented to help improve performance on future projects, and **project documents** are organized and **archived**.

INITIATING

This first phase of the project life cycle involves the identification of a need, problem, or opportunity and can result in the sponsor authorizing a project to address the identified need or solve the problem. Projects are initiated when a need is identified by a sponsor—the people or the organization willing to provide funds to have the need satisfied. For example, a company may need to reduce the high scrap rate from its manufacturing process that makes its costs higher and production times longer than those of its competitors, or a community with a growing population may need to build a new school. In some cases, it could take several months to clearly define a need, gather data, and define the project objective. For example, the management of a hospital may want to establish an on-site day care center for the children of its employees as part of its strategy to attract and retain employees. However, it may take some time to gather data regarding the need and analyze various approaches to addressing the need. It is important to define the right need. For example, is the need to provide an on-site day care center, or is it to provide child care for the children of the hospital's employees? That is, is "on-site" necessarily part of the need?

The need for projects is often identified as part of an organization's strategic planning process. Projects are a means to implement elements of specific strategies or actions, such as build an offshore wind farm, deploy a nutrition assistance program in a developing country, construct a new manufacturing facility in

Reinforce Your Learning

4. Match the phases of the project life cycle, listed first, with the descriptions that follow:

___ First phase
___ Second phase
___ Third phase
___ Fourth phase
A. Planning
B. Performing
C. Initiating
D. Closing

South America, or implement a corporate-wide online training program. Organizations may have many projects they would like to pursue, but they may be limited by the amount of available funds. Although an individual may need an addition to his house, need a new car, and want to go on a two-week vacation, he may not have the money to do all of those things. Therefore, organizations must employ a process to select which projects to pursue. Once projects are selected, they are formally authorized using a document referred to as a *project charter*. The charter may include the rationale or justification for the project; project objective and expected benefits; general requirements and conditions such as amount of funds authorized, required completion date, major deliverables, and required reviews and approvals; and key assumptions.

Reinforce Your Learning

5. A project is authorized using a document called a

_____ .

If the organization decides to use external resources (a contractor) to perform the project, the organization will prepare a document called a *request for proposal (RFP)* that defines the project requirements and is used to solicit proposals from potential contractors to do the project. Through the RFP, the sponsor or customer asks contractors to submit proposals on how they might address the need and the associated costs and schedule to do so. An individual who needs a new house may spend time identifying requirements for the house—size, style, number of rooms, location, maximum amount she wants to spend, and date by which she would like to move in. She may then write down these requirements and ask several contractors to provide house plans and cost estimates. A company that has identified a need to develop a multifaceted advertising campaign for a new food product might document its requirements in an RFP and send it to several advertising firms. The advertising firms would submit proposals to the company. The company would then evaluate the competing proposals and select an advertising firm (the contractor) to do the advertising campaign (the project) and sign an agreement or contract with that firm.

PLANNING

Before jumping in and starting the project, the project team or contractor must take sufficient time to properly plan the project. It is necessary to lay out a roadmap, or game plan, that shows how the project scope will be accomplished within budget and on schedule. Trying to perform a project without a plan is like attempting to assemble a backyard grill without first reading the instructions. Individuals who think planning is unnecessary or a waste of time invariably need to find time later on to redo things. It is important to *plan the work and then work the plan*. Otherwise, chaos and frustration will result, and the risk of project failure will be higher. Once a project is authorized and/or a contract is signed with an external contractor, the next phase of the project life cycle is to do detailed planning for how to accomplish the project. The planning involves determining *what* needs to be done (scope, deliverables), *how* it will get done (activities, sequence), *who* will do it (resources, responsibility), *how long* it will take (durations, schedule), *how much* it will cost (budget), and what the *risks* are. The result of this effort is a *baseline plan* that is a set of integrated documents that shows how the project scope will be accomplished within budget and on schedule and is used as a benchmark to which actual performance can be compared.

Reinforce Your Learning

6. The result of the planning phase is a

_____ .

Taking the time to develop a well-thought-out plan is critical to the successful accomplishment of any project. Many projects have overrun their budgets, missed their completion dates, or only partially satisfied their technical specifications because there was no viable baseline plan in place before they were started.

It is important that the people who will be involved in performing the project also participate in planning the work. They are usually the most knowledgeable about which detailed activities need to be done. Also, by participating in the planning of the work, these individuals become committed to accomplishing it according to the plan. Participation builds commitment.

PERFORMING

The third phase of the project life cycle is performing the project. Once the baseline plan has been developed, work can proceed. The project team, led by the project manager, will execute the plan and perform the activities to produce all the deliverables and to accomplish the project objective. The pace of project activity will increase as more and various resources become involved in performing the project tasks. During the course of performing the project, different types of resources will be utilized. For example, if the project is to design and construct an office building, the project effort might first involve a few architects and engineers in developing the building plans. Then, as construction gets under way, the resources needed will substantially increase to include steelworkers, carpenters, electricians, painters, and the like. The level of effort will decrease after the building is finished, and a smaller number of different workers will finish up the landscaping and final interior touches.

This phase results in the accomplishment of the project objective, leaving the customer satisfied that the full scope of the work and deliverables were completed according to specifications, within budget, and on time. For example, the performing phase is complete when a project team within a company has completed a project that consolidated two of its facilities into one, or when an external contractor has completed the design and installation of a customized information system that satisfactorily passes performance tests and is accepted by the customer.

While the project work is being performed, it is necessary to *monitor and control the progress* of the project work to ensure that everything is going according to plan and the project objective will be accomplished. This involves measuring actual progress and comparing it to planned progress according to the baseline plan. To measure actual progress, it is important to keep track of which tasks have actually been started and completed, when they were started and completed, the earned value of the work completed, if the project deliverables are meeting the expected quality criteria, and how much money has been spent or committed. If, at any time during the project, comparison of actual progress to planned progress reveals that the project is behind schedule, overrunning the budget, or not meeting the technical specifications, corrective action must be taken to get the project back on track.

Before a decision is made to implement corrective action, it may be necessary to evaluate several alternative actions to make sure the corrective action will bring the project back within the scope, schedule, and budget constraints of the project objective. Be aware, for instance, that adding resources to make up time and get back on schedule may result in overrunning the planned budget. If a project gets too far out of control, it may be difficult to accomplish the project objective without sacrificing the scope, budget, schedule, or quality. The key to effective project control is measuring actual progress and comparing it to planned progress on a timely and regular basis throughout the performing phase and taking any needed corrective action immediately. Hoping that a

Reinforce Your Learning

7. In the performing phase, the project plan is _____ to produce all the _____ and to accomplish the _____.

problem will go away without corrective intervention is naive. The earlier a problem is identified and corrected, the better. Based on actual progress, it is possible to forecast a schedule and budget for completion of the project. If these parameters are beyond the limits of the project objective, corrective actions need to be implemented at once.

Changes are going to occur during the performing phase. So it is important to *manage and control changes* to minimize any negative impact on the successful accomplishment of the project objective. A change control system needs to be established for the process and procedures that define how changes will be documented, approved, and communicated. Agreement must be reached between the sponsor or customer and the project manager or contractor, as well as between the project manager and the project team, regarding the way changes will be handled. These procedures should address communication between the project manager and the sponsor or customer and between the project manager and the project team. If changes are consented to verbally rather than approved in writing and there is no indication given of the impact the changes will have on the work scope, budget, or schedule, there are bound to be problems down the road. Project team members should be careful about casually agreeing to changes without knowing whether they will necessitate additional person-hours of work. If the customer does not agree to pay for extra effort, the contractor must absorb the additional costs and also risk overrunning costs for a particular activity or the project.

Some changes are trivial, but others may significantly affect the project work scope, budget, or schedule. Deciding to change the color of a room before it is painted is a trivial change. Deciding that you want a two-story house after the contractor has already put up the framing for a single-story house is a major change, and would certainly increase the cost and probably delay the completion date.

The impact a change has on accomplishing the project objective may be affected by when the change is identified. Generally, *the later in the project that changes are identified, the greater their effect on accomplishing the project objective.* The aspects most likely to be affected are the project budget and the completion date. This is particularly true when work that has already been completed needs to be "undone" to accommodate the required change. For example, it would be very expensive to change the plumbing or wiring in a new office building after the walls and ceilings are completed because some of them would need to be torn out and new ones installed. However, if such a change was made much earlier in the project—for instance, while the building was still being designed—the accommodation would be easier and less costly. The drawings could be changed so that the plumbing and wiring would be installed correctly the first time.

The project manager, project team, contractor, or sponsor/customer may initiate changes. Some changes could be necessary as a result of the occurrence of a previously defined risk, such as a new product development not meeting certain test criteria, which would mean additional redesign work.

When it is determined that corrective actions or changes are necessary, decisions must be made regarding how to update the baseline plan. These decisions often mean a trade-off involving time, cost, scope, and quality. For example, reducing the duration of an activity may require either increasing costs to pay for more resources or reducing the scope of the activity (and possibly not

meeting the customer's technical requirements). Similarly, reducing project costs may require using materials of a lower quality than originally planned. Once a decision is made on which actions to take, they must be incorporated into the schedule and budget. It is necessary to develop a revised schedule and budget to determine whether the planned corrective measures or changes result in an acceptable schedule and budget. If not, further revisions must be made until an acceptable revised baseline plan is agreed upon.

The performing phase of the project life cycle ends when the sponsor or customer is satisfied that the project objective has been accomplished and that the requirements have been met, and accepts the project deliverables.

CLOSING

The final phase of the project life cycle is closing the project. The process of closing the project involves various actions, including collecting and making final payments, evaluating and recognizing staff, conducting a postproject evaluation, documenting lessons learned, and archiving project documents.

The project organization should ensure that copies of appropriate project documentation are properly organized, filed, and archived so that they can be readily retrieved for use in the future. For example, using some actual cost and schedule information from a completed project may be helpful when developing the schedule and estimated costs for a proposed project.

An important task during this phase is evaluating performance of the project. The project team should identify lessons learned and make recommendations for improving performance on future projects. To encourage the use of this information, a knowledge base system should be established that includes an easily accessible repository to retrieve lessons learned and information from previous projects.

Feedback should also be obtained from the sponsor or customer to determine whether the anticipated benefits from the project were achieved, assess the level of customer satisfaction, and obtain any feedback that would be helpful in future business relationships with this customer or other customers.

Project Management Process

Project management is planning, organizing, coordinating, leading, and controlling resources to accomplish the project objective. The project management process involves *planning the work and then working the plan*. A coaching staff may spend hours preparing a unique plan for a game; the team then executes the plan to try to accomplish the objective—victory. Similarly, the project management process involves two major functions: first *establishing a plan* and then *executing that plan* to accomplish the project objective.

Once the sponsor has prepared a project charter to authorize going forward with a project, the front end effort in managing a project must be focused on establishing a realistic baseline plan that provides a set of integrated documents that shows how the project scope will be accomplished within budget and on schedule. The project objective establishes what is to be accomplished. The **planning** process determines *what* needs to be done (scope, deliverables), *how* it will get done (activities, sequence), *who* will do it (resources, responsibility),

how long it will take (durations, schedule), and *how much* it will cost (budget). It includes the following steps:

1. *Establish project objective.* The objective must be agreed upon by the sponsor or customer and the organization that will perform the project.
2. *Define scope.* A project scope document must be prepared. It should include customer requirements, a statement of work, as well as a list of deliverables and associated acceptance criteria that can be used to validate that the work and deliverables meet specifications.
3. *Create a work breakdown structure.* Subdivide the project scope into pieces or **work packages**. Although projects may seem overwhelming when viewed as a whole, one way to conquer even the most monumental endeavor is to break it down into smaller components. A **work breakdown structure (WBS)** is a hierarchical decomposition of the project work scope into work packages to be executed by the project team that will produce the project deliverables. Figure 1.3 is an example of a WBS.
4. *Assign responsibility.* The person or organization responsible for each work item in the WBS must be identified in order to inform the project team of who is responsible and accountable for the performance of each work package and any associated deliverables. For example, Figure 1.3 indicates who is responsible for each work item.
5. *Define specific activities.* Review each work package in the WBS and develop a list of the detailed activities that need to be performed for each work package and to produce any required deliverables.
6. *Sequence activities.* Create a **network diagram** that shows the necessary sequence and dependent relationships of the detailed activities that need to be performed to achieve the project objective. Figure 1.4 is an example of a network diagram.
7. *Estimate activity resources.* Determine the types of resources, such as the skills or expertise required to perform each activity, as well as the quantity of each resource that may be needed. Resources include people, materials, equipment, and so on that may be required to perform each activity. Resource estimates must consider the availability of each type of resource, whether it is internal or external (such as subcontractors), and the quantity available over the duration of the project. Designate a specific individual to be responsible for each activity.
8. *Estimate activity durations.* Make a time estimate for how long it will take to complete each activity, based on the estimate of the resources that will be applied.
9. *Develop project schedule.* Based on the estimated duration for each activity and the dependent relationships of the sequence of activities in the network diagram, develop the overall project schedule, including when each activity is expected to start and finish, as well as the latest times that each activity must start and finish in order to complete the project by the required completion date. Figure 1.5 is an example of a project schedule.
10. *Estimate activity costs.* Activity costs should be based on the types and quantities of resources estimated for each activity as well as the appropriate labor cost rate or unit cost for each type of resource.
11. *Determine budget.* A total budget for the project can be developed by aggregating the cost estimates for each activity. Similarly, budgets can be determined for each work package in the WBS by aggregating the cost estimates

FIGURE 1.3 Work Breakdown Structure

Level 0

Festival
Lynn

Level 1

1 Promotion — Lynn
2 Volunteers — Beth
3 Games — Steve
4 Rides — Pat

Level 2

1.1 Newspaper Ads — Lynn
1.2 Posters — Keith
1.3 Tickets — Andrea
3.1 Booths — Jim
3.2 Games — Steve
3.3 Prizes — Jeff
4.1 Amusement Contractor — Pat
4.2 Permits — Neil

Level 3

for the detailed activities for each work package. Other costs, such as project or organizational administrative, indirect, or overhead costs should also be included in the budget and be appropriately allocated to each activity or work package. Once the total budget is determined for the overall project or

for each work package, a time-phased budget needs to be developed to distribute the budget over the duration of the project or work package based on the project schedule for when each activity is expected to start and finish. Figure 1.6 is an example of a time-phased project budget.

FIGURE 1.4 Network Diagram

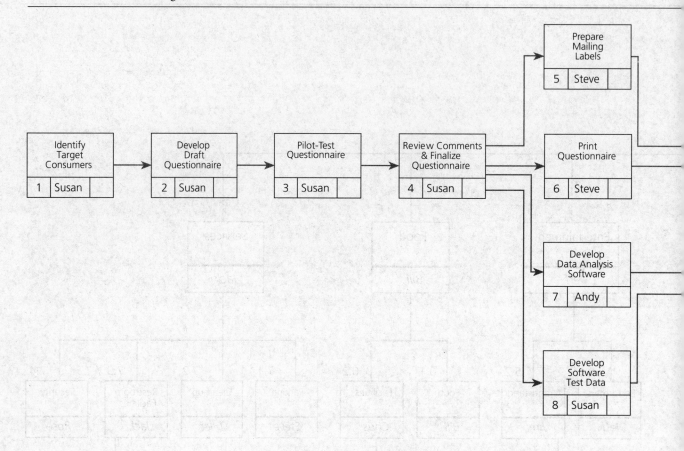

Once the project schedule and budget are developed, it must be determined whether the project can be completed within the required time, with the allotted funds, and with the available resources. If not, adjustments must be made to the project scope, activity resource or duration estimates, or resource assignments until an achievable, realistic **baseline plan** for accomplishing the project scope within budget and on schedule can be established.

The result of the planning process is a **baseline plan**. Taking the time to develop a well-thought-out plan is critical to the successful accomplishment of any project. Many projects have overrun their budgets, missed their completion dates, or only partially met their requirements because there was no viable baseline plan before the project was started.

The baseline plan for a project can be displayed in graphical or tabular format for each time period (week, month) from the start of the project to its completion. Plans are discussed and illustrated in Chapters 4 to 7. Information should include:

- The start and completion dates for each activity
- The amounts of the various resources that will be needed during each time period

- The budget for each time period, as well as the cumulative budget from the start of the project through each time period

Once a baseline plan has been established, the plan must be executed. The executing process involves performing the work according to the plan, monitoring and controlling the work, and managing changes so that the project scope is achieved within the budget and schedule, to the customer's satisfaction. It includes the following elements:

1. *Perform the work*. All the activities in the baseline plan, as depicted in the network diagram, must be performed in accordance with the project schedule and technical specifications. All deliverables must be produced and meet their acceptance criteria. Accomplishing this requires coordination of the project team, including external resources, and regular communication with all stakeholders, including the sponsor or customer, to make sure that expectations are being met.
2. *Monitor and control progress*. While the project work is being performed, it is necessary to monitor progress to ensure that everything is going according to

FIGURE 1.5 **Project Schedule Consumer Market Study Project**

Consumer Market Study Project

	Activity	Respon.	Dur. Estim.	Earliest Start	Earliest Finish	Latest Start	Latest Finish	Total Slack
1	Identify Target Consumers	Susan	3	0	3	−8	−5	−8
2	Develop Draft Questionnaire	Susan	10	3	13	−5	5	−8
3	Pilot-Test Questionnaire	Susan	20	13	33	5	25	−8
4	Review Comments & Finalize Questionnaire	Susan	5	33	38	25	30	−8
5	Prepare Mailing Labels	Steve	2	38	40	38	40	0
6	Print Questionnaire	Steve	10	38	48	30	40	−8
7	Develop Data Analysis Software	Andy	12	38	50	88	100	50
8	Develop Software Test Data	Susan	2	38	40	98	100	60
9	Mail Questionnaire & Get Responses	Steve	65	48	113	40	105	−8
10	Test Software	Andy	5	50	55	100	105	50
11	Input Response Data	Jim	7	113	120	105	112	−8
12	Analyze Results	Jim	8	120	128	112	120	−8
13	Prepare Report	Jim	10	128	138	120	130	−8

FIGURE 1.6 **Time-phased Project Budget**

Cumulative Budgeted Cost ($ in thousands)

plan. It is also necessary to measure actual progress and compare it to planned progress. If, at any time during the project, the comparison of actual progress to planned progress reveals that the project is behind schedule, overrunning the budget, or not meeting the technical specifications, corrective action must be taken to get the project back on track within the scope, schedule, and budget constraints of the project objective. Be aware, for instance, that adding resources to make up time and get back on schedule may result in overrunning the planned budget. If a project gets too far out of control, it may be difficult to achieve the project objective without sacrificing the scope, budget, schedule, or quality. The key to effective project control is measuring actual progress and comparing it to planned progress on a timely and regular basis and taking any needed corrective action immediately. Hoping that a problem will go away without corrective intervention is naive. Based on actual progress, it is possible to forecast a schedule and budget for completion of the project. If these parameters are beyond the limits of the project objective, corrective actions need to be implemented at once.

3. *Control changes.* During the performance of the project work, changes will occur for a variety of unexpected reasons, such as some activities taking longer than expected to complete, resources not being available when needed, materials costing more than anticipated, or the occurrence of identified risks. Also, the project manager, contractor, or the sponsor/customer can request changes to the project scope based on new information or the result of project reviews. Changes are fine if the customer and the project manager or contractor agree on them, and both parties are aware of the impact the changes may have on the scope, schedule, budget, and accomplishment of the project objective. It is important to manage and control changes to minimize any negative impact on the successful accomplishment of the project objective. A change control system needs to be established for the process and procedures that define how changes will be documented, approved, and communicated. Agreement must be reached with the sponsor or customer on such a system, and it must be communicated to all project participants.

Attempting to perform a project without first establishing a baseline plan is foolhardy. It is similar to starting a vacation without a roadmap, itinerary, and budget. You may end up in the middle of nowhere—out of money and out of time!

Stakeholder Engagement

Project **stakeholders** are individuals or entities involved in, or who may influence, or may be affected by a project, such as the customer/sponsor; project team, including the project manager, subcontractors, and consultants; end users or consumers; and advocacy groups. In addition to the customer/sponsor and the project team including subcontractors and suppliers, stakeholders can be organizations or groups of people who may be supportive or adversarial or may want to be kept informed about the project because of potential impact.

Examples of stakeholders for various projects include:

Staff of a medical practice who will use a new electronic health records system

Community or neighborhood that will be affected by the route of a new highway

Small retailers near the construction of a new shopping mall

Advocacy group that is concerned about the environmental and safety impact of a new chemical facility

Advisory groups such as parents who provide input to the design of new playground at a childcare center, or emergency room staff who provide input to the redesign and expansion of an emergency room

Government regulatory agencies that are concerned about code enforcement, pharmaceutical drug trials, or conducting public forums to solicit citizen comments for certain types of projects

It is important to identify a project's stakeholders as early as possible in the project life cycle. The project sponsor may identify specific stakeholders in the project charter authorizing the project. Additionally the project manager can ask, or have a brainstorming session, with the project team to identify stakeholders, or perhaps to create advisory groups to provide input and guidance to the project or portions of a project. The project manager can also network with other organizations, such as community groups, nonprofit organizations, professional organizations, or local government officials, to help identify potential stakeholders. Identifying potential stakeholders as early as possible in the project will help to avoid surprises later. For example, if a certain group finds out about a particular issue with a project, and they were not informed about it beforehand or included, it can create an adversarial situation and make it more difficult to build a trust relationship.

As potential stakeholders are identified, a list should be created that includes key contact information, role or specific topics of interest, expectations, any known issues, and areas of potential influence for each stakeholder. Such a document is sometimes referred to as a **stakeholder register**. During the performance of the project, information about stakeholders may change or additional stakeholders may be identified. The stakeholder register is a convenient tool to keep all stakeholder information consolidated and up-to-date.

The project manager and team need to build a relationship with each stakeholder that is tailored to each stakeholder's specific interests in the project. The project team needs to be proactive and take the initiative to contact and engage each stakeholder, listen to their interests, needs, expectations and concerns, rather than waiting for the stakeholders to approach and then be in a reactive or defensive mode. Good relationships are built on trust and respect; and trust and respect are built on being honest, ethical, and delivering on promises. The project team should welcome stakeholder input, involvement, discussions, and debate. It will build support for the project. Stakeholders' concerns should be addressed early, positively, and in a timely manner; and not confrontationally, put off, ignored, or dismissed. The project manager needs to provide opportunities for regular two-way communication with each stakeholder, not just when an issue or concern is identified. The project manager and team need to listen, be open-minded, thoughtful, and behave professionally; and not dominate the

discussions, overreact, become defensive, or lose control of their emotions. In most situations each stakeholder should be dealt with separately because each has their unique interests and concerns, rather than dealing with all stakeholders as a group.

An **issue log** should be created of specific issues or concerns or questions that various stakeholders identify so that the project manager, project team, or sponsor/customer can address them and make sure they are not forgotten or dismissed without an adequate follow up and response. The project team should keep the issue log up-to-date indicating the status of which issues have been addressed or resolved, new issues added, and those that may require negotiation to resolve specific disputes. If any stakeholder's specific issue cannot be satisfied or resolved, it is important that a detailed clear explanation be provided, so that the stakeholder knows the reasons or rationale behind the decision, even if they may not agree with it.

Stakeholder engagement and support are important to the successful performance of a project and accomplishment of the project objective. Regular and open communication, trust, respect, open-mindedness, and a positive win-win attitude are keys to successful stakeholder engagement.

Reinforce Your Learning

10. What are the keys to successful stakeholder engagement?

Global Project Management

Globalization adds a unique dimension to managing projects. It changes the dynamics of the project and adds a layer of complexity that can adversely affect the project outcome if the project participants are not aware of what they might encounter regarding cultural differences and multinational economic transactions. For example, there could be a project contractual outsourcing requirement to spend a percentage of the project budget on wages and materials in the customer's country by employing indigenous labor to perform certain project tasks and using in-country suppliers for project materials. Factors external to the project itself, or to the project or customer organizations, can create a dynamic and perhaps unstable environment over the life of the project, introduce sources of risk, and affect the success of the project. Such influencing factors can include:

- Currency fluctuations and exchange rates
- Country-specific work codes and regulations, such as hours per day, holidays, and religious observances
- Corporate joint ventures and partnerships creating entities with a presence and facilities in multiple countries
- Political relations between countries
- Availability of high-demand workforce skills

Large international events, such as the Olympics or rebuilding a region after a natural disaster, require multilingual project teams. Global projects can be multinational and multilingual, with participants who are located in various countries and who speak different languages. These aspects can create barriers to communication, team development, and project performance.

Global project management requires an additional set of competencies. It is helpful for the project manager and team to have foreign language skills and also knowledge and understanding of other countries and cultures, as well as geography, world history, and international economics (currencies, exchange rates, export/import transactions, and so forth). There is a need to have

awareness and understanding of the culture and customs (meal times, eye contact, possible differing roles of men and women, dress codes, religious practices, lines of authority, communication protocol, and so forth) and etiquette (for example, in some countries crossing your legs when sitting is considered an insult, or shaking hands or touching someone of the opposite sex is frowned upon) of the countries of the various project participants (project team, customer, subcontractors, and suppliers). It is also vital to have an awareness of the geopolitical environment of the countries of the various project participants, in particular the country of the customer, or where the project is being delivered or implemented.

Technology enables project participants to be just a "click" away, despite being thousands of miles apart physically. It also helps to reduce the impact that time zone differences among the locations of various project participants can have on project communication. One way to facilitate communication in multilingual project teams is to utilize software that translates e-mails and documents among the languages of the various project participants.

Globalization and the Internet have also brought new opportunities for firms, as seen in multisourcing project work elements to more competitive participants worldwide as well as in purchasing materials and services from suppliers around the globe.

Cultural awareness and sensitivity are not only important but also imperative for successful global project management. Learning and understanding the culture and customs of other project participants demonstrate respect, help build trust, aid in developing an effective project team, and are critical for successful global project management.

See the section on Valuing Team Diversity in Chapter 11 and the section on Collaborative Communication Tools in Chapter 12 for additional related information. Also see Appendix C for a list of project management associations around the globe.

Reinforce Your Learning

11.

and sensitivity are not only important but also

for successful

project management.

Project Management Associations

The Project Management Institute (PMI) is a premier worldwide not-for-profit association for practitioners in the project management profession and individuals who want to learn more about the profession. Founded in 1969, PMI is approaching 500,000 members in nearly 200 countries and has about 270 chapters worldwide. Additionally, the association has over 30 online communities of practice where peers can collaborate on specific topics of interest.

PMI publishes *A Guide to the Project Management Body of Knowledge (PMBOK® Guide)*, which provides a framework of processes and guidelines for the application of project management concepts, practices, and techniques. The association also created the *PMI Code of Ethics and Professional Conduct*, which sets standards and establishes expectations for professional behavior.

PMI offers a certification program that provides the opportunity to earn credentials in various project management disciplines. There are well over 500,000 individuals worldwide who are PMI credential holders. Additional and current information about the Project Management Institute can be found at http://www.pmi.org.

There are also many other project management associations around the globe. Appendix C provides a list of approximately 60 such associations. Their website addresses can be found on this book's student companion website.

Benefits of Project Management

The ultimate benefit of implementing project management techniques is having a satisfied customer—whether you are the customer of your own project, such as remodeling your basement, or a business (contractor) being paid by a customer to perform a project. Completing the full project scope in a quality manner, on time, and within budget provides a great feeling of satisfaction. For a contractor, it could lead to additional business from the same customer in the future or to business from new customers referred by previously satisfied customers.

"Hey! Great for the customer, but what about me? What's in it for me?" If you are the project manager, you have the satisfaction of knowing you led a successful project effort. You also have enhanced your reputation as a project manager and positioned yourself for expanded career opportunities. If you are a member of a project team that successfully accomplished a project, you feel the satisfaction of being on a winning team. You not only contributed to the project's success but also probably expanded your knowledge and enhanced your skills along the way. If you choose to remain an individual contributor, you will be able to make a greater contribution to future, more complex projects. If you are interested in eventually managing projects, you will be in a position to take on additional project responsibilities. When projects are successful, everybody wins!

 REAL WORLD PROJECT MANAGEMENT

Hoover Dam Generates Project Management Techniques in Addition to Hydroelectricity

The 1930s in the United States was experiencing a time of depression, limited project implementation, and reduced production of goods and services. Issues related to flooding and silt accumulation in canals influenced the study and approval to complete the construction of the Hoover Dam in Black Canyon. The $165 million project finished two years ahead of schedule and $15 million under budget. The collaboration of Six Companies, Inc. successfully balanced resources to manage the challenges of completing one of the largest infrastructure projects ever built in the United States.

Contributions to the success of the project include thorough analysis of the need, development of the proposed solution to establish the feasibility, strong oversight of the project performance, and innovative funding to secure adequate resources. Much of this success was due to an experienced project manager, close relationships with government officials, and a supply of workers and materials necessary to complete the project.

Financial planning to overbid the creation of the tunnels and the rock removal and a low bid for concrete installation allowed for increased cash income up front to fund the surety bond required for the project. The entire project was planned as 119 separate projects. A $3,000-per-day fine was imposed for any delays. An incentive bonus was negotiated for completing the project early and under budget. The small projects allowed for aspects of the overall project to be completed years in advance.

Salaries paid to the workers were greater than other skilled workers in the United States in the 1930s. This wage rate attracted large numbers of workers to the region.

Electric lights allowed for three 8-hour shifts per day. The project manager, Frank Crowe, devised timesaving and efficient construction methods using workers and machinery, and outsourcing where appropriate, to avoid delays. Rigorous scheduling seven days a week supplemented with the use of heavy machinery and innovative technology pushed the project toward early completion.

Lessons learned from the project management techniques used in the construction of Hoover Dam are still utilized today in Department of Energy megaprojects. Project sponsors must know what they can afford. The Hoover Dam project was funded over 50 years by the sale of electricity through contracts worth nearly double the costs to build the dam. Project sponsors must have open communications, trust, and coordination with the contractor. The contractor for the dam and the government agencies had a strong relationship that was maintained throughout the project. Project leaders must be dedicated to the success of the project. The project manager was an experienced manager who was a project team builder as well as a project builder. Contract incentives must be clear and provide adequate compensation for risks and resources used. Incentive bonuses for early completion and planning strategies to avoid risks contributed to an accelerated schedule and a completion two years before the scheduled deadline.

The completion of Hoover Dam resulted from managing challenges and applying project management techniques and strategies. Application of these project management principles increases the probability of future successful project management.

Based on information from Kwak, Y. H., J. Waleski, D. Sleeper, and H. Sadatsafavi (2013). "What Can We Learn from the Hoover Dam Project That Influenced Modern Project Management?" *International Journal of Project Management*, http://dx.doi.org.ezaccess.libraries.psu.edu/10.1016/j.ijproman.2013.04.002.

CRITICAL SUCCESS FACTORS

- Planning and communication are critical to successful project management. They prevent problems from occurring or minimize their impact on the accomplishment of the project objective when they do occur.

- Taking the time to develop a well-thought-out plan before the start of the project is critical to the successful accomplishment of any project.

- A project must have a clear objective of what is to be accomplished and defined in terms of end product or deliverable, schedule, and budget, and agreed upon by the customer.

- Involve the sponsor or customer as a partner in the successful outcome of the project through active participation during the project.

- Achieving customer satisfaction requires ongoing communication to keep the customer informed and to determine whether expectations have changed.

- The key to effective project control is measuring actual progress and comparing it to planned progress on a timely and regular basis and taking any needed corrective action immediately.

- After the conclusion of a project, the project performance should be evaluated to learn what could be improved if a similar project were to be done in the future. Feedback should be obtained from the sponsor or customer and the project team.

- Identify, engage, and build relationships with stakeholders as early as possible to gain their support.

- Learning and understanding the culture and customs of other project participants will demonstrate respect, help build trust, and aid in developing an effective project team, and it is critical for successful global project management.

SUMMARY

A project is an endeavor to accomplish a specific objective through a unique set of interrelated activities and the effective utilization of resources. It has a clear objective that establishes what is to be accomplished in terms of the end product or deliverable, schedule, and budget. A project also has interdependent activities, uses various resources, has a specific time frame, is a unique one-time endeavor, has a sponsor or customer, and involves a degree of uncertainty. The successful accomplishment of the project objective could be constrained by many factors, including scope, quality, schedule, budget, resources, risks, customer satisfaction, and stakeholder support.

The project life cycle has four phases: initiating, planning, performing, and closing the project. In the initiating phase, projects are identified and selected. They are then authorized using a document referred to as a project charter. The planning phase includes defining the project scope, identifying resources, developing a schedule and budget, and identifying risks, all of which make up the baseline plan for doing the project work. In the performing phase, the project plan is executed and activities are carried out to produce all the project deliverables and to accomplish the project objective. During this phase, the project progress is monitored and controlled to assure the work remains on schedule and within budget, the scope is fully completed according to specifications, and all deliverables meet acceptance criteria. Also, any changes need to be documented, approved, and incorporated into an updated baseline plan if necessary. In the closing phase, project evaluations are conducted, lessons learned are identified and documented to help improve performance on future projects, and project documents are organized and archived.

Project management is planning, organizing, coordinating, leading, and controlling resources to accomplish the project objective. The project management process involves two major functions: first establishing a plan and then executing that plan to accomplish the project objective. The planning process includes the following steps: establish the project objective, define scope, create a work breakdown structure, assign responsibility, define specific activities, sequence activities, estimate activity resources, estimate activity durations, develop a project schedule, estimate costs, and determine the budget. The executing process involves three elements: perform the work, monitor and control progress, and control changes.

Project stakeholders are individuals or entities involved in, or who may influence, or may be affected by a project. They can be organizations or groups of people who may be supportive or adversarial or may want to be kept informed about the project because of potential impact. It is important to identify a project's stakeholders as early as possible in the project life cycle. A stakeholder register should be created that includes key contact information, role or specific topics of interest, expectations, any known issues, and areas of potential influence for each stakeholder. The project manager and team need to build a relationship with each stakeholder that is tailored to each stakeholder's specific interests in the project. Stakeholder engagement and support are important to the successful performance of a project and accomplishment of the project objective. Regular and open communication, trust, respect, open-mindedness, and a positive win-win attitude are keys to successful stakeholder engagement.

Globalization changes the dynamics of a project and adds a layer of complexity that can adversely affect the project outcome if the project participants are not aware

of what they might encounter regarding cultural differences and multinational economic transactions. Factors external to the project itself, or to the project or customer organizations, can create a dynamic and perhaps unstable environment over the life of the project, introduce sources of risk, and affect the success of the projects. Global projects can be multinational and multilingual, with participants who are located in various countries and who speak different languages. Technology (for example, computers, Internet access) enables project participants to be just a mouse-click away, despite being thousands of miles apart physically. Global project management requires an additional set of competencies. Cultural awareness and sensitivity are not only important but also imperative for successful global project management. Learning and understanding the culture and customs of other project participants demonstrate respect, help build trust, aid in developing an effective project team, and are critical for successful global project management.

The Project Management Institute is a premier worldwide not-for-profit association for practitioners in the project management profession. It publishes *A Guide to the Project Management Body of Knowledge (PMBOK® Guide)*, which provides a framework of processes and guidelines for the application of project management concepts, practices, and techniques.

The ultimate benefit of implementing project management techniques is having a satisfied customer—whether you are the customer of your own project or a business (contractor) being paid by a customer to perform a project. Completing the full project scope in a quality manner, on time, and within budget provides a great feeling of satisfaction to everyone involved in the project.

QUESTIONS

1. Define project.
2. Define the term project objective, and give some examples.
3. List some examples of resources that are used on a project.
4. What role does a customer have during the project life cycle? Why is it important to satisfy the customer?
5. What aspects of a project might involve some degree of uncertainty? Why?
6. Define scope, schedule, cost, and customer satisfaction. Why are these considered to be constraints?
7. List and describe the main phases of the project life cycle.
8. List and describe the steps required to develop a baseline plan.
9. Why must a manager monitor the progress of a project? What can be done if a project is not proceeding according to plan?
10. Think of a project in which you were involved and identify the stakeholders and what "stake" each had in the project.
11. Describe how a global project can be more complex than a project performed within just one country. How might these elements affect the successful outcome of the global project?
12. List some benefits of using project management techniques.
13. Consider a project in which you are currently involved (or in which you have recently been involved).
 a. Describe the objectives, scope, schedule, cost, and any assumptions made.
 b. Where are you in the project life cycle?

c. Does this project have a baseline plan? If yes, describe it. If not, create it.
d. Are you or is anyone else monitoring the progress of the project? If so, how? If not, how could you do so?
e. Describe some unexpected circumstances that could jeopardize the success of the project.
f. Describe the anticipated benefits of the project.

INTERNET EXERCISES

For the website addresses of the organizations mentioned in these exercises, make an Internet connection and go to www.cengagebrain.com. At the Cengagebrain.com home page, search for the ISBN of your title (from the back cover of your book) using the search box at the top of the page. This will take you to the product page where free companion resources can be found. It is suggested that you save this website in your "Favorites" list for easy access in the future.

1. Using your favorite Web search engine, perform a search for "project management." Be sure to look at video sites during your search; a number of videos related to project management processes and techniques are available online and embedded on websites. Explore at least five of the links that your search produces. Give the Web address for each site and describe what information each site contains.

2. Do several additional Web searches by adding, after the words "project management," some of the key words listed in this chapter. For example, search for "project management objectives," "project management life cycle," "project management process," "project management work breakdown structures," and so on. What did you find?

3. Since it was founded in 1969, the Project Management Institute (PMI) has grown to almost 500,000 members in nearly 200 countries. The Pennsylvania-based PMI is, by far, the leading not-for-profit professional association in the area of project management. It establishes standards, sponsors seminars, develops educational programs, has a professional certification program, and publishes *Project Management Journal* and *PM Network*. Check out the PMI website for information regarding memberships, certification, education, and publications. Describe the benefits of having a membership. Apply for membership online if you are interested (student rates are available).

4. PMI is an international organization with chapters worldwide. Search for PMI Global Congresses and Events. Describe what you find, including upcoming international conferences. Also, explore the link for your local PMI chapter. Print out the information for PMI chapters in your local area. In addition, explore the link for Resources. Browse through the Virtual Library, Research, Publications, and Standards links. *PM Network, PMI Today*, and the *Project Management Journal* are excellent sources of project management information published by PMI. Select an article that interests you, locate it in the library or online, and provide a one-page summary.

5. Executive Planet™ provides valuable tips on business etiquette, customs, and protocol for doing business worldwide. Go to the organization's website and

explore the business culture guides for three different countries. Summarize key points regarding etiquette and customs for each of the three countries.

CASE STUDY 1 A Not-for-Profit Organization

At a local college, the officers of the student community service organization—which collects and buys food and distributes it to people in need—are having their February meeting. Sitting in the meeting room are Beth Smith, the organization's president, and two officers: Rosemary Olsen, vice president, and Steve Andrews, volunteer coordinator. Beth announces, "Our funds are almost exhausted. The demands on the food bank have been increasing. We need to figure out how to get more funds."

"We need to have a fund-raising project," responds Rosemary.

Steve suggests, "Can't we ask the city government if they can increase their allocation of funds to us?"

"They're strained. They may even cut our allocation next year," replies Beth.

"How much do we need to get us through this year?" asks Rosemary.

"About $10,000," answers Beth, "and we are going to start needing that money in about two months."

"We need a lot of things besides money. We need more volunteers, more space for storage, and more food donations," says Steve.

"Well, I guess we can make that all part of the fund-raising project. This is going to be fun!" says Rosemary excitedly.

"This project is growing. We'll never get it done in time," Beth says.

Rosemary responds, "We'll figure it out and get it done. We always do."

"Is a project what we need? What are we going to do next year—another project?" asks Steve. "Besides, we're having a hard time getting volunteers anyway. Maybe we need to think about how we can operate with less money. For example, how can we get more food donations on a regular basis so we won't have to buy as much food?"

Rosemary jumps in. "Great idea! You can work on that while we also try to raise funds. We can't leave any stone unturned."

"Time out," says Beth. "These are all very good ideas, but we have limited funds and volunteers and a growing demand. We need to do something now to make sure we don't have to close our doors in two months. I think we all agree we need to undertake some type of initiative. But I'm not sure we all agree on the objective."

CASE QUESTIONS
1. What are the needs that have been identified?
2. What is the project objective?
3. What assumptions, if any, should be made regarding the project to be undertaken?
4. What are the risks involved in the project?

GROUP ACTIVITY
Contact a local not-for-profit organization in your community. Tell its officers that you are interested in learning about their operations. Ask them to describe a project that they are currently working on. What are the objectives? The constraints? The resources?

If possible, have your team contribute a few hours to the project. Through this process, you will be helping someone in need and learning about a real-world project at the same time. Prepare a report summarizing the project and what you learned from this experience.

CASE STUDY 2 E-Commerce for a Small Supermarket

Matt and Grace own a small supermarket in a rural town with a large and growing elderly population. Because of their remote location, they don't have any competition from the large chain stores. A small private liberal arts college, with about 1,500 students, is also located in the town.

"I think we need a website for our store," Matt tells Grace.

"Why?" asks Grace.

"Everybody has one. It's the wave of the future," responds Matt.

"I'm still not clear, Matt. What would be on our website?" Grace asks.

"Well, for one thing we could have a picture of our market with me and you standing in front of it," says Matt.

"What else?" asks Grace.

Matt answers, "Ah, maybe people could look up stuff and order it through the website. Yeah, those college kids would think that's great; they're into using computers all the time. That will increase our business. They'll buy food from our store rather than the pizza and burgers they always eat or get delivered from Sam's Sub Shop. And those people who live in the senior citizens' apartments would use it, too. I heard they're teaching them how to use computers. And maybe we can even set up a delivery service."

"Hold on," says Grace. "Those college students get pizza and subs from Sam's at all hours of the night, long after we're closed. And I think the senior citizens enjoy getting out. They have a van that brings some of them here each day to shop, and they really don't buy much anyway. And how will they pay for what they order through the website? I'm all for keeping up with things, but I'm not sure this makes sense for our little supermarket, Matt. What would we be trying to accomplish with a website?"

"I just explained it to you, Grace. It's the way all businesses are going. We either keep up with things or we'll be out of business," replies Matt.

"Does this have anything to do with that Chamber of Commerce meeting you went to in Big Falls last week, where you said they had some consultant talking about e-business or something?" asks Grace.

"Yeah, maybe," Matt says. "I think I'll give him a call and tell him to stop by and tell him what I want."

"How much is all this going to cost us, Matt?" asks Grace. "I think we need to think about this some more. You know we are probably going to have to pave the parking lot this summer."

Matt answers, "Don't worry. It'll all work out. Trust me. Our business will increase so much, it'll pay for itself in no time. Besides, it can't cost that much; this consultant probably does these kinds of projects all the time."

CASE QUESTIONS

1. What are the needs that have been identified?
2. What is the project objective?

3. What are some things Matt and Grace should do before they talk with the consultant?
4. What should the consultant tell Matt and Grace?

GROUP ACTIVITY

Select two course participants to use this case script to role-play Matt and Grace in front of the class. Then divide the course participants into groups of three or four to discuss the case questions. Each group must choose a spokesperson to present its responses to the entire class.

OPTIONAL ACTIVITY

Have each course participant contact a business that went "online" and ask the business what led it to that decision and if the project met its initial expectations.

REFERENCES

A Guide to the Project Management Body of Knowledge (PMBOK® Guide) Fifth Edition. Newtown Square, PA: Project Management Institute, 2013.

De Mascia, S. (2013). "Project Psychology: Using Psychological Models and Techniques to Create a Successful Project," *Project Management Journal,* *44*(2), 99.

Hermano, V., A. Lopez-Paredes, N. Martin-Cruz, and J. Pajares (2013). "How to Manage International Development (ID) Projects Successfully. Is the PMD Pro1 Guide Going in the Right Direction?" *International Journal of Project Management, 31,* 22–30.

Kwak, Y. H., J. Waleski, D. Sleeper, and H. Sadatsafavi (2013). "What can we Learn from the Hoover Dam Project that Influenced Modern Project Management?" *International Journal of Project Management,* http://dx.doi.org.ezaccess .libraries.psu.edu/10.1016/j.ijproman.2013.04.002.

Lavagnon, A. I., D. Amadou, and D. Thuillier (2012). "Critical Success Factors for World Bank Projects: An Empirical Investigation," *International Journal of Project Management, 30,* 105–116.

Levinson, M. "Why Project Management Certifications Matter," http://www.cio .com/article/519213/Why_Project_Management_Certifications_Matter. January 20, 2010.

Meng, X. (2012). "The Effect of Relationship Management on Project Performance in Construction," *International Journal of Project Management, 30,* 188–198.

Nag, B., J. Singh and V. M. Tiwari (2012). "Choosing the Appropriate Project Management Structure, Project Financing, Land Acquisition and Contractual Process for Indian Railway Mega-Projects: A Case Study of the Dedicated Freight Corridor Project," *Project, Program & Portfolio Management Journal,* *3*(2), 39–54.

Nash, K. (2012). "Busting up Gangs: A Local Police Force Built a Mobile-data System to Quickly Access the Records Officers Need to Make Arrests," *CIO, 26*(6), 6.

Project Management Institute, Inc., http://www.pmi.org. 2013.

Silvius, G., R. Schipper, J. Planko, J. van den Brink, and A. Köhler (2013). "Sustainability in Project Management," *Project Management Journal, 44*(2), 101.

Tang, L. and Q. Shen (2013). "Factors Affecting Effectiveness and Efficiency of Analyzing Stakeholders' Needs at the Briefing Stage of Public Private Partnership Projects," *International Journal of Project Management, 31*, 513–521.

Vanhoucke, M. (2012). "Measuring the Efficiency of Project Control Using Fictitious and Empirical Project Data," *International Journal of Project Management, 30*, 252–263.

Young, M. (2012). "The Rise and Fall of Project Management: Are We Observing the Birth of a New Discipline," *Journal of Project, Program & Portfolio Management, 3*(1), 58–77.

Zhang, F., J. Zuo, and G. Zillante (2013). "Identification and Evaluation of the Key Social Competencies for Chinese Construction Project Managers," *International Journal of Project Management, 31*, 748–759.

PART 1

Initiating a Project

Concepts in the chapters in this part of the book support the following Project Management Knowledge Areas of *A Guide to the Project Management Body of Knowledge* (*PMBOK® Guide*):

Project Integration Management (Chapter 2)

Project Procurement Management (Chapters 2 and 3)

The initiating phase of the project life cycle involves identifying a need, problem, or opportunity and can result in the sponsor's authorizing a project to address the identified need or solve the problem. Projects are initiated when a need is identified by the sponsor—the people or the organization willing to provide funds to have the need satisfied. The need for projects is often identified as part of an organization's strategic planning process. Organizations may have many projects they would like to pursue, but they may be limited by the amount of available funds. Therefore, organizations need to employ a project selection process. Once projects are selected, they are formally authorized using a document referred to as a project charter. If the organization decides to use external resources (a contractor) to perform the project, it will prepare a document called a request for proposal (RFP). Interested contractors submit proposals to the customer, who then decides which contractor to engage to perform the project and signs an agreement (contract) with the selected contractor.

Chapter **2**

Identifying and Selecting Projects

Discusses how projects are identified, selected, authorized, and outsourced.

Chapter **3**

Developing Project Proposals

Discusses building relationships with customers and explains the development of winning proposals.

CHAPTER 2

Identifying and Selecting Projects

Alexander McClearn/Alamy

Concepts in this chapter support the following Project Management Knowledge Areas of *A Guide to the Project Management Body of Knowledge (PMBOK® Guide)*:

Project Integration Management
Project Procurement Management

REAL WORLD PROJECT MANAGEMENT

Hornet's Nest

Canada's defense system is in need of upgrades in their military aircraft fleet, specifically the CF-18 Hornet fighter fleet. Discussions within Canada's Public Works and Government Services Canada (PWGSC) have been taking place with the Fixed-Wing Search and Rescue (FWSAR) Secretariat and the industry. The FWSAR Secretariat is responsible for the development of the draft request for proposal (RFP) to replace the CF-18s. One difficulty in the RFP development is communication of the requirements, details that are proprietary and classified.

The first CF-18 Hornet fighters were placed into service in October 1982. The aging fleet has interoperability with the U.S. military fighters and other allied forces. In the past, Canada's leadership has selected their military equipment with interoperability in mind in addition to the needs of the military personnel. Stealth and aerial refueling capabilities have been crucial.

The majority of the CF-18 Hornets have one pilot and one engine. Survivability by a lone pilot in the northernmost regions of Canada in the case of emergency is a concern for those deciding what features are needed in the draft RFP. If the single engine were to catch fire or have other problems, the pilot would have to eject in the bitter north. The harsh cold and the lack of shelter would leave the pilot stranded and difficult to rescue in the Arctic. Other potential problems that could cause engine failure endangering the pilot include birdstrikes, damage due to foreign objects, airframe ice ingestion into the engines, or damage from battle. The team is calculating the risks and the benefits of having a second engine and a second pilot.

A plane with two engines and two seats has less range and less stealth. If a larger plane were to be involved in coalition operations, there is the potential the opposition could detect the larger plane before the pilots could identify the opposition. This risk is balanced against the benefits of having a second engine in case of engine failure and the ability to limp back to safety. The second pilot could help with survival in the far north regions.

Another concern for the PWGSC is financial. The government experienced surplus budgets for several decades and has faced budget shortfalls for the last five years. The RFP must reflect all of the priorities for military capability with the safety for the personnel and the funding that is available. The PWGSC and FWSAR Secretariat are systematically approaching a solution to balance the risk of failure with operational cost and range of the aircraft to develop a draft RFP. When the RFP is finalized, a formal competition would be announced. Canada's leadership is working to determine if the replacement of the CF-18s is a project that will be completed. The identification and selection for this project is a hornet's nest, complete with all the problems with and hazards of replacing or not replacing the CF-18 fighter fleet.

Based on information from Majumdar, D. (2013). "Hornets' Nest," *Flight International*, 183, 32–35.

This chapter discusses the initiating phase of the project life cycle. You will become familiar with

- How projects are identified and selected
- A project charter
- Outsourcing projects using a request for proposal
- The proposal solicitation process

Project Identification

Reinforce Your Learning

1. The initiating phase of the project life cycle starts with the recognition of a

_____,

_____,

or

_____.

The initiating phase of the project life cycle starts with recognizing a need, problem, or opportunity for which a project or projects are identified to address the need. Projects are identified in various ways: during an organization's strategic planning, as part of its normal business operations, in response to unexpected events, or as a result of a group of individuals deciding to organize a project to address a particular need.

Business strategies can be driven by the market opportunities, competition, and/or technology. For example, there may be an emerging market opportunity for a project to develop a new educational product for preschool-age children. Or a company that is losing market share to a competitor may need a project to redesign its product in order to incorporate the latest technology and more customer-friendly features. Another business may see a rapidly growing market for its products in Asia, and thus it identifies a project to build a factory in India to meet the demand for its products. Not-for-profit organizations or associations can also define strategies to advance their mission. Based on a survey of its members, a national association may need a project to develop a new website to better serve its members. A philanthropic foundation may want to address a critical health care need in a particular country and therefore identifies a project to build a clinic.

Projects can also be identified as part of a company's normal operational or maintenance needs. As an example, a business needs to reduce its indirect costs and identifies a project to consolidate its office space from several locations into one. In order to reduce the risk of noncompliance with new government regulations, a company identifies a project to install a new wastewater treatment system.

There are circumstances when projects are identified as a result of unexpected events—such as an earthquake that caused the collapse of a bridge—that create the need for a project to be undertaken—in this case, to build a new bridge. Another situation would be if a fire destroyed an elementary school, and projects were needed to determine how to continue to provide instruction for the students and to build a new school.

In some cases, volunteers may come together and decide they want to do a project for a particular reason. It could be to raise funds for a local food bank or to organize a festival to celebrate the anniversary of the town's founding.

Projects are identified in various ways by different organizations. It is important to clearly define the need. This may require gathering data about the need or opportunity to help determine if it is worth pursuing. For example, if a company needs to change the layout of its manufacturing facility to make room for new production equipment that has to be incorporated into the production flow, the manufacturing manager may simply ask one of the supervisors to put together a proposal for "what it's going to take to reconfigure the production line." Or if a business wants to pursue a new market for one of its products, it may first conduct a market assessment or survey. It is important to try to quantify the need to help evaluate whether the expected benefits from implementing a project outweigh the costs or consequences of conducting the project. Once the magnitude of the expected benefit or improvement has been estimated, the organization needs to estimate the cost for a project to implement the improvement. For example, if a business estimates that it could save $100,000 a year by reducing its scrap rate from 5 percent to 1 percent, it might be willing to make an investment of $200,000 for new automated production equipment, thus breaking even after two years of operation. However, the business may not be willing to spend $500,000 for a solution. Businesses have a limited amount of funds available and, therefore, usually want to spend those funds on projects that will provide the greatest return on investment or overall benefit.

Sometimes organizations identify several or many needs but have limited funds and people available to pursue potential projects to address all of those needs. In such cases, the company must go through a decision-making process to prioritize and select those projects that will result in the greatest overall benefit.

Project Selection

Project selection involves evaluating potential projects, and then deciding which of these should move forward to be implemented. The benefits and consequences, advantages and disadvantages, plusses and minuses of each project need to be considered and evaluated. They can be quantitative and qualitative, tangible and intangible. Quantitative benefits could be financial, such as an increase in sales or a reduction in costs. There also may be intangible benefits associated with a project, such as improving the company's public image or employee morale. On the other hand, there are quantitative consequences associated with each project, such as the cost required to implement the project or disruption to work throughput while the project is being implemented. Some consequences may be less tangible, such as legal barriers or reaction from a particular advocacy group.

The steps in the project selection process include:

1. *Develop a set of criteria against which the project will be evaluated.* These criteria will be used to evaluate potential projects and support project selection and probably include both quantitative and qualitative factors. For example, if a pharmaceutical company has identified several potential projects to develop new products, it might evaluate each potential project against the following criteria:

 - Alignment with company goals
 - Anticipated sales volume

Reinforce Your Learning

2. Project selection involves _____ potential projects, and then _____ which of these should move forward to be _____ .

- Increase in market share
- Establishment of new markets
- Anticipated retail price
- Investment required
- Estimated manufacturing cost per unit
- Technology development required
- Return on investment
- Human resources impact
- Public reaction
- Competitors' reaction
- Expected time frame
- Regulatory approval
- Risks

Sometimes the potential projects may not all be similar, such as several alternative new products. They could be very different and all compete for a company's limited funds. One project may be to put a new roof on the factory, another to implement a new information system, and a third to develop a new product to replace one that is outdated and for which sales are rapidly declining.

2. *List assumptions* that will be used as the basis for each project. For example, if one project is to build an on-site day care center for children and elderly relatives of company employees, one assumption might be that the company would be able to obtain a bank loan to build such a center.

3. *Gather data and information for each project* to help ensure an intelligent decision regarding project selection. For example, it may be necessary to gather some preliminary financial estimates associated with each project, such as estimated revenue projections and implementation and operating costs. These data may then be analyzed using certain mathematically based financial models so that the projects can be compared on an equal basis. Such financial or economic models can include methodologies used to calculate simple payback, discounted cash flow, net present value, internal rate of return, return on investment, or life cycle costs associated with each project being considered.

 In addition to gathering quantitative data, it may also be necessary to obtain other information regarding each potential project. This could include getting information from various stakeholders who would be affected by the project. These stakeholders could be employees, consumers, or community residents, depending on the specific project. Methods of gathering this information could include surveys, focus groups, interviews, or analysis of available reports. For example, if the projects being considered have to do with introducing several alternative food preparation products into the market, it may be valuable to conduct some focus groups with consumers to determine their needs and preferences. In the case of building an on-site day care center, it may be worthwhile to survey employees to determine how many employees would use the day care center for children or elderly relatives, and how often (all day, second shift, before or after school), ages of children, the health care needs of elderly relatives, and so forth.

4. *Evaluate each project against the criteria.* Once all the data and information have been collected, analyzed, and summarized for each potential project, they should be given to all the individuals who are responsible for

performing the evaluation. It is beneficial to have several individuals involved in the evaluation and selection process in order to get various viewpoints. Each person on the evaluation and selection team or committee should have a different background and experiences to bring to the decision-making process. There may be someone from marketing who knows consumer preferences; someone from finance who knows costs and the company's financial condition; someone from production who understands what process and equipment changes may be needed; someone from research and development who can provide expertise on how much additional technology development may be required; and someone from human resources to represent any impact on the workforce or the community.

Although it may take longer and be more stressful to gain group consensus on project priorities and selection, it will most likely be a better quality decision than if the decision is made by just one individual. Acceptance of the decision will also be greater.

One approach to the evaluation and selection process would be to have the evaluation and selection committee meet to develop a set of evaluation criteria. They may also develop some type of rating system (such as High-Medium-Low, 1 to 5, 1 to 10) against which to rate each potential project against each criterion. Then each committee member should be provided with any data and information that have been collected, analyzed, and summarized. Before the entire committee meets, each member can individually assess the benefits and consequences of each project against the evaluation criteria. This will give each member sufficient time for thoughtful preparation prior to a meeting of the entire committee.

It is advisable to develop a project evaluation form listing the criteria with space for comments and a rating box for each criterion. Each evaluation and selection committee member could then complete a form for each project prior to coming to a meeting of the entire committee. Figure 2.1 is an example of a project evaluation and selection form that is suitable for comparing and selecting among projects that are *similar*, such as if a company is deciding to select one of three potential product development projects for three of its houseware appliance product lines. Which one of the three potential product development projects in Figure 2.1 would you select? When the potential projects are not similar, such a form may not be useful since the evaluation criteria may be different for each project, and it may be difficult to identify a set of criteria that is appropriate for all potential projects being evaluated. An example would be trying to identify common criteria for evaluating and comparing dissimilar projects such as a marketing campaign, a production control system, refurbishing the company's offices, a website, building a new warehouse, and development of a new pharmaceutical product.

In most cases, the project selection will be based on a combination of quantitative evaluation and what each person feels in her or his "gut" based on experience. Although the final decision may be the responsibility of the company owner, president, or department head, having a well-understood evaluation and selection process and a well-rounded committee will increase the chances of making the best decision that will result in the greatest overall benefit.

Once the project selection decision has been made, the next step is for the sponsor to prepare a project charter to authorize moving forward with the project. If it is determined that project work should be outsourced to a contractor or consultant rather than using the organization's own internal resources, then an RFP will also need to be prepared to solicit proposals from potential contractors.

FIGURE 2.1 Project Evaluation and Selection Form

PROJECT EVALUATION AND SELECTION			
EVALUATION CRITERIA	PROJECT A	PROJECT B	PROJECT C
Investment ($)	$700,000	$2,100,000	$1,200,000
Return on Investment	9.1%	18.3%	11.5%
Time to Market	10 months	16 months	12 months
Increase in Market Share	2%	5%	3%
Risk	Low	High	Medium
Chance of Success	High	Medium	High

Comments

Project A: Major competitor already has similar product and may reduce price.
Project B: New technology may not work as expected.
Project C: Product features may not be accepted in some international markets.

Project Charter

Once a project is selected, it is formally authorized using a document referred to as a **project charter**, sometimes called a *project authorization* or *project initiation document*. In this document, the sponsor provides approval to go forward with the project and commits the funding for the project. The project charter also summarizes the key conditions and parameters for the project and establishes the framework for developing a detailed baseline plan for performing the project. The content and format of the charter or authorization is not standard, but varies depending on the company or organization. It usually includes many of the following elements:

Reinforce Your Learning

4. A

is used to formally

a project and
summarize the key

and

for the project.

1. *Project title* should be concise and create a vision for the end result of the project, such as Implement a Customer Relationship Management System, or Install Wind Farm to Support Energy Needs of Bioprocessing Facility in Europe. If there is a concern about confidentiality or proprietary competitive information, a company many give the project a generic title such as Capacity Expansion, or a government military agency may refer to a project as Project 824 for security reasons.
2. *Purpose* summarizes the need and justification for the project. It may reference prior documents regarding the rationale for selecting the project.
3. *Description* provides a high-level description of the project. It may include a description of the major tasks or phases of the project or even a preliminary work breakdown structure delineating the major work items. For a project to develop and launch a new food product, the major work items may be Concept Development, Feasibility Assessment, Ingredients Selection, Preliminary Formulation, Prototype Development, Final Formulation, Produce Sample Lot, Test Market, Final Reformulation, Production, Marketing Support, Training, and Distribution and Logistics. The project charter may reference other more detailed documents that are available regarding key performance requirements, prior studies, and so forth.
4. *Objective* is a statement of what is expected to be *accomplished*—the end product or deliverable. It can indicate the amount of funds authorized for the

project and the expected completion time (either as a specific date or length of time in weeks, months, and so forth). An objective might be to launch a new website in eight months for an amount not to exceed $100,000.

5. *Success criteria or expected benefits* indicate the outcomes or expected quantitative benefits that will result from implementation of the project. They describe the sponsor's expectations regarding measures that will define success for the project. Examples include achieving a sales volume of 500,000 units within 12 months after the launch of a product, reducing the waiting time for patients in the emergency room by 40 percent, reducing annual energy costs by 50 percent after installation of wind farm, or handling 10,000 cases in a new clinic in the first year after it opens.

6. *Funding* indicates the total amount of money the sponsor authorizes for the project. Sometimes the funds are released in stages depending on the progress of the project. For example, a project may be authorized for $2,000,000 with $500,000 released for phase 1 up through preliminary design. Funding for subsequent phases will be based on satisfactory progress and results of prior phases.

7. *Major deliverables* are the major end products or tangible items that are expected to be produced during and at the completion of the performance of the project, such as concept sketches for a new zoo, a website, a simulation of the workflow for the production system in a new motorcycle manufacturing plant, the photos or final text for an annual report, an electronic medical records system, or a promotional video.

8. *Acceptance criteria* describe the quantitative criteria for each major deliverable that the sponsor will use to validate that each deliverable meets certain performance specifications and are the basis for the sponsor's accepting that the deliverable is indeed done correctly and meets the sponsor's expectations. For example, a new production line will achieve 99 percent uptime during a 30-day acceptance test period, an information system will process up to 10,000 transactions per second without any degradation of response time, or the text for a marketing brochure does not exceed 400 words and is written at a fifth-grade reading and comprehension level.

9. *Milestone schedule* is a list of target dates or times (also referred to as *milestone dates*) for the occurrence of key events (also referred to as *milestones*) in the project timetable. For constructing a new office building, the key milestones and their target times might be:

Baseline plan	month 1
Architectural concepts	month 2
Preliminary design and specifications	month 4
Order long lead items	month 5
Final design specifications	month 8
Complete excavation and foundation	month 10
Complete steelwork and concrete work	month 14
Complete exterior	month 16
Complete utilities	month 18
Complete interior	month 20

Complete landscaping	month 20
Complete furnishing	month 22
Move in	month 24

Some projects are segmented into phases. For example, a project to develop and build a website might have the following milestone targets for completion of each phase:

Phase 1 Preliminary design	March 31
Phase 2 Detail design	June 30
Phase 3 Construct website	August 31
Phase 4 Test and accept	September 15

10. *Key assumptions* include those that the project rationale or justification is based on, such as a new medical device will receive approval from the regulatory agency. Or an assumption could be about resources for the project, such as the company will be able to secure financing for the construction project at an interest rate of 5 percent or lower.

11. *Constraints* could include such things as a requirement to complete the project without disrupting the current workflow, or the necessity to outsource a project because the organization does not have the appropriate expertise or capacity to perform the project with its own staff. Another constraint might be that certain project team members will have to obtain a specific level of government security clearance to work on secret portions of the project.

12. *Major risks* identify any risk that the sponsor thinks has a high likelihood of occurrence or a high degree of potential impact that could affect the successful accomplishment of the project objective. As an example, if a project requires the integration of several technologies in a way that has not been done before, there could be a significant risk that it may not work and cause a delay and additional costs to the project because of redesign, or even result in terminating the project.

13. *Approval requirements* define the limits of authority of the project manager, such as the approval of all purchase orders or subcontracts of more than $25,000 require the approval of the board of directors. Approvals may also be required for a project to move from one phase to the next. As an example, at the completion of phase 1, the external contractor must present the results of phase 1 to the sponsor's executive committee and obtain the committee's approval before starting work on phase 2 of the project.

14. *Project manager* is an individual in the organization who has been identified to be the manager for the project. The project manager's initial work is to organize a core team to do the planning for the project. If the project will be outsourced to an external resource (contractor), then the sponsor's project manager will prepare an RFP. It is also not unusual for the sponsor to identify the project manager early in the initiating phase of the project life cycle; the project manager would participate in preparing the project charter.

15. *Reporting requirements* state the frequency and content of project status reports and reviews. For example, the project manager must provide monthly written status reports to the sponsor or have quarterly status review meetings with the sponsor.

16. *Sponsor designee* is the person who the sponsor designates to act on behalf of the project sponsor. The designee is the individual with whom the project manager would communicate and to whom the project manager is accountable. The sponsor may also authorize the designee to sign off on the acceptance of the project deliverables. If a corporation's board of directors sponsors a $10 million project to implement a new financial reporting system, the board may designate the corporation's chief information officer to be its designee to oversee the project on the board's behalf; the project manager would be accountable to this person.

17. *Approval signature and date* indicate that the sponsor has officially or formally authorized the project. Depending on the funding amount of the project, level of risk, or organizational reporting structure, the signature might be that of the company president, marketing director, or manager of the information technology department, for example; or it might be that of a not-for-profit organization's executive director or the deputy secretary of a government agency. The approval date on the project charter is significant because it is considered to be when the clock starts for accomplishing the key milestones by their target dates.

Reinforce Your Learning

5. List at least eight elements that could be included in a project charter.

The project charter is an important document. It not only authorizes going forward with a project but also provides the key conditions and parameters that are the framework for the project manager and team to develop a detailed baseline plan for performing the project. Figure 2.2 shows an example of a project charter.

FIGURE 2.2 Project Charter

Project Charter

Project Title: Create ASTRA Corporation Online University

Purpose: Currently ASTRA Corporation offers and provides education and training programs for its employees that are delivered face-to-face in classroom settings. Online training has been requested by ASTRA employees at the company's six locations in North America and five locations in Europe. This project is authorized to create ASTRA Corporation Online University, an education and training component that will provide online training programs for employees.

Description: ASTRA will issue a request for proposal to select an external contractor to design, develop, deliver, and evaluate the online environment for 20 courses that have been identified as critical information for the majority of ASTRA employees. ASTRA has identified the 20 courses from the current face-to-face course offerings in the corporate training catalog. The language of instruction will be English. Feedback for the initial six courses available online will be evaluated for availability, requirements for synchronous and asynchronous experiences, and effectiveness during the initial three-month pilot. At the conclusion of the six-course pilot, the contractor will provide a written report and a presentation to ASTRA's Vice President for Human Resources of the results of the evaluation and recommended changes for availability, training experience, and effectiveness. The remaining 14 courses will be available online at the conclusion of the pilot. At six months, nine months, and the conclusion of the first year of training offerings, the contractor will present reports of enrollments and course evaluations.

Objective: The objectives of the implementation of the 20 critical courses are twofold:

1. To provide a consistent training message for the courses through the online delivery using the ASTRA course management system; and,

(continued)

FIGURE 2.2 *(continued)*

2. To reduce costs related to providing training for the courses by incorporating Web 2.0 technologies and other appropriate instructional strategies into the course design and removing the requirement of a face-to-face instructor.

Success Criteria or Expected Benefits: The implementation of the courses are expected to reduce the costs of presenting the information for the 20 courses by 26 % in the first year and provide training to all new employees within their probation period and recertification for all other employees once per year.

Funding: The total amount of funds authorized for this project is $200,000 for the design and development of the 20 courses and $25 per enrollment for delivery. The projected enrollments are 15,000 (3,000 employees, 5 courses each).

Major Deliverables: The contractor is to design, develop, deliver, and evaluate 20 online courses; provide written and presented quarterly reports; and provide technical support at all times during the year after the initial pilot.

Acceptance Criteria: The online training environment will meet the ASTRA standards in AOU Publication #7. Training will be in English. The Vice President for Human Resources for ASTRA has the final approval for all courses before they go online.

Milestone Schedule: The project timetable for key milestones in calendar months after the contract is signed with the contractor:

1. Baseline project plan prepared month 1
2. Pilot courses designed month 3
3. Pilot courses developed month 7
4. Evaluation designed month 7
5. Start delivery of six pilot courses month 8
6. Remaining 14 courses designed month 10
7. Complete evaluation of six pilot courses month 11
8. Remaining 14 courses developed month 12
9. Start delivery of remaining courses month 12
10. Evaluation of all courses month 15
11. Evaluation of all courses month 18
12. Evaluation of all courses month 21

Key Assumptions: The contractor will use the course management system already developed and tested by ASTRA Corporation information systems.

Constraints: Courses must present the information within the developed courses selected by ASTRA. Appropriate instructional strategies are to be used for the presentation of the information within the online environments. The ASTRA course management system contains Web 2.0 technologies, quiz mechanisms, calendaring system, video capacity, and participant activity monitoring.

Major Risks: The contractor must sign a nondisclosure agreement to not reveal any proprietary information within the 20 courses to avoid disclosure of processes and practices ASTRA Corporation has developed to have a competitive edge.

Approval Requirements: All courses are to be approved by the ASTRA Vice President for Human Resources at milestones and before their initial offering activation.

(continued)

FIGURE 2.2 *(continued)*

Project Manager: Marie Kerba is the assigned ASTRA project manager and is responsible for the project. She is ASTRA's point of contact with the contractor and will oversee the performance of the contractor.

Reporting Requirements: The ASTRA project manager must prepare written reports and submit them electronically to the ASTRA Vice President for Human Resources one week before the oral presentation. The oral presentation may use electronic presentation techniques from a distance.

Authorized by: Ida Trayna, Vice President for Human Resources **Date:** June 1

It should be noted that not all projects use a project charter. Projects that are informal (not done within a formal business environment) or done in response to an unexpected event may not be appropriate for a project charter. Examples are a home remodeling project, a wedding, organizing a community event, or responding to a natural disaster.

Preparing a Request for Proposal

In some cases, an organization does not have the expertise or staff capacity to plan and perform the project or major portions of the project, and therefore it decides to outsource the work to an external resource (**contractor**). A **request for proposal (RFP)** is a document, prepared by the sponsor/customer, which defines the project requirements and is used to solicit proposals from potential contractors to do the project. A **proposal** is a document that includes a proposed approach, schedule, and budget for meeting the project requirements and accomplishing the project scope.

A good RFP allows contractors to understand what the customer expects so that they can prepare a thorough proposal that will satisfy the customer's requirements at a realistic price. For example, an RFP that simply requests contractors to submit a proposal for building a house is not specific enough. Contractors could not even begin to prepare proposals without information about the kind of house that is wanted. An RFP should be comprehensive and provide sufficiently detailed information so that a contractor or project team can prepare an intelligent proposal that is responsive to the customer's needs.

Reinforce Your Learning

6. What is the purpose of a request for proposal?

Following are some guidelines for drafting a formal RFP to external contractors:

1. *The RFP must state the **project objective** or purpose*, including any rational or background information that may be helpful to contractors so that they can prepare thorough and responsive proposals.
2. *An RFP must provide a **statement of work (SOW)*** that outlines the major tasks the customer wants the contractor or project team to perform to accomplish the project scope and produce all the deliverables. For example, if the RFP is for a house, the contractor needs to know whether he should design and build the entire house, build it according to the customer's design, or include finishing the basement and installing the carpeting. If a customer needs a marketing brochure, the RFP must state whether the contractor is just to design the brochure or design, print, and mail it.
3. *The RFP must include the **customer requirements***, which define functional, operational, and performance *specifications* or *capabilities* that must be met. Requirements cover size, quantity, color, weight, speed, and other physical or operational parameters the contractor's proposed solution must satisfy.

For the marketing brochure, the requirements might be for a trifold self-mailer, printed on card stock in two colors, with a print run of 10,000. Requirements for the house might include an overall size of 3,000 square feet with four bedrooms, two baths, a two-car garage, central air-conditioning, and a fireplace.

Some requirements address performance. If the RFP is for an automated billing and collection system, performance requirements might include the capacity to process 12,000 transactions a day and provisions for special functions such as consolidated multiple invoices for individual customers and automatic generation of second invoices for payments not received within 30 days of the initial invoice.

The requirements may also reference standards and codes that must be used and met.

4. *The RFP should state what* **deliverables** *the customer expects the contractor to provide.* Deliverables are the tangible items that the contractor is to provide during and at the completion of the project. With the brochure example, there might be two deliverables: the concept layout and the 10,000 copies of the brochure. With the billing and collection system, the contractor may be expected to provide the hardware (computers), software, operator manuals (electronic and hardcopies), and training sessions. Deliverables could also include regular progress reports or a final report that the customer requires the contractor to provide.

5. *The RFP should state the* **acceptance criteria** *the customer will use to determine if the project deliverables are completed according to the customer's requirements.* For example, the project contractor will have to run tests on the automated billing and collection system to validate to the customer that it meets the performance requirements before the customer accepts the system and makes the final payment to the contractor.

6. *The RFP should list any customer-supplied items.* For example, the RFP might state that the customer will supply a copy of its logo for use on the brochure. If the RFP is for a piece of automated equipment for testing electronic circuit boards, it may state that the customer will provide a certain quantity of the boards for the contractor to use during factory testing of the equipment before it is shipped to the customer.

7. *The RFP might state the approvals required by the customer.* For example, the housing customer may want to review and approve the plans before construction is started. The brochure customer may want to review and approve the brochure's layout before printing is started.

8. *Some RFPs mention the type of contract the customer intends to use.* It could be a fixed-price contract, in which case the customer will pay the contractor a fixed amount, regardless of how much the work actually costs the contractor. (The contractor accepts the risk of taking a loss.) Or the contract might be for time and materials. In this case, the customer will pay the contractor whatever the actual costs are. For example, if the RFP is to remodel a basement, the RFP might state that the contractor will be paid for the hours expended and the cost of materials.

9. *An RFP might state the payment terms the customer intends to use.* For example, the brochure customer may intend to make one payment at the end of the project. On the other hand, the customer for the house may specify progress payments, based on a percentage of the total price, that are made as

certain milestones are accomplished—25 percent when the foundation is complete, another 25 percent when the framing is complete, and so on, until the entire project is finished.

10. *The RFP should state the **required schedule** for completion of the project and key milestones.* It might state simply that the house must be completed within six months, or it might include a more detailed schedule. For example, the billing and collection system must be designed and developed and a design review meeting conducted within four months of the start of the project; then, the system must be installed and tested within four months of the design review; and, finally, the contractor must provide all system documentation and operator training within one month of the system's installation. In addition to the required project completion date, the RFP may also indicate required dates for key milestones during the project.

11. *The RFP should provide instructions for the format and content of the contractor proposals.* If the customer is going to compare and evaluate proposals from several contractors, it is important that they be consistent in format and content so that a fair evaluation can be made. Instructions might state a required outline or table of contents, the maximum number of pages, specific requirements to provide a detailed breakdown of cost elements, or even the font size and margins for the proposal.

12. *The RFP should indicate the **due date** by which the customer expects potential contractors to submit proposals.* Customers want to receive all proposals by a certain date so that they can compare and evaluate them at the same time. For example, a customer may give potential contractors 30 calendar days from the time the RFP is formally issued to submit a proposal. Customers usually state in the RFP that any proposals submitted after the due date will not be accepted for consideration, because it would be unfair to give some contractors extra time.

13. *An RFP may include the **evaluation criteria**.* These are the criteria that the customer will use to evaluate proposals from competing contractors in order to select the one to perform the project. Criteria might include the following:
 a. The contractor's experience with similar projects. How recently has the contractor completed similar projects? Were they completed within budget and on schedule? Were the customers satisfied?
 b. The technical approach proposed by the contractor. What technology will be used? What type and configuration of computer hardware will be used? What is the design approach for the database? Which software language will be used for developing the management information system?
 c. The schedule. Will the contractor be able to meet or beat the required schedule?
 d. The costs. If the estimate is based on time and materials, are the costs reasonable? Have any items been left out? Does it appear that the contractor has submitted a low cost estimate but will add costs after the project is under way, resulting in final costs that are much higher than the original estimate?

14. *In rare cases, an RFP will indicate the funds the customer has available to spend on the project.* Usually, the customer expects contractors to submit a proposal that meets the requirements in the RFP at the most reasonable cost. In some situations, however, it may be helpful for the customer to indicate a "ballpark" amount to be spent. For example, stating in the RFP that the cost

Reinforce Your Learning

7. What are some elements that may be included in a request for proposal?

of building the house should be about $300,000 would be helpful. Contractors can then submit proposals that are appropriate to that level of funding, rather than submitting proposals for houses that cost far more than the customer has available. Otherwise, all the contractors might submit proposals with prices much higher than the available funding, and the disappointed customer will have to ask all the contractors to resubmit proposals for a less expensive house.

A sample RFP is shown in Figure 2.3. Additional examples of requests for proposals can be found by using a search engine to search the Web for "Request for Proposals."

FIGURE 2.3 Request for Proposal

February 1st
To Whom It May Concern:
AJACKS Information Services Company is seeking proposals from contractors with relevant experience to conduct a market survey of the technical information needs of manufacturing firms nationwide. The objectives of this project are:

1. To determine the technical information needs of manufacturing firms nationwide, and
2. To recommend approaches to promote the purchase and utilization of AJACKS Information Services by such firms.

This project must provide adequate information for AJACKS Information Services Company to determine

- Future information products or services, and
- The best methods for delivering these products or services to its customers.

The contents of this request for proposal (RFP) are to be considered confidential information.

1. **Statement of Work**
 The contractor will perform the following tasks:
 Task 1: Identify Technical Information Needs of Manufacturing Firms
 Conduct a survey of manufacturing firms nationwide to determine their specific needs for external (to their firms) technical information. The assessment should determine the various specific types of technical information needed and the frequency with which each type of information is needed.
 Task 2: Determine the Best Approaches to Promote the Purchase and Utilization of AJACKS Information Services by Businesses
 The survey should include an identification of the firms' perceptions of the most effective direct and indirect marketing approaches that influence the firms' decisions to both purchase and utilize specific services or products, in particular, information services.
2. **Requirements**
 The survey should determine the various specific types of technical information needed and the frequency with which each type of information is needed.
 The survey should identify the current sources for the various types of technical information that are used by manufacturing firms, their frequency of use, and the firms' perception of the value (benefit, cost, accuracy, timeliness) of each source. It should determine the various methods the firms currently use to access these sources of information. The survey should determine the average and range of funds (both internal to the firm and external fees) that firms currently expend for obtaining the various types of technical information.

(continued)

FIGURE 2.3 *(continued)*

The assessment must provide sufficient detail to permit demand-driven product planning by AJACKS Information Services Company. Therefore, it must include: (1) the information content most frequently needed by firms; (2) the applications for which the firms use the information; (3) the persons (title, skill level) responsible for both accessing and utilizing the information; and (4) the channels that firms use to access the various types of information.

AJACKS Information Services Company is interested in developing and delivering products and services that are valued by the users (manufacturing firms). With these interests in mind, the contractor must generate information about which firms (as distinguished by size, sector, location, or other important factors) may benefit most from information products and services or represent the most appropriate markets for such products and services.

The contractor should determine the size of the market for the various types of technical information and determine market sensitivity to price, timeliness, accuracy, and delivery mechanisms for such information. The survey methodology should include both focus groups and mail surveys.

The focus groups should be categorized by major manufacturing sectors and by multisector firm size (large, medium, small).

Based on the results from the focus groups, a draft mail survey questionnaire should be developed and pretested on representative firms. This survey instrument should be finalized after sufficient pretesting.

The contractor should provide a sampling design for the mail survey that is stratified by sector and firm size, is representative of the entire population of manufacturing firms, and is sufficiently large to present the survey results for each stratum at the 90% confidence level.

3. **Deliverables**
 a. A detailed report of the results of Task 1 must be prepared that identifies and analyzes the results for all respondents and also provides detailed analyses (1) for each sector and (2) by firm size. The contractor must provide an electronic copy and 20 hardcopies of the report.

 The database of the survey responses used in the analysis must be delivered in a format suitable for further analysis by AJACKS Information Services Company.
 b. Based on the analyses of Tasks 1 and 2, provide a detailed report of recommendations of the most effective approaches, and associated costs, to promoting technical information services to manufacturing firms with the objective of getting such firms to purchase and use such services. Discuss any differences in approaches based on sector or size of business. The contractor must provide an electronic copy and 20 hardcopies of the report.
 c. Status reports on project progress must be e-mailed to AJACKS Information Services Company on the 15th and 30th of each month. Reports should be brief and focus on progress compared to the contractor's original plan and schedule. These reports should cover activities, milestones achieved, plans for the next month, obstacles encountered or anticipated, and hours and dollars expended. For any work items where progress is behind schedule, a plan must be proposed to complete the project within the original schedule and budget.

4. **Acceptance Criteria**
 Reports identified in items A and B of section 3, Deliverables, must contain all the information mentioned in section 2, Requirements, in order to be accepted by AJACKS Information Services Company. Final payment as stated in section 10, Payment Terms, will not be made until AJACKS is satisfied that reports in items A and B of section 3 are inclusive of all the required information and supporting data and in a format suitable to AJACKS.

5. **Items Supplied by AJACKS Information Services Company**
 AJACKS will provide the contractor with detailed information about its current information services and products, as well as statistical information regarding its current customer base.

(continued)

FIGURE 2.3 *(continued)*

6. **Approvals Required**

 The contractor must obtain the approval of AJACKS for the final version of the survey instrument before it is implemented.

7. **Type of Contract**

 The contract will be for a fixed price for all of the work the contractor proposes to meet all the requirements of this RFP.

8. **Due Date**

 The contractor must submit an electronic copy and five hardcopies of the proposal to AJACKS Information Services Company on or before February 28.

9. **Schedule**

 AJACKS Information Services Company expects to select a contractor by March 30. The required period of performance of this project is six months, from May 1 to October 30. Report identified in item A of section 3, Deliverables must be provided to AJACKS by September 30, and the report identified in item B of section 3, Deliverables, must be provided to AJACKS by October 15.

10. **Payment Terms**

 AJACKS Information Services Company will make payments to the contractor according to the following schedule:

 • 20% of total amount upon approval by AJACKS of the final survey instrument
 • 35% of the total amount when report identified in item A of section 3, Deliverables, is accepted by AJACKS
 • 35% of total amount when report identified in item B of section 3, Deliverables, is accepted by AJACKS
 • 10% of total amount when AJACKS Information Services Company is satisfied that the project is 100% complete and that the contractor has fulfilled all contractual obligations

11. **Proposal Contents**

 As a minimum, the contractor's proposal must include the following:

 a. **Approach**

 A discussion that indicates the contractor clearly understands the RFP and what is expected. Also, a detailed discussion of the contractor's approach to conducting the project and a detailed description of each task and how it will be accomplished.

 b. **Deliverables**

 A description of each deliverable the contractor will provide.

 c. **Schedule**

 A bar chart or network diagram showing the weekly schedule of the detailed tasks to be performed in order to complete the project by the required project finish date.

 d. **Experience**

 A discussion of recent similar projects the contractor has performed, including customer names, addresses, and phone numbers.

 e. **Staffing**

 The names and detailed resumes of the specific individuals who will be assigned to work on the project and highlights of their experience on similar projects.

 f. **Costs**

 The total fixed price must be stated and supported by a detailed breakdown of hours and an hourly cost rate for each person who will be assigned to the project. Additionally, an itemized list of all direct expenses must be included.

(continued)

FIGURE 2.3 *(continued)*

12. Proposal Evaluation Criteria

AJACKS Information Services Company will evaluate all contractor proposals according to the following criteria:

a. **Approach (30%)**

The approach and methodology the contractor proposes to conduct the survey and analyze the results.

b. **Experience (30%)**

The experience of the contractor and the staff assigned to the project in performing similar projects.

c. **Price (30%)**

The fixed price of the contractor's proposal.

d. **Schedule (10%)**

The detail and overall duration of the contractor's proposed schedule to complete the project on or before the required project finish date.

Soliciting Proposals

Once the RFP has been prepared, the customer solicits proposals by notifying potential contractors that the RFP is available. One way for customers to do this is by identifying a selected group of contractors in advance and sending each of them a copy of the RFP. For example, a customer who has prepared an RFP for designing and building a customized piece of automated testing equipment might send it to several well-known companies (contractors) that specialize in producing such equipment. Another approach to soliciting potential contractors is for the customer to provide information on certain websites and in relevant business newspapers that the RFP is available and give instructions on how interested contractors can obtain or download a copy. For example, federal government agencies announce their RFPs on the *Federal Business Opportunities* website.

Business customers and contractors consider the RFP/proposal process to be a competitive situation. Customers should be careful not to provide one or more of the contractors with information that is not provided to all interested contractors. Therefore, during the proposal development phase, customers may not want to answer questions from individual contractors who are preparing proposals for fear of giving those contractors an unfair competitive advantage over other contractors who do not have the same information. Business or government customers may hold a bidders' meeting to explain the RFP and answer questions from interested contractors.

It must be noted that *not all project life cycles include the preparation of a written RFP by a customer and subsequent submittal of proposals from contractors.* Some endeavors move right from the initiating phase where a project is identified and selected into the planning and performing phases of the life cycle. This process bypasses the RFP and proposal steps. For instance, when a company decides to initiate and implement a project to meet a certain need or solve a particular problem, it may use its own staff and project team rather than external contractors. Or when a group of volunteers decides to put on a county-wide weeklong arts festival, the volunteers may elect to do all the work themselves. When an accident victim requires a series of reconstructive surgeries, a

Reinforce Your Learning

8. Care should be taken not to provide

_____ to only some of the _____ that is not provided to all interested contractors because it would give some of them an

_____.

team of surgeons may determine what needs to be done and then plan and perform a series of operations spanning several years. In all these examples, requests for proposals from contractors would not be appropriate.

There are other projects in which requirements are not written down in a formal RFP, but are communicated to several providers or suppliers (contractors). For example, in planning a wedding, the bride and groom may define their requirements for the reception, dinner, flowers, and other items and then shop around to select the providers that most closely match their requirements and budget.

Although projects can be businesslike or informal, they all start with the identification of a need, problem, or opportunity and then proceed to the sponsor defining (in writing or verbally) the scope, requirements, budget, and schedule for what is to be accomplished.

 REAL WORLD PROJECT MANAGEMENT

To Outsource or Not to Outsource

When Elizabeth Linck was hired as a manager for fleet operations, everything was done manually. Imagine the bookkeeping associated with tracking 500 vehicles and pieces of equipment for all a town's departments'—fire, police, public water, parks and recreation, education, and administration—repair, use, maintenance, and fueling. Programs and systems for fleet maintenance, automated fueling, preventative care, and perpetual inventory were implemented as the first projects.

Elizabeth chose these first projects to get the time required for fleet operations under control. Integrated with the maintenance and care were projects to train staff to operate computerized technician workstations and the automated fueling system. Fully automated devices were installed in each vehicle to enhance the automated fueling system. Outcome-based budgeting was built on measurement of key outcomes for the fleet management department. Other projects undertaken were purchasing hybrid vehicles, establishing car pools, constructing a truck washing facility, and complying with environmental rules and regulations.

All these successful projects resulted in repair and service satisfaction ratings of almost 98 percent and membership in the top 15 of the Top 100 Best Fleets award to recognize peak performing public sector fleet operations. Not satisfied, Elizabeth evaluated the fleet department for additional projects. The goal was to do more with less and maximize existing resources. An inventory of the parts room revealed over $300,000 of value. Even though the extensive inventory was available, critical parts had to be ordered for the many different types and ages of the vehicles and equipment. The waiting created downtime and the necessity for redundancy.

Elizabeth and her team completed an analysis to identify the issues and objectives associated with streamlining the parts room operations. Key objectives included increased productivity for operations and technicians, increased on-demand availability of parts, reduced downtime, reduced paperwork, improved monitoring, reduced administration, and eliminated inventory and inventory control (especially obsolete parts). The team asked other fleet managers about their experiences managing and outsourcing parts room operations to establish the feasibility of the project. The costs and the benefits were evaluated to inform their decision about outsourcing.

Timelines for implementation and stakeholders were identified. The team created a communication plan to inform the employees, departments, town officials, and other stakeholders of the project objectives. Details related to the physical inventory, change over, projections and actual costs, emergency coverage, and personnel were the highest concerns for the stakeholders and addressed within the costs and benefits analysis.

After much analysis and communication with stakeholders, Elizabeth developed an RFP to secure a vendor to supply the parts room operations for the fleet management team. To determine if the project to outsource the parts room operations should continue, Elizabeth completed comparison analyses at three months and six months. Continuous analysis was necessary to insure that the vendor maintained the expected averages for the project.

The success of the projects was due to careful costs and benefits analysis, communications with stakeholders, and project selection. Not all projects considered were completed. Those projects deemed feasible resulted in thousands of labor hours redirected to core functions and reduction of administrative paperwork.

Anonymous (2012). "Should the Parts Room Be Outsourced?" *Fleet Maintenance, 17*, 2.

CRITICAL SUCCESS FACTORS

- The need must be clearly defined before preparing a request for proposal (RFP).

- When selecting a project from among several needs or opportunities, the decision should be based on which project will provide the greatest overall benefits compared to its costs and possible consequences.

- Having a well-understood evaluation and selection process and a well-rounded committee will increase the chances of making the best project selection decision.

- Establish quantitative project success criteria or expected benefits.

- A good RFP allows contractors to understand what the customer expects so that they can prepare a thorough proposal that addresses the customer's needs and requirements.

- A request for proposal should include a statement of work, customer requirements, expected deliverables, and the criteria by which the customer will evaluate proposals.

- An RFP should provide instructions for the format and content of contractor proposals so that the customer will be able to make a consistent and fair comparison and evaluation of all the proposals.

- Customers must be careful not to provide information to only some of the contractors because it would give these contractors an unfair competitive advantage in preparing their proposals.

SUMMARY

The initiating phase of the project life cycle starts with recognizing a need, problem, or opportunity for which a project or projects are identified to address the need. Projects are identified in various ways: during an organization's strategic planning, as part of its normal business operations, in response to unexpected events, or as a result of a group of individuals deciding to organize a project to address a particular need.

Sometimes organizations identify several or many needs but have limited funds and people available to pursue potential projects to address all of those needs. In such cases, the company must go through a decision-making process to prioritize and select those projects that will result in the greatest overall benefit.

Project selection involves evaluating potential projects and then deciding which of these should move forward to be implemented. The steps in the project selection process are developing a set of criteria against which the project will be evaluated, listing assumptions about each project, gathering data and information about each project, and evaluating each project against the criteria. Having a well-understood evaluation and selection process and a well-rounded committee will increase the chances of making the best decision that will result in the greatest overall benefit.

Once a project is selected, it is formally authorized using a document referred to as a project charter, sometimes called a project authorization or project initiation document. In this document, the sponsor provides approval to go forward with the project and commits the funding for the project. The project charter also summarizes the key conditions and parameters for the project and establishes the framework for developing a detailed baseline plan for performing the project.

In some cases, an organization does not have the expertise or staff capacity to plan and perform the project or major portions of the project, and therefore decides to have the project done by an external resource (contractor). A request for proposal is a document, prepared by the sponsor/customer, which defines the project requirements and is used to solicit proposals from potential contractors to do the project. A proposal is a document that includes a proposed approach, schedule, and budget for meeting the project requirements and accomplishing the project scope. A good RFP allows contractors to understand what the customer expects so that they can prepare a thorough proposal that will satisfy the customer's requirements at a realistic price.

RFPs may include the project objective or purpose; a statement of work; customer requirements for the functional, operational, and performance specifications or capabilities that must be met; deliverables the customer expects the contractor to provide; acceptance criteria for the deliverables; a list of any customer-supplied items; any approvals the customer requires; the type of contract the customer intends to use; the payment terms; the required schedule for completion of the project; instructions for the format and content of the contractor proposals; the due date by which the customer expects potential contractors to submit proposals; and criteria by which the proposals will be evaluated.

Once the RFP has been prepared, the customer solicits proposals by notifying potential contractors that the RFP is available. Business customers and contractors consider the RFP/proposal process to be a competitive situation. Customers should be careful not to provide one or more contractors with information that is not provided to all interested contractors.

Not all project life cycles include the preparation of a written request for proposal by a customer and subsequent submittal of proposals from contractors. Some endeavors move right from the initiating phase, where a project is identified and selected, into the planning and performing phases of the life cycle.

QUESTIONS

1. Why is it important to do a thorough and detailed job of needs identification?
2. Describe a situation in your life in which you performed needs identification.
3. Why is it important to select the right project before you begin working?
4. Describe how a business selects which projects to work on when there are numerous projects that could be done.
5. Which elements of a project charter would you use to help plan if you have a project that does not require a project charter? Why?
6. Give examples of situations in which a business might develop a request for proposal.
7. Give examples of situations in which an individual might develop a request for proposal.
8. Why is it important for a business to try to quantify the expected benefits of implementing a solution to a problem?
9. What should be contained in a statement of work?
10. What is meant by customer requirements? Why must they be precise?
11. Why would an RFP state the approvals that will be required during the project? Give some examples.
12. Why would a customer give contractors instructions in the RFP to submit their proposals according to a standard format?
13. Develop an RFP for a real-world project such as landscaping the grounds surrounding a nearby business office, building a deck for your house, or holding a big graduation celebration. Be creative in specifying your needs. Feel free to come up with unique ideas for the RFP.

INTERNET EXERCISES

For the website addresses of the organizations mentioned in these exercises, go to "Internet Exercises" at the book's companion website at www.cengagebrain.com. It is suggested that you save this website in your "Favorites" list for easy access in the future.

In order to answer the following questions, perform a search for "Requests for Proposals," using your favorite search engine.

1. Based on the results of your search, find an RFP that has been posted on the Web. What company developed the RFP, and what is the company looking to accomplish?
2. Evaluate the effectiveness of this RFP based on information you have studied in this chapter. Discuss the strengths and weaknesses of the RFP. Are there any items missing from the RFP that should have been included?
3. Download the RFP, and based on what you learned in this chapter, revise it. Highlight the areas you revised. What makes your revised RFP better than the original?
4. Locate a website that provides suggestions for developing RFPs. Compare and contrast this with what was presented in the chapter.
5. Perform a Web search for software systems that can help you develop an RFP. Provide the Web address and a brief summary for three of the systems you found. Download a demo copy of at least one, if possible.

CASE STUDY 1 A Midsize Pharmaceutical Company

Jennifer Childs is the owner and chief executive officer of a midsize global pharmaceutical company with sales offices or manufacturing plants in eight countries. At an October staff meeting she tells her managers that company profits for the year are expected to be $2,000,000 more than anticipated. She tells them she would like to reinvest this additional profit by funding projects within the company that will either increase sales or reduce costs. She asks her three key managers to get together to develop a prioritized list of potential projects and then to meet with her to "sell" her on their ideas. She mentions that they should not assume the funds will be divided equally among the three of them. She also mentions that she is willing to put all of the funds into just one project if it seems appropriate.

Julie Chen, manager of product development, has had a team of scientists working on a new prescription drug. This effort has been taking much longer than expected. She is worried that larger firms are working on a similar prescription drug and that these firms might get it to the marketplace first. Her team has not made any major breakthroughs yet, and some tests are not producing the expected results. She knows this is a risky project but feels that she cannot stop it now. Julie believes the company's long-term growth depends on this new drug, which can be sold worldwide. She has tried to be optimistic at staff meetings about progress on this development project, but she knows that Jennifer is growing impatient and that her peers believe she should have terminated the project after the initial tests were less than promising. Julie would like to use the additional funds to accelerate the development project. She would hire a highly respected scientist from a larger firm and buy more sophisticated laboratory equipment.

Tyler Ripken, manager of production at the firm's largest and oldest manufacturing facility, has been with the company only six months. His early observation is that the production flow is very inefficient. He believes this is the result of poor planning when additions were made to the plant over the years as the company grew. Tyler would like to form several employee teams to implement a better layout of the equipment in the plant. He thinks this would increase plant capacity while reducing costs. When Tyler mentions this idea to some of his supervisors, they remind him that when Jennifer's father ran the business, Jennifer was in charge of production, and she was responsible for the design of the current plant layout. They also remind Tyler that Jennifer is not a fan of using employee teams. She believes production employees are paid to do their jobs, and she expects her managers to be the ones to come up with and implement new ideas.

Jeff Matthews, manager of operations, is responsible for the company's computers and information systems as well as its accounting operations. Jeff believes that the company's computer systems are outdated, and as the business has grown with locations worldwide, the older computer equipment has been unable to handle the volume of transactions. He thinks that a new computer system could keep better track of customer orders, reduce customer complaints, and issue more timely invoices, thus improving cash flow. The employees in Jeff's operation joke about their outdated computer systems and put pressure on Jeff to buy newer equipment. Jennifer has told Jeff in the past that she is not

interested in spending money on new computers just for the sake of having the latest equipment, especially if the current system is working all right. She had suggested that Jeff look into hiring an outside service to do the accounting operations and reduce his own staff. Jeff would like to use this year's excess profits to buy new computers and to hire a computer programmer to upgrade the software to run on the new computers. He feels that this would be cost-effective.

After Jennifer's October staff meeting, Joe Sanchez, manager of marketing, stops by Jennifer's office. He says that although he has not been asked to come up with project ideas for the extra profits, his feeling is that she should forget this project nonsense and just give him a larger budget to hire more sales representatives in several additional countries. "That would increase sales faster than anything else," Joe tells her. "And besides, that's what your father would have done!" Joe is counting on disagreements among the other three managers in establishing priorities. He hopes that if Jennifer sees a lack of consensus, she might give him funds to hire the additional sales representatives.

CASE QUESTIONS
1. How should Jennifer go about making her decision?
2. What kind of additional data or information should she collect?
3. What exactly should Jennifer require the others to submit in the way of proposals?
4. What do you think Jennifer should do with the $2,000,000? In explaining your answer, address the concerns and positions of Julie, Tyler, Jeff, and Joe.

GROUP ACTIVITY
Select five course participants to play the roles of Jennifer, Julie, Tyler, Jeff, and Joe. While Jennifer and Joe leave the room, have Julie, Tyler, and Jeff role-play (preferably in front of the remaining course participants) a meeting in which they discuss their proposed projects and develop a prioritized list to "sell" to Jennifer.

After Jennifer and Joe reenter the room, have all five participants role-play (preferably in front of the class) a meeting with Jennifer in which Julie, Tyler, and Jeff try to sell her on the prioritized list of projects and Joe promotes his agenda.

Discuss what took place. What positions did the players take? How was the final decision made? What was the final decision?

CASE STUDY 2 Transportation Improvements

Polk County is the largest county in the state, yet it is one of the most sparsely populated. The fairly mountainous terrain is home to a number of lakes and forests, which provide great fishing and hunting for many of its residents as well as for visitors. Winters can be pretty rough. Both the average age of its population and the percentage of people over the age of 65 are substantially higher than the state statistics.

The county seat, Mainville, is located in the eastern side of the county. With a population of 15,000, it is the largest town in the county. Most of the people from Mainville work for the hospital, the town school system, the town government, or the Big John's superstore just outside the town limits. The largest employer in the county is the state correctional institution for female offenders located in the southwestern part of the county.

A three-member board of commissioners governs the county. The current members are Commissioners Thomas, Richardson, and Harold, all from remote regions of the county. Each receives a minimal stipend for serving on the board and travel to Mainville once a week for the commissioners' meeting at the county office building. Commissioners Thomas and Harold are retired. Commissioner Richardson lives on the western edge of the county and is a foreman at Ye Olde Saw Mill in the adjacent western county.

JR is the supervisor for the county Transportation Department; he lives in Mainville. Most of the department's budget is used to clear and salt the roads during the long winters, and for minimal maintenance. Until about five years ago, when Mainville resident and state senator Joe Schmooze passed away, the Transportation Department received a special allocation of state funds. JR worked for Joe, the prior supervisor for the county Transportation Department, and they became friends. Joe, after years of being reelected and gaining seniority in the Senate, was named the head of the Transportation Committee. With his position, Joe was able to make sure funds were available each year for Polk County. The new state senator representing Polk County is focused on economic development for the county, not on transportation.

Without the special state allocation, county roads have progressively deteriorated. Several critical projects need to be done: the entrance to Big John's superstore, Elk Mountain Road, and a bridge on County Route 1045. With the budget situation, JR is worried that none of the projects may get done. The commissioners will not be willing to raise taxes, but they may allocate funds from another department's budget to pay for such projects. The final decision is to be made by the commissioners at their September 15 budget meeting.

JR is working with his summer intern, Zachary, a resident of Mainville, to pull together information about each of the projects by August 15. Zachary is starting his senior year as a civil engineering major at the state university this fall. JR is worried if he does not present a good case for at least one of the projects, then the commissioners probably will not fund any of them. He is very concerned that all three are disasters waiting to happen.

"Why don't the commissioners just give you the money for all three projects?" Zachary asked JR.

"I wish it was that simple," replied JR. "They don't want to raise taxes, and even if they did, we are a poor county and the people probably wouldn't have the money to pay any more taxes anyway. They also have other budgets to think about besides just the Transportation Department. I'm sure all the other county departments would like more money, too."

"Zachary, I'm hoping that some of what you learned at that university is going to help you put together what I need—a priority ranking of the three projects and the information on each one to back it up. I know the commissioners are going to ask a lot of questions, and I need to be prepared. If we're lucky, they'll approve the project we recommend. If we don't have a good story to help them with a decision, they may just argue about it and deadlock with no decision. And we won't get any money for any of the projects. Yep, I think this will give you an opportunity to get a different kind of education than you get at the university. Why don't we get together next week, and you can give me your ideas about how you'll tackle this? This may be a bigger job than you think. I want you to work on it full-time for the next two months. This is very important, and I want you to do a thorough job."

Zachary pulled together the following information for the meeting with JR about the three projects. Zachary realized that he had a personal connection to each.

The first project, the entrance to Big John's superstore, is off a two-lane highway at the base of the hill. It is difficult for cars traveling in one direction to see cars traveling in the opposite direction until they come over the crest. This makes it difficult for the cars turning left into the store and for those pulling out of the parking lot. A number of accidents have occurred. Just months ago, Peggy Sue Suite, one of Zachary's best friends from high school, was seriously hurt when a pick-up truck struck her car from behind as she was waiting to turn left into the store's entrance.

The number of cars traveling on the road has increased over the last three years since the store opened. Several residents have raised concerns at the commissioners' meetings in the past. The commissioners just said people have to be careful. JR had approached the store manager about helping to pay for the road improvements to widen the road to add a turning lane or install a traffic light. JR is concerned if something is not done, someone will get killed there eventually. The manager replied, "Big John's superstore has been a good community citizen for the county because it has created jobs, kept its prices low, gave discounts to senior citizens, and donated a percentage of its sales receipts to various charities and fund raisers in the county. We are barely making a profit. If we don't make a profit, corporate headquarters will close it down, and a lot of people will lose their jobs." The manager did sympathize with JR about the highway safety issue.

Zachary also learned that many people go to the store because there are no other shopping malls in the county and that Commissioner Thomas's wife works at the store part time.

The second project is to widen and repair Elk Mountain Road in the northwest part of the county. The winters have taken their toll on the road and left it with large, deep potholes. The increase in unemployment in the county has led to an increase in independent loggers using the road to bring logs from Elk Mountain to several sawmills, including Ye Olde Saw Mill in the adjacent county. The lack of repair over the years and the heavy trucks are causing the road to deteriorate even faster. Both Commissioners Thomas and Richardson have seen the worsening conditions of the road; they use it frequently to go hunting and fishing on Elk Mountain. Each has received an earful of complaints from friends who use the road.

Zachary knows how bad the road is from personal experience. Last week, he had to wire his car's muffler and tailpipe to the frame because the bracket had rusted. While driving up Elk Mountain Road, Zachary was nearly sideswiped by a logging truck that was much bigger than his little car; he was forced off the side of the road. The low-hanging tailpipe and muffler were ripped off Zachary's car as he hit a large pothole.

The third project, County Road 1045, is the main road to the state correctional institution in the southwestern part of the county. Near the prison is a bridge over Crockett Creek that barely passed the last state inspection four years ago. Each spring during the winter thaw, Crockett Creek threatens to wash out the bridge. If the bridge washes out or is closed, the detour would be nearly 15 miles for most of the people who work at the prison.

Commissioner Thomas suggested at a meeting last year, "Let's wait until the bridge washes out and then maybe the state will give the county money to build

a new bridge. Besides, all those people who work at the prison make a lot of money compared to all the retired people on a fixed income." Commissioner Harold, whose daughter is a correctional officer at the prison, was quite angry and got into a shouting match at the meeting with Commissioner Thomas.

Zachary's brother is also a correctional officer at the prison. He has said to Zachary, "It is just a matter of time until Crockett Creek bridge collapses or is washed out. I swear I can feel it shake when I go over it. I just hope that I am not on it or my girlfriend (Commissioner Harold's daughter) isn't on it at the moment it happens."

CASE QUESTIONS

1. What criteria should Zachary use to evaluate the projects?
2. What assumptions should he make?
3. What additional data and information should he gather, and how should he go about gathering the data and information?
4. After he has evaluated each project against the evaluation criteria, how should he decide the priority of the three projects?

GROUP ACTIVITY

Ask each course participant to individually answer the first case question. Then, divide the course participants into groups of three or four to discuss the case questions. Each group must select a spokesperson to present its answers to the entire class.

REFERENCES

A Guide to the Project Management Body of Knowledge (PMBOK® Guide) Fifth Edition. Newtown Square, PA: Project Management Institute, 2013.

Anonymous (2012). "Should the Parts Room Be Outsourced?" *Fleet Maintenance, 17*, 2.

Ballesteros-Pérez, P., M. C. González-Cruz, and A. Cañavate-Grimal (2012). "Mathematical Relationships Between Scoring Parameters in Capped Tendering," *International Journal of Project Management, 30*, 850–862.

Ballesteros-Pérez, P., M. C. González-Cruz, and A. Cañavate-Grimal (2013). "On Competitive Bidding: Scoring and Position Probability Graphs," *International Journal of Project Management, 31*, 434–448.

Ben-David, A., R. Gelbard, and I. Milstein (2012). "Supplier Ranking by Multi-alternative Proposal Analysis for Agile Projects," *International Journal of Project Management, 30*, 723–730.

Boonstra, A. (2013). "How Do Top Managers Support Strategic Information System Projects and Why Do They Sometimes Withhold Support?" *International Journal of Project Management, 31*, 498–512.

Gale, S. F. (2013). "Wind Farms Go the Distance," *PM Network, 27*(4), 10.

Jones, A. (2013). "Marriages Made in Heaven," *E.learning Age, 8*.

Majumdar, D. (2013). "Hornets' Nest," *Flight International, 183*, 32–35.

Overby, S. (2012). "Getting Control Over Spending: The Sporting Goods Unit in Latin America Implemented Cloud-Based Procurement Software in a Multinational Environment. It Wasn't Easy." *CIO, 26*, 5.

Peled, M. and D. Dvir (2012). "Towards a Contingent Approach of Customer Involvement in Defence Projects: An Exploratory Study," *International Journal of Project Management*, *30*, 317–328.

Phelps, M. (2013). "Who's in Charge Here?" *Airport Business*, *27*, 3.

Schachter, D. (2004). "How to Manage the RFP Process," *Information Outlook*, *8*(11), 10–12.

Schuurman, D., B. Baccarne, and P. Mechant (2013). "Open Innovation: A Typology of User Involvement in the Context of the Web 2.0-paradigm," *Communications & Strategies*, *89*, 17–36.

Sweeney, B. (2013). "Megaprojects in Micro Living," *PM Network*, *27*(5), 10–13.

Yogalingam, M. M. (2013, May 17). "Basically It All Boils Down to Decision-Making," *The Business Times*. Retrieved from http://search.proquest.com/docview/1352468009?accountid=13158.

CHAPTER 3

Developing Project Proposals

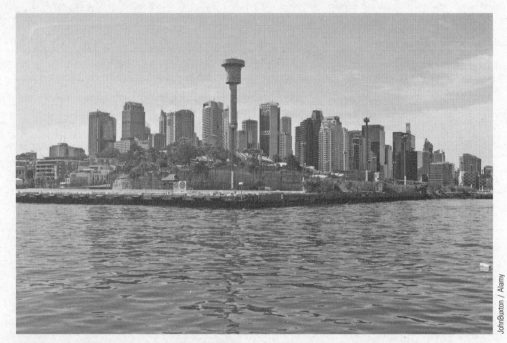

JohnBuxton / Alamy

Concepts in this chapter support the following Project Management Knowledge Areas of
A Guide to the Project Management Body of Knowledge (PMBOK® Guide):

Project Procurement Management

 REAL WORLD PROJECT MANAGEMENT

Sea Green, Redeveloping for Sustainability

To redevelop Barangaroo Harbor in the area of Sydney, New South Wales, Australia,
would be to remove the dismal disused container wharves of the once bustling har-
bor front and transform the area into an urban destination. Started in 2003 with an
expected end date of 2020, bidding opened globally for development rights in 2008.
Sustainability was core to the aesthetic and commercial goals in the proposal

requirements. Development director of Barangaroo Delivery Authority, Phil Paris, stated, "Sustainable designs and initiatives have served as instrumental project components at each delivery stage—environmentally, socially, and economically."

A long analysis period was part of the delay from the project start in 2003 to the global call for proposals in 2008. Phil Paris commented, "Headland Park is not a business-as-usual product, and therefore detailed design studies have been undertaken in relation to how it will be built. We are setting a project culture plan dedicated to ensuring that we create a high-performance team from the top down, with all members being inducted into the culture and understanding the project vision, values, and objectives."

A number of proposals were received and were subjected to a comprehensive review process. Within the proposals were requirements related to finance, risk, design, sustainability, planning and delivery, marketing and promotion, and capability for each of the three aspects of the phased project. Slated to start and end at different times, Headland Park, Barangaroo Central, and Barangaroo South were three major developments within the proposed project. To ensure sustainability, in addition to renewable energy adoption the proposals needed to include a workforce participation program to train workers and apprentices on sustainability and sustainable practices.

Evaluation reduced the competition to two organizations, which were requested to further develop their proposals and display them for public comment. Project spokesperson, Natalie Soltyszewski commented, "Given its scale and importance, Barangaroo has and will continue to attract a variety of opinions and ideas. We welcome those ideas and have a comprehensive engagement program in place to capture them. The public displays of proposals was to share with the community the designs submitted by both proponents."

Once a winning proposed solution is visualized and communicated in the written proposal, the project continues to be evaluated and changes are managed. The proposal is not a final document; it is a continuation of a relationship. One that began in the pre-RFP (request for proposal) stages of a project and lasts through the project completion and follow-up. As a project manager, you will manage relationships with clients and other stakeholders to understand their needs and provide a solution within your project proposal. Maintain a long-term relationship, even if your organization is not chosen to provide the solution. There may be opportunities in the future to propose another solution.

Fretty, P. (2013). "Sea Green," *PM Network, 27(3), 56–59.*

This chapter covers the development of proposals by interested contractors in response to a customer's request for proposal (RFP). A proposal is a document that includes a proposed approach, schedule, and budget for meeting the project requirements and accomplishing the project scope. When the customer decides which contractor to engage to perform the project, the customer and the contractor sign an agreement (contract).

In many situations, an RFP does not involve soliciting competitive proposals from external contractors. For example, suppose company management sees a need to develop new marketing materials (brochures, videos, websites, TV ads, or sample CDs of software) or to reconfigure the office layout. Management may simply ask someone on its own staff or internal team to prepare a proposal that defines what should be done, what company resources would be needed, how much it would cost, and how long it would take. Once the individual or team has prepared the proposal, management can decide whether to go forward with the project, maybe modifying it in the process. Once a decision is made to go forward, the project proceeds directly to the planning and performing phases of the project life cycle: creating a detailed plan for the project and then implementing that plan to accomplish the project objective.

For some projects, there is neither an RFP nor an actual proposal; rather, after the need is identified, the project moves right into the planning and performing phases of the project life cycle. Examples include a project that one or two individuals do by themselves, such as remodeling their basement into a family room, or a project carried out by a volunteer group, such as organizing a fundraising event. You will become familiar with:

- Building relationships with customers and partners
- Proposal marketing strategies
- Decision making to develop a proposal
- Creating winning proposals
- The proposal preparation process
- Elements that may be included in a proposal
- Pricing considerations
- Customer evaluation of proposals
- Types of contracts between the customer and the contractor
- Measuring success of proposal efforts

LEARNING OUTCOMES

After studying this chapter, the learner should be able to:

- Develop relationships with customers and partners
- Decide whether to prepare a proposal in response to a customer's RFP

- Create a credible proposal
- Determine a fair and reasonable price for a proposal
- Discuss how customers evaluate proposals

- Explain types of contracts and various terms and conditions
- Measure the success of proposal efforts

Reinforce Your Learning

1. _____ establish the foundation for successful funding and contract _____.

Building Relationships with Customers and Partners

Customers (clients) and partner organizations prefer to work with people they know and trust.

Relationships establish the foundation for successful funding and contract opportunities. Relationship building requires being proactive and engaged. In many ways, it is a contact sport. It requires getting out of the office and having face to face contact. It cannot be done as effectively through electronic

Reinforce Your Learning

2. Relationship building requires being

and

communications or phone conversations. For example, if you were soliciting proposals from several contractors for a house you wanted them to build, would you make a final decision of which contractor to select based solely on exchanges of electronic messages or phone conversations? Probably not. You would want to meet the contractors face to face.

Contractors should get to know people in potential customer organizations on a personal basis. Relationship building necessitates being a good listener and a good learner. When you are with clients, ask questions and listen. Make the discussion about them, not about you. You will learn more from listening than from telling. Try to learn some personal information about them—where they are from, their career and prior work assignments, where they may have gone to college, their hobbies or interests, their family, and so forth—without seeming intrusive. Look for things that you may have in common: do you know people from the same city or have common interests (sports, gardening, books, children of similar ages, and so forth), or did you attend the same university? You can store this information for later recall in future encounters with them. Start every dialogue by showing a personal interest and making a personal inquiry such as, "How is your daughter's soccer team doing?" or "How is your mother recovering from her hip surgery?" If you show a genuine interest, they will be impressed or flattered that you remembered. Make clients feel good. Empathize with their issues whether they are business or personal. Look for opportunities to congratulate or console them. If they just got married, had a baby, or had a death in their family, send them a card with a handwritten note. If you know that a client has a particular personal or business interest, such as mountain climbing, collecting antiques, the American Civil War, or a technology such as digital media or biofuels, send her any articles you may come across, along with a handwritten note stating, "I thought this might be of interest to you." The personal touch is special and endearing. Sending an electronic message with a link to an article on a website would also be a nice gesture.

Contacts with potential clients should be frequent and not just when there is a current opportunity for funding or just before they will be issuing an RFP. Whenever you are in the city where a client is located, plan ahead to schedule a lunch, or perhaps just stop by the office to say "Hello." If you stop by for an impromptu visit and the client is not available, make sure you leave your business card and a note to let him know that you stopped by. During these lunches or brief encounters, do not just talk all business, but also discuss personal interests that you have in common, such as specific sports, movies, recent vacations, current news events, and so on. However, you may want to avoid some topics, such as politics, which could lead to strong disagreements, unless you get to know the client's views better.

During contacts, do not focus on discussing potential contract opportunities. If you talk too much business or ask too many questions about upcoming RFPs or funding opportunities, the client will know you are just trying to pry information from her. When business is discussed, try to listen and understand the client's needs and determine if you or your organization can help the client organization achieve its goals and be successful. After meeting with a client, always express your appreciation and thank her for making the time to meet with you. You may want to follow up with a brief electronic message saying thanks. Offer to provide any help or information the client may need, or extend an invitation to visit you and your organization. Leave the door open for continuing the dialogue and developing a stronger relationship.

Establishing and building trust is key to developing effective and successful relationships with clients and partners. One way to foster this is to always keep your word; be reliable and responsive. If you tell a client that you will send him particular information by the end of the week, make sure you do it. Deliver on what you promise, but make realistic promises.

Ethical behavior in dealing with clients and partners is also imperative for building trust. Nothing can sour a business relationship faster than doing or saying something that the client may perceive as unethical. In encounters with clients and partners, do not do anything that would give the impression that you are trying to get away with something or acting shady or under- handed. Do not exaggerate or stretch the truth. Be fair and always do the right thing. Do not be nosy or try to pry insider or confidential information from them. For example, do not ask a client about the detailed budget for a recent contract that the client awarded to one of your competitors. Similarly, if the client asks you for information that is confidential, you should tell her that you cannot divulge it; she will respect you for being honest and truthful, and it will build her trust in you. Do not pass along gossip, rumors, or hearsay and then tell the client that she should keep it confidential or not tell anyone else. You are asking her to do something that you yourself could not do—keep a secret—and the client will lose trust in you. Also do not make negative com- ments about other people or organizations, even if the client does; do not join the feeding frenzy.

The first impression you make on a client is pivotal to developing a continu- ing and fruitful relationship. Make direct eye contact and exhibit a positive, friendly, courteous, respectful, and professional demeanor and behavior in the ensuing interaction or discussion. It is important to control your emotions and be tactful and not confrontational in discussions with clients. Do not make quick knee-jerk responses that you may regret later. It is better to sleep on a contradictory issue and provide a more thoughtful response the next day. Learn to guide the conversations with the client by knowing when to keep quiet, when not to respond, when to give your opinion (or not to give it pre- maturely), and when to change the topic of discussion. If you prematurely respond to a client's comment before he is finished with it, your response can be totally off-base from where he was going with his comments. Also be careful and sensitive to making, or responding to, comments or jokes that may be inappropriate. For example, telling a joke about a person of a certain religious faith or about a person with a certain disability or an off-color remark about the opposite gender may strike a discord with the client and could end the rela- tionship, closing your firm out of future business opportunities with that client. Avoid foul language, slang, and jargon.

Maintain a positive and can-do attitude in your dealings with clients and part- ners. Do not be negative and dwell on why things will not work or cannot be done. Rather, try to suggest creative approaches of how things can be done. Cli- ents want to work with people who can solve problems, not with those who merely identify them.

Build credibility based on performance. Do not just say you can deliver; prove it. Go the extra mile, make the extra effort, and exceed expectations.

Always put the client first. Clients want to be confident that any projects they do with a contractor will be successful, involve a good working relationship with the contractor, and help the clients achieve their business goals.

Reinforce Your Learning

3. Establishing and building

is key to developing

and successful

_____.

Reinforce Your Learning

4. Building effective and successful relationships takes

and

_____ .

It is advisable not to rely on a good relationship with just one individual in a client or partner organization, but rather to build relationships with several key people, because key individuals may leave and others may become more influential.

Building effective and successful relationships takes time and work; it does not happen overnight.

Pre-RFP/Proposal Marketing

Contractors whose livelihood depends on creating winning proposals in response to business or government RFPs should not wait until formal RFP solicitations are announced by customers before starting to develop proposals. Rather, such contractors need to develop relationships with potential customers long before the customers prepare an RFP.

Reinforce Your Learning

5. Contractors need to

with potential customers long

customers prepare an RFP.

Contractors should maintain frequent contacts with past and current customers and initiate contacts with potential customers. During these contacts, contractors should help customers identify areas in which they might benefit from the implementation of projects that address needs, problems, or opportunities. Working closely with a potential customer puts a contractor in a better position to be selected eventually as the winning contractor when the customer does issue an RFP. A contractor who is familiar with a customer's needs, requirements, and expectations can prepare a more clearly focused proposal in response to the customer's RFP. These pre-RFP or preproposal efforts by a contractor are considered marketing or business development and are performed at no cost to the customer. The payoff to the contractor for these efforts is expected to come later—when the contractor is selected as the winning contractor in response to the customer's RFP.

During this pre-RFP/proposal activity, the contractor should learn as much as possible about the customer's needs, problems, and decision-making process. The contractor should ask the customer for information, data, and documentation about the identified need or problem. The contractor may then develop some preproposal concepts or approaches and present them to or review them with the customer. By getting the customer's reactions to such concepts, the contractor can begin to understand and clarify what the customer expects, as well as develop a responsive and favorable image in the eyes of the customer. The contractor may invite the customer to visit another of the contractor's clients who had a similar need or problem for which the contractor proposed and implemented a successful solution. Such a visit can enhance the contractor's reputation with the customer.

Reinforce Your Learning

6. What is the outcome of a successful pre-RFP/ proposal marketing effort?

In some cases, the contractor may prepare an *unsolicited proposal* and present it to the customer. If the customer is confident that the proposal will address their need or solve their problem at a reasonable cost, the customer may simply negotiate a contract with the contractor to implement the proposed project, thus eliminating the preparation of an RFP and the subsequent competitive proposal process. By doing a good job in pre-RFP/proposal marketing, the contractor may obtain a contract from a customer without having to compete with other contractors.

Whether the goal is winning a competitive RFP or obtaining a noncompetitive contract from a customer, *a contractor's pre-RFP/proposal efforts are crucial to establishing the foundation for eventually winning a contract from the customer.*

Decision to Develop a Proposal

Because the development and preparation of a proposal takes time and can be costly, contractors interested in submitting a proposal in response to an RFP must be realistic about the probability of being selected as the winning contractor. Evaluation by a contractor of whether to go forward with the preparation of a proposal is sometimes referred to as the **bid/no-bid decision**. A contractor might consider the following factors in deciding whether to develop a proposal in response to an RFP:

1. *Competition.* Which other contractors might also submit a proposal in response to the RFP? Do any of these contractors have a competitive advantage, because of either pre-RFP marketing efforts or their previous work for or reputation with the customer?

2. *Risk.* Is there a risk that the project will be unsuccessful—technically or financially? For example, are there too many uncertainties regarding the technological feasibility of developing an integrated electronic circuit that will meet the customer's requirements? Or, does the customer want contractors to submit a proposal based on a fixed-price contract for a project that involves a research and development effort with only a 50 percent chance of technical success?

3. *Mission.* Is the proposed project consistent with the contractor's business mission? For example, if a contractor's business is to develop and implement automated systems for business-oriented applications, such as accounting, order tracking, or financial reporting, developing an automated system for monitoring, testing, and controlling a chemical process for a pharmaceutical company would not be within this contractor's business mission.

4. *Extension of capabilities.* Would the proposed project provide the contractor with an opportunity to extend and enhance its capabilities? For example, if a contractor has been providing automated inventory control systems to individual food markets, an RFP to provide an integrated inventory control system for a supermarket chain of 10 stores might provide the contractor with an opportunity to extend its capabilities and expand its business to a larger customer base.

5. *Reputation.* Has the contractor successfully completed projects for the same customer in the past, or were there problems that left the customer dissatisfied? Has the contractor unsuccessfully bid on RFPs from the customer in the past?

6. *Customer funds.* Does the customer really have funds available to go forward with the project? Or is the customer on a "fishing expedition"—issuing an RFP although unsure whether the project will ever be funded? A customer may issue an RFP with the best of intentions but do so prematurely, anticipating that the board of directors will approve funding. However, if the company is having financial difficulties, the board may decide to postpone the project indefinitely, even after proposals have been received from interested contractors. Good pre-RFP marketing by the contractor will help to determine the viability of a project. Contractors should not spend time responding to RFPs by developing proposals for projects that probably will not be funded.

7. *Proposal resources.* Are appropriate resources available to prepare a quality proposal? It is not enough for a contractor to just prepare a proposal. It is imperative that the proposal be of sufficient quality to have a good chance

of winning. To prepare a quality proposal, a contractor must have the appropriate people—that is, resources—to work on it. If the contractor's organization does not have the right resources available to prepare a quality proposal, the contractor should make arrangements to secure other resources to ensure the best possible proposal. A contractor should not use inappropriate resources to prepare a proposal just for the sake of submitting a proposal. Submitting a poor quality proposal can leave the customer with a negative impression, which can hurt the contractor's chances of winning future contracts from that customer.

8. *Project resources.* Are appropriate resources available to perform the project if the contractor is selected as the winner? Contractors need to be sure that the appropriate individuals within their organization will be available to work on the project. If, after being awarded the contract, the contractor discovers that the team must be made up of individuals other than those originally planned for the project, the chances of successfully completing the project may diminish. The result could be a dissatisfied customer who will not ask the contractor to respond to future RFPs. If a contractor is not sure that it has the resources to perform the project, it must have a plan for securing the resources needed to perform the project successfully (such as hiring new people, outsourcing some work elements to subcontractors, or partnering with other contractors).

Reinforce Your Learning

7. What are some factors that a contractor should consider when deciding whether to respond to an RFP?

Reinforce Your Learning

8. Contractors need to be

about their ability to prepare proposals and about the

of winning the contract.

Contractors need to be realistic about their ability to prepare proposals and about the probability of winning the contract. The proposal selection process is competitive—the customer will select one winner from among competing proposals. For a contractor, success is winning the contract, not merely submitting a proposal. Submitting a lot of nonwinning proposals in response to RFPs can hurt a contractor's reputation. So, although it is often the right thing to do, sometimes the hardest thing for a contractor to do is to decide to *no-bid* an RFP.

Figure 3.1 is an example of a bid/no-bid checklist that a contractor might use in deciding whether to submit a proposal in response to an RFP. Such a checklist might be used by the decision makers in the contractor's organization to reach a consensus. The checklist in Figure 3.1 illustrates the consensus of key individuals from a training consulting firm. It summarizes their deliberations over whether to bid on an RFP from ACE Manufacturing, Inc. to conduct a substantial supervisory training program for employees at seven plant locations nationwide. Do you think they should submit a proposal to ACE?

Creating a Winning Proposal

It is important to remember that *the proposal process is competitive*. A customer uses an RFP to solicit competing proposals from contractors. Each contractor, therefore, must keep in mind that its proposal will be competing with other contractors' proposals to be selected by the customer as the winner. Submitting a proposal that meets the customer's statement of work and requirements in the RFP is not sufficient to guarantee selection as the winning contractor. Many or all of the proposals will likely meet the requirements. The customer will select the one that it expects will provide the best value.

FIGURE 3.1 Bid/No-Bid Checklist

Bid/No-Bid Checklist		
Project Title: Supervisory Training Program		
Customer: ACE Manufacturing, Inc. Due Date: 5/31		
Score each factor as High (H), Medium (M), or Low (L)		
Factor	**Score**	**Comments**
1. Competition	H	Local university has been providing most of the training to ACE in the past
2. Risk	L	Requirements in RFP are well defined
3. Consistent with our mission	H	Training is our business
4. Opportunity to extend our capabilities	H	Some tasks require videoconferencing, which we haven't done before
5. Reputation with customer	L	Have not done any training for ACE before
6. Availability of funds	H	ACE has funds budgeted to implement the training
7. Resources available to prepare quality proposal	M	Lynn will have to reschedule her vacation. Will probably need to work over Memorial Day weekend to finish proposal
8. Resources available to perform project	M	Will have to hire subcontractors for several specific training topics

Our advantages, strengths, or distinct capabilities:

• Good track record in supervisory training—we have many repeat customers
• More flexible than local university in meeting ACE's need for on-site training during 2nd and 3rd shift operations

Our weaknesses:

• Most of our customers have been in the service sector, such as hospitals. ACE is a manufacturer
• President of ACE is a graduate of local university and a large contributor to it

A *proposal is a selling document*; it is not a technical report. In the proposal, the contractor must convince the customer that the contractor

Reinforce Your Learning

9. The proposal process is a

process. A proposal is a

document.

- Understands what the customer is looking for.
- Can carry out the proposed project.
- Will provide the greatest value to the customer.
- Is the best contractor to address the need or solve the problem.
- Will capitalize on its successful experience with previous, related projects.
- Will do the work professionally.
- Will achieve the intended results.
- Will complete the project within budget and on schedule.
- Will satisfy the customer.

In the proposal, the contractor must highlight the unique factors that differentiate it from competing contractors. The proposal must emphasize the benefits to the customer if the customer selects the contractor to perform the project.

Key partners and subcontractors can complement a contractor's expertise. Identifying and including appropriate partners or subcontractors to perform specific key tasks on a proposed project can provide a significant competitive advantage, especially if those organizations have specific technical expertise that is crucial to the project, have an excellent reputation, or perhaps already have good credibility with the customer.

Reinforce Your Learning

10. In a proposal, the contractor must highlight the

factors that

it from

proposals.

Proposals should be written in a simple, concise manner; they should not be wordy or redundant. They should use terminology with which the customer is familiar and avoid abbreviations, acronyms, jargon, and other words that the customer may not know or understand. Simple illustrations and graphics should be used when possible. Overly complex illustrations should be avoided; several simple graphics will likely be easier for the customer to understand than one complicated graphic. When a point is made or an approach or concept proposed, it should be supported with logic, rationale, and/or data. Proposals must specifically address the customer's requirements as laid out in the RFP. Proposals written in generalities will cause the customer to question whether the contractor really understands what needs to be done and how to do it. For example, suppose one of the requirements in a customer's RFP is the design of a specialized piece of machinery that will produce 20 parts per minute. A contractor proposal stating that "the machine to be designed will, in fact, produce 20 parts per minute" is more convincing than one stating that "the machinery will be designed to produce the maximum number of parts per minute." The customer will be doubtful about the latter statement because "maximum" could mean something less than 20 parts per minute.

Finally, proposals must be realistic in terms of the proposed scope, cost, and schedule in the eyes of the customer. Proposals that promise too much or are overly optimistic may seem unbelievable and again raise doubt about whether the contractor understands what needs to be done and how to do it.

Proposal Preparation

The preparation of a proposal can be a straightforward task performed by one person, or it can be a resource-intensive effort requiring a team of organizations and individuals with various expertise and skills. In the simple case of designing and printing an annual report, an experienced commercial printer

(the contractor), after meeting with the customer regarding the requirements, may be able to prepare a proposal within a short period of time without involving other individuals. However, in the case where a government agency has issued an RFP for a multimillion-dollar project to design and construct a new regional rapid transit system, each interested contractor may have to assemble a team of many individuals, subcontractors, and/or partners to help develop the proposal. In such situations, the contractor may designate a *proposal manager* who coordinates the efforts of the proposal team to ensure that a consistent, comprehensive proposal is prepared by the due date stated in the RFP.

Developing a comprehensive proposal for a large project should be treated as a project in itself; thus, the proposal manager needs to meet with the proposal team to develop a schedule for completing the proposal by the customer's due date. The schedule should include the dates by which various individuals will have drafts of their assigned portions of the proposal, dates for conducting reviews with appropriate people on the proposal team, and the date on which the proposal will be finalized. The proposal schedule must allow time for review and approval by management within the contractor's organization. Time must also be provided for preparing any graphic illustrations, typing, copying, and delivery of the proposal to the customer, who may be hundreds of miles away from the contractor.

Proposals in response to RFPs for very large technical projects can be multivolume documents that include engineering drawings and hundreds of pages of text. And, yes, such proposals are often due within 30 calendar days of the RFP's issuance! Contractors who bid on such large projects usually do pre-RFP marketing, and so they may have a draft proposal prepared before the customer even issues a formal RFP. In such cases, during the 30-day response period, the contractor can first revise the draft proposal to incorporate any unanticipated requirements and then use any remaining time to "package" a first-class professional proposal.

Customers do not pay contractors to prepare proposals. Contractors absorb such costs as normal marketing costs of doing business, in anticipation of winning contracts and making profits on them.

As stated previously, a proposal is a selling document, not a technical report. It may consist of several pages or several volumes, containing hundreds of pages, illustrations, and tabulations. A proposal should contain sufficient detail to convince the customer that the contractor will provide the best value to the customer. Too much detail in a proposal, however, may overwhelm the customer and needlessly increase the proposal preparation costs for the contractor.

Proposal Contents

Proposals are often organized into three sections: technical, management, and cost. For large proposals, these sections could comprise three separate volumes. The amount of detail the contractor includes will depend on the complexity of the project and the contents of the RFP. Some RFPs state that contractor proposals that exceed a certain number of pages will not be accepted by the customer. After all, customers are anxious to do an expeditious evaluation of all proposals submitted, and they may not have the time to review a large number of voluminous proposals.

TECHNICAL SECTION

Reinforce Your Learning

11. A proposal should address three topics or contain three sections. What are they?

The objective of the technical section of the contractor proposal is to *convince the customer that the contractor understands the need or problem and can provide the least risky and most beneficial solution.* The technical section should contain the following elements:

1. *Understanding of the need.* The contractor should state its understanding of the customer's problem or need in its own words. The contractor should not merely restate the problem statement that appears in the customer's RFP. This first part of the technical section must show the customer that the contractor thoroughly understands the problem to be solved or the need to be addressed and establish the basis for the solution proposed later in the technical section. The contractor may want to describe, in narrative or graphic form, the customer's current condition. For example, if the problem is a high reject rate from a manufacturing process, the contractor may want to incorporate a flowchart of the customer's current manufacturing process that indicates where the rejects are occurring and what other problems they may be causing, such as production bottlenecks. Customers will feel more confident working with a contractor who, they believe, really understands their need.

2. *Proposed approach or solution.* Some needs lend themselves to a specific proposed solution—for example, an RFP to reconfigure a large office to accommodate 10 percent more people. Other problems, however, do not. A problem may require that an analysis and development task be conducted as part of the proposed project before a specific solution can be described in detail. In such cases, the contractor proposal must describe the approach or methodology that would be used in developing the solution. For example, if an RFP is for a specialized noncontact inspection system to measure certain characteristics of a complexly shaped product made of an advanced material, it would be unrealistic for the customer to expect the contractors to design such a system as part of the proposal itself; rather, such engineering design and development would be done as part of the proposed project. However, in the proposal, the contractor must convince the customer that the approach proposed for designing, developing, and building such a system is logical and realistic and would lead to the contractor supplying a system that would successfully meet the customer's requirements. This part of the technical section might contain the following:

 a. A description of how the contractor would collect, analyze, and evaluate data and information about the need or problem.

 b. A description of the methods that would be used by the contractor to evaluate alternative solutions or further develop the proposed solution to the problem. This portion could include a discussion of various experiments, tests, or physical or computer models the contractor would use or has used on similar projects.

 c. The rationale for the proposed approach or solution. This rationale could be based on experiments previously conducted by the contractor, the contractor's experience in solving similar problems, or a unique patented technology the contractor would use to address the need.

 d. Confirmation that the proposed solution or approach would meet each of the functional, operational, and performance requirements stated in the customer's RFP. For example, if the RFP for the design and construction

of a day care center states that certain furnishings must be at a specific height to accommodate children under 48 inches tall, the proposal must state that the contractor will meet that requirement. Not addressing each of the customer's requirements will raise doubt in the customer's mind about the proposed solution and could hurt a contractor's chances of winning the contract, especially if competing contractors' proposals state that they will meet the requirements.

If the contractor cannot meet a specific customer requirement, that fact should be stated in the contractor proposal. A variation from specified requirements is known as an **exception**. For each exception taken to a customer requirement, the contractor should explain why the requirement will not or cannot be met and propose an alternative. Although contractors should avoid taking exceptions to customer requirements, there may be circumstances where an exception is appropriate. For example, if the customer requires an electric heating system for an office building, the contractor may take exception and show in the proposal that the initial and operating costs for a natural gas heating system would be less expensive for the customer. However, the customer may have very good reasons beyond cost for requiring an electric heating system and may reject proposals that take exception to that requirement.

3. *Benefits to the customer.* The contractor should state how the proposed approach or solution would benefit the customer and achieve the project's success criteria or expected outcomes. Benefits could be quantitative or qualitative and could include cost savings; reduced processing time; reduced inventory; better customer service; less scrap, rejects, or errors; improved safety conditions; more timely information; and reduced maintenance. This portion of the proposal should help convince the customer of the value of the proposed approach compared with proposals the customer may receive from competing contractors.

Reinforce Your Learning

12. What is the objective of the technical section of a proposal?

MANAGEMENT SECTION

The objective of the management section of the contractor proposal is to *convince the customer that the contractor can do the proposed work (the project) and achieve the intended results*. The management section should contain the following elements:

1. *Description of major tasks.* The contractor should define the major tasks that will be performed in carrying out the project and provide a brief description of what each major task includes. It is important that the contractor not merely restate the statement of work that may be included in the customer's RFP. The proposal need not include a lengthy list of detailed activities; such an activity list would be developed during the detailed planning phase, after the contract has been awarded.

2. *Deliverables.* The contractor should include a list of all deliverables (tangible products or items) that will be provided during the project, such as reports, drawings, manuals, and equipment.

3. *Project schedule.* The contractor should provide a schedule for performing the major tasks required to complete the project. The schedule must show that the contractor can complete the project within the time frame stated in the RFP. The task schedule can be given in any one of several formats:

a list of tasks with their estimated start and completion dates; a bar chart, often called a Gantt chart, with the estimated duration of each task represented by a bar along a horizontal timeline; or a network diagram in which the tasks are portrayed graphically, showing the sequence of and the dependent relationships among the tasks.

In addition to the major tasks, the schedule might include dates for other key milestone events such as important review meetings, customer approval activities, and completion of deliverable items such as progress reports, concept sketches, drawings, manuals, databases, or equipment.

4. *Project organization.* The contractor should describe how the work and resources will be organized to perform the project. For large projects involving many people and subcontractors or partners, it may be appropriate to include an organization chart that shows the major project functions along with the name of the specific individual who will be assigned responsibility for each function. Resumes of the key people who will be assigned to the project should be included to convince the customer that their significant related experience will be brought to bear to ensure the project's success. In addition to or in place of an organization chart, the contractor may include a responsibility assignment matrix that lists the major project tasks and designates the individual, organization, or subcontractor responsible for the accomplishing each task.

5. *Related experience.* To help convince the customer that the contractor can do the project, the contractor should provide a list of similar projects it has completed. The contractor should briefly describe each past project and explain how the experience from that project will be helpful in successfully performing the proposed project. The contract dollar value of each project should also be provided to give the customer a sense of the contractor's ability to manage projects the size of the proposed one. The probability of a contractor winning a contract for a $1,000,000 project is not very high if all its previous related experience is on projects of $20,000 or less. For each previous similar project, the contractor might want to include the name, title, and contact information of an individual the current customer could contact to check on the contractor's performance. Reference letters from satisfied customers might also be included. This type of information will be particularly helpful if the contractor has a strong performance record.

Additionally, if key tasks are proposed to be outsourced to subcontractors or partners, the relevant experience of those organizations should also be stated, including why they were selected to be part of the proposed project team. Resumes of their key people might also be included.

6. *Equipment and facilities.* Some projects require the contractor to use or have access to unique equipment or materials, such as high-performance computers, proprietary software, manufacturing equipment, or testing facilities. In these cases, the contractor may want to provide a list of the equipment and special facilities it has, in order to convince the customer that it has the necessary resources.

Reinforce Your Learning

13. What is the objective of the management section of a proposal?

COST SECTION

The objective of the cost section of the contractor proposal is to *convince the customer that the contractor's price for the proposed project is realistic and reasonable.* Often the customer requires the contractor to provide a detailed breakdown

of the various cost elements. However in some cases, the customer may want only the bottom line total price of the project. Some customers also want to see the costs of optional items. For example, a couple who is asking several contractors for proposals for building a house may be looking for the total cost plus costs of options such as landscaping, a deck, a finished basement, a built-in swimming pool, and a fence around the backyard.

The cost section usually consists of tabulations of the contractor's estimated costs of elements such as the following:

1. *Labor.* This portion gives the estimated costs of the various types or classifications of people who are expected to work on the project. It might include the estimated hours and hourly labor rate for each person or classification, such as senior engineer, graphic designer, machinist, programmer, electrician, or painter. The estimated hours must be realistic. If they are too high and have too much "fat" in them, the total estimated costs may be higher than what the customer is willing to pay. On the other hand, if the estimated hours are too low, the contractor may lose money on the project. The hourly labor rate is usually based on the annual salary for each person or the average annual salary for each classification plus an additional percentage to cover employee fringe benefits (health insurance, retirement, and so forth). These salaries are then divided by the number of normal work hours in a year (for example, 40 hours a week times 52 weeks equals 2,080 hours) to determine the hourly labor rate for each person or classification.

2. *Materials.* This portion gives the cost of materials the contractor needs to purchase for the project. For example, the cost of materials for a remodeling project might include lumber, new windows, electrical and plumbing supplies, and carpeting.

3. *Equipment.* Some projects require equipment that must be purchased as part of the project. Equipment can include items such as computers and machinery. For example, a project to construct a clinic would include the purchase of various types of medical equipment. Or a project to upgrade a manufacturing facility may include the purchase of new production machinery. Or an office renovation project might include the purchase of new furniture.

4. *Facilities.* Some projects may require special facilities or additional space for the project team, for security reasons, to store materials, or to build, assemble, and test the project end item (deliverable). If such facilities are required, the estimated cost for renting the space needs to be included.

5. *Subcontractors and consultants.* When contractors do not have the expertise or resources to do certain project tasks, they may outsource some of the work to subcontractors or consultants to perform those tasks. For example, a project to remodel a church basement into a day care center might require that the contractor hire a subcontractor to remove any asbestos and a consultant to provide advice on state regulations and codes for day care facilities. The contractor usually asks the subcontractors and consultants to submit a proposal of work scope and cost for their tasks. The contractor then includes these costs in the overall cost of the project.

6. *Travel.* If travel (other than local travel) is required during the project, the costs of travel such as air fare, lodging, and meals need to be included. The contractor must first estimate the number and duration of trips. For example,

if the customer is a government agency in Washington, DC, and the contractor is in California, the costs associated with travel to Washington for review meetings with the customer need to be included.

7. *Documentation*. Some customers want the contractor to show separately the costs associated with the project documentation deliverables. This would be the cost of printing manuals, drawings, or reports or the cost of producing videos or DVDs, for example.

8. *Overhead*. Contractors will add a percentage to costs in items 1 through 7 to cover their normal **overhead**—the **indirect costs** of doing business, such as insurance, depreciation, accounting, general management, marketing, and human resources. Of course, in informal projects, such as organization of a town celebration by volunteers, such overhead costs are not applicable.

9. *Escalation*. For large projects that are expected to take several years to complete, the contractor needs to include the costs of escalation in wage rates and materials costs over the duration of the project. For example, for a three-year project, the contractor may want to anticipate a 3 percent wage increase in each of the final two years of the project. If the same project requires that the contractor purchase most of the materials during the third year, the current materials cost estimates may need to be increased by a certain percentage to cover the expected cost of the materials at the time they will be purchased.

10. *Reserve*. Also referred to as **management reserve** or **contingency reserve**, is an amount the contractor may want to include to cover unexpected situations that may come up during the project, such as items that may have been overlooked when the initial project scope was defined, activities that may have to be redone because they may not work the first time (redesigns), or the costs to cover a high probability or high impact risk that may occur.

11. *Profit*. Items 1 through 10 are costs. The contractor must aggregate the cost elements and then add an amount for its desired profit. The total aggregated cost of items 1 through 10 plus the profit is the contractor's **price** for the proposed project.

Reinforce Your Learning

14. What is the objective of the cost section of a proposal?

If possible, it is good practice to have the person who will be responsible for each of the major work tasks estimate the associated costs. This generates a commitment from that person and avoids any bias that may be introduced by having one person estimate all the costs for the entire project. In other cases, the contractor may designate several experienced individuals to estimate the costs for certain groups or types of tasks. If a contractor has performed similar projects in the past and has kept records of the actual costs for various items, these historical data can be used as a guide in estimating costs for the proposed project.

Cost estimates should be reasonable and realistic. They should not be so heavily "padded" that they include reserve funds for every conceivable thing that might come up or go wrong. If cost estimates are overly conservative, the price for the project may be more than the customer has authorized for the project or higher than that of competing contractors. On the other hand, if the estimated costs are overly optimistic and some unexpected expenditures arise, the contractor is likely to either lose money (on a fixed-price contract) or have to suffer the embarrassment of going back to the customer to request additional funds to cover cost overruns.

Reinforce Your Learning

15. What elements might each of the three sections of a proposal contain?

Pricing Considerations

When contractors prepare a proposal, they are generally competing with other contractors to win a contract. Therefore, they need to be careful not to overprice the proposed project, or the customer may select a lower-priced contractor. However, contractors must be equally careful not to underprice the proposed project; otherwise, they may lose money rather than making a profit or may have to request additional funds from the customer, which could be embarrassing and hurt the contractor's reputation.

The contractor must consider the following items when determining the price for the proposed project:

1. *Reliability of the cost estimates.* Does the contractor have confidence that the total cost of the proposed project is complete and accurate? The contractor should take the time to think through the project and estimate costs at a detailed level, rather than making a ballpark estimate. Ideally the costs should be based on a recent similar project or, in the case of materials costs, on current price lists, catalogues, or quotations. It may be advisable to ask experienced individuals or specialists to help estimate the labor effort. In general, the more detailed the cost estimates, the better.

2. *Risk.* If the proposed project involves an endeavor that has not been undertaken before, such as a research and development project to come up with a drug to control a disease, it may be necessary to include a large amount of management or contingency reserve funds.

3. *Value of the project to the contractor.* There may be situations in which the contractor is willing to live with a tight or low price. For example, if the contractor has few other projects, it may need to lay off workers unless new contracts are obtained. In such a case, the contractor may include a smaller than normal profit to increase the chances of winning the contract and avoid having to lay off people. Another example of a project that may be particularly valuable to the contractor is a project that provides an opportunity to extend capabilities or expand into new types of projects. For example, a building contractor who has been doing only remodeling projects may want to get into building complete houses and be willing to make a smaller profit in order to gain entry into the market and establish a reputation.

4. *Customer's budget.* A contractor who knows how much money the customer has budgeted for a project should not submit a price that exceeds what the customer has available. This is where good pre-RFP marketing is important. By helping a potential customer identify a need or submitting an unsolicited proposal with estimated costs, a contractor can help the customer determine a budget for the project. Then, if the customer issues a competitive RFP (and does not disclose the amount budgeted for the project), the contractor with the customer budget "intelligence" information may be in a better position to submit a proposal with an acceptable price than are contractors who have not done similar homework.

5. *Competition.* If many contractors are expected to submit proposals in response to a *customer* RFP or if some competing contractors are hungry for work, it may be necessary to submit a price that includes only a small profit in order to increase the chances of winning the contract.

Reinforce Your Learning

16. What are some items a contractor needs to consider when determining a price for a proposed project?

Simplified Project Proposal

Large, complex megadollar projects that are outsourced by customers using an RFP result in contractors preparing and submitting comprehensive proposals that can be voluminous and detailed and include much of the information discussed in the previous section (Proposal Contents). However, many smaller or less complex projects may not require such extensive proposals. In other cases, contractors may even submit an unsolicited proposal prior to the customer's preparation of an RFP. In both of these situations, a simplified or basic proposal may be appropriate and sufficient. Such a proposal should include the following elements as a minimum:

1. *Statement of customer's need.* This should clearly describe the contractor's understanding of the customer's need or problem and reference any information or data to support the need. For example, if the customer has a need to expand by building a retail outlet in a certain geographic region, the contractor may reference some data on the emerging trends for such a retail outlet or the demographic data for the region where the store will be located. This will demonstrate to the customer that the contractor has made the effort to gather background data relative to the customer's need. In this section of the proposal, the contractor should try to quantify the customer's current condition or opportunity in order to establish a baseline for measuring project success.

2. *Assumptions.* Sometimes the customer may not provide certain information in defining their need, may be unintentionally ambiguous about an item, or perhaps may not even address an issue at all that the contractor thinks is significant and necessary to performing the project successfully. In such instances, it is appropriate for the contractor to state any assumptions that may affect the contractor's scope, schedule, or price. An example might be that the customer would accept upgrading the user interface of all workstations from the current keypads to touch screen technology. Another case may be an assumption that all work regarding reconfiguring office space would be done on weekends to minimize disruption to workflow during normal work hours. Listing assumptions can also be a way for the contractor to address topics that might make its proposal more competitive than that of another contractor.

3. *Project scope.* This should describe the contractor's approach to addressing the customer's need or solving the problem, define specifically what major tasks the contractor proposes to do, and outline how the contractor expects the customer to be involved throughout the project. This is the critical section of the proposal. It should be in sufficient detail to convince the customer that the contractor has a well-thought-out approach that is feasible, is practical, and will be successful. It should highlight the unique features of the contractor's approach and how they will benefit the customer. An example is the contractor's stating that it will incorporate a unique design technique or use proprietary materials that will result in significantly lower life cycle costs for the new system. Or it may be the contractor's mentioning how it will capitalize on its knowledge gained from successfully completing similar projects in the last five years.

4. *Deliverables.* The contractor must list all the tangible products or items it will provide to the customer during the performance of the project. Depending on the project, these can include such items as progress reports, concept designs, prototypes or mock-ups, specifications, reports, workbooks, videos, brochures, a website, a database, hardware, a building, furniture, workshops, equipment, and so on. The contractor needs to assure that all deliverables will be done in accordance with the customer's specifications, building codes, or industry standards, and so forth, and that they will pass the customer's acceptance criteria. The more descriptive and quantitative the contractor can be regarding the deliverables, the better it will demonstrate its knowledge and confidence in accomplishing the customer's project objective.

5. *Resources.* This discusses the types of expertise and skills that the contractor will utilize on the project, including any key subcontractors, consultants, or suppliers. This section provides another opportunity for the contractor to state any unique or competitive advantages, such as by highlighting the well-regarded expertise or experience of specific individuals who will be assigned to the project. Other resources to mention might include the availability of unique equipment such as high-precision production equipment to manufacture components that must meet the customer's rigorous specifications or a proprietary environmental testing chamber to perform required acceptance tests. This portion of the proposal is very important because it provides an opportunity for the contractor to persuade the customer that the contractor has the right type of resources available and the project management wherewithal to successfully perform the project, and that an excellent working relationship will be established with the customer that will be based on timely and open communication and avoidance of any unpleasant surprises.

6. *Schedule.* This should include a list of key milestones with their target dates or cycle time from the start of the project. The more detailed it is, the easier it will be for the customer to see the well-thought-out plan. Providing a graphic depiction of the schedule in the form of a network diagram or bar chart could increase the customer's confidence in the contractor's ability to manage the project and provide all the deliverables in accordance with the customer's requirements.

7. *Price.* The contractor needs to indicate the bottom line price to perform the project. It is also important to include a discussion to convince the customer that the price is fair and reasonable for the work the contractor is proposing to do. The emphasis should be on the value provided and not on how low, or "cheap," the price is. For example, the contractor should describe the unique things it brings to the project that add value.

 Sometimes the contractor may suggest several alternatives or options to the customer's basic requirements, and therefore also provide a price for each option or alternative for the customer to consider. An example may be an option to increase the structural strength of a building during construction in order to make it less expensive to add several more floors in the future.

8. *Risks.* If the contractor has concern about any risks that have a high likelihood of occurrence or a high degree of potential impact, then these risks should be pointed out to the customer. This will show the customer that the contractor has experience and a realistic approach to performing the project and wants to avoid surprises. An example of such a risk is that the location where the customer wants to build a child care center has a high likelihood

of large rock formations under the top soil, which may prolong the excavation of the foundation, impact drainage, and affect the cost of the project. Another case may be the customer's requirement to use its existing software language in a project to upgrade its information system, which may create a risk of the system becoming obsolete; this would make the information system more expensive to maintain, and it might be more expensive to hire people with knowledge of the outdated software.

9. *Expected benefits.* This is an important section of the proposal because the contractor can pull together information from the preceding sections and make a case to justify the "value" of its proposal in terms of expected quantitative benefits, such as return on investment, payback, cost savings, an increase in productivity, reduced processing times, faster time-to-market, and so on. This is an excellent way to conclude the proposal on a positive note, emphasize the distinguishing features of the contractor's proposal, and indicate the qualitative and quantitative benefits the customer will obtain if they select the contractor to perform the project.

Reinforce Your Learning

17. The focus of a proposal should be on _____ of the _____ rather than the _____ of pages.

The focus of the proposal should be on quality of the content—clear, concise, and convincing—rather than quantity or number of pages. Many simplified project proposals range from 4 to 8 pages, and they are usually less than 20 pages. It is appropriate to attach appendices for items such as resumes of key people who will be assigned to the project, back-up details for cost estimates, or a list of past related projects and associated references.

Proposal Submission and Follow-Up

The customer's RFP will usually provide instructions regarding the due date by which proposals must be submitted and the name and contact information of the person to whom the proposals should be submitted. Some customers want the contractor to provide an electronic copy and/or several hard copies of the proposal because the proposal will be distributed to various individuals within the customer's organization for review and evaluation. From the customer's point of view, it is easier and less costly to have the contractor make the necessary copies. This is especially true for large projects, where proposals may be several hundred pages and may include large drawings or color graphics. Government agencies are very strict about having proposals submitted on time; those submitted late will not be accepted—and the contractor's efforts will have been wasted. Rather than trust the mail, some contractors hand-deliver proposals to ensure that they arrive on time. Other contractors have been known to send two sets of proposals by different express mail services to ensure that at least one set arrives at its destination on time. Such precautions are usually taken for multimillion-dollar projects or when thousands of hours have been spent in pre-RFP marketing and proposal preparation. Customers may request that proposals be submitted only electronically. This approach can save both the customer and bidding contractors time and costs associated with printing, mailing, and distribution.

Contractors must continue to be proactive even after the proposal is submitted. The contractor should call the customer to confirm that the proposal was received. After several days, the contractor should contact the customer again and ask whether the customer has any questions or needs clarification of

anything in the proposal. Such follow-up needs to be done in a professional manner in order to make a favorable impression on the customer. If the contractor appears aggressive rather than responsive, the customer may view the contractor as an intrusive element trying to influence the proposal evaluation process. A contractor must always consider whether and how aggressively other competing contractors are following up with the customer after proposals have been submitted.

Industrial and, especially, government customers usually do not respond to attempted follow-up communications from contractors so that no contractor gains an unfair advantage in influencing the proposal evaluation process. Such customers will initiate any needed communication. It will usually be in the form of a list of specific questions that need to be answered or points that need to be clarified about a particular contractor's proposal, and it requires a written response from the contractor by a specific date.

Reinforce Your Learning

18. Contractors must continue to be

even after the proposal is submitted.

Customer Evaluation of Proposals

Customers evaluate contractors' proposals in many different ways. Some customers first look at the prices of the various proposals and select, for example, only the three lowest-priced proposals for further evaluation. Other customers initially screen out those proposals with prices above their budget or those whose technical section does not meet all the requirements stated in the RFP. Other customers, especially on large projects, create a proposal review team that uses a scorecard to determine whether each proposal meets all requirements in the RFP and to rate the proposal against predefined evaluation criteria.

Figure 3.2 illustrates a proposal evaluation scorecard. This scorecard was used by AJACKS Information Services Company to review contractor proposals submitted in response to the RFP in Chapter 2 (Figure 2.3). It is an evaluation of a proposal from Galaxy Market Research, Inc. one of five contractors that submitted proposals to AJACKS. Each person on the customer's proposal evaluation team completes a scorecard for each of the contractor proposals. These scorecards are then used by the proposal evaluation team to reach a consensus on which contractor, if any, to select as the winner. The scorecards are not the sole mechanism for evaluating proposals and selecting the winner. They are usually used as input to the decision-making process.

Sometimes the technical and management proposals are evaluated first, without consideration of cost. Those proposals with the highest points on the technical/management review are then evaluated for their costs. The customer weighs the technical/management merit against the costs to determine which proposal offers the best value.

Some of the criteria that might be used by customers in evaluating contractor proposals include the following:

- Compliance with the customer's statement of work and requirements in the RFP.
- Contractor's understanding of the customer's need or problem.
- Soundness and practicality of the contractor's proposed approach to solving the problem.
- Contractor's experience and success with similar projects.
- The experience of key individuals who will be assigned to work on the project.

FIGURE 3.2 **Proposal Evaluation Scorecard**

AJACKS Information Services Company
Proposal Evaluation

Project Title: Technical Information Needs of Manufacturers

Contractor: Galaxy Market Research Inc.

Score all criteria on a scale from 1 (low) to 10 (high)

Evaluation Criteria	Weight A	Score B	Points A x B	Comments
1. Approach	30	4	120	Shallow description of methodology
2. Experience	30	3	90	Little experience with manufacturing firms
3. Price	30	9	270	Lowest price bid Supported by details
4. Schedule	10	5	50	Schedule is overly optimistic
Total	100		530	

Advantages of this proposal:

• This is the lowest price proposal received. It appears the salaries of Galaxy's staff are low compared to those of other proposers.

Concerns about this proposal:

• Galaxy may not fully comprehend the requirements.

• Low salaries in its budget may reflect low levels of experience of the staff Galaxy plans to use.

• Optimistic schedule (3 months) to complete project may indicate Galaxy doesn't fully comprehend the work scope.

- Management capability, including the contractor's ability to plan and control the project to ensure that the work scope is completed within budget and on schedule.
- Realism of the contractor's schedule. Is it realistic, considering the resources the contractor plans to assign to the project? Does it meet the customer's schedule as stated in the RFP? How detailed is the schedule?
- Price. Customers may evaluate not only the contractor's total price for the project but also the detailed costs in the cost section of the proposal. Customers are concerned about the reasonableness, realism, and completeness of the contractor's costs. Did the contractor use sound cost-estimating methodology? Are the labor hours, classifications, and rates appropriate for the type of project? Were any items left out? The customer wants to be sure that a contractor is not "lowballing" the price to win the contract, expecting to come back to the customer for additional funds if the project overruns its proposed cost. It is unethical and may be illegal for contractors to intentionally lowball their price.

In some instances, especially when a large number of proposals are received, the proposal evaluation process will produce a short list of proposals the customer considers to be acceptable and of good value. The customer may then ask each of these contractors to give an oral presentation of its proposal. This provides a final opportunity for each contractor to convince the customer that its proposal will provide the best value. The customer may also ask each of these contractors to submit a **best and final offer (BAFO)** that is a final price from each contractor that the customer will consider. This gives the contractor one last chance to reduce its price and possibly win the contract. However, the customer usually requires the contractor to provide a written rationale for any cost reductions to make sure that they are reasonable. The contractor, for instance, might review the people to be assigned to the project and determine that for some tasks individuals with lower labor cost rates could be used, or the contractor might decide that some travel to meetings could be eliminated by videoconferencing.

Once the customer has selected the winning contractor, the contractor is informed that it is the winner, subject to successful negotiation of a contract.

Contracts

Just because the contractor has been selected as the winner does not mean the contractor can start doing the work. Before the project can proceed, a contract must be signed between the customer and the contractor. It is a vehicle for establishing good customer–contractor communications and arriving at a mutual understanding and clear expectations to ensure project success.

A **contract** is an agreement between the contractor, who agrees to perform the project and to provide a product or service (deliverables), and the customer, who agrees to pay the contractor a certain amount in return. The contract must clearly spell out the deliverables the contractor is expected to provide. For example, a contract will state that the project result will meet certain specifications or that certain documentation will be provided. The contract must also state the terms by which the customer will make payments to the contractor. There are basically two types of contracts: fixed-price and cost-reimbursement.

FIXED-PRICE CONTRACTS

In a **fixed-price contract**, the customer and the contractor agree on a price for the proposed work. The price remains fixed unless the customer and the contractor agree on changes. This type of contract provides low risk for the customer because the customer will not pay more than the fixed price, regardless of how much the project actually costs the contractor. However, a fixed-price contract is high risk for the contractor because if the cost of completing the project is more than originally planned, the contractor will make a lower profit than anticipated or may even lose money.

A contractor bidding on a fixed-price project must develop accurate and complete cost estimates and include sufficient reserves. However, the contractor needs to be careful not to overprice the proposed project, or a competing contractor with a lower price may be selected.

Fixed-price contracts are most appropriate for projects that are well defined and entail little risk. Examples include the construction of a standard model house or the design and production of a brochure for which the customer has provided detailed specifications regarding format, content, photos, color, number of pages, and number of copies.

Reinforce Your Learning

19. A contractor bidding on a fixed-price contract must develop

and

cost estimates and include sufficient

COST-REIMBURSEMENT CONTRACTS

In a **cost-reimbursement contract**, the customer agrees to pay the contractor for all actual costs (labor, materials, and so forth), regardless of amount, plus some agreed-upon profit. This type of contract is high risk for the customer because contractor costs can overrun the proposed price—as when a car repair service provides an estimate for repairing a transmission but presents a final bill that is higher than the original estimate. In cost-reimbursement contracts, the customer usually requires that, throughout the project, the contractor regularly compares actual expenditures with the proposed budget and reforecasts cost at completion, comparing it with the original proposed price. This allows the customer to take action if it looks as if the project will overrun the original proposed budget. This type of contract is low risk for the contractor because all costs will be reimbursed by the customer. The contractor cannot lose money on this type of contract. However, if the contractor's costs do overrun the proposed budget, the contractor's reputation will be hurt, in turn reducing the contractor's chances of winning contracts in the future.

Cost-reimbursement contracts are most appropriate for projects that involve risk. Examples include the development of a new robotics device to assist during surgery or the environmental cleanup of a contaminated site.

Reinforce Your Learning

20. Write the word low or high in each box, depending on the degree of risk for the customer and contractor associated with each type of contract.

	Customer Risk	Contractor Risk
Fixed price		
Cost reimbursement		

CONTRACT TERMS AND CONDITIONS

The following are some miscellaneous terms and conditions that may be included in project contracts:

1. *Misrepresentation of costs.* States that it is illegal for the contractor to overstate the hours or costs expended on the project.
2. *Notice of cost overruns or schedule delays.* Outlines the circumstances under which the contractor must notify the customer immediately of any actual or anticipated cost overruns or schedule delays, submitting in writing both the reason and a plan for corrective action to get the costs back within budget or the schedule back on track.

3. *Approval of subcontractor.* Indicates when the contractor needs to obtain advance approval from the customer before hiring a subcontractor to perform a project task.
4. *Customer-furnished equipment or information.* Lists the items (such as parts for conducting tests) that the customer will provide to the contractor throughout the project and the dates by which the customer will make these items available. This provision protects the contractor from incurring schedule slippage caused by customer delays in furnishing information, parts, or other items.
5. *Patents.* Covers ownership of patents that may result from performing the project.
6. *Disclosure of proprietary information.* Prohibits one party from disclosing confidential information, technologies, or processes utilized by the other party during the project to anyone else or using it for any purpose other than work on the project.
7. *International considerations.* Specifies accommodations that must be made for customers from other countries. Contracts for projects that are done for a foreign customer or are conducted in part in a foreign country may require the contractor to make certain accommodations, such as

 - Observing certain holidays or work rules
 - Spending a certain percentage of the contract costs for labor or materials within the customer's country
 - Providing project documentation, such as manuals, specifications, training materials, and reports, in the customer's language

8. *Termination.* States the conditions under which the customer can terminate the contract, such as nonperformance by the contractor.
9. *Terms of payment.* Addresses the basis on which the customer will make payments to the contractor. Some types of payments are

 - Monthly payments, based on actual costs incurred by the contractor
 - Equal monthly or quarterly payments, based on the expected overall duration of the project schedule
 - Percentages of the total contract amount, paid when the contractor completes predefined milestones or when the customer accepts specific deliverables
 - Single payment at completion of the project

 In some cases, such as when the contractor needs to purchase a significant amount of materials and supplies during the early stages of the project, the customer provides an initial down payment at the start of the contract.

10. *Bonus/penalty payments.* Some contracts have a bonus clause, whereby the customer will pay the contractor a bonus if the project is completed ahead of schedule or exceeds other customer performance requirements. On the other hand, some contracts include a penalty clause, whereby the customer can reduce the final payment to the contractor if the project is not completed on schedule or if performance requirements are not met. Some of these penalties can be substantial, such as 1 percent of the total contract price for each

week the project extends beyond the required project completion date, up to a maximum of 10 percent. A 10-week schedule overrun could wipe out the contractor's profit and cause a loss.

11. *Changes*. Covers the procedure for proposing, approving, and implementing changes to the project scope, schedule, or budget. Changes can be initiated by the customer or be proposed by the contractor. Some changes may necessitate a change in price (increase or decrease); others may not. All changes must be documented and approved by the customer before they are incorporated into the project. Customers usually want the contractor to provide a price estimate, along with an indication of the schedule impact, for a proposed change before they will allow the contractor to implement the change. If a contractor makes changes without the customer's approval or with only verbal approval from someone in the customer's organization who may not be authorized to give it, the contractor runs the risk of being unable to collect payment for the work associated with the changes made.

Measuring Proposal Success

Contractors measure the success of their proposal efforts by the number of times their proposals are selected by customers and/or by the total dollar value of their proposals that are selected. A measure that is often used is known as the **win ratio**, which is the percentage of the number or dollar value of the contractor's proposals that result in contractual agreements with customers. The win ratio can be expressed as the percentage of the number of proposals a contractor won out of the total number of proposals the contractor submitted to various customers over a particular time period. An alternative method of determining the win ratio is to base it on the total dollar value of proposals that the contractor won as a percentage of the total dollar value of all the proposals the contractor submitted to various customers during a specific time period. The former approach gives equal weight to all proposals, whereas the later approach gives more weight to proposals with larger dollar amounts. For example, assume that a contractor submits four different proposals to four different customers in a particular month, for the amounts of $120,000, $50,000, $250,000, and $80,000; however, only one of their proposals, the one valued at $250,000, was selected by a client. The contractor's win ratio based on the number of proposals submitted is 0.25 or 25 percent (1 of 4), but their win ratio based on dollar value is 50 percent ($250,000 of $500,000).

Some contractors have a strategy of submitting proposals in response to as many RFPs as they can with the hope that they will eventually win their fair share. Their philosophy is that if they do not submit a proposal, then they do not have any chance to win, but by submitting more proposals, they increase their chances of winning more contracts. Other contractors are more selective in submitting proposals; they respond to only those RFPs where they think they have a better-than-average chance of winning the contract. These contractors seriously consider the bid/no-bid decision process in responding to RFPs and submit fewer proposals but attempt to have a high win ratio.

Reinforce Your Learning

21. A measure used to determine the success of proposal efforts is known as the

REAL WORLD PROJECT MANAGEMENT

Project Proposals Nurture the Next Big Thing

Projects come in all shapes and sizes. They range from being completed by a small team internally in an organization to externally by large collaborative groups. One aspect, innovation, is a must-have if an organization is to remain competitive in a volatile global economy.

All projects, whether they are research and development for new innovative products or internal projects to an organization, require project proposals and project management. Shibab Kuran, CEO and president of Petra Solar, stated, "The world is full of prototypes, but turning them into business solutions is very challenging. Without proper project management, good ideas will never make it to market."

One company, Associated Bank, in Green Bay, Wisconsin, USA, evaluates every project against the organization's vision statement's four principles: customer focus, innovation, partnering, and value. The first slide of every project proposal demonstrates how the project links to the company's goals and vision. Potential innovative product projects are also assessed for meeting the market's needs.

Execution of a review strategy determines if a project is not up to par and evaluates projects in process for continuation or termination. "Project management isn't free, and some ideas don't deserve to get past the prototype phase," states Paul Williams, PMP, vice president, and technology infrastructure project manager at Associated Bank. "If something isn't going to deliver benefit and you can't fix it, you need to have the courage to kill it. Otherwise it's just going to limp along, taking up valuable resources that could be better used."

A recent Associated Bank project team proposed implementing a "bring your own device" policy to allow employees to use their personal smartphones for work tasks to stay connected. The proposal addressed common concerns for IT—cost and data security—and defined the innovative value proposition related to communications with a focus on customer service and innovation. Solving customer problems during the off-hours has been problematic and costly. The ability to be connected during and after office hours addressed the customer service issues and demonstrated a return on investment by eliminating company-provided technology and its costs.

Implementing innovations is more than coming up with a new idea. Proof of concept and alignment with strategic business goals must be described in every project proposal. Steering committees and proposal review teams determine from the project description in the proposal if the process will manage risks and can achieve the anticipated outcome. Stringent processes in proposal development and management of project implementation are necessary to deliver demonstrable value. Project managers are responsible for shepherding the best innovations to market while ceasing activity on those projects that are not viable. Ultimately, the next big thing starts with an innovative idea and a project proposal.

Gale, S. F. (2013). "Nurturing the Next Big Thing," *PM Network, 27*(3), 28–37.

CRITICAL SUCCESS FACTORS

- Customers and partner organizations prefer to work with people they know and trust. Relationships establish the foundation for successful funding and contract opportunities.

- Establishing and building trust is key to developing effective and successful relationships with clients and partners.

- The first impression one makes on a client is pivotal to developing a continuing and fruitful relationship.

- Pre-RFP/proposal efforts are crucial to establishing the foundation for eventually winning a contract from the customer.

- Do not wait until formal RFP solicitations are announced by customers before starting to develop proposals. Rather, develop relationships with potential customers long before they prepare their RFPs.

- Working closely with a potential customer puts a contractor in a better position to be selected as the winning contractor. Learn as much as possible about the customer's needs, problems, and decision-making process during the pre-RFP/proposal marketing.

- Becoming familiar with the customer's needs, requirements, and expectations will help in preparing a more clearly focused proposal.

- Be realistic about the ability to prepare a quality proposal and about the probability of winning the contract. It is not enough just to prepare a proposal; rather, the proposal must be of sufficient quality to have a chance of winning.

- A proposal is a selling document, not a technical report. It should be written in a simple, concise manner and should use terminology with which the customer is familiar.

- In a proposal, it is important to highlight the unique factors that differentiate it from competitors' proposals.

- Proposals must be realistic. Proposals that promise too much or are overly optimistic may be unbelievable to customers, and may raise doubt about whether the contractor understands what needs to be done or how to do it.

- When bidding on a fixed-price project, the contractor must develop accurate and complete cost estimates and include sufficient reserves.

SUMMARY

Interested contractors develop proposals in response to a customer's request for proposal. When the customer decides which contractor to engage to perform the project, an agreement (contract) is signed by the customer and contractor.

Customers (clients) and partner organizations prefer to work with people they know and trust. Relationships establish the foundation for successful funding and contract opportunities. Relationship building requires being proactive and engaged. Establishing and building trust is key to developing effective and successful relationships with clients and partners. Ethical behavior in dealing with clients and partners is also imperative for building trust. The first impression one makes on a client is pivotal to developing a continuing and fruitful relationship. Building effective and successful relationships takes time and work.

Contractors should develop relationships with potential customers long before customers prepare a request for proposal. Contractors should maintain frequent contacts with past and current customers and initiate contacts with potential customers. During these contacts, contractors should help customers identify areas in which the customers might benefit from the implementation of projects that address needs, problems, or opportunities. These pre-RFP/proposal efforts are crucial to establishing the foundation for eventually winning a contract from the customer.

Because the development and preparation of a proposal take time and money, contractors interested in submitting a proposal in response to an RFP must be realistic about the probability of being selected as the winning contractor. Evaluation of whether to go forward with the preparation of a proposal is sometimes referred to as the bid/no-bid decision. Some factors that a contractor might consider in making a bid/no-bid decision are the competition, the risk, its business mission, the ability to extend its capabilities, its reputation with the customer, the availability of customer funds, and the availability of resources for the proposal and the project.

It is important to remember that the proposal process is competitive and that the proposal is a selling document that should be written in a simple, concise manner. In the proposal, the contractor must highlight the unique factors that differentiate it from competing contractors. The contractor proposal must also emphasize the benefits to the customer if the customer selects the contractor to perform the project. The customer will select the contractor that it expects will provide the best value.

Proposals are often organized into three sections: technical, management, and cost. The objective of the technical section of the contractor proposal is to convince the customer that the contractor understands the need or problem and can provide the least risky and most beneficial solution. The technical section should show an understanding of the need, a proposed approach or solution, and the benefits to the customer. The objective of the management section of the contractor proposal is to convince the customer that the contractor can do the proposed work and achieve the intended results. The management section should contain a description of major tasks, a list of deliverables, a project schedule, a description of the organization of the project, a synopsis of related experience, and a list of any special equipment and facilities the contractor has. The objective of the cost section of the contractor proposal is to convince the customer that the contractor's price for the proposed project is realistic and reasonable. The cost section usually consists of tabulations of the contractor's estimated costs of such elements as labor, materials, equipment, facilities, subcontractors and consultants, travel, documentation, overhead, escalation, reserve, and a profit.

When contractors prepare proposals, they are generally competing with other contractors to win a contract. Therefore, they must consider the reliability of the cost estimates, the risk, the value of the project to the contractor, the customer's budget, and the competition when determining the price for the proposed project.

Many projects that are small or not complex may not require an extensive proposal. In other cases, contractors may even submit an unsolicited proposal prior to the customer preparing an RFP. In both of these situations, a simplified or basic proposal may be appropriate and sufficient. Such a proposal should include the following elements: statement of the customer's need, assumptions, project scope, deliverables, resources, schedule, price, risks, and expected benefits. The focus of the proposal should be on quality of the content—clear, concise, and convincing—rather than quantity or number of pages.

Customers evaluate contractors' proposals in many different ways. Sometimes the technical and management proposals are evaluated first, without consideration of cost. Those proposals with the highest points on the technical/management review are then evaluated for their costs. The customer weighs the technical/management merit against the costs to determine which proposal offers the best value. Some of the criteria that might be used by customers in evaluating

contractor proposals include compliance with the customer's statement of work, the contractor's understanding of the customer's need or problem, the soundness and practicality of the contractor's proposed solution to the project, the contractor's experience and success with similar projects, the experience of key individuals who will be assigned to work on the project, the contractor's ability to plan and control the project, the realism of the contractor's schedule, and the price.

Once the customer has selected the winning contractor, the contractor is informed that it is the winner, subject to successful negotiation of a contract. A contract is an agreement between the contractor, who agrees to perform the project and to provide a product or service (deliverables), and the customer, who agrees to pay the contractor a certain amount in return.

There are basically two types of contracts: fixed-price and cost-reimbursement. In a fixed-price contract, the customer and the contractor agree on a price for the proposed work. The price remains fixed unless the customer and the contractor agree on changes. This type of contract provides low risk for the customer and high risk for the contractor. In a cost-reimbursement contract, the customer agrees to pay the contractor for all actual costs (labor, materials, and so forth), regardless of amount, plus some agreed-upon profit. This type of contract provides low risk for the contractor and high risk for the customer, because contractor costs can overrun the proposed price.

A contract may include miscellaneous terms and conditions covering misrepresentation of costs, notice of cost overruns or schedule delays, approvals for any subcontractors, customer-furnished equipment or information, patent ownership, disclosure of proprietary information, international considerations, termination, terms of payment, bonuses or penalties, and procedures for making changes.

Contractors measure the success of their proposal efforts by the number of times their proposals are selected by customers and/or by the total dollar value of their proposals that are selected. A measure that is often used is known as the win ratio.

QUESTIONS

1. Describe why building relationships with customers and partners is important. How is this accomplished?
2. Describe what is meant by pre-RFP/proposal marketing. Why should contractors do it?
3. Discuss why contractors must make bid/no-bid decisions and the factors involved in making these decisions. Give an example of when a contractor should bid and when a contractor should not bid.
4. Define proposal and describe the purpose of a proposal. In addition, list the three major sections of a proposal and the purpose and elements of each.
5. What factors must be considered when a contractor develops the proposal price? Why is this not an easy task?
6. Should a contractor try to contact a customer after a proposal has been submitted? Why or why not?
7. How do customers evaluate proposals? What factors might they consider?
8. Should the lowest-priced proposal always be selected as the winner? Why or why not? Give examples.

9. Describe two different types of contracts, when each should be used, and the risks associated with each.
10. Give examples of some miscellaneous provisions that might be found in a contract.
11. Describe two methods for measuring the effectiveness of your proposal efforts.
12. Develop a complete proposal in response to the RFP you created for question 13 at the end of Chapter 2.

INTERNET EXERCISES

For the website addresses of the organizations mentioned in these exercises, go to "Internet Exercises" at the book's companion website at www.cengagebrain.com. It is suggested that you save this website in your "Favorites" list for easy access in the future.

To answer the following questions, perform a Web search for sample proposals, using your favorite search engine.

1. Based on the results of your search, find a sample proposal that has been posted on the Web. What company or organization developed the proposal, and what objective was it trying to accomplish?
2. Evaluate the effectiveness of this proposal based on information you have studied in this chapter. Discuss the strengths and weaknesses of the proposal. Are there any items missing from the proposal that should have been included?
3. Based on what you have learned in this chapter, download the proposal and revise it. Highlight the areas you revised. What makes your revised proposal better than the original?
4. Locate a website that provides suggestions for developing effective proposals. Compare and contrast this information with what was presented in the chapter.
5. Explore and describe at least three software packages that can help you write effective proposals. What features do these packages provide? Download a demo copy of at least one, if possible.

CASE STUDY 1 Medical Information Systems

Maggie Pressman, Paul Goldberg, and Steve Youngblood are equal partners in their own consulting business, which specializes in designing and installing computer-based information systems for physicians. These systems usually include patient records, prescriptions, billings, and medical insurance processing. In some cases, the physician customers have a manual system and want to computerize it; in other situations, they have an existing computer system that needs to be upgraded and enhanced.

In most cases, the consulting firm purchases the necessary hardware as well as some packaged software. They add some of their own customized software to meet the specific requirements of the physician, and they install the complete, integrated system. They also provide training for the employees in the

physician's office. The cost of most of these projects ranges from $10,000 to $40,000, depending on the amount of hardware needed. Most physicians are willing to spend such amounts rather than hire an additional office person to keep up with the ever-increasing paperwork.

Dr. Houser, one of the physicians for whom Paul had done a project in the past, left her private practice to join a large regional medical practice. This organization has six offices throughout the region, with an average of eight physicians in each office. Two of the offices also include a pharmacy. The organization employs a total of 200 people. Dr. Houser contacted Paul and asked if his consulting firm would be interested in submitting a proposal to upgrade the information system for the entire regional medical practice. The project will include integrating the six offices and two pharmacies into one system; the physicians will eventually hire an information systems person to oversee the operation of the system. Presently, each office has its own system.

Paul learns from Dr. Houser that some of the other physicians have patients who work for large consulting firms that they think could also do the job. She says that a team of representatives from the six offices and two pharmacies, with the help of the organization's purchasing manager, has prepared a request for proposal. The proposals are due in two weeks. The RFP was issued two weeks ago to the larger consulting firms, which are already working on their proposals. The purchasing manager was not familiar with Paul's consulting firm, and that is why he did not receive a copy of the RFP.

Dr. Houser tells Paul that she is sorry she cannot talk to him more about this, but she has not been involved like some of the other physicians, who discussed ideas with their patients who work at the larger consulting firms before the RFP was issued. Dr. Houser says that she will have the purchasing manager send Paul the RFP if he is interested and will be able to submit a proposal within two weeks.

"Sure," Paul says. "I'll drive over this afternoon and pick it up!" He asks if she knows how much money the medical practice has allocated for the project, but she does not. Paul picks up the RFP and makes copies for Maggie and Steve. Paul is enthusiastic about the opportunity when he meets with them. "If we do this project, it will propel us into a whole new business arena," Paul tells them. "This is the big break we've been waiting for!" he shouts.

Maggie moans, "This couldn't have come at a worse time. I'm working on three projects for other physicians, and they're all hounding me to finish up. In fact, one of them is not very satisfied. He said that if I don't finish his project in two weeks, he doesn't want it and won't recommend us to other physicians. I'm working 16 hours a day to keep up. I'm just overcommitted. I agree with you, Paul, it is a great opportunity, but I'm afraid I won't be able to spend any time helping with the proposal."

Steve wonders out loud, "Preparing the proposal is one thing, but can we do the project? I think we have the expertise among the three of us to do such a project, but this is a really big one, and we have other customers, too."

Paul replies, "We can hire more people. I have a few friends who would probably want some part-time work. We can do it! If we don't go after projects like this, we'll always be a small firm, each of us working 12-hour days for peanuts. And these small jobs for individual offices aren't going to last forever. Someday they'll all be computerized, and we'll be out of business. What do we have to lose by submitting a proposal? We can't win if we don't submit one!"

CASE QUESTIONS

1. Why did this team not receive the RFP at the same time the larger consulting firms did?
2. Why is this team being considered as a candidate to submit a proposal?
3. Develop a bid/no bid checklist to help determine if they should submit a proposal.
4. What should Maggie, Paul, and Steve do? In explaining your answer, address the concerns of each of the three team members.

GROUP ACTIVITY

Divide the course participants into teams of three or four to discuss the case and decide whether the consulting firm should submit a proposal. Each team must provide reasons for its decision. Have each team choose a spokesperson to present its decision and reasons for that decision to the entire class.

CASE STUDY 2 New Manufacturing Facility in China

At its January 15 meeting, the board of directors of Omega Consolidated Industries made a decision to build a new manufacturing facility in China and approved funding up to $180 million for construction and start-up activities. It wants the new facility completed within two years from the date that a contractor is selected to design and build the facility. Omega is a worldwide corporation with its headquarters in London.

The board asked I. M. Uno, Omega's president, to assign a team to develop a request for proposal (RFP) and solicit proposals from contractors to design and build the facility, including installation of all production equipment, offices, and an integrated information system. The team would also be responsible for monitoring the performance of the selected contractor to ensure the contractor fulfills all contractual requirements and performance specifications.

Ms. Uno selected four members of her management team:

- Alysha Robinson, who will be the plant manager of the new facility
- Jim Stewart, Chief Financial Officer
- Olga Frederick, Vice President of Engineering
- Willie Hackett, Procurement Manager

The team chose Alysha as their team leader. By April 30, they developed a comprehensive RFP that included:

- A statement of work describing the major tasks that the contractor must complete, as well as the performance specifications for the production capacity of the facility
- A requirement that the contractor complete the project within 24 months after a contract is signed
- Criteria by which the team would evaluate proposals:

Related experience	30 points
Cost	30 points
Schedule	30 points
Innovative design	30 points

- That the contract would be a fixed-price contract

The RFP did *not* state how much funding Omega had available for the project.

On May 15, the team announced the RFP in various trade publications and websites and required that interested contractors submit a proposal no later than June 30.

On June 30, the Omega team received three proposals:

1. J&J, Inc. an American firm, submitted a proposal for $150 million. However, the proposal stated that they would require 30 months to complete the project.
2. ROBETH Construction Company of Ireland submitted a proposal for $175 million. They had built several other facilities for Omega in the past, and its officers felt they had a good relationship with Ms. Uno, Jim Stewart, and Olga Frederick's predecessor, who recently left Omega to become president of one of Omega's competitors, which is also considering building a facility in China.
3. Kangaroo Architects and Engineers of Australia submitted a proposal for $200 million. Although Kangaroo has never done a project for Omega, they are one of the largest contractors in the world, have designed and built many and various types of facilities, and have a great reputation for innovative concepts, such as "green" environmentally friendly designs, and for building award-winning showcase facilities. They had built facilities for several of Omega's competitors.

The team was disappointed that they received only three proposals; they had expected at least eight.

On July 5, a fourth proposal was received from Asia General Contractors, a company based in China. The proposal was for $160 million. They had built many facilities in China for other global corporations and stated that they have good knowledge of many credible trade subcontractors in China that would be needed to build the facility. The proposal also stated that they could complete the project in 20 months.

The team scheduled a meeting for July 15 to discuss the proposals and, as a team, to score each of the proposals with respect to the evaluation criteria. That provided the team members with two weeks to individually read the proposals and develop their individual comments about each proposal, but they agreed not to individually score the proposals prior to the July 15 meeting.

At the July 15 meeting, Alysha opened the meeting and stated, "I like the proposal from Kangaroo because it would provide a showcase state-of-the-art facility."

Jim interrupted her, saying, "Their proposal is for more than the board has allocated for this project, I don't think we should consider them any further. In my mind, they are out."

Alysha responded, "Even though it would require some additional funding beyond what the board originally approved, I feel confident that I can persuade I. M. and the board to approve the additional amount required."

Jim said, "I like the proposal from ROBETH. We have worked with them in the past during my 30 years here at Omega, and their proposal cost is just about what the board has allocated. I know a lot of the people at ROBETH."

Olga mentioned, "I have only been here at Omega for less than a year, but I took it upon myself to review the final reports of the previous projects that ROBETH did for Omega and found that ROBETH missed their proposed schedules on most of the projects or that some of the production systems never met all the performance specifications." She continued, "I am also concerned about

ROBETH's continuing relationship with my predecessor who is now president at one of our major competitors and the potential conflict of interest if they would also be the contractor selected by our competitor to build the plant they are considering in China. They might use some of our proprietary processes in their design for our competitor's facility. I think it would be too risky to use them."

She continued, "I think the proposal from Asia General Contractors should be seriously considered, even though it arrived a few days after the required due date."

Willie spoke up. "I strongly disagree. It would be unfair to the other three contractors."

Olga replied, "I think it is our job to select the contractor that will provide the best value and not be concerned about some silly rules about being a few days late; who cares? Besides, they state that they can complete the project in 20 months, which means we will get the facility fully operational sooner than with any of the other contractors. And that means more products out the door sooner, more revenues and cash flow earlier, and a better return on our investment."

After everyone's initial comments, Alysha stated, "Okay, I guess we have to score these four proposals against the evaluation criteria."

Jim interrupted, "You mean three proposals."

Olga spoke up loudly, "I think she said the four proposals, not three. Let's not get bogged down in bureaucratic games; we have an important decision to make."

I. M. Uno is expecting the team to recommend a contractor to her by July 31 so that she can review it and present it to the board of directors at their August 15 meeting.

CASE QUESTIONS

1. Is there anything the team should have done when they received only three proposals by June 30?
2. Should the team consider the proposal from Asia General Contractors? Why or why not?
3. After sharing their individual comments at the start of the July 15 meeting, how should the team proceed with the rest of the meeting and any follow-up?
4. How could the selection process have been improved? Is there anything the board, I. M. Uno, Alysha, or the team could have done differently?

GROUP ACTIVITY

Divide the course participants into teams of three or four to discuss this case and decide which contractor should be selected to design and build the new manufacturing facility in China. Each team must provide reasons for its decision. Have each team select a spokesperson to present its decision and reasons for that decision to the entire class.

REFERENCES

A Guide to the Project Management Body of Knowledge (PMBOK® Guide) Fifth Edition. Newtown Square, PA: Project Management Institute, 2013.

Anonymous (2013). "Atkins to Help Explore Airport Options for South East England," *The Engineer (online)*. Retrieved from: http://search.proquest.com.ezaccess.libraries.psu.edu/docview/1285534729?accountid=13158.

Anonymous (2012). "Promising Protection," *PM Network, 26*(2), 9.

Corporation for Entertainment and Learning (1982). "Fred Smith: Corporate Creativity (The Story of Federal Express)," Creativity Series with Bill Moyer: Independent Production Fund (video).

Fretty, P. (2013). "Sea Green," *PM Network*, *27*(3), 56–59.

Gale, S. F. (2012a). "Coral Cops," *PM Network*, *26*(10), 13–14.

Gale, S. F. (2012b). "Ports Prep for Panama's Megaships," *PM Network*, *26*(5), 8–11.

Gale, S. F. (2013). "Nurturing the Next Big Thing," *PM Network*, *27*(3), 28–37.

Glowacki, J. J. (2012). "Willing to Change," *Residential Systems*, *13*(9), 36.

Hoyle, C. (2013). "Out with the Old," *Flight International*, 182.5377, 3335.

Massey, N. (2013). "Quietly, Kinder Morgan Withdraws Bid to Build Coal Terminal in Oregon," *Climate Wire*, May 13.

Rees-Caldwell, K. and A. H. Pinnington (2013). "National Culture Differences in Project Management: Comparing British and Arab Project Managers' Perceptions of Different Planning Areas," *International Journal of Project Management*, *31*, 212–227.

Schultz, B. (2013). "Going to the Chapel," *Mix*, *37*, 2.

Swartz, T. (2012). "Remodeler's Exchange: To Build or Design-build, That Is the Question," *Professional Remodeler*. Retrieved from: http://search.proquest.com.ezaccess.libraries.psu.edu/docview/1276844320?accountid=13158.

PART 2

Planning, Performing, and Controlling the Project

Concepts in the chapters in this part of the book support the following Project Management Knowledge Areas of *A Guide to the Project Management Body of Knowledge (PMBOK® Guide)*:

Project Integration Management (Chapters 4, 5, 7, and 9)
Project Scope Management (Chapter 4)
Project Time Management (Chapters 4, 5, and 6)
Project Cost Management (Chapter 7)
Project Quality Management (Chapter 4)
Project Human Resource Management (Chapter 6)
Project Risk Management (Chapter 8)

The chapters in Part 2 address techniques and tools for planning, performing, and controlling a project in order to accomplish the project objective successfully. The project objective establishes what is to be accomplished. Planning determines exactly what needs to be done, how it will get done, who will do it, how long it will take, how much it will cost, and what the risks are. Taking the time to develop a well-thought-out plan is critical to the successful accomplishment of the project objective. Developing a detailed plan includes (1) defining the project scope and deliverables, (2) defining the specific activities needed to perform the project and assigning responsibility, (3) determining the sequence in which those activities must be accomplished, (4) estimating the resources that will be required and duration for each activity, (5) developing the project schedule, (6) estimating costs and determining the project budget, and (7) identifying and assessing risks and developing a risk response plan. Many projects have overrun their budgets, missed their completion dates, or only partially met their technical specifications or quality standards because no viable plan was created before the project was started. To avoid this, you must *plan the work and then work the plan.*

In the initiating phase, the project charter or request for proposal establishes the framework for the project. During the planning phase, the detailed baseline plan for performing the project is developed. At the beginning of the project, it is not always possible to define all the details for planning purposes, especially for projects with long durations. It is easier to define the details for near-term efforts, and as the project progresses, the project team or contractor can *progressively elaborate* the plan as more information is known or becomes clear.

It is important that the people who will be involved in performing the work are also involved in planning the work. They are usually the most knowledgeable about what detailed activities need to be done and how long each should take. By participating in the planning of the work, individuals will become committed to accomplishing it according to the plan and within the schedule and budget. *Participation builds commitment.*

Once a baseline plan has been established, it must be executed. In the performing phase, work tasks are carried out to produce all the project deliverables and to accomplish the project objective. It involves performing the work according to the plan and controlling the work so that the project scope is accomplished on schedule and within budget. While the project work is being performed, it is necessary to monitor progress to ensure that everything is going according to the plan. This involves measuring actual progress and comparing it to planned progress. If, at any time, the project is not proceeding according to plan, corrective action must be taken and replanning must be done. The key to effective project control is measuring actual progress and comparing it to the planned progress on a timely and regular basis and taking any needed corrective action immediately.

donding/Alamy

Chapter **4**

Defining Scope, Quality, Responsibility, and Activity Sequence

Discusses the project scope document, quality, defining what activities need to be done, will be responsible for them, and in what sequence they will be performed.

AP Photo

Chapter **5**

Developing the Schedule

Deals with estimating the resources and durations for all activities and developing a detailed project schedule that determines when each activity should start and finish. Also discusses monitoring and controlling the progress of the project, replanning, and updating the project schedule.

Huntstock/Getty Images

Chapter **6**

Resource Utilization

Explains the incorporation of resource requirements and constraints into the project plan and schedule.

Jon Brenneis/Time Life Pictures/ Getty Images

Chapter **7**

Determining Costs, Budget, and Earned Value

Includes estimating project costs, developing a project budget, determining the earned value of the work completed, analyzing project cost performance, and forecasting total costs at project completion.

Caro/Alamy

Chapter **8**

Managing Risk

Covers identifying, assessing, and controlling risks, as well as developing response plans.

© Eastimages/Shutterstock.com

Chapter **9**

Closing the Project

Discusses what actions should be taken during the final phase of the project life cycle.

CHAPTER 4

Defining Scope, Quality, Responsibility, and Activity Sequence

donding/Alamy

Concepts in this chapter support the following Project Management Knowledge Areas of *A Guide to the Project Management Body of Knowledge (PMBOK® Guide)*:

Project Integration Management
Project Scope Management
Project Quality Management
Project Time Management

 REAL WORLD PROJECT MANAGEMENT

Project Runaway

Many organizations turn to the Chief Financial Officer of the organization to lead projects. Their intricate knowledge of how their business works and deep understanding

of the organization provide a perspective necessary to examine the technical details of a project and translate them into clear communication and project plan.

David English, CFO for Ryan LLC, a Dallas-based global tax firm, has learned from experience, sometimes the hard way. His fast growing company was using software that was 15 years old and operated in a rudimentary manner. A project was needed to help the $150 million company with 750 employees in 45 cities in Canada and the United States to integrate finance, customer relationship, and human resource management systems.

After receiving the green light for the project, English assembled the right members to create a cross-functional team. Understanding the composition was critical, he assessed the strengths of the potential team members to get the right people assigned to the right slots. "I knew we needed to have the currency-conversion feature of the expense-reporting tool working by a certain date, and I could tell them how it should work and where the rate tables resided in our accounting system," English says. "But I couldn't write the code myself or even be sure they were writing it the most efficient way."

The team members had the expertise he lacked. Subject-matter experts were assigned oversight on the portions of the project of their expertise with English providing overall project management of the team. English also understood that all the team members were assigned to his project for only a portion of their workweek.

A common impedance of project progress is the distraction of tasks required by the team member's regular workweek. The project manager must work to motivate his team members to keep the project on track. English understood the significant communication necessary and the concern for the team members' time. Wanting to make sure that his team would keep progressing and not be mired in the planning, English recalled, "I know a CFO who got so fed up with all the time eaten up at project meetings that he took the chairs out of the room. That got those meetings down to 10 minutes fast."

Activity sequence and assigning responsibility were in the forefront of English's plan. "You want to set a hard date, but build in a cushion that allows for contingencies," says English. "Obviously, you don't want to be perpetually resetting dates. There is a fine line between a legitimate cushion and sandbagging." A good definition of the project scope with stated quality plans helps to secure a green light for the project from management. Careful selection of the project team, assigned responsibility, and an appropriate activity sequence will help to avoid a project runaway.

Based on information from Banham, R. and N. Webb (2012). "Project Runaway," *CFO*, *28*(4), 46–51.

This chapter discusses the project scope document, quality, how to define what activities need to be done, who will be responsible for them, and in what sequence they will be performed. It describes techniques and tools used to plan the work and activities that need to be performed in order to accomplish the project objective successfully. The

project scope defines what work needs to be done and what deliverables need to be produced. Then, specific activities are defined and arranged in a sequence of dependent relationships to determine how the work will be performed. You will become familiar with

- Clearly defining the project objective
- Preparing a project scope document
- Understanding the importance of planning for quality
- Creating a work breakdown structure
- Assigning responsibility for work items
- Defining specific activities
- Creating a network diagram
- Utilizing a project management methodology called the systems development life cycle for information systems development projects

LEARNING OUTCOMES

After studying this chapter, the learner should be able to:

- Establish a clear project objective
- Prepare a project scope document
- Discuss the importance and elements of a project quality plan
- Develop a work breakdown structure
- Prepare a responsibility assignment matrix
- Describe how to define specific activities
- Create a network diagram

Establish Project Objective

The planning process is based on the **project objective**, which establishes what is to be accomplished. Often the project objective is stated in the project charter or request for proposal (RFP). The objective is the tangible end product that the project team or contractor must produce and deliver in order for the sponsor or customer to achieve the expected benefits from implementing the project. The project objective is usually defined in terms of the end product or deliverable, schedule, and budget. It requires completing the project work scope and producing all the deliverables by a certain time and within budget. It should also include the expected benefits that will result from implementing the project and define the success of the project. The project objective must be clearly defined and agreed upon by the sponsor or customer and the project team or contractor that will perform the project. The project objective must be clear, attainable, specific, and measurable. The project objective should include the following elements:

- *Expected benefits* that will result from implementation of the project and define success. This element establishes *why* the project is being done. It may include verbs, such as to increase, to expand, to reduce, to save, to establish, and so on. This element should also include a quantified measure if appropriate, such as a percent, dollar amount, or absolute number. Examples

Reinforce Your Learning

1. The project _____ establishes _____ is to be _____.

Reinforce Your Learning

2. The project objective is usually defined in terms of the _____, _____, and _____.

include: to increase sales volume by 5,000 units annually, to expand customer base in European markets by 60 percent, to reduce the number of patients that contract postsurgical infections by 50 percent, to double the number of donors, or to reduce annual overhead costs by $150,000.

- *Primary project end product or deliverable,* such as a mobile app shopping capability, a nationwide marketing campaign, a dormitory complex, or a noninvasive medical monitoring device.
- *Date* by which the project is required to be completed, such as by June 30, 2015, or in 18 months.
- *Budget* within which the project must be completed.

Some examples of project objectives are:

- To increase emergency room capacity by 20 percent and reduce average patient waiting time by 50 percent through a reconfiguration, and process improvement project to be completed in 12 months and within a budget of $400,000.
- To reduce outstanding accounts payable by $20 million by implementing a new billing, collection, and receiving system by May 31 with a budget not to exceed $220,000.
- To raise $40,000 for hunger relief by organizing a community festival for the last weekend in September within a budget of $3,000.
- To double annual sales revenue by creating an online shopping and fulfillment capability by April 30 with a budget not to exceed $40,000.
- To expand market share by 3 percent by introducing a new portable food preparation appliance within 10 months with a budget of $2 million.
- To increase August sales revenue by 10 percent above that of last August by producing and distributing a back-to-school catalog by July 15 with a budget not to exceed $40,000.
- To meet new environmental regulatory requirements by installing a new filtration system within 15 months and with a budget of $3.2 million.
- To obtain information about consumer preferences by conducting a consumer market study to be completed in 26 weeks with a budget of $40,000.

A project objective such as "complete the house" is too ambiguous because the customer and the contractor may have different views of what is meant by "complete." A better objective is to "complete the house by May 31 in accordance with the floor plans and specifications dated October 15 and within a budget of $200,000." The specifications and floor plans provide the details as to the scope of the work that the contractor agreed to perform. Therefore, no arguments should arise about whether the landscaping and carpeting were to be included or about the size of the entrance door, the color of paint in the bedrooms, or the style of lighting fixtures. All of these should have been spelled out in the specifications.

The project objective should be clear and concise at the beginning of the project. However, there can be situations where the project objective needs to be modified as the project proceeds because of extenuating circumstances or new information. The project manager and the customer must agree on all changes to the project objective. Any such changes might affect the remaining work scope, deliverables, completion date, and final cost.

Define Project Scope

The **project scope** defines *what* needs to be done. It is all the work that must be done to produce all the project deliverables, satisfy the sponsor or customer that all the work and deliverables meet the requirements and acceptance criteria, and accomplish the project objective. The project charter or RFP establishes the framework for further elaboration of the project scope.

The project team or contractor prepares a **project scope document** that includes many of the items contained in the project charter, RFP, or contractor's proposal, but in much greater detail. The document is valuable for establishing a common understanding among project stakeholders regarding the scope of the project.

The project scope document usually contains the following sections:

1. *Customer requirements* define the functional, operational, and performance specifications or capabilities that must be met for the project's end product and other project deliverables. The requirements can include specifications regarding size, color, weight, or performance parameters, such as speed, uptime, throughput, processing time, or operating temperature range, that the project result must satisfy. Some of a customer's requirements for a new house might include five bedrooms, a two-car attached garage, a fireplace, and a geothermal system. One of the requirements for a commercial security system might be eight hours of battery backup power in case of an outage of the primary power source.

 In many cases, the customer states high-level requirements in the project charter or RFP, but the project team or the contractor may need to collect more information from the customer or end users to further refine the requirements. This information can be obtained or collected using interviews, surveys, or focus groups. It is typical in process improvement projects or information systems projects to obtain input for requirements from the end users who are most familiar with and knowledgeable about the existing process or system and may have specific requirements or suggestions for improving the process or enhancing the current system. These requirements could include items such as consolidation of documents, data elements to include or exclude from databases, formats or contents of reports, or human factors such as the design or location of workstations. For product development projects, such as a new food product or vehicle, focus groups are often used to help determine customer preferences and requirements.

 This requirements section should also include or reference applicable technical specifications, standards, and codes that must be used and met regarding quality and performance of the project work and deliverables. As an example, for a project to construct a child care center, the requirements might state that the design must meet government specifications for certain physical parameters (square feet of space per child, number of restrooms, and so forth), and also must meet local building codes (use of fire retardant materials for interior walls, floor height for electric outlets, and so forth). Or if an internal project team is developing a new website for a company that was acquired by a parent corporation, they may be required to design the website in accordance with the corporation's technical specifications for websites to assure consistency, compatibility, and integration with the parent corporation's other websites.

Reinforce Your Learning

3. The project scope defines

needs to be done.

It is important to document the detailed requirements in the project scope document in order to establish a clear understanding with the sponsor or customer.

2. *Statement of Work (SOW)* defines the major tasks that will need to be performed to accomplish the work that needs to be done and produce all the project deliverables. The SOW defines what the project team or contractor will do. If something is not included in the SOW, then it should be assumed that it will not be done or provided. Having the contractor or project team review the SOW with the sponsor or customer provides an opportunity to make sure everything that the customer expects is included. For example, if training users how to operate or maintain a new system was not stated in the project charter or RFP, or was ambiguous, then including it in the SOW provides an opportunity to clarify or determine if the contactor should or should not provide training. Similarly, if landscaping was not stated in the homeowner's requirements and therefore not included in the contractor's SOW, it will not be provided, even though the homeowner may assume that it will be included. The SOW section of the project scope document is where the contractor or project team can state and clarify exactly what is included in the work scope and provide an opportunity to reconsider items that are not stated but that the customer may have forgotten to include in her requirements or RFP.

For a project of designing, building, and installing a specialized automated high-speed packaging machine in the customer's factory, the SOW might include the following major work tasks:

a. Develop preliminary and detailed designs, including preparation of specifications, drawings, flowcharts, and a list of materials.

b. Prepare plans for testing of the components, subsystems, and system by the contractor, before shipping the equipment to the customer's plant and after it has been installed at the customer's plant, to ensure that the equipment meets the customer's acceptance criteria. The customer may want to review and approve the test plans before the start of testing.

c. Conduct design review meetings, both internally and with the customer. Based on these design review meetings, the customer may initiate or approve changes to the original plan. These changes could have an impact on the scope, schedule, and price. The customer may need to amend the contract, and the contractor may have to do some replanning of the project to incorporate any changes and establish a new baseline plan for the remainder of the project work.

d. Order materials and parts.

e. Fabricate components and parts.

f. Develop and test software.

g. Assemble and test hardware, including testing components, assembling components into subassemblies, testing subassemblies, assembling subassemblies into the system, and testing the entire hardware system.

h. Integrate hardware and software and test the system. The customer may want to witness and document the test results to ensure that they meet the customer's specifications.

i. Prepare installation requirements, such as floor plans and utility requirements (electrical, plumbing, and so forth), and identify which items the customer will be responsible for during installation.

 j. Develop training materials (workbooks, videos, computer simulations) to train the customer to operate and maintain the new equipment.
 k. Ship the equipment to the customer's factory and install it.
 l. Conduct training for the customer's employees who will operate and maintain the new equipment.
 m. Conduct final acceptance tests to demonstrate that the equipment meets the customer's specified requirements and acceptance criteria.

For a project to put on a community festival, the major work elements might include the following:

 a. Prepare promotions—newspaper advertisements, posters, tickets, and so forth.
 b. Solicit volunteers.
 c. Organize games, including constructing booths and acquiring prizes.
 d. Contract for amusement rides and obtain the necessary permits.
 e. Obtain performers to entertain and workers to construct the grandstand stage.
 f. Arrange for food, including making or purchasing the food and building concession stands.
 g. Organize all the support services, such as parking, cleanup, security, and restroom and first aid facilities.

3. *Deliverables* are the products or outputs that the project team or contractor will produce and provide to the customer during and at the completion of the performance of the project. Although major or key deliverables may be stated in the project charter or RFP, they need to be expanded in greater detail in the project scope document. A detailed description of each deliverable should be stated to provide a basis for agreement between the project team/contractor and the customer of exactly what will be provided. This will help to manage stakeholder expectations. It would be embarrassing if a customer is expecting the contractor to provide a concept of a new office building as a three-dimensional physical model, but the contractor provides a pencil sketch on paper. Not only would the customer not accept the sketch, but the contractor would also have to spend additional time and money to construct the three-dimensional model, and would probably delay the project schedule. It would also be a setback to developing a good working relationship with the customer.

4. *Acceptance criteria* for all project deliverables must be described in greater detail than what is stated in the project charter or RFP. For each deliverable, the quantitative measures or references to specifications, standards, or codes that will be used should be stated, as the criteria will be the basis for the customer agreeing that a deliverable is acceptable. The inclusion of specifications or standards will help assure quality of the deliverable. In some cases, the acceptance criteria may need to describe certain inspection techniques (such as sampling), testing procedures (length of testing period, use of external laboratory), or specific testing equipment or facilities that must be used (calibrated to industry standards, environmental chamber). A clear description of the acceptance criteria with quantitative measures will help to avoid misunderstandings. For example, if the acceptance criteria for testing a prototype of a new product are not clear and only state that the prototype must be tested for a sufficient period of time without failing, the development team

may test the prototype for 2 days and expect the sponsor to approve and accept the prototype design and specifications; however, the sponsor may have expected the test period to be 10 days. In this case, the acceptance criteria should have stated that the prototype must be tested to show that it operates continuously over a 10-day period without failing, rather than merely stating "for a sufficient period of time."

For some projects, the terms of payment may be tied to the customer's acceptance of certain deliverables, such as 20 percent of the total project amount is paid to the contractor upon customer approval and acceptance of the detail design specifications for the customer relationship management system.

Clear, unambiguous acceptance criteria for all deliverables are important because they are the basis for *validating* that the project scope has been completed in accordance with the customer's requirements and expectations.

5. *Work Breakdown Structure (WBS).* The major work tasks defined in the SOW section along with the detailed list of deliverables provide the basis for creating a WBS, which is a hierarchical decomposition of the project work scope into work packages that produce the project deliverables. It is a technique for organizing and subdividing all the project work and deliverables into more manageable components. The WBS establishes the framework for further planning to create a baseline plan for performing the project work. *The project scope document may include a high-level WBS* in a graphic chart format or as an indentured list of the work items and associated deliverables. This WBS will be used as the basis for creating a more detailed WBS in the next step of the planning process.

It should be noted that at the beginning of the project it might not be possible to define all of the requirements, work items, and deliverables at a detailed level. This is especially the case for a project with a long duration, such as a multiyear project, or a project that has several phases. It is easier to define the details for the near-term efforts, but as the project progresses or moves from phase to phase, the project team or contractor can *progressively elaborate* the details as more information is known or becomes clear.

The project scope document is valuable for establishing a common understanding among project stakeholders regarding the scope of the project. The contractor or project team needs to gain agreement from the sponsor or customer on the project scope document. If the scope seems much greater than originally anticipated by the customer, it may affect the budget and schedule for performing the work and jeopardize accomplishing the project objective. In such a case, the customer and contractor would have to agree on increasing the budget, extending the schedule, reducing the scope, or some combination thereof.

The agreed-upon project scope document establishes the baseline for any changes that may be made to the scope during the performance of the project. A change control system needs to be established for the process and procedures that define how changes will be documented, approved, and communicated. The project team or contractor *must avoid* **scope creep,** which is informally making changes to the project scope without appropriate approval. Many projects overspend their budget or are not completed on time because of scope creep caused by additional work that was not documented or approved, or that was not communicated and in turn caused errors or rework for other work items of the project. See the section on managing changes in Chapter 10, and the section on control document changes in Chapter 12 for further information.

Plan for Quality

It is important to plan for quality in performing the project to assure that the work is done according to specifications and applicable standards and that deliverables meet acceptance criteria. Planning for quality is a necessary, yet often forgotten or dismissed, function on a project. It is essential to have a plan for assuring the quality of project deliverables and results rather than waiting until the end of the project to check if the sponsor/customer requirements and expectations have been met regarding the quality of the project deliverables. For example, if a new homeowner required the contractor to paint the interior walls of all the rooms, but the work was done in a sloppy manner and the paint showed streaks, the rooms were painted, but the quality was below customer expectations. If 20,000 merchandise catalogs were printed but the photo images were fuzzy or blurred, the quantity of deliverables was accomplished, but the quality was not.

In order to prevent poor quality and avoid quality problems, there needs to be a **project quality plan.** The quality plan must include or reference the specifications, industry or government standards (for design, testing, safety, construction, and so forth), and codes that must be used and met during the performance of the project work. For example, in construction projects, appropriate industry standards should be used for building design and for materials, along with local building codes. Similarly, on projects that involve developing electrical-based products, industry standards regarding safety should be used and the product tested in accordance with specified testing procedures to assure it meets these safety standards. Quality standards that will be used should also be stated and referenced in other appropriate project documents, such as technical specifications and acceptance criteria, and communicated to members of the project team at the outset of the project *before* the work begins. The quality plan may also state that suppliers must provide documentation certifying that the materials they supply meet certain required specifications.

To help **assure quality**, the project quality plan should contain written procedures for using various quality tools and techniques, such as audits, inspections, testing, checklists, and so on. The plan should also state which tools and techniques to use and when. Techniques such as audits and inspections are often used. For military contracts that use contractors to develop or build weapon systems for example, it is normal for the government agency to have a quality representative reside at the contractor's facility for the duration of the project to regularly review and inspect the contractor's work. In the case of building a house, the contractor is required to have a local building inspector check certain types of work (foundation, framing, plumbing, electrical) at different times throughout the construction. If the work does not comply with the codes or meet required specifications, then the contractor has to redo the work until it passes inspection. For some projects, the customer may hire an independent third party or laboratory to be its representative or perform tests rather than relying on the contractor's inspecting and testing its own work. In other situations, the customer may make unannounced visits to the contactor's facility or work site and randomly select certain work elements to review in order to determine whether they are being done in conformance with quality standards and requirements.

With the quality plan in place including procedures for the application of appropriate quality tools and techniques, quality can then be controlled. The key to **quality control** is to monitor the quality of the work early and regularly throughout the performance of the project, compare results with quality standards, and make any necessary corrective actions immediately, rather than

Reinforce Your Learning

6. To avoid quality problems, there needs to be a

_____ .

waiting until all the work is completed before checking or inspecting for quality. If, in the house painting example, there had been written quality procedures that stated the project manager must inspect the paint work after the first room is painted and before painting is started in the remaining rooms, it might have minimized the impact of the shoddy paint job by making sure the painting of the remaining rooms would be done correctly—only the first room would have had to be repainted, rather than all the rooms.

Having a written quality plan at the outset of a project is extremely beneficial because it helps prevent incurring additional costs and schedule extensions due to rework caused by work and deliverables that fail to meet quality requirements and customer expectations. The focus must be on *doing it right the first time* by doing the work in accordance with quality standards, and therefore preventing quality problems, rather than relying on after-the-fact inspections or testing and then having to do additional work to correct quality problems.

It is often said that some people think they never have enough time to do the work right the first time, but then must take the time later to redo it correctly— *haste makes waste!*

Create Work Breakdown Structure

Once the project scope document has been prepared and agreed on, the next step in the planning phase is to create a detailed **work breakdown structure (WBS)**, which is a deliverable-oriented hierarchical decomposition of the project work scope into work packages that produce the project deliverables. Having a comprehensive project scope document is important because it is the foundation for creating the WBS. The project scope document defined *what* needs to be done in terms of the SOW and deliverables, and the WBS establishes the framework for *how* the work will get done to produce the project deliverables.

Creating a WBS is a structured approach for organizing all the project work and deliverables into logical groupings and subdividing them into more manageable components to help ensure that all the work and deliverables to complete the project are identified and included in the baseline project plan. It is a hierarchical tree of deliverables or end items that will be accomplished or produced by the project team or contractor during the project. The WBS subdivides the project into smaller pieces called *work items.* The lowest-level work item of any one branch is called a **work package**. The work package includes all of the specific work activities that need to be performed to produce the deliverable associated with that work package. The WBS should be decomposed to a level that identifies individual work packages for each specific deliverable listed in the project scope document. Often the WBS includes a separate work package labeled "project management" that is for all the work associated with managing the project such as preparing progress reports; conducting review meetings; planning, monitoring, and tracking schedules and budgets, and so on. The accomplishment or production of all of these lowest-level work packages in the WBS constitutes completion of the project work scope.

The WBS can be created using a graphic chart format or as an indentured list. Figure 4.1 shows a WBS in a graphic chart format for a community festival project. Not all branches of the WBS have to be broken down to the same level. Most work packages shown in Figure 4.1 are at the second level, but four work items are further divided into a more detailed third level; one work item (Volunteers) is not broken down beyond the first level.

Reinforce Your Learning

7. The key to quality control is to monitor the quality of the work

_____ and

_____ .

Reinforce Your Learning

8. The work

_____ structure is a

_____ oriented

_____ of the project

_____ .

Reinforce Your Learning

9. The work

_____ structure establishes the

_____ for

_____ the work will get done to produce the project

_____ .

Reinforce Your Learning

10. The lowest-level work item of any given branch of the WBS is called a

_____ .

FIGURE 4.1 **Work Breakdown Structure for Festival Project**

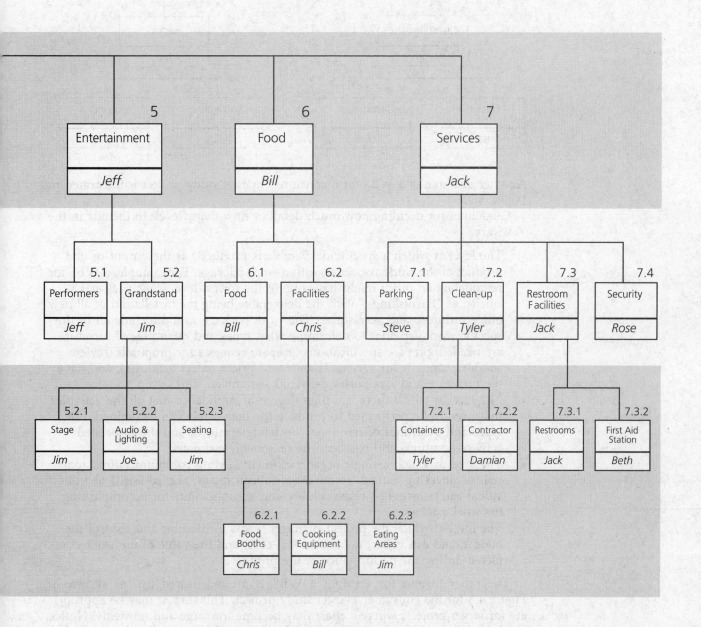

FIGURE 4.2 **Work Breakdown Structure for Consumer Market Study Project**

Another example of a WBS for a consumer market study project is illustrated in Figure 4.2.

Guidelines for deciding how much detail or how many levels to include in the WBS are:

- The level at which a specific deliverable is produced as the output or end product of the work associated with a work package. For example, a WBS for remodeling an office might have one of the lowest-level work packages labeled as "Furnishings," with the deliverable being the installation of all new office furniture and accessories. The work package would include all of the specific work activities to determine what types and quantities of furniture are needed, prepare specifications, prepare requests for proposals, review vendor proposals for various layouts and prices, select vendor(s), and have the furniture and accessories delivered, assembled, and set up.
- The level at which there is a high degree of confidence that all the activities that need to be performed to produce the deliverable can be defined, the types and quantities of resources can be determined, and the associated activity durations and costs can be reasonably estimated.
- The level at which a single organization (marketing communications, materials engineering, human resources, a subcontractor, and so forth) or individual can be assigned responsibility and accountability for accomplishing the work package.
- The level at which the project manager wants to monitor and control the budget, and can collect data on actual costs and the value of the work completed during the performance of the project.

The other format for creating a WBS is an indentured list, as shown in Figure 4.3 for the consumer market study project. This format may be appropriate for larger projects where a chart may become too large and unwieldy. Notice on the indentured list that it also states the specific deliverable that is expected to be completed from the work activities associated with each lowest-level work package. For example, the deliverable for the work package 1.1 (Design) is Questionnaire approved; for 1.2 (Responses), the deliverable is All completed

FIGURE 4.3 **Work Breakdown Indentured List for Consumer Market Study Project**

WBS #	DESCRIPTION	RESPONSIBLE	DELIVERABLES
	Consumer Market Study	Jim	
1.0	Questionnaire	Susan	
1.1	Design	Susan	Questionnaire approved
1.2	Responses	Steve	All completed responses received
2.0	Report	Jim	
2.1	Software	Andy	Application software working
2.2	Report	Jim	Final report

responses received; for 2.1 (Software), the deliverable is Application software working; and for 2.2 (Report), the deliverable is Final report.

For large or complex projects, it may be difficult for one individual to determine all the work items to include in the WBS. Therefore, the project manager should involve key team members in developing the WBS. They may have special expertise, knowledge, or experience that will help develop a more comprehensive and complete WBS. Having other project team members participate in developing the project scope document and WBS will also build teamwork, commitment to the project plan, and commitment to completing the project successfully.

The WBS usually indicates the organization or individual assigned responsibility for performance and completion of each work item. However, the WBS is *not* the same thing as the project organization chart or structure. In some cases, it could be—but not usually. See Chapter 13, Project Management Organizational Structures, for more discussion on this topic.

The WBS establishes the framework for further planning to create a baseline plan for performing the project work. There is not a single ideal WBS for any project. Different project teams might create somewhat different WBSs for the same project.

Assign Responsibility

A **responsibility assignment matrix (RAM)** illustrates *who* will be responsible for the work. It is a tool used to designate the individuals responsible for accomplishing the work items in the WBS. It is a useful tool because it emphasizes who is responsible for each work item and shows each individual's role in supporting the overall project. Figure 4.4 shows the RAM associated with the WBS in Figure 4.1 for the community festival project.

The RAM may use a P to designate primary responsibility and an S to indicate support responsibility for a specific work item. The RAM shows all the individuals associated with each work item in the WBS, as well as all the work items associated with each individual. For example, Figure 4.4 indicates that Jim has primary responsibility for the game booths, with Chris and Joe supporting this effort. The figure also shows all the work items with which Joe is involved, for example. Only one individual should be designated as the lead, or primary, person responsible for each work item. Designating two or more individuals as having primary responsibility can cause confusion and increase the risk that some work will "fall through the cracks," because each person may assume that the other person is going to do it.

FIGURE 4.4 Responsibility Assignment Matrix for Festival Project

WBS Item	Work Item	Andrea	Beth	Bill	Chris	Damian	Jack	Jeff	Jim	Joe	Keith	Lynn	Neil	Pat	Rose	Steve	Tyler
	Festival		S	S			S	S				P		S		S	
1	**Promotion**	S									S	P					
1.1	Newspaper Ads											P					
1.2	Posters										P						
1.3	Tickets	P	S									S					
2	**Volunteers**		P						S						S		
3	**Games**							S	S								P
3.1	Booths				S				P	S							
3.2	Games														S		P
3.3	Prizes							P							S		
4	**Rides**												S	P			
4.1	Amusement Contractor													P			
4.2	Permits												P	S			
5	**Entertainment**							P	S	S							
5.1	Performers					S		P									
5.2	Grandstand								P	S							
5.2.1	Stage								P	S							
5.2.2	Audio & Lighting									P							
5.2.3	Seating					S				P							
6	**Food**			P	S												
6.1	Food			P											S		
6.2	Facilities			S	P				S								
6.2.1	Food Booths				P				S	S							
6.2.2	Cooking Equipment			P													
6.2.3	Eating Areas									P					S		
7	**Services**						P								S	S	S
7.1	Parking														P		
7.2	Clean-up				S												P
7.2.1	Containers																P
7.2.2	Contractor				P												
7.3	Restroom Facilities		S				P										
7.3.1	Restrooms						P										
7.3.2	First Aid Stations		P														
7.4	Security				S				S						P		

KEY: **P** = Primary responsibility; S = Support responsibility.

Define Activities

Using the WBS, the individual or team responsible for each work package must next define all the specific activities that need to be performed to produce the end product or deliverable for the work package. Activities define more specifically *how* the work will get done. An **activity**, also referred to as a *task,* is a defined piece of work that consumes time. It does not necessarily require the expenditure of effort by people—for example, waiting for concrete to harden can take several days but does not require any human effort.

For work package 3.1 in Figure 4.1, game booths, the following eight specific activities may be defined:

- Design booths
- Specify materials
- Buy materials
- Construct booths
- Paint booths
- Dismantle booths
- Move booths to festival site and reassemble
- Dismantle booths and move to storage

In Figure 4.5, the WBS for a consumer market study project, the specific activities that need to be performed for each work package are defined.

Reinforce Your Learning

12. An activity is also called a
_____.

FIGURE 4.5 **Work Breakdown Structure for Consumer Market Study Project**

When all the specific activities have been defined for all of the work packages, they should be consolidated into a comprehensive *activity list* of all the specific activities that need to be performed to produce all the project deliverables and accomplish the project objective. The next step is to create a network diagram that shows their appropriate sequence and defines the dependent relationships indicating how the activities need to be performed to accomplish the overall project work scope and produce the deliverables.

It should be noted that at the beginning of the project it might not be possible to define all of the specific activities. This is especially the case for a project with a long duration. It is easier to define the specific activities for near-term work; but as more information is known or becomes clear, the project team can *progressively elaborate* the specific activities.

Sequence Activities

A **network diagram** is a tool for arranging the specific activities in the appropriate sequence and defining their dependent relationships. It defines the sequence of *how* the activities will get done.

Two network planning techniques, program evaluation and review technique (PERT) and the critical path method (CPM), were developed in the 1950s. Since that time, other forms of network planning, such as the precedence diagramming method (PDM), have been developed. All of these fall under the general category of network planning techniques, because they all make use of a network diagram to show the sequential flow and interrelationships of activities. In the past, there were distinguishable methodological differences between PERT and CPM. Today, however, when most people refer to a CPM diagram or PERT chart, they mean a generic network diagram. See Figures 4.9 and 4.13 for examples of network diagrams for a project to conduct a consumer market study and for a project to develop a Web-based reporting system.

NETWORK PRINCIPLES

There are a few basic principles that must be understood and followed in creating a network diagram. Each activity is represented by a box in the network diagram, and the description of the activity is written within the box, as shown below.

```
Get
Volunteers

7
```

Activities consume time, and their description usually starts with a verb. Each activity is represented by one and only one box. In addition, each box is assigned a *unique* activity number. In the above example, the activity "Get Volunteers" has been given activity number 7.

Activities have a **dependent relationship**, also referred to as a *precedence relationship*—that is, they are linked in a logical sequence to show which activities must be finished before others can start. Arrows linking the activity boxes show the direction of the dependent relationship. *An activity cannot start until all of the preceding activities that are linked to it by arrows are finished.*

Reinforce Your Learning

13. A _____ defines the _____ of _____ the activities will get done.

Reinforce Your Learning

14. A network diagram _____ activities in the appropriate sequence and defines their _____ _____.

Certain activities have to be done in serial sequence. For example, as shown below, only after "Wash Car" is finished can "Dry Car" start.

Some activities may be done concurrently. For example, as shown below, "Get Volunteers" and "Buy Materials" can be performed concurrently; when they are *both* finished, "Construct Booth" can start. Similarly, when "Paint Booth" is finished, *both* "Dismantle Booth" and "Clean Up" can start and be performed concurrently.

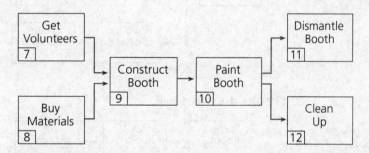

Shown below is an illogical relationship among activities known as a *loop*. In preparing a network diagram, drawing activities in a loop is not acceptable because it portrays a path of activities that perpetually repeats itself.

Some projects have a set of activities that are repeated several times. For example, consider a project involving the painting of three rooms. Painting each room requires: (1) preparing the room to be painted, (2) painting the ceiling and walls, and (3) painting the trim. Assume that three experts will be available—one to do the preparation, one to paint the ceilings and walls, and one to do the trim.

It may seem logical to draw a network diagram for the project like the one shown in Figure 4.6 or 4.7. However, Figure 4.6 indicates that all the activities must be done in serial sequence, which means that at any one time only one person is working while two other people are waiting. Figure 4.7, on the other hand, indicates that all three rooms can be done concurrently, which is not possible because only one expert is available for each type of activity.

Figure 4.8 shows a technique known as **laddering**, which is used to show the dependent relationship of a set of activities that is repeated several consecutive times and allows the activities to be completed in the shortest possible time while making the best use of available resources. It indicates that each expert,

FIGURE 4.6 **Activities Performed Serially**

FIGURE 4.7 **Activities Performed Concurrently**

FIGURE 4.8 **Laddering**

after finishing one room, can start working on the next room. This approach will allow the project to be completed in the shortest possible time while making the best use of available resources (the experts).

CREATE NETWORK DIAGRAM

With the list of specific activities and knowledge of network principles, a network diagram can now be created. Start by drawing the activities in boxes in their logical sequence and connecting them with arrows to show the required dependent relationships, as the project should be performed from start to completion. When deciding on the sequence in which the activities should be drawn to show their dependent relationships to one another, ask the following three questions regarding each individual activity:

1. Which activities must be finished *immediately* before this activity can be started?
2. Which activities can be done concurrently with this activity?
3. Which activities cannot be started until *immediately* after this activity is finished?

By answering these questions for each activity, you should be able to draw a network diagram that portrays the sequence and dependent relationships of activities needed to accomplish the project work scope.

The entire network diagram should flow from left to right, although some arrows may flow from right to left to prevent the overall diagram from becoming too long or unwieldy. It is easier to visualize the entire project if the network diagram can be drawn to fit on a large sheet of paper. If the network is very large, however, it may require multiple sheets. In such cases, it may be necessary to create a reference system or set of symbols to show the linkages between activities on different sheets.

When initially drawing the network diagram for a project, do not be too concerned about drawing it neatly. It is better to sketch out a rough draft of the diagram and make sure the sequence and dependent relationships among the activities are correct. Then, go back later and draw it more neatly (or preferably generate the diagram on the computer if you are using project management software).

The following guidelines should be considered in deciding how detailed (in terms of number of activities) a network diagram for a project should be:

1. Based on the WBS for a project, specific activities should be defined for each work package. For example, Figure 4.5 shows a WBS for a project involving a consumer market study and the specific activities that have been defined for each work package.
2. It may be preferable to draw a summary-level network first and then expand it to a more detailed network. A *summary network* contains a small number of higher-level activities rather than a large number of detailed activities. In some cases, a summary network may suffice for use throughout a project.
3. The level of detail may be determined by certain obvious interface or transfer points:
 - If there is a change in responsibility—that is, a different person or organization takes over responsibility for continuing the work—it should define the end of one activity and the start of other activities. For example, if one person is responsible for building an item and another person is responsible for packaging it, these should be two separate activities.
 - If there is a tangible output or product or deliverable as a result of an activity, it should define the end of one activity and the start of other activities. Some examples of outputs include a report, a drawing, the shipment of a piece of equipment, and the costumes for a theatrical production. In the case of a brochure, the production of a draft brochure should be defined as the end of one activity; another activity, perhaps "Approve Draft Brochure," would follow.
4. Activities should not be longer in estimated duration than the time intervals at which actual project progress will be reviewed and compared to planned progress. For example, if the project is a three-year endeavor and the project team plans to review project progress monthly, then the network diagram should contain no activities with estimated durations greater than one month. If there are activities with estimated durations longer than one month, they should be broken into more detailed activities with durations of one month or less.

Whatever the level of detail of the initial network diagram, some activities may be broken down further as the project progresses. It is always easier to identify activities that need to be done in the near term (the next several weeks or months) than to identify activities that are a year in the future. It is not unusual

FIGURE 4.9 Network Diagram for Consumer Market Study Project

to *progressively elaborate* the network diagram as the project progresses and more information is known or becomes clear.

In some cases, an organization may do similar projects for different customers, and certain portions of these projects may include the same types of activities in the same sequence and dependent relationships. If so, it may be worthwhile to develop standard *subnetworks* for these portions of the projects. A subnetwork is a portion of a network diagram that represents a specific work package or a somewhat standard or well-established set and sequence of activities. Having standard subnetworks can save effort and time when a network diagram is developed for an overall project. Standard subnetworks should be developed for those portions of projects for which the dependent relationships among the activities have been well established through historical practice. These subnetworks may, of course, be modified as necessary for a particular project.

Finally, when the entire network diagram has been drawn, it is necessary to assign a unique activity number to each activity (box).

Figure 4.9 shows a complete network diagram for the consumer market study project. Notice the inclusion of the person responsible for each activity on this diagram.

The network diagram is a roadmap that displays how all the specific activities fit together to accomplish the project work scope. It also is a communication tool for the project team because it shows who is responsible for each activity and how each person's work fits into the overall project.

Reinforce Your Learning

15. Refer to Figure 4.9.
a. When "Prepare Mailing Labels" and "Print Questionnaire" are finished, what activity can be started?
b. In order to start "Input Response Data," which activities must have been finished immediately beforehand?

KEY:

Activity
Description

Activity
Number

Person
Responsible

REAL WORLD PROJECT MANAGEMENT

Building Abroad

Projects are guided by unique circumstances, especially if they are in foreign countries. Ales Ertis, senior project manager at Alfa Tech, notes that issues in India are different than Singapore and both are different than other countries. "One thing that is constant, however, is relationship is king. You have to be comfortable with your local representative. You can't be cavalier about contracts. If you think they carry the same weight as they do in the U.S., you're wrong."

Ertis advises other project managers about the critical steps and considerations when planning a construction project outside the United States. The project scope is the critical first step. The subsequent critical steps are dependent upon the project scope and dictate the project planning. Protocols for following government regulations define quality requirements to ensure the proper infrastructure. All construction projects require detailed due diligence on the building process to meet regulations and entitlement and are dependent upon having a strong in-country advocate and foreign team.

Although the critical steps sound similar to U.S.-based construction projects, Ertis reinforces that plans for quality, responsibility, and activity sequence are subject to

Reinforce Your Learning

16. Refer to Figure 4.9.
 a. In order to start "Test Software," which activities must have been completed immediately beforehand?
 b. True or false: Once "Print Questionnaire" is finished, "Mail Questionnaire & Get Responses" can start immediately.

the quality standards and the speed of construction. Some fast growing economies have alarming rates and minor changes may be made without formal design review and approval. A clean set of plans and a conscious decision of responsibility for change approvals are necessary to help mitigate later risks once the project is started.

Requirements such as immigration implications, regulations, submission processes, and substitutions all impact project quality. Ertis cautions project managers to develop procedures to have an in-country advocate inspect materials and processes to ensure each is adequate and correct for the project requirements. The same goes for contractors on the project. Hiring an international firm quite possibly will result in paying higher rates, similar to union rates in the United States, for contracted labor in the country. Often, these international firms will hire lower cost contractors as subcontractors to complete the work. A local partner could help assign the responsibility of the tasks to the small- and medium-sized contractors who would be subcontractors to other international firms and save significant costs of construction.

The preconstruction effort is necessary to define the roles and responsibilities in a clear and explicit manner. If the level of definition for the project scope, quality, responsibilities, and activity sequence is not maximized in detail, the potential for failures related to time, budget, and quality are increased. Something as simple as having a permit could have lagging impacts if not acquired in the correct time frame. Assignment of responsibility to an in-country partner is a means of improving the likelihood of meeting deadlines and having a successful project outcome.

Based on information from Ertis, A. (2012). "Building Abroad," *Smart Business Northern California*, *5*(10), 12.

Planning for Information Systems Development

Because of the rapidly increasing number of information technology-related projects that are being undertaken, it seems appropriate to include a section in each of the next few chapters on project management practices in information systems development. An **information system** is a computer-based system that accepts data as input, processes the data, and produces useful information for users. Information systems include computerized order entry systems, e-commerce systems, automated teller machines, and billing, payroll, and inventory systems. The development of an information system is a challenging process that requires extensive planning and control to ensure that the system meets user requirements and is finished on time and within budget.

A project management planning tool, or methodology, called the **systems development life cycle (SDLC)** is often used to help plan, execute, and control information system development projects. The SDLC consists of a set of phases or steps that need to be completed over the course of a development project.

Many people view the SDLC as a classic problem-solving approach. It consists of the following steps:

1. *Problem definition.* Data are gathered and analyzed, and problems and opportunities are clearly defined. Technical, economic, operational, and other feasibility factors are defined and studied to determine, at least initially, whether the information system can be successfully developed and used.

2. *System analysis.* The development team defines the scope of the system to be developed, interviews potential users, studies the existing system (which might be manual), and defines user requirements.

3. *System design.* Several alternative conceptual designs are produced that describe input, processing, output, hardware, software, and the database at a high level. Each of these alternatives is then evaluated, and the best one is selected for further design and development.

4. *System development.* The actual system is brought into existence. Hardware is purchased, and software is purchased, customized, or developed. Databases, input screens, system reports, telecommunication networks, security controls, and other features are also developed.

5. *System testing.* After individual modules within the system have been developed, testing can begin. Testing involves looking for logical errors, database errors, errors of omission, security errors, and other problems that might prevent the system from being successful. After the individual modules are tested and problems are corrected, the entire system is tested. Once the users and the developers are convinced that the system is error-free, the system can be implemented.

6. *System implementation.* The existing system is replaced with the new, improved system, and users are trained. Several methodologies exist for converting from the existing system to the new system with minimal interruption to the users.

The SDLC concludes with implementation of the system. The system life cycle itself continues with a formal review of the development process after the system is up and running, and then continues with maintenance, modifications, and enhancements to the system.

AN INFORMATION SYSTEM EXAMPLE: INTERNET APPLICATIONS DEVELOPMENT FOR ABC OFFICE DESIGNS

A corporation called ABC Office Designs has a large number of sales representatives who sell office furniture to major corporations. Each sales representative is assigned to a specific state, and each state is part of one of four regions in the country. To enable management to monitor the number and amount of sales for each representative, for each state, and for each region, ABC has decided to build a Web-based information system that will track prices, inventory, and the competition.

The Information System department within the corporation has assigned Beth Smith to be the project manager of the Web-based reporting system

FIGURE 4.10 **Work Breakdown Structure for Web-based Reporting System Project**

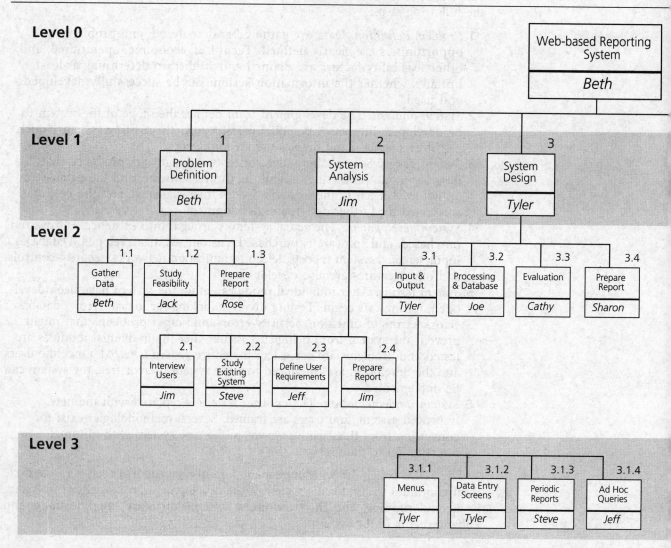

development project. With the help of her staff, Beth identified all of the major tasks that need to be accomplished and developed the WBS shown in Figure 4.10. Notice that the WBS follows the steps of the SDLC. At level 1, the major tasks are problem definition, analysis, design, development, testing, and implementation. Each of these tasks is further broken down into level 2 tasks, and a few are broken down further into level 3 tasks.

After the project team created the WBS, the RAM shown in Figure 4.11 was developed. Notice that this table reflects all of the activities shown in the WBS. In addition, it shows who has primary and secondary responsibilities for each task.

Next, Beth wanted to develop a network diagram to show the interdependencies that exist among tasks. Before Beth did this, however, she and the project team created a list of all tasks to be done, with the immediate predecessor for each task listed to the right of the task, as shown in Figure 4.12. Notice that before "Prepare (Problem Definition) Report" can start, both "Gather Data" and "Study Feasibility" must be finished. Similarly, before "Prepare (System Analysis) Report" can start, both "Study Existing System" and "Determine User Requirements" must be completed.

With this list, Beth then created the network diagram shown in Figure 4.13.

FIGURE 4.11 **Responsibility Assignment Matrix for Web-based Reporting System Project**

WBS Item	Work Item	Beth	Jim	Jack	Rose	Steve	Jeff	Tyler	Cathy	Sharon	Hannah	Joe	Gerri	Maggie	Gene	Greg
	Web-based Reporting System	P	S					S			S			S		
1	**Problem Definition**	P		S	S											
1.1	Gather Data	P	S										S			
1.2	Study Feasibility			P		S	S	S	S							
1.3	Prepare Report	S			P											
2	**System Analysis**		P			S	S									
2.1	Interview Users		P		S						S			S		
2.2	Study Existing System					P										
2.3	Define User Requirements						P									
2.4	Prepare Report		P													
3	**System Design**							P	S	S	S					
3.1	Input & Output					S	S	P								
3.1.1	Menus		S					P								
3.1.2	Data Entry Screens		S					P								
3.1.3	Periodic Reports					P	S						S			
3.1.4	Ad Hoc Queries					S	P						S			
3.2	Processing & Database											P			S	S
3.3	Evaluation	S	S	S					P							
3.4	Prepare Report									P	S					
4	**System Development**			S							P	S	S			
4.1	Software										P	S	S	S		
4.1.1	Packaged Software										P	S	S	S		
4.1.2	Customized Software											S	S	P		
4.2	Hardware							S				P				
4.3	Network												P			
4.4	Prepare Report		P													
5	**Testing**				S									P	S	S
5.1	Software					S	S							P		
5.2	Hardware											S	S		P	
5.3	Network									S	S					P
5.4	Prepare Report				P									S	S	S
6	**Implementation**	P	S	S												
6.1	Training		P									S	S			
6.2	System Conversion	P										S	S			
6.3	Prepare Report	S	S	P												

KEY: **P** = Primary responsibility; S = Support responsibility.

FIGURE 4.12 List of Activities and Immediate Predecessors

Web-based Reporting System Project

Activity	Immediate Predecessors
1. Gather Data	—
2. Study Feasibility	—
3. Prepare Problem Definition Report	1, 2
4. Interview Users	3
5. Study Existing System	3
6. Define User Requirements	4
7. Prepare System Analysis Report	5, 6
8. Input & Output	7
9. Processing & Database	7
10. Evaluation	8, 9
11. Prepare System Design Report	10
12. Software Development	11
13. Hardware Development	11
14. Network Development	11
15. Prepare System Development Report	12, 13, 14
16. Software Testing	15
17. Hardware Testing	15
18. Network Testing	15
19. Prepare Testing Report	16, 17, 18
20. Training	19
21. System Conversion	19
22. Prepare Implementation Report	20, 21

Project Management Information Systems

A wide variety of affordable project management information systems are available for purchase. These systems can help and support the project manager and the project team in planning, monitoring, and controlling projects.

Common features of project management information systems allow the user to:

- Create lists of tasks with their estimated durations
- Establish dependencies among tasks
- Work with a variety of time scales, including hours, days, weeks, months, and years
- Handle certain constraints—for example, a task cannot start before a certain date, a task must be started by a certain date, labor unions allow no more than two people to work on the weekends
- Track team members, including their pay rates, hours worked thus far on a project, and upcoming vacation dates
- Incorporate company holidays, weekends, and team member vacation days into calendaring systems
- Handle shifts of workers (day, evening, night)

FIGURE 4.13 Network Diagram for Web-based Reporting System Project

- Monitor and forecast budgets
- Look for conflicts—for example, over-allocated resources and time conflicts
- Generate a wide variety of reports
- Interface with other software applications such as spreadsheets and databases
- Sort information in a variety of ways—for example, by project, by team member, or by work package
- Handle multiple projects
- Work online and respond quickly to changes in schedule, budget, or team task assignments
- Compare actual costs with budgeted costs
- Display data in a variety of ways, including both network diagrams and Gantt or bar charts

See Appendix A in the back of the book for a thorough discussion of project management information systems.

KEY:

Activity Description

Activity Number →

Person Responsible

CRITICAL SUCCESS FACTORS

- Plan the work and then work the plan. It is important to develop a plan before starting to perform the project. Taking the time to develop a well-thought-out plan is critical to the successful accomplishment of any project.

- Participation builds commitment. By participating in the planning of the work, individuals will become committed to accomplishing it according to the plan.

- The project must have a clear objective of what is to be accomplished and defined in terms of end product or deliverable, schedule, and budget, and it must be agreed upon by the customer and the project team that will perform the project.

- The project scope document is valuable for establishing a common understanding and

agreement among project stakeholders regarding the scope of the project.

- Having a quality plan at the outset of the project is extremely beneficial because it will help prevent incurring additional costs and schedule extensions due to rework caused by work and deliverables that fail to meet quality requirements and customer expectations.

- The key to quality control is to monitor the quality of the work early and regularly throughout the performance of the project, rather than waiting until all the work is completed before checking or inspecting for quality.

- The network diagram is also a communication tool for the project team because it shows who is responsible for each activity and how each person's work fits into the overall project.

SUMMARY

The planning process is based on the project objective, which establishes what is to be accomplished. The project objective is usually defined in terms of the end product or deliverable, schedule, and budget. It requires completing the work and producing all the deliverables by a certain time and within budget. It should also include the expected benefits that will result from implementing the project and that will define the success of the project.

The project scope defines *what* needs to be done. It is all the work that must be done to produce all the project deliverables, satisfy the sponsor or customer that all the work and deliverables meet the requirements and acceptance criteria, and accomplish the project objective. The project scope document usually contains the customer requirements, statement of work, deliverables, acceptance criteria, and a work breakdown structure. The project scope document is valuable for establishing a common understanding among project stakeholders regarding the scope of the project. The contractor or project team needs to gain agreement from the sponsor or customer on the project scope document.

It is important to plan for quality in performing the project to assure that the work is done according to specifications and applicable standards and that deliverables meet acceptance criteria. The quality plan must include or reference the specifications, industry or government standards, and codes that must be used and met during the performance of the project work. To help assure quality, the project quality plan should contain written procedures for using various quality tools and techniques. The key to quality control is to monitor the quality of the work early and regularly throughout the performance of the project, rather than waiting until all the work is completed before checking or inspecting for quality. Having a written quality plan at the outset of the project is extremely beneficial because it will help prevent incurring additional costs and schedule extensions due to rework caused by work and deliverables that fail to meet quality requirements and customer expectations.

A work breakdown structure is a deliverable-oriented hierarchical decomposition of the project work scope into work packages that produce the project deliverables. The work breakdown structure establishes the framework for *how* the work will get done to produce the project deliverables. A WBS is a structured approach for organizing all the project work and deliverables into logical groupings and subdividing them into more manageable components to help ensure that all the work and deliverables to complete the project are identified and included in the baseline project plan.

A responsibility assignment matrix illustrates *who* will be responsible for the work. It shows all the individuals associated with each work item in the work breakdown structure, as well as all the work items associated with each individual.

Using the work breakdown structure, the individual or team responsible for each work package must define all the specific activities that need to be performed to produce the end item or deliverable for the work package. Activities define more specifically *how* the work will get done.

A network diagram is a tool for arranging the specific activities in the appropriate sequence and defining their dependent relationships. It defines the sequence of *how* the activities will get done. The network diagram is a roadmap that displays how all the specific activities fit together to accomplish the project

work scope. It also is a communication tool for the project team because it shows who is responsible for each activity and how each person's work fits into the overall project.

Project planning is a critical activity in developing an information system. A project management planning tool, or methodology, called the systems development life cycle is often used to help plan, execute, and control information system development projects. The SDLC consists of a set of phases or steps: problem definition, system analysis, system design, system development, system testing, and system implementation. All of these steps need to be completed over the course of a development project.

A variety of project management information systems are available to help and support the project manager and project team in planning, monitoring, and controlling projects.

QUESTIONS

1. What is meant by planning a project? What does this encompass? Who should be involved in planning the work?
2. What is meant by the term project objective? What might happen if a project objective is not clearly written? Give three examples of clearly written project objectives.
3. Describe a project scope document. Why is it important to clearly define the project scope?
4. What is a work breakdown structure? What is a responsibility assignment matrix? How are they related?
5. Why is creating a plan for quality important? From your experience, give an example of how having and controlling a quality plan could have prevented (or did prevent) quality problems in a project.
6. What is an activity? Does it always require human effort? Refer to Figure 4.1. Provide a detailed list of activities needed to accomplish work package 3.3. Do the same for work package 4.2.
7. Refer to Figure 4.9. What activities must be accomplished before "Input Response Data" can start? What activities can start after "Review Comments & Finalize Questionnaire" has finished? List two activities that can be done concurrently.
8. When would you use laddering in a network diagram? Give an example, different from the one provided in the chapter, and draw the corresponding network diagram.
9. Why would you recommend project management software to someone involved in project management? What features and benefits does it provide?
10. Draw a network diagram representing the following logic: as the project starts, activities A and B can be performed concurrently. When activity A is finished, activities C and D can start. When activity B is finished, activities E and F can start. When activities D and E are finished, activity G can start. The project is complete when activities C, F, and G are finished.
11. Draw a network diagram representing the following information: the project starts with three activities—A, B, and C—which can be done concurrently. When A is finished, D can start; when B is finished, F can start; when B and D are finished, E can start. The project is complete when C, E, and F are finished.

Draw a network diagram that represents the following information system development task list.

Activity	Immediate Predecessor
Problem Definition	—
Study Current System	1
Define User Requirements	1
Logical System Design	3
Physical System Design	2
System Development	4, 5
System Testing	6
Convert Database	4, 5
System Conversion	7, 8

INTERNET EXERCISES

For the website addresses of the organizations mentioned in these exercises, go to "Internet Exercises" at the book's companion website at www.cengagebrain.com. It is suggested that you save this website in your "Favorites" list for easy access in the future.

1. Search the Web for project planning tools and describe at least three sites that you find.
2. Visit the website of the International Project Management Association (IPMA). Explore the site to learn more about certifications, memberships, publications, awards, events, and educational opportunities.
3. Look at the IPMA link called "Young Crew." Young Crew is a key component of IPMA's strategy for nurturing the project management leaders of tomorrow. Describe what you found.
4. The *International Journal of Project Management* is an IPMA publication. Go to the journal's home page or go to the website of Elsevier Science Direct and search for the journal. Click on the "Free Tables of Contents and Abstracts" link. Print out a list of articles from the current edition.
5. Within the "Free Tables of Contents and Abstracts" link, perform a quick search using the keyword "Planning." Provide a list of what you found. Next, click on "View Related Articles" and describe what you found.

CASE STUDY 1 A Not-for-Profit Medical Research Center

You are Alexis, the director of external affairs for a national not-for-profit medical research center that does research on diseases related to aging. The center's work depends on funding from multiple sources, including the general public, individual estates, and grants from corporations, foundations, and the federal government.

Your department prepares an annual report of the center's accomplishments and financial status for the board of directors. It is mostly text with a few charts and tables, all black and white, with a simple cover. It is voluminous and pretty dry reading. It is inexpensive to produce other than the effort to pull together the content, which requires time to request and expedite information from the center's other departments.

At the last board meeting, the board members suggested the annual report be "upscaled" into a document that could be used for marketing and promotional purposes. They want you to mail the next annual report to the center's various stakeholders, past donors, and targeted high-potential future donors. The board feels that such a document is needed to get the center "in the same league" with other large not-for-profit organizations with which it feels it competes for donations and funds. The board feels that the annual report could be used to inform these stakeholders about the advances the center is making in its research efforts and its strong fiscal management for effectively using the funding and donations it receives.

You will need to produce a shorter, simpler, easy-to-read annual report that shows the benefits of the center's research and the impact on people's lives. You will include pictures from various hospitals, clinics, and long-term care facilities that are using the results of the center's research. You also will include testimonials from patients and families who have benefited from the center's research. The report must be "eye-catching." It needs to be multicolor, contain a lot of pictures and easy-to-understand graphics, and be written in a style that can be understood by the average adult potential donor.

This is a significant undertaking for your department, which includes three other staff members. You will have to contract out some of the activities and may have to travel to several medical facilities around the country to take photos and get testimonials. You will also need to put the design, printing, and distribution out to bid to various contractors to submit proposals and prices to you. You estimate that approximately 5 million copies need to be printed and mailed.

It is now April 1. The board asks you to come to its next meeting on May 15 to present a detailed plan, schedule, and budget for how you will complete the project. The board wants the annual report "in the mail" by November 15, so potential donors will receive it around the holiday season when they may be in a "giving mood." The center's fiscal year ends September 30, and its financial statements should be available by October 15. However, the nonfinancial information for the report can start to be pulled together right after the May 15 board meeting.

Fortunately, you are taking a project management course in the evenings at the local university and see this as an opportunity to apply what you have been learning. You know that this is a big project and that the board has high expectations. You want to be sure you meet their expectations, and get them to approve the budget that you will need for this project. However, they will only do that if they are confident that you have a detailed plan for how you will get it all done. You and your staff have six weeks to prepare a plan to present to the board on May 15. If approved, you will have six months, from May 15 to November 15, to implement the plan and complete the project.

Your staff consists of Grace, a marketing specialist; Levi, a writer/editor; and Lakysha, a staff assistant whose hobby is photography (she is going to college part-time in the evenings to earn a degree in photojournalism, and has won several local photography contests).

CASE QUESTIONS
You and your team need to prepare a plan to present to the board. You must:

1. Establish the project objective, and make a list of your assumptions about the project.
2. Develop a work breakdown structure.
3. Prepare a list of the specific activities that need to be performed to accomplish the project objective.
4. For each activity, assign the person who will be responsible.
5. Create a network diagram that shows the sequence and dependent relationships of all the activities.

Note: This case study will continue in Chapters 5 through 8, so save the results of your work.

GROUP ACTIVITY
Divide the course participants into groups of four, with the people in each group assuming the role of Alexis, Grace, Levi, or Lakysha. Then address each of the steps listed above.

CASE STUDY 2 The Wedding

Tony and Peggy Sue graduated from a university in Texas last May. She received a degree in elementary education, and he graduated from the culinary school. They both now work in the Dallas area. Peggy Sue teaches, and Tony is a chef at a resort hotel restaurant.

It is Christmas Day and Tony asks Peggy Sue to marry him. She excitedly accepts. They set a wedding date of June 30.

Tony is from New York City. He is the only son of "Big Tony" and Carmella. He is known as "Little Tony" to his family. He has three younger sisters, none of whom are yet married. The family owns a restaurant called Big Tony's, and all four children have worked in the restaurant since they were young. They have a large extended family with many relatives, most of whom live in New York City. They also have many friends in the neighborhood.

Peggy Sue is from Cornfield, Nebraska. She is the youngest of four sisters. She and her sisters worked on the family farm when they were young. Her father passed away several years ago. Her mother, Mildred, now lives alone in the family farmhouse and leases the farmland to a neighboring farmer. Peggy Sue's sisters all married local men and all live in Cornfield. All of their weddings were small (about 50 people), simple, and pretty much the same. Mildred has the wedding plans down to almost a standard operating procedure—9:00 A.M. ceremony at the small church, followed by a buffet brunch in the church hall, and that is about it. They really could not afford much more elaborate

weddings because the income from the farm had been pretty meager. Peggy Sue's sisters did not go to college, and she had to take out loans to pay for her college expenses.

Tony and Peggy Sue decide to call home and announce the good news about their engagement and the forthcoming wedding.

Tony calls home and tells his mom, Carmella, the news. She replies, "That's great, honey! I've been waiting for this day. I can't believe my little baby is getting married. I'm so excited. We're going to have the biggest, best wedding ever. All our friends and family will come to celebrate. We'll probably have 300 people. And, of course, we'll have the reception at our restaurant; the banquet room should be big enough. I'll tell your cousin Vinnie that you want him to be best man. You grew up together, although you haven't seen much of each other since you went off to college in Texas. I'll call Aunt Lucy as soon as we're done talking and tell her that we want her little Maria and Teresa to be flower girls and little Nicky to be ring bearer. And, oh, I almost forgot the most important thing—your sisters, they'll all be bridesmaids. I already know what color their gowns will be—a deep rose; they'll be gorgeous. And sweetie, I didn't ask your papa yet, but I know he'll agree with me—on Monday, I'm going to call my friend Francine, the travel agent, and get two tickets for you for a two-week honeymoon in Italy. You've never been there, and you must go. It will be a gift from your papa and me. And tell Peggy Lee or Peggy Susie or whatever congratulations. We are so happy for both of you. It's your wedding, and I don't want to interfere. I'll just be here to help. You know what I'm saying. So, my little Tony, whatever you want me to do, you just tell me. And one more thing, I'll see Father Frank after Mass on Sunday and tell him to mark his calendar already for a two o'clock ceremony on June 30. Goodbye, my big boy. I'll tell Papa you called. And I can't wait to start telling everybody to get ready to party on June 30."

Peggy Sue also calls her mom to tell her the news about the upcoming wedding. Mildred responds, "That's wonderful, dear. I'm glad you're finally getting married. You waited so long with going off to college and everything. I'll start getting everything ready. I know how to do this in my sleep by now. I'll mention it to Reverend Johnson after Sunday service. I'll tell your sisters to expect to be bridesmaids again in keeping with the family tradition. I guess Holley will be the matron of honor; it's her turn. By the way, she's expecting her third child probably right around the same time as your wedding, but I don't think that will matter. Well, I guess pretty soon you'll be having babies of your own, like all your sisters. I'm glad you are finally settling down. You should really be thinking about moving back home, now that you are done with college. I saw Emma Miller, your second-grade teacher, at the grocery store the other day. She told me she is retiring. I told her you would be excited to hear that and probably want to apply for her job."

"She said she didn't think they would have too many people applying so you would have a good chance. You could move in with me. The house is so big and lonely. There is plenty of room, and I can help you watch your babies. And your boyfriend, Tony—isn't he a cook or something? I'm sure he could probably get a job at the diner in town. Oh dear, I'm so happy. I've been praying that you would come back ever since you left. I'll tell all your sisters the news when they all come over for family dinner tonight. It won't be long before we're all together again. Goodbye, my dear, and you be careful in that big city."

Tony and Peggy Sue start discussing their wedding. They decide they want a big wedding—with their families and friends, including a lot of their college friends. They want an outdoor ceremony and outdoor reception, including plenty of food, music, and dancing into the night. They are not sure how much it will cost, though, and realize Peggy Sue's mother cannot afford to pay for the wedding, so they will have to pay for it themselves. Both Tony and Peggy Sue have college loans to pay back, but they hope that the money gifts they get from the wedding guests will be enough to pay for the wedding expenses and maybe have some left over for a honeymoon.

It is now New Year's Day, and Tony and Peggy Sue decide to sit down and start laying out the detailed plan of all the things they need to do to get ready for their wedding.

CASE QUESTIONS

1. Make a list of assumptions that will be used as the basis for planning the wedding. And no, it is not acceptable to assume that Tony and Peggy Sue will just elope, no matter how tempting that may be!
2. Develop a work breakdown structure.
3. Make a list of the specific activities that need to be done between now and the wedding day.
4. For each activity, identify the person (Tony, Peggy Sue, and so forth) who will be responsible for seeing that the activity is accomplished.
5. Create a network diagram that shows the sequence and dependent relationships of all the activities.

Note: This case study will continue in Chapters 5 through 8, so save the results of your work.

GROUP ACTIVITY

Divide the course participants into groups of three or four, then address each of the steps listed above.

REFERENCES

A Guide to the Project Management Body of Knowledge (PMBOK® Guide) Fifth Edition. Newtown Square, PA: Project Management Institute, 2013.

Altuwaijri, M. M. and M. S. Khorsheed (2012). "InnoDiff: A Project-based Model for Successful IT Innovation Diffusion," *International Journal of Project Management, 30,* 37–47.

Banham, R. and N. Webb (2012). "Project Runaway," *CFO, 28*(4), 46–51.

Chen, C., L. Heng-An, and J. Song (2013). "Integrated Projects Planning in IS Departments: A Multi-Period Multi-Project Selection and Assignment Approach with a Computerized Implementation," *European Journal of Operational Research, 229*(3), 683.

de Vries, J. (2013). "The Influence of Power and Interest on Designing Inventory Management Systems," *International Journal of Production Economics, 143*(2), 233.

de Waal, B., P. Breman, and R. Batenburg (2012). "Do Employees Accept the Information Systems That Management Buy? A BPM Implementation Case Study," *European Conference on Management, Leadership & Governance*, 110-X. Kidmore End: Academic Conferences International Limited.

Doloi, H., A. Sawhney, K. C. Iyer, and S. Rentala (2013). "Analysing Factors Affecting Delays in Indian Construction Projects," *International Journal of Project Management*, 30(4), 479–489.

Ertis, A. (2012). "Building Abroad," *Smart Business Northern California*, 5(10), 12.

Gale, S. F. (2013). "Climate Chaos Demands New Infrastructure," *PM Network*, 27(3), 18–19.

Gutjahr, W. J. and K. A. Froeschl (2013). "Project Portfolio Selection Under Uncertainty with Outsourcing Opportunities." *Flexible Services and Manufacturing Journal*, 25(1–2), 255–281.

Jørgensen, M. (2013). "The Influence of Selection Bias on Effort Overruns in Software Development Projects." *Information and Software Technology*, 55(9), 1640.

Killen, C. and C. Kjaer (2012). "Understanding Project Interdependencies: The Role of Visual Representation, Culture and Process," *International Journal of Project Management*, 30, 545–566.

Li, Q., M. Syal, N. Turner, and M. Arif (2013). "Constructors and Innovation Credits in Green Building Projects," *Construction Innovation*, 13(3), 320–338.

Parker, D., J. Charlton, A. Ribeiro, and R. D. Pathak (2013). "Integration of Project-based Management and Change Management," *International Journal of Productivity and Performance Management*, 62(5), 534–544.

Sleesman, D. J., D. E. Conlon, G. McNamara, and J. E. Miles (2012). "Cleaning Up the Big Muddy: A Meta-Analytic Review of the Determinants of Escalation of Commitment," *Academy of Management Journal*, 55(3), 541–562.

Sundic, M. and K. Leitner (2013). "Crowdsourcing as an Innovation Strategy: A Study on Innovation Platforms in Austria and Switzerland." *Communications & Strategies*, 89, 55–72.

Vogel, B. (2013). "Winter Planning Brings Benefits," *Jane's Airport Review*, 25(7), np.

APPENDIX | Microsoft Project

Microsoft Project is the most widely used project management software system in the business environment today. It is powerful, easy to use, and available at a very reasonable price. **A free trial version is included with new copies of this text**. In this appendix, we will briefly discuss how Microsoft Project can be used to support the techniques discussed in this chapter, based on the consumer market study example.

Becoming oriented with the Microsoft Project 2013 environment: Open Microsoft Project 2013. Notice the Gantt Chart View and the Task ribbon in the main workspace. If you do not see Gantt Chart Tools above Format in the Menu or the Task ribbon, click on Task to open the Task ribbon, then in the Tasks View group, click Gantt Chart. Above the main workspace are the ribbons for Task, Resource, Report, Project, View, and Format. To view any of the ribbons, click on the tab with the ribbon's name. To the left of the ribbon titles

is the File tab, which contains links to Microsoft Office Online in the Help link, a list of the previously opened Microsoft Project files, and options to save or print the current project or to begin a New Project.

A quick link to Microsoft Online is available in the upper right corner of the project window as a Question Mark button. The Format ribbon changes to include groups related to the view selected. The Gantt Chart Tools Format ribbon contains Format, Columns, Bar Styles, Gantt Chart Style, Show/Hide, and Drawings groups with selections that format the Gantt Chart. The Resource Usage Tools Format ribbon contains Format, Columns, Details, and Assignments groups that format the Resource Usage chart.

Visit Microsoft Office Online for online tutorials and more: If you have not already explored Microsoft Office Online, set aside some time to do so. There you will find tutorials, tips, templates, news, and other valuable information about Microsoft Project 2013. The link to Microsoft Office Online is provided in the Help link on the File tab or as the quick link on the project window as a Question Mark button.

Let's begin building the Consumer Market Study Project:
The Consumer Market Study project will continue through Chapter 7. In this appendix, you will enter the work breakdown structure in a hierarchical indentured list format, determine predecessors for tasks, assign responsibility for each activity, and create the network diagram.

On the File tab, click New to begin a new project. Then, from the available templates, select Blank Project and click on Create. Save the file as Consumer Market Study by clicking on the File tab and the Save As link. After choosing a location and entering the name of the file, click Save.

First, set some properties to describe the project file. On the File tab, click on the Info link. On the right side of the page will be the name Project Information with a drop-down arrow. Click on Project Information. Two choices will appear in a pop-up window: Advanced Properties and Project Statistics. Click on Advanced Properties. In the Advanced Properties window, click on the Summary tab and enter "Consumer Market Study" as the title, as shown in Figure 4A.1. You can enter other information, such as Subject, Author, Manager, Company, and other related comments. Click on OK to save, and close the Advanced Properties window. Click the Arrow in the upper left corner to return to the Project ribbon and the entry view.

You also need to enter time-related information so that the software can automatically build project schedules and calculate costs.

On the Project ribbon, click on the Project Information link in the Properties group to view the Project Information window, and enter the Start date: Mon 1/12/15, as in Figure 4A.2. Click on OK to close the Project Information window.

Click on the Task ribbon to display the Task ribbon tools. You should see the Gantt Chart View with the Entry Table on your screen. Here you will display the project title and enter the names for the work packages and their activities into the Task Name column on the level at which you want to monitor and control the budget, and can collect data on actual costs and the value of the work

FIGURE 4A.1 Project Properties

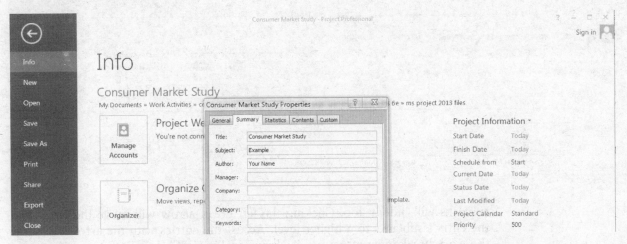

completed during the performance of the project. To display the project name as Task 0, on the Gantt Chart Tools Format ribbon, click on Project Summary Task in the Show/Hide group (as shown in Figure 4A.3). Next enter the names of the work packages to be completed in the Task Name column. Please refer to Figure 4A.4 for the names to enter.

After you enter a name, notice the Task Mode column has questions about the type of Task Mode automatically entered. Leave these as the default values for now.

You can easily create subsets of the work packages and their activities. In the Task ribbon in the Schedule group, you should see two green arrows. You can use these arrows to create subtasks and to bring a task to a higher level of organization. Highlight the row you want to indent. Click the green arrow to the right once to indent the work packages. Notice that all the highlighted row's

FIGURE 4A.2 Project Information

FIGURE 4A.3 **Project Summary Task**

subtasks will indent, too. Clicking the left green arrow will move the entry and the entry's subtasks to a higher level. Adjust the entries with the arrows to show the work breakdown structure, as shown in Figure 4A.4.

Next, you will enter the predecessor data directly into the Predecessor column to show dependencies among the activities for the work packages. Please see Figure 4A.5 for this data. Each row has a task number along the left column.

FIGURE 4A.4 **Work Package and Activity Entry**

#	Task Name	Duration	Start	Finish
0	⊿ Consumer Market Study	1 day?	Mon 1/12/15	Mon 1/12/15
1	⊿ Questionnaire	1 day?	Mon 1/12/15	Mon 1/12/15
2	⊿ Design	1 day?	Mon 1/12/15	Mon 1/12/15
3	Identify Target Consumers			
4	Develop Draft Questionnaire			
5	Pilot-Test Questionnaire			
6	Review Comments & Finalize Questionnaire			
7	Develop Software Test Data			
8	⊿ Responses	1 day?	Mon 1/12/15	Mon 1/12/15
9	Print Questionnaire			
10	Prepare Mailing Labels			
11	Mail Questionnaire & Get Responses			
12	⊿ Report	1 day?	Mon 1/12/15	Mon 1/12/15
13	⊿ Software	1 day?	Mon 1/12/15	Mon 1/12/15
14	Develop Data Analysis Software			
15	Test Software			
16	⊿ Report	1 day?	Mon 1/12/15	Mon 1/12/15
17	Input Response Data			
18	Analyze Results			
19	Prepare Report			

FIGURE 4A.5 Tasks—Entering Predecessor Data

You will use this number to identify the task for the dependencies. For example, Task 3 is the predecessor for Task 4 or, in other words, Task 4 is dependent on the completion of Task 3. If a task has more than one predecessor, use a comma to separate the task number entries.

The Consumer Market Study project team consists of Susan, Steve, Andy, and Jim. You can show who will perform each activity by entering the name in the Resource Names column for the activity in the Entry Table. Please refer to Figure 4A.6 for name-activity assignments in this exercise. Names are assigned to the activities to monitor and control the project's budget and collect data for the actual costs and performance. Names assigned to a work package will cue Microsoft Project to assign costs and time to the work package in addition to its activities and are likely to result in incorrect reports for the project's costs and workers' performance.

To view the network diagram shown in Figure 4A.7, on the Task ribbon, click on the View group down arrow and select Network Diagram.

Saving a project with a baseline plan before the project starts is highly recommended so that you can compare actual progress versus planned progress once the project has started. To set a baseline, click on the Project ribbon and select

FIGURE 4A.6 Resources

FIGURE 4A.7 Network Diagram

FIGURE 4A.8 **Set Baseline for Project**

Set Baseline in the Schedule group, as shown in Figure 4A.8. Click OK after making your choice in the Set Baseline window. You can also use this tool to clear a baseline. It is helpful to save your project as you work. To save your project information, on the File tab, click on Save.

Developing the Schedule

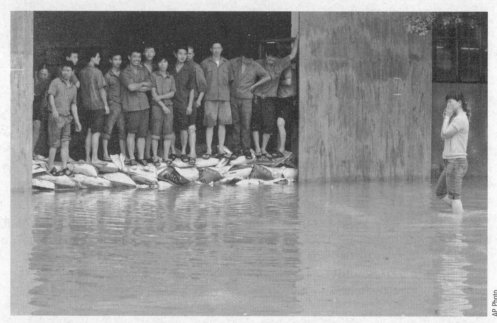

AP Photo

Concepts in this chapter support the following Project Management Knowledge Areas of *A Guide to the Project Management Body of Knowledge (PMBOK® Guide)*:

Project Integration Management
Project Time Management

 REAL WORLD PROJECT MANAGEMENT

More than Rain Delays Construction in Taiwan

Weather has always played a part in the scheduling of construction projects. Typhoons in Taiwan are known to suspend or extend project schedules. Delayed starts and extended durations have pushed activities on the critical paths to cause project delays on hundreds of construction projects in Taiwan. These scheduling

delays are resulting in litigation, an average of 1.3 claims for each of the Taiwan Area National Expressway Engineering Bureau's 300 construction projects.

Project scheduling by experienced project managers and teams had taken into account potential causes for delays and had planned for predictable causes. The litigation claims in Taiwan are due to delays in precedent activities that impacted the work to be performed by contractors assigned to the delayed subsequent activities. These costly delays are a lesson for all who schedule the activities of any type of project and, in particular, construction projects.

Two main causes of critical path delays were identified—delayed start of the project and extended duration of activities. The challenges for the project delay causes were exclusive to each delay type.

Delayed starts were caused by public resistance, delayed site handover, change orders, government regulation changes, and delayed precedent activities. In addition to weather, extended duration delays were caused by changed site conditions, changed scope of work, shortages of materials, contractor financial difficulties, delayed inspections and acceptance by owner, inadequate construction approaches and methods, poor site management, and ambiguous definition and approval of calendar working days. A lesser extent of causes for extended duration of project activities include interference by the owner, contract issues, accidents, and price escalations.

A further examination into the causes reveals a common theme—change management. The team developing the schedule should use the lessons learned to include the expected impacts of changes to the orders and scope of work to limit the delays and the litigations. Even though the weather remains a leading cause for delays of the project's critical path, approaches to mitigate the other causes of delays in the project schedule are necessary to develop the most realistic schedule. Contingency inclusions within contracts are one method of mitigation, contingency scheduling is another.

Many lessons related to scheduling are to be learned from these 300 construction projects and their delays. A proactive approach to scheduling delay mitigation could offset the vast number of claims made in Taiwan and increase the probability of completing projects on time and within the planned schedule. Careful schedule planning to include the weather and expected changes are important to future planning efforts for successful project management in Taiwan or in your projects.

Based on information from Jyh-Bin, Y., C. Mei-Yi, and K. Huang (2013). "An Empirical Study of Schedule Delay Causes Based on Taiwan's Litigation Cases," *Project Management Journal, 44*(3), 21–31. doi:10.1002/pmj.21337.

The previous chapter discussed what work needs to be done in terms of scope and deliverables. It also discussed how that work will get done by defining specific activities and arranging them in a sequence of dependent relationships to create a network plan. This network plan is a roadmap for how all the activities fit together to accomplish the project work scope and objective. When network planning techniques are used, the scheduling function depends on the planning function. A *schedule* is a timetable for the plan and, therefore, cannot be established until the network-based plan has been created. In this chapter, we will develop a schedule for that plan. This chapter deals



with estimating the resources and durations for all the specific activities, and developing a detailed project schedule that determines when each activity should start and finish.

This chapter also discusses monitoring and controlling the progress of the project, replanning, and updating the project schedule. Once a project actually starts, it is necessary to monitor progress to ensure that everything is going according to schedule. This involves measuring actual progress and comparing it to the schedule. If at any time during the project it is determined that the project is behind schedule, corrective action must be taken to get back on schedule, which may be very difficult if a project gets too far behind.

The key to effective project control is measuring actual progress and comparing it to planned progress on a timely and regular basis and taking any needed corrective action immediately. A project manager cannot simply hope that a problem will go away without corrective intervention—it will not. Based on actual progress and on consideration of other changes that may occur, an updated project schedule can be generated regularly that forecasts whether the project will finish ahead of or behind its required completion time. You will become familiar with,

- Estimating the resources required for each activity
- Estimating the duration for each activity
- Establishing the estimated start time and required completion time for the overall project
- Calculating the earliest times at which each activity can start and finish, based on the project estimated start time
- Calculating the latest times by which each activity must start and finish to complete the project by its required completion time
- Determining the amount of positive or negative slack between the time each activity can start or finish and the time it must start or finish
- Identifying the critical (longest) path of activities
- Performing the steps in the project control process
- Determining the effects of actual schedule performance on the project schedule
- Incorporating changes into the schedule
- Developing an updated project schedule
- Determining approaches to controlling the project schedule
- Implementing agile project management

LEARNING OUTCOMES

After studying this chapter, the learner should be able to:

- Estimate the resources required for activities
- Estimate the duration for an activity
- Determine the earliest start and finish times for activities
- Determine the latest start and finish times for activities

- Explain and determine total slack
- Prepare a project schedule
- Identify and explain the critical path
- Discuss the project control process

- Develop updated schedules based on actual progress and changes
- Discuss and apply approaches to control the project schedule
- Explain agile project management

Estimate Activity Resources

It is necessary to estimate the types and quantities of resources that will be required to perform each specific activity to subsequently estimate how long it will take to perform the activity. Resources include people, materials, equipment, facilities, and so forth. The **estimated resources** required for an activity will influence the estimated duration to perform the activity and the estimated cost of the activity.

When estimating resources for activities, the *availability* of each resource has to be taken into account. It is important to know what types of resources are available, in what quantities, and during what time periods to determine if the right types of resources will be available in sufficient quantities during the time periods that they are needed for specific activities. For example, a project for a new building requires architects and engineers during the design phase at the front end of the project, and then requires crafts and tradespeople during the construction phase. So the architect-engineering firm needs to have architects and engineers available when they will be needed to design the new office building. If they will not be available because they are assigned to work on other projects, it could delay the design of the office building or may require outsourcing the design activities to a subcontractor. When considering the availability of resources, it may be necessary to make some assumptions, such as the ability to hire additional individuals with the appropriate expertise in time for when they will be required to work on a project. For example, a project to develop a new information system to track product recalls may require more software developers than are currently available on staff. So when resources are estimated for specific software development activities, it may be determined that a certain quantity of software developers are required, along with the assumption that additional developers will be hired and available by the time they are required.

With an understanding of the availability of the types and quantities of various resources during the period the project will be performed, it is necessary to *estimate the types and quantities of resources required to perform each specific activity*. In many cases, especially for smaller projects, most activities involve people resources—that is, the members of the project team who may be utilized full time or part time during the project. For example, it is estimated that four painters are needed to paint the interior of a new house. If four painters are not available during the period they will be needed, then some of the painters may have to work extra hours or some of the work may have to be subcontracted. On the other hand, if too many painters are estimated, it would cause a problem of inefficiency because they would be bumping into each other, or they might have an excessive amount of idle time. In addition to people resources, specific activities may also require an estimate of equipment resources, such as the types and quantities of earth-moving equipment required to clear the land for an expansion of a school building. Similarly, there may be specific activities that require an estimate of materials or supplies needed for performing an activity, such as the lumber needed to frame a house, or the shingles needed to install a roof, or the furniture needed to be installed at a new day care center. Sometimes, estimating the types and quantities of materials that will be required for a specific activity provides an opportunity or reminder to include some related activities that may have been unintentionally forgotten when the specific activities were defined for a work package. In the case of the furniture, maybe the materials estimate was for the activity to install furniture, but then it was realized that several other preceding activities

associated with the furniture had been left out, including requesting bids or quotes for the furniture, reviewing proposals, and ordering the furniture, as well as the supplier's task of making and/or delivering the furniture.

The estimated types and quantities of resources required for an activity together with the availability of those resources will influence the estimated duration for how long it will take to perform the activity.

When estimating the types and quantities of resources required for each specific activity, it is valuable to involve a person who has expertise or experience with the activity to help make the estimate. The estimated activity resources will also be used later for estimating activity costs and determining the project budget. See the section on estimating activity costs in Chapter 7 for further information.

See Chapter 6, Resource Utilization, for further discussion of this topic.

Estimate Activity Durations

Once the types and quantities of resources are estimated for each activity, estimates can be made for *how long* it will take to perform each activity. The **estimated duration** for each activity must be the *total elapsed time*—the time for the work to be done plus any associated waiting time. In Figure 5.1, for example, the estimated duration for activity 1, "Varnish Floors," is five days, which includes both the time to varnish the floors and the waiting time for the varnish to dry.

The activity's estimated duration is shown in the lower right-hand corner of the box.

It is a good practice to have the person who will be responsible for performing a specific activity estimate the duration for that activity. This generates a commitment from that person and avoids any bias that may be introduced by having one person estimate the durations for all of the activities. In some cases, though—such as for large projects that involve several hundred people performing various activities over several years—it may not be practical to have each person estimate activity durations at the beginning of the project. Rather, each organization or subcontractor responsible for a group or type of activities may designate an experienced individual to estimate the durations for all the activities for which the organization or subcontractor is responsible. If an organization or subcontractor has performed similar projects in the past and has kept records of how long specific activities actually took, these historical data can be used as a guide in estimating the durations of similar activities for future projects.

FIGURE 5.1 Activity Estimated Duration

The estimated duration for an activity must be based on the estimated quantity of resources required to perform the activity. The estimated duration should be aggressive, yet realistic. It should not include time for a lot of things that could possibly go wrong. Nor should it be too optimistically short. It is generally better to be somewhat aggressive and estimate a duration for an activity at 5 days, say, and then actually finish it in 6 days, than to be overly conservative and estimate a duration at 10 days and then actually take 10 days. People sometimes perform to expectations—if an activity is estimated to take 10 days, their effort will expand to fill the whole 10 days allotted, even if the activity could have been performed in a shorter time.

Playing the game of inflating estimated durations in anticipation of the project manager negotiating shorter durations is not a good practice. Nor is padding estimates with the vision of becoming a hero when the activities are completed in less time than estimated.

Throughout the performance of the project, some activities will take longer than their estimated duration, others will be done in less time than their estimated duration, and a few may conform to the estimated duration exactly. Over the life of a project that involves many activities, such delays and accelerations will tend to cancel one another out. For example, one activity may take two weeks longer than originally estimated, but this delay may be offset by two other activities that each takes a week less than originally estimated.

It should be noted that at the beginning of the project, it may not be possible to estimate the durations for all activities with a level of confidence regarding their accuracy. This is especially true for longer-term projects. It may be easier to estimate the durations for near-term activities, but as the project progresses, the project team can *progressively elaborate* the estimated durations as more information is known or becomes clear to allow for more accurate estimated durations.

Figure 5.2 shows the network diagram for a consumer market study, with the estimated durations in days for each activity. A consistent time base, such as hours or days or weeks, should be used for all the estimated durations of activities in a network diagram.

With projects for which there is a high degree of uncertainty about the estimated durations for activities, it is possible to use three time estimates: an optimistic estimate, a pessimistic estimate, and a most likely estimate. For a discussion of this probabilistic technique, see Appendix 1 at the end of this chapter.

Establish Project Start and Completion Times

To establish a basis from which to calculate a schedule using the estimated durations for the activities, it is necessary to select an **estimated start time** for when the project is expected to begin and a **required completion time** for when the project must be done. These two times (or dates) define the overall window, or envelope, of time in which the project must be completed.

The sponsor or customer often states the project required completion time in the project charter, request for proposal (RFP), or contract—for example, the project must be finished by June 30, the feasibility study must be completed in time for the board meeting on September 30, or the annual reports must be in the mail by January 15.

The contractor, however, may not want to commit to completing the project by a specific date until the customer has approved the contract. In such cases, the contract may state, "The project will be completed within 90 days after signing of

FIGURE 5.2 Network Diagram for Consumer Market Study Project, Showing Estimated Durations

the contract." Here, the overall project time is stated in terms of a cycle time (90 days) rather than in terms of specific calendar dates.

Assume that the consumer market study project shown in Figure 5.2 must be completed in 130 working days. If we establish the project estimated start time as 0, then its required completion time is day 130.

Develop Project Schedule

Once you have an estimated duration for each activity in the network and have established an overall window of time in which the project must be completed, you must determine (based on durations and sequence) whether the project can be done by the required completion time. To determine this, you can develop a project schedule that provides a timetable for each activity and shows:

1. The earliest times (or dates) at which each activity can start and finish, based on the project estimated start time (or date).
2. The latest times (or dates) by which each activity must start and finish to complete the project by its required completion time (or date).

EARLIEST START AND FINISH TIMES

Given an estimated duration for each activity in the network and using the project estimated start time as a reference, you can calculate the following two times for each activity:

KEY:

Activity
Description

Activity
Number

Estimated
Duration

Person
Responsible

1. **Earliest start (ES) time** is the earliest time at which a specific activity can begin, calculated on the basis of the project estimated start time and the estimated durations of preceding activities.
2. **Earliest finish (EF) time** is the earliest time by which a specific activity can be completed, calculated by adding the activity's estimated duration to the activity's earliest start time:

$$EF = ES + \text{Estimated Duration}$$

The ES and EF times are determined by calculating *forward*—that is, by working through the network diagram from the beginning of the project to the end of the project. There is one rule that must be followed in making these forward calculations:

Rule 1: The earliest start time for a specific activity must be the same as or later than the latest of all the earliest finish times of all the activities leading directly into that specific activity.

Figure 5.3 shows three activities leading directly into "Dress Rehearsal." "Practice Skit" has an EF of day 5, "Make Costumes" has an EF of day 10, and "Make Props" has an EF of day 4. "Dress Rehearsal" cannot start until all three of these activities are finished, so the latest of the EFs for these three activities determines the ES for "Dress Rehearsal." The latest of the three EFs is day 10—the EF time for "Make Costumes." Therefore, "Dress Rehearsal" cannot start any earlier than day 10. That is, its ES must be day 10 or later. Even though "Practice Skit" and "Make Props" may finish sooner than "Make Costumes," "Dress Rehearsal" cannot start because the network dependent relationships indicate that *all three activities* must be finished before "Dress Rehearsal" can start.

Reinforce Your Learning

7. What is the equation for calculating an activity's earliest finish time?

Reinforce Your Learning

8. The earliest start and earliest finish times for activities are determined by calculating

through the network diagram.

FIGURE 5.3 Earliest Start Times

Figure 5.4 shows the forward calculations for the consumer market study project. The project estimated start time is 0. Therefore, the earliest "Identify Target Consumers" can start is time 0, and the earliest it can finish is 3 days later (because its estimated duration is 3 days). When "Identify Target Consumers"

FIGURE 5.4 Network Diagram for Consumer Market Study Project, Showing Earliest Start and Finish Times

Reinforce Your Learning

9. Refer to Figure 5.4. What are the earliest start and earliest finish times for "Pilot-Test Questionnaire"?

Reinforce Your Learning

10. What determines a particular activity's earliest start time?

is finished on day 3, "Develop Draft Questionnaire" can start. It has an estimated duration of 10 days, so its ES is day 3 and its EF is day 13. The calculations of ES and EF for subsequent activities are done similarly, continuing forward through the network diagram.

Look for a moment at "Test Software." It has an ES of day 50 because, according to Rule 1, it cannot start until the two activities leading directly into it are finished. "Develop Data Analysis Software" does not finish until day 50, and "Develop Software Test Data" does not finish until day 40. Because "Test Software" cannot start until both of these are finished, "Test Software" cannot start until day 50.

As a further illustration of Rule 1, refer once more to Figure 5.4. To start "Mail Questionnaire & Get Responses," the two activities immediately preceding it, "Prepare Mailing Labels" and "Print Questionnaire," must be finished. The EF of "Prepare Mailing Labels" is day 40, and the EF of "Print Questionnaire" is day 48. According to Rule 1, it is the later of the two EFs, which is day 48, that determines the ES of "Mail Questionnaire & Get Responses."

If you continue calculating the ES and the EF for each remaining activity in the network diagram in Figure 5.4, you will see that the very last activity, "Prepare Report," has an EF of day 138. That is 8 days beyond the project required completion time of 130 days. At this point, we know there is a problem.

It should be noted that although the ES and EF times for each activity are shown on the network diagram in Figure 5.4, this is *not* normally the case. Rather, the ES and EF times (and the LS and LF times, which are explained in

Required Completion = 130 Working Days

FIGURE 5.5 **Schedule for Consumer Market Study Project, Showing Earliest Start and Finish Times**

Consumer Market Study Project								
	Activity	Respon.	Estim. Dur.	Earliest				
				Start	Finish			
1	Identify Target Consumers	Susan	3	0	3			
2	Develop Draft Questionnaire	Susan	10	3	13			
3	Pilot-Test Questionnaire	Susan	20	13	33			
4	Review Comments & Finalize Questionnaire	Susan	5	33	38			
5	Prepare Mailing Labels	Steve	2	38	40			
6	Print Questionnaire	Steve	10	38	48			
7	Develop Data Analysis Software	Andy	12	38	50			
8	Develop Software Test Data	Susan	2	38	40			
9	Mail Questionnaire & Get Responses	Steve	65	48	113			
10	Test Software	Andy	5	50	55			
11	Input Response Data	Jim	7	113	120			
12	Analyze Results	Jim	8	120	128			
13	Prepare Report	Jim	10	128	138			

the following section) are listed in a separate schedule table, like the one in Figure 5.5. Separating the schedule table from the network logic diagram makes it easier to generate revised and updated schedules (perhaps using project management software), without continually making changes to the ES, EF, LS, and LF times on the network diagram itself.

LATEST START AND FINISH TIMES

Given an estimated duration for each activity in the network and using the project required completion time as a reference, you can calculate the following two times for each activity:

1. **Latest finish (LF) time** is the latest time by which a specific activity must be completed for the entire project to be finished by its required completion time. It is calculated on the basis of the project required completion time and the estimated durations of succeeding activities.
2. **Latest start (LS) time** is the latest time by which a specific activity must be started for the entire project to be finished by its required completion time. It is calculated by subtracting the activity's estimated duration from the activity's latest finish time:

$$LS = LF - \text{Estimated Duration}$$

FIGURE 5.6 **Latest Finish Times**

The LF and LS times are determined by calculating *backward*—that is, by working through the network diagram from the end of the project to its beginning. There is one rule that must be followed in making these backward calculations:

Rule 2: The latest finish time for a specific activity must be the same as or earlier than the earliest of all the latest start times of all the activities emerging directly from that specific activity.

Figure 5.6 shows two activities emerging directly from "Print Posters & Brochures." This project is required to be completed by day 30. Therefore, "Distribute Posters" must be started by day 20 because it has an estimated duration of 10 days, and "Mail Brochures" must be started by day 25 because it has an estimated duration of 5 days. The earlier of these two LSs is day 20. Therefore, the latest that "Print Posters & Brochures" must finish is day 20, so that "Distribute Posters" can start by day 20. Even though "Mail Brochures" does not have to start until day 25, "Print Posters & Brochures" must finish by day 20 or else the whole project will be delayed. If "Print Posters & Brochures" does not finish until day 25, then "Distribute Brochures" will not be able to start until day 25. Because "Distribute Brochures" has an estimated duration of 10 days, it will not finish until day 35, which is 5 days beyond the project required completion time.

Figure 5.7 shows the backward calculations for the consumer market study project. The required completion time for the project is 130 working days. Therefore, the latest that "Prepare Report," the last activity, can finish is day 130, and the latest that it can start is day 120 because its estimated duration is 10 days. For "Prepare Report" to start on day 120, the latest that "Analyze Results" must finish is day 120. If the LF for "Analyze Results" is day 120, then its LS is day 112 because its estimated duration is 8 days. The calculations of LF and LS for prior activities are done similarly, continuing backward through the network diagram.

Look at "Review Comments & Finalize Questionnaire." For the four activities emerging from this activity to start by their LS times (so that the project can finish by its required completion time of 130 days), "Review Comments & Finalize Questionnaire" must be finished by the earliest LS of all four activities, according to Rule 2. The earliest of the four LSs is day 30, the latest time by which "Print Questionnaire" must start. Therefore, the latest that "Review Comments & Finalize Questionnaire" must finish is day 30.

If you continue calculating the LF and the LS for each activity in the network diagram in Figure 5.7, you will see that the very first activity, "Identify Target

Reinforce Your Learning

12. The latest finish and latest start times are determined by calculating

through the network diagram.

Reinforce Your Learning

13. Refer to Figure 5.7. What are the latest finish and latest start times for "Input Response Data"?

Reinforce Your Learning

14. What determines a particular activity's latest finish time?

FIGURE 5.7 **Network Diagram for Consumer Market Study Project, Showing Latest Start and Finish**

Consumers," has an LS of −8! This means that, in order to complete the entire project by its required completion time of 130 days, the project must start 8 days earlier than it is estimated to start. Note that this difference of 8 days is equal to the difference we got when calculating forward through the network diagram to obtain the ES and EF times. In essence, what we have found is that this project may take 138 days to complete, even though its required completion time is 130 days.

Like the ES and EF times, the LS and LF times are usually not shown on the network diagram itself, but rather in a separate schedule table as shown in Figure 5.8.

TOTAL SLACK

In the consumer market study project, there is a difference of eight days between the calculated EF time of the very last activity ("Prepare Report") and the project required completion time. This difference is the **total slack (TS)**, also referred to as *total float*. When the TS is a negative number, as in this example, it indicates a lack of slack over the entire project.

If TS is positive, it represents the maximum amount of time that the activities on a particular path can be delayed without jeopardizing completion of the project by its required completion time. On the other hand, if TS is negative, it represents

Required Completion = 130 Working Days

KEY:

the amount of time that the activities on a particular path must be accelerated to complete the project by its required completion time. If TS is zero, the activities on the path do not need to be accelerated but cannot be delayed.

*The total slack for a particular path of activities is common to and **shared** among all the activities on that path.* Consider the example below.

Required Completion = 20 Days

The earliest the project can finish is day 15 (the sum of the estimated durations of the three activities, 7 + 5 + 3). However, the required completion time for the project is 20 days. The three activities on this path can therefore be delayed up to 5 days without jeopardizing completion of the project by the required time. This does *not* mean that each activity on the path can be delayed 5 days (because this would create a total delay of 15 days); rather, it means that

FIGURE 5.8 Schedule for Consumer Market Study Project, Showing Latest Start and Finish Times

Consumer Market Study Project			Estim. Dur.	Earliest		Latest			
	Activity	Respon.		Start	Finish	Start	Finish		
1	Identify Target Consumers	Susan	3	0	3	–8	–5		
2	Develop Draft Questionnaire	Susan	10	3	13	–5	5		
3	Pilot-Test Questionnaire	Susan	20	13	33	5	25		
4	Review Comments & Finalize Questionnaire	Susan	5	33	38	25	30		
5	Prepare Mailing Labels	Steve	2	38	40	38	40		
6	Print Questionnaire	Steve	10	38	48	30	40		
7	Develop Data Analysis Software	Andy	12	38	50	88	100		
8	Develop Software Test Data	Susan	2	38	40	98	100		
9	Mail Questionnaire & Get Responses	Steve	65	48	113	40	105		
10	Test Software	Andy	5	50	55	100	105		
11	Input Response Data	Jim	7	113	120	105	112		
12	Analyze Results	Jim	8	120	128	112	120		
13	Prepare Report	Jim	10	128	138	120	130		

all the activities that make up the path can have a total delay of 5 days among them. For example, if "Remove Old Wallpaper" actually takes 10 days (3 days longer than the estimated duration of 7 days), then it will use up 3 of the 5 days of TS, and only 2 days of TS will remain.

TS is calculated by subtracting the activity's EF time from its LF time or its ES time from its LS time. That is, the slack is equal to either the latest finish time (LF) minus the earliest finish time (EF) for the activity, or the latest start time (LS) minus the earliest start time (ES) for that activity. The two calculations are equivalent.

$$\text{Total Slack} = \text{LF} - \text{EF}, \quad \text{or} \quad \text{Total Slack} = \text{LS} - \text{ES}$$

CRITICAL PATH

Not all networks are as simple as the one just used to illustrate TS. In large network diagrams, there may be many paths of activities from the project start to the project completion, just as there are many routes you can choose from to get from New York City to Los Angeles. If 20 friends were going to leave at the same time from New York City and each was going to drive a different route to Los Angeles, they could not get together for a party in Los Angeles until the last person had arrived—the one who took the longest (most time-consuming) route. Similarly, a project cannot be completed until the longest (most time-consuming) path of

activities is finished. This longest path in the overall network diagram is called the **critical path**.

One way to determine which activities make up the critical path is to find which ones have the least slack. Subtract the EF time from the LF time for each activity (or subtract the ES time from the LS time—both calculations will result in the same value), and then look for all the activities that have the lowest value (either least positive or most negative). All the activities with this value are on the critical path of activities.

The values of TS for the consumer market study project are shown in Figure 5.9. The lowest value is −8 days. The activities that have this same value of TS make up the path 1–2–3–4–6–9–11–12–13. These nine activities comprise the critical, or most time-consuming, path. The estimated durations of the activities on this path add up to 138 days (3 + 10 + 20 + 5 + 10 + 65 + 7 + 8 + 10). Among them, these activities need to be accelerated 8 days to complete the project by its required completion time of 130 days. Figure 5.10 highlights the activities that make up the critical path.

To eliminate the −8 days of slack, the estimated durations of one or more activities on this critical path need to be reduced. Suppose we reduce the estimated duration of "Mail Questionnaire & Get Responses" from 65 days to 55 days by reducing the time respondents are given to return the questionnaire. Because the estimated duration of an activity on the critical path is being reduced

FIGURE 5.9 **Schedule for Consumer Market Study Project, Showing Total Slack Values**

Consumer Market Study Project			Estim. Dur.	Earliest		Latest		Total Slack	
	Activity	Respon.		Start	Finish	Start	Finish		
1	Identify Target Consumers	Susan	3	0	3	−8	−5	−8	
2	Develop Draft Questionnaire	Susan	10	3	13	−5	5	−8	
3	Pilot-Test Questionnaire	Susan	20	13	33	5	25	−8	
4	Review Comments & Finalize Questionnaire	Susan	5	33	38	25	30	−8	
5	Prepare Mailing Labels	Steve	2	38	40	38	40	0	
6	Print Questionnaire	Steve	10	38	48	30	40	−8	
7	Develop Data Analysis Software	Andy	12	38	50	88	100	50	
8	Develop Software Test Data	Susan	2	38	40	98	100	60	
9	Mail Questionnaire & Get Responses	Steve	65	48	113	40	105	−8	
10	Test Software	Andy	5	50	55	100	105	50	
11	Input Response Data	Jim	7	113	120	105	112	−8	
12	Analyze Results	Jim	8	120	128	112	120	−8	
13	Prepare Report	Jim	10	128	138	120	130	−8	

FIGURE 5.10 Network Diagram for Consumer Market Study Project, Showing the Critical Path

by 10 days, the TS changes from −8 days to +2 days. The revised estimated duration of 55 days can be used to prepare a revised project schedule, as shown in Figure 5.11. This schedule shows that the critical path now has a TS of +2 days, and the project is now estimated to finish in 128 days, which is 2 days earlier than the required completion time of 130 days.

As stated earlier, a large network diagram can have many paths or routes from its beginning to its end. Some of the paths may have positive values of TS; others may have negative values of TS. Those paths with positive values of TS are sometimes referred to as **noncritical paths**, whereas those paths with zero or negative values of TS are referred to as **critical paths**. The longest path is often referred to as the **most critical path**.

*It is not unusual that the initial project schedule that is developed may have negative total slack, and it may then take several **iterations** of revising the estimated resources and estimated durations of specific activities and/or changing the sequence or dependent relationships among activities to arrive at an acceptable baseline schedule.*

Sometimes the project team or contractor reacts to the project required completion date by force-fitting the schedule to meet the project required end date by arbitrarily reducing the estimated durations of specific activities and convincing themselves that somehow (by luck) the activities will get done in the reduced amount of time. Then, when the project does not get completed on time, they seem astonished! Instead, they should develop a realistic schedule, and then

Required Completion = 130 Working Days

KEY:

determine how much negative TS there is based on the customer's required completion date. At that point, they can *rationally* determine how to reduce the negative slack to come up with an acceptable schedule that meets the project required completion date. This is done by making decisions about *how* to reduce the estimated durations of specific activities on the paths with negative slack. This may mean making trade-off decisions to add more resources; working overtime; subcontracting certain tasks; reducing scope/specifications; replacing some resources with higher-cost, more experienced resources; and so forth. As a last resort, it may mean going back to the sponsor or customer and asking for an extension of the project required completion date, for more money for the extra resources to accelerate the schedule, or for approval to reduce scope. It is better to inform the customer early in the project rather than surprising him or her later. It is important to manage the customer's expectations.

FREE SLACK

Another type of slack that is sometimes calculated is **free slack (FS)**, also referred to as *free float*, which is the amount of time a specific activity can be postponed without delaying the ES time of its immediately succeeding activities. It is the *relative difference* between the amounts of TS for activities entering into the same activity. FS is calculated by finding the lowest of the values of TS for all the activities entering into a specific activity and then subtracting it from the values of TS for the other activities also entering into that same activity. Because FS is the relative difference between values of

FIGURE 5.11 Revised Schedule for Consumer Market Study Project

| Consumer Market Study Project | | | Earliest | | Latest | | | |
Activity	Respon.	Estim. Dur.	Start	Finish	Start	Finish	Total Slack	
1 Identify Target Consumers	Susan	3	0	3	2	5	2	
2 Develop Draft Questionnaire	Susan	10	3	13	5	15	2	
3 Pilot-Test Questionnaire	Susan	20	13	33	15	35	2	
4 Review Comments & Finalize Questionnaire	Susan	5	33	38	35	40	2	
5 Prepare Mailing Labels	Steve	2	38	40	48	50	10	
6 Print Questionnaire	Steve	10	38	48	40	50	2	
7 Develop Data Analysis Software	Andy	12	38	50	88	100	50	
8 Develop Software Test Data	Susan	2	38	40	98	100	60	
9 Mail Questionnaire & Get Responses	Steve	55	48	103	50	105	2	
10 Test Software	Andy	5	50	55	100	105	50	
11 Input Response Data	Jim	7	103	110	105	112	2	
12 Analyze Results	Jim	8	110	118	112	120	2	
13 Prepare Report	Jim	10	118	128	120	130	2	

TS for activities entering into the same activity, it will exist only when two or more activities enter into the same activity. Also, because FS is a relative difference between values of TS, *it is always a positive value.*

For an illustration of FS, consider Figures 5.9 and 5.10. In the network diagram in Figure 5.10, there are three instances where a particular activity has more than one activity entering into it:

- Activity 9, "Mail Questionnaire & Get Responses," has activities 5 and 6 entering into it.
- Activity 10, "Test Software," has activities 7 and 8 entering into it.
- Activity 11, "Input Response Data," has activities 9 and 10 entering into it.

In the schedule in Figure 5.9, the values of TS for activities 5 and 6 are 0 and −8 days, respectively. The lesser of these two values is −8 days for activity 6. The FS for activity 5 is the relative difference between its TS, 0, and −8. This relative difference is 8 days: 0 − (−8) = 8 days. This means that activity 5, "Prepare Mailing Labels," already has a FS of 8 days and can slip by up to that amount without delaying the ES time of activity 9, "Mail Questionnaire & Get Responses."

Similarly, the values of TS for activities 7 and 8 are 50 and 60 days, respectively. The lesser of these two values is 50 days. Therefore, activity 8, "Develop Software Test Data," has an FS of 10 days (60 − 50 = 10) and can slip by up to that amount without delaying the ES time of activity 10, "Test Software."

Reinforce Your Learning

18. Refer to Figures 5.9 and 5.10. Of the two activities entering into activity 11, "Input Response Data," which activity has free slack? What is its value?

BAR CHART FORMAT

Network-based planning and scheduling techniques are often compared to another somewhat familiar tool known as a **bar chart**, sometimes referred to as a *Gantt chart*, that displays activities along a *time scale*. This is an older planning and scheduling tool; however, it remains popular because of its simplicity.

Figure 5.12 shows a bar chart for the consumer market study. Activities are listed on the left-hand side, and a *time scale* is shown along the bottom. The estimated duration for each activity is indicated by a bar spanning the period during which the activity is expected to be accomplished. A column that indicates who is responsible for each task can be added to the chart.

Project management software can automatically generate a time-scaled bar chart from the schedule table that is based on the network diagram. These bar charts can display arrows that connect the bars to show the dependent relationships among the activities. The bar chart can be based on the ES and EF times or on the LS and LF times. Figure 5.12 is a bar chart based on the ES and EF times in Figure 5.9.

However, bar charts are sometimes used *instead of* a network-based schedule. This has a shortcoming. When using *only* a bar chart for scheduling, without first creating a network-based schedule, the planning and scheduling of activities

FIGURE 5.12 **Bar Chart for Consumer Market Study Project**

Activity	Person Responsible	Estim. Dur.
Identify Target Consumers	Susan	3
Develop Draft Questionnaire	Susan	10
Pilot-Test Questionnaire	Susan	20
Finalize Questionnaire	Susan	5
Print Questionnaire	Steve	10
Prepare Mailing Labels	Steve	2
Mail Questionnaire & Get Responses	Steve	12
Develop Data Analysis Software	Andy	2
Develop Software Test Data	Susan	65
Test Software	Andy	5
Input Response Data	Jim	7
Analyze Results	Jim	8
Prepare Report	Jim	10

Days

is done simultaneously. The person draws the activity bars proportionate to the estimated durations for each activity and must be aware of the dependent relationships among the activities—that is, which activities must be finished before others can start and which activities can be performed concurrently. A major drawback of using only a traditional bar chart is that it does not graphically display those dependent relationships of activities. Therefore, it is not obvious which activities will be affected when a given activity is delayed.

Project Control Process

Figure 5.13 illustrates the steps in the project control process. It starts with establishing a baseline plan that shows how the project scope will be accomplished on schedule and within budget. Once this baseline plan is agreed upon by the customer and the contractor or project team, the project work can be performed. Then it is necessary to monitor the progress to ensure that everything is going according to the plan. The **project control process** involves regularly gathering data on project performance, comparing actual performance to planned performance, and taking corrective action immediately if actual performance is behind planned performance. This process must occur regularly throughout the project.

A regular **reporting period** (time interval) should be established for comparing actual progress with planned progress. Reporting may be daily, weekly, biweekly, or monthly, depending on the complexity or overall duration of the project. If a project is expected to have an overall duration of a month, the reporting period might be as short as a day. On the other hand, if a project is expected to run five years, the reporting period might be a month.

During each reporting period, two kinds of data or information need to be collected:

1. *Data on actual performance.* This includes

 * The actual time that activities were started and/or finished
 * The actual costs expended and committed
 * The earned value of the work completed

2. *Information on any changes to the project scope, schedule, and budget.* These changes could be initiated by the customer or the project team, or they could be the result of an unanticipated occurrence.

It should be noted that once changes are incorporated into the plan and agreed upon by the sponsor or customer, a new baseline plan has to be established. The scope, schedule, and budget of the new baseline plan may be different from those of the original baseline plan.

It is crucial that the data and information discussed above be collected in a timely manner and used to calculate an updated project schedule and budget. For example, if project reporting is done monthly, data and information should be obtained as late as possible in that monthly period so that when an updated schedule and budget are calculated, they are based on the latest possible information. In other words, a project manager should not gather data at the beginning of the month and then wait until the end of the month to use it to calculate an updated schedule and budget because the data will be outdated and may cause incorrect decisions to be made about the project status and corrective actions.

Reinforce Your Learning

19. If actual _____ is behind _____ performance, _____ should be taken _____.

Reinforce Your Learning

20. What are the two kinds of data or information that need to be collected during each reporting period?

FIGURE 5.13 **Project Control Process**

```
                    ┌─────────────────────────┐
                    │        Establish         │
                    │      baseline plan       │
                    │ (scope, schedule, budget)│
                    └────────────┬─────────────┘
                                 │
                    ┌────────────▼─────────────┐
                    │     Perform project      │
   ┌──────────┐     └────────────┬─────────────┘
   │Wait until│                  │
   │next report◄─────┐  ┌────────▼─────────┐
   │  period  │      │  │   During each    │
   └────┬─────┘      │  │   report period  │
        │            │  └──┬────────────┬──┘
        │            │     │            │
   ┌────▼──────────┐ │ ┌───▼────────┐ ┌─▼──────────────┐
   │ Collect data  │ │ │            │ │Incorporate     │
   │ on actual     │ │ │            │ │changes into    │
   │ performance   │ │ │            │ │project plan    │
   │(schedule,costs)│ │ │            │ │(scope,sched,bud)│
   └───────────────┘ │ └────────────┘ └────────────────┘
```

Once an updated schedule and budget have been calculated, they need to be compared to the baseline schedule and budget and analyzed for variances to determine whether a project is ahead of or behind schedule and under or over budget. If the project status is okay, no corrective actions are needed; the status will be analyzed again for the next reporting period.

The key to effective project control is measuring actual progress and comparing it to planned progress on a timely and regular basis and taking any needed corrective action immediately.

If it is determined that corrective actions are necessary, however, decisions must be made regarding how to revise the scope, schedule, or the budget. These

decisions often involve a trade-off of scope, time, and cost. For example, reducing the estimated duration of an activity may require either increasing costs to pay for more resources or reducing the scope of the task (and possibly not meeting the customer's technical requirements). Similarly, reducing project costs may require using materials of a lower quality than originally planned. Once a decision is made on which corrective actions to take, they must be incorporated into the schedule and budget. It is then necessary to calculate a revised schedule and budget to determine whether the planned corrective measures result in an acceptable schedule and budget. If not, further revisions will be needed.

The project control process continues throughout the project. In general, the shorter the reporting period, the better the chances of identifying problems early and taking effective corrective actions. If a project gets too far out of control, it may be difficult to accomplish the project objective without sacrificing the scope, quality, schedule, or budget. There may be situations in which it is wise to increase the frequency of reporting until the project is back on track. For example, if a five-year project with monthly reporting is endangered by a slipping schedule or an increasing budget overrun, it may be prudent to reduce the reporting period to one week to monitor the project and the impact of corrective actions more closely.

The project control process is an important and necessary part of project management. Just establishing a sound baseline plan is not sufficient because even the best-laid plans do not always work out. *Project management is a proactive approach to controlling a project* to ensure that the project objective is accomplished, even when things do not go according to plan.

Reinforce Your Learning

21. True or false: In general, it is better to have a shorter reporting period during a project.

Reinforce Your Learning

22. Project

is a

approach to

the project to accomplish the project

_____ .

Reinforce Your Learning

23. What three schedule elements will be affected by the actual finish times of completed activities?

Effects of Actual Schedule Performance

Throughout a project, some activities will be completed on time, some will be finished ahead of schedule, and others will be finished later than scheduled. Actual progress—whether faster or slower than planned—will have an effect on the schedule of the remaining, uncompleted activities of the project. Specifically, the **actual finish (AF) times** at which activities are actually completed will determine the ES and EF times for the remaining activities in the network diagram, as well as the TS.

Part (a) of Figure 5.14 is a network diagram for a simple project. It shows that the earliest the project can finish is day 15 (the sum of the estimated durations of the three activities, $7 + 5 + 3$). Given that the required completion time is day 20, the project has a TS of +5 days.

Suppose that activity 1, "Remove Old Wallpaper," is *actually* finished on day 10, rather than on day 7 as planned, because it turns out to be more difficult than anticipated. See part (b) of Figure 5.14. This means that the ES and EF times for activities 2 and 3 will be 3 days later than on the original schedule. Because "Remove Old Wallpaper" is actually finished on day 10, the ES for "Patch Walls" will be day 10 and its EF will be day 15. Following through with the forward calculations, we find that "Put Up New Wallpaper" will have an ES of day 15 and an EF of day 18. Comparing this new EF of the last activity to the required completion time of day 20, we find a difference of 2 days. The TS got worse—it changed in a negative direction, from +5 days to +2 days. This example illustrates how the AF times of activities have a ripple effect, altering the remaining activities' ES and EF times and the TS.

FIGURE 5.14 **Effect of Actual Finish Times**

(a)

(b)

Crossed-out boxes indicate completed activities

It is helpful to indicate on the network diagram, in some manner, which activities have been completed. One method is to shade or crosshatch the activity box, as was done in part (b) of Figure 5.14.

Incorporate Changes into Schedule

Throughout a project, changes may occur that have an impact on the schedule. As was noted earlier, these changes might be initiated by the customer or the project team, or they might be the result of an unanticipated occurrence. Here are some examples of changes initiated by the customer:

- A home buyer tells the builder that the family room should be larger and the bedroom windows should be relocated.
- A customer tells the project team developing an information system that the system must have the capability to produce a previously unmentioned set of reports and graphics, which requires additional new elements in the database.

These types of changes represent revisions to the original project scope and will have an impact on the schedule and budget. The degree of impact, however, may depend on when the changes are requested. If they are requested early in the project, they may have less impact on schedule and budget than if they are requested later in the project. For example, changing the size of the family room and relocating the bedroom windows would be relatively easy if the house was still being designed and the drawings being prepared. However, if the changes are requested after the framing is put up and the windows are installed, the impact on schedule and budget will be much greater.

When the customer requests a change, the contractor or project team should estimate the impact on the project schedule and budget and then obtain customer approval *before* proceeding. If the customer approves the proposed revisions to the project schedule and budget, then any additional activities, revised estimated durations, and revised estimated resources and associated costs should be incorporated into the project schedule and budget.

An example of a change initiated by a project team is the decision by a team that is planning a community festival to eliminate all amusement rides for adults because of space limitations and insurance costs. The project plan would then have to be revised to delete or modify all those activities involving adult rides. An example of a change initiated by a project manager would be, rather than develop customized software for an automated invoicing component of a system, to use standard available software to reduce costs and accelerate the schedule.

Some changes involve the addition of activities that may have been overlooked when the original plan was developed. For example, the project team may have forgotten to include activities associated with developing training materials and conducting training for a new information system. Or the customer or contractor may have failed to include the installation of gutters and downspouts in the work scope for the construction of a restaurant.

Other changes become necessary because of unanticipated occurrences, such as a snowstorm that slows down construction of a building, the failure of a new product to pass quality tests, or the untimely resignation of a key member of a project team. These events will have an impact on the schedule and/or budget and will require that the project plan be modified.

Still other changes can result from progressive elaboration of adding more detail as the project moves forward. No matter what level of detail is used in the initial network diagram, there will be activities that can be broken down into greater detail as the project progresses.

Any type of change—whether initiated by the customer, the contractor, the project manager, a team member, or an unanticipated event—will require a modification to the plan in terms of scope, schedule, and/or budget. When such changes are agreed upon, a new baseline plan is established and used as the benchmark against which actual project performance will be compared.

With respect to the project schedule, changes can result in the addition or deletion of activities, resequencing of activities, changes to estimated durations for specific activities, or a new required completion time for the project.

See the section on managing changes in Chapter 10, and the section on track document changes in Chapter 12 for further discussion of managing and controlling changes.

Update Project Schedule

Based on actual progress and on consideration of other changes that may occur, an updated project schedule can be generated regularly that forecasts whether the project will finish ahead of or behind its required completion time. Once data have been collected on the AF times of completed activities and the effects of any project changes, an updated project schedule can be calculated. These calculations are based on the methodology explained in this chapter:

- The ES and EF times for the remaining, uncompleted activities are calculated by working forward through the network, but they are based on the *actual finish times* of completed activities and the estimated durations of the uncompleted activities.
- The LS and LF times for the uncompleted activities are calculated by working backward through the network.

As an illustration of the calculation of an updated schedule, let us consider the network diagram shown in Figure 5.15 for the consumer market study project. Assume the following:

1. Completed activities:
 a. Activity 1, "Identify Target Consumers," actually finished on day 2.
 b. Activity 2, "Develop Draft Questionnaire," actually finished on day 11.
 c. Activity 3, "Pilot-Test Questionnaire," actually finished on day 30.

2. Project changes:
 a. It was discovered that the database to be used to prepare the mailing labels was not up to date. A new database needs to be purchased before the mailing labels can be prepared. This new database was ordered on day 23. It will take 21 days to get it from the supplier.
 b. A preliminary review of comments from the pilot test of the questionnaire indicates that substantial revisions to the questionnaire are required. Therefore, the duration estimate for activity 4 needs to be increased from 5 days to 15 days.

The network diagram in Figure 5.15 incorporates the above information. Figure 5.16 shows the updated schedule. Note that the TS for the critical path is now −5 days, instead of the +2 days in the baseline schedule in Figure 5.11. The anticipated project completion time is now day 135, which is beyond the required completion time of 130 days.

Control Schedule

Schedule control involves four steps:

1. Analyzing the schedule to determine which areas may need corrective action
2. Deciding what specific corrective actions should be taken
3. Revising the plan to incorporate the chosen corrective actions
4. Recalculating the schedule to evaluate the effects of the planned corrective actions

If the planned corrective actions do not result in an acceptable schedule, these steps need to be repeated.

Throughout a project, each time a schedule is recalculated—whether it is after actual performance data or project changes are incorporated or after corrective actions are planned—it is necessary to analyze the newly calculated schedule to determine whether it needs further revision. The schedule analysis should include identifying the critical path and any paths of activities that have negative slack, as well as those paths where slippages have occurred (the slack got worse) compared with the previously calculated schedule.

A concentrated effort to accelerate project progress must be applied to the paths with negative slack. The amount of slack should determine the priority with which these concentrated efforts are applied. For example, the path with the most negative slack should be given top priority.

Corrective actions that will eliminate the negative slack from the project schedule must be identified. These corrective actions must reduce the estimated durations of activities on the negative-slack paths. Remember, the slack for a path of activities is shared among all the activities on that path. Therefore, *a change in the estimated duration of any activity on that path will cause a corresponding change in the slack for that path.*

Reinforce Your Learning

25. In analyzing a project schedule, it is important to identify all the paths of activities that have

slack.

FIGURE 5.15 **Network Diagram for Consumer Market Study Project, Incorporating Actual Progress and Changes**

When analyzing a path of activities that has negative slack, you should focus on two kinds of activities:

1. *Activities that are near term (that is, in progress or to be started in the immediate future).* It is much wiser to take aggressive corrective action to reduce the estimated durations of activities that will be done in the near term than to plan to reduce the estimated durations of activities that are scheduled sometime in the future. If you postpone until the distant future taking corrective action that will reduce the estimated durations of activities, you may find that the negative slack has deteriorated even further by that time. As the project progresses, there is always less time remaining in which corrective action can be taken.

 Looking at Figure 5.16, we can see that it would be better to try to reduce the durations of the near-term activities on the critical path, such as "Review Comments & Finalize Questionnaire" or "Print Questionnaire," than to put off corrective action until the last activity, "Prepare Report."

2. *Activities that have long estimated durations.* Taking corrective action that will reduce a 20-day activity by 20 percent (that is, by four days) has a greater impact than totally eliminating a 1-day activity. Usually, longer-duration activities present the opportunity for larger reductions.

 Look again at Figure 5.16. There may be more opportunity to reduce the 55-day duration estimate for "Mail Questionnaire & Get Responses" by five days (9 percent) than to reduce the shorter estimated durations of other activities on the critical path.

Reinforce Your Learning

26. When analyzing a path of activities that has negative slack, what two kinds of activities should you look at carefully?

Required Completion = 130 Working Days

KEY:

Activity Description

Activity Number

Estimated Duration

Person Responsible

Crossed-out boxes indicate completed activities

There are various approaches to reducing the estimated durations of activities. One obvious way is to apply more resources to accelerate an activity. This could be done by assigning more people to work on the activity or asking the people working on the activity to work more hours per day or more days per week. Additional appropriate resources might be transferred from concurrent activities that have positive slack. Sometimes, however, adding people to an activity may, in fact, result in the activity taking longer, because the people already assigned to the activity are diverted from their work to help the new people get up to speed. Another approach is to assign a person with greater expertise or more experience to perform or help with the activity, to get it done in a shorter time than was possible with the less experienced people originally assigned to it.

Reducing the scope or requirements for an activity is another way to reduce its estimated duration. For example, it might be acceptable to put only one coat of paint on a room rather than two coats, as originally planned. In some cases, a decision might be made to totally eliminate some activities, deleting them and their durations from the schedule, such as deciding not to install a fence around the property.

Increasing productivity through improved methods or technology is yet another approach to reducing the estimated durations of activities. For example, instead of having people keyboard data from patient medical forms into a computer database, optical scanning equipment might be used.

Once specific corrective actions to reduce the negative slack have been decided, the estimated durations for the appropriate activities must be revised

Reinforce Your Learning

27. List four approaches to reducing the estimated durations of activities.

FIGURE 5.16 **Updated Schedule for Consumer Market Study Project**

Consumer Market Study Project		Estim. Dur.	Earliest		Latest		Total Slack	Actual Finish	
#	Activity	Respon.		Start	Finish	Start	Finish		
1	Identify Target Consumers	Susan							2
2	Develop Draft Questionnaire	Susan							11
3	Pilot-Test Questionnaire	Susan							30
4	Review Comments & Finalize Questionnaire	Susan	15	30	45	25	40	−5	
5	Prepare Mailing Labels	Steve	2	45	47	48	50	3	
6	Print Questionnaire	Steve	10	45	55	40	50	−5	
7	Develop Data Analysis Software	Andy	12	45	57	88	100	43	
8	Develop Software Test Data	Susan	2	45	47	98	100	53	
9	Mail Questionnaire & Get Responses	Steve	55	55	110	50	105	−5	
10	Test Software	Andy	5	57	62	100	105	43	
11	Input Response Data	Jim	7	110	117	105	112	−5	
12	Analyze Results	Jim	8	117	125	112	120	−5	
13	Prepare Report	Jim	10	125	135	120	130	−5	
14	Order New Database for Labels	Steve	21	23	44	27	48	4	

in the network plan. Then a revised schedule needs to be calculated to evaluate whether the planned corrective actions reduce the negative slack as anticipated.

In most cases, eliminating negative slack by reducing durations of activities will involve a trade-off in the form of an increase in costs or a reduction in scope. (For a further discussion of this topic, see the appendix on Time–Cost Trade-Off at the end of Chapter 07.) If the project is way behind schedule (has substantial negative slack), a substantial increase in costs and/or reduction in work scope or quality may be required to get it back on schedule. This could jeopardize elements of the overall project objective, such as scope, schedule, budget, and/or quality. In some cases, the customer and the contractor or project team may have to acknowledge that one or more of these elements cannot be achieved; therefore, the customer may have to extend the required completion time for the entire project, or there may be a dispute over who should absorb any increased cost to accelerate the schedule—the contractor or the customer.

Some contracts include a bonus provision, whereby the customer will pay the contractor a bonus if the project is completed ahead of schedule. Conversely, some contracts include a penalty provision, whereby the customer can reduce the final payment to the contractor if the project is not completed on time. Some of these penalties can be substantial. In either of these situations, effective schedule control is crucial.

The key to effective schedule control is to aggressively address any paths with negative or deteriorating slack values as soon as they are identified, rather than hoping that things will improve as the project goes on. Addressing schedule problems early will minimize the negative impact on budget and scope. If a project falls too far behind, getting back on schedule becomes more difficult, and it does not come free. It requires spending more money or reducing the scope or quality.

On projects that do not have negative slack, it is important not to let the slack deteriorate by accepting delays and slippages. If a project is ahead of schedule, a concentrated effort should be made to *keep* it ahead of schedule.

Project meetings are a good forum for addressing schedule control issues. See the section on meetings in Chapter 12, and the section on problem solving in Chapter 11 for related information.

 REAL WORLD PROJECT MANAGEMENT

Big Delivery in Small Packages

Genesis Consulting had a portfolio of 10 projects to be completed. Their budget and time constraints allowed only 2 of those 10 projects to be scheduled to be completed in the next fiscal year. The team led by Jason Fair, CEO of Genesis Consulting in Glen Allen, Virginia, USA, knew they needed to do something different with their schedule. After a meeting with a colleague who had successfully implemented agile techniques into her company's projects and considering the potential payoffs and pitfalls, Fair decided to try.

With a schedule set to 15-day sprints instead of months, the team worked to address the most important deliverables at the front of the schedule to make sure they were completed first. As noted by Alan Campbell, PMP, senior consultant at ERP consultancy ArcherPoint, Atlanta, Georgia, USA, "Traditional projects will go along, then they'll start to run out of money, so they cut things out of the scope. What happens then is something at the very end of the project plan doesn't get delivered because of time and budget constraints, even though it was really important."

"With agile, you can visibly see what all the different pieces of work are, where they are, and who's working on what. You can very quickly identify where there are constraints, and that makes people very uncomfortable in the beginning," said Fair. Team meetings were limited to 15 minutes with a report by each member of the team stating, 'I did this yesterday, this is what I am doing today, and these are the obstacles that I need help with to complete my work.'

In addition to the quick meetings each day, communication with the stakeholders occurred at the end of each sprint instead of the more traditional quarterly update. Any miscommunications were handled in 15 days instead of waiting for 3 months; avoiding extensive cost and schedule delays to make changes or to clarify the miscommunication.

With each project, the potential benefits and pitfalls were evaluated to assess the risk of implementing agile project management techniques. Consideration of the best tools from the many techniques of project management was necessary to ensure implementation of the tools in the most appropriate situations to help increase the probability of successfully completing a project.

An evaluation of the projects' progress resulted in a productivity increase of 250 percent. The elimination of waste and increased collaboration allowed the team to complete two more projects the next year as they became more efficient. Jason Fair's decision to try agile project management techniques resulted in payoffs and avoided pitfalls to give Genesis Consulting big deliveries through the small packages completed during the 15-day sprints.

Based on information from Alderton, M. (2013), "Big Delivery in Small Packages," *PM Network*, *27*(3), 60–65.

Scheduling for Information Systems Development

Chapter 4 defined an information system as a computer-based system that accepts data as input, processes the data, and produces information required by users. Scheduling the development of an information system is a challenging process. Such scheduling is often done in a haphazard manner, and, as a result, a large number of information system projects are finished much later than originally promised or never finished at all. One of the most important factors in effective scheduling is estimating activity durations that are as realistic as possible. This is not an easy task; however, it does become easier with experience.

Among the common problems that often push information system development projects beyond their required completion time are the following:

- Failure to identify all user requirements
- Failure to identify user requirements properly
- Continuing growth of project scope
- Underestimating learning curves for new software packages
- Incompatible hardware
- Logical design flaws
- Poor selection of software
- Failure to select the best design strategy
- Data incompatibility issues
- Failure to perform all phases of the systems development life cycle

Controlling the schedule for the development of an information system is a challenge. Numerous unexpected circumstances might arise that can push an information system development project well beyond its originally required completion date. However, just as with any other type of project, the key to effective project control is measuring actual progress and comparing it to planned progress on a timely and regular basis and taking any necessary corrective action immediately.

Like other forms of project control, schedule control for information system development projects is carried out according to the steps discussed earlier in this chapter. A project control process such as the one illustrated in Figure 5.13 should be used for comparing actual performance with the schedule. Once the customer and the project team agree on changes, these changes should be recorded and the schedule should be revised.

Among the changes that commonly become necessary during information system development projects are the following:

- *Changes to the interface*—such as added fields, different icons, different colors, different menu structures or buttons, or completely new screens.

FIGURE 5.17 List of Activities, Immediate Predecessors, and Estimated Durations

Web-based Reporting System Project

Activity	Immediate Predecessors	Estimated Duration (days)
1. Gather Data	—	3
2. Study Feasibility	—	4
3. Prepare Problem Definition Report	1, 2	1
4. Interview Users	3	5
5. Study Existing System	3	8
6. Define User Requirements	4	5
7. Prepare System Analysis Report	5, 6	1
8. Input & Output	7	8
9. Processing & Database	7	10
10. Evaluation	8, 9	2
11. Prepare System Design Report	10	2
12. Software Development	11	15
13. Hardware Development	11	10
14. Network Development	11	6
15. Prepare System Development Report	12, 13, 14	2
16. Software Testing	15	6
17. Hardware Testing	15	4
18. Network Testing	15	4
19. Prepare Testing Report	16, 17, 18	1
20. Training	19	4
21. System Conversion	19	2
22. Prepare Implementation Report	20, 21	1

- *Changes to reports*—such as added fields, different subtotals and totals, different sorts, different selection criteria, different order of fields, or completely new reports.
- *Changes to online queries*—such as different ad hoc capabilities, access to different fields or databases, different query structures, or additional queries.
- *Changes to database structures*—such as additional fields, different data field names, different data storage sizes, different relationships among the data, or completely new databases.
- *Changes to software processing routines*—such as different algorithms, different interfaces with other subroutines, different internal logic, or new procedures.
- *Changes to processing speeds*—such as higher throughput rates or response times.
- *Changes to storage capacities*—such as an increase in the maximum number of data records.
- *Changes to business processes*—such as changes in work or data flow, addition of new clients that must have access, or completely new processes that must be supported.
- *Changes to software resulting from hardware upgrades* or, conversely, *hardware upgrades resulting from the availability of more powerful software.*

FIGURE 5.18 Network Diagram for Web-based Reporting System Project, Showing Earliest Start and Finish Times

AN INFORMATION SYSTEM EXAMPLE: INTERNET APPLICATIONS DEVELOPMENT FOR ABC OFFICE DESIGNS (CONTINUED)

Recall from Chapter 4 that ABC Office Designs has a large number of sales representatives who sell office furniture to major corporations. Each sales representative is assigned to a specific state, and each state is part of one of four regions in the country. To enable management to monitor the number and amount of sales for each representative, for each state, and for each region, ABC has decided to build a Web-based information system. In addition, the information system needs to be able to track prices, inventory, and the competition.

The Information System department within the corporation assigned Beth Smith to be the project manager of the Web-based reporting system development project. Previously, Beth had identified all of the major tasks that needed to be accomplished and developed the work breakdown structure (WBS), responsibility assignment matrix, and network diagram. Her next step was to come up with estimated durations for the activities. After consulting extensively with the project team, she derived the estimates shown in Figure 5.17.

The project is required to be completed in 50 days, and it needs to be started as soon as possible. Having the estimated durations for each activity and the project required start and finish times, Beth was ready to perform the calculations for the ES and EF times for each activity. These values are shown above each activity in Figure 5.18.

Beth calculated the ES and EF times by going forward through the network. The first tasks, "Gather Data" and "Study Feasibility," have ES times of 0. Because "Gather Data" is estimated to take 3 days, its EF is 0 + 3 = 3 days. Because "Study Feasibility" is estimated to take 4 days, its EF is 0 + 4 = 4 days. Beth continued this process, moving forward through the network diagram until all activities had been assigned ES and EF times.

Required Completion = 50 Days

KEY:

Earliest Start | Earliest Finish

Activity Number → Activity Description ← Estimated Duration

Person Responsible

After the ES and EF times were calculated, Beth calculated the LS and LF times. The starting point here is the time by which the project must be completed—50 days. The LS and LF times are shown below each activity in Figure 5.19.

Beth calculated the LF and LS times by going backward through the network. The last task, "Prepare Implementation Report," has an LF time of 50—the time by which the project needs to be completed. Because "Prepare Implementation Report" is estimated to take 1 day to perform, its LS is $50 - 1 = 49$ days. This means that "Prepare Implementation Report" must be started by day 49 at the latest, or the project will not finish by its required completion time. Beth continued this process, moving backward through the network diagram until all activities had been assigned LF and LS times.

After the ES, EF, LS, and LF times were calculated, Beth calculated the TS. These values are shown in Figure 5.20. Recall that the TS is calculated by either subtracting ES from LS or subtracting EF from LF for each activity.

After she calculated the TS for each activity, Beth had to identify the critical path. For the Web-based reporting system development project, any activity with a slack of −9 is on the critical path. Figure 5.21 shows the critical path for this

FIGURE 5.19 Network Diagram for Web-based Reporting System Project, Showing Latest Start and Finish Times

development project. At this point, Beth and her team must determine a way to reduce the development time by 9 days, request that the project completion date be extended from 50 to 59 days, or find some compromise.

However, after extensive discussions with upper management, in which she stressed the importance of developing the system right the first time and not having to rush through some critical phases of the SDLC, Beth convinced her superiors to extend the project completion time to 60 days.

Beth and her team proceeded with the project and completed activities 1 through 6:

- Activity 1, "Gather Data," actually finished on day 4.
- Activity 2, "Study Feasibility," actually finished on day 4.
- Activity 3, "Prepare Problem Definition Report," actually finished on day 5.
- Activity 4, "Interview Users," actually finished on day 10.
- Activity 5, "Study Existing System," actually finished on day 15.
- Activity 6, "Define User Requirements," actually finished on day 18.

They then discovered that, by using some reusable software for the database, they could reduce the estimated duration of activity 9, "Processing & Database," from 10 days to 8 days.

Figures 5.22 and 5.23 show the updated network diagram and project schedule, respectively, after these changes have been incorporated. Notice that because of the above occurrences, the critical path now has a TS of 0.

Project Management Information Systems

Almost all project management information systems allow you to perform the scheduling functions identified in this chapter. Specifically, activity estimated durations can be in hours, days, weeks, months, or years, and with a click of

the mouse, time scales can easily be converted from days to weeks, weeks to days, and so on. The estimated durations can easily be updated and revised. In addition, calendaring systems provide the project manager with the ability to handle weekends, company holidays, and vacation days.

Project start and finish times can be entered as specific calendar dates (for example, June 1, 2015 or December 31, 2015), or an overall number of days (or weeks or months), without specific calendar dates assigned, can be entered (for example, the project needs to finish by week 50). Given the project required completion date and the list of activities with their estimated durations, the software will calculate the date by which a project needs to start. Similarly, it will calculate the earliest project completion date, based on the actual start date and the list of activities with their estimated durations.

The software will also calculate ES, EF, LS, and LF times, TS and FS, and the critical path, all with a click of the mouse. It is important, however, for the project manager to understand what these terms are and what the calculations mean.

Most project management information systems have the ability to provide Gantt or bar charts that display the dependencies among tasks by connecting

FIGURE 5.20 **Schedule for Web-based Reporting System Project**

Web-based Reporting System Project		Respon.	Estim. Dur.	Earliest		Latest		Total Slack	
	Activity			Start	Finish	Start	Finish		
1	Gather Data	Beth	3	0	3	–8	–5	–8	
2	Study Feasibility	Jack	4	0	4	–9	–5	–9	
3	Prepare Problem Definition Report	Rose	1	4	5	–5	–4	–9	
4	Interview Users	Jim	5	5	10	–4	1	–9	
5	Study Existing System	Steve	8	5	13	–2	6	–7	
6	Define User Requirements	Jeff	5	10	15	1	6	–9	
7	Prepare System Analysis Report	Jim	1	15	16	6	7	–9	
8	Input & Output	Tyler	8	16	24	9	17	–7	
9	Processing & Database	Joe	10	16	26	7	17	–9	
10	Evaluation	Cathy	2	26	28	17	19	–9	
11	Prepare System Design Report	Sharon	2	28	30	19	21	–9	
12	Software Development	Hannah	15	30	45	21	36	–9	
13	Hardware Development	Joe	10	30	40	26	36	–4	
14	Network Development	Gerri	6	30	36	30	36	0	
15	Prepare System Development Report	Jack	2	45	47	36	38	–9	
16	Software Testing	Maggie	6	47	53	38	44	–9	
17	Hardware Testing	Gene	4	47	51	40	44	–7	
18	Network Testing	Greg	4	47	51	40	44	–7	
19	Prepare Testing Report	Rose	1	53	54	44	45	–9	
20	Training	Jim	4	54	58	45	49	–9	
21	System Conversion	Beth	2	54	56	47	49	–7	
22	Prepare Implementation Report	Jack	1	58	59	49	50	–9	

tasks and their predecessors with lines and arrowheads. The user can click back and forth between the Gantt or bar charts and the network diagrams.

Virtually all project management information systems allow you to perform the control functions identified in this chapter. Specifically, while an activity is

in progress or once an activity has been completed, current information can be entered into the system and the software will automatically revise the project schedule. Likewise, if the estimated durations for any future activities change, these changes can be entered into the system and the information system will automatically update the schedule. All network diagrams, tables, and reports produced by the software will be updated to reflect the most recent information.

See Appendix A in the back of the book for a thorough discussion of project management information systems.

Agile Project Management

Agile project management is an approach to reduce product development time while minimizing risk through continuous interaction between the customer and small self-organized teams that produce increments of working product features in short time iterations while rapidly adapting to changes in requirements. It is applicable to projects for which the requirements are difficult to define at the beginning or may change quickly or often during the project. It emphasizes short term planning and intense work efforts in short fixed time cycles. Agile project management is sometimes used for software product development projects during which the final system product is completed in increments by developing sets or modules of specific product requirements and features in short timeframes.

There are various methodologies for implementing agile project management. One of the more popular methodologies is **Scrum**, a term derived from the game of rugby.

The roles of the participants involved in this approach include:

- A *product owner*, also referred to as the *customer representative*, is responsible for defining the customer requirements and product features and for ensuring that the development team delivers an end product with the required features. Sometimes product features may be defined by "stories" that are descriptions by end users of features they would like changed or added to an existing product or included in a new product. The product owner also prioritizes the requirements based on their value and dependent relationships or required sequence. She then creates a **product backlog** that is an ordered list of requirements or features from which the specific sets of items will be selected and released to the development team to produce and to demonstrate at the end of a fixed timeframe. These sets of features are referred to as a *releases* (similar to work packages) because the items are released from the product backlog to the team to produce a working product increment that is a portion of the overall end product that is being developed. The product owner is encouraged to collocate with the development team to enable regular discussions and clarifications of customer requirements, to review and provide comments and feedback on the work of the development team, and to specify any modifications that need to be made so the development team can adapt their work efforts during the remaining fixed time period to accommodate any changes; otherwise the changes will need to be incorporated in future releases.

FIGURE 5.21 Network Diagram for Web-based Reporting System Project, Showing the Critical Path

- The *development team* develops, delivers, and demonstrates working **product increments** (portions or modules of the overall end product that is being developed) for specific product features or requirements during a fixed timeframe, called a *sprint*, also referred to as an *iteration*. A sprint is usually one to four weeks. The development teams are cross-functional and include all the expertise and skills to produce the deliverable product increment by the end of the particular sprint. The goal for each sprint is to create and demonstrate a working product increment toward the completion of the final end product. The teams are also small, usually no more than about eight people, to ensure a high level of communication and collaboration. There is a strong emphasis on face-to-face communication and on an open office environment where people can readily interact with each other. Teams are self-organizing and do not have a leader. Rather they select and perform specific work tasks based on each person's skills and availability during the sprint.

- A *Scrum master* is a facilitator for the Scrum development process during a sprint whose primary job is to take actions to remove or reduce any obstacles, barriers, or constraints that are impeding progress of the development team toward accomplishing their work tasks and that may negatively impact the successful production and demonstration of a deliverable working product increment by the end of the sprint time. Sprint cycle times are fixed. If all the work is not completed within the fixed timeframe of a sprint, the uncompleted items are added back to the product backlog to be performed during a future sprint. The Scrum master is not the same as a project manager in that he does not have direct responsibility for the people on the development team. Team members do not work for the Scrum master; rather they are self-organized and self-directed.

Required Completion = 50 Days

KEY:

Activity
Description

Activity
Number — | | | — Estimated
Duration

Earliest Start / Earliest Finish (top)
Latest Start / Latest Finish (bottom)
Person Responsible

The agile project management process includes:

1. Establishing the rationale, description, funding amount, and target completion date for the final end product (deliverable) and authorizing the project. This is similar to a project charter.
2. Defining the product requirements and creating an ordered product backlog of prioritized specific requirements and product features. This is similar to a project scope document.
3. At the beginning of each sprint the product owner and the development team have a *sprint planning meeting* to select a set of requirements or features from the top of the product backlog that will be released to the team and that can be produced and demonstrated by the team during the fixed timeframe for the sprint cycle. The development team then identifies the specific tasks, and estimates their durations, that it needs to perform to produce the product increment that demonstrates the features. Tasks are usually between four and twelve hours in duration. This sprint planning meeting usually takes one day or less. Once the team identifies the specific tasks to be

FIGURE 5.22 Network Diagram for Web-based Reporting System Project Incorporating Actual Progress and Changes

performed during the sprint, the list of tasks is referred to as the **sprint backlog**, which is used to monitor work progress. The Scrum master may create some project monitoring and control tools such as a *task board* that is used to display which tasks have been completed, are in-progress, or not yet started, and/or a *burn down chart* that shows the effort and work to date and the remaining effort in the sprint backlog. Often these tools are on large displays in the open office area and visible to the entire team to see their progress toward the completion of the sprint.

For large projects there may be multiple development teams working concurrently in different sprints on various releases from the product backlog to produce specific product increments. In such cases, it is important that the development teams communicate regularly to ensure there is appropriate integration among the product increments and also that there is no overlap or duplication of effort. The sprint Scrum masters should facilitate such efforts.

4. At the start of each day the development team has a *daily Scrum meeting*, also referred to as the *daily standup* as these meetings are usually limited to 15 minutes. During these meetings each team member is expected to come prepared to state

- what they did the previous day
- what they plan to do today
- any obstacles that are impeding their work. If impediments are identified, they are not solved at these Scrum meetings, rather the Scrum master and the appropriate team members will resolve those items during the workday. The Scrum meetings are not intended to be problem solving meetings.

During the daily Scrum meeting, if any team members state that they had completed a task, they then select another task from the sprint backlog of tasks on which they will work based on their skills.

Required Completion = 60 Days

KEY:

Activity Description

Activity Number

Estimated Duration

Person Responsible

Crossed-out boxes indicate completed activities

These daily meetings provide a mechanism for accountability and motivation for the development team members.

Based on which tasks have been completed, the Scrum master will update the task board or burn down chart each day.

5. At the end of the sprint, there is a *sprint review meeting* at which the development team reviews the work that has been accomplished as well as which items were not completed. They also demonstrate their completed working product increment to the product owner and other appropriate stakeholders. If the product owner determines that changes need to be made to some features of the product increment, those changes are documented and added to the product backlog, along with any items that were not completed, and will be included in future releases and sprints. This meeting usually is no more than about four hours.

6. At the end of the sprint, there is also a *sprint retrospective meeting* during which the Scrum team, including the product owner, evaluates performance during the sprint regarding what went well and what could be improved in future sprints. This meeting is facilitated by the Scrum master and should take about two or three hours.

FIGURE 5.23 Updated Schedule for Web-based Reporting System Project

Web-based Reporting System Project

	Activity	Respon.	Estim. Dur.	Earliest Start	Earliest Finish	Latest Start	Latest Finish	Total Slack	Actual Finish
1	Gather Data	Beth							4
2	Study Feasibility	Jack							4
3	Prepare Problem Definition Report	Rose							5
4	Interview Users	Jim							10
5	Study Existing System	Steve							15
6	Define User Requirements	Jeff							18
7	Prepare System Analysis Report	Jim	1	18	19	18	19	0	
8	Input & Output	Tyler	8	19	27	19	27	0	
9	Processing & Database	Joe	8	19	27	19	27	0	
10	Evaluation	Cathy	2	27	29	27	29	0	
11	Prepare System Design Report	Sharon	2	29	31	29	31	0	
12	Software Development	Hannah	15	31	46	31	46	0	
13	Hardware Development	Joe	10	31	41	36	46	5	
14	Network Development	Gerri	6	31	37	40	46	9	
15	Prepare System Development Report	Jack	2	46	48	46	48	0	
16	Software Testing	Maggie	6	48	54	48	54	0	
17	Hardware Testing	Gene	4	48	52	50	54	2	
18	Network Testing	Greg	4	48	52	50	54	2	
19	Prepare Testing Report	Rose	1	54	55	54	55	0	
20	Training	Jim	4	55	59	55	59	0	
21	System Conversion	Beth	2	55	57	57	59	2	
22	Prepare Implementation Report	Jack	1	59	60	59	60	0	

CRITICAL SUCCESS FACTORS

- The person who will be responsible for performing the activity should estimate the duration for that activity. This generates commitment from the person.

- The estimated duration for an activity must be based on the types and quantities of resources required to perform the activity.

- Activity estimated durations should be aggressive yet realistic.

- Activities should not be longer in estimated duration than the time intervals at which the actual progress will be reviewed and compared to planned progress.

- Project management involves a proactive approach to controlling a project to ensure that the project objective is accomplished, even when things do not go according to plan.

- Once the project starts, it is important to monitor progress to ensure that everything is going according to plan.

- The key to effective project control is measuring actual progress and comparing it to planned progress on a timely and regular basis and taking any needed corrective action immediately.

- The key to effective schedule control is to address any paths with negative or deteriorating slack values aggressively as soon as they are identified. A concentrated effort to accelerate project progress must be applied to these paths. The amount of negative slack should determine the priority for applying these concentrated efforts.

- When attempting to reduce the duration of a path of activities that has negative slack, focus on activities that are near term and on activities that have long estimated durations.

- Addressing schedule problems early will minimize the negative impact on scope and budget. If a project falls too far behind, getting it back on schedule becomes more difficult and usually requires spending more money or reducing the scope or quality.

- If corrective actions are necessary, decisions must be made regarding a trade-off of scope, time, and cost.

- A regular reporting period should be established for comparing actual progress to planned progress.

- The shorter the reporting period, the better the chances of identifying problems early and taking corrective actions.

- During each reporting period, data on actual performance and information on changes to the project scope, schedule, and budget need to be collected in a timely manner and used to calculate an updated schedule and budget.

SUMMARY

When network planning techniques are used, the scheduling function depends on the planning function. A schedule is a timetable for the plan and, therefore, cannot be established until the network-based plan has been created.

It is necessary to estimate the types and quantities of resources that will be required to perform each specific activity in the network diagram to subsequently estimate how long it will take to perform the activity. When estimating resources for activities, the availability of each resource has to be taken into account. The estimated types and quantities of resources required for an activity together with the availability of those resources will influence the estimated duration for how long it will take to perform the activity.

Once the types and quantities of resources are estimated for each activity, estimates can then be made for how long it will take to perform each activity. The estimated duration for each activity must be the total elapsed time—the time for the work to be done plus any associated waiting time. An activity's estimated

duration must be based on the quantity of resources required to perform the activity. The estimate should be aggressive, yet realistic. At the beginning of the project, it may not be possible to estimate durations for all activities with a level of confidence regarding their accuracy. This is especially true for longer-term projects. It may be easier to estimate the durations for near-term activities, but as the project progresses, the project team can progressively elaborate the estimated durations as more information is known or becomes clear to allow for more accurate estimated durations.

To establish a basis from which to calculate a schedule using the estimated durations for the activities, it is necessary to select an estimated start time for when the project is expected to begin and a required completion time for when the project must be done. These two times define the overall window, or envelope, of time in which the project must be completed.

A project schedule provides a timetable for each activity and shows the earliest start (ES) and earliest finish (EF) times and the latest start (LS) and latest finish (LF) times for each activity. The ES and EF times are calculated by working forward through the network. The ES time for an activity is calculated on the basis of the project estimated start time and the estimated durations of preceding activities. The EF time for an activity is calculated by adding the activity's estimated duration to the activity's ES time. The ES time for a specific activity must be the same as or later than the latest of all the EF times of all the activities leading directly into that specific activity.

The LS and LF times are calculated by working backward through the network. The LF time for an activity is calculated on the basis of the project required completion time and the estimated durations of succeeding activities. The LS time is calculated by subtracting the activity's estimated duration from the activity's LF time. The LF time for a specific activity must be the same as or earlier than the earliest of all the LS times of all the activities emerging directly from that specific activity.

The TS for a particular path of activities through the network is common to and shared among all activities on that path. If it is positive, it represents the maximum amount of time that the activities on a particular path can be delayed without jeopardizing completion of the project by the required time. If TS is negative, it represents the amount of time that the activities on that path must be accelerated to complete the project by the required time. If it is zero, the activities on that path do not need to be accelerated but cannot be delayed. The critical path is the longest (most time-consuming) path of activities in the network diagram.

Once a project actually starts, it is necessary to monitor the progress to ensure that everything is going according to the plan. The key to effective project control is measuring actual progress and comparing it to planned progress on a timely and regular basis and taking any needed corrective action immediately. A regular reporting period should be established for comparing actual progress with planned progress. During each reporting period, two kinds of data or information need to be collected: data on actual performance and information on any changes to the project scope, schedule, and budget. The project control process continues throughout the project. In general, the shorter the reporting period, the better the chances of identifying problems early and taking effective corrective actions. If a project gets too far out of control, it may be difficult to achieve the project objective without sacrificing the scope, quality, schedule, or budget.

Throughout a project, some activities will be completed on time, some will be finished ahead of schedule, and others will be finished later than scheduled. Actual progress—whether faster or slower than planned—will have an effect on the schedule of the remaining, uncompleted activities of the project. Specifically, the AF times of completed activities will determine the ES and EF times for the remaining activities in the network diagram, as well as the TS.

Throughout a project, changes may occur that have an impact on the schedule. These changes might be initiated by the customer or the project team, or they might be the result of an unanticipated occurrence. Any type of change—whether initiated by the customer, the contractor, the project manager, a team member, or an unanticipated event—will require a modification to the plan in terms of scope, schedule, and/or budget. When such changes are agreed upon, a new baseline plan is established and used as the benchmark against which actual project performance will be compared.

Based on actual progress and on consideration of other changes that may occur, an updated project schedule can be generated regularly that forecasts whether the project will finish ahead of or behind its required completion time. Once data have been collected on the AF times of completed activities and the effects of any project changes, an updated project schedule can be calculated.

Schedule control involves four steps: analyzing the schedule to determine which areas may need corrective action, deciding what specific corrective actions should be taken, revising the plan to incorporate the chosen corrective actions, and recalculating the schedule to evaluate the effects of the planned corrective actions. Corrective actions that will eliminate the negative slack from the project schedule must be identified. These corrective actions must reduce the estimated durations of activities on the negative-slack paths. When analyzing a path of activities that has negative slack, the focus should be on two kinds of activities: activities that are near term and activities that have long estimated durations.

There are various approaches to reducing the estimated durations of activities. These include applying more resources to accelerate an activity, assigning individuals with greater expertise or more experience to work on the activity, reducing the scope or requirements for the activity, and increasing productivity through improved methods or technology.

Scheduling the development of an information system is a challenging process. Such scheduling is often done in a haphazard manner, and as a result, a large number of information system projects are finished much later than originally promised. One of the most important factors in effective scheduling is estimating activity durations that are as realistic as possible. The project manager should be aware of the common problems that often push information system development projects beyond their scheduled completion dates. Project management information systems can help with the scheduling process.

Agile project management is an approach to reduce product development time while minimizing risk through continuous interaction between the customer and small self-organized teams that produce increments of working product features in short time iterations while rapidly adapting to changes in requirements. It is applicable to projects for which the requirements are difficult to define at the beginning or may change quickly or often during the project. It emphasizes short term planning and intense work efforts in short fixed time cycles.

QUESTIONS

1. Why does the scheduling function depend on the planning function? Which one must be done first? Why?
2. Describe what an activity estimated duration is. How is it determined?
3. Why might a contractor prefer to state a project completion time in terms of number of days after the project starts rather than a specific date? Give some examples of instances when this would be appropriate.
4. Refer to Figure 5.4. Why is the earliest start time for "Review Comments & Finalize Questionnaire" day 33? Why is the earliest finish time day 38?
5. Refer to Figure 5.7. Why is the latest start time for "Mail Questionnaires & Get Responses" day 40? Why is the latest finish time day 105?
6. Describe the different types of project slack and how each is calculated.
7. Why is it important to determine the critical path of a project? What happens if activities on this path are delayed? What happens if activities on this path are accelerated?
8. From your experience, describe how you have used a project control process. If you did not use continual monitoring of the progress, how would it have helped improve the project's success if you did use it?
9. Why should a project have a regular reporting period? Should all projects have the same reporting period? Why or why not? What types of data should be collected during each reporting period?
10. Who can initiate changes to a project schedule? Describe why and when changes would occur in a project. How are the network diagram and schedule updated to reflect the changes?
11. Describe how you would apply the four steps of schedule control to a project. If the project needs to be accelerated, what kinds of activities would be the primary focus? Why?
12. Why is the scheduling of information system projects so challenging? What are some of the common problems that push information system projects beyond their due dates? How could using agile project management techniques help control a project's progression?
13. Calculate the ES, EF, LS, and LF times and the slack for each activity in the figure below, and identify the critical path for the project. Can the project be completed in 40 weeks? Assume that activity A actually finished at 3 weeks,

activity B actually finished at 12 weeks, and activity C actually finished at 13 weeks. Recalculate the expected project completion time. Which activities would you focus on to get the project back on schedule?

14. Calculate the ES, EF, LS, and LF times and the slack for each activity in the figure below, and identify the critical path for the project. Can the project be completed in 30 weeks? Assume that "Systems Analysis" actually finished at 8 weeks, "Design Input & Output" actually finished at 15 weeks, and "Design Database" actually finished at 19 weeks. Recalculate the expected project completion time. Which activities would you focus on to get the project back on schedule?

15. Calculate the ES, EF, LS, and LF times and the slack for each activity in the figure below, and identify the critical path for the project. Can the project be completed in 30 weeks? Assume that activity A actually finished at 5 weeks and activity B actually finished at 5 weeks. Recalculate the expected project completion time. Which activities would you focus on to get the project back on schedule?

INTERNET EXERCISES

For the website addresses of the organizations mentioned in these exercises, go to "Internet Exercises" at the book's companion website at www.cengagebrain.com. It is suggested that you save this website in your "Favorites" list for easy access in the future.

1. Search the Web for "project schedule." Describe at least three sites that you find. Search with additional terms such as "tools" and "control." List the terms that you have added, and describe at least three sites that you find.
2. For exercises 2 through 5, visit the website for the organization Mind Tools™. Explore the site. What kind of information does it provide?
3. On the "Home" page, explore the "Hot Tools and Resources" links. Describe what you find.
4. Explore the topics in the "Toolkit" link for Project Management. Read through a topic that interests you. Provide a one-page summary.
5. Click on the "News" link to subscribe to the free newsletter. In addition, under the "More Resources" link, click on "Videos," read an article and watch a video that interests you and provide a one-page summary.

CASE STUDY 1 A Not-for-Profit Medical Research Center

This case study is a continuation of the case study started in Chapter 4.

CASE QUESTIONS

1. Develop an estimated duration for each activity.
2. Using a project start time of 0 (or May 15) and a required project completion time of 180 days (or November 15), calculate the ES, EF, LS, and LF times and TS for each activity. If your calculations result in a project schedule with negative TS, revise the project scope, activity estimated durations, and/or sequence or dependent relationships among activities to arrive at an acceptable baseline schedule for completing the project within 180 days (or by November 15). Describe the revisions you made.
3. Determine the critical path, and identify the activities that make up the critical path.
4. Produce a bar chart (Gantt chart) based on the ES and EF times from the schedule in item 2.

Note: This case study will continue in Chapters 6 through 8, so save the results of your work.

GROUP ACTIVITY

Divide the course participants into the same groups as for the previous chapter's group activity. Then address each of the steps listed above.

CASE STUDY 2 The Wedding

This case study is a continuation of the case study started in Chapter 4.

CASE QUESTIONS

1. Develop an estimated duration for each activity.
2. Using a project start time of 0 (or January 1) and a required project completion time of 180 days (or June 30), calculate the ES, EF, LS, and LF times

and TS for each activity. If your calculations result in a project schedule with negative TS, revise the project scope, activity estimated durations, and/or sequence or dependent relationships among activities to arrive at an acceptable baseline schedule for completing the project within 180 days (or by June 30). Describe the revisions you made.

3. Determine the critical path, and identify the activities that make up the critical path.
4. Produce a bar chart (Gantt chart) based on the ES and EF times from the schedule in item 2.

Note: This case study will continue in Chapters 6 through 8, so save the results of your work.

GROUP ACTIVITY
Divide the course participants into the same groups as for the previous chapter's group activity. Then address each of the steps listed above.

REFERENCES

A Guide to the Project Management Body of Knowledge (PMBOK® Guide) Fifth Edition. Newtown Square, PA: Project Management Institute, 2013.

Alderton, M. (2013). "Big Delivery in Small Packages," *PM Network, 27*(3), 60–65.

Anonymous (2013). "Oracle International Corporation; 'Real-Time Project Progress Entry: Applying Project Team Member-Entered Progress Immediately to the Project Plan' in Patent Application Approval Process," *Computer Weekly News,* July 4, 236.

Cantwell, P. R., S. Sarkani, and T. A. Mazzuchi (2013). "Dynamic Consequences of Cost, Schedule, and Performance Within DoD Project Management," *Defense Acquisition Research Journal: A Publication of the Defense Acquisition University, 20*(1), 89–106.

Chang, A., C. Hatcher, and J. Kim (2013). "Temporal Boundary Objects in Megaprojects: Mapping the System with the Integrated Master Schedule," *International Journal of Project Management, 31*(3), 323–332. doi:10.1016/j.ijproman.2012.08.007

Gapuz, C. and F. Gapuz (2013). "Silk Technology Promotion and Commercialization: Corporate Social Responsibility Towards Livelihood Generation, Gender, Development and Climate Change Adaptation," *International Conference on Management, Leadership & Governance,* 126-IX. Kidmore End: Academic Conferences International Limited.

Göbel, H. and S. Cronholm (2013). "Towards an Agile Method for ITSM Self-Assessment: A Design Science Research Approach," *International Conference on Management, Leadership & Governance,* 135-IX. Kidmore End: Academic Conferences International Limited.

Hamid, S., H. Ghafoor, and T. Shah (2012). "Work Environment and Its Impact on Triple Constraint of Project Management," *Information Management & Business Review, 4*(10), 545–552.

Hartmann, S. (2013). "Project Scheduling with Resource Capacities and Requests Varying with Time: A Case Study," *Flexible Services and Manufacturing Journal, 25*(1–2), 74–93.

Hwang, B. and L. Leong (2013). "Comparison of Schedule Delay and Causal Factors Between Traditional and Green Construction Projects," *Technological & Economic Development of Economy, 19*(2), 310–330.

Judy, S. (2013). "GAO Faults VA for Project Overruns," *ENR: Engineering News-Record, 270*(14), 22.

Jyh-Bin, Y., C. Mei-Yi, and K. Huang (2013). "An Empirical Study of Schedule Delay Causes Based on Taiwan's Litigation Cases," *Project Management Journal, 44*(3), 21–31. doi:10.1002/pmj.21337

Kanaracus, C. (2013). "Audit: Tech Overhaul for Police, Fire Three Years Behind Schedule," *CIO* (13284045), 3.

Khamooshi, H. and D. F. Cioffi (2013). "Uncertainty in Task Duration and Cost Estimates: Fusion of Probabilistic Forecasts and Deterministic Scheduling," *Journal of Construction Engineering & Management, 139*(5), 488–497. doi:10.1061/(ASCE)CO.1943-7862.0000616

Killen, C. P. (2013). "Evaluation of Project Interdependency Visualizations Through Decision Scenario Experimentation," *International Journal of Project Management, 31*(6), 804.

Love, P., C. Sing, X. Wang, D. Edwards, and H. Odeyinka (2013). "Probability Distribution Fitting of Schedule Overruns in Construction Projects," *Journal of the Operational Research Society, 64*(8), 1231–1247. doi:10.1057/jors.2013.29

Martinsuo, M. (2013). "Project Portfolio Management in Practice and in Context," *International Journal of Project Management, 31*(6), 794.

McCarthy, D. (2013). "Automation Project Road Map: Advice for the Journey," *Control Engineering*, April 2013, 44.

Shaw, M. and E. Joyce (2013). "Dearth of CPM Schedule Experts Still Bedevils," *ENR: Engineering News-Record, 270*(13), 25.

Zhou, J., P. Love, X. Wang, K. Teo, and Z. Irani (2013). "A Review of Methods and Algorithms for Optimizing Construction Scheduling," *Journal of the Operational Research Society, 64*(8), 1091–1105. doi:10.1057/jors.2012.174

APPENDIX 1 Probabilistic Activity Durations

ESTIMATE ACTIVITY DURATIONS

Recall that the estimated duration for each activity is the estimated total elapsed time from when the activity is started until it is finished. With projects for which there is a high degree of uncertainty about the estimated duration for activities, it is possible to use three estimates for each activity:

1. *Optimistic time (t_o)* is the time in which a specific activity can be completed if everything goes perfectly well and there are no complications. A rule of thumb is that there should be only one chance in ten of completing the activity in less than the optimistic time estimate.

2. *Most likely time (t_m)* is the time in which a specific activity can most frequently be completed under normal conditions. If an activity has been repeated many times, the actual duration that occurs most frequently can be used as the most likely time estimate.

3. *Pessimistic time (t_p)* is the time in which a specific activity can be completed under adverse circumstances, such as in the presence of unusual or unforeseen

complications. A rule of thumb is that there should be only one chance in ten of completing the activity in more than the pessimistic time estimate.

Establishing three time estimates makes it possible to take uncertainty into account when estimating how long an activity will take. The most likely time must be longer than or equal to the optimistic time, and the pessimistic time must be longer than or equal to the most likely time.

It is not required that three time estimates be made for each activity. If someone has experience or data on how long it took to perform very similar activities in completed projects, it may be preferable to make only one estimated duration for how long an activity will take (as discussed in this chapter). However, using three time estimates (t_o, t_m, and t_p) can be helpful when there is a high degree of uncertainty as to how long an activity may take.

THE BETA PROBABILITY DISTRIBUTION

When three time estimates are used for each activity, it is assumed that the three estimates follow a **beta probability distribution** which is a distribution that is frequently used to determine the expected duration and variance for an activity. Based on this assumption, it is possible to calculate an **expected duration**, t_e (also called *mean* or *average* time), for each activity from the activity's three time estimates. The **expected duration** is calculated using the following formula:

$$t_e = \frac{t_o + 4(t_m) + t_p}{6}$$

Assume that the optimistic time for an activity is 1 week, the most likely time is 5 weeks, and the pessimistic time is 15 weeks. The beta probability distribution for this activity is shown in Figure 5.24. The expected duration for this activity is

$$t_e = \frac{1 + 4(5) + 15}{6} = 6 \text{ weeks}$$

Assume that the optimistic time for another activity is 10 weeks, the most likely time is 15 weeks, and the pessimistic time is 20 weeks. The beta probability

FIGURE 5.24 **Beta Probability Distribution**

FIGURE 5.25 **Beta Probability Distribution**

distribution for this activity is shown in Figure 5.25. The expected duration for this activity is

$$t_e = \frac{10 + 4(15) + 20}{6} = 15 \text{ weeks}$$

Coincidentally, this happens to be the same as the most likely time estimate.

The peaks of the curves in Figures 5.24 and 5.25 represent the most likely times for their respective activities. The expected duration, t_e, divides the total area under the beta probability curve into two equal parts. In other words, 50 percent of the area under any beta probability curve will be to the left of t_e and 50 percent will be to the right. For example, Figure 5.24 shows that 50 percent of the area under the curve is to the left of 6 weeks and 50 percent of the area is to the right of 6 weeks. Thus, *there is a 50–50 chance that an activity will actually take more or less time than its expected duration.* Stated another way, there is a probability of 0.5 that an activity will take more time than t_e, and a probability of 0.5 that it will take less time than t_e. In Figure 5.24, there is a 50 percent chance that the activity will take longer than 6 weeks and a 50 percent chance that it will take less than 6 weeks.

It is assumed that, as a project progresses, some activities will take less time than their expected duration and some activities will take more time than their expected duration. It is further assumed that, by the time the entire project is completed, the total net difference between all *expected* durations and all *actual* durations will be minimal.

Reinforce Your Learning

28. Calculate the expected duration for an activity having the following time estimates: $t_o = 8$, $t_m = 12$, and $t_p = 22$.

PROBABILITY FUNDAMENTALS

Network planning in which three time estimates are used for each activity can be considered a *stochastic or probabilistic technique*, because it allows for uncertainty in activity duration by incorporating three estimates that are assumed to be distributed according to the beta probability distribution. Any technique that uses only one estimated duration is considered a *deterministic* technique. Because it is assumed that the three time estimates for each activity follow a beta probability distribution, it is possible to calculate the probability, or

likelihood, of actually completing the project before the required time. If only one estimated duration is used for each activity, probability calculations cannot be made.

When three time estimates are used, all of the activities on the critical path of the network diagram can be added together to obtain a total probability distribution. The central limit theorem of probability theory states that this total probability distribution is not a beta probability distribution but a **normal probability distribution**, which is bell-shaped and symmetrical around its mean (or expected) value. Furthermore, this total normal probability distribution has an expected duration that is equal to the sum of the expected durations of all of the activities that make up the total distribution.

Whereas the expected duration, which divides the area under a probability distribution into two equal parts, is a measure of the central tendency of a distribution, the **variance**, σ^2, is a measure of the dispersion, or spread, of a distribution from its expected value. The variance for the beta probability distribution of an activity is calculated using the following formula:

$$\text{Variance} = \sigma^2 = \left[\frac{t_p - t_o}{6}\right]^2$$

Reinforce Your Learning

29. Compute the expected duration (t_e) and the variance (σ^2) for the following beta probability distribution.

The variance of the total normal probability distribution is equal to the sum of the variances of all of the activities that make up the total normal distribution.

The **standard deviation**, σ, is another measure of the dispersion of a distribution and *is equal to the square root of the variance*. The standard deviation gives a better visual representation of the spread of a distribution from its mean or expected value than does the variance. For a normal distribution (see Figure 5.26), the area within one standard deviation of the mean (to both sides) includes approximately 68 percent of the total area under the curve, the area within two standard deviations includes approximately 95 percent of the total area under the curve, and the area within three standard deviations includes approximately 99 percent of the total area under the curve.

As noted above, the standard deviation is a measure of the dispersion of a distribution. Figure 5.27 shows two normal distributions. The distribution in

Reinforce Your Learning

30. What percentage of the area under this normal curve is shaded?

FIGURE 5.26 Normal Probability Distribution

FIGURE 5.27 Normal Probability Distributions

(a) (b)

(a) of Figure 5.27 is more widespread and thus has a larger standard deviation than that in (b). However, for both distributions 68 percent of the area under the curve is included within one standard deviation of the mean.

The total probability distribution of all the activities on the critical path of a network diagram is a normal distribution, with a mean or expected value equal to the sum of the individual activity expected durations and a variance equal to the sum of the individual activity variances. Consider the simple network in Figure 5.28. Assume that the project can start at time 0 and must be completed by day 42. The probability distributions for the activities in Figure 5.28 are shown in Figure 5.29.

FIGURE 5.28 Example Project

Required Completion = 42 Days

The expected duration for each activity is as follows.

$$\text{Activity A} \quad t_e = \frac{2 + 4(4) + 6}{6} = 4 \text{ days}$$

$$\text{Activity B} \quad t_e = \frac{5 + 4(13) + 15}{6} = 12 \text{ days}$$

$$\text{Activity C} \quad t_e = \frac{13 + 4(18) + 35}{6} = 20 \text{ days}$$

$$\text{Total} = 36 \text{ days}$$

FIGURE 5.29 **Probability Distributions**

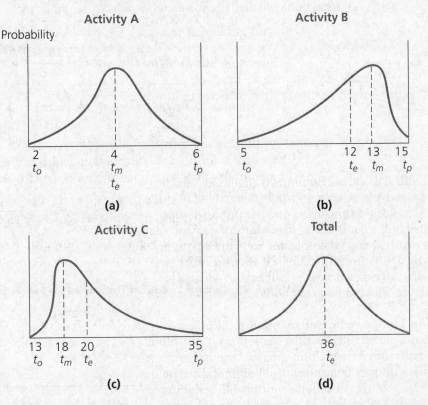

(a) Activity A — Probability; t_o = 2, t_m = 4, t_e = 4, t_p = 6

(b) Activity B — t_o = 5, t_e = 12, t_m = 13, t_p = 15

(c) Activity C — t_o = 13, t_m = 18, t_e = 20, t_p = 35

(d) Total — t_e = 36

If we sum the three distributions, we obtain a total mean, or total t_e:

Activity	t_o	t_m	t_p
A	2	4	6
B	5	13	15
C	13	18	35
Total	20	35	56

$$t_e = \frac{20 + 4(35) + 56}{6} = 36 \text{ days}$$

This result is the same as the sum of the three individual expected durations calculated previously: $4 + 12 + 20 = 36$ days. The total probability distribution is shown in (d) of Figure 5.29. The total expected duration for path 1–2–3–4 is 36 days. Thus, the project has an earliest expected completion time of day 36. As previously stated, the project has a required completion time of day 42.

The total distribution has a mean elapsed time equal to the sum of the three individual means, or expected durations. There is a probability of 0.5 that the project will be completed before day 36 and a probability of 0.5 that it will be completed after day 36.

For the simple example in Figure 5.28, the variances for the beta distributions of the three activities are as follows.

$$\text{Activity A} \quad \sigma^2 = \left(\frac{6-2}{6}\right)^2 = 0.444$$

$$\text{Activity B} \quad \sigma^2 = \left(\frac{15-5}{6}\right)^2 = 2.778$$

$$\text{Activity C} \quad \sigma^2 = \left(\frac{35-13}{6}\right)^2 = 13.444$$

$$\text{Total} = 16.666$$

The variance for the total distribution, which is a normal probability distribution, is the sum of the three individual variances, or 16.666. The standard deviation, σ, of the total distribution is

$$\text{Standard deviation} = \sigma = \sqrt{\sigma^2} = \sqrt{16.666} = 4.08 \text{ days}$$

Figure 5.30, like (d) of Figure 5.29, shows the total probability curve, with the addition of the standard deviations.

FIGURE 5.30 **Normal Probability Distribution for Sample Project**

Figure 5.30 is a normal curve, so 68 percent of its total area is contained within $\pm 1\sigma$ (standard deviation) of t_e, or between 31.92 days and 40.08 days; 95 percent of its area is between 27.84 days and 44.16 days; and 99 percent of its area is between 23.76 days and 48.24 days. This probability distribution can be interpreted as follows:

- There is a 99 percent chance (0.99 probability) of completing the project in 23.76 to 48.24 days.
- There is a 95 percent chance (0.95 probability) of completing the project in 27.84 to 44.16 days.
- There is a 47.5 percent chance (0.475 probability) of completing the project in 27.84 to 36 days.
- There is a 47.5 percent chance (0.475 probability) of completing the project in 36 to 44.16 days.
- There is a 68 percent chance (0.68 probability) of completing the project in 31.92 to 40.08 days.
- There is a 34 percent chance (0.34 probability) of completing the project in 31.92 to 36 days.
- There is a 34 percent chance (0.34 probability) of completing the project in 36 to 40.08 days.

- There is a 13.5 percent chance (0.135 probability) of completing the project in 27.84 to 31.92 days.
- There is a 13.5 percent chance (0.135 probability) of completing the project in 40.08 to 44.16 days.
- There is a 0.5 percent chance (0.005 probability) of completing the project before 23.76 days.
- There is a 0.5 percent chance (0.005 probability) of completing the project after 48.24 days.

Thus, it can be stated that the ratio of the area under certain parts of the normal curve to the total area under the curve is related to the probability.

CALCULATING PROBABILITY

The earliest expected finish time for a project is determined by the critical path through the network diagram. It is equal to the project estimated start time plus the sum of the expected durations of the activities on the critical path leading from project start to project completion. As stated previously, the probability of actually completing a project before its earliest expected finish time is 0.5, because half of the area under the normal distribution curve is to the left of this expected time; the probability of actually completing a project after its earliest expected finish time is also 0.5, because half of the area under the normal curve is to the right of this expected time. Knowing the required completion time for a project makes it possible to calculate the probability of actually completing the project before this time.

To find the probability of actually completing a project before its required completion time, the following formula is used:

$$Z = \frac{LF - EF}{\sigma_t}$$

The elements in this formula are as follows:

- LF is the required completion time (latest finish) for the project.
- EF is the earliest expected finish time for the project (mean of the normal distribution).
- σ_t is the standard deviation of the total distribution of the activities on the longest (most time-consuming) path leading to project completion.

In the above equation, Z measures the number of standard deviations between EF and LF on the normal probability curve. This Z value must be converted into a number that gives the proportion of the area under the normal curve that lies between EF and LF. Because the total area under a normal curve is equal to 1.0, the probability of finishing the project before its required completion time is equal to the proportion of the area under the curve that is to the left of LF.

The EF time for the simple three-activity network in Figure 5.28 was calculated to be 36 days. Recall that the required completion time (LF) for the project is 42 days, or 6 days later than the EF. Figure 5.31 shows the normal curve for the project, with EF = 36 days and LF = 42 days.

The proportion of the area under the curve to the left of LF is equal to the probability of completing the project before 42 days. EF divides the area under the curve into two equal parts, each containing half of the area, so we know that the proportion of the area to the left of EF is 0.5. We must now find the proportion of the area between EF and LF and add this to 0.5 to obtain the

FIGURE 5.31 Normal Probability Distribution for Sample Project

proportion of the total area to the left of LF. Using the previous equation to find the proportion of the area between EF and LF, we can calculate Z:

$$Z = \frac{\text{LF} - \text{EF}}{\sigma_t} = \frac{42 - 36}{4.08} = \frac{6}{4.08} = 1.47$$

The Z value of 1.47 indicates that there are 1.47 standard deviations (1 standard deviation = 4.08 days) between EF and LF. However, the Z value does not directly give the proportion of the area under the curve between EF and LF. To find this area, we must convert the Z value to a number that gives the area directly, using a standard conversion table such as Table 5.1.

The first column and top row of the table are used to find the desired Z value with a significance of 0.01. To find the area for a Z value of 1.47, first go down the column on the far left to 1.4, then go across this row to the 0.07

TABLE 5.1 Table of Areas of the Normal Curve Between the Maximum Ordinate and Values of *Z*

Z	0.00	0.01	0.02	0.03	0.04	0.05	0.06	0.07	0.08	0.09
0.0	.00000	.00399	.00798	.01197	.01595	.01994	.02392	.02790	.03188	.03586
0.1	.03983	.04380	.04776	.05172	.05567	.05962	.06356	.06749	.07142	.07535
0.2	.07926	.08317	.08706	.09095	.09483	.09871	.10257	.10642	.11026	.11409
0.3	.11791	.12172	.12552	.12930	.13307	.13683	.14058	.14431	.14803	.15173
0.4	.15542	.15910	.16276	.16640	.17003	.17364	.17724	.18082	.18439	.18793
0.5	.19146	.19497	.19847	.20194	.20540	.20884	.21226	.21566	.21904	.22240
0.6	.22575	.22907	.23237	.23565	.23891	.24215	.24537	.24857	.25175	.25490
0.7	.25804	.26115	.26424	.26730	.27035	.27337	.27637	.27935	.28230	.28524
0.8	.28814	.29103	.29389	.29673	.29955	.30234	.30511	.30785	.31057	.31327
0.9	.31594	.31859	.32121	.32381	.32639	.32894	.33147	.33398	.33646	.33891
1.0	.34134	.34375	.34614	.34850	.35083	.35314	.35543	.35769	.35993	.36214
1.1	.36433	.36650	.36864	.37076	.37286	.37493	.37698	.37900	.38100	.38298
1.2	.38493	.38686	.38877	.39065	.39251	.39435	.39617	.39796	.39973	.40147
1.3	.40320	.40490	.40658	.40824	.40988	.41149	.41309	.41466	.41621	.41774
1.4	.41924	.42073	.42220	.42364	.42507	.42647	.42786	.42922	.43056	.43189
1.5	.44319	.43448	.43574	.43699	.43822	.43943	.44062	.44179	.44295	.44408
1.6	.44520	.44630	.44738	.44845	.44950	.45053	.45154	.45254	.45352	.45449

1.7	.45543	.45637	.45728	.45818	.45907	.45994	.46080	.46164	.46246	.46327
1.8	.46407	.46485	.46562	.46638	.46712	.46784	.46856	.46926	.46995	.47062
1.9	.47128	.47193	.47257	.47320	.47381	.47441	.47500	.47558	.47615	.47670
2.0	.47725	.47778	.47831	.47882	.47932	.47982	.48030	.48077	.48124	.48169
2.1	.48214	.48257	.48300	.48341	.48382	.48422	.48461	.48500	.48537	.48574
2.2	.48610	.48645	.48679	.48713	.48745	.48778	.48809	.48840	.48870	.48899
2.3	.48928	.48956	.48983	.49010	.49036	.49061	.49086	.49111	.49134	.49158
2.4	.49180	.49202	.49224	.49245	.49266	.49286	.49305	.49324	.49343	.49361
2.5	.49377	.49396	.49413	.49430	.49446	.49461	.49477	.49492	.49506	.49520
2.6	.49534	.49547	.49560	.49573	.49585	.49598	.49609	.49621	.49632	.49643
2.7	.49653	.49664	.49674	.49683	.49693	.49702	.49711	.49720	.49728	.49736
2.8	.49744	.49752	.49760	.49767	.49774	.49781	.49788	.49795	.49801	.49807
2.9	.49813	.49819	.49825	.49831	.49836	.49841	.49846	.49851	.49856	.49861
3.0	.49865	.49869	.49874	.49878	.49882	.49886	.49889	.49893	.49897	.49900
3.1	.49903	.49906	.49910	.49913	.49916	.49918	.49921	.49924	.49926	.49929
3.2	.49931	.49934	.49936	.49938	.49940	.49942	.49944	.49946	.49948	.49950
3.3	.49952	.49953	.49955	.49957	.49958	.49960	.49961	.49962	.49964	.49965
3.4	.49966	.49968	.49969	.49970	.49971	.49972	.49973	.49974	.49975	.49976
3.5	.49977	.49978	.49978	.49979	.49980	.49981	.49981	.49982	.49983	.49983
3.6	.49984	.49985	.49985	.49986	.49986	.49987	.49987	.49988	.49988	.49989
3.7	.49989	.49990	.49990	.49990	.49991	.49991	.49992	.49992	.49992	.49992
3.8	.49993	.49993	.49993	.49994	.49994	.49994	.49994	.49995	.49995	.49995
3.9	.49995	.49995	.49996	.49996	.49996	.49996	.49996	.49996	.49997	.49997
4.0	.49997	.49997	.49997	.49997	.49997	.49997	.49998	.49998	.49998	.49998

column. The number there is 0.42922. This means that for a Z value of 1.47, the proportion of the area under a normal curve is 0.42922. This number tells us that the probability of actually completing the project between EF and LF, or in 36 to 42 days, is 0.42922; thus, there is a 42.922 percent chance. However, because we are interested in finding the probability of actually completing the project any time before 42 days, we must add the probability of finishing before 36 days. The probability of finishing the project any time before 42 days is equal to the probability of finishing before 36 days plus the probability of finishing between 36 days and 42 days:

$$0.50000 + 0.42922 = 0.92922$$

The probability of actually completing the project before its required completion time of 42 days is 0.92922; there is a 92.922 percent chance.

SUMMARY

If each activity in the network diagram for a project has three time estimates (optimistic, most likely, and pessimistic), it is possible to calculate the probability of actually completing the project before its required completion time using the methods discussed in this appendix. However, you should be careful in interpreting this probability, especially when there are several paths that are nearly as

long as the critical path. If the standard deviations of these alternative paths are substantially different from that of the critical path, the probability of the project actually being finished before its required completion time may be lower when these paths are used in the probability calculations than when the critical path is used. This discrepancy usually arises only when two or more paths that are equal or nearly equal in length lead to project completion.

QUESTIONS

1. True or false: To calculate the probability of finishing a project by its required completion time, it is necessary to have three time estimates for each activity and the required completion time for the project.
2. What are the expected duration, variance, and standard deviation for an activity whose three time estimates are $t_o = 2$, $t_m = 14$, and $t_p = 14$?
3. Which of the following is *not* a measure of the dispersion, or spread, of a distribution: variance, mean, or standard deviation?
4. The earliest expected finish time for a project is 138 days, and its required completion time is 130 days. What is the probability of completing the project before its required time if σ_t (the standard deviation of the total distribution of the activities on the longest path) is 6?

APPENDIX 2 Microsoft Project

In this appendix, we will discuss how Microsoft Project can be used to support the techniques discussed in this chapter based on the consumer market study example. To retrieve your project information, on the File menu, click Open and locate the consumer market study file you saved in Chapter 4. We are now ready to enter the estimated durations for each task, examine the project schedule, produce a Gantt chart, determine the critical path, set a baseline to help track the project, monitor and control the schedule, edit task information, and produce reports.

Enter duration data directly into the Duration column in the Gantt Chart View. If you are not in the Gantt Chart View, click on Gantt Chart in the Task Views group on the Task ribbon. Check that the words "Gantt Chart Tools" are above the Format tab on the menu. Please see Figure 5A.1 for the duration data to enter. Note that when you enter the duration for each task, the default time unit is "d" for days. You can enter "m" after the number to represent minutes; "h" for hours; "d" for days; "w" for weeks; or "mon" for months. For example, an entry of "2w" would equal a two-week duration estimate. As you modify the duration estimates, the system automatically updates the start and finish dates for each task if Auto Schedule is selected in the Task group on the Task ribbon for a task. The icon next to each task in the Task Mode column will display if the task is set to Manually Schedule or Auto Schedule. For this example, select Auto Schedule for each task.

As you enter durations, the durations for the work packages total the duration for their activities. The task row for the title shows the total of the durations for all the activities in the project. The work packages and the project title operate as summary tasks. Note the total duration of the project is 138 days.

Microsoft Project 2013 has already calculated the ES, EF, LS, and LF times, FS, and TS for each task. To see these values, you need to view the Schedule Table from the Gantt Chart View. On the View ribbon, click on Tables in the Data group. Then, click on Schedule in the menu. You should see the table shown in

FIGURE 5A.1 Add Duration Data

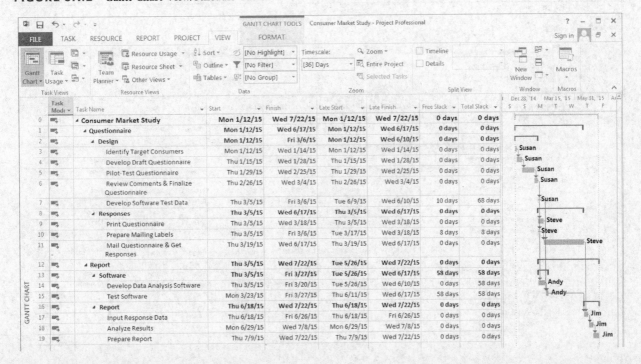

Figure 5A.2. Note that the Timeline has been unchecked in the Split View group
on the View ribbon.

Microsoft project automatically creates the Gantt chart to the right of the tables
in the Gantt Chart View as you enter tasks and their task information. The Gantt

FIGURE 5A.2 Gantt Chart View/Schedule Table

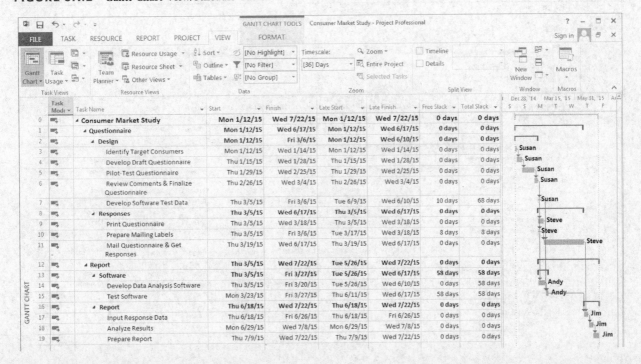

chart displays the dependencies between tasks with arrows. To highlight the critical path in red, on the Format ribbon for Gantt Chart Tools, click in the box to put a check mark next to Critical Tasks in the Bar Styles group. Figure 5A.3 shows the Gantt chart with the critical path highlighted.

You can request a report of all critical tasks in the Consumer Market Study project. On the Report ribbon in the View Reports group, click on In Progress. You should see the drop-down menu of report types. Click on Critical Tasks to select the Critical Tasks Report. You should see the Critical Tasks Report as in Figure 5A.4.

Recall the total duration for the project is 138 days. The project needs to be completed in 130 days. Note that the Schedule view shows the earliest day the project can be completed and the latest start dates for each task. To reduce the total duration of the project, the duration of at least one task on the critical path needs to be reduced. It is decided that the Mail Questionnaire & Get Responses task will be reduced from 65 days to 55 days. Change the duration of the task on the Entry Table in the Gantt Chart View. The Entry Table is accessed by clicking on Entry Table in the Tables menu in the Data group on the View ribbon. Microsoft Project automatically updates the Gantt Chart, network diagram, and the schedule with the change. Note that the total duration of the project reduces to 128 days, as shown in Figure 5A.5.

It is important to periodically save the baseline of your project to monitor changes. To save baseline project data, on the Project ribbon, click on Set Baseline in the Schedule group, and click on Set Baseline. *Save your file at this point with the file name Consumer Market Study to continue the planning presented in Chapters 6 and 7.*

Microsoft Project helps to determine the effects of actual performance on the project completion date. AF dates are entered in the task information window. Susan completed the Identify Target Consumers in two days instead of three days.

FIGURE 5A.3 Gantt Chart with Critical Path

FIGURE 5A.4 **Critical Tasks Report**

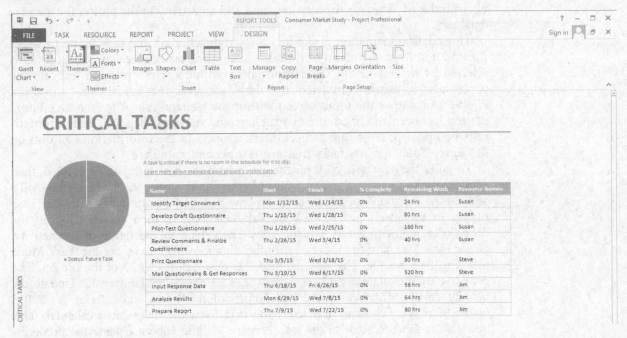

FIGURE 5A.5 **Edit Activity Duration**

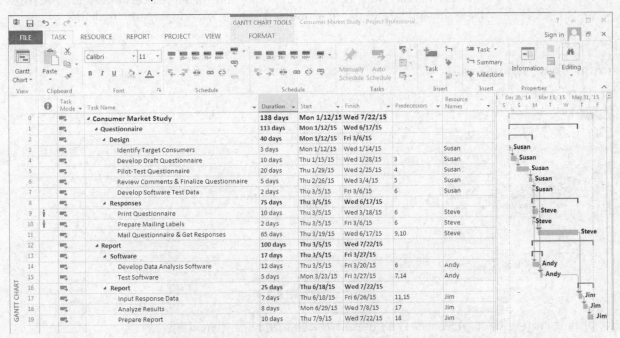

She developed the draft questionnaire in 9 days and pilot-tested the questionnaire in 19 days. Susan discovered that she needed to make substantial revisions to the questionnaire and changed the duration to finish the revisions from 5 days to 15 days. Steve had to order a new database for the labels on day 23 of the project because the database was not up to date. The time for Steve to receive the database is 21 days and

the activity is a predecessor to the Prepare Mailing Labels activity. Update the schedule with the AF dates for the activities, and add an activity to the project for the new database.

To update information about any task, right-click on the task name to select Information from the menu or double-click on the task name. The General tab is selected by default in the Task Information window. Here you can indicate the percentage of work completed for that task and the actual time duration. Figure 5A.6 shows the input screen within the General tab. After the task information has been modified, the Gantt chart and network diagrams will automatically be updated. Note that a check mark appears in the Information Column on the Entry Table for any tasks that are 100 percent complete.

To enter the new task, click on the row where the new task will be entered, then click on the top part of the Task button in the Insert group on the Task ribbon. To add the new activity for Steve, click on row 9, Print Questionnaire. On the Task ribbon in the Insert group, click on the Task button, then choose Task in the drop-down menu to insert a blank row. Then, type in the name of the activity, Order New Database for Labels. Enter the duration of 21 days. Set the Task Mode to Manually Schedule. The start date for this new task is day 23 of the project. The project started on January 12. February 12 is 23 days after January 12. Update the task information by opening the Task Information window and entering 2/12/2015 in the Start box. You can also select the date from the drop-down calendar. This new task is a predecessor to the task Prepare Mailing Labels. Update the predecessors for Prepare Mailing Labels. Note that Microsoft Project automatically adjusted the task numbers for the remaining tasks and their predecessors. Figure 5A.7 displays the addition of the new task and Figure 5A.8 displays the updates.

FIGURE 5A.6 Task Information

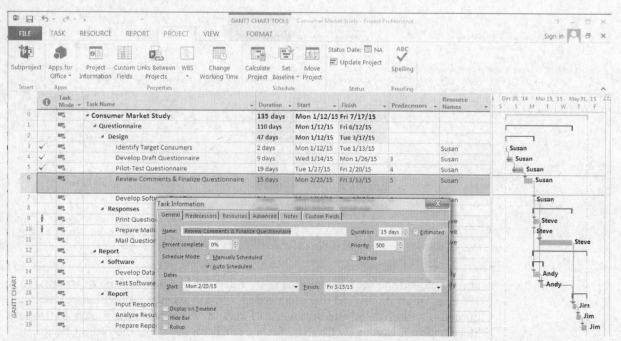

FIGURE 5A.7 Insert New Manually Scheduled Activity

FIGURE 5A.8 Updated Predecessors

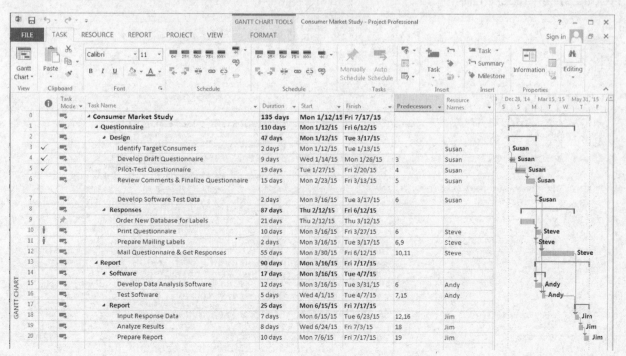

Valuable tracking data can be displayed through the Tracking Table. While in the Gantt Chart View, on the View ribbon, click on Table in the Data group, and click on Tracking in the menu. This table, as seen in Figure 5A.9, shows actual start and finish times, percent complete, actual duration, remaining duration, actual costs, and actual work time for each activity. Note the AF times are reflected for the three tasks Susan has completed.

To get a visual representation of actual versus planned progress, on the Task ribbon, click on the down arrow on the Gantt Chart icon in the View group, and select Tracking Gantt from the menu. The Tracking Gantt chart, shown in Figure 5A.10, displays two bars for each task. The lower bar shows the baseline start and finish dates, and the upper bar shows the current start and finish dates, so that you can see the difference between your baseline plan and the current schedule.

To obtain information on variances within your project, you need to select a table that will display variance values. On the View ribbon, click on Tables in the Data group, and select Variance from the menu. You should see the table that is shown in Figure 5A.11. This table shows the actual start and finish times compared to the baseline start and finish times for each activity, along with any variances. Note that at this point we see the results of the three tasks Susan has completed. The times will change as your project progresses and you update the percent complete and the AF dates for tasks.

It is helpful to save your project as you work. To save your project information, on the File tab, click on Save As and enter the file name *Consumer Market Study with Actual Finish Entries*.

FIGURE 5A.9 **Tracking Table**

FIGURE 5A.10 Tracking Gantt Chart

#	Task Name	Act. Start	Act. Finish	% Comp	Phys. %	Act. Dur.	Rem. Dur.	Act. Cost	Act. Work
0	**Consumer Market Study**	Mon 1/12/15	NA	17%	0%	88 days	12 days	$0.00	240 hrs
1	**Questionnaire**	Mon 1/12/15	NA	22%	0%	44 days	15.56 days	$0.00	240 hrs
2	**Design**	Mon 1/12/15	NA	64%	0%	30 days	17 days	$0.00	240 hrs
3	Identify Target Consumers	Mon 1/12/15	Tue 1/13/15	100%	0%	2 days	0 days	$0.00	16 hrs
4	Develop Draft Questionnaire	Wed 1/14/15	Mon 1/26/15	100%	0%	9 days	0 days	$0.00	72 hrs
5	Pilot-Test Questionnaire	Tue 1/27/15	Fri 2/20/15	100%	0%	19 days	0 days	$0.00	152 hrs
6	Review Comments & Finalize Questionnaire	NA	NA	0%	0%	0 days	15 days	$0.00	0 hrs
7	Develop Software Test Data	NA	NA	0%	0%	0 days	2 days	$0.00	0 hrs
8	**Responses**	NA	NA	0%	0%	0 days	87 days	$0.00	0 hrs
9	Order New Database for Labels	NA	NA	0%	0%	0 days	21 days	$0.00	0 hrs
10	Print Questionnaire	NA	NA	0%	0%	0 days	10 days	$0.00	0 hrs
11	Prepare Mailing Labels	NA	NA	0%	0%	0 days	2 days	$0.00	0 hrs
12	Mail Questionnaire & Get Responses	NA	NA	0%	0%	0 days	55 days	$0.00	0 hrs
13	**Report**	NA	NA	0%	0%	0 days	90 days	$0.00	0 hrs
14	**Software**	NA	NA	0%	0%	0 days	17 days	$0.00	0 hrs
15	Develop Data Analysis Software	NA	NA	0%	0%	0 days	12 days	$0.00	0 hrs
16	Test Software	NA	NA	0%	0%	0 days	5 days	$0.00	0 hrs
17	**Report**	NA	NA	0%	0%	0 days	25 days	$0.00	0 hrs
18	Input Response Data	NA	NA	0%	0%	0 days	7 days	$0.00	0 hrs
19	Analyze Results	NA	NA	0%	0%	0 days	8 days	$0.00	0 hrs
20	Prepare Report	NA	NA	0%	0%	0 days	10 days	$0.00	0 hrs

FIGURE 5A.11 Variance Table

CHAPTER 6

Resource Utilization

Huntstock/Getty Images

Concepts in this chapter support the following Project Management Knowledge Areas of *A Guide to the Project Management Body of Knowledge (PMBOK® Guide):*

**Project Time Management
Project Human Resource Management**

 REAL WORLD PROJECT MANAGEMENT

The New House Call

The statistics for chronic diseases are alarming. An estimated 60 percent of deaths around the globe are attributed to chronic diseases such as heart disease and cancer. Low- and middle-income countries account for 80 percent of these chronic

disease-related deaths. Chronic disease care in the United States has been reported to be 75 percent of the total healthcare costs.

The solution expected is development of mobile healthcare apps. The prognosis is a surge from US$1.2 billion in 2011 to US$11.8 billion in 2018 for expenditures related to mobile healthcare app development and implementation. The authors of a 2012 Ernst & Young report on healthcare costs noted, "A critical component for bringing these costs under control will be the move to a 'healthcare everywhere' future in which care is more patient-centric, self-managed, and delivered in more disaggregated settings."

Investments in projects and the resources for mobile healthcare app development are expected to be spent for software and services (80 percent), hardware (12 percent), and networks and connectivity (8 percent). Project managers are considering how the mobile apps will influence the future expectation of healthcare everywhere. A primary goal of the projects is to help reduce the occurrence of chronic diseases.

In an effort to provide more accessible healthcare, project teams have identified emerging and developed markets. By capitalizing on these markets, project managers are assembling teams of mobile app developers to meet the rising demand.

The market for patients using apps to monitor their health has been developed; 37 percent of all patients are interested in tracking their weight or caloric intake within a mobile app. A 20 percent increase in adoption is expected as more patients want to track their personal habits and their consequences. Devices that send personal health reports and data to healthcare professionals are expected to be adopted by more than half of all patients, 51 percent. General healthcare information gathering apps are used by 44 percent of all patients and adoption is expected to reach 57 percent of all patients.

This potential 10-fold investment will require an increase in resources to shape the healthcare everywhere in future. Project teams are addressing the current mobile healthcare app requirements and are planning for future use. Reduction in healthcare costs and incidence of chronic diseases is expected by having patients make the new house call to their healthcare professionals with a mobile healthcare app. Maybe the new statement will be, "An app a day keeps the doctor away."

Based on information from Anonymous (2013). "The New House Call," *PM Network, 27*(3), 13.

The consideration of resources adds another dimension to planning and scheduling. It is necessary to estimate the types and quantities of resources required to perform each activity. These resources can include people, materials, equipment, tools, facilities, and so forth. A resource requirements plan illustrates the expected utilization of resources by time period during the time span of the project.

In many projects, the quantities of the various types of resources available to perform the project activities are limited. Several activities may require the same resources at the same time, and there may not be sufficient resources available to satisfy all the demands. In a sense, these activities are *competing* for the use of the same resources. If sufficient resources are not available when required, some activities may have to be delayed until a later time when resources *are* available for them. Therefore, resources can constrain the project schedule. They can also be a constraint to completing the

project within budget if it is determined that additional resources are needed to complete the project by its required completion time.

This chapter covers several approaches to incorporating resource considerations into the project plan and schedule. You will become familiar with,

- Taking resource constraints into account when developing a network diagram
- Determining the resource requirements plan for a project
- Leveling the use of resources within the required time frame of the project
- Determining the shortest project schedule with the limited resources available

LEARNING OUTCOMES

After studying this chapter, the learner should be able to:

- Create a network diagram that takes resource constraints into account
- Prepare a resource requirements plan
- Explain resource leveling
- Discuss resource-limited scheduling

Resource-Constrained Planning

One way to consider resources is to take them into account when establishing the dependent relationships among activities in the network diagram. At a minimum, network diagrams illustrate the *technical constraints* among activities. Activities are drawn in a serial relationship because, from a technical standpoint, they must be performed in that sequence. For example, Figure 6.1 shows that the three house-building activities—building the foundation, building the frame, and putting on the roof—must be done serially. Technically, these activities must be performed in this sequence. The roof cannot be put on before the frame is built!

Reinforce Your Learning

1. At a minimum, network diagrams illustrate the _____ constraints among activities. However, when limited resources are available, the network diagram can be drawn to also reflect _____ constraints.

FIGURE 6.1 Technically Constrained Activity Sequence

Resource-constrained planning is an approach to creating a network diagram and schedule in which the sequence and dependent relationships of activities are based on *resource constraints* that take into account the availability of a limited quantity of resources. Part (a) of Figure 6.2 shows that, technically, three activities—paint living room, paint kitchen, and paint bedroom—could be performed concurrently; that is, there is no technical reason why the start of any one of these activities should depend on the completion of any other one. Suppose, however, that there is only one person available to do all the painting;

FIGURE 6.2 **Resource-Constrained Planning**

(a) Activity Sequence without Resource Constraints

(b) Activity Sequence Based on Resource Constraints

this limitation would introduce a resource constraint on the painting activities. That is, although technically all three activities could be performed concurrently, they would have to be performed in series because only one painter would be available to do all three. To incorporate this resource constraint, the diagram will have to be drawn as shown in part (b) of Figure 6.2. The exact sequence of these three activities—which particular rooms get painted first, second, and third—is another decision that must be made when the network diagram is created.

This example illustrates how resource limitations can be considered when a network plan is prepared. This approach of incorporating resource constraints into the dependent relationships among activities in the network diagram is feasible for small projects involving few resources. However, it becomes complicated for large projects and for projects in which several different resources are needed for some of the activities.

Reinforce Your Learning

2. A resource

plan illustrates the expected

of

by time period during the time span of the project.

Resource Requirements Plan

As discussed in the previous chapter, it is necessary to estimate the types and quantities of resources required to perform each activity. A **resource requirements plan** illustrates the expected utilization of resources by time period during the time span of the project.

Using the consumer market study project as an example, refer to Figure 5.10, which shows the network diagram for the project, and to Figure 5.11, which is the revised baseline schedule. Let us consider the utilization of the human

resources—the project team: Susan, Steve, Andy, and Jim. Several assumptions need to be mentioned:

- None of the four team members are required for the entire estimated duration of the project (128 days).
- Activity 6, "Print Questionnaire," will be subcontracted to a vendor. So although it has an estimated duration of 10 days, it will require only one day of work by Steve. However, Steve is still the project team member assigned responsibility for the activity.
- Activity 9, "Mail Questionnaire & Get Responses," has an estimated duration of 55 days. However, Steve will only work on it for the first 5 days to mail the questionnaires. The remaining 50 days are waiting time for the questionnaires to be returned and require no work by Steve.
- For all other activities, when the assigned person is working on an activity, he or she will work full time on it for its estimated duration.

With the above assumptions in mind and referring to the earliest start (ES) and earliest finish (EF) times in the schedule in Figure 5.11, we can determine the planned resource requirements for each member of the project team:

- Susan's five activities (1, 2, 3, 4, and 8) are all on the front end of the project and will require 40 work days during the period 0 to 40.
- Steve's three activities (5, 6, and 9) require 8 work days during the period 38 to 53. Remember the last 50 days (53 to 103) of the estimated duration for activity 9 is just elapsed time waiting for the questionnaires to be returned. Also, Steve is performing only one day of work on activity 6 because it is being subcontracted to a vendor.
- Andy's two activities (7 and 10) require 17 work days during the period 38 to 55.
- Jim's three activities (11, 12, and 13) are all at the end of the project and require 25 work days during the period 103 to 128.

Figure 6.3 shows the estimated required work days for each team member and the time period during which each will be utilized. Although the project estimated completion time is 128 days, the four project team members will perform 90 days of work during that period.

FIGURE 6.3 **Estimated Resource Requirements for Consumer Market Study Project**

NAME	ACTIVITIES	WORK DAYS	PERIOD
Susan	1, 2, 3, 4, 8	40	0 to 40
Steve	5, 6, 9	8	38 to 53
Andy	7, 10	17	38 to 55
Jim	11, 12, 13	25	103 to 128
		90	**0 to 128**

For an example that illustrates the utilization of a multiple quantity of a particular resource, consider the painting project in Figure 6.4. Each activity shows its estimated duration, as well as the quantity of painters required to accomplish the activity within its estimated duration.

Using the information in Figure 6.4, we can prepare a resource requirements plan, as shown in Figure 6.5, that indicates how many painters are required each

FIGURE 6.4 Required Resources for Painting Project

day based on the ES and EF times for each activity. This resource requirements plan shows that four painters are required on days 1 through 4, three painters are required on days 5 and 6, two painters are required on days 7 through 10, and only one painter is required on days 11 and 12. A total of 32 painter-days are required. The resource requirements graph for painters is illustrated in Figure 6.6. It shows an uneven utilization of painters. A peak of four painters is required during one portion of the project, and a low of only one painter is required during another portion of the project.

FIGURE 6.5 Resource Requirements Plan for Painting Project

													Painter Days
First-Floor Rooms (2 Painters)													16
								Stairs & Hall (1 Painter)					4
							Bathroom (1 Painter)						2
Basement Rooms (1 Painter)													4
Bedrooms (1 Painter)													6
Day	1	2	3	4	5	6	7	8	9	10	11	12	
Painters	4	4	4	4	3	3	2	2	2	2	1	1	32

FIGURE 6.6 Resource Utilization for Painters

Resources cannot usually be hired on a day-to-day basis to meet fluctuating requirements. If the same quantity of painters must be employed throughout the project, it may be necessary to pay some painters to work overtime during periods of peak demand and to pay some painters when they are idle during periods of low demand. Thus, it is preferable to have a more uniform, or level, application of resources.

It should be noted that the resource requirements graphs shown in Figures 6.5 and 6.6 are based on each activity's earliest start time. Such resource requirements graphs are said to be based on an **as-soon-as-possible (ASAP) schedule**. Resource requirements graphs based on each activity's latest start time are said to be based on an **as-late-as-possible (ALAP) schedule**.

Also see the section on assign responsibility in Chapter 4 and the section on estimate activity resources in Chapter 5 for additional related information.

Resource Leveling

Reinforce Your Learning

3. Resource-leveling attempts to establish a schedule in which resource utilization is made as level as possible

extending the project beyond its

time.

Resource leveling, or **smoothing**, is a method for developing a schedule that attempts to minimize the fluctuations in requirements for resources. This method levels the resources so that they are applied as uniformly as possible without extending the project schedule beyond its required completion time. It is a trial-and-error method in which the start of noncritical activities (those with positive slack values) are delayed beyond their earliest start times (but not beyond their latest start times) to maintain a uniform level of required resources. Activities can be delayed only to the point where all their positive slack is used up, as any further delays would cause the project to extend beyond the project required completion time. *Resource leveling attempts to establish a schedule in which resource utilization is made as level as possible without extending the project beyond its required completion time.*

Let us look at the painting project in Figures 6.4, 6.5, and 6.6 to determine whether resource utilization can be leveled. Figures 6.4 and 6.5 show that the critical path for the project is made up of two activities and is 12 days long (8 days to paint the first-floor rooms, plus 4 days to paint the stairs and hall). Therefore, these two activities cannot be delayed without extending the project completion

time beyond 12 days. Looking at Figure 6.5, however, we can see that "Bathroom" could be delayed up to 2 days, "Basement Rooms" could be delayed up to 8 days, and "Bedrooms" could be delayed up to 6 days—all without extending the project completion time beyond 12 days. Looking again at Figure 6.5, we can see that two alternative actions could be taken to level the daily resource requirements for painters:

Alternative 1: Delay the activity with the most positive slack—"Basement Rooms" (+8 days slack)—by six days so that it will start after "Bedrooms" is finished. Rather than have two separate painters paint the basement rooms and bedrooms concurrently, the resource-leveled schedule will use the same painter to first paint the bedrooms and then paint the basement rooms.

Alternative 2: Delay "Bedrooms" so that it will start on day 4, after "Basement Rooms" is completed. This alternative will use the same painter to first paint the basement rooms and then paint the bedrooms (the reverse of alternative 1, achieving the same result).

Figures 6.7 and 6.8 illustrate the resource profile for the resource-leveled schedule if we choose alternative 1. Comparing Figure 6.7 with Figure 6.5, we see that the ES time for "Basement Rooms" has been delayed from time 0 to day 6, and its EF time is now day 10 rather than day 4. Figure 6.8 shows a more uniform utilization of painters than Figure 6.6, except for days 11 and 12, which remain the same. In both cases, 32 painter-days are required, but in the resource-leveled schedule, they are utilized with less fluctuation.

For a large project with many different resources, resource leveling can get very complicated. Various project management information systems are available that will assist in generating a resource-leveled schedule and resource requirements graphs and tables.

FIGURE 6.7 Resource-leveled Requirements Plan for Painting Project

Activity			Painter Days
First-Floor Rooms (2 Painters)			16
Stairs & Hall (1 Painter)			4
Bathroom (1 Painter)			2
Basement Rooms (1 Painter)			4
Bedrooms (1 Painter)			6

Day	1	2	3	4	5	6	7	8	9	10	11	12	
Painters	3	3	3	3	3	3	3	3	3	3	1	1	32

FIGURE 6.8 **Resource-leveled Utilization for Painters**

Resource-Limited Scheduling

Resource-limited scheduling is a method for developing the shortest schedule when the quantity of available resources is fixed. This method is appropriate when the resources available for the project are limited and these resource limits cannot be exceeded. This method *will extend the project completion time, if necessary, to keep within the resource limits*. It is an iterative method in which resources are allocated to activities based on the least slack. When several activities need the same limited resource at the same time, the activities with the least slack have first priority. If resources are left over, the activities with the second-least slack have the next priority, and so forth. If other activities need the resource but the resource has been totally allocated to higher-priority activities, the lower-priority activities get delayed; as their slack becomes worse, they eventually move up the priority ladder. This delaying of activities can extend the project completion time.

Figure 6.9 illustrates what would happen if only a limited quantity of painters—two—were available to do the painting project. When we push down on the level of resources because no more than two painters can be used, we push out the project completion time. If only two painters are available at any time, the project completion time has to be extended from day 12 to at least day 16, to utilize the 32 painter-days required.

Let us apply resource-limited scheduling to the painting project shown in Figure 6.4. Figure 6.10, which is based on Figure 6.5, is our original resource requirements plan, but it shows total slack based on a project completion time of 12 days. Let us now assume, however, that we are limited to only two painters.

Figure 6.10 shows that, as the project starts, three activities require a total of four painters ("First-Floor Rooms," "Basement Rooms," and "Bedrooms"). Only two painters are available, though, so they will be allocated to the activities based on a priority determined by slack.

"First-Floor Rooms" has a slack of 0, whereas "Basement Rooms" has a slack of +8 days and "Bedrooms" has a slack of +6 days. Therefore, the two painters will be allocated to the first-floor rooms and will continue to be assigned to that activity until it is finished. (In this example, it is assumed that, once an activity starts, it continues until it is finished and cannot be stopped and restarted.) Because all the available resources are assigned to "First-Floor Rooms" from time 0 through day 8, the other two activities ("Basement Rooms" and

FIGURE 6.9 **Effect of Limited Resource Availability**

FIGURE 6.10 **Resource Requirements Plan for Painting Project**

Day	1	2	3	4	5	6	7	8	9	10	11	12
Painters	4	4	4	4	3	3	2	2	2	2	1	1

"Bedrooms") will have their starts delayed until after day 8. This first resource allocation is shown in Figure 6.11.

The result of this first iteration of allocating the painters is extension of project completion from day 12 to day 14 because of the delay of "Bedrooms." Additionally, there is still a problem on days 9 through 12 because the resource requirements exceed the limit of two painters. So it is now necessary to do a

FIGURE 6.11 **First Resource Allocation**

															Slack
First-Floor Rooms (2 Painters)															0
								Stairs & Hall (1 Painter)							0
								Bathroom (1 Painter)							2
								Basement Rooms (1 Painter)							0
								Bedrooms (1 Painter)							−2
Day	1	2	3	4	5	6	7	8	9	10	11	12	13	14	
Painters	2	2	2	2	2	2	2	2	4	4	3	3	1	1	

second allocation of painters on day 9. "Bedrooms" has the least slack, with −2 days; its earliest expected finish time is now day 14, and the required project completion time is 12 days. "Bedrooms" requires one painter, so one of the two available painters is allocated to it. One painter is still to be allocated. Two activities, "Stairs & Hall" and "Basement Rooms," have the same next lowest value of slack (0). One way to choose between these two is to determine which has been critical for a longer time. Looking back, we see that "Stairs & Hall" was more critical (0 slack) than "Basement Rooms" (+8 days slack) in Figure 6.10. Therefore, the remaining painter should be allocated to "Stairs & Hall." "Bedrooms" will start after day 8 and will continue through day 14. "Stairs & Hall" will also start after day 8 and will continue through day 12. The next time a painter will become available is after "Stairs & Hall" is finished on day 12. Therefore, the remaining two activities, "Basement Rooms" and "Bathrooms," will have their starts delayed until after day 12. This second resource allocation is shown in Figure 6.12.

The result of this second iteration of allocating the painters is another extension of project completion, this time from day 14 to day 16, because of the delay of "Basement Rooms." There is still a problem on days 13 and 14 because the resource requirements exceed the limit of two painters. So it is now necessary to do a third allocation of painters on day 13, when one painter becomes available after finishing "Stairs & Hall." (Remember that the second painter is still working on "Bedrooms.") Two activities, "Bathrooms" and "Basement Rooms," need a painter on day 13. "Basement Rooms" has less slack (−4 days) than the other activity, so the available painter will be allocated to it. "Basement Rooms" will start after day 12 and will continue through day 16. The next time a painter will become available is after "Bedrooms" is finished on day 14. Therefore, "Bathroom" will have its start delayed until after day 14. This third resource allocation is shown in Figure 6.13.

FIGURE 6.12 Second Resource Allocation

	Slack
First-Floor Rooms (2 Painters)	0
Stairs & Hall (1 Painter)	0
Bathroom (1 Painter)	−2
Basement Rooms (1 Painter)	−4
Bedrooms (1 Painter)	−2

Day	1	2	3	4	5	6	7	8	9	10	11	12	13	14	15	16
Painters	2	2	2	2	2	2	2	2	2	2	2	2	3	3	1	1

FIGURE 6.13 Third Resource Allocation

	Slack
First-Floor Rooms (2 Painters)	0
Stairs & Hall (1 Painter)	0
Bathroom (1 Painter)	−4
Basement Rooms (1 Painter)	−4
Bedrooms (1 Painter)	−2

Day	1	2	3	4	5	6	7	8	9	10	11	12	13	14	15	16
Painters	2	2	2	2	2	2	2	2	2	2	2	2	2	2	2	2

As a result of this third iteration of allocating the painters, the project completion time is still four days beyond its required completion time, but all the activities have been scheduled to start and finish so as to stay within the limit of two painters. No further iterations are needed.

To accelerate the schedule to complete the project by day 12, it would be necessary to implement one or more of the approaches to schedule control

mentioned in Chapter 5, such as adding more painters, working overtime, reducing the scope of work or the requirements for some of the activities, or increasing productivity.

For a large project that requires many different resources, each of which has a different limit of availability, resource-limited scheduling can get very complicated. Various project management information systems are available that will perform resource-limited scheduling.

 REAL WORLD PROJECT MANAGEMENT

Industrial Sites Get a New Look

An inactive quarry in Shanghai. A decommissioned military base in Germany. An abandoned industrial district in London. All different, yet the same. These locations identified as in need of transformation are resources within projects meant to reclaim and rejuvenate areas that have served their initial purpose.

Visitors to Shanghai, China, will soon be able to stay in a 300-room luxury hotel that extends 200 feet below the surface. This hotel is much different than recent innovative hotel construction projects reaching thousands of feet into the sky. Of the 18 floors in the US$190 million project, only 2 of the floors will be above ground. The project team finds the project motivating as evidenced by a comment by Baet Yeok-Hoon, senior associate director of architecture at Atkins, Epsom, Surrey, England, "The unusual nature of the quarry project has been a great incentive to all team members. Everyone is very keen to face up to the challenges."

With "little or no precedent for an 'upside-down' hotel on a cliff face," according to Baet, the obstacles are interesting. The resources necessary to complete the project extend beyond people and materials; they include the site-specific issues that can add to the schedule and the budget. Toxic chemicals, machinery needing disassembling, fire-safety, seismic activity, and storm-water management require resources for their mitigation.

Baumholder, Germany, had the potential to suffer the fate of becoming a ghost town after the closing of a U.S. military base. More than 500 registrants from 74 countries designed solutions to repurpose abandoned military sites around the world, including Baumholder, into civic spaces that respect the communities' physical, cultural, and socioeconomic characteristics. "Former military installations offer an opportunity to reenvision the future of a community and positive social good," states T. Luke Young, program coordinator at Architecture for Humanity, San Francisco, California, USA, the company sponsoring a contest for project designs.

London's transformation of the abandoned industrial district spotlighted during the 2012 Summer Olympics employed numerous human and material resources to upgrade rail lines, clean contaminated soil, build more than 2,800 homes, and create a vibrant region for use after the closing ceremonies. The regional revamp project plan was the heart of the proposal for the Games. As a result, the blighted region was turned into a booming commercial and residential community.

The goals for these creative projects in unlikely spaces included positive community impact, economic viability, and sustainable ecological footprints. Constraints for the planning for these and other similar projects do not follow standard requirements for resources. Complexity, vision, and site-specific solutions are challenging to project teams and investors as the clients and design teams generate sustainable and responsible solutions. The field of project management successfully applies techniques to address the complexity and will continue to lead in the field of opportunities for out of the ordinary projects and for helping former industrial sites get a new look.

Based on information from La Plante, L. (2012). "Industrial Sites Get a New Look," *PM Network, 26*(7), 12–13.

Resource Requirements for Information Systems Development

Information systems development includes people, hardware, software, data, and network resources as the five basic required resources. The people resources include end users and information system specialists. Hardware resources consist of the computer systems, computer peripherals, and the media required to store information. Programs and the procedures to instruct users on how to operate the programs are the software resources. Information system development creates data that are organized in databases and knowledge bases that are used to support all the phases of the project. Network resources are composed of communications media and network support.

Each of these resources is assigned to the activities to complete the tasks. The more accurately the activities are assessed for the needed resources, the more likely it is that the development projects can be completed on time. The majority of information system projects assign resources to multiple tasks at the same time without considering the overallocation and the conflict that the work resources face to complete the project work. The overallocation forces the resources to be overextended and increases the probability of project failure. A more careful analysis during the problem definition step in the classic systems development life cycle problem-solving approach introduced in Chapter 4 could improve assigning work, material, and cost resources in a manner that increases the probability of project success.

AN INFORMATION SYSTEM EXAMPLE: INTERNET APPLICATIONS DEVELOPMENT FOR ABC OFFICE DESIGNS (CONTINUED)

Recall from Chapters 4 and 5 that Beth Smith of ABC Office Designs was assigned as project manager for the development of a Web-based reporting system project. Beth has identified the major tasks to be completed and the project schedule. Management has agreed to the project team's plan for 60 days to complete the development. Beth has 14 staff members on the project team. Each staff member has been assigned to have primary responsibility for at least one activity as shown in the responsibility assignment matrix for the project (Figure 4.11). Most activities include support responsibility by the project team members.

Beth Smith begins her resource requirements plan by seeking input from the person assigned primary responsibility for each of the major tasks that need to be accomplished. Beth had previously consulted with the project team to develop the responsibility matrix to have enough resources to complete the tasks. Beth initially allocates each primary and support resource at 100 percent effort for the duration of their assigned activities.

Beth noticed if every resource is assigned to 100 percent of all the tasks according to the responsibility matrix, some of the resources would be overal-located in the project. The overallocated resources are assigned to the subtasks necessary to complete the major task Software Development and major tasks for Training and System Conversion. Beth evaluates each of the tasks with the project team, and together they set priorities for assignments to determine if all the primary and support resources are needed on every activity to complete the work.

Even though Joe and Gerri were assigned support responsibility for the sub-tasks Packaged Software and Customized Software, for Software Development, their primary responsibilities for Hardware Development and Network Develop-ment take priority according to Hannah, who has primary responsibility for the Software Development activity. Hannah has support help from Maggie for these subtasks and decides that if she and Maggie need any additional help from Joe and Gerri to support their work on the Software Development task, Joe and Gerri would be assigned on an overtime basis.

For the other overallocation, Hannah and Gerri are assigned to Training and System Conversion with Jim and Beth. The two days of work to complete the System Conversion occur during the four days of work necessary for Training. Hannah and Gerri are assigned to Training with Jim. Beth and Jim agree that Hannah and Gerri could be removed from Training for two days if Beth cannot complete the System Conversion in the two days assigned. Hannah and Gerri would still be able to work for two days with Jim. They could plan to have more training events while Hannah and Gerri are available if Beth needs them for the system conversion. The development team suggested they could prepare for a single resource to be able to complete the system conversion during their work on System Development and Testing to help the overallocation.

Beth finalized the resource requirements table to share with management in her project report. The total working time necessary to complete the Web-based reporting system project is 2,040 working hours. The project team is confident they can complete the task in the 60-day time frame. Figure 6.14 shows the resource names, activities as shown in the responsi-bility assignment matrix in Figure 4.11, and the amount of time for each, as well as total work hours for each resource and the period of performance for the resources. Beth also included the material and cost resources in her report.

Project Management Information Systems

Project management information systems provide excellent features for handling resource considerations within a project. Most systems allow you to create and maintain a list of resources that can be accessed by all of the tasks within a proj-ect. The list typically allows you to store the resource name, maximum quantity

FIGURE 6.14 **Resource Requirements for Web-based Reporting System Project**

RESOURCE NAME	ACTIVITIES	ACTIVITY WORK HOURS	TOTAL WORK HOURS	PERIOD
Beth	1.1 Gather Data	24	72	1–3
	1.3 Prepare Problem Definition Report	8		55–56
	3.3 Evaluation	16		5
	6.2 System Conversion	16		31–32
	6.3 Prepare Implementation Report	8		59
Jim	1.1 Gather Data	24	192	16
	2.1 Interview Users	40		6–10
	2.4 Prepare Systems Analysis Report	8		16
	3.1.1 Menus	32		17–20
	3.1.2 Data Entry Screens	32		21–24
	3.3 Evaluation	16		31–32
	6.1 Training	32		55–58
	6.3 Prepare Implementation Report	8		59
Jack	1.2 Study Feasibility	32	72	1–4
	3.3 Evaluation	16		31–32
	4.4 Prepare Software Development Report	16		50–51
	6.3 Prepare Implementation Report	8		59
Rose	1.3 Prepare Problem Definition Report	8	56	55–56
	2.1 Interview Users	40		6–10
	5.4 Prepare Testing Report	8		33
Steve	1.2 Study Feasibility	32	208	1–4
	2.2 Study Existing System	64		6–13
	3.1.3 Periodic Reports	32		17–20
	3.1.4 Ad Hoc Queries	32		21–24
	5.1 Software Testing	48		48–53
Jeff	1.2 Study Feasibility	32	184	1–4
	2.3 Define User Requirements	40		11–15
	3.1.3 Periodic Reports	32		17–20
	3.1.4 Ad Hoc Queries	32		21–24
	5.1 Software Testing	48		48–53
Tyler	3.1.1 Menus	32	144	16
	3.1.2 Data Entry Screens	32		21–24
	4.2 Hardware Development	80		31–40
Cathy	1.2 Study Feasibility	32	80	1–4
	3.3 Evaluation	16		31–32
	5.3 Network Testing	32		48–51
Sharon	1.2 Study Feasibility	32	48	1–4
	3.4 Prepare Systems Design Report	16		29–30
Hannah	2.1 Interview Users	40	136	6–10
	3.4 Prepare Systems Design Report	16		29–30
	4.1.1 Packaged Software	16		31–32
	5.3 Network Testing	32		48–51
	6.1 Training	32		55–58

FIGURE 6.14 *(Continued)*

RESOURCE NAME	ACTIVITIES	ACTIVITY WORK HOURS	TOTAL WORK HOURS	PERIOD
Joe	3.2 Processing & Database	80	192	17–26
	4.2 Hardware Development	80		31–40
	5.2 Hardware Testing	32		48–51
Gerri	1.1 Gather Data	24	200	1–3
	3.1.3 Periodic Reports	32		17–20
	3.1.4 Ad Hoc Queries	32		21–24
	4.3 Network Development	48		31–36
	5.2 Hardware Testing	32		48–51
	6.1 Training	32		55–58
Maggie	2.1 Interview Users	40	216	6–10
	4.1.1 Packaged Software	16		31–32
	4.1.2 Customized Software	104		33–45
	5.1 Software Testing	48		48–53
	5.4 Prepare Testing Report	8		54
Gene	3.2 Processing & Database	80	120	17–26
	5.2 Hardware Testing	32		48–51
	5.4 Prepare Testing Report	8		54
Greg	3.2 Processing & Database	80	120	17–26
	5.3 Network Testing	32		48–51
	5.4 Prepare Testing Report	8		54
Training materials	6.1 Training			55–58
Packaged software	4.1.1 Packaged Software			31–32
Travel	2.1 Interview Users			6–10
		2,040	**2,040**	

of units available, standard and overtime rates, and costs. In addition, because the expenses for resources can be accrued at different times throughout a project, most systems allow you to create charges for a resource at the beginning of its use, at fixed intervals, or at the end of the project. Each resource can also be assigned a calendar of its availability over a specified period of time.

The information systems typically inform the user if any resources have time conflicts or if any resources are overallocated within a project or among concurrent projects. Tables and graphs of resource utilization are often available.

To resolve any conflicts or to level, or smooth, the resources, the information systems typically provide two options. The first is to correct the situation manually. With this option, the user modifies the task information and requirements or the resource list, and then determines whether the situation has been resolved. The second option is to allow the information systems to perform this process automatically. If the automatic process is selected, the information systems typically ask the user whether the deadline can be extended if that is the only way to resolve the conflict or smooth the resources.

See Appendix A in the back of the book for a thorough discussion of project management information systems.

CRITICAL SUCCESS FACTORS

- Resources can constrain the project schedule because the quantities of various types of resources available to perform the project activities may be limited.

- It is necessary to estimate the types and quantities of resources required to perform each activity.

- If sufficient resources are not available when required, some activities may have to be delayed until a later time when resources become available to perform the activities.

- Resource leveling, or smoothing, is a method for developing a schedule that attempts to minimize the fluctuations in requirements for resources. It levels the resources so that they are applied as uniformly as possible without extending the project schedule beyond its required completion time.

- Resource-limited scheduling is a method for developing the shortest schedule when the quantity of resources is fixed. It will extend the project completion time, if necessary, to keep within the resource limits.

SUMMARY

The consideration of resources adds another dimension to planning and scheduling. It is necessary to estimate the types and quantities of resources required to perform each activity. Resources can include people, materials, equipment, tools, facilities, and so forth. A resource requirements plan illustrates the expected utilization of resources by time period during the time span of the project.

In many projects, the quantities of the various types of resources available to perform the project activities are limited. Several activities may require the same resources at the same time, and there may not be sufficient resources available to satisfy all the demands. If sufficient resources are not available when required, some activities may have to be delayed until a later time when resources are available. Therefore, resources can constrain the project schedule.

Resource-constrained planning is an approach to creating a network diagram and schedule in which the sequence and dependent relationships of activities are based on resource constraints that take into account the availability of a limited quantity of resources.

Resource leveling, or smoothing, is a method for developing a schedule that attempts to minimize the fluctuations in requirements for resources. Resource leveling attempts to establish a schedule in which resource utilization is made as level as possible without extending the project beyond its required completion time. In resource leveling, the required project completion time is fixed, and the resources are varied in an attempt to eliminate fluctuation.

Resource-limited scheduling is a method for developing the shortest schedule when the quantity of available resources is fixed. This method is appropriate when the resources available for the project are limited and these resource limits cannot be exceeded. This method will extend the project completion time, if necessary, to keep within the resource limits. It is an iterative method in which resources are allocated to activities based on the least slack. The steps are repeated until all resource constraints have been satisfied. In resource-limited scheduling, the resources are fixed, and the project completion time is varied (extended) in order not to exceed the resource limits.

Figure 6.15 shows the differences between resource leveling and resource-limited scheduling.

FIGURE 6.15 Fixed and Variable Elements for Resource Leveling and Resource-limited Scheduling

	Fixed	**Variable**
Resource Leveling	Project Required Completion Time	Resources
Resource-limited Scheduling	Resources	Project Required Completion Time

For a large project that requires many different resources, each of which has a different limit of availability, resource-limited scheduling can get very complicated. Various project management information systems are available that can assist with this process.

QUESTIONS

1. Give at least 10 examples of resources.
2. Think about a project that you are currently working on or have worked on. List all of the resources used in this project.
3. Discuss why resources need to be considered when developing a schedule.
4. Describe how resources can be considered when creating a network diagram.
5. What are technical constraints? Give some examples.
6. What are resource constraints? Give some examples.
7. Describe what is meant by resource leveling or smoothing. Why is it used? When is it used?
8. Does resource leveling keep a project on schedule? If so, how?
9. Describe what is meant by resource-limited scheduling. Why is it used? When is it used?
10. Does resource-limited scheduling keep a project on schedule? If so, how?
11. Using the following figure, perform resource leveling. Assume that each task can be performed independently of the other tasks.

Day	1	2	3	4	5	6	7	8	9	10
Workers	6	6	6	4	2	3	3	4	3	3

12. Using the figure in question 11, perform resource-limited scheduling. Assume that you have only three workers available at any given time. What is the new completion date for the project?

INTERNET EXERCISES

For the website addresses of the organizations mentioned in these exercises, go to "Internet Exercises" at the book's companion website at www.cengagebrain.com. It is suggested that you save this website in your "Favorites" list for easy access in the future.

1. Search the Web for resource leveling or resource-limited scheduling and describe what you find.
2. Find and describe how at least one project management software package handles the resource considerations discussed in this chapter.
3. For exercises 3 through 5, visit the website of the Association for Project Management. Click on the "About Us" link and describe the mission of the organization.
4. Click on the "Resources" link. Explore the resources offered on this website and summarize one that interests you.
5. Explore either the "News" or "Events" link. Describe what you find.

CASE STUDY 1 A Not-for-Profit Medical Research Center

This case study is a continuation of the case study from Chapters 4 and 5.

CASE QUESTION
Using the responsibility assignments you made in Chapter 4 and the baseline schedule you developed in Chapter 5, now develop a resource requirements table (similar to Figure 6.3).

Note: This case study will continue in Chapters 7 and 8, so save the results of your work.

GROUP ACTIVITY
Divide the course participants into the same groups as for the previous chapter's group activity, and answer the question listed above.

CASE STUDY 2 The Wedding

This case study is a continuation of the case study from Chapters 4 and 5.

CASE QUESTION
Using the responsibility assignments you made in Chapter 4 and the baseline schedule you developed in Chapter 5, now develop a resource requirements table (similar to Figure 6.3).

Note: This case study will continue in Chapters 7 and 8, so save the results of your work.

GROUP ACTIVITY

Divide the course participants into the same groups as for the previous chapter's group activity, and answer the question listed above.

REFERENCES

A Guide to the Project Management Body of Knowledge (PMBOK® Guide) Fifth Edition. Newtown Square, PA: Project Management Institute, 2013.

Anonymous (2013). "The New House Call," *PM Network*, 27(3), 13.

Beringer, C., D. Jonas, and A. Kock (2013). "Behavior of Internal Stakeholders in Project Portfolio Management and Its Impact on Success," *International Journal of Project Management*, 31(6), 830.

Bianco, L. and M. Caramia (2013). "A New Formulation for the Project Scheduling Problem under Limited Resources," *Flexible Services and Manufacturing Journal*, 25(1–2), 6–24.

Fretty, P. (2012). "The Rise of VoIP," *PM Network*, 26(3), 66–67.

Gale, S. F. (2013). "Let Us Entertain You," *PM Network*, 27(5), 30–39.

Gamble, B. (2013). "Labor Shortage Hammers U.S. Construction Industry," *PM Network*, 27(4), 4.

Jia, Q. and Y. Seo (2013). "Solving Resource-Constrained Project Scheduling Problems: Conceptual Validation of FLP Formulation and Efficient Permutation-Based ABC Computation," *Computers & Operations Research*, 40(8), 2037.

Killen, C. P. (2012). "Evaluation of Project Interdependency Visualizations through Decision Scenario Experimentation," *International Journal of Project Management,* http://dx.doi.org.ezaccess.libraries.psu.edu/10.1016/j.ijproman.2012.09.005.

Koné, O., C. Artigues, P. Lopez, and M. Mongeau (2013). "Comparison of Mixed Integer Linear Programming Models for the Resource-Constrained Project Scheduling Problem with Consumption and Production of Resources," *Flexible Services and Manufacturing Journal*, 25(1–2), 25–47.

La Plante, L. (2012). "Industrial Sites Get a New Look," *PM Network*, 26(7), 12–13.

Moore, J. (2013). "Enterprise Software Gets a Consumer Makeover: When It Comes to Developing Enterprise Applications, Organizations Are Increasingly Realizing that User Experience Is As Important As Functionality. In Response, Vendors Are Taking a More Agile Approach to Building Those Apps in order to Better Meet Users' Need," *CIO*, 26, 16.

Ranjbar, M. (2013). "A Path-relinking Metaheuristic for the Resource Levelling Problem," *The Journal of the Operational Research Society*, 64(7), 1071–1078.

Voss, M. (2012). "Impact of Customer Integration on Project Portfolio Management and Its Success—Developing a Conceptual Framework," *International Journal of Project Management*, 30, 567–581.

Voss, M. and A. Kock (2013). "Impact of Relationship Value on Project Portfolio Success—Investigating the Moderating Effects of Portfolio Characteristics and External Turbulence," *International Journal of Project Management*, 31(6), 847.

Zamani, R. (2013). "A Competitive Magnet-based Genetic Algorithm for Solving the Resource-Constrained Project Scheduling Problem," *European Journal of Operational Research*, 229(2), 552.

APPENDIX

Microsoft Project

In this appendix, we will discuss how Microsoft Project can be used to support the techniques discussed in this chapter based on the Consumer Market Study example. To retrieve your project information, on the File menu, click Open and locate the consumer market study file you saved in Chapter 5 when you set the baseline before adding the actual finish dates and the new task. We are now ready to add additional resources, manage the time assignment on a task for a resource, evaluate task usage, level resources that are overallocated, and create resource reports.

Figure 6A.1 shows a resource sheet for the consumer market study. To obtain the resource sheet, on the View ribbon, click on Resource Sheet in the Resource Views group. The Resource Sheet allows you to enter information about your resources, including specific work calendars for each of your resources. Resources other than human resources can also be entered into this table. Human resources are entered as Work resources. Other types of resources are entered as Material or Cost resources. The Type column of the Resource Sheet shows the type of resource as Work, Material, or Cost.

Material and cost resources are added by entering the name in the Resource Name column and selecting the type as material or cost in the Type column by clicking on the down arrow in the Type column for the entry. The Consumer Market Study requires two material resources and one cost resource, in addition to the four work resources.

Additional information can be entered about each resource by double-clicking on a resource name in the Resource Name column. You will see the Resource Information window with four tabs: General, Costs, Notes, and Custom Fields, as shown in Figure 6A.2, where a note has been added to provide additional information about the cost resource.

Assign the new material and cost resources to tasks in the Consumer Market Study by viewing the task list in the Gantt Chart Entry Table view. Recall the Gantt Chart Entry Table can be viewed by clicking on Gantt Chart on the View ribbon in the Task Views group, then clicking on Tables in the Data group and selecting Entry in the menu. To add a material or cost resource to a task, double-click the task name to open the Task Information window. On the Resources tab, enter the resource name or select from the resource list by clicking on the down arrow in the cell. Note in Figure 6A.3 that the duration for the

FIGURE 6A.1 **Resource Sheet**

FIGURE 6A.2　Resource Notes

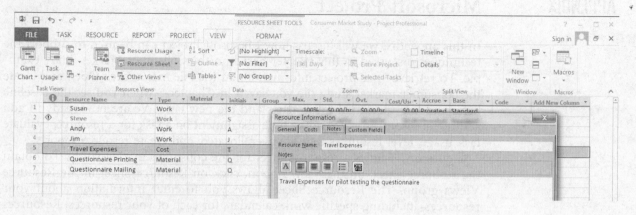

FIGURE 6A.3　Adding a Resource to a Task

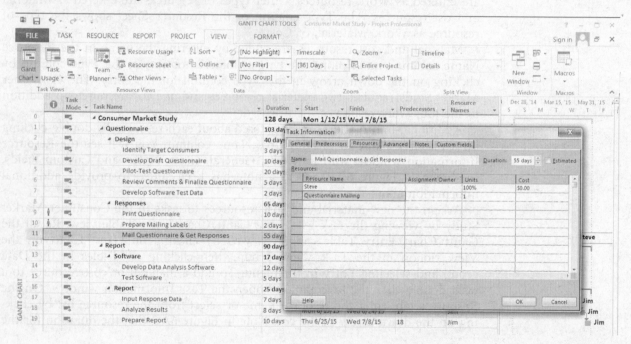

Mail Questionnaire & Get Responses activity had been reduced to 55 days in Chapter 5, and Questionnaire mailing has been added as a material resource to the project. Add the cost resource, Travel Expenses, to the Pilot-Test Questionnaire activity. Add the material resource, Questionnaire printing, to the Print Questionnaire activity. Add the material resource, Questionnaire mailing, to the Mail Questionnaire & Get Responses activity.

For the Consumer Market Study, not all of the work resources will work the entire duration of a task. For the activities Print Questionnaire and Mail Questionnaire & Get Responses, Steve will not work the entire duration of the tasks. For the Print Questionnaire activity, he will work one day, and for the Mail Questionnaire & Get Responses activity, he will work five days. Microsoft Project has the option to make the duration of a task dependent on the effort necessary to complete the task

and to set the type of task as Fixed Units, Fixed Work, or Fixed Duration. Setting a task's Effort Driven category to No and its Type to Fixed Duration, the number of hours of actual work on a task can be set without affecting the duration of a task.

In the Gantt Chart Table Entry View, enter three new columns. Click on the Add New Column and select Effort Driven from the menu for the first column. Click on Add New Column and select Type for the second column. Click on Add New Column and select Work for the third column. Change the Type column for the tasks Print Questionnaire and Mail Questionnaire & Get Responses to Fixed Duration by clicking on the down arrow in the cell. Edit the time in the Work column for Steve to work on the Print Questionnaire activity to 8 hours and on the Mail Questionnaire & Get Responses activity to 40 hours, as shown in Figure 6A.4.

Microsoft Project will enter in the time for each of these times to be a percentage of time. Both of these tasks need to be completed As-Soon-As-Possible. Open the Task Usage sheet by clicking on Task Usage on the View ribbon in the Task Views group. Check that the activities Print Questionnaire and Mail Questionnaire & Get Responses are not effort driven, have fixed duration, and have the correct amount of work assigned by adding the columns Effort Driven, Type, and Work to the Task Usage screen. Scroll across to March 5 in the schedule details, enter 8h for the work to be completed by Steve for the Print Questionnaire activity, and delete other times entered across the duration of the activity. Check that the time for Questionnaire printing remains at 1 unit. For the Mail Questionnaire & Get Responses activity, scroll across to the activity start date, March 19, enter 8h in each cell for March 19 to March 25 for Steve, and delete the remaining times for the task. Check that Questionnaire mailing remains at 1 unit. Figure 6A.5 displays the changes in work times for Steve, the number of units for the material resources, and the number of hours for work on the schedule details.

Resource Overview and Overallocated Resources reports are available in the Resources link on the Report ribbon in the View Reports group. The indicator

FIGURE 6A.4 **Assignment of Work Time to Fixed Duration Tasks**

FIGURE 6A.5 **Task Usage**

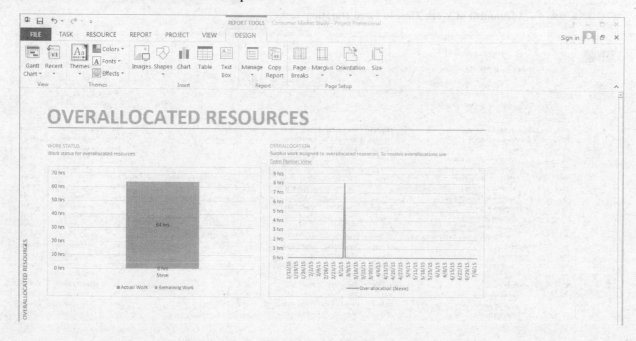

column on the Gantt Chart View includes two red figures for tasks 9 and 10 alerting you that the resources for these tasks are overallocated. To view the Overallocated Resources report, on the Report ribbon, click on Resources in the View Reports group, then choose Overallocated Resources in the drop-down menu. This report (Figure 6A.6) provides information about any resources that are overallocated.

To view details of the overallocation, click on the link in the Overallocated Resources report for the Team Planner view. Scroll to the dates indicated for the overallocation, the week beginning March 2, 2015 (Figure 6A.7). In this

FIGURE 6A.6 **Overallocated Resources Report**

FIGURE 6A.7 **Team Planner View of Overallocated Resources**

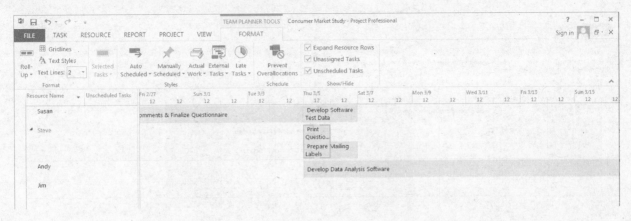

example, note that Steve is assigned to Prepare Mailing Labels on Thursday 3/5/15 for 8 hours each day. He is also assigned to Print Questionnaire on the same day. In other words, this report indicates that Steve is assigned to work 8 hours per day on Thursday (March 5) on two different tasks. The overallocated resource needs to be leveled.

To perform Microsoft's version of resource leveling, on the Resource ribbon, click on Level Resource to open the Level Resource window (Figure 6A.8). In Microsoft Project, the resource-leveling tool basically just looks at overallocated resources and typically resolves those overallocations by extending the project deadline. When this leveling is done, Microsoft Project does not change resource assignments, and it does not change task information; it only delays tasks that have resources that are overallocated. The leveling can be performed by selecting the name of the resource to be leveled and clicking on the Level Now button. Leveling can be removed by clicking on the Clear Leveling button in the Level group on the Resource ribbon. Another technique in Microsoft Project 2013 is to click on Level All in the Level group on the Resource ribbon. Options for how Microsoft Project levels the resources can be selected by clicking on Leveling Options in the Level group on the Resource ribbon.

FIGURE 6A.8 **Resource Leveling**

FIGURE 6A.9 Resources Leveled

Note on the Team Planner view, as shown in Figure 6A.9, that the time for Steve to work on Prepare Mailing Labels has shifted to start on Friday, March 6.

The Resource Overview report displays an overview of all Work resources on your project along with the number of hours of work assigned, percent of work completed, and the number of hours of remaining work. To display the overview of your work resources, first click on Resources in the View Reports group on the Report ribbon, then choose Resource Overview from the drop down menu. The Resource Overview report is displayed in Figure 6A.10.

The Resource Usage sheet displays an overview per day of the total amount of work assigned to a work resource and the number of units assigned to a material resource. To display the Resource usage sheet as shown in Figure 6A.11, first click on View to navigate to the View ribbon, then click on Resource Usage in Resource Views group. Compare the Resource Usage sheet to the Task Usage sheet in Figure 6A.5. Note that Steve is now assigned 8 hours each day.

It is important to periodically save the baseline of your project to monitor changes. To save baseline project data, on the Project ribbon, click on Set Baseline in the Schedule group, and click on Set Baseline. *Save your file at this point to continue the planning presented in* Chapter 7.

FIGURE 6A.10 Resource Overview Report

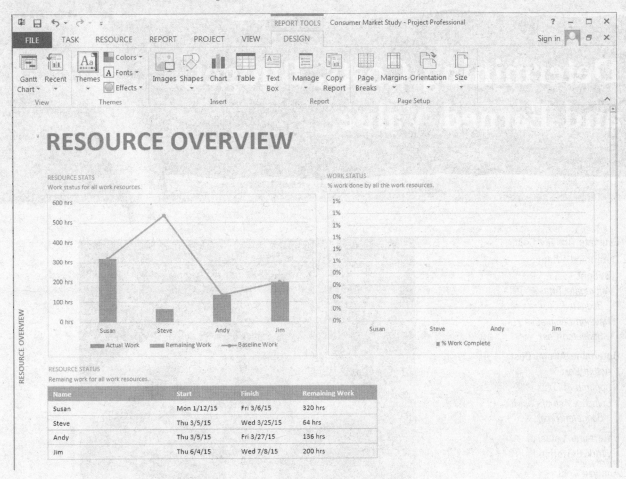

FIGURE 6A.11 Resource Usage Sheet

Determining Costs, Budget, and Earned Value

Jon Brenneis/Time Life Pictures/Getty Images

Concepts in this chapter support the following Project Management Knowledge Areas of *A Guide to the Project Management Body of Knowledge (PMBOK® Guide)*:

<p style="text-align:center">**Project Integration Management**
Project Cost Management</p>

REAL WORLD PROJECT MANAGEMENT

Dynamic Consequences of Cost, Schedule, and Performance

Department of Defense (DoD) projects have used project management techniques formally beginning in the 1950s within the U.S. Polaris missile development project.

Critical paths were examined and managed. Although there are core practices to project management and earned value calculations, it seems that managing DoD projects requires additional factors to be considered, quite possibly because of the long time span from conception to production.

The U.S. Government Accountability Office (GAO) has reported that half of major defense programs are not meeting costs goals and 98 projects between 2008 and 2010 experienced a growth in budget by 9 percent. The most common reasons for failure to stay on time and within budget include budget pressure, schedule pressure, and changing user requirements. These are quite familiar challenges to all project managers regardless if the project is a large DoD project or a commercial project or completing a small backyard project.

In an effort to avoid the age-old problem of DoD project managers underestimating their costs and schedules because of misunderstandings of the complexity required to design and develop the product, researchers have examined hundreds of projects and developed a work flow process to help forecast the earned value and future costs of DoD projects more accurately. To determine if the project should continue, the planned schedule and budget is compared to the actual performance and a number of ratios are calculated. Depending upon positive or negative magnitude of the ratios, a change in schedule or budget is implemented.

In 1999, a Future Combat System was designed by the U.S. Army. An expectation was for the first unit to be equipped by 2011 and the entire army by 2032. Key to the project was multiple networked and interoperable ground and air systems. Smaller in mass to facilitate logistics and rapid deployment, the highly technical and revolutionary system-of-systems was assessed using the work flow model developed for defense projects. Cost estimates using the baseline in 2005 for 2025 were $161 billion. The initial project budget was $130 billion.

Total costs, delivered performance percentages, the amount of work expected to be completed by 2025, and an estimate of the time scale for the project to actually be completed were assessed. After analysis that resulted in an estimate of $210 billion with only 86 percent of the performance delivered and a potential completion date of 2022, the U.S. Army decided that the initial project for developing a Future Combat System for the entire army was not a feasible project. A change in project scope was implemented after termination in 2009 to complete the development of 14 units by 2021.

Earned value methods are a valuable asset in the tool set of a project manager. Using the cost estimates at completion in comparison to schedule, costs, and performance are good strategies to determine if a project should continue or be terminated. One of the most difficult decisions by a project manager is to terminate a project or limit its scope. The U.S. Army project managers made this difficult decision based on analysis of the costs, schedule, performance, and earned value.

Based on information from Cantwell, P. R., S. Sarkani, and T. A. Mazzuchi (2013). "Dynamic Consequences of Cost, Schedule, and Performance Within DoD Project Management," *Defense Acquisition Research Journal: A Publication of the Defense Acquisition University*, 20(1), 89–106.

In addition to establishing a baseline schedule for a project, it is also necessary to develop a baseline budget. Estimates must be made of the costs for each specific activity. The project budget is determined by aggregating the estimated costs for all the activities. The budget must then be spread over the expected time span of the project to create a time-phased baseline budget that is used to analyze cost performance of the project. Once the project starts, it is important to monitor actual costs and earned value of the work performed. At regular intervals during the project, the following cost-related parameters should be monitored:

- Cumulative actual amount spent since the start of the project
- Cumulative earned value of the work performed since the start of the project
- Cumulative budgeted amount planned to be spent, based on the project schedule, from the start of the project

Comparisons must be made among these three parameters to evaluate whether the project is being accomplished within budget and whether the earned value of the work performed is in line with the actual cost expended.

If at any time during the project it is determined that the project is overrunning the budget or the value of the work performed is not keeping up with the actual cost expended, corrective action must be taken immediately. Once project costs get out of control, it will be very difficult to complete the project within budget. As you will see in this chapter, the key to effective cost control is to analyze cost performance on a timely and regular basis. Early identification of cost variances allows corrective action to be taken before the situation gets worse. Based on the actual cost expended and the earned value of the work performed, you will learn how to regularly forecast whether the entire project will be completed within budget. You will become familiar with

- Estimating the costs of activities
- Determining a time-phased baseline budget
- Determining the earned value of the work performed
- Analyzing cost performance
- Forecasting project cost at completion
- Controlling project costs
- Managing cash flow

Estimate Activity Costs

The total project cost is often estimated during the initiating phase of the project or when the project charter or a proposal is prepared, but detailed plans are not usually prepared at that time. However, during the planning phase of the project, specific activities are defined and a network plan is created. Once specific activities are defined, then estimates can be made of resources, durations, and costs for each specific activity. Resources include people, materials, equipment, facilities, and so forth. The estimated activity resources are used for estimating activity costs. *The **estimated cost** of an activity is based on an estimate of the types and quantities of resources required to perform the activity*, as mentioned in the section on estimating activity resources in Chapter 5. The estimated cost for each specific activity can include the following elements:

1. *Labor costs.* These are the estimated costs for the various types or classifications of people who are expected to work on the project, such as painters, designers, and computer programmers. The labor costs are based on the estimated *work time* (not necessarily the same as the activity estimated duration) and the dollar labor rate for each person or classification.
2. *Materials costs.* These are the estimated costs of materials that the project team or contractor needs to purchase for the project, such as paint, lumber, piping, shrubbery, carpeting, electrical cable, paper, art supplies, food, computers, and application software.
3. *Equipment costs.* Some projects require equipment that must be purchased as part of the project. Equipment can include items such as computers and machinery. For example, a project to construct a clinic would include the purchase of various types of medical equipment. Or a project to upgrade a manufacturing facility may include the purchase of new production machinery. Or a new office might include the purchase of new computer systems.
4. *Facilities costs.* Some projects may require special facilities or additional space for the project team, for security reasons, to store materials, or to build, assemble, and test the project end item (deliverable). If such facilities are required, the estimated costs for renting the space need to be included.
5. *Subcontractors and consultants costs.* When project teams or contractors do not have the expertise or resources to do certain project tasks, they may outsource some of the work to subcontractors or consultants to perform those activities. Examples of such tasks include designing a brochure, developing a training manual, developing software, and catering a reception.
6. *Travel costs.* If travel (other than local travel) is required during the project, the costs for travel, such as airfare, lodging, and meals, need to be included.
7. *Reserve.* In addition to the above items, the project team or contractor may include an estimated amount for contingencies to cover unexpected situations that may come up during the project, such as items that may have been overlooked when the initial project scope was defined, activities that may have to be redone because they may not work the first time (redesigns), or a high probability or high impact risk that may occur. Often there is a separate budget (*management reserve*) set aside for contingencies at the project level rather than for specific activities.

Figure 7.1 shows the estimated costs for each activity in the consumer market study project. The labor costs in the example are based on the estimated work

FIGURE 7.1 Estimated Activity Costs for Consumer Market Study Project

ACTIVITY	NAME	WORK DAYS	LABOR $ RATE	LABOR COSTS	MATERIALS COSTS	TRAVEL COSTS	TOTAL COSTS
1. Identify Target Consumers	Susan	3	$260	$780			$780
2. Develop Draft Questionnaire	Susan	10	260	2,600			2,600
3. Pilot-Test Questionnaire	Susan	20	260	5,200		$3,000	8,200
4. Review Comments & Finalize Questionnaire	Susan	5	260	1,300			1,300
5. Prepare Mailing Labels	Steve	2	200	400			400
6. Print Questionnaire	Steve	1	200	200	$1,700		1,900
7. Develop Data Analysis Software	Andy	12	300	3,600			3,600
8. Develop Software Test Data	Susan	2	260	520			520
9. Mail Questionnaire & Get Responses	Steve	5	200	1,000	7,800		8,800
10. Test Software	Andy	5	300	1,500			1,500
11. Input Response Data	Jim	7	400	2,800			2,800
12. Analyze Results	Jim	8	400	3,200			3,200
13. Prepare Report	Jim	10	400	4,000			4,000
		90		**$27,100**	**$9,500**	**$3,000**	**$39,600**

days discussed in the section on resource requirements plan in Chapter 6. Several additional assumptions need to be mentioned:

- Activity 3, "Pilot-Test Questionnaire," requires some travel to conduct focus groups to obtain feedback and comments about the draft questionnaire, and therefore the estimated costs for travel are included
- Activity 6, "Print Questionnaire," will be subcontracted to a vendor so an estimated cost for the vendor is included
- Activity 9, "Mail Questionnaire & Get Responses," includes an estimated cost for postage
- The sponsor has approved a budget of $40,000 for the project

It is good practice to have the person who will be responsible for performing a specific activity estimate the costs associated with the activity. This generates a commitment from that person and avoids any bias that may be introduced by having one person estimate all the costs for all the activities. In some cases, though, such as for large projects involving several hundred people performing various activities over several years, it may not be practical to have each person estimate activity costs. Rather, each organization or subcontractor responsible for a group or type of activities may designate an experienced individual to estimate the costs for all the activities for which that organization or subcontractor is responsible. If an organization or contractor has performed similar projects in the past and has kept records of the actual costs for various items, these historical data can be used as a guide in estimating the costs of similar items for future projects.

The estimated costs for an activity should be reasonable and realistic. They should not be so heavily "padded" that they include reserve funds for every conceivable thing that might come up or go wrong. If cost estimates are overly conservative, the total estimated cost for the project is likely to be more than

Reinforce Your Learning

3. The estimated cost for an activity should be

and

_____ .

the sponsor or customer has budgeted for the project. On the other hand, if estimated costs are overly optimistic and some unexpected expenditures arise, the project team or contractor may have to suffer the embarrassment of going back to the sponsor or customer to request additional funds.

It should be noted that at the beginning of the project, it may not be possible to estimate the costs for all activities with a level of confidence regarding their accuracy. This is especially true for longer-term projects. It may be easier to estimate the costs for near-term activities, but as the project progresses, the project team can *progressively elaborate* the estimated costs as more information is known or becomes clear to allow for more accurate estimated costs.

Determine Project Budget

The project budgeting process involves two steps. The first step is to determine the **total budgeted cost (TBC)**, which is the aggregate amount of the estimated costs of all the specific activities to perform and complete a work package or the project. The second step is to develop a **time-phased budget,** which is the distribution by time period of the total budgeted cost for a work package or project over its expected time span based on when specific activities are scheduled to be performed.

AGGREGATE TOTAL BUDGETED COST

Reinforce Your Learning

4. The first step in the project budgeting process is to

the

costs for each

in the work breakdown structure and establish a

for each work package.

Aggregating the estimated costs of all the specific activities to perform and complete each work package in the work breakdown structure will establish a total budgeted cost (TBC), also referred to as *budget at completion (BAC)* for each work package. The TBC for each work package is the sum of the estimated costs of all the specific activities that make up that work package. *When the budgets for all the work packages are aggregated, they cannot exceed the total amount of funds the sponsor or customer budgeted for the project.*

*It is not unusual for the initial sum of the estimated costs of all the work packages or activities to be greater than the amount of funds the sponsor or customer has budgeted for the project, and it may then take several **iterations** of revising the estimated costs of specific activities to arrive at an acceptable baseline budget.*

Sometimes the project team or contractor reacts to the customer's budget amount by force-fitting the activity cost estimates to meet the customer's total budget amount by just arbitrarily reducing the estimated costs of specific activities and convincing themselves that somehow (by luck) the activities will get accomplished with the reduced amount of costs. Then when the project does not get completed within budget, they seem astonished! Instead, they should develop realistic estimated activity costs, and then determine how much the aggregate of the estimated costs is over the amount of funds the customer budgeted for the project. At that point, they can *rationally* determine how to reduce the costs to come up with a TBC that is within the customer's budget amount. This is done by making decisions about *how* to reduce the estimated costs of specific activities. This may mean making trade-off decisions to replace some resources with lower-cost or more efficient resources; subcontracting certain tasks; reducing scope/specifications; and so forth. As a last resort, it may mean going back to the sponsor or customer and asking for additional funds or approval to reduce scope. It is better to inform the customer early in the project rather than surprising him or her later. It is important to manage the customer's expectations.

Reinforce Your Learning

5. Referring to Figures 7.1 and 4.5, what is the total budgeted cost for each work package?

Figure 7.2 shows the TBCs of individual work packages in the work breakdown structure for a $600,000 project. The amount for each work package represents the TBC for performing and completing all the specific activities associated with the work package.

FIGURE 7.2 **Work Breakdown Structure with Work Package Budgets**

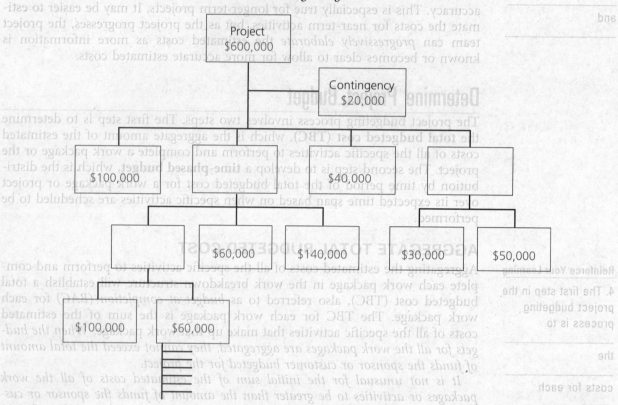

Figure 7.3 is a network diagram for a project to design and build a specialized automated packaging machine and install it at the customer's factory. The machine will insert the customer's product into boxes rolling by at high speed on a conveyor. This project will be used as an example throughout the remainder of this chapter, so it has been kept simple. The project consists of three activities, and the network diagram shows the duration (in weeks) for each activity. Figure 7.4 shows the work breakdown structure with the TBC for each work package.

DEVELOP CUMULATIVE BUDGETED COST

Once a TBC has been established for each work package, the second step in the project budgeting process is to distribute or spread each TBC over the expected time span of its work package. A cost is determined for each period within the time span, based on when the specific activities that make up the work package are scheduled to be performed. When the TBC for each work package is spread out by time period, a *time-phased budget* is created so that it can be determined how much of the budget should have been spent at any point in time. This amount is calculated by adding up the budgeted costs for each time period up to that point in time. This amount, known as the **cumulative budgeted cost (CBC)**, also referred to as the

FIGURE 7.3 Network Diagram for the Packaging Machine Project

FIGURE 7.4 Work Breakdown Structure for the Packaging Machine Project

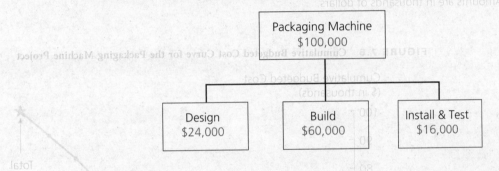

planned value (PV) or *budgeted cost of work scheduled (BCWS)*, is the amount that is budgeted to accomplish all the work that is scheduled to be performed up to a specific point in time. The CBC is the *time-phased baseline budget* that will be used to analyze the cost performance of the project.

For the packaging machine project, Figure 7.5 shows how the TBC for each work package is spread over the time periods, based on the estimated durations shown in Figure 7.3. Also shown is the period-by-period budgeted cost for the entire project, as well as its CBC. Figure 7.5 indicates that $32,000 is budgeted to accomplish the work that is scheduled to be performed through week 5. The periods over which budgeted costs are spread usually are determined by the earliest start and finish times for the activities in the baseline project schedule (adjusted to take into account resource leveling or resource-limited scheduling).

With the CBC values, it is possible to draw a CBC curve to illustrate budgeted expenditures over the duration of the project. Figure 7.6 shows the CBC curve for the packaging machine project. Although the table in Figure 7.5 and the cost curve in Figure 7.6 display CBC for the total project, a similar cumulative table and curve can be made for each work package, if desired.

The CBC for the entire project or each work package provides a baseline against which actual cost and work performance can be compared at any time during the project. It would be misleading to merely compare actual amounts expended to the TBC for the project or work package, as cost performance will always look good as long as actual costs are below the TBC. In the packaging machine example, we would think that the project cost was under control as long as the total actual cost was below $100,000. But what happens when one

FIGURE 7.5 Budgeted Cost by Period for the Packaging Machine Project

	TBC	Week											
		1	2	3	4	5	6	7	8	9	10	11	12
Design	24	4	4	8	8								
Build	60					8	8	12	12	10	10		
Install & Test	16											8	8
Total	100	4	4	8	8	8	8	12	12	10	10	8	8
Cumulative		**4**	**8**	**16**	**24**	**32**	**40**	**52**	**64**	**74**	**84**	**92**	**100**

Amounts are in thousands of dollars.

FIGURE 7.6 Cumulative Budgeted Cost Curve for the Packaging Machine Project

day the total actual cost exceeds the $100,000 TBC, and the project is not finished? By that time, it is too late to control the project to complete it within budget—the project budget has been exceeded and work remains to be done, so more costs will yet have to be incurred to complete the project!

To avoid such nightmares, it is important to use the CBC, rather than the TBC, as the baseline against which actual cost is compared. This way, if at any

time actual cost begins to exceed the CBC, corrective action can be taken immediately, before it is too late.

For large projects involving many work packages or activities, project management software is available that can assist with project budgeting.

Determine Actual Cost

Once the project starts, it is necessary to keep track of the amount of actual cost expended and committed costs so that they can be compared to the CBC.

ACTUAL COST

To keep track of **actual cost** on a project, it is necessary to establish a system to collect, on a regular and timely basis, data on costs actually expended. Such a system might include processes, procedures, and forms for gathering data. An accounting structure should be established based on the work breakdown structure numbering system so that each item of actual cost can be charged to the appropriate work package. Each work package's actual cost can then be summed and compared to its CBC.

Weekly timesheets are often used to collect actual labor hours. Individuals working on the project indicate the numbers of the work packages on which they worked and the amount of hours they spent on each work package. These hours are then multiplied by the hourly cost rate for each individual to determine the actual dollar cost. In cases where individuals may be assigned to several projects concurrently, the person would indicate the proper project number as well as the work package number on the timesheet to ensure that the actual labor costs are charged to the appropriate project. When invoices are received for materials, equipment, or services that were purchased for use on the project, they, too, have to be charged to the proper work package number.

COMMITTED COSTS

Committed costs are funds that have been obligated for an item that has been ordered or purchased but not yet paid for, and therefore are not available to be spent elsewhere on the project because they will be needed some time later to pay for the item. Committed costs are *also referred to as commitments, obligated costs,* or *encumbered costs.*

Costs are committed when an item (material, subcontractor) is ordered, usually by means of a purchase order, even though actual payment may take place at some later time—when the material or equipment has been delivered or the service has been completed, and it has been invoiced. When a purchase order is issued to a supplier or subcontractor for an item, the funds for that purchase order are "committed" and are no longer available to be spent on other project activities. The committed amount must be considered as encumbered, or set aside, because funds will be needed to pay the supplier or subcontractor at some time in the future, when an invoice is received. For example, if you hire a contractor to paint your home for $5,000, you have committed $5,000, even though you may not actually pay the contractor until the work is finished.

These committed costs need to be treated in a special way so that the accounting system periodically assigns a portion of their total cost to actual cost, rather than waiting until all the materials are delivered or services are totally completed to charge their total actual costs. To permit a realistic comparison of actual cost to

CBC, *portions of the committed amount should be assigned to actual cost while the work is being performed.* In some cases, the supplier or subcontractor may require progress payments, rather than waiting until all the work is finished before being paid. In such situations, when an invoice is received from the supplier or subcontractor for a partial or progress payment, the amount of that invoice should be charged to the actual cost for the proper work package. Suppose a project to develop an inventory control system includes a subcontract with a consultant to develop six different software modules for $120,000. As each module is completed and delivered, the consultant submits an invoice for $20,000. When the invoice is received, the $20,000 should be considered an actual cost.

Now let us consider a different scenario in which the subcontractor or supplier does not issue invoices for partial or progress payments, but rather waits until all the work is finished and/or delivered and then submits one invoice for the total amount. Even in such a case, a portion of the total committed amount should be periodically assigned as an actual cost, because work is actually being performed. For example, suppose a project to remodel an office building includes a subcontract with a heating contractor to install new heating units in each office throughout the building over four months for $80,000. Even though the subcontractor will submit only one invoice for $80,000 when all the work has been completed, $20,000 should be assigned to actual cost each month, because work is actually being performed.

COMPARE ACTUAL COST TO BUDGETED COST

Reinforce Your Learning

8. Look at Figures 7.5 and 7.7. How much did the "Design" work package and the "Build" work package each contribute to the $4,000 cost overrun at the end of week 8?

As data are collected on *actual cost, including portions of any committed costs,* they need to be summed by work packages so that they can be compared to the CBC for the work package. The **cumulative actual cost (CAC)**, also referred to as the *actual cost of work performed (ACWP),* is the amount of costs actually expended and committed to accomplish all the work performed up to a specific point in time. For the packaging machine project, Figure 7.7 shows actual cost by time period for each work package through week 8. Also shown is the total period-by-period actual cost, as well as the CAC for the project through week 8.

Figure 7.7 indicates that, at the end of week 8, $68,000 has actually been expended on this project. The CBC in Figure 7.5 reveals that only $64,000 was

FIGURE 7.7 Actual Cost by Period for the Packaging Machine Project

	Week								Total Expended
	1	2	3	4	5	6	7	8	
Design	2	5	9	5	1				22
Build				2	8	10	14	12	46
Install & Test									0
Total	2	5	9	7	9	10	14	12	**68**
Cumulative	**2**	**7**	**16**	**23**	**32**	**42**	**56**	**68**	**68**

Amounts are in thousands of dollars.

FIGURE 7.8 Cumulative Budgeted and Actual Costs for the Packaging Machine Project

budgeted to have been spent by the end of week 8. There is a variance of $4,000—the project is overrunning its budget.

With the CAC values, it is possible to draw a CAC curve. Drawing this curve on the same graph as the CBC curve, as shown in Figure 7.8, provides a good visual comparison.

Although the table in Figure 7.7 and the cost curves in Figure 7.8 display data for the total project, similar cumulative tables and curves can be made for each work package, if desired. Generating individual curves will help pinpoint the particular work packages that are contributing to the overrun.

Determine Value of Work Performed

Consider a project that involves painting 10 similar rooms over 10 days (one room per day) for a TBC of $2,000. The budget is $200 per room. At the end of day 5, you determine that $1,000 has actually been spent. When you compare the actual expenditures to the CBC of $1,000 for five days, it looks as if actual costs are tracking the budget. But that is only part of the story. What if, at the end of day 5, only 3 rooms have been painted? That would not be very good, because half of the budget has been spent on only 3 of the 10 rooms that need to be painted. On the other hand, what if, at the end of day 5, 6 rooms have been painted? That would be excellent, because only half of the budget has been spent and 6 of the 10 rooms have been painted. This example introduces the concept of *earned value* of the work performed. The fact that half the budget was actually expended does not necessarily mean that half the work was

performed. If the work performed is not keeping up with the actual cost, there is trouble, even if the actual cost is in line with the CBC.

Earned value (EV), also referred to as the *budgeted cost of work performed (BCWP)*, is the value of the work actually performed; it is a key parameter that must be determined throughout the project. Comparing the CAC to the CBC tells only part of the story and can lead to wrong conclusions about the status of the project.

Just as it is important to track actual cost for a project, it is also necessary to set up a companion system to collect, on a regular and timely basis, data regarding the EV of the work performed on each work package. *Determining the earned value involves collecting data on the **percent complete*** for each work package and then converting this percentage to a dollar amount by multiplying the TBC of the work package by the percent complete.

The percent complete data usually are obtained each period from the individual responsible for the work package. In many cases, the estimate is subjective. It is extremely important that the person who comes up with the percent complete estimate makes an honest assessment of the work performed relative to the entire work scope for the work package. There often seems to be an inclination to be overly optimistic and make a high percent complete estimate too early. For example, suppose the team leader of a work package with a 20-week duration reports at the end of week 10 that the work is 90 percent complete. If this report is unrealistic, it will create a false sense of confidence that work performance is outpacing actual cost. An unrealistic report will lead the project manager to conclude that project performance is better than it actually is and keep her or him from taking any corrective action. As the percent complete begins to stretch out while the actual cost continues to accumulate, it will appear that project performance is deteriorating over the final weeks. By week 20, the percent complete may be only 96 percent, and the CAC may have exceeded the CBC. If corrective action had been taken earlier, problems could have been prevented. One way to prevent premature inflated percent complete estimates is to keep the work packages or activities small in terms of scope and estimated duration. Activities should not be longer in estimated duration than the time intervals at which actual project performance will be reviewed and compared to planned progress. It is important that the person estimating the percent complete not only assess how much work has been performed but also consider what work remains to be done.

Reinforce Your Learning

9. Cumulative earned value is calculated by first determining the

for each work package and then multiplying it by the

for the work package.

Once the percent complete data have been collected, the earned value must be determined. The **cumulative earned value (CEV)**, which is the *value* of the work actually performed up to a specific point in time, is calculated by multiplying the TBC by the percentage of the work estimated to be complete. For example, in the project involving painting 10 rooms for $2,000, if 3 rooms were completed, it is safe to say that 30 percent of the work has been performed. The CEV is

$$0.30 \times \$2,000 = \$600$$

Let us now return to the example of the packaging machine project. At the end of week 8, the "Build" work package is the only one in progress, and it is estimated to be 50 percent complete. The "Design" work package had previously been finished, so it is 100 percent complete; and the "Install & Test" work package has not yet started, so it is 0 percent complete. Figure 7.9 shows the cumulative percent complete estimates reported during each of the first eight weeks for

FIGURE 7.9 Cumulative Percent Complete by Period for the Packaging Machine Project

	Week							
	1	2	3	4	5	6	7	8
Design	10	25	80	90	100	100	100	100
Build	0	0	0	5	15	25	40	50
Install & Test	0	0	0	0	0	0	0	0

Amounts are cumulative percent complete.

FIGURE 7.10 Cumulative Earned Value by Period for the Packaging Machine Project

	TBC	Week							
		1	2	3	4	5	6	7	8
Design	24	2.4	6	19.2	21.6	24	24	24	24
Build	60				3	9	15	24	30
Install & Test	16								
Cumulative	100	**2.4**	**6**	**19.2**	**24.6**	**33**	**39**	**48**	**54**

Amounts are in thousands of dollars.

each work package. Figure 7.10 shows the associated CEV for each work package, calculated by multiplying each percent complete by the TBC for that work package. Figure 7.10 indicates that, at the end of week 8, the CEV of the work performed on this project is $54,000.

With the CEV values, it is possible to draw a CEV curve. Drawing this curve on the same graph as the CBC and CAC curves, as shown in Figure 7.11, provides an excellent visual comparison. Although the cost curves in Figure 7.11 illustrate the CBC, CAC, and CEV for the entire project, similar curves can be made for each work package, if desired. Generating individual curves will help identify how much each work package is affecting project cost performance.

Analyze Cost Performance

The following four cost-related measures are used to analyze project cost performance:

- TBC: Total Budgeted Cost
- CBC: Cumulative Budgeted Cost
- CAC: Cumulative Actual Cost
- CEV: Cumulative Earned Value

They are used to determine whether the project is being performed within budget and whether the value of the work performed is in line with the actual cost.

FIGURE 7.11 **Cumulative Budgeted and Cumulative Actual Costs and Cumulative Earned Value for the Packaging Machine Project**

In analyzing Figures 7.5, 7.7, and 7.10 for the packaging machine project at the end of week 8, we see that

- $64,000 was *budgeted* through the end of week 8 to perform all the work scheduled to be performed during the first eight weeks
- $68,000 was *actually expended* by the end of week 8
- $54,000 was the *earned value of work actually performed* by the end of week 8

A quick analysis indicates that the actual cost is exceeding the budgeted cost. Aggravating the situation further is the fact that the value of the work performed is not keeping up with the actual cost.

It is a good idea to plot CBC, CAC, and CEV curves on the same graph, as shown in Figure 7.11, at the end of each report period. This will reveal any trends toward improving or deteriorating cost performance.

Another way to approach the situation is to analyze progress in terms of percentages of the TBC of $100,000 for the project. Using the format in Figure 7.12, we could say that, at the end of week 8,

- 64 percent of the total budget for the project was to have been spent to perform all the work scheduled to be performed during the first eight weeks
- 68 percent of the total budget was actually expended by the end of week 8
- 54 percent of the total project work was actually performed by the end of week 8

In addition to plotting the dollar values of CBC, CAC, and CEV curves on the same graph, it may be useful to tabulate or draw curves for the percentages. This, too, will indicate any trends toward improving or deteriorating cost performance.

FIGURE 7.12 Packaging Machine Project Status as of Week 8

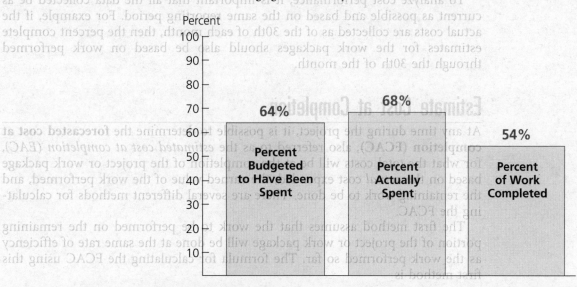

COST PERFORMANCE INDEX

Another indicator of cost performance is the **cost performance index (CPI)**, which is a measure of the cost efficiency with which the project is being performed. The formula for determining the CPI is

$$\text{Cost performance index} = \frac{\text{Cumulative earned value}}{\text{Cumulative actual cost}}$$

$$\text{CPI} = \frac{\text{CEV}}{\text{CAC}}$$

Reinforce Your Learning

11. What is the cost performance index for the "Design" work package in the packaging machine project at the end of week 5?

In the packaging machine project, the CPI as of week 8 is given by

$$\text{CPI} = \frac{\$54,000}{\$68,000} = 0.79$$

This ratio indicates that for every $1.00 actually expended, only $0.79 of earned value was accomplished. Trends in the CPI should be watched carefully. When the CPI goes below 1.0 or gradually decreases, corrective action should be taken.

COST VARIANCE

Another indicator of cost performance is **cost variance (CV)**, which is the difference between the CEV of the work performed and the CAC. The formula for determining the CV is

$$\text{CV} = \text{CEV} - \text{CAC}$$

Reinforce Your Learning

12. What is the cost variance for the "Build" work package in the packaging machine project at the end of week 8?

Like the CPI, this indicator shows the gap between the value of the work performed and the actual cost, but the CV is expressed in terms of dollars.

In the packaging machine project, the CV as of week 8 is given by

$$\text{CV} = \$54,000 - \$68,000 = -\$14,000$$

This calculation indicates that the value of the work performed through week 8 is $14,000 less than the amount actually expended. It is another indication that the work performed is not keeping pace with the actual cost.

To analyze cost performance, it is important that all the data collected be as current as possible and based on the same reporting period. For example, if the actual costs are collected as of the 30th of each month, then the percent complete estimates for the work packages should also be based on work performed through the 30th of the month.

Estimate Cost at Completion

At any time during the project, it is possible to determine the **forecasted cost at completion (FCAC)**, also referred to as the *estimated cost at completion (EAC)*, for what the total costs will be at the completion of the project or work package based on the *actual* cost expended, the earned value of the work performed, and the remaining work to be done. There are several different methods for calculating the FCAC.

The first method assumes that the work to be performed on the remaining portion of the project or work package will be done at the same rate of efficiency as the work performed so far. The formula for calculating the FCAC using this first method is

$$\text{Forecasted cost at completion} = \frac{\text{Total budgeted cost}}{\text{Cost performance index}}$$

$$\text{FCAC} = \frac{\text{TBC}}{\text{CPI}}$$

Reinforce Your Learning

13. Using the first forecasting method described, calculate the forecasted cost at completion for the "Build" work package in the packaging machine project.

For the packaging machine project, the FCAC is given by

$$\text{FCAC} = \frac{\$100,000}{0.79} = \$126,582$$

As of week 8, the project has a cost efficiency, or CPI, of 0.79, and if the remainder of the project continues to be performed at this same efficiency rate, then the entire project will actually cost $126,582. If this forecast is correct, there will be an overrun of $26,582 beyond the TBC for the project of $100,000.

A second method for determining the FCAC assumes that, regardless of the efficiency rate the project or work package has experienced in the past, the work to be performed on the remaining portion of the project or work package will be done according to its budget. The formula for calculating the FCAC using this method is

$$\text{Forecasted cost at completion} = \frac{\text{Cumulative actual cost}}{} + (\text{Total budgeted cost} - \text{Cumulative earned value})$$

$$\text{FCAC} = \text{CAC} + (\text{TBC} - \text{CEV})$$

Reinforce Your Learning

14. Using the second forecasting method described, calculate the forecasted cost at completion for the "Build" work package in the packaging machine project.

For the packaging machine project, the FCAC is given by

$$\text{FCAC} = \$68,000 + (\$100,000 - \$54,000)$$
$$= \$68,000 + \$46,000$$
$$= \$114,000$$

As of week 8, the CAC was $68,000, but the CEV of the work performed was only $54,000. Therefore, work with an earned value of $46,000 still needs to be performed to complete the project. This method assumes that the remaining work will be performed at an efficiency rate of 1.0, even though the project has

been experiencing an efficiency rate of 0.79 as of the end of week 8. This method results in a FCAC of $114,000, a forecasted overrun of $14,000 beyond the TBC for the project of $100,000.

A third method for determining the FCAC is to reestimate the costs for all the remaining work to be performed, and then add this reestimate to the CAC. The formula for determining the FCAC using this third method is

$$FCAC = CAC + \text{Reestimate of remaining work to be performed}$$

This approach can be time consuming, but it may be necessary if the project experiences persistent deviations from the plan or if there are extensive changes.

As part of the regular cost performance analysis, the FCAC for the project should be calculated using the first or second method described above. The forecasted overrun or underrun can then be determined. When cost is forecasted to the completion of the project or work package, a small variance in a given reporting period can expand to a much greater overrun as the work continues; therefore, corrective action should be taken early.

Another measure that may be of interest is the **to-complete performance index (TCPI)**. It is the rate of performance required for the remaining work to complete the project or work package within its TBC. The formula for calculating the TCPI is

$$TCPI = (TBC - CEV)/(TBC - CAC)$$

The numerator of the equation, $TBC - CEV$, is the amount earned value of work remaining that needs to be done. The denominator of the equation, $TBC - CAC$, is the amount of budget still left. So for the packaging machine project, the TCPI is

$$\begin{aligned} TCPI &= (\$100,000 - \$54,000)/(\$100,000 - \$68,000) \\ &= \$46,000/\$32,000 \\ &= 1.44 \end{aligned}$$

It indicates that there is $46,000 of remaining earned value of work to be done, and only $32,000 of budget still left to do that remaining work. So the remaining work must be done at an efficiency rate of 1.44 to complete the project within the budget of $100,000.

Control Costs

The key to effective cost control is to analyze cost performance on a regular and timely basis. It starts with establishing a baseline time-phased budget that shows how the costs are expected to be expended during the time span of the project. Then it is necessary to monitor the actual cost expended and the earned value of the work performed. It is crucial that cost variances and inefficiencies be identified early so that corrective action can be taken immediately, before the situation gets worse. Once project costs get out of control, it may be very difficult to complete the project within budget.

Cost control involves the following:

1. Analyzing cost performance to determine which work packages may require corrective action.
2. Deciding what specific corrective action should be taken.

3. Revising the project plan, including estimated durations and costs, to incorporate the planned corrective action.

The cost performance analysis should include identifying those work packages that have a negative CV or a CPI of less than 1.0. Also, those work packages for which the CV or CPI has deteriorated since the prior reporting period should be identified. A concentrated effort must be applied to the work packages with negative variances to reduce cost or improve the efficiency of the work performed. The amount of CV should determine the priority for applying these concentrated efforts; that is, the work package with the largest negative CV should be given top priority.

When evaluating work packages that have a negative CV, you should focus on taking corrective actions to reduce the costs of two types of activities:

1. *Activities that will be performed in the near term.* It is much wiser to take aggressive corrective action to reduce the estimated costs of activities that will be done in the near term than to plan to reduce the costs of activities that are scheduled sometime in the distant future. You will get more timely feedback on the effects of corrective actions if they are done in the near term. If you postpone corrective actions until the distant future, the negative CV or CPI may deteriorate even further by that time. As the project progresses, there is always less time remaining in which corrective action can be taken.

2. *Activities that have a large estimated cost.* Taking corrective actions that will reduce the cost of a $20,000 activity by 10 percent will have a greater impact than totally eliminating a $300 activity. Usually, the larger the estimated cost for an activity, the greater the opportunity for a large cost reduction.

There are various ways to reduce the costs of activities. One way is to substitute less expensive materials that meet the required specifications. Maybe another supplier can be found who can supply the same material but at a lower cost. Another approach is to assign a person with greater expertise or more experience to perform or help with the activity to get it done more efficiently.

Reducing the scope or requirements for the work package or specific activities is another way to reduce estimated costs. For example, a contractor might decide to put only one coat of paint on a room rather than two coats, as originally planned. In some cases, a decision might be made to totally eliminate some activities, such as deciding not to install a fence around the property.

Increasing productivity through improved methods or technology is yet another approach to reducing the estimated costs of activities. For example, by renting automatic paint-spraying equipment, a contractor may substantially lower the cost and duration of painting a room below what it would be for painters working with rollers and brushes.

In many cases, there will be a trade-off—reducing cost variances will involve a reduction in project scope or a delay in the project schedule. If the negative CV is very large, a substantial reduction in the work scope or quality may be required to get the project back within budget. This could jeopardize elements of the overall project objective, such as scope, schedule, budget, and/or quality. In some cases, the customer and contractor or project team may have to acknowledge that one or more of these elements cannot be achieved. Therefore, the sponsor or customer may have to provide additional funds to cover the forecasted overrun, or there may be a dispute over who should pay for it—the customer or the contractor.

The key to effective cost control is to aggressively address negative cost variances and cost inefficiencies as soon as they are identified, rather than hoping that things will improve as the project goes on. Addressing cost problems early will minimize the negative impact on scope and schedule. Once costs get out of control, getting back within budget becomes more difficult and is likely to require reducing the project scope or quality, or extending the project schedule.

Even when projects have only positive cost variances, it is important not to let the cost variances deteriorate. If a project's cost performance is positive, a concentrated effort should be made to *keep* it under budget. Once a project gets in trouble with cost performance, it becomes difficult to get it back on track.

Project meetings are a good forum for addressing cost control issues. See the section on meetings in Chapter 12 and the section on problem solving in Chapter 11 for related information.

For a further discussion of an approach to project control, see Appendix 1, Time–Cost Trade-Off, at the end of this chapter.

Manage Cash Flow

It is important to manage the cash flow on a project. Managing cash flow involves making sure that sufficient funds or payments are received from the customer in time so that you have enough money to cover the costs of performing the project—employee payroll, invoices for materials, invoices from subcontractors, and travel expenses, for example.

The key to managing cash flow is to ensure that cash comes in faster than it goes out. If sufficient cash is not available to meet expenses, money must be borrowed. Borrowing increases project cost because any money borrowed must be paid back to the lender, along with a charge for borrowing the money—the interest.

The flow of cash coming in from the customer can be controlled by the terms of payment in the contract. From the contractor's point of view, it is desirable to receive payments from the customer early in the project rather than later. The contractor might try to negotiate payment terms that require the customer to do one or more of the following:

- Provide a down payment at the start of the project. This requirement is reasonable when the contractor needs to purchase a significant amount of materials, equipment, and supplies during the early stages of the project.
- Make equal monthly payments based on the expected duration of the project. Cash outflow usually is smaller in the early stages of a project. If more cash is coming in than is going out during the early part of the project, the contractor may be able to invest some of the excess cash and earn interest. The saved funds can then be withdrawn to meet the greater cash outflow requirements later in the project.
- Provide frequent payments, such as weekly or monthly payments rather than quarterly payments.

The worst scenario from the contractor's point of view is to have the customer make only one payment at the end of the project. In this situation, the contractor will need to borrow money to have cash available to meet expenses throughout the project.

The contractor's outflow of cash can also be controlled by the terms of payment, in this case in contracts with suppliers or subcontractors. The contractor

wants to delay payments (cash outflow) as long as possible. For example, a contractor who has ordered $100,000 worth of material would want to wait until it has all been delivered before paying the supplier. If the supplier's invoice states that it must be paid within 30 days, the contractor would probably hold off until about the 27th day before making the payment.

REAL WORLD PROJECT MANAGEMENT

Power Transmission Project Cost Management

Crisscrossing Canada are high-voltage power transmission lines. Over the last 25 years, overloading the national grid has revealed the insufficiencies of the system. A need to execute power transmission line replacement projects to upgrade the lines is increasing in urgency. Transmission facility owners, industry regulators, and the public have a growing concern for the upcoming projects. Fortunately, they have two project teams from western Canada who have recently completed two major transmission line projects to guide the new projects on controlling costs, overcoming problems, and estimating budgets.

Problems were identified by each of the western Canadian power transmission project teams. Topping both project teams' lists of problems for their transmission line installation projects was high employee turnover, especially the turnover in the engineering and procurement aspects of the project. The continuing training of new personnel not only was a problem for engineering and procurement, a shortage of staff in general and changes in key project personnel and senior team members in the middle of the project caused milestones to not be met and increased project costs.

The personnel problems compounded other problems related to costs and schedule. The budgets for each project were subjected to inaccurate estimates of the work to be done by the project team and subcontractors submitted bids for work with inflated bid prices. Misunderstanding of the scope of the project and insufficient detail of the required work led to additional issues. Heavily imposed restrictions by the industry on the project team related to permits, licenses, landowners, and the environment were beyond the control of the project team yet delayed project progress as hearings had to be held and approvals obtained before work could be completed.

Doomed as these projects seemed to have been, both projects did finish their scheduled tasks. The teams offered solutions to future project teams. The top rated solution suggested future teams acquire a clear understanding of the scope of work and the client's requirements and suggested they include sufficient time to spend with the subcontractors to clarify the scope of work and requirements necessary to complete all the work needed for the subtasks. This increased planning and clarification translates into spending more time creating realistic schedule and cost estimates based upon sound conceptual design with visits to the project sites and upon budget development by lead engineers, project managers, and key project personnel.

To help control costs and reduce turnover, the project teams recommended that future project teams should be established that completed a specific project task

before they were assigned to another task. These assigned teams should have better integration between departments and input by stakeholders to increase the communication within the project.

These lessons learned are a valuable resource for the project planning teams for the new power transmission line upgrades. Using lessons learned from your prior projects will help you accurately estimate costs, budget, and schedules. Project cost control is complex owing to many internal and external factors. Involvement and collaboration of the project team and stakeholders will help minimize cost overruns by being proactive using cost controls and earned value calculations to ensure your projects are progressing according to plan.

Based on information from Gharaibeh, H. (2013). "Managing the Cost of Power Transmission Projects: Lessons Learned," *Journal of Construction Engineering & Management, 139*(8), 1063–1067.

Cost Estimating for Information Systems Development

Chapter 4 defined the information system as a computer-based system that accepts data as input, processes the data, and produces information required by users. Chapter 5 revealed that scheduling is often done in a haphazard manner, resulting in a large number of information system projects not finishing on time. Chapter 6 reinforced the resource requirements planning necessary for people, hardware, software, data, and network resources. Accurately estimating costs and including an amount for reserve are essential in creating a realistic budget to complete the work without cost overruns. Having a good plan and schedule helps to develop cost estimates and a baseline budget.

Estimating costs too optimistically leaves the development team without enough funds to cover the costs of the labor, materials, equipment, and/or subcontractors. Adding expenses for every contingency results in a total estimated cost for the project that is more than expected and may cause no-go decisions to be made for projects because of the high estimated costs. Common errors in estimating costs include:

- Underestimating the work time necessary to complete an activity
- Requiring rework to meet the user requirements
- Underestimating growth in the project scope
- Not anticipating new hardware purchases
- Making corrections to flaws in excess of the contingency planning
- Changing the design strategy
- Increasing resources to fast-track phases of the systems development life cycle

AN INFORMATION SYSTEM EXAMPLE: INTERNET APPLICATIONS DEVELOPMENT FOR ABC OFFICE DESIGNS (CONTINUED)

Recall from Chapters 4, 5, and 6 that Beth Smith was assigned to be the project manager by the Information System Department of ABC Office Designs. Chapter 5 described how Beth had scheduled the ES, EF, LS, and LF times for the activities necessary to complete the Web-based reporting system development project for ABC Office Designs. Chapter 6 described how Beth and the project team

planned the resources for the 60-day schedule they have to complete the project. Management approved a budget of $125,000 to complete the project and train the sales staff.

After confirming with the primary responsible resources that the tasks could be completed with the estimated level of effort on each task, Beth worked with the human resources team to use the hourly wage for each of the employees to determine the labor costs for each of the Web-based Reporting System project activities. Beth and the project team estimated the costs associated with traveling to complete the interviews of users ($3,000), the price of the packaged software ($500), and the costs of the training materials ($1,300).

The budgeted costs of the work to complete the project were near the $125,000 limit without training the sales staff. Beth realized that there was not enough in the budget to have centralized face-to-face training for all of the staff members. A project team member commented that if the sales team traveled to the training offices, then each would lose at least two days of sales opportunities. This was a cost that could not be quantified as a project cost.

The project team discussed options for training the sales staff members on how to use the Web-based reporting system. They decided the training would best be presented through a Web-based system instead of having the entire sales team travel to the home office for face-to-face training. The Web-based system could be recorded for later viewing by new sales staff members and those who would like to review the training. The costs of the Web-based system were much less than the travel costs and helped to keep the costs of the project below the budget. The team confirmed that the price for the Web-based system was $300. This was less than a single airline ticket for one of the sales staff members. The estimated cost for other additional training materials is $1,000.

Beth's estimated activity costs for completing the Web-Based Report System Development project are shown in Figure 7.13. The cost estimate allowed for a small, almost 5 percent, contingency amount for cost overruns, fast-tracking of the project, or increased costs of materials or travel for the interviews.

Project Management Information Systems

Project management information systems make it fairly easy to handle the cost considerations of a project. All costs associated with each resource in a project can be stored, and the system will calculate the budget for each work package and for the entire project. It will calculate the actual costs as the project proceeds and will forecast the final costs as well. Because various resources have different rate structures and charge their rates at various points in the project, project management information systems usually allow the user to define different rate structures for each resource and determine when charges for those resources will actually be accrued. At any time during a project, cost estimates, aggregated TBC, CBC, actual cost, committed costs, EV, a CPI, CV, and a cost forecast can be calculated for each task, each work package, or the entire project, with a click of the mouse. Cost tables and graphs are often available to help analyze cost performance.

See Appendix A in the back of the book for a thorough discussion of project management information systems.

FIGURE 7.13 Estimated Activity Costs for Web-based Reporting System Project

ACTIVITY	PRIMARY RESPONSIBILITY	WORK DAYS	LABOR COSTS	MATERIALS COSTS	TRAVEL COSTS	TOTAL COSTS
1. Gather Data	Beth	3	$4,440			$4,440
2. Study Feasibility	Jack	4	7,360			7,360
3. Prepare Problem Definition Report	Rose	1	1,000			1,000
4. Interview Users	Jim	5	9,200		$6,000	15,200
5. Study Existing System	Steve	8	3,200			3,200
6. Define User Requirements	Jeff	5	1,600			1,600
7. Prepare System Analysis Report	Jim	1	480			480
8. Input & Output	Tyler	8	17,280			17,280
9. Processing & Database	Joe	10	13,600			13,600
10. Evaluation	Cathy	2	3,760			3,760
11. Prepare System Design Report	Sharon	2	1,760			1,760
12. Software Development	Hannah	15	7,120	$500		7,620
13. Hardware Development	Joe	10	9,600			9,600
14. Network Development	Gerri	6	2,400			2,400
15. Prepare System Development Report	Jack	2	960			960
16. Software Testing	Maggie	6	6,720			6,720
17. Hardware Testing	Gene	4	5,120			5,120
18. Network Testing	Greg	4	5,440			5,440
19. Prepare Testing Report	Rose	1	1,760			1,760
20. Training	Jim	4	5,760	1,300		7,060
21. System Conversion	Beth	2	1,200			1,200
22. Prepare Implementation Report	Jack	1	1,560			1,560
Total		**104**	**$111,320**	**$1,800**	**$6,000**	**$119,120**

CRITICAL SUCCESS FACTORS

- Estimated activity costs must be based on the estimated activity resources.

- The person who will be responsible for performing the activity should estimate the costs for that activity. This generates commitment from the person.

- Cost estimates should be reasonable and realistic.

- Once the project starts, it is important to monitor actual costs and work performance to ensure that everything is within budget.

- A system should be established to collect, on a regular and timely basis, data on costs actually expended and committed, and the earned value (percent complete) of the work performed, so that they can be compared to the cumulative budgeted cost (CBC).

- If at any time during the project it is determined that the project is overrunning the budget, or the value of the work performed is not keeping up with the actual amount of costs expended, corrective action must be taken immediately.

- It is important to use the time-phased cumulative budgeted cost (CBC), rather than the total budgeted cost (TBC), as the baseline against which cumulative actual cost (CAC) is compared. It would be misleading to compare the actual costs expended to the total budgeted cost, because cost performance will always look good as long as actual costs are below the TBC.

- To permit a realistic comparison of cumulative actual cost to cumulative budgeted cost, portions of the committed costs should be assigned to actual costs while the associated work is in progress.

- The earned value of the work actually performed is a key parameter that must be determined and reported throughout the project.

- For each reporting period, the percent complete data should be obtained from the person responsible for the work. It is important that the person make an honest assessment of the work performed relative to the entire work scope.

- One way to prevent inflated percent complete estimates is to keep the work packages or activities small in terms of scope and duration. It is important that the person estimating the percent complete assess not only how much work has been performed but also what work remains to be done.

- The key to effective cost control is to analyze cost performance on a timely and regular basis. Early identification of cost variances (CV) allows corrective actions to be taken immediately, before the situation gets worse.

- For analyzing cost performance, it is important that all the data collected be as current as possible and based on the same reporting period.

- Trends in the cost performance index (CPI) should be monitored carefully. If the CPI goes below 1.0 or gradually decreases, corrective action should be taken.

- As part of the regular cost performance analysis, the estimated or forecasted cost at completion (FCAC) should be calculated.

- The key to effective cost control is to aggressively address work packages or activities with negative cost variances and cost inefficiencies as soon as they are identified. A concentrated effort must be applied in these areas. The amount of negative cost variance should determine the priority for applying these concentrated efforts.

- When attempting to reduce negative cost variances, focus on activities that will be performed in the near term and on activities that have large estimated costs.

- Addressing cost problems early will minimize the negative impact on scope and schedule. Once costs get out of control, getting back within budget becomes more difficult and is likely to require reducing the project scope or quality, or extending the project schedule.

- The key to managing cash flow is to ensure that cash comes in faster than it goes out.

- It is desirable to receive payments (cash inflow) from the customer as early as possible, and to delay making payments (cash outflow) to suppliers or subcontractors as long as possible.

SUMMARY

The total project cost is often estimated during the initiating phase of the project or when the project charter or a proposal is prepared, but detailed plans are not usually prepared at that time. However, during the planning phase of the project, specific activities are defined and a network plan is created. Once specific activities are defined, then estimates can be made of resources, durations, and costs for each specific activity. Resources include people, materials, equipment, facilities, subcontractors, and consultants. The estimated activity resources are used for estimating activity costs. The estimated cost of an activity is based on an estimate of the types and quantities of resources required to perform the activity. The estimated costs for an activity should be reasonable and realistic.

The project budgeting process involves two steps. The first step is to determine the total budgeted cost (TBC) which is the aggregate amount of the estimated costs of all the specific activities to perform and complete a work package

or the project. The second step is to develop a time-phased budget, which is the distribution by time period of the TBC for a work package or project over its expected time span based on when specific activities are scheduled to be performed.

Aggregating the estimated costs of all the specific activities to perform and complete each work package in the work breakdown structure will establish a TBC, also referred to as budget at completion (BAC), for each work package. The TBC for each work package is the sum of the estimated costs of all the specific activities that make up that work package. When the budgets for all the work packages are aggregated, they cannot exceed the total amount of funds the sponsor or customer budgeted for the project. It is not unusual that the initial sum of the estimated costs of all the work packages or activities may be greater than the amount of funds the sponsor or customer has budgeted for the project, and it may then take several iterations of revising the estimated costs of specific activities to arrive at an acceptable baseline budget.

Once a TBC has been established for each work package, the second step in the project budgeting process is to distribute or spread each TBC over the expected time span of its work package. A cost is determined for each period within the time span, based on when the specific activities that make up the work package are scheduled to be performed. When the TBC for each work package is spread out by time period, a time-phased budget is created so that it can be determined how much of the budget should have been spent at any point in time. This amount is calculated by adding up the budgeted costs for each time period up to that point in time. This amount, known as the cumulative budgeted cost (CBC), is the amount that is budgeted to accomplish all the work that is scheduled to be performed up to a specific point in time. The CBC is the time-phased baseline budget that will be used to analyze the cost performance of the project. The CBC for the entire project or each work package provides a baseline against which actual cost and work performance can be compared at any time during the project.

Once the project starts, it is necessary to keep track of actual cost expended and committed costs so that they can be compared to the CBC. In addition, it is also necessary to monitor the earned value of the work that has been performed. Determining the earned value involves collecting data on the percent complete for each work package and then converting this percentage to a dollar amount by multiplying the TBC of the work package by the percent complete. This figure can then be compared to the CBC and the CAC.

After this has been done, the project cost performance can be analyzed by looking at the TBC, the CBC, the CAC, and the cumulative earned value (CEV). They are used to determine whether the project is being performed within budget and whether the value of the work performed is in line with the actual cost.

An indicator of cost performance is the cost performance index (CPI), which is a measure of the cost efficiency with which the project is being performed. The CPI is calculated by dividing the CEV by the CAC. Another indicator of cost performance is cost variance (CV), which is the difference between the CEV of the work performed and the CAC.

At any time during the project, it is possible to determine the forecasted cost at completion (FCAC), also referred to as estimated cost at completion (EAC), for what the total costs will be at the completion of the project or work package

based on the actual cost expended, the earned value of work performed, and the remaining work to be done. There are several different methods for calculating the FCAC. The first method assumes that the work to be performed on the remaining portion of the project or work package will be done at the same rate of efficiency as the work performed so far. The second method assumes that, regardless of the efficiency rate the project or work package has experienced in the past, the work to be performed on the remaining portion of the project or work package will be done according to budget. The third method for determining the FCAC is to reestimate the costs for all the remaining work to be performed and then add this reestimate to the CAC.

The key to effective cost control is to analyze cost performance on a regular and timely basis. It is crucial that cost variances and inefficiencies be identified early so that corrective action can be taken immediately, before the situation gets worse. Cost control involves analyzing cost performance to determine which work packages may require corrective action, deciding what specific corrective action should be taken, and revising the project plan, including estimated durations and costs, to incorporate the planned corrective action.

It is important to manage the cash flow on a project. Managing cash flow involves making sure that sufficient payments are received from the customer in time so that you have enough money to cover the costs of performing the project (employee payroll, invoices for materials, invoices from subcontractors, and travel expenses, for example). The key to managing cash flow is to ensure that cash comes in faster than it goes out.

QUESTIONS

1. Describe why it is necessary to develop a baseline budget for a project.
2. List and describe items that should be included when estimating activity costs.
3. What does the term reserve mean? Should a reserve amount be included in a project proposal? Explain your answer.
4. What is the problem with making cost estimates too conservative or too aggressive?
5. Describe the project budgeting process.
6. Define the following: TBC, CBC, CAC, CEV, CPI, CV, FCAC, and TCPI. How is each calculated?
7. Why is it necessary to track actual and committed costs once a project starts?
8. Why is it necessary to calculate the earned value of work performed? How is this done?
9. Give an example of calculating a cost performance index. What does it mean when the CPI is below 1.0? What does it mean when the CPI is above 1.0?
10. What does it mean when cost variance is negative? What does it mean when cost variance is positive? When evaluating a work package with a negative cost variance, on what two types of activities should you focus? Why?
11. What is the key to managing cash flow? How can this goal be accomplished?
12. a. Refer to the table below. What is the cumulative budgeted cost at the end of week 6?

	TBC	Week									
		1	2	3	4	5	6	7	8	9	10
Task 1	30	10	15	5							
Task 2	70		10	10	10	20	10	10			
Task 3	40					5	5	25	5		
Task 4	30								5	5	20
Total	170	10	25	15	10	25	15	35	10	5	20
Cumulative											

Amounts are in thousands of dollars.

b. Below is a table of actual costs. What is the cumulative actual cost at the end of week 6? Determine whether there is a cost overrun or underrun. What is causing it?

	Week					
	1	2	3	4	5	6
Task 1	10	16	8			
Task 2		10	10	12	24	12
Task 3					5	5
Task 4						
Total	10	26	18	12	29	17
Cumulative						

Amounts are in thousands of dollars.

c. Below is a table of the cumulative percentages of work completed by the end of week 6. What is the cumulative earned value of the project at the end of week 6? Is it good?

	Week					
	1	2	3	4	5	6
Task 1	30	80	100			
Task 2		10	25	35	55	65
Task 3					10	20
Task 4						

Amounts are cumulative percent complete.

d. What is the CPI at the end of week 6? What is the CV?

e. Calculate the FCAC using the first two methods described in the chapter.

In addition, describe a third FCAC method you could use.

INTERNET EXERCISES

For the website addresses of the organizations mentioned in these exercises, go to "Internet Exercises" at the book's companion website at www.cengagebrain.com. It is suggested that you save this website in your "Favorites" list for easy access in the future.

1. Search the Web for cost analysis tools. Provide a description of what you find. If possible, download a demo copy of a software package that provides some cost analysis tools.

2. Search the Web for "Cost Forecasting" and discuss how what you find is similar to and/or different from the methods described in the chapter.

3. For Exercises 3 through 5, visit the website of Project Smart. Click on the "Cost Management" or "Earned Value Management" link and explore the articles listed. Read an article and provide a one-page summary.

4. Click on the "Methods & Tools" link, then explore the methods and tools presented. Review at least one method or tool. How would you use this method or tool in your projects?

5. Search the website for "Cost Planning." Describe what you find and how it relates to this chapter.

CASE STUDY 1 A Not-for-Profit Medical Research Center

This case study is a continuation of the case study from Chapters 4, 5, and 6.

CASE QUESTIONS

1. Using the schedule from Chapter 5, estimate the cost for each activity.

2. Determine the total budgeted cost for the project.

3. Prepare a budgeted cost by period table (similar to Figure 7.5) and a cumulative budgeted cost (CBC) curve (similar to Figure 7.6) for the project.

Note: This case study will continue in Chapter 8, so save the results of your work.

GROUP ACTIVITY

Divide the course participants into the same groups as for the previous chapter's group activity. Then address each of the steps listed above.

CASE STUDY 2 The Wedding

This case study is a continuation of the case study from Chapters 4, 5, and 6.

CASE QUESTIONS

1. Using the schedule from Chapter 5, estimate the cost for each activity.

2. Determine the total budgeted cost for the project.

3. Prepare a budgeted cost by period table (similar to Figure 7.5) and a cumulative budgeted cost (CBC) curve (similar to Figure 7.6) for the project.

Note: This case study will continue in Chapter 8, so save the results of your work.

GROUP ACTIVITY
Divide the course participants into the same groups as for the previous chapter's group activity. Then address each of the steps listed above.

REFERENCES

A Guide to the Project Management Body of Knowledge (PMBOK® Guide) Fifth Edition. Newtown Square, PA: Project Management Institute, 2013.

Almahmoud, E. S., H. K. Doloi, and K. Panuwatwanich (2012). "Linking Project Health to Project Performance Indicators: Multiple Case Studies of Construction Projects in Saudi Arabia," *International Journal of Project Management*, 30, 296–307.

Al-Tmeemy, S. M. H., H. Abdul-Rahman, and Z. Harun (2013). "Contractor's Perception of the Use of Costs of Quality System in Malaysian Building Construction Projects," *International Journal of Project Management*, 30, 827–838.

Anonymous (2013). "Environment; Project Insight Drives Budget Management Success at Stillwater Associates," *Computer Weekly News*, 1042.

Cantwell, P. R., S. Sarkani, and T. A. Mazzuchi (2013). "Dynamic Consequences of Cost, Schedule, and Performance Within DoD Project Management," *Defense Acquisition Research Journal: A Publication of the Defense Acquisition University*, 20(1), 89–106.

Chen, H. L., C. Chen, and N. Wei (2013). "Estimating a Project's Profitability: A Longitudinal Approach," *International Journal of Project Management*, 31, 400–410.

Chou, J. and C. Wu (2013). "Estimating Software Project Effort for Manufacturing Firms," *Computers in Industry*, 64(6), 732.

Doloi, H. (2013). "Cost Overruns and Failure in Project Management: Understanding the Roles of Key Stakeholders in Construction Projects," *Journal of Construction Engineering & Management*, 139(3), 267–279.

Elshaer, R. (2013). "Impact of Sensitivity Information on the Prediction of Project's Duration Using Earned Schedule Method," *International Journal of Project Management*, 31(4), 579–588.

Gharaibeh, H. (2013). "Managing the Cost of Power Transmission Projects: Lessons Learned," *Journal of Construction Engineering & Management*, 139(8), 1063–1067.

Halawa, W. S., A. M. K. Abdelalim, and I. A. Elrashed (2012). "Financial Evaluation Program for Construction Projects at the Pre-investment Phase in Developing Countries: A Case Study," *International Journal of Project Management*, 31(6), 912–923.

Kanaracus, C. (2013). "Military IT Projects Wracked with Delays, Increased Costs, GAO Finds," *CIO* (13284045), 22.

Keegan, A., M. Huemann, and J. R. Turner (2012). "Beyond the Line: Exploring the HRM Responsibilities of Line Managers, Project Managers and the HRM Department in Four Project-Oriented Companies in the Netherlands, Austria, the UK and the USA," *Academy of Management Journal*, 23(15), 3085–3104.

Maravas, A. and J. Pantouvakis (2012). "Project Cash Flow Analysis in the Presence of Uncertainty in Activity Duration and Cost," *International Journal of Project Management*, 30(3), 374–384.

Sharma, V. K. (2013). "Earned Value Management: A Tool for Project Performance," *Advances in Management*, 6(5), 37–42.

Wang, Y., C. Yu, and H. Chan (2012). "Predicting Construction Cost and Schedule Success Using Artificial Neural Networks Ensemble and Support Vector Machines Classification Models," *International Journal of Project Management*, 30, 470–478.

APPENDIX 1 Time–Cost Trade-Off

The time–cost trade-off methodology, also referred to as *crashing*, is used to reduce the project duration incrementally with the smallest associated increase in incremental cost. It is based on the following assumptions:

1. Each activity has two pairs of duration and cost estimates: normal and crash. **Normal time** is the estimated length of time required to perform the activity under normal conditions, according to the plan. **Normal cost** is the estimated cost to complete the activity in the normal time. **Crash time** is the shortest estimated length of time in which the activity can be completed. **Crash cost** is the estimated cost to complete the activity in the crash time. In Figure 7.14, each of the four activities has a pair of normal time and cost estimates and a pair of crash time and cost estimates. The estimated normal time to perform activity A is seven weeks, and its estimated normal cost is $50,000. The crash time for this activity is five weeks, and the cost to complete the activity in this duration is $62,000.

2. An activity's duration can be incrementally accelerated from its normal time to its crash time by applying more resources—assigning more people,

Reinforce Your Learning

19. What are the normal and crash times and costs for activities B, C, and D in Figure 7.14?

	Normal Time	Normal Cost	Crash Time	Crash Cost
Activity B	___	___	___	___
Activity C	___	___	___	___
Activity D	___	___	___	___

FIGURE 7.14 Network with Normal and Crash Times and Their Costs

KEY:
N = Normal estimates
C = Crash estimates
Time is estimated in weeks.

working overtime, using more equipment, and so on. Increased costs will be associated with expediting the activity.

3. An activity cannot be completed in less than its crash time, no matter how many additional resources are applied. For example, activity A cannot be completed in less than five weeks, no matter how many more resources are used or how much money is spent.
4. The resources necessary to reduce an activity's estimated duration from its normal time to its crash time will be available when needed.
5. Within the range between an activity's normal and crash points, the relationship between time and cost is linear. Each activity has its own *cost per time period* for accelerating the activity's duration from its normal time to its crash time. This acceleration cost per time period is calculated as follows:

$$\frac{\text{Crash cost} - \text{Normal cost}}{\text{Normal time} - \text{Crash time}}$$

Reinforce Your Learning

20. What are the cost-per-week rates to accelerate activities B, C, and D in Figure 7.14?

For example, in Figure 7.14, the cost per week to accelerate activity A from its normal time to its crash time is

$$\frac{\$62,000 - \$50,000}{7 \text{ weeks} - 5 \text{ weeks}} = \frac{\$12,000}{2 \text{ weeks}} = \$6,000 \text{ per week}$$

The network diagram in Figure 7.14 has two paths from start to finish: path A–B and path C–D. If we consider only the normal duration estimates, path A–B will take 16 weeks to complete, whereas path C–D will take 18 weeks to complete. Therefore, the earliest the project can be finished based on these time estimates is 18 weeks—the length of its critical path, made up of activities C and D. The total project cost, based on the cost associated with performing each activity in its normal time, is

$$\$50,000 + \$80,000 + \$40,000 + \$30,000 = \$200,000$$

Reinforce Your Learning

21. If all the activities in Figure 7.14 were performed in their crash times, what would be the total project cost?

If all the activities were performed in their respective crash times, path A–B would take 11 weeks and path C–D would take 15 weeks. The earliest the project can be finished based on the crash time estimates is 15 weeks, which is 3 weeks earlier than if the activities were performed in their normal times.

It is usually not necessary or even constructive to crash all the activities. For example, in Figure 7.14, we want to crash only the appropriate activities by the amount necessary to accelerate project completion from 18 weeks to 15 weeks. Any additional crashing of activities will merely increase total project cost; it will not reduce the total project duration any further because that is determined by the length of the critical path. In other words, expediting activities not on the critical path will not reduce the project completion time but will increase total project cost.

The objective of the time–cost trade-off method is to determine the shortest project completion time based on crashing those activities that result in the smallest increase in total project cost. To accomplish this, it is necessary to shorten the total project duration, one time period at a time, crashing only those activities that are on the critical path(s) and have the lowest acceleration cost per time period. From Figure 7.14, we previously determined that, based on normal time and cost estimates, the earliest the project could be completed is 18 weeks

(as determined by the critical path C–D), at a total project cost of $200,000. The cost per week of accelerating each of the activities is

Activity A	$6,000 per week
Activity B	$10,000 per week
Activity C	$5,000 per week
Activity D	$6,000 per week

To reduce the total project duration from 18 weeks to 17 weeks requires first identifying the critical path, which is C–D, and then determining which activity on the critical path can be accelerated at the lowest cost per week. Activity C costs $5,000 per week to accelerate, and activity D costs $6,000 per week to accelerate. Therefore, it is less expensive to expedite activity C. If activity C is crashed 1 week (from 10 weeks to 9 weeks), the total project duration is shortened from 18 weeks to 17 weeks, but the total project cost increases by $5,000 to $205,000.

To shorten the total project duration by one more time period, from 17 weeks to 16 weeks, we must again identify the critical path. The durations of the 2 paths are 16 weeks for A–B and 17 weeks for C–D. Therefore, the critical path is still C–D, and it must be reduced again. Looking at path C–D, we see that although activity C has a lower acceleration cost per week than activity D, we cannot accelerate activity C any further because we reached its crash time of 9 weeks when the project was reduced from 18 weeks to 17 weeks. Therefore, the only choice is to accelerate activity D by 1 week, from 8 weeks to 7 weeks. This reduces the duration of critical path C–D to 16 weeks, but the total project cost increases by $6,000 (the cost per week for accelerating activity D), from $205,000 to $211,000.

Once again, let us reduce the project duration another week, from 16 weeks to 15 weeks. If we look at our 2 paths, we see that they are now of equal duration (16 weeks), so we now have 2 critical paths. To reduce the total project duration from 16 weeks to 15 weeks, it is necessary to accelerate each path by 1 week. In looking at path C–D, we see that the only activity with any remaining time to be crashed is activity D. It can be crashed 1 more week, from 7 weeks to 6 weeks, at an additional cost of $6,000. To accelerate path A–B by 1 week, we have a choice of crashing activity A or activity B. Activity A has a $6,000 cost per week to accelerate, compared with a $10,000 per week rate for activity B. Therefore, to reduce the total project duration from 16 weeks to 15 weeks, we need to crash activities D and A 1 week each. This increases the total project cost by $12,000 ($6,000 + $6,000), from $211,000 to $223,000.

Let us try again to shorten the total project duration by 1 week, from 15 weeks to 14 weeks. We again have two critical paths with the same duration, 15 weeks. Therefore, they must both be accelerated by 1 week. However, in looking at path C–D, we see that both activities are already at their crash time—9 weeks and 6 weeks, respectively—and therefore cannot be expedited any further. Accelerating path A–B would thus be of no value, because it would increase the total project cost but not reduce the total project duration. Our ability to reduce the total project duration is limited by the fact that path C–D cannot be reduced any further.

Table 7.1 displays the incremental acceleration in total project completion and the associated incremental increase in total project cost. It indicates that reducing the total project duration by 1 week would increase the total project cost by

TABLE 7.1 Time–Cost Trade-Off

PROJECT DURATION (WEEKS)	CRITICAL PATH(S)	TOTAL PROJECT COST
18	C–D	$200,000
17	C–D	$200,000 + $5,000 = **$205,000**
16	C–D	$205,000 + $6,000 = **$211,000**
15	C–D, A–B	$211,000 + $6,000 + $6,000 = **$223,000**

$5,000. To reduce it by 2 weeks would cost $11,000, and to reduce it by 3 weeks would cost $23,000.

If all four activities were crashed, the total cost of the project would be $259,000, but it would still not be completed any earlier than 15 weeks. Using the time–cost trade-off method, we were able to reduce the project duration from 18 weeks to 15 weeks at an additional cost of $23,000 by selectively crashing the critical activities with the lowest acceleration cost per time period. Crashing all the activities would have resulted in a waste of $36,000 because no reduction in total project duration beyond 15 weeks could be achieved.

SUMMARY

The time–cost trade-off methodology is used to reduce the project duration incrementally with the smallest associated increase in incremental cost. It is based on the assumptions that each activity has a normal and a crash duration and a normal and a crash cost estimate, that an activity's duration can be incrementally accelerated by applying more resources, and that the relationship between time and cost is linear. Normal time is the estimated length of time required to perform the activity under normal conditions; normal cost is the estimated cost to complete the activity in the normal time. Crash time is the shortest estimated length of time in which the activity can be completed; crash cost is the estimated cost to complete the activity in the crash time.

QUESTIONS

1. What is the time–cost trade-off methodology, and when is it used?
2. Why do you need both normal and crash times and costs for this procedure?
3. Assume that an activity has a normal time of 20 weeks, a normal cost of $72,000, a crash time of 16 weeks, and a crash cost of $100,000. By how many weeks, at most, can this activity's duration be reduced? What is the cost per week to accelerate this activity?
4. Why is it not appropriate to crash all of the activities in a project to achieve the shortest project schedule?

APPENDIX 2 Microsoft Project

In this appendix, we will discuss how Microsoft Project can be used to support the techniques discussed in this chapter, based on the Consumer Market Study example. To retrieve your project information, on the File menu, click Open and

locate the consumer market study file you saved in Chapter 6 when you set the baseline after resource leveling. We are now ready to enter costs for resources, produce cost reports, and examine cash flow and earned value.

Microsoft Project calculates the costs of the project by using rates for work, material, and cost resources that are entered on the Resource Sheet or on the Resources Tab in the Task Information window after double-clicking on the task name. Recall that to access the Resource Sheet, click on Resource Sheet in the Resource Views group on the View ribbon. The rates for work resources and for material resources are recorded on the Resource Sheet by entering in the standard rate in the Std. Rate column for each resource and overtime rates, if they apply. The rate for work resources is cost per hour. The rate for material resources is cost per use. Figure 7A.1 shows the standard and overtime rates on the Resources Sheet in Entry View for the work resources and standard rates for material resources necessary for the Consumer Market Study.

The cost of a cost resource is assigned at the task level by double-clicking on the task name in the Gantt Chart Entry View and editing the cost value on the Resources tab as shown in Figure 7A.2.

FiGURE 7A.1 **Resource Sheet with Work and Material Rates**

FIGURE 7A.2 **Cost Resource Entry for Task**

Examine the Resources for the tasks Print Questionnaire and Mail Questionnaire & Get Responses to be sure that you are using only one unit of the material resources assigned to each task. In the Resource Names column in Figure 7A.2, you can see a number 1 in brackets to show the number of the material resource you are using. If you need to change the number of units, double click on the task name and change the number of units on the Resource tab in the Task Information window.

To get the Work Overview Report shown in Figure 7A.3, on the Report ribbon, click on Dashboards in the View Reports group, choose Work Overview from the drop-down menu. If you have been updating your task resource information, then this report will show you the actual versus baseline for work resources. The Work Overview report provides a quick report for stakeholders about the key performance information for the project.

Five different standard cost reports can be obtained in Microsoft Project: Cash Flow, Cost Overruns, Earned Value Report, Resource Cost Overview, and Task Cost Overview. To view the drop-down menu to select one of these reports, on the Report ribbon click on Costs in the View Reports group. Choose Cash Flow in the Costs reports drop-down menu to generate a Cash Flow Report. The Cash Flow Report in Figure 7A.4 provides a breakdown of costs on a quarterly basis.

A visual Cash Flow Report can be created by choosing Visual Reports in the Export group on the Report ribbon, then selecting Cash Flow Report for Excel from the All tab and clicking View. Visual reports will open in Microsoft Excel or Microsoft Visio. The Visual Cash Flow Report from Microsoft Excel displays the flow of cash over time for the project, as shown in Figure 7A.5.

Let us examine what happens to the project when actual finish dates are entered. Save your Consumer Market Study project file before completing this example. Be sure to set the baseline before entering these actual finish durations and dates.

As you did in Chapter 5, enter the actual finish dates and mark the three tasks Susan completed as 100 percent complete. Recall that Susan completed the Identify Target Consumers in 2 days, developed the draft questionnaire in 9 days, and pilot-tested the questionnaire in 19 days. Figure 7A.6 displays the Tracking Gantt view of the project with the actual finish dates for Tasks 4, 5, and 6.

The Task Cost Overview Report is selected on the Costs menu on the Report ribbon in the View Reports group. Figure 7A.7 shows cost status, distribution, and details for the top-level tasks in the consumer market study project. The actual cost, remaining cost, total cost, baseline cost, and cost variance for the top-level activities are displayed. Note that Susan finished each of the tasks one day early. The budget report indicates that the project is currently operating under budget.

To get a cost table similar to the one shown in Figure 7A.8, on the View ribbon click on Gantt Chart in the Task Views group and select Tracking Gantt from the menu. Then on the View ribbon, click on Tables in the Data group and choose Cost from the menu. For each task, this table provides information about total, baseline, actual, and remaining costs, along with any variances. Recall, the Tracking Gantt chart displays a pair of bars for each task with a bar on the top for the time to complete the task and a bar on the bottom for the baseline time for the task.

You can also generate a cost variance table for resources. To do this, you would need to view the resource sheet (on the View ribbon, click on Resource

FIGURE 7A.3 Work Overview Report

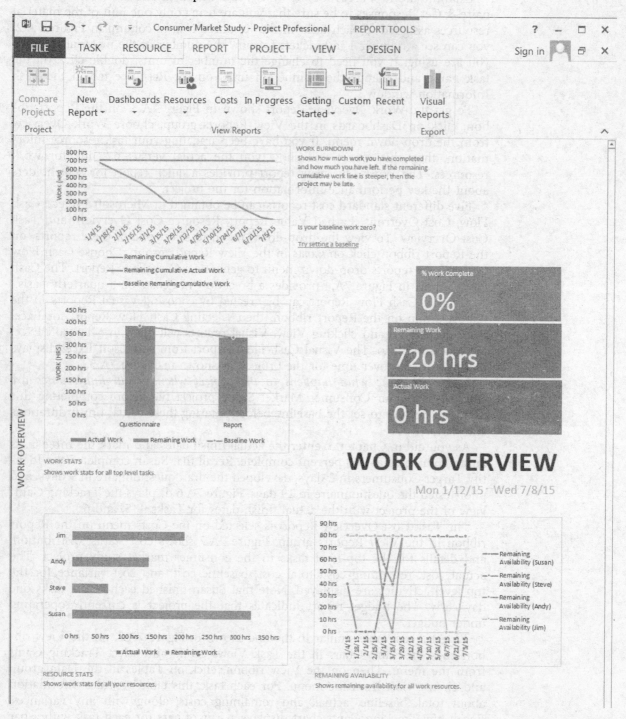

Sheet in the Resource Views group) and then view the cost table (on the View ribbon, click on Tables in the Data group and choose Cost from the menu). Examine the entries for Susan in the table shown in Figure 7A.9.

FIGURE 7A.4 Cash Flow Report

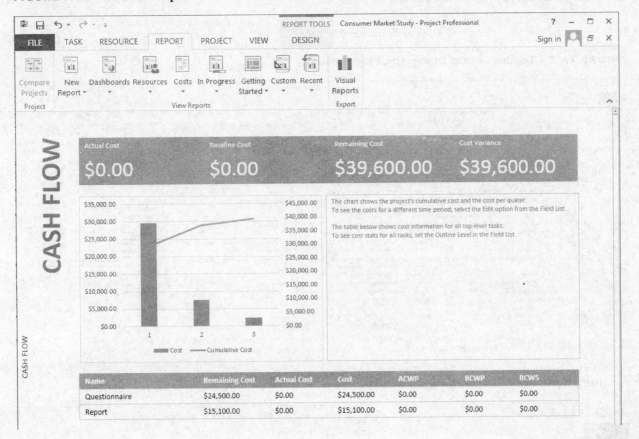

FIGURE 7A.5 Visual Cash Flow Report, Displayed in Microsoft Excel

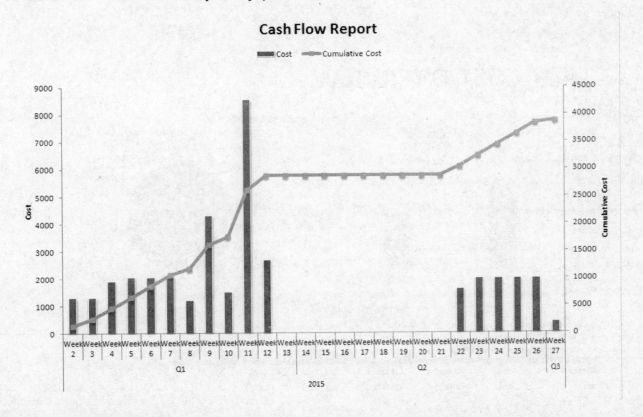

FIGURE 7A.6 Tracking Gantt to Display Actual Finish Dates

FIGURE 7A.7 Task Cost Overview Report

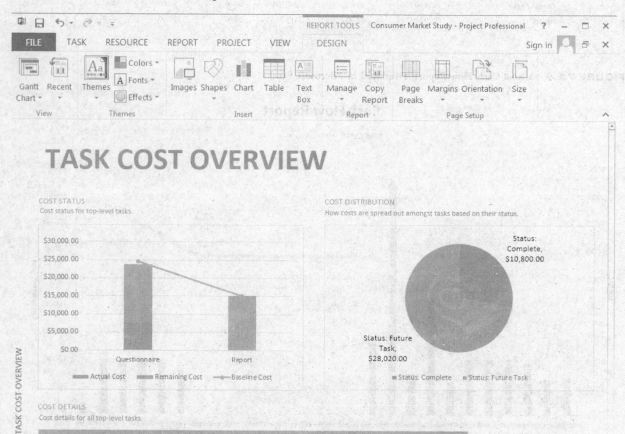

TASK COST OVERVIEW

COST STATUS
Cost status for top-level tasks.

COST DISTRIBUTION
How costs are spread out amongst tasks based on their status.

COST DETAILS
Cost details for all top-level tasks.

Name	Fixed Cost	Actual Cost	Remaining Cost	Cost	Baseline Cost	Cost Variance
Questionnaire	$0.00	$7,800.00	$15,920.00	$23,720.00	$24,500.00	($780.00)
Report	$0.00	$0.00	$15,100.00	$15,100.00	$15,100.00	$0.00

FIGURE 7A.8 Cost Variance Table for Tasks

ID	Task Name	Fixed Cost	Fixed Cost Accrual	Total Cost	Baseline	Variance	Actual	Remaining
0	◢ Consumer Market Study	$0.00	Prorated	$38,820.00	$39,600.00	($780.00)	$7,800.00	$31,020.00
1	◢ Questionnaire	$0.00	Prorated	$23,720.00	$24,500.00	($780.00)	$7,800.00	$15,920.00
2	◢ Design	$0.00	Prorated	$12,620.00	$13,400.00	($780.00)	$7,800.00	$4,820.00
3	Identify Target Consumers	$0.00	Prorated	$520.00	$780.00	($260.00)	$520.00	$0.00
4	Develop Draft Questionnaire	$0.00	Prorated	$2,340.00	$2,600.00	($260.00)	$2,340.00	$0.00
5	Pilot-Test Questionnaire	$0.00	Prorated	$7,940.00	$8,200.00	($260.00)	$4,940.00	$3,000.00
6	Review Comments & Finalize Questionnaire	$0.00	Prorated	$1,300.00	$1,300.00	$0.00	$0.00	$1,300.00
7	Develop Software Test Data	$0.00	Prorated	$520.00	$520.00	$0.00	$0.00	$520.00
8	◢ Responses	$0.00	Prorated	$11,100.00	$11,100.00	$0.00	$0.00	$11,100.00
9	Print Questionnaire	$0.00	Prorated	$1,900.00	$1,900.00	$0.00	$0.00	$1,900.00
10	Prepare Mailing Labels	$0.00	Prorated	$400.00	$400.00	$0.00	$0.00	$400.00
11	Mail Questionnaire & Get Responses	$0.00	Prorated	$8,800.00	$8,800.00	$0.00	$0.00	$8,800.00
12	◢ Report	$0.00	Prorated	$15,100.00	$15,100.00	$0.00	$0.00	$15,100.00
13	◢ Software	$0.00	Prorated	$5,100.00	$5,100.00	$0.00	$0.00	$5,100.00
14	Develop Data Analysis Software	$0.00	Prorated	$3,600.00	$3,600.00	$0.00	$0.00	$3,600.00
15	Test Software	$0.00	Prorated	$1,500.00	$1,500.00	$0.00	$0.00	$1,500.00
16	◢ Report	$0.00	Prorated	$10,000.00	$10,000.00	$0.00	$0.00	$10,000.00
17	Input Response Data	$0.00	Prorated	$2,800.00	$2,800.00	$0.00	$0.00	$2,800.00
18	Analyze Results	$0.00	Prorated	$3,200.00	$3,200.00	$0.00	$0.00	$3,200.00
19	Prepare Report	$0.00	Prorated	$4,000.00	$4,000.00	$0.00	$0.00	$4,000.00

FIGURE 7A.9 Cost Variance Table for Resources

ID	Resource Name	Cost	Baseline	Variance	Actual Cost	Remaining
1	Susan	$9,620.00	$10,400.00	($780.00)	$7,800.00	$1,820.00
2	Steve	$1,600.00	$1,600.00	$0.00	$0.00	$1,600.00
3	Andy	$5,100.00	$5,100.00	$0.00	$0.00	$5,100.00
4	Jim	$10,000.00	$10,000.00	$0.00	$0.00	$10,000.00
5	Travel Expenses	$3,000.00	$3,000.00	$0.00	$0.00	$3,000.00
6	Questionnaire Printing	$1,700.00	$1,700.00	$0.00	$0.00	$1,700.00
7	Questionnaire Mailing	$7,800.00	$7,800.00	$0.00	$0.00	$7,800.00

You can create a table that shows earned value for each task. Earned Value is calculated based upon the status date of the project. Susan's third task was finished on February 23. To set the status date to February 23, 2015, on the Project ribbon in the Properties group click on Project Information to open the Project Information window, then enter 2/23/15 or select the date from the drop-down calendar. The status date can be set to the current date or any date before the current date. See Figure 7A.10.

On the View ribbon, click on Gantt Chart and choose Gantt Chart from the menu, then on the View ribbon, point to Tables in the Data group, and choose Entry. This will put you back in the default display mode. To view the Earned Value table, on the View ribbon click on Tables in the Data group, and select More Tables to open the menu of additional tables available. Scroll down the list, choose Earned Value and click Apply.

FIGURE 7A.10 Change in Status Date

You should see the table shown in Figure 7A.11. This table will provide a variety of information, including budgeted cost of work scheduled, earned value of work performed, actual cost of work performed, budgeted cost at completion, estimated cost at completion, and any variances.

A visual Earned Value Report is also available. On the Project ribbon, click on Visual Reports in the Reports group, then choose Earned Value Over Time from the All tab, choose Day for the level of usage data to include in the report, and click View. Figure 7A.12 displays the Visual Reports-Create Report window. See Figure 7A.13 for the visual Earned Value Over Time Report. From this data and graph, you can make new cost projections.

FIGURE 7A.11 Earned Value Table

Task Name	Planned Value - PV (BCWS)	Earned Value - EV (BCWP)	AC (ACWP)	SV	CV	EAC	BAC	VAC
0 ▲ Consumer Market Study	$8,060.00	$8,580.00	$7,800.00	$520.00	$780.00	$36,000.00	$39,600.00	$3,600.00
1 ▲ Questionnaire	$8,060.00	$8,580.00	$7,800.00	$520.00	$780.00	$22,272.73	$24,500.00	$2,227.27
2 ▲ Design	$8,060.00	$8,580.00	$7,800.00	$520.00	$780.00	$12,181.82	$13,400.00	$1,218.18
3 Identify Target Consumers	$780.00	$780.00	$520.00	$0.00	$260.00	$520.00	$780.00	$260.00
4 Develop Draft Questionnaire	$2,600.00	$2,600.00	$2,340.00	$0.00	$260.00	$2,340.00	$2,600.00	$260.00
5 Pilot-Test Questionnaire	$4,680.00	$5,200.00	$4,940.00	$520.00	$260.00	$7,790.00	$8,200.00	$410.00
6 Review Comments & Finalize Questionnaire	$0.00	$0.00	$0.00	$0.00	$0.00	$1,300.00	$1,300.00	$0.00
7 Develop Software Test Data	$0.00	$0.00	$0.00	$0.00	$0.00	$520.00	$520.00	$0.00
8 ▲ Responses	$0.00	$0.00	$0.00	$0.00	$0.00	$11,100.00	$11,100.00	$0.00
9 Print Questionnaire	$0.00	$0.00	$0.00	$0.00	$0.00	$1,900.00	$1,900.00	$0.00
10 Prepare Mailing Labels	$0.00	$0.00	$0.00	$0.00	$0.00	$400.00	$400.00	$0.00
11 Mail Questionnaire & Get Responses	$0.00	$0.00	$0.00	$0.00	$0.00	$8,800.00	$8,800.00	$0.00
12 ▲ Report	$0.00	$0.00	$0.00	$0.00	$0.00	$15,100.00	$15,100.00	$0.00
13 ▲ Software	$0.00	$0.00	$0.00	$0.00	$0.00	$5,100.00	$5,100.00	$0.00
14 Develop Data Analysis Software	$0.00	$0.00	$0.00	$0.00	$0.00	$3,600.00	$3,600.00	$0.00
15 Test Software	$0.00	$0.00	$0.00	$0.00	$0.00	$1,500.00	$1,500.00	$0.00
16 ▲ Report	$0.00	$0.00	$0.00	$0.00	$0.00	$10,000.00	$10,000.00	$0.00
17 Input Response Data	$0.00	$0.00	$0.00	$0.00	$0.00	$2,800.00	$2,800.00	$0.00
18 Analyze Results	$0.00	$0.00	$0.00	$0.00	$0.00	$3,200.00	$3,200.00	$0.00
19 Prepare Report	$0.00	$0.00	$0.00	$0.00	$0.00	$4,000.00	$4,000.00	$0.00

FIGURE 7A.12 Visual Reports—Create Report Window

FIGURE 7A.13 Visual Earned Value Over Time Report, Displayed in Microsoft Excel

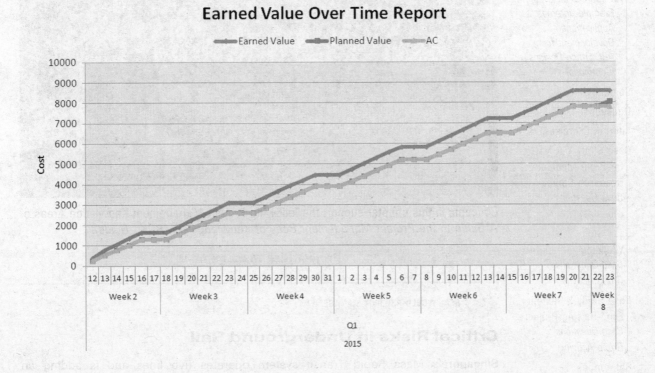

CHAPTER 8

Managing Risk

Caro/Alamy

Concepts in this chapter support the following Project Management Knowledge Areas of *A Guide to the Project Management Body of Knowledge (PMBOK® Guide)*:

Project Risk Management

 REAL WORLD PROJECT MANAGEMENT

Critical Risks in Underground Rail

Singapore's Mass Rapid Transit system operates five lines and is adding an additional three fully underground lines by 2020. Unpredictable ground conditions leading to ground settlement control issues is one of the risks the international joint ventures teams are facing. Too great a project for a single civil engineering firm, this

large-scale project garnered the collaboration of firms from a number of countries to create a multifaceted team that matches the complexity of the project and adds additional management risks.

With a limited number of Singapore-based construction firms eligible to bid on projects greater than $50 million SGD (~$40 million USD), foreign contractors were invited to collaborate with local contractors to bid on major public projects. Even though the partnerships reduced some of the potential risk associated with the lack of regional knowledge and awareness of customs, communication problems related to social and cultural misunderstandings still plague the project progress.

Risks related to differences in management styles, procurement methods, and expectations are catalysts for project failure. The detailed contracts preferred by European contractors do little to curb conflicts associated with roles and responsibilities and level of commitment by the partners. Mutual trust and verbal communications used by the Japanese contractors result in fewer conflicts, joint decision-making, and more success completing the tasks.

An outcome of earlier failed projects by international joint venture teams was the proposition of three practical risk management strategies: cooperation with government offices, proper risk allocation within the contracts, and technical risk control. Leading risks identified by the joint venture teams included accounting profit and loss disagreements, financial distress, lack of competence, overinterference by parent companies of the contractors, and work allocation disagreements.

As with all projects, the risks of the project can and most likely will change as the project progresses. A more in depth look at the project's risks revealed some risks that were not associated with the actual work being completed to construct the underground rail. Risks such as policy changes in a contractor's parent company, exchange rate fluctuations, language barriers, social and cultural customs differences, labor and equipment import restrictions, governmental cash flow issues, and technology transfer disputes all cause delays, conflict, and failure to complete tasks within the project.

These risks and those directly related to the work being completed must be managed in order for the underground rail project to be completed by its projected 2020 date. Every risk raises the probability that the underground rail will not be operational when expected. The completion of the construction of the underground rail is dependent upon managing risk.

Based on information from Zhao, X., B. Hwang, and G. S. Yu (2013). "Identifying the Critical Risks in Underground Rail International Construction Joint Ventures: Case Study of Singapore," *International Journal of Project Management, 31*(4), 554–566.

As mentioned in Chapter 1, one attribute of a project is that it involves a degree of uncertainty. Such uncertainty can impact the outcome of a project. Risk is an uncertain event that, if it occurs, can jeopardize accomplishing the project objective. **Risk management** involves identification, assessment, control, and response to project risks to minimize the likelihood of occurrence and/or potential impact of adverse events on the accomplishment of the project objective. Addressing risks proactively will increase the

chances of accomplishing the project objective. Waiting for unfavorable events to occur and then reacting to them can result in panic and costly responses. Managing risk includes taking action to prevent or minimize the likelihood of occurrence or the impact of such unfavorable events.

Some level of risk planning should be done during the initiating phase of the project life cycle to make sure, for example, that a contractor understands the risks involved with bidding on a proposed project. With knowledge of potential risks, the contractor can include contingency reserve amounts in the bid price. On the other hand, if the risks seem too great, the contractor may decide to not bid on a proposed project, as discussed in the decision to develop a proposal section in Chapter 3. Subsequently, more detailed risk planning should be done during the planning phase of a project.

A project manager cannot be risk averse. She must accept that risk is a part of project management and has to address it head-on. Furthermore, the project manager needs to set the tone for encouraging open and timely discussion of risks among the project team. You will become familiar with:

- Identifying risks and their potential impact
- Assessing the likelihood of occurrence and degree of impact of risks
- Risk response planning
- Controlling risks

LEARNING OUTCOMES

After studying this chapter, the learner should be able to:

- Discuss what is involved in managing risks
- Identify and categorize risks
- Assess and prioritize risks
- Prepare a risk response plan
- Develop a risk assessment matrix
- Control risks

Identify Risks

A **risk** is an uncertain event that, if it occurs, can jeopardize accomplishing the project objective. **Risk identification** includes determining which risks may adversely affect the project objective and what the impact of each risk might be if it occurs.

Sometimes a sponsor identifies major risks in the project charter when the project is authorized. A contractor may also identify risks in a proposal to a customer. It can show the customer that the contractor has experience and a realistic approach to performing the project and wants to avoid surprises. It is also a means of managing customer expectations.

A common approach to identifying the sources of risks is brainstorming. See the section on brainstorming in Chapter 11 for further discussion. The project manager should involve key project team members in identifying potential sources of risk—things that could happen that would negatively impact

accomplishing the project objective. Each member of the project team can bring his or her experience and insight to help develop a comprehensive list of risks. How many risks should be identified? A team can go overboard and come up with hundreds of possible risks. For example, there is a chance that every activity can take longer than estimated or cost more than estimated. Common sense and reasonableness must prevail when identifying risks. The risks should be those that are somewhat likely to occur and/or can have a significant negative impact on accomplishing the project objective.

Another approach is to establish *risk categories*, which are groupings of potential sources of risk by topic, and then identify risks that might occur for each category. Examples of risk categories along with some risks for each are:

- *Technical*
 - Failure to meet customer performance requirements
 - New application for technology
 - May not be able to meet quality standards or codes

- *Schedule*
 - Vendor delay in delivery of critical equipment

- *Cost*
 - Material costs escalate more than anticipated

- *Human resources*
 - May not have people available when required to staff the project

- *External*
 - Inclement weather
 - Changes in government regulations
 - Change in consumer preferences
 - Local protesters file legal action to delay project

- *Sponsor/customer*
 - Delays in approvals
 - Security of sponsor funding

Another source that can be helpful in identifying possible risks is historical information from past projects. If postproject evaluations (discussed in Chapter 9) are done on completed projects, they could be a good source for identifying possible risks, as well as for getting information on how to address such risks if they occur again.

Additional examples of specific risks are:

- Incorporating advanced technology in a new product
- Performance requirements for taking measurements 10 times faster than can be done currently
- Technological advances that could make the originally selected technology obsolete before the project is completed
- First-time use of new robotic equipment for a rare and complex surgical procedure

- Nonavailability of labor force of certain craftspeople when required because of a strong local economy and low unemployment rate
- Encountering more than expected rock formations when excavating
- Excessive number of revisions to a website design before it is acceptable to the customer
- Labor strike may occur during the peak of a construction project
- Severe weather (early snow) may hit during the construction phase of a facility expansion
- Bank may not approve full amount of the loan for the project
- Significant price escalation for rare fire-retardant coating material
- Patient may hemorrhage during surgery
- Sufficient vaccine may not be available to meet emergency needs
- New product may not pass certification tests
- Longer-than-anticipated delivery of key subassembly from overseas supplier
- Customer will not provide sample parts for testing when needed
- Rain on the days of a weekend community festival

For each risk that is identified, the potential impacts must be estimated. Such impacts could include schedule delays, substantial additional expenditures, the project end deliverable not meeting acceptance criteria, the lack of consumer acceptance of new product, the customer's enforcement of penalty terms in a contract, or the sponsor's termination of the contract.

It should be noted that at the beginning of the project, it may not be possible to identify all risks. This is especially true for longer-term projects, such as multiyear projects or projects that have several phases. It may be easier to identify risks associated with near-term efforts, but as the project progresses, the project team can *progressively elaborate* the identification of new risks as well as the estimated impacts of previously identified risks as more information is known or becomes clear.

Assess Risks

Risk assessment involves determining the likelihood that a risk event will occur and the degree of impact the event will have on the project objective. Each of these factors can be assigned a rating of high, medium, or low, for example, or some other rating scale (1--5, 1–10, percentages, etc.). The project manager, in consultation with appropriate team members or other experts who are most knowledgeable about the potential risk, should determine ratings for each risk. Historical data from prior similar projects can also be helpful. For example, if severe weather is a risk, historical daily weather data or consultation with a weather forecasting service may be useful.

Based on the likelihood of occurrence and degree of impact, the risks can then be *prioritized*. For example, those with a high likelihood of occurrence *and* a high degree of impact should be assigned a higher priority for more serious consideration than risks that have a low likelihood of occurrence *and* a low degree of impact.

Another factor to consider in prioritizing risks is whether a risk is related to activities that are on critical paths. If so, perhaps such risks should be given higher priority because if the risk occurs, it would have a greater impact on the schedule than if it was associated with activities on a path that has a large positive value of total slack.

Reinforce Your Learning

2. For each risk that is _____, the potential _____ must be _____.

Reinforce Your Learning

3. Risk assessment involves determining the _____ that a risk will _____ and the _____ of _____ it will have on the project _____.

Plan Risk Responses

A **risk response plan** is a defined set of actions to prevent or reduce the likelihood of occurrence or the impact of a risk, or to implement if the risk event occurs. Risk response planning involves developing an action plan to reduce the likelihood of occurrence or potential impact of each risk, establishing a trigger point for when to implement the actions to address each risk, and assigning responsibility to specific individuals for implementing each response plan.

A risk response plan can be to *avoid* the risk, *mitigate* the risk, or *accept* the risk. Avoidance means to eliminate the risk by choosing a different course of action. Examples of avoiding risk would be to decide to use conventional technology rather than advanced state-of-the-art technology in a new product, or deciding to hold a weekend festival indoors to avoid the possibility of a rainout. Mitigating the risk involves taking action to reduce the likelihood that the risk event will occur or to reduce the potential impact. For example, reducing the risk of multiple redesigns of a customer's website might require reviewing other sample designs with the client earlier in the project. Accepting a risk means dealing with it if and when it occurs, rather than taking actions to avoid or reduce the impact.

A risk response plan should include a trigger point or warning flag for when to implement the action plan for each risk. A trigger point for when to purchase a rare material may be if the current price increases more than 5 percent above the amount budgeted for purchasing the material. The trigger point for deciding to incorporate advanced technology in a new product may be the completion of an engineering feasibility study. Another example would be to authorize overtime if the project falls behind schedule by more than 5 percent of the remaining project duration.

A tool for assessing and managing risks is a **risk assessment matrix**, also referred to as a *risk register*, which includes potential risks, their potential impact, likelihood of occurrence, and response plan. Figure 8.1 shows the more significant risks and their associated information for an outdoor concert.

FIGURE 8.1 Risk Assessment Matrix

RISK	IMPACT	LIKELIHOOD OF OCCURRENCE (L, M, H)	DEGREE OF IMPACT (L, M, H)	ACTION ON TRIGGER	RESPONSIBILITY	RESPONSE PLAN
Rain on Day of Event	• Low attendance • Incur financial loss	M	H	Weather forecast two days before event	Laura	• Reserve indoor space now • Recruit extra volunteers to work around the clock to set up indoors • Develop detailed plan
Road Construction	• Reduced attendance • Reduced revenue	H	H	Highway Dept. publishes construction schedule	Allison	• Identify alternate routes • Have signs made • Post signs along all routes • Announce in news media

Control Risks

Risk control includes implementing risk response plans and monitoring risks. Risk response plans should be implemented as appropriate when their trigger point is reached. Implementing risk response plans often requires spending additional funds for additional resources, working overtime, paying for expedited shipments, purchasing additional materials, and so forth. Project prices and budgets should include a contingency reserve to pay for additional costs associated with implementing response plans.

Risk monitoring involves regularly reviewing the risk assessment matrix throughout the project. During the project, it is important to regularly review and evaluate all risks to determine if there are any changes to the likelihood of occurrence or the potential impact of any of the risks. These factors can determine if a particular risk has increased in priority for attention or if the risk has diminished in importance. Furthermore, new risks may be identified that were not considered as risks earlier in the project but now need to be added to the risk assessment matrix. For example, early tests of the prototype of a new product indicate the product may now not meet the original performance specifications. Another situation may be that because of previous delays in the design phase, the construction phase of a facility expansion is now scheduled to take place in the middle of the hurricane season. During a project, the customer may initiate changes to the project work scope, schedule, or budget that could also affect the assessment of previously defined risks or result in the identification of new risks.

Project meetings are a good forum for regularly reviewing, updating, and addressing risks. The agenda for project status review meetings should include an item regarding risk assessment. Particular attention should be given to reviewing the trigger points for each risk to determine if any risk response plans are on the verge of having to be implemented. See the section on meetings in Chapter 12 and the section on problem solving in Chapter 11 for related information.

It is also helpful to track and document which risks actually occurred and the impact of those risks. This information is an excellent source of lessons learned for managing risks on future projects.

Reinforce Your Learning

6. _____ _____ are a good forum for _____ reviewing, _____, and _____ risks.

REAL WORLD PROJECT MANAGEMENT

Wrestling with the Grand Challenges of IT

One generally doesn't think of the author Shakespeare when thinking about project management. Catherine Bessant, Bank of America's Global Technology and Operations Executive, does. Bessant says, "Shakespeare's lessons, every one of them, are timeless lessons." Her goal is to build systems that are elastic and foundationally strong yet nimble enough to last for 30 years and through the challenges of hurricanes, tsunamis, earthquakes, cyber attacks, and other risks.

To stand the test of time, every decision must manage and mitigate risks. "A key to success is using appropriate speed in decision making and execution," states Bessant. "Sticking to those strategies over time is not for the faint of heart at all. It takes guts, it takes deep understanding of both the business and IT, and it takes a bull-doggedness to say 'no, we're not going to be distracted by the feature of the day.'"

Attention to risk management and mitigation decisions is an even greater challenge when the team is more than 100,000 employees and contractors who handle all the technology and operations for the financial services giant. Technology continues to be advancing rapidly and regulatory requirements are ever changing. Bessant's team must maintain the robustness in their systems necessary to withstand every potential devastating event that puts Bank of America's customers at risk of not achieving their business objectives.

"It's very hard to get a process of prioritization or to figure out what work to take on or to have a long-term strategy," added Bessant. To have the firm function at world class levels, a priority was to unify the management team. The unification has worked to simplify processes for risk mitigation through a series of boot camps to intensely focus on creating risk management strategies. The first boot camp reduced risks and increased understanding of operational risks for the capabilities of the technology and its operations. Controls were examined process-by-process during the second boot camp to analyze the procedures for any risks. During the third boot camp, the project team identified specific issues, including business continuity and cyber security, and ways to mitigate risks.

Tests such as Hurricane Sandy, the earthquakes and tsunami in Japan, and cybersecurity attacks have shown the developed risk mitigation strategy has performed extraordinarily. A timeless characteristic of project management is risk management. Proactive risk identification, assessment, and response helps increase the probability of success. The Global Technology and Operations team of Bank of America wrestled the challenges in their risk management and mitigation plan. They reversed the negative potential effects of the challenges and escaped the serious consequences of the events and incidents, which might have caused the customers to fall. You, too, can be successful controlling risks through management and mitigation plans.

Based on information from Gallant, J. (2013). "Wrestling with the Grand Challenges of IT: Bank of America's Catherine Bessant Talks about the Advantages, and Challenges, of Being a Non-technologist Leading IT. She looks at the lessons she's learned from navigating the company's super-sized acquisitions. Bessant also talks about her team's bold plan to simplify dramatically the IT environment while reducing risk through design, aggressive training and more." *CIO, 26*(9), n/a.

Managing Risks for Information Systems Development

Risks are inherent in all aspects of an information system development project. The risks can be categorized into seven types of risks: technological risk, human risk, usability risk, project team risk, project risk, organizational risk, and strategic and political risk. These categories help to explain the risks associated with developing systems that accept data inputs, process those inputs, and produce information to be used by users. Chapters 4, 5, 6, and 7 provided foundation information about the definition, scheduling, resources, and costs associated with information systems development projects.

Recall from Chapter 6 that the five basic types of resources used in an information system development project are people, hardware, software, data, and network resources. Technological risk is a critical project risk factor for the hardware and software used in the project. Complexities associated with integration, functionality, and compatibility impact the success of an information system

development project, as do processing speed and system security. The technology risks require resources and are directly related to the human, usability, organizational, and strategic and political risks for the project.

The project team and the project have risks associated with the implementation of project management skills in addition to the information system knowledge and skills necessary to complete the project. Improvements in technology capabilities pose problems. A decision to incorporate the latest technology may lead to a lack of integration of the hardware or software into the organization's systems. The new technology advancements may have project scope creep and the potential to cause changes in project requirements that are not well managed.

Having categories to guide the brainstorming sessions for the project team to list potential risks is helpful. Keep the list of project risks within the lessons learned to also help with the brainstorming of the list. Use experience and historical evidence to assess the risks in the categories to rate and prioritize those that are most likely to occur and will have the greatest impact, especially for those on the critical path of the information system development project.

AN INFORMATION SYSTEM EXAMPLE: INTERNET APPLICATIONS DEVELOPMENT FOR ABC OFFICE DESIGNS (CONTINUED)

Recall from Chapters 4 through 7 that Beth Smith of ABC Office Designs is the project manager for the development of a Web-based reporting system project. Beth and the project team have planned for a $125,000 project that is to be completed in 60 days. The project team members with primary responsibility have assured Beth that the project could be completed with the current resources and schedule. Beth wants to prepare for potential risks for the project so that the team can take care of them early and not impact the delivery date for the system. The sales staff members are already holding the training dates in their schedules. If the project is delayed, these times would be missed opportunities for the sales staff and the company.

Beth held a project update meeting. In her agenda, she included time to discuss possible risks. For each risk, she planned for the team to determine the impact of the risk, the likelihood of occurrence, the degree of impact if it does occur, the action trigger that will serve as a warning flag for the risk, who is responsible for the risk, and the response plan to avoid, mitigate, or accept the risk. Together, the project team and Beth created the risk assessment matrix. Figure 8.2 is their first draft of the risk assessment matrix.

The team discussed that these risks would change as the project progressed. With only 60 days to complete the project, Beth and the team knew that they had several tasks with slack in the project. Beth did identify that she could assign resources from tasks with slack to those tasks on the critical path if she had to fast-track the critical path tasks to finish on time. The increased costs would be covered by the contingency reserve funds to support the effort, if necessary.

Beth reviewed the lessons learned from other projects again to make sure that the project team discussed the risks from the other projects at the next team project update meeting. Learning the lessons from the successes and failures of other projects is one of Beth's goals as the project manager. Beth sees no need to repeat any earlier mistakes; those are risks that Beth has decided the team can avoid.

FIGURE 8.2 Risk Assessment Matrix for Web-based Reporting System Project

RISK	IMPACT	LIKELIHOOD OF OCCURRENCE (L, M, H)	DEGREE OF IMPACT (L, M, H)	ACTION ON TRIGGER	RESPONSIBILITY	RESPONSE PLAN
Lack of cooperation and commitment from users	Incorrect sales records in reporting system	M	H	Sales staff have difficulty using system during training	Jim	Have additional training materials to describe how to use
High number of ad hoc queries	Systems design not completed on time	L	H	More queries to be answered than time remaining to complete	Jeff	Have assigned staff work longer on tasks; staff have at least seven days of slack
Testing reveals design problems	Rework the design and development	M	H	Evaluation reveals problems	Cathy	Examine for design flaws during Evaluation task
Customized software has integration problem	System not working and no information recorded	L	H	Study of existing system identifies potential problems	Steve	Develop system with compatible programming, possibly not latest technology
Changes in membership of the project team	Lack of proper skills and knowledge to do task	L	M	Resignation statement by staff member	Beth	Assign another project team member to learn task during notice period

CRITICAL SUCCESS FACTORS

- Identify risks and their potential impacts before the project starts.
- Involve the project team or experts in assessing risks.
- Assign high priority to managing risks that have a high likelihood of occurrence and a high potential impact on the project outcome.
- Develop response plans for addressing high-priority risks.

SUMMARY

Risk is an uncertain event that, if it occurs, can jeopardize accomplishing the project objective. Risk management involves identification, assessment, control, and response to project risks to minimize the likelihood of occurrence and/or potential impact of adverse events on the accomplishment of the project objective. Risk identification includes determining which risks may adversely affect the project objective and estimating what the potential impacts of each risk might be if they occur. Assessing each risk involves determining the likelihood that the risk event will occur and the degree of impact the event will have on the project objective,

and then prioritizing the risks. A risk response plan is a defined set of actions to prevent or reduce the likelihood of occurrence or the impact of a risk, or to implement if the risk event occurs. Risk response planning involves developing an action plan to reduce the likelihood of occurrence or potential impact of each risk, establishing a trigger point for when to implement the actions to address each risk, and assigning responsibility to specific individuals for implementing each response plan. During the project, it is important to regularly review and evaluate all risks to determine if there are any changes to the likelihood of occurrence or the potential impact of any of the risks; also, new risks may be identified that were not considered to be risks earlier in the project. Project meetings are a good forum in which to review, update, and address risks.

QUESTIONS

1. Describe what needs to be done to manage risk on a project. When should this be done? How can a risk assessment matrix help in this process?
2. From your experience working on projects, list and categorize three risks. Was the response plan for those projects adequate to mitigate these risks? How would you respond to these risks now?
3. What risks for a project have the highest priority? Does the priority for a risk change as the project progresses?
4. How does project risk change as a project progresses? What changes are made to the risk assessment matrix as the changes occur?

INTERNET EXERCISES

For the website addresses of the organizations mentioned in these exercises, go to "Internet Exercises" at the book's companion website at www.cengagebrain.com. It is suggested that you save this website in your "Favorites" list for easy access in the future.

1. Search the Web for "project risk management" and describe at least three sites that you find.
2. For exercises 2 through 5, visit the website for the Software Program Managers Network (SPMN). Why was the SPMN established, and what is its mission?
3. Click on the "16 Critical Software Practices" link. Briefly describe those 16 factors. Identify the factors that you think are relevant to all types of projects, not just software projects.
4. Click on the "Lessons Learned" section. Explore several of the links. Explore the links related to risk management and describe what you discover.
5. Click on the "Web Links" button. Explore and describe at least three of these links.

CASE STUDY 1 A Not-for-Profit Medical Research Center

This case study is a continuation of the case study from Chapters 4 through 7.

CASE QUESTIONS
1. Identify at least four risks that could jeopardize the project.
2. Create a risk assessment matrix including a response plan for each of the risks.

GROUP ACTIVITY
Divide the course participants into the same groups as for the previous chapter's group activity and answer the questions listed above.

Congratulations on completing this case study! If you developed the work breakdown structure, network diagram, schedule, bar chart, resource plan, and budget table and graph manually using pencil and paper, it was probably tedious, prone to errors, frustrating, and time consuming. Application software, such as Microsoft Project, Word, and Excel, can automate many of these tasks and allow you to use your time more effectively to analyze the project schedule and cost performance and manage the project successfully.

CASE STUDY 2 The Wedding

This case study is a continuation of the case study from Chapters 4 through 7.

CASE QUESTIONS
1. Identify at least four risks that could jeopardize the wedding.
2. Create a risk assessment matrix including a response plan for each of the risks.

GROUP ACTIVITY
Divide the course participants into the same groups as for the previous chapter's group activity and answer the questions listed above.

Congratulations on completing this case study! If you developed the work breakdown structure, network diagram, schedule, bar chart, resource plan, and budget table and graph manually using pencil and paper, it was probably tedious, prone to errors, frustrating, and time consuming. Application software, such as Microsoft Project, Word, and Excel can automate many of these tasks and allow you to use your time more effectively to analyze the project schedule and cost performance and manage the project successfully.

CASE STUDY 3 Student Fund-Raising Project

In September at its initial meeting of the academic year, the Council of Fraternities and Sororities (CFS) at Mount Clement University decided to organize a project to raise funds to help upgrade the pediatric intensive care unit at the local hospital. The CFS consists of representatives from each of the 24 fraternities and sororities. There were 15 representatives at the meeting.

Although the council members who were at the meeting expressed enthusiasm for such an endeavor, they also raised some concerns, including:

- What kind of project should we do?
- When would be the best time of the year to do it?
- Do we have a goal for how much money we should try to raise?
- How should we assign responsibilities to all the fraternities and sororities?
- What about the council members who are not at the meeting? What if they do not support the idea?

- Are we going to need any money at the beginning to get things going and pay for things like advertising and other necessities?
- Do we need any kind of approvals?

Hannah said, "This is getting complicated. There are a lot of questions and unknowns."

Marcus added, "What if we don't raise a lot of money? That will be embarrassing, especially if we have to do a lot of work."

Teresa responded, "Sure it may be a lot of work, but we have a lot of people in our fraternities and sororities who we can get to help."

Cathy said, "Maybe we should try to identify what the risks may be, then see if we still think we can do it?"

Meghan said, "I'm not going to stand on corners with a can collecting money."

Wendy added, "Me either, but there are a lot of other things we can do to raise money that could be fun for all the students."

"Maybe even get the community to come, too. That will help us raise more money than just from students," added Sophie.

Suli spoke up, "I'm willing to chair a planning committee. Who else wants to be on it? We'll meet here tomorrow at 5:00. I'll send an e-mail to the CFS members who aren't here, inviting them to come. We are going big time and are going to raise a lot of money. Hey, there are risks in anything we do, but they'll work out. We have got to have a can-do attitude."

CASE QUESTIONS
1. What would you recommend for the next possible steps?
2. Identify three potential projects to raise funds for the hospital pediatric intensive care unit.
3. Select one of the three projects and identify four risks that could jeopardize the success of the project.
4. Develop a response plan for how each of the four risks can be either avoided or mitigated.

GROUP ACTIVITY
Divide the course participants into teams of three or four. Have them:

- Brainstorm a list of eight possible projects to raise funds for the hospital.
- Agree on one of the eight projects.
- For the selected project, identify six risks that could jeopardize the success of the project.
- Develop a response plan for how each of the six risks can be either avoided or mitigated.

Have each team select a spokesperson to present their responses to the entire class.

REFERENCES

A Guide to the Project Management Body of Knowledge (PMBOK® Guide) Fifth Edition. Newtown Square, PA: Project Management Institute, 2013.

Andruszkiewicz, G., M. Davis, and S. Lleo (2013). "Taming Animal Spirits: Risk Management with Behavioural Factors," *Annals of Finance*, 9(2), 145–166.

Anonymous (2012). "Augmenting Public Private Partnership (PPP) in Infrastructure Projects Through Project Management and Accountable Governance in India," *NBM & CW*. Retrieved from: http://search.proquest.com/docview/1031184305?accountid=13158.

Chronopoulos, M., B. De Reyck, and A. Siddiqui (2013). "The Value of Capacity Sizing Under Risk Aversion and Operational Flexibility," *IEEE Transactions on Engineering Management, 60*(2), 272–288.

Donkor, E. A. and M. Duffey (2013). "Optimal Capital Structure and Financial Risk of Project Finance Investments: A Simulation Optimization Model with Chance Constraints," *Engineering Economist, 58*(1), 19–34.

El-adaway, I. H. (2013). "Promoting the Sustainability of Relational Contracting through Addressing Third Party Insurance Obstacles," *Journal of Management in Engineering, 29*(3), 216–223.

Gallant, J. (2013). "Wrestling with the Grand Challenges of IT: Bank of America's Catherine Bessant Talks about the Advantages, and Challenges, of Being a Non-technologist Leading IT. She looks at the lessons she's learned from navigating the company's super-sized acquisitions. Bessant also talks about her team's bold plan to simplify dramatically the IT environment while reducing risk through design, aggressive training and more." *CIO, 26*(9), n/a.

Goh, C. S., H. Abdul-Rahman, and Z. Abdul Samad (2013). "Applying Risk Management Workshop for a Public Construction Project: Case Study," *Journal of Construction Engineering & Management, 139*(5), 572–580.

Hwang, B., X. Zhao, and L. P. Toh (2013). "Risk Management in Small Construction Projects in Singapore: Status, Barriers and Impact," *International Journal of Project Management*, http://dx.doi.org/10.1016/j.ijproman.2013.01.007.

Joshi, C. S. and P. G. Dangwal (2012). "Management of Business Process Reengineering Projects: A Case Study," *Journal of Project, Program, & Portfolio Management, 3*(1), 78–89.

Kuo, Y. and S. Lu (2013). "Using Fuzzy Multiple Criteria Decision Making Approach to Enhance Risk Assessment for Metropolitan Construction Projects," *International Journal of Project Management, 31*(4), 602–614.

Lee, C. K. M., Y. Lv, and Z. Hong (2013). "Risk Modelling and Assessment for Distributed Manufacturing System," *International Journal of Production Research, 51*(9), 2652–2666.

Smith, K. J. (2013). "Collaboration Enables Operational and Cultural Change on a Shoestring," *Public Manager, 42*(2), 40–42.

Taroun, A. (2013). "Towards a Better Modelling and Assessment of Construction Risk: Insights from a Literature Review," *International Journal of Project Management*, http://dx.doi.org/10.1016/j.ijproman.2013.03.004.

Teller, J. and A. Kock (2013). "An Empirical Investigation on How Portfolio Risk Management Influences Project Portfolio Success," *International Journal of Project Management, 31*(6), 817.

Vizcaíno, A., F. García, J. C. Villar, M. Piattini, and J. Portillo (2013). "Applying Q-Methodology to Analyse the Success Factors in GSD," *Information and Software Technology, 55*(7), 1200.

Zhao, X., B. Hwang, and G. S. Yu (2013). "Identifying the Critical Risks in Underground Rail International Construction Joint Ventures: Case Study of Singapore," *International Journal of Project Management, 31*(4), 554–566.

CHAPTER 9

Closing the Project

© Eastimages/Shutterstock.com

Concepts in this chapter support the following Project Management Knowledge Areas of *A Guide to the Project Management Body of Knowledge (PMBOK® Guide)*:

Project Integration Management

REAL WORLD PROJECT MANAGEMENT

Lessons Learned in the Bird's Nest

The 29th Olympic Games opened on August 8, 2008, in the National Stadium in Beijing, China. A capacity-crowd of 100,000 attendees took their places in the Bird's Nest to witness the opening of the games. Over the course of the games, track and field events, the final game of the football (soccer) events, and the closing ceremonies brought hundreds of thousands to the National Stadium to experience the construction marvel.

By hosting of the Olympic Games, a host country has an opportunity to raise the awareness of their country's attributes and to positively strengthen the attitudes held about their country around the world. The design of the Bird's Nest was meant to showcase China's construction abilities, infrastructure development, and economic success. The initial design included a retractable roof to permit indoor events after the Olympic Games were completed, 2,000 parking spaces, and commercial areas within the stadium.

The innovative project to design and build the stadium in a bird's nest style began in October 2002, nearly six years before the lighting of the Olympic flame at the start of the games. Seven companies applied for prequalification and five were accepted. Bids were received and opened on June 30, 2003. Concession agreements were signed and the project company was established by September 2003. An aggressive construction schedule was planned to have a completed building by December 31, 2006.

But later on, changes to the design eliminated the retractable roof, slashed the number of parking spaces in half to 1,000 spaces, and reduced the number of commercial areas within the arena. The result was a significant reduction in the sources of revenue for the project company. Even though each of these changes led to waste of funding, resources, manpower, and time, the elimination of the 1,700-ton retractable roof led to increased safety for the operation of the stadium and savings of another 2,000 tons of high quality expensive steel that would have been part of the supporting structure.

Evaluation of the project and its prospects for use after the Olympic Games have presented many valuable lessons for cities seeking to host future games.

The first lesson was that government support and commitment to a project are essential when opting for innovative and complex designs. Colossal edifices such as the Bird's Nest should never be ventured without government support because of their lack of financial viability after their primary use. Temporary seating in the Bird's Nest was removed to have a 91,000-person seating capacity for other sporting events. Between 3,000 and 10,000 visitors have attended football (soccer) games. Team sponsors consider the attendance figures to be embarrassingly small fractions of the Bird's Nest's capacity.

The second lesson learned was that strategic planning and community interests must be part of the planning for short-term national esteem projects associated with hosting of Olympic Games or other international contests. A clearly defined project scope should be included within the project company's shareholder agreements and

contracts for the design, construction, and insurance. Shareholders are stakeholders in the project and their involvement could reduce future disagreements and disputes during the execution of the project.

Project aims and objectives for the entire life cycle of the project should focus on high efficiency, international safety standards, cost containment, and project completion. This third lesson reinforced the comprehensive nature of projects and how stakeholder concerns for any one aspect and lack of concern for others threaten the integrity and viability of the entire project.

The fourth lesson learned pertained to alignment of public and private sector interests, especially as the interest alignment impacted risk management. Development of an attraction that has no future benefit to the community or one that puts community members at risk during construction is a source of poor rapport between business developers and community members. A potential future use of the Bird's Nest is its conversion into a shopping center. The lack of a roof limited its use to a traditional open air stadium rather than outdoor exhibitions or indoor events such as sporting games, cultural shows, or musicals.

The National Stadium demonstrated to the world the innovative design and construction capabilities of China and provided some very important lessons. Redesign delays of six months caused an already tight schedule to be even more severe. Hopefully, the lessons learned in Beijing will provide guidance to other cities developing showcase facility projects for large international events.

Based on information from Chinyere, I. (2013). "Comprehensive Objectives for PPP Projects: Case of Beijing Olympic Stadium," *International Journal of Business & Management, 8*(9), 88–110.

After the project work is completed and all the deliverables are accepted by the customer, the performing phase of the project is ended. The project then moves into the fourth and final phase of the project life cycle—closing the project. This chapter discusses the various activities involved in the process of closing the project. You will become familiar with

- Actions that should be taken when closing a project
- Conducting a postproject evaluation
- The importance of documenting lessons learned
- The need to organize and archive project documents
- Obtaining feedback from the customer about the project
- Early termination of projects

LEARNING OUTCOMES

After studying this chapter, the learner should be able to:

- Identify actions that should be taken during the process of closing a project
- Conduct a postproject evaluation
- Discuss the value and use of lessons learned
- Explain the importance of organizing and archiving project documents
- Obtain customer feedback about the project
- Describe situations that could result in early project termination

Project Closing Actions

The fourth and final phase of the project life cycle is closing the project, as shown in Figure 9.1. It starts after the project work has been completed and the sponsor or customer has accepted the project deliverables. When a project team or contractor completes a project for a customer, they must verify that all the agreed-upon deliverables were, in fact, provided. Such deliverables might include training or procedure manuals, drawings, flowcharts, equipment, a building, software, brochures, a conference, reports, videos, or data. In some situations, this might be a somewhat formal event in which an automated system satisfies a set of acceptance criteria or passes tests that were stated in the contract. Other projects, such as a weekend of homecoming activities at a university, are completed merely with the passage of time.

The process of closing the project involves various actions, including:

- Collecting and making final payments
- Recognizing and evaluating staff
- Conducting a postproject evaluation
- Documenting lessons learned
- Organizing and archiving project documents

The activities associated with closing the project should be identified and included in the project baseline plan—they should not be done merely as spontaneous afterthoughts.

FINAL PAYMENTS

An activity that must be performed during the closing phase is assuring that all payments have been collected from the customer. Many contracts include a progress payment clause, which states that the customer will make the final

FIGURE 9.1 Project Life Cycle

payment at the completion of the project. In some cases, the final payment is a high percentage (for example, 25 percent) of the total project price. Likewise, it should be verified that all payments have been made to any subcontractors, consultants, vendors, or suppliers for any purchased materials or services. Once all payments have been received and made, the project "books," or accounting records, can be closed, and a financial analysis of the project can be made in which final actual costs are compared to the project baseline budget.

STAFF RECOGNITION AND EVALUATION

Reinforce Your Learning

2. Successful projects should end with some type of

and

_____ .

An important project closing action is staff recognition and evaluation. Successful projects should end with some type of recognition and celebration. This can range from an informal pizza party after work to a more formal event, with speakers from the customer's organization and awards or certificates of recognition for project participants.

During the closing phase of the project, the project manager should prepare a written performance evaluation of each member of the project team that mentions how each has expanded her or his knowledge as a result of the project assignment and identifies areas she or he needs to develop further. If a project team member does not report directly to the project manager within the company's organizational structure, the project manager should provide a copy of the performance evaluation to the person's immediate supervisor.

POSTPROJECT EVALUATION

Another significant activity during the closing phase is conducting postproject evaluation meetings within the project team or organization that performed the project. The purpose of such meetings is to review and evaluate performance of the project and to identify what can be done to improve performance on future projects.

There should be two types of meetings: individual meetings with team members and a group meeting with the project team. They should be held as soon as possible after the completion of the project, and they should be announced in advance so that people can be prepared.

The project manager should have an individual meeting with each of the team members. These meetings allow team members to give their personal impressions of performance of the project and what can be done better on future projects. Such individual meetings allow people to speak openly, without the constraints of a group meeting. For example, they can mention any problems in working relationships with other team members. Of course, the project manager must assure team members that any such disclosures will be kept confidential. Once the individual meetings with team members are complete, the project manager can identify common issues brought up in those meetings. With this information, the project manager can then develop an agenda for a group meeting with the entire project team.

Reinforce Your Learning

3. What are the two types of internal postproject evaluation meetings the project manager should have?

At the group meeting with the project team, the project manager should lead a discussion of what happened during performance of the project and solicit specific recommendations for improvement. A sample agenda for such a *postproject evaluation team meeting* is shown in Figure 9.2.

Following are some topics that might be discussed under each of the agenda items:

1. *Technical performance.* How did the final scope of the work compare to the scope of the work at the start of the project? Were there many changes to the work scope? Were the changes handled properly in terms of documentation, approvals, and communication? What impact did the changes have on project

FIGURE 9.2 Postproject Evaluation Team Meeting Agenda

POSTPROJECT EVALUATION
Team Meeting

Agenda

1. Technical performance
 - Work scope
 - Quality
 - Managing changes

2. Budget performance

3. Schedule performance

4. Project planning and control

5. Risk management

6. Customer relationships

7. Stakeholder engagement

8. Team relationships

9. Communications

10. Problem identification and resolution

11. Lessons learned

12. Recommendations for future projects

budget and schedule? Was the work scope totally completed? Were the project work and deliverables completed in a quality manner, and did they meet the expectations of the customer?

2. *Budget performance.* How did the final project actual costs compare with the original project baseline budget and with the final project budget, which included any changes in project scope? If there was a fixed-price contract, was it profitable, or did the project organization lose money? If there was a cost-reimbursement contract, was the project completed within the customer's budget? Were there any particular work packages that overran or underran their budgets by more than 10 percent? If so, why? What were the causes of any cost overruns? Were the estimated activity costs realistic?

3. *Schedule performance.* How did the actual project schedule compare with the original schedule? If the project was late, what were the causes? How was performance on the schedule associated with each work package? Were the estimated activity durations realistic?

4. *Project planning and control.* Was the project planned in sufficient detail? Were the plans updated in a timely manner to incorporate changes? Was actual performance compared with planned performance on a regular basis?

Were data on actual performance accurate and collected in a timely manner? Was the planning and control system used on a regular basis by the project team? Was it used for decision making?

5. *Risk management.* Was the project outcome impacted by the occurrence of any unexpected events? If so, were they identified in the risk plan? Were the high-probability and high-impact risks adequately identified at the beginning of the project? Were there any risks that should have been, but were not, identified at the beginning of the project? What risks were identified during the project that were not identified at the beginning, and why were they not identified at the beginning? For identified risks that occurred, were the response plans adequate? Were there unexpected events that occurred for which there were no response plans?

6. *Customer relationships.* Was every effort made to make the customer a participant in the success of the project? Was the customer asked on a regular basis about the level of satisfaction with the performance and progress of the project? Were there regularly scheduled face-to-face meetings with the customer? Was the customer informed of potential problems in a timely manner and asked to participate in the problem-solving process?

7. *Stakeholder engagement.* Were all key stakeholders identified early? Were the roles and expectations of each stakeholder clear and unambiguous? Were good working relationships developed with each stakeholder? Was there regular communication with all stakeholders? Were stakeholder input, involvement, and discussions welcome? Were stakeholders' concerns addressed early, positively, and in a timely manner?

8. *Team relationships.* Did the team participate in planning the project? Was there a "team" feeling and a commitment to the success of the project? Were there any conditions that impeded teamwork?

9. *Communications.* Was the team kept informed of the project status and potential problems in a timely manner? Was the project environment conducive to open, honest, and timely communications? Were project meetings productive? Were written communications within the team and with the customer sufficient, insufficient, or overburdening?

10. *Problem identification and resolution.* Were mechanisms in place for team members to identify potential problems early? Did appropriate team members participate in problem solving? Was problem solving done in a thorough, rational manner?

11. *Lessons learned.* What worked and what did not? What particular things were done well on the project that helped the project and should be done on other projects? What things were done that hindered the project and should be eliminated or changed on future projects? If there would be an opportunity to start over and do this project again, what should be done differently?

12. *Recommendations.* Based on the team's discussion and evaluation of the above items, what specific recommendations can be made to help improve performance on future projects?

After the evaluation meetings, the project manager should prepare a written report of project performance including lessons learned and recommendations. Project organizations must be proactive and timely in communicating such postproject reports, excluding any confidential information, to key people in the project organization and ensure that the reports are taken into consideration by project managers and teams on future projects.

LESSONS LEARNED

The purpose of identifying and documenting lessons learned is to capitalize on the knowledge and experience gained on the project to improve performance on future projects. The project organization should establish a knowledge base system that includes an easily accessible repository that encourages project managers and teams to retrieve lessons learned and information from previous projects. The system should organize information so that it is easily retrievable by category or subject of lesson learned or by key words.

The project team should not wait until the end of the project to capture and document lessons learned; it should be done on an ongoing basis throughout the planning and performing phases of the project. This can also help to improve performance during the remainder of performing the project. A system should be established to capture these learning moments and to maintain a list of lessons learned during performance of the project. With such a system, some items will not be forgotten. Otherwise, if the project was for a long duration—for example, several years—some key people involved in situations that might have provided good lessons learned early in the project may no longer be associated with the project when the project moves into the closing phase, and therefore might not be available to share their experience.

Information regarding lessons learned and associated recommendations from internal postproject evaluation meetings and from feedback from the customer or sponsor should also be incorporated into the organization's lessons learned knowledge base.

An important consideration regarding lessons learned is to ensure that they are documented, communicated, and used by project managers and teams on future projects. One way to do this might be to require it to be an agenda item at the initial kickoff meeting for a new project. Lessons learned can also be a good topic for any internal project management training that is conducted by the project organization.

ARCHIVE PROJECT DOCUMENTS

During project closing, the project team or contractor should ensure that copies of appropriate project documentation are properly organized, filed, and archived so that they can be readily retrieved for future use. For example, the contractor may want to use some of the actual cost and schedule information from a completed project to help develop the schedule and estimated costs for a proposed project. Or, if the project involved, say, staging a community festival, the project team should organize all its documentation—including suggestions for improving aspects of the festival—for use by the project team that will plan and organize the festival the following year.

Some organizations have a standard checklist or index of items to ensure all important project documents and records are retained, including technical, financial, approvals, contracts, reports, and so forth. Most documents can probably be saved in electronic format, but in some cases hard copies may be required. For safety and security purposes, it is also a good practice to retain a backup copy of all documents in a separate archive.

As part of, or in addition to, the documents in the archive, it can be valuable to create a database of common data elements from past projects to analyze and determine if there are trends or correlations that could be helpful in bidding, planning, and/or performing future projects. Such analyses might show a tendency to

Reinforce Your Learning

4. The purpose of identifying and documenting

is to capitalize on the

and

gained on the project to

on

projects.

Reinforce Your Learning

5. The project team should

wait until the

of the project to capture and

Reinforce Your Learning

6. During project closing, copies of project

should be properly

_____,

_____,

and

underestimate costs for certain types of activities or materials, for example, or underestimate durations for certain categories of activities.

Customer Feedback

Just as important as having the internal postproject meetings within the project organization is having a postproject evaluation meeting with the customer or sponsor. The purposes of this meeting should be to determine whether the project provided the customer with the expected benefits, assess the level of customer satisfaction, and obtain any feedback that would be helpful in future business relationships with this customer or with other customers. Meeting participants should include the project manager, key project team members, and key representatives of the customer's organization who were involved with the project. The project manager should schedule the meeting for a time when the customer is in a position to really determine whether the project met expectations and achieved the anticipated benefits. In the case of a project to develop an eight-page color brochure for a customer, a meeting can be held shortly after the final printed brochure is given to the customer, because the customer will know immediately whether the brochure met expectations. However, in the case of a project that supplied a customer with a specialized automated assembly machine expected to reduce the product defect rate from 10 percent to 2 percent, it could be several months after the machine is installed before the customer can verify whether the defect rate was reduced. This time may be needed for the operators to learn how to operate the equipment properly or for the company to verify a reduction in returned merchandise. If a project to develop a new product had an objective to achieve a sales volume of 2,000,000 units within 12 months after the launch of the new product, the sponsor may not know whether the project of developing and launching the new product achieved its expected benefit until 12 months after the product was launched.

Ideally, the contractor or project team should sit down with the customer or sponsor and ask open-ended questions, and then *listen* with an open mind. This provides an opportunity for customers not only to express their level of satisfaction but also to provide detailed comments about the parts of the project with which they were satisfied or dissatisfied. These comments will not come as a surprise if the project manager has been continually monitoring the level of customer satisfaction throughout the project and communicating regularly with the customer.

If the customer provides comments that are critical of the contractor's or project team's performance, the project manager or team should not attempt to argue or debate with the customer. Doing so may inhibit the customer from honestly expressing their true feelings during the rest of the meeting; and some valuable feedback may be lost. On the other hand, if the customer is satisfied with the project, the contractor or project team is presented with several opportunities.

First, the contractor should ask the customer about any other projects the contractor could do—perhaps without going through a competitive RFP (request for proposal) process. If the customer is satisfied with a brochure, for instance, the contractor should ask if any other brochures, annual reports, or marketing materials are needed. Likewise, if the customer is satisfied with an automated assembly machine, the contractor should ask whether other parts of the

manufacturing process need to be studied for additional productivity improvements.

Second, the contractor should ask permission to use the customer as a reference with potential customers. The contractor may even want to feature the customer in a brochure or on a website, maybe with a picture and a quote or a video stating how satisfied the customer was with the contractor's performance. Another way to capitalize on the success of a project is for the contractor to write a news article about the project in collaboration with the customer and issue it as a press release to the appropriate news media.

Another method of getting feedback from the customer regarding satisfaction with the results of the project is through a postproject customer evaluation survey, as shown in Figure 9.3. The project manager provides this survey form to the sponsor or customer and, possibly, other project stakeholders to complete and return. For large projects, several individuals in the customer's organization may contribute to formulating the responses. After receiving the completed evaluation survey back from the customer, the project manager may then want to schedule a follow-up meeting with the customer to obtain more detailed feedback. Having a system to organize and retain such customer evaluation and feedback information could be very valuable if the contractor or project organization might develop proposals for other projects for the same customer in the future.

When there are multiple customers or end users of the results of a project, it may be difficult to get feedback from them. For example, after a volunteer group organizes a week-long community festival, how does it get feedback from the people who attended about their level of satisfaction and their suggestions for improving next year's event? Or consider a project in which a new software product was developed. The immediate sponsor is the company's product manager, but the true end customers are the people who eventually purchase the software. The product manager may be satisfied with the resultant product, but how does the project team determine whether the end users are satisfied? In both of these cases—the community festival and the new software product—the project team may use some type of survey or focus group to obtain feedback from the end users.

Early Project Termination

There may be circumstances that require a project to be terminated before it is completed. For example, suppose a company is working on a research and development project with an advanced material that has certain properties at extremely low temperatures. After some development work and testing, it is determined that further development of the material could cost much more and take far longer than originally thought. If the company determines that the probability is low that further expenditures on the project will yield a successful outcome, then the project will be stopped, even though the company may have several million dollars invested in it. Another circumstance that can cause a project to be terminated early is a change in a company's financial situation, such as if a company's revenues or sales are shrinking, or if the company is acquired by another company.

Projects also can be terminated by the sponsor or customer because of dissatisfaction. For example, if the buyers of a house are not satisfied with the quality of the contractor's work or are frustrated with schedule delays, they may terminate the agreement with the contractor and hire another contractor to finish the

FIGURE 9.3 Postproject Customer Evaluation Survey

Postproject Customer Evaluation Survey

Please complete this brief survey to help us evaluate and improve our project management performance. If more space is needed for responses, please attach additional pages.

Project Title: _____

	Degree of Satisfaction
	Low 1 2 3 4 5 6 7 8 9 10 High

1. Completeness of Work Scope 1 2 3 4 5 6 7 8 9 10
 Comments _____

2. Quality of Work 1 2 3 4 5 6 7 8 9 10
 Comments _____

3. Schedule Performance 1 2 3 4 5 6 7 8 9 10
 Comments _____

4. Budget Performance 1 2 3 4 5 6 7 8 9 10
 Comments _____

5. Communications 1 2 3 4 5 6 7 8 9 10
 Comments _____

6. Customer Relations 1 2 3 4 5 6 7 8 9 10
 Comments _____

7. Overall Performance 1 2 3 4 5 6 7 8 9 10
 Comments _____

What **benefits** did you _____ actually realize or _____ anticipate as a result of this project?

A. Quantitative Benefits

B. Qualitative Benefits

Suggestions on how we can improve our performance on future projects:

Name: _____ Date: _____

project. Similarly, if the government is funding the design and production of new military aircraft and project costs begin to significantly overrun the budget, the government may terminate the contract.

Having a project terminated early by a customer that is not satisfied can really hurt a contractor's business. The contractor may incur a financial loss because of early termination and may have to lay off some of the employees who were working on the project. More important, the contractor's reputation may be damaged. There will likely be no future business from a customer who was not satisfied, and a tarnished reputation could make it difficult for the contractor to obtain business from other customers. One way to avoid early termination of a project due to customer dissatisfaction is to monitor the level of customer satisfaction continually throughout the project and take corrective action at the first hint of any dissatisfaction.

 REAL WORLD PROJECT MANAGEMENT

Lessons Learned Help CSP Department Operate

Operating rooms rely on sterile processing and distribution departments to sterilize and maintain a broad range of complex instruments. Used instruments are brought into one area of the sterilization department and cleaned in another. The Sanford Medical Center in Sioux Falls, South Dakota, was facing the challenge of sterilizing and packaging instruments in a timely manner for their surgical procedures. The facility was so small that only sterilization could occur in the central sterile processing (CSP) department. The operating room staff had to process and package their own instruments after sterilization. With the construction of a new medical tower, the medical center needed to expand and redesign its CSP department.

The new CSP facility had 17,000 square feet, more than three times its size before the expansion. Unlike the small facility, the staff of the new CSP department was tasked to perform all the instrument processing. The members of the CSP department worked with the vendors to create a project plan for the design of the new department that did not include the operating room staff processing and packaging instruments. To help with the cultural change, the project plan included tasks to change the expectations of the operating room staff. "At first, the operating room staff had trouble believing that we could do the job," commented Gail Doyle, CSPDM, CRCST, and manager of the CS/SPD.

The vendor supplied Sanford Medical Center staff and management with computer-aided design (CAD) drawings and 3-D images to provide a preview of the process and technology improvements. Steve Dillon, vice president of surgical instruments for Integrated Medical Systems International, Inc. stated, "Vendors can play a tremendous role in these renovations. They have insight of working with several, sometime hundreds of other facilities facing the same challenges. They can advise in areas such as shelving design and needs, equipment needs, and department layout infrastructure challenges."

The project plan incorporated best practices, optimized workflows, and the appropriate mix of equipment to meet the current and future needs. The medical center

staff worked closely with the vendor and the architect to complete a survey of the needs of the medical center CSP. The project team answered questions related to the number of surgical suites in operation and planned for the future, the number of procedures performed during peak periods, what clinical services were associated with the procedures, and what instruments were in inventory and what were needed to meet the future needs.

The plans included lessons learned from other CSP redesign projects. Suggested best practices for the final design included adequate storage of contaminated equipment that did not impede on the washing areas, large sinks with sufficient depth and width for the instruments, pressurized air and water to help remove difficult debris, flat surfaces for preparation, storage areas for cleaning supplies and brushes, separate air and water supplies for the contaminated equipment and sterilization areas, washable rubber floor mats to protect dropped instruments, and space for sonic cleaning technology.

To further help with the speed and efficiency of the CSP, Sanford Medical Center implemented an instrument tracking system. The technology kept track of what instrument types should be part of a surgical set, tracked the instruments through processing, logged sterilization records, and tracked the instruments' real time location. The technology helped to better manage their assets and implement proactive maintenance programs.

The Sanford Medical Center CSP team used their knowledge of the processes and design of their small unit and the experiences of other sterile processing departments to create a project to meet their current and future needs. At the close of their expansion project, Sanford Medical Center staff shared their lessons learned with other CSP planning teams to help in their design projects.

Based on information from Della Vecchia, K. (2013). "SPDs Share Renovation Best Practices and Lessons Learned." *Healthcare Purchasing News, 37*(6), 50–57.

CRITICAL SUCCESS FACTORS

- Recognize the project team and celebrate accomplishments throughout the project.
- Regularly ask the customer about the level of satisfaction with the performance and progress of the project and take corrective action at the first hint that the customer is not satisfied.
- After the conclusion of a project, the project performance should be evaluated to learn what could be improved if a similar project were to be done in the future. Feedback should be obtained from the customer and the project team.
- Capture and document lessons learned throughout the performance of the project.
- Establish a knowledge base of lessons learned and ensure that they are communicated and used on future projects.
- Organize and archive project documentation and analyze key data that could be helpful in bidding, planning, or performing future projects.
- Retain customer evaluation and feedback information that could be valuable in developing proposals for other projects for the same customer in the future.

SUMMARY

After the project work is completed and all the deliverables are accepted by the customer, the performing phase of the project is ended. The project then moves into the fourth and final phase of the project life cycle—closing the project. The process of closing the project involves various actions, including collecting and making final payments, recognizing and evaluating staff, conducting a postproject evaluation, documenting lessons learned, and organizing and archiving project documents.

An important project closing action is staff recognition and evaluation. Successful projects should end with some type of recognition and celebration. During the closing phase of the project, the project manager should prepare a written performance evaluation of each member of the project team.

Another significant activity during the closing phase is conducting postproject evaluation meetings within the project team or organization that performed the project. The purpose of such meetings is to review and evaluate performance of the project and to identify what can be done to improve performance on future projects. There should be two types of meetings: individual meetings with team members and a group meeting with the project team. Project organizations must be proactive and timely in communicating such postproject reports to key people in the project organization and ensure that the reports are taken into consideration by project managers and teams on future projects.

The purpose of identifying and documenting lessons learned is to capitalize on the knowledge and experience gained on the project to improve performance on future projects. The project organization should establish a knowledge base system that includes an easily accessible repository that encourages project managers and teams to retrieve lessons learned and information from previous projects.

During project closing, the project team or contractor should ensure that copies of appropriate project documentation are properly organized, filed, and archived so that they can be readily retrieved for future use.

A postproject evaluation meeting should be held with the customer or sponsor to determine whether the project provided the customer with the expected benefits, assess the level of customer satisfaction, and obtain any feedback that would be helpful in future business relationships with this customer or with other customers. Another method of getting feedback from the customer regarding satisfaction with the results of the project is through a postproject customer evaluation survey.

Projects may be terminated before completion for various reasons. They may be terminated by the customer because of dissatisfaction. This can result in a financial loss and damage the reputation of the contractor or organization performing the project. One way to avoid early termination due to customer dissatisfaction is to monitor the level of customer satisfaction continually throughout the project and take corrective action at the first hint that the customer is not satisfied.

QUESTIONS

1. Discuss what needs to be done as part of closing a project. Why are these activities important?
2. Discuss the internal postproject evaluation process and the two types of meetings involved.

3. What are some ways you can obtain feedback from a customer after a project has been completed? How would you use this information?
4. Why are some projects terminated before they are completed? When would it be wise to do so?
5. List several lessons learned from a project in which you were a project team member or project manager. How will these lessons learned inform your future projects?

INTERNET EXERCISES

For the website addresses of the organizations mentioned in these exercises, go to "Internet Exercises" at the book's companion website at www.cengagebrain.com. It is suggested that you save this website in your "Favorites" list for easy access in the future.

1. Search the Web for a project that was completed successfully. Write a three-page summary of the project, including the critical factors that made this project a success. Search the Web for a project that was not completed successfully. Write a three-page summary of the project, including the reasons why you think this project failed.
2. Search the Web for "project lessons learned." Record how lessons learned were used to inform projects. How does this compare to what was discussed in this chapter?
3. Search the Web for "postproject evaluations." Try to find a write-up of a project that was completed. Evaluate the strengths and weaknesses of the postproject review.
4. Search the Web for "project management standards." Provide a list of the standards that you find. Describe three that you feel are the most important.
5. Search the Web and your library for project management journals. Provide a list of these journals and some of their recent articles. If possible, request a free sample from one or more of these journals.

CASE STUDY 1 Factory Expansion Project

Jacob Clemson is the owner of Digitsig, Inc., a growing Canadian electronics company. The company has been receiving orders from customers worldwide, and sales have been expanding rapidly. The factory is now working three shifts and is at capacity. Jacob had to lease additional space in a building several miles away. He knows he must expand his factory to keep up with growing demand, to increase efficiency, and to reduce the costs associated with trucking materials and product back and forth between his factory and the building he is leasing. The cost of the lease was very high because there just was not much good available space in the area and Jacob was desperate to get additional space right away, or he would not be able to keep up with demand and customers would go to his competitors.

Jacob met Andy Gibson, part-owner of AG Contractors, at a recent business networking event. He told Andy about his expansion needs. Andy said, "We can do that for you, Mr. Clemson. We've done many similar projects. As you may know, business is booming in the region, and getting a contractor won't be

easy. But it could be lucky we met because we are just finishing up another project and could probably get working on yours if we can get an agreement soon. I've got four other proposals pending, and if they come in, we won't be able to handle any other projects. And like I said, I understand all the other contractors are just as busy. It sounds like you really need to start on this factory expansion right away, and I think we can help you out."

Jacob became worried that he might not be able to get another contractor, and he did not want to waste any more time. So he signed a contract with AG Contractors, for what he thought was a reasonable price, to design and build the expansion to his factory. The expansion space would be used primarily for inventory storage of incoming materials and finished goods. He agreed to a bonus clause in the contract to pay AG Contractors a 10 percent bonus if it completed the building in 12 months rather than the 15 months Andy told him it would normally take.

It is now 14 months later. Andy Gibson and Gerri Penk, a recently hired project manager for AG Contractors, walked into Jacob Clemson's office. The receptionist asked, "May I help you?"

Andy asked, "Is Jacob in?"

"Yes, he is. Do you have an appointment?" responded the receptionist. Andy hurried by the receptionist, saying, "I don't need one. This will only take a minute." A surprised Gerri followed after him. He knocked on Mr. Clemson's door once, opened it, and walked in without waiting for a response.

Astonished, Jacob Clemson looked up and said, "I'm right in the middle of this important"

Andy interrupted. "This will only take a minute. I just wanted to say that we got your factory expansion project completed on time and within budget. We finished in 12 months, just like I knew we, I mean, like I hoped we would. I had to kick butt with some of our subcontractors, but that's the way it goes in this business. Sometimes you've got to be an SOB to get the job done. I'm sure you're the same way, Jacob, or you wouldn't be where you're at."

Jacob Clemson spoke up. "Well, there were some problems"

But Andy interrupted again. "In a big project like this, there are always problems, and some people's feathers get ruffled. But that always happens. Don't be concerned about that. In the end, it all worked out. I thought maybe we could go to lunch to celebrate, but we have another meeting across town. Give me a call sometime, and maybe we can get together and see if I can help you with any other projects you might have." Andy then turned and quickly left Jacob's office, walking right past Gerri, who ran to catch up with him.

After they left, Jacob was somewhat stunned and became furious. He thought to himself, "Another project? Over my dead body. An SOB? What kind of person does he think I am? Getting the project done on time and within budget—does he think that is all that it's about? This project was a nightmare. It finished up costing about 50 percent more than AG's original price because of all the changes they came back with. They never asked, never listened, never told me what was going on, and never returned my phone calls. What a bunch of jerks! I'll never do business with them again."

As Andy and Gerri walked to Andy's car, he told Gerri, "There you go, another satisfied AG customer. And a pretty naive one too," Andy chuckled. "I knew we could get the project done in 12 months. But I knew he was desperate, and I told him it would take 15 months, and then got him to agree to a bonus payment if we got it done in 12 months."

Gerri asked, "Andy, isn't that unethical?"

"Hey, business is booming for Digitsig; they have plenty of money. Besides, it's his problem for waiting so long before deciding on doing the expansion anyway. He was lucky we helped him out of a bind. But I've got to tell you, Gerri, I wondered why he was building all that warehouse space for inventory when most other businesses are going to just-in-time deliveries. But I wasn't about to tell him that. It's amazing he's in business at all. Oh, well, you'll find out it's a dog-eat-dog world out there, Gerri."

Gerri responded, "Andy, I got a sense that maybe Mr. Clemson wasn't totally satisfied. I mean he really didn't say he was."

"He didn't say he wasn't either," snapped Andy. "Besides, he never seemed interested in the project, he never asked to have any meetings, and when I tried to schedule a meeting, he was too busy. And then his payments were always late—like he was anal or something. Believe me, he's tickled with what AG did. He was desperate to get the project done, and we did it for him—on time and within budget. And made a bunch of money on the project. So we both came out winners."

"In fact, I'll use old Jacob as a reference with the new customer we'll be meeting this afternoon to review their RFP. Customers always ask for references from previous projects, but quite frankly, they hardly ever call them."

"Hey, Gerri, you'll learn that you've got to focus on the next customer and not worry about the old ones. It works, believe me, or I wouldn't be driving this Porsche. Maybe they didn't teach you that in MBA school, Gerri, but I learned from the school of hard knocks when I took this business over from my father. He was well liked in the community, and I'm just following in his footsteps."

CASE QUESTIONS
1. What should Andy Gibson have done differently in his meeting with Jacob Clemson in Jacob's office?
2. What are some things Andy could have done differently in his initial contact with Jacob and during the project?
3. What are some things Jacob could have done differently from the time he met Andy Gibson initially and during the project?
4. What should Gerri do?

GROUP ACTIVITY
Divide the course participants into groups of three or four to develop responses to the case questions. Each group must choose a spokesperson to present its responses to the entire class.

CASE STUDY 2 Market Research Report Project

Meghan has been a project manager for more than 10 years for Effective Market Research. The president of the company, Allison, is very pleased with Meghan's careful attention to detail on every project. The portfolio of projects for Effective Market Research has more than tripled since Meghan was hired as the project manager.

Meghan's project team is composed of eight members, each with a specialty for market research. In addition to doing excellent market research, the team's

customer comments on the project evaluations usually have included a statement specifically related to how well informed they were during the course of the project. Meghan is very careful about the communication plan for each project. She gathers information from the client and makes sure the client is satisfied with the project at each project update meeting.

Christine, a director for the Upper Region Workforce Development Group, was at a meeting and saw a copy of one of the reports for market research completed by Meghan's team. Funding was available for Christine to contract with a group to do market research in her region. Several proposals that Christine wanted to write to get funding for workforce development required the same type of information that was in the market research report.

Christine contacted the sales department for Effective Market Research to inquire about purchasing a market research report for her region. The sales department confirmed a face-to-face meeting time for Allison and Meghan to meet with Christine to discuss the project requirements.

At the meeting, Christine described her information needs. Meghan listened carefully and crafted a list of project deliverables. At the conclusion of the meeting, Allison and Meghan developed a project proposal and sent the document to Christine for her review and authorization. The Effective Market Research finance team worked with the Upper Region Workforce Development Group finance group to secure a fixed-price contract for the work.

Meghan and her team attended the first meeting with Christine and Christine's new project manager, Sarah. At the meeting, Christine stated, "My duties at Upper Region have increased, and I am putting Sarah in charge of the market research project. Sarah is the contact person for you and should receive all the communications. I just don't have time to deal with this project now." Meghan updated the communication plan to have all communications with Sarah for the remaining scheduled project time.

Three weeks before the final report was due, Meghan sent a copy of the draft report to Sarah to review. Three days later, Meghan received a note that said, "Meghan, the report looks great! Christine and I talked about having a few more of the pictures from the region that you took included in the report and having a short two-page summary document that we could share with the region commissioners and local supervisors. I think that is all that they will review."

Meghan updated the project schedule and set a meeting with Sam, the graphic specialist on the team, for the next day. "Sam, I received feedback from Upper Region to include more of the images into the report. What do you think is best?" The two-page summary was already being completed as one of the project deliverables. It was not part of the three-week prior review documents.

"In the file, there are seven graphics that we haven't used in the report. We can include them as a collage on the cover and put each one on the page that shows the data for the type of work being performed in the image. The report is being distributed electronically according to the project communication plan, so the additional graphics will not raise the production costs," suggested Sam. Meghan and Sam agreed on the technique.

Meghan sent Sarah the two-page summary and the new report for the final approval. Sarah confirmed that all was good to go. The final report was sent to Sarah for distribution within the Upper Region Workforce Development Group more than a week before the due date. The finance team for Effective Market Research sent the final invoice for the last 25 percent of the project costs.

Meghan sent the project evaluation form to Sarah and met with her project team members.

Two days later, Meghan received the following e-mail, "Meghan, I did not approve this report, and it cannot be distributed. I see all kinds of problems in the report that must be corrected before the report is OK." The e-mail was from Christine.

Meghan was very careful to follow the directions of Christine and had approval from Sarah for the final report. Meghan sent a note, "Christine, Please let me know the problems that are in the report so that we can make corrections." Meghan was a bit concerned that Christine had responded in such a manner when the communication from Sarah had suggested that Christine had approved the report. Sarah was supposed to be Meghan's contact.

CASE QUESTIONS

1. Did Meghan's team satisfy the customer? Why or why not?
2. How should Meghan respond to the comments from Christine after Sarah had given feedback and approval for the final report?
3. The project team had gone through the steps of closing this project. They have one week of slack in the schedule before they would be causing another project to be delayed. What should Meghan do with her team?
4. What should Meghan have done differently in the project?

GROUP ACTIVITY

Divide the course participants into groups of three or four to develop responses to the case questions. Each group must choose a spokesperson to present its responses to the entire class.

REFERENCES

A Guide to the Project Management Body of Knowledge (PMBOK® Guide) Fifth Edition. Newtown Square, PA: Project Management Institute, 2013.

Adegoke, Y. (2013). "Questions Answered," *Billboard*, *125*(27), 14.

Al-Nammari, F. (2013). "Participatory Urban Upgrading and Power: Lessons Learnt from a Pilot Project in Jordan," *Habitat International*, *39*, 224–231.

Braun, T., A. I. Ferreira, and J. Sydow (2013). "Citizenship Behavior and Effectiveness in Temporary Organizations," *International Journal of Project Management*, *31*(6), 862.

Carrillo, P., K. Ruikar, and P. Fuller (2013). "When Will We Learn? Improving Lessons Learned Practice in Construction," *International Journal of Project Management*, *31*(4), 567–578.

Chinyere, I. (2013). "Comprehensive Objectives for PPP Projects: Case of Beijing Olympic Stadium," *International Journal of Business & Management*, *8*(9), 88–110.

Della Vecchia, K. (2013). "SPDs Share Renovation Best Practices and Lessons Learned," *Healthcare Purchasing News*, *37*(6), 50–57.

Doelle, M., N. Bankes, and L. Porta (2013). "Using Strategic Environmental Assessments to Guide Oil and Gas Exploration Decisions: Applying Lessons Learned from Atlantic Canada to the Beaufort Sea," *Review of European Community & International Environmental Law*, *22*(1), 103–116.

Donaldson, R. and D. Du Plessis (2013). "The Urban Renewal Programme as an Area-Based Approach to Renew Townships: The Experience from Khayelitsha's Central Business District, Cape Town," *Habitat International, 39*, 295–301.

Gharaibeh, H. M. (2013). "Managing the Cost of Power Transmission Projects: Lessons Learned," *Journal of Construction Engineering & Management, 139*(8), 1063–1067.

Gillis, C. (2013). "Waterlogged," *Maclean's, 126*(28), 1.

Heerkens, G. (2012). "Longer-Lasting Measures," *PM Network, 26*(10), 75.

Jyh-Bin, Y., C. Mei-Yi, and K. Huang (2013). "An Empirical Study of Schedule Delay Causes Based on Taiwan's Litigation Cases," *Project Management Journal, 44*(3), 21–31.

Lewis, K. (2013). "Four Lessons Learned Building a Data Warehouse in the Real World," *Business Intelligence Journal, 18*, 1.

Mathur, S. (2013). "Use of Land Pooling and Reconstitution for Urban Development: Experiences from Gujarat, India," *Habitat International, 38*, 199–206.

Miguel, P. (2013). "Benchmarking QFD Application for Developing Packaging Products: A Comparison Between a Company in Italy and One in Brazil," *Benchmarking: An International Journal, 20*(3), 419–433.

Mora-Soto, A., M. Sanchez-Segura, A. Ruiz-Robles, and F. Medina-Dominguez (2012). "Organizational Knowledge Management to Increase Productivity," *European Conference on Knowledge Management, 792-XXVII*. Kidmore End: Academic Conferences International Limited.

Osipova, E. and P. Eriksson (2013). "Balancing Control and Flexibility in Joint Risk Management: Lessons Learned from Two Construction Projects," *International Journal of Project Management, 31*(3), 391–399.

Shiferaw, A. and O. Klakegg (2013). "Project Evaluation: Accomplishments, Shortfalls, and Lessons Learned in Housing Development Projects in Ethiopia," *Journal of Management in Engineering, 29*(3), 289–301.

Williams, P. (2013). "A Job Like Mine," *E.Learning Age, April 2013*, 23.

PART 3

People: The Key to Project Success

Concepts in the chapters in this part of the book support the following Project Management Knowledge Areas of *A Guide to the Project Management Body of Knowledge (PMBOK® Guide)*:

Project Integration Management (Chapters 10, 12, and 13)

Project Human Resource Management (Chapters 10, 11, 12, and 13)

Project Communications Management (Chapter 12)

Project Stakeholder Management (Chapters 10 and 12)

The chapters in Part 3 focus on the importance of the people involved in a project. It is the people, not the procedures and techniques, who are critical to accomplishing the project objective. Procedures and techniques are merely tools that help people do their jobs.

The project manager provides leadership to the project team—leadership in planning, organizing, and controlling the work effort to accomplish the project objective. The ultimate responsibility of the project manager is to make sure that the customer is satisfied that the work scope is completed in a quality manner, within budget, and on time. The project manager must possess the skills needed to inspire the project team to succeed and to win the confidence of the customer.

The project team is a group of individuals working interdependently to accomplish the project objective. Teamwork is the cooperative effort by members of the project team to accomplish this common goal. The effectiveness of the project team can make the difference between project success and project failure. Although plans and project management techniques are necessary, it is the people—the project manager and the project team—who are the key to project success.

To ensure the success of projects, various structures are used to organize people to work on projects. Regardless of how the project team is organized, though, communication between the project team and the customer and other stakeholders, within the project team, and between the project team and its upper management is critical to success.

Chapter **10**

The Project Manager

Discusses the responsibilities of the project manager, the skills needed to manage projects successfully, how to develop project manager competence, and managing changes.

Chapter **11**

The Project Team

Covers the formation and development of teams, characteristics of effective project teams and effective team members, team building, valuing team diversity, ethical behavior, conflict resolution, problem solving, and time management.

Chapter **12**

Project Communication and Documentation

Discusses the importance of effective verbal and written communication, effective listening, project meetings, presentations and reports, tracking changes to project documents, as well as a project communication plan and collaborative communication.

Chapter **13**

Project Management Organizational Structures

Explains the various configurations in which people can be organized to work on projects.

CHAPTER 10

The Project Manager

Andrea Matone/Alamy

Concepts in this chapter support the following Project Management Knowledge Areas of *A Guide to the Project Management Body of Knowledge (PMBOK® Guide)*:

Project Integration Management
Project Human Resource Management
Project Stakeholder Management

Mind Your Business

Organizational planning and decision making by project managers is more than choosing between which team member should be assigned a task or implementing a change that will impact the project's progress. Planning and decisions include understanding what drives business objectives and how the marketing, finance, operations, and other functions of an organization impact how a project meets the organization's long-term objectives and strategic plans.

In addition to the project's budget, schedule, and scope, awareness of the strategic side of organizations—a fourth dimension to project management—must be considered by project managers as they develop their business acumen. Mark Rogers, director, Xafinity, Manchester, England, advises project managers that "building business acumen is a never-ending process that should allow you to challenge whether the objectives provided are actually sensible, or whether something else would be better to deliver what the business needs."

Shilpa Eguvanti, PMP, assistant project manager, ValueNotes, a research and analytics firm in Pune, India, commented, "Business acumen represents overall strategy that helps employees learn how their organization generates revenues and what key role they play in it. It is about awareness of what drives business objectives and plays an instrumental role in bridging the communication gap between project managers and executives." Having well-informed business acumen helps increase the confidence and credibility project managers exhibit when communicating with upper management.

A project manager's development of business acumen extends to learning about the clients' business objectives. "Every day is a test, and it's very important for us to understand the business acumen of the client so we can align the project to provide the necessary recommendations to help their business stay ahead of the competition. We have to continually talk in terminology the clients use to negate any communication gap," stated Eguvanti.

To gain valuable insight about a company, project managers could review public documents, listen to shareholder reports, or pay attention to competitors to spot successes and failures. President of Roeder Consulting, Cleveland, Ohio, USA, Tres Roeder, PMP, suggested to project managers, "You can learn a lot by hearing the CEO and CFO explain business performance to analysts and by paying attention to the types of questions analysts ask. This helps in understanding the key issues the executive leadership team is facing and how your project is going to address those issues."

Project managers serve as the glue between the individuals involved in a project and the members of an organization's many departments. Informal discussions with customers, one-on-one meetings with executives and team leaders, and water-cooler conversations with coworkers help to develop an increased understanding of what

really matters to an organization. The development of relationships and increased communication help a project manager more easily describe how their projects deliver value to an organization.

Minding the business helps the project manager to avoid inadvertently making a decision that could negatively impact a project's success in meeting the needs of the organization.

Based on information from Fretty, P. (2012). "Mind Your Business," *PM Network, 26*(8), 50–54.

It is the people, not the procedures and techniques, who are critical to accomplishing the project objective. Procedures and techniques are merely tools that help people do their jobs. For example, an artist needs to have paint, canvas, and brushes to paint a portrait, but it is the skills and knowledge of the artist that allow a portrait to be created with these tools. So, too, in project management are the skills and knowledge of the people involved vital for producing the desired result. This chapter focuses on one very important person: the project manager. You will become familiar with

- The responsibilities of the project manager
- The skills needed to successfully manage projects and ways to develop project manager competence
- Approaches to effective delegation
- How the project manager can manage and control changes to the project

LEARNING OUTCOMES

After studying this chapter, the learner should be able to:

- Discuss three responsibilities of a project manager
- Identify, explain, and practice at least five skills and abilities a project manager should have
- Describe and take actions to develop project manager competence
- Discuss and practice effective delegation
- Explain how to manage changes

Project Manager Responsibilities

It is the responsibility of the project manager to make sure that the customer is satisfied that the work scope is completed in a quality manner, within budget, and on time. The project manager has primary responsibility for providing leadership in planning, organizing, and controlling the work effort to accomplish the project objective. In other words, *the project manager provides leadership to the project team to accomplish the project objective.* If the project team were an athletic team, the project manager would be the coach; if it were an orchestra, the project manager would be the conductor. The project manager coordinates the activities of the various team members

to ensure that the right people perform the right tasks at the right time, as a cohesive group.

PLANNING

First, the project manager clearly defines the project objective and reaches agreement with the customer on this objective. The manager then communicates this objective to the project team in such a manner as to create a vision of what will constitute successful accomplishment of the objective. The project manager spearheads development of a plan to achieve the project objective. By involving the project team in developing this plan, the project manager ensures a more comprehensive plan than he or she could develop alone. Furthermore, such participation gains the commitment of the team to accomplish the plan. The project manager reviews the plan with the customer to gain endorsement and then sets up a project management information system—either manual or computerized—for comparing actual progress to planned progress. It is important that this system be explained to the project team so that the team can use it properly to manage the project.

ORGANIZING

Organizing involves securing the appropriate resources to perform the work. First, the project manager must decide which tasks should be performed by internal staff and which tasks should be outsourced to subcontractors or consultants. For tasks that will be carried out internally, the project manager gains a commitment from the specific people who will work on the project. For tasks that will be performed by subcontractors, the project manager clearly defines the work scope and deliverables and negotiates a contract with each subcontractor. He also assigns responsibility and delegates authority to specific individuals or subcontractors for the various tasks, with the understanding that they will be accountable for the accomplishment of their tasks within the assigned budget and schedule. For large projects involving many individuals, the project manager may designate leaders for specific work packages or groups of tasks. Finally, and most important, the task of organizing involves creating an environment in which the individuals are highly motivated to work together as a project team.

CONTROLLING

To control the project, the project manager implements a project management information system designed to track actual progress and compare it with planned progress. Such a system helps the manager distinguish between busyness and accomplishment. Project team members monitor the progress of their assigned tasks and regularly provide data on actual progress, schedule, costs, and earned value of the work performed. These data are supplemented by regular project review meetings. If actual progress falls behind planned progress or unexpected events occur, the project manager takes immediate action. She or he obtains input and advice from team members regarding appropriate corrective action and how to replan those parts of the project. It is important that problems, and even potential problems, be identified early and corrective action taken. The project manager cannot take a "let's wait and see how things work out" approach—things never work out on their

own. The project manager must intervene and be proactive, resolving problems before they become worse.

The project manager plays the leadership role in planning, organizing, and controlling the project but does not try to do it alone. She or he involves the project team in these functions to gain the members' commitment to successful completion of the project.

Reinforce Your Learning

4. The project manager has primary responsibility for providing leadership for what three management functions?

Project Manager Skills

The project manager is a key ingredient in the success of a project. In addition to providing leadership in planning, organizing, and controlling the project, the project manager should possess a set of skills and abilities that will both inspire the project team to succeed and win the confidence of the customer. Effective project managers have strong leadership ability, the ability to develop people, excellent communication skills, good interpersonal skills, the ability to handle stress, problem-solving skills, negotiating skills, and time management skills.

LEADERSHIP ABILITY

Leadership is getting things done through others; the project manager achieves results through the project team. Project leadership involves inspiring the people assigned to the project to work as a team to implement the plan and accomplish the project objective successfully. The project manager needs to create for the team a vision of the result and expected benefits of the project. For example, the project manager may describe a new layout for a plant that will be the result of a project and articulate the benefits of this project, such as the elimination of bottlenecks, increased throughput, and reduced inventory. When project team members can envision the results, they will be more motivated to work as a team to complete the project successfully.

Effective project management requires a participative and consultative leadership style, in which the project manager provides guidance and coaching to the project team. This style is preferred over a hierarchical, autocratic, and directive management approach. Leadership requires that the project manager provide *direction*, not *directions*. He establishes the parameters and guidelines for what needs to be done, and the project team members determine how to get it done. The effective manager does not tell people how to do their jobs.

Project leadership requires involvement and empowerment of the project team. Individuals want to have ownership and control of their own work. They want to show that they can accomplish goals and meet challenges. The project manager should involve individuals in decisions affecting them and should empower them to make decisions within their assigned areas of responsibility. Creating a project culture that empowers the project team means not only assigning responsibility for tasks to team members but also delegating the authority to make decisions regarding the accomplishment of those tasks. Team members will embrace the responsibility for planning their work, deciding how to accomplish their tasks, controlling the progress of their work, and solving problems that may impede progress. They will accept accountability for performing their work scope within budget and on schedule.

Reinforce Your Learning

5. Project leadership involves _____ the people assigned to the project to work as a team to implement the _____ and accomplish the _____ successfully.

Reinforce Your Learning

6. Project leadership requires _____ and _____ of the project team.

In empowering individuals to make decisions affecting their work, the project manager should establish clear guidelines and, if appropriate, any limits. For example, team members may be authorized to implement their own remedy for solving a problem as long as the decision does not result in overrunning the budget or schedule; otherwise, consultation with a team leader or the project manager may be required. Likewise, when a decision by an individual or group of individuals within the team could have a negative impact on the work, budget, or schedule of other team members, consultation with the project manager would be required. For example, suppose one team member wants to hold up ordering certain materials until he confirms particular test results, but doing so will cause the work of other team members to fall behind schedule. In this instance, the project manager might want to involve all appropriate team members in a problem-solving meeting.

The capable project manager understands what motivates team members and creates a supportive environment in which individuals work as part of a high-performing team and are energized to excel. The manager can create such an environment by encouraging participation and involvement by all members of the project team. Techniques include facilitating project meetings to draw all individuals into the discussions, soliciting an individual's ideas when meeting separately with that person, and having various team members participate in presentations to the customer or the project organization's upper management. The project manager shows that she values the contributions of each team member by seeking advice and suggestions and should make an extra effort to involve team members who may be less outspoken. By example, the project manager encourages team members to seek advice from one another. In addition to allowing each member to tap into the knowledge and expertise of other team members, this approach creates a sense of support and mutual respect within the team for the unique expertise each person brings to the team.

The project manager must be careful not to create situations that cause individuals to become discouraged. When expectations are unclear, discouragement is likely to result. Consider the following example. On Monday, the project manager tells Gayle to get a specific task done as soon as possible. Then, on Friday, he asks her whether the task is done yet. When Gayle says she will not have it done until next Friday, he looks annoyed and says, "I really needed it done by today!" If he had a specific deadline, he should have communicated it to Gayle at the start.

Another way of discouraging a project team is to subject members to unnecessary procedures, such as the weekly preparation of written status reports that basically duplicate what is verbalized at the weekly project meetings. Unproductive team meetings can also decrease motivation.

The under-utilization of individuals creates another problematic situation. Assigning people to work that is well below their level of competence and not challenging will decrease their motivation. Even more detrimental is "overmanaging" people by telling them how to do their work. Such an approach will cause individuals to think that the project manager does not trust them; it will create a feeling of "If you're going to tell me how to do my job, why don't you just do it yourself!" So, effective project managers not only do things that establish a supportive environment, but also are careful not to do things that can have the opposite effect.

Reinforce Your Learning

7. The capable project manager understands what

team members and creates a

environment in which individuals work as part of a high-performing team.

The project manager can foster motivation through recognition of the project team as a whole and of individual members. Always give credit to people for their ideas, special efforts, and accomplishments. This should be done throughout the project, not just at the end of the project. People want to feel that they are contributing to the project and need to be recognized. Recognition can take many forms—it need not be monetary. It can come in the form of verbal encouragement, praise, a sign of appreciation, or rewards. Such positive reinforcement helps stimulate desired behavior; behavior that is recognized or rewarded is repeated. A project team might be recognized for completing a major task under budget and ahead of schedule or for identifying an innovative way to accelerate the project schedule. Such recognition will encourage the team to try to repeat such feats in the future.

One way the project manager provides recognition is by exhibiting a genuine interest in the work of each person on the project team. This can be accomplished by focusing full and undivided attention on individuals when they are explaining their work and then asking them questions about the work. A brief concluding comment such as "thank you," "good job," or "sounds great" will show the person that her or his contributions are recognized and appreciated. Showing appreciation and complimenting individuals will motivate them to be more engaged in contributing to the success of the project. Other forms of recognition include a phone call to express appreciation for an extraordinary effort; a congratulatory or "thanks for the nice job" email; some publicity, such as an article or photograph in the company newsletter; a presentation of a certificate or plaque; or assigning the person a more responsible position on the project team.

Recognition should be carried out as soon as possible after the contribution is made. If too much time elapses between the good deed and the recognition, there will be little impact on future performance. In fact, the individual may feel that the project manager is not interested in the contribution that he or she made. When possible, recognition activities should involve other people in addition to the person being recognized. Individuals appreciate being acknowledged in front of their peers. The project manager, for example, might make a positive comment about the team or specific individuals during a project meeting or in front of the customer or the project organization's upper management. The project manager should try to make the recognition event fun, perhaps by presenting the person with some type of novelty award or taking the person to lunch. The effective project manager never monopolizes the spotlight or tries to take credit for the work of others.

The project manager sets the tone for the project team by establishing an environment of trust, high expectations, and enjoyment. To foster an atmosphere of trust, the project manager lives up to his word and follows through on commitments. By doing so, the project manager sets an example, demonstrating that follow-through is expected of everyone on the project team. If the project manager fails to follow up on any suggestions, questions, or concerns, he will lose credibility. In cases where things cannot or do not work out as intended or expected, the project manager needs to provide an explanation so that his or her credibility is not damaged.

Capable project managers have high expectations of themselves and of each person on the project team. They believe that people tend to live up to what is expected of them. If the project manager shows confidence in the team members and has high expectations for their performance, team members will usually rise

to the occasion and deliver. Project managers tend to be optimistic that, at times, even apparently insurmountable obstacles to accomplishing the project can be overcome. If the project manager does not balance her or his high expectations and optimism with reality, however, the project team can become frustrated. Examples of unrealistic expectations include committing to an overly ambitious schedule for completing a complicated task or expecting a newly developed sophisticated software product to work right the first time without any glitches. A project manager who is perceived as foolhardy or reckless will not win the confidence of the project team or the customer.

Projects should be fun. Project managers should enjoy their work and encourage the same positive attitude on the part of the project team members. Most people working on projects look for affiliation and socialization; they do not want to work in isolation. The project team needs to go through socialization before it can function effectively as a high-performing team. The project manager can facilitate this socialization process by creating a sense of camaraderie among team members. One technique is to initiate periodic social gatherings, such as lunches or pizza parties for the project team; organizing events that include team members' families, such as picnics, hikes, bike rides, or going to a sports event or concert; or organizing a group of volunteers to help with a community event to support a specific cause or charity. Another technique is to try to place all the project team members in one office location, if feasible. Having an open office environment, rather than having everyone behind a closed door, will further foster socialization by making it easier for people to interact. Finally, the project manager should look for opportunities to celebrate successes, especially early in the project. As early milestones are achieved, the project manager might bring donuts to a team meeting or order boxed lunches for everyone at the conclusion of a staff meeting. Such activities create a forum for socialization, informal chatter, and team building, and they make the job enjoyable. Who said work should not be fun!

The project manager can influence the behavior of the team to accomplish the project objective. Leadership requires that the project manager be highly motivated and set a positive example for the project team—in other words, practice what she preaches. If a project manager expects people to stay late to finish up work to keep the project on schedule, she has to be there, too; the manager cannot leave early. Everything the project manager does and says sets an example for the team in terms of expected behavior. A project manager must maintain a positive attitude—no negative comments, no whining, no bad-mouthing or blaming, and no derogatory remarks—and make it clear that such behavior is not acceptable while working on the team. Effective project managers have a "can do" attitude— a desire to overcome obstacles and achieve. They thrive on challenges and getting things done. They focus on ways to get the job done rather than on reasons why it cannot be done. A good project manager is not deterred by barriers or excuses, and has self-confidence and exhibits confidence in the project team members.

It is said …

There are those who make things happen,
those who let things happen, and
those who wonder what happened.

The project manager leads by making things happen!

Reinforce Your Learning

11. People working on projects look for

and

_____ ;

they do not want to work in

_____ .

Reinforce Your Learning

12. Leadership requires that the project manager be highly

and set a

for the project team.

ABILITY TO DEVELOP PEOPLE

The effective project manager has a commitment to the training and development of people working on the project. She or he uses the project as an opportunity to add value to each person's experience base so that all members of the project team are more knowledgeable and competent at the end of the project than when they started it. The project manager should establish an environment where people can learn from the tasks they perform and the situations they experience or observe, and he or she must communicate to the team the importance of continuous self-development activities. One way of encouraging such activities is to talk about the importance of self-development at project team meetings. Another way is to meet with project team members individually at the start of their project assignments and encourage them to take advantage of their assignments to expand their knowledge and skills. A good project manager believes that all individuals are valuable to the organization and that they can make greater contributions through continuous learning. He or she stresses the value of self-improvement by encouraging individuals to take the initiative—for example, to ask for new or challenging assignments or to participate in seminars. A project presents many opportunities for people to expand their technical knowledge as well as further develop skills in communication, problem solving, leadership, negotiating, and time management.

A capable project manager provides opportunities for learning and development by encouraging individuals to assume the initiative, take risks, and make decisions. Rather than create a fear of failure, the manager acknowledges that mistakes are part of the learning and growth experience. The project manager can try to provide "stretch" assignments that require individual team members to extend their knowledge and accomplish more than they may think they can. For instance, a design task that involves the use of optics technology for sensors may be assigned to an engineer who has only limited familiarity with optics technology. This will require the engineer to learn more about optics, making her more valuable to the organization on future projects.

Another thing the project manager can do is identify situations in which less experienced people can learn from more experienced people. For example, a person who has been compiling test data may be assigned to work with an analyst in order to learn how to analyze and interpret the data. In such situations, the project manager should tell the experienced people that part of their job on the project is to mentor, coach, and teach the less experienced people.

A final way in which the project manager can develop people is by having them attend formal training sessions. For example, if an individual on the project team has no experience in making presentations or has poor presentation skills, the project manager might have that person attend a seminar on how to make effective presentations. The individual might then be given opportunities to apply what he has learned by making presentations at team meetings. The project manager might even provide coaching to help him improve to the point where he can make an effective presentation to the customer.

During discussions with individual team members, the project manager should ask, "What have you learned from working on the project?" Each response will help the manager determine what further development activities or learning opportunities are needed. Asking such questions also sends the message that the project manager values and expects continuous self-improvement.

Reinforce Your Learning

13. A good project manager believes that all individuals are

to the organization and that they can make greater contributions through

_____.

Reinforce Your Learning

14. Rather than create a fear of
_____,
the project manager acknowledges that mistakes are part of the

and

experience.

Reinforce Your Learning

15. A good project manager values and expects continuous
_____.

COMMUNICATION SKILLS

Project managers must be good communicators. They need to communicate *regularly* with the project team, as well as with any subcontractors, the customer, their own organization's upper management, and other stakeholders. Effective and frequent communication is crucial for keeping the project moving, identifying potential problems, soliciting suggestions to improve project performance, keeping abreast of customer satisfaction and stakeholder issues, and avoiding surprises. A high degree of communication is especially important early in the project to build a good working relationship with the project team and to establish clear expectations with the customer and other stakeholders, especially as it relates to developing a clear understanding and agreement on the project scope document.

Effective project managers communicate and share information in a variety of ways. They have meetings and informal conversations with the project team, the customer, stakeholders, and their organization's upper management. They also provide written reports to the customer and their own upper management. All these tasks require that the project manager have good verbal and written communication skills. We learn more by listening than by talking; therefore, good project managers spend more time listening than talking. They listen to the expectations and needs expressed by the customer or sponsor and the ideas and concerns expressed by the project team and stakeholders. They do not dominate a conversation; rather they initiate, stimulate, and facilitate communication. To initiate dialogue on important issues, they start discussions and conversations; to stimulate dialogue, they ask questions and solicit comments and ideas. For example, when a project manager introduces a topic at a team meeting, she might ask for others' reactions or ideas, rather than just giving her views on the topic and then moving to the next agenda item. Every project manager should get out of the office on a regular basis and drop in on individual team members—for instance, to follow up on a comment or idea that the person expressed at a team meeting but that was not pursued at the meeting.

The project manager establishes ongoing communication with the customer and other stakeholders to keep them informed and to determine whether there are any changes in expectations. The project manager needs to keep abreast of the degree of customer satisfaction throughout the project by regularly talking with the customer—for example, scheduling a phone discussion with the customer every Friday afternoon.

Communication by project managers needs to be timely, honest, and unambiguous, while maintaining discretion regarding any confidential information. Effective communication establishes credibility and builds trust. It is the foundation for managing the expectations of stakeholders, including the sponsor or customer, end users of the project deliverable, subcontractors, vendors, the project team, and the project organization's upper management. Withholding information or delaying communication can mislead stakeholders into incorrect expectations about performance or results.

Timely and honest communication also prevents rumors from starting. Suppose a team member is temporarily assigned to another project where her expertise is needed to help solve a critical problem. When the project team discovers that one of the members is no longer working on the project, rumors may start that she was let go for overrunning her budget or that she quit because she was unhappy. The project manager needs to call a team meeting to inform

Reinforce Your Learning

20. Give three reasons the project manager should establish on-going communication with the customer.

the other team members that she was temporarily reassigned and will return to the project in a couple of weeks.

It is important for the project manager to provide timely feedback to the team and customer. Both the good news and the bad news should be shared promptly. For the project team to be effective, members need to have up-to-date information—especially customer feedback that may necessitate changes to the project work scope, budget, or schedule. When communicating bad news to the customer or sponsor, the project manager should also provide recommendations and a plan for addressing the issue(s), along with supporting data and rationale.

Reinforce Your Learning

21. Why does communication by project managers need to be timely, honest, and unambiguous?

The project manager should create an atmosphere that fosters timely and open communication without any fear of reprisal, and must be open to differing viewpoints. For example, an individual who is having difficulty completing a task should feel that he can bring the problem to the attention of the project manager without being penalized.

See Chapter 12, Project Communication and Documentation, for further discussion.

INTERPERSONAL SKILLS

Interpersonal skills are essential for a project manager. Such skills depend on good verbal and written communication skills, as discussed in the previous section. The project manager needs to establish clear expectations of members of the project team so that everyone knows the importance of his or her role in accomplishing the project objective. The project manager can do so by involving the team in developing a project plan that shows which people are assigned to which tasks and how those tasks fit together. Much like the coach of an athletic team, the project manager should emphasize that everyone's contribution is valuable to executing the plan successfully.

Reinforce Your Learning

22. The project manager should have an informal

with each person on the project team and with each key individual in the

organization.

It is important that the project manager develops a relationship with each person on the project team. This may sound like a time-consuming activity, but it is not necessarily so. It requires making the time to have an informal conversation with each person on the project team and with each key individual in the customer's organization. These conversations, initiated by the project manager, can take place during work or outside the office. They can occur over lunch, while traveling with the person on a business trip, or while sitting next to the individual at a Little League game. Such situations provide an opportunity for the project manager to get to know the various people on the project team—what motivates them, how they think things are going, what concerns they have, and how they feel about things. For example, suppose Carlos mentions that he enjoys doing demonstrations but would like to further develop his formal presentation skills. With such knowledge, the project manager can ask Carlos to provide a demonstration at the next customer review meeting of the graphics software he has developed. Or, the project manager might ask Carlos to give a presentation at the next internal project review meeting, which Carlos may find a less stressful forum for practicing his presentation skills. Carlos's self-improvement goal might not have been uncovered in any situation other than an informal conversation initiated by the project manager.

The project manager should try to learn about the personal interests of each individual without being intrusive. The project manager might mention her own hobbies or family and see whether the team member picks up on the

topic. With each individual, it is important that the project manager look for areas of common interest, such as tennis, cooking, books, college sports, children, or hometown.

In informal conversations, the project manager should use open-ended questions and do a lot of listening. It is amazing how much information can be obtained from a response to a simple question like "How are things going?" Show genuine interest in what an individual says, however; if you seem disinterested, the person will not pursue the conversation. Thus, it is important to provide feedback and encouraging comments, such as "That's interesting" or "Tell me more about that."

Good interpersonal skills enable a project manager to empathize with individuals when special circumstances arise—whether a team member is discouraged because of technical problems in developing software or is distracted by the stress of a spouse's recuperation from an automobile accident. Of course, the project manager must be genuine in offering encouragement and support. He or she must also use good judgment in treating as confidential any private or personal information an individual may confide.

Reinforce Your Learning

23. The project manager should use

questions and do a lot of

When the project manager encounters a member of the project team, whether in the hallway or at the supermarket, he or she should capitalize on the opportunity. Rather than make do with a mere "Hi" or "Good afternoon," the manager should try to engage the team member in a conversation, even if it is brief. It can be on any topic, from "Are you ready for our meeting with the customer next week?" to "Did your daughter's soccer team win yesterday?" An effective project manager develops and maintains these interpersonal relationships throughout the duration of the project and afterward.

Good interpersonal skills are necessary when trying to influence the thinking and actions of others. Throughout the project, the project manager will have to persuade and negotiate with the customer, the project team, subcontractors, stakeholders, and his or her organization's upper management. For example, the manager of a construction project might need to try to persuade the customer to forgo a change in the project scope that would require an increase in costs. Or the manager of a project to present a talent show for the benefit of a local charity might have to use her interpersonal skills to persuade a local celebrity to work on the project. These situations cannot be dealt with in a heavy-handed manner; good interpersonal skills are required to bring about the desired outcome.

A project manager also needs good interpersonal skills to deal with disagreement or divisiveness among team members or with stakeholders. Such situations can require delicate handling on the project manager's part in order to mediate a resolution in which no one loses face, relationships do not deteriorate, and the project work is not affected. See the section on conflict on projects in Chapter 11 for further discussion.

ABILITY TO HANDLE STRESS

Project managers need to be able to handle the stress that can arise from work situations. Stress is likely to be high when a project is in jeopardy of not meeting its objective because of a cost overrun, a schedule delay, or technical problems with the equipment or system; when changes in scope are requested by the customer; or when conflict arises within the project team regarding the most appropriate solution to a problem. Project activity can get both tense and intense at

times. The project manager cannot panic; she or he has to remain unruffled. The effective project manager is able to cope with constantly changing conditions. Even with the best-laid plans, projects are subject to unforeseen events that can cause immediate turmoil. The project manager needs to remain composed and make sure that panic and frustration do not beset the project team, the customer, or the organization's upper management.

In certain situations, the project manager needs to act as a buffer between the project team and either the customer, stakeholders, or upper management. If the customer or upper management is not satisfied with the progress of the project, the project manager has to take the criticism and make sure that the project team does not become discouraged. She or he needs to communicate any discontent to the project team in a manner that will inspire the team to meet the challenge. Similarly, there may be times when the project team has complaints about the customer's requirements or unwillingness to make changes. Here, too, the project manager needs to act as a buffer, absorbing the complaints and redirecting them into challenges for the project team to overcome.

The project manager also needs to protect team members from external interferences that may divert their attention, impede their performance, and be a source of unnecessary stress.

A good sense of humor is a requirement for a project manager. Used appropriately, humor can help a manager handle the stress and break the tension. Because the project manager sets an example for the project team and demonstrates what acceptable behavior on the project is, any humor must be in good taste. A manager should not tell inappropriate jokes or have improper items hanging on the office wall, and he or she must make it known to the project team right from the beginning that such behavior is unacceptable and will not be tolerated.

The project manager can improve her or his ability to handle stress by keeping physically fit through regular exercise, good nutrition, and a healthy lifestyle. She or he also can organize stress relief activities for the project team, such as a softball game, golf outing, biking or hiking trip, or brief after-lunch walks.

Reinforce Your Learning

24. The project manager needs to have a good sense of

and needs to stay

fit.

PROBLEM-SOLVING SKILLS

A project manager needs to be a good problem solver. Although it is easier to identify problems than to solve them, good problem solving starts with the early identification of an actual problem or a potential problem. Early identification of a problem will allow more time to develop a well-thought-out solution. In addition, if a problem is identified early, it may be less costly to solve and may have less impact on other parts of the project. Good problem identification requires a timely and accurate data-driven information system; open and timely communication among the project team, the subcontractors, and the customer; and some "gut feelings," based on experience.

The project manager should encourage project team members to identify problems early and solve them on their own. The project team needs to be self-directed in solving problems and not wait for or depend on the project manager to get them started.

When a problem is potentially critical and likely to jeopardize accomplishment of the project objective, team members need to communicate this information to the project manager early so that he or she can lead the problem-solving effort. Once such a problem has been identified, the project manager may need

to seek additional data and ask clarifying questions to really understand the problem and its magnitude. Team members should be asked whether they have any suggestions for how the problem might be solved. An effective project manager recognizes that the best solution often emerges from differences of ideas, viewpoints, experiences, and opinions. Working with the appropriate members of the project team, the project manager should then use analytical skills to assess the information and develop the optimal solution. It is important that the project manager possesses the ability to see the "big picture" and how potential solutions might affect other parts of the project, including relationships with the customer, other stakeholders, or upper management. After the optimal solution has been developed, the project manager delegates implementation of the solution to the appropriate individuals on the project team.

See the section on problem solving in Chapter 11 for further discussion.

NEGOTIATING SKILLS

Good negotiating skills are essential for project managers. During the project life cycle, project managers encounter many occasions to employ their negotiating skills in interactions with the sponsor or customer, the project organization's management, subcontractors, vendors, end users of the project's end product, and other stakeholders. The subject of negotiations can be contract terms and conditions, obtaining specific resources to staff the project, subcontractor prices, vendor delivery schedules, payment for damages, the cost or schedule impact of changes, customer approval of designs, the need for rework if quality standards were not met, the best approach to resolve a technical performance issue, interpretation of acceptance criteria or test results, approaches to get the project back on track if it is behind schedule and/or over budget, stakeholder concerns about the impact or safety of a project, and so forth.

The goal of a negotiation is for two people or parties to arrive at a mutually acceptable agreement on an issue. It is a form of problem solving. Negotiating effectively requires good listening skills. The other person has to feel that his or her position or viewpoint has been heard and *understood*. The project manager should take the time to listen and ask questions for clarification or to get more information. See the section on effective listening in Chapter 12 for related information.

It is helpful if the project manager has developed a trusting relationship with the other person or party because this can provide a strong foundation for positive and robust negotiations. In addition to effective listening, the project manager needs to be able to make a persuasive case and clearly articulate her position on issues. That requires taking the time to prepare for negotiations and developing a persuasive rationale for her positions on the various issues that are being negotiated.

Negotiations cannot be approached as a "win or lose," "take it or leave it," or "all or nothing" contest. Rather, effective negotiations result in a win-win outcome for both parties. This requires the project manager to be flexible and willing to compromise. The manager must be careful not to make knee-jerk comments, but rather contemplate responses and not feel pressure to respond to the other party immediately. That requires having patience. The manager has to know when to say that she wants to take some time to think about the proposal and will get back to the other party later. A project manager should be proactive in trying to gain agreement on various issues with tactics such as

Reinforce Your Learning

25. In solving problems, the project manager needs to be able to see the _____ _____ and how potential solutions might affect other parts of the project.

Reinforce Your Learning

26. Effective negotiations result in a _____ outcome for _____ parties. It requires the project manager to be _____ and willing to _____.

saying, "Yes, I can do that *if* you could...." Such a conciliatory overture can set the tone for the other party to make concessions. If some items are at an impasse, the project manager may suggest setting them aside and moving forward with other items that are less contentious so that progress can be made and momentum built for addressing the more difficult issues.

Negotiating with customers or subcontractors involved in global projects can be particularly challenging. The project manager must take cultural differences into consideration when negotiating. Individuals from various cultural backgrounds have different approaches to conducting negotiations; for example, some may be anxious to reach an immediate agreement, whereas others may think that it is appropriate for negotiations to proceed at a slower pace. Here again, the project manager has to take the time to properly prepare and understand the cultural differences to ensure he can negotiate a mutually acceptable agreement. For example, an awareness of nonverbal cues or body language can be helpful in understanding the other party's position or reaction to a comment or proposal.

It is important that all parties save face in negotiations and that neither party feels resentful at the conclusion of an agreement. The project manager must set the example in maintaining integrity and respect for the other party throughout the negotiating process. Effective negotiations strengthen relationships, not erode them. When negotiating with the customer, the project manager must keep in mind that maintaining a good relationship is critical to having an opportunity to do additional business or projects with the same customer in the future.

TIME MANAGEMENT SKILLS

Effective project managers manage their time well. Projects require a lot of energy because they involve many concurrent activities and unexpected events. To make optimal use of the time available, project managers need to have self-discipline, be able to prioritize, and show a willingness to delegate.

See the section on time management in Chapter 11 for further discussion.

Developing Project Manager Competence

People are not born with the knowledge, skills, and abilities to be effective project managers; rather, they need to develop them. There are various ways to develop the competence necessary to be an effective project manager.

1. *Gain experience.* Work on as many projects as you can. Each project presents a learning opportunity. It is helpful if the projects are not all the same. For example, if you are a civil engineer with a large architectural firm and you just worked on a project to design a high school, you might then look for an opportunity to be assigned to another type of project, such as designing a museum or a church. Also, look for different assignments on each project. On one project, you might develop software, whereas on another project, you might ask to be a group leader or to have an opportunity to interact more with the customer. The purpose of varying projects and assignments is to gain exposure to as many project managers, customers, and other experienced project people as possible. Each experience

presents an opportunity to learn from other people and gain valuable knowledge and skills.

2. *Learn from others.* You should also observe how the other project participants employ their skills. See what they do—right and wrong. For example, suppose you want to develop your presentation skills. When people make presentations on the project, observe what they do right (such as showing enthusiasm or engaging the audience) and what they do wrong (such as blocking the view of the slides so that not everyone can see them, or telling an inappropriate joke at the start of the presentation). Making mental notes of such things will help you when you have to make a presentation. It is less painful to learn from others' mistakes than from your own.

3. *Interview project managers who have skills that you want to develop in yourself.* If you want to develop leadership skills, for example, seek out project managers who you think are effective leaders. Ask them how they developed their skills and what suggestions they have. Offer to buy them lunch, if that is the only time you can meet them. It could be a worthwhile investment.

4. *Conduct a self-evaluation, and learn from your mistakes.* If you completed a project task but overran the budget or were behind schedule, for example, ask yourself what happened, what you could have done differently, and what you will do differently the next time. Maybe you need to work on time management—focusing on the most important activities first.

5. *Get a mentor.* You can ask someone to be your mentor while you work on a project. This should be someone who you think has the skills that you are trying to develop. Seek out feedback from others. If you want to improve your problem-solving skills, for example, ask a mentor whether he or she has observed anything you could do better in problem-solving situations. If the project manager tells you that you have a tendency to jump to conclusions prematurely, you can work on taking more time to find out all the facts or listen to others' viewpoints. Prepare a personal development plan, and ask your mentor or other successful project managers to review it and provide suggestions.

6. *Participate in education and training programs.* There are many workshops, webinars, and self-study materials on all of the skills discussed in the previous section. Also, various universities and other education service providers offer noncredit, certificate, and degree programs in project management, including many that are available online. When participating in workshops, look for opportunities to learn from three sources: the instructor, the materials, and the other participants.

7. *Join organizations.* For example, membership in the Project Management Institute will provide opportunities for you to participate in meetings and conferences with other people involved in project management. See the section on project management associations in Chapter 1, as well as Appendix C at the back of the book, for related information. Joining professional organizations, such as Toastmasters International, will give you a chance to develop effective presentation skills.

8. *Read.* Subscribe to journals or look up articles related to the skills you want to develop. There are plenty of articles on improving your skills. Ask other people if they know of any good books or articles on a specific topic; their endorsement may save you time searching for good materials.

9. *Earn a credential.* Another way to develop project manager competence is to earn a credential in a specific project management discipline. The Project Management Institute offers the following credentials:

- Project Management Professional (PMP)®
- Certified Associate of Project Management (CAPM)®
- Program Management Professional (PgMP)®
- PMI Scheduling Professional (PMI-SP)®
- PMI Risk Management Professional (PMI-RMP)®
- PMI Agile Certified Practitioner (PMI-ACP)®
- OPM3® Professional Certification

For additional information about eligibility requirements and the steps to obtain the appropriate credential, go to the Project Management Institute website at http://www.pmi.org and click on the Certification tab.

10. *Volunteer.* The workplace is not the only place where you can develop skills. Consider getting involved with a volunteer organization, in which you not only can contribute to the community or a specific cause but also can try your hand at developing leadership skills.

Learning and development are lifetime activities—there is no finish line. Your employer can support and encourage you and provide the resources (time and money). The organization has to budget funds for training and staff development activities. You, however, have the primary responsibility for developing your competence. You have to take the initiative and have the desire. You have to make it happen.

Delegation

Delegation involves empowering the project team to accomplish the project objective and empowering each team member to achieve the expected results for his or her area of responsibility. It is the act of allowing individuals to carry out assigned tasks successfully. Delegation implies more than just assigning tasks to specific members of the project team. It includes giving team members responsibility for accomplishing job objectives and the authority to make decisions and take actions to achieve the expected results, as well as accountability for accomplishing those results.

Members of the project team are given specific results to achieve in terms of the work scope, tangible results or products to be delivered, the available budget, and the allowable time frame or schedule for their assigned areas of responsibility. They plan their own methods for accomplishing the desired results, and they exercise control over the resources they need to do the work.

Delegation is a must for an effective project manager. It is part of the project manager's responsibility for organizing the project. Delegation is *not* "passing the buck." The project manager is still ultimately responsible for achieving the project results. The project manager who understands and practices delegation ensures effective performance by the project team and creates the conditions necessary for cooperation and teamwork.

Effective delegation requires effective communication skills. The project team members need to realize that the job of implementing the project has been delegated to them. The project manager has the responsibility for providing a clear

understanding of what is expected in terms of specific results. It is not sufficient for the project manager to say, "Rashid, you work on the mechanical design" or "Rosemary, you handle the publicity." Rather, the manager needs to define what specifically constitutes each task and what the desired result of the task is. The work scope, tangible results or products to be delivered, expected quality, budget, and schedule should be defined and agreed upon by the project manager and project team members before any work begins. However, the project manager *should not tell the individuals how to do the task.* That should be left up to the team members so that they can be creative. If people are told how to do tasks, they will not be as committed to achieving the desired result and will feel that the project manager lacks confidence in their capabilities.

If team members are to accomplish their tasks successfully, they need to be given the necessary resources and authority to exercise control over those resources. Resources can include people, money, and facilities. Team members should be able to call on other team members' expertise, purchase materials, and have access to facilities as needed. Team members should be given the authority to make decisions regarding the use of resources as long as they stay within the constraints of the budget and schedule.

Delegation involves selecting the project team members who are best qualified to perform each task and then empowering them to do it. Because the project manager makes such selections and assignments based on each person's capabilities, potential, and workload, she needs to know the capabilities, capacity, and limitations of each member of the project team when making assignments. The project manager cannot delegate to a particular individual a set of tasks that requires more person-days than the individual has available. For example, one person, working alone, cannot be expected to paint six rooms in a week when it is estimated that it takes two days to paint each room. Similarly, the project manager cannot expect individuals to perform tasks for which they do not have the appropriate expertise. For example, an individual without the appropriate knowledge of chemistry or analysis techniques cannot be expected to perform a chemical analysis. Delegation, however, does provide an opportunity to give challenging, or "stretch," assignments to individuals in order to develop and extend their expertise and skills. Therefore, a project manager, when delegating, considers not only the person's current capabilities but also the person's potential. Stretch assignments energize people to take on the challenge and show that they can meet the project manager's expectations.

When a project manager empowers team members to make decisions associated with performing their work, he gives them freedom to take action to accomplish the work without interference. However, the project manager should realize that in performing the work and making decisions, people may make errors and failure may occur. A project manager who is critical of mistakes will train people to seek him out to review and approve every little thing they do. Such fear of failure will paralyze the project team. Effective delegation requires that the project manager have confidence in each member of the project team.

When the project team is carrying out its tasks, the project manager should let team members do their jobs; however, she or he should be available to coach and advise individuals when needed. An effective project manager is careful not to disempower individuals by giving them directives, by telling them how to do

things, or by making decisions for them. Rather, he or she shows confidence in their capabilities and encourages them.

Delegation requires that individuals be accountable for achieving the expected results of their tasks. To support team members in controlling their work efforts, the project manager needs to establish a project management information and control system. This system should keep the project manager and the team informed and support decision making. The system may include a computerized information reporting system and the requirement that regular meetings be held with the project team or individual team members to check on progress. Such a system should focus on measuring and evaluating progress toward the expected result of each task, not merely on monitoring busyness. The project manager is interested in knowing whether the work scope for each task is progressing according to plan and whether it will be completed within the available budget and on the required schedule. She cannot accept a report that "the team worked until 10:00 P.M. all week" as an indication that the work is on track. The project manager makes it known that delegation requires team members to be accountable for achieving the expected results, not just to keep busy. Empowered individuals accept this accountability. When monitoring progress, the project manager should offer encouragement to team members. She should show genuine interest in their work and offer recognition and appreciation of their progress.

Following are some common barriers to effective delegation and what can be done to overcome them.

Reinforce Your Learning

34. Delegation requires that individuals be

for achieving the expected results.

- The project manager has a personal interest in the task or thinks she can do it better or faster herself. In this case, the manager must force herself to let go and have confidence in other individuals. She needs to understand that other people may not do things in exactly the same way she would.
- The project manager lacks confidence in the capability of others to do the work. In this case, he should be sure that he knows the capabilities, potential, and limitations of each member of the project team so that he can select the most appropriate person for each task.
- The project manager is afraid that she will lose control of the work and not know what is going on. In this case, the manager should set up a system for regularly monitoring and evaluating progress toward the expected results.
- Team members fear criticism for mistakes or lack self-confidence. In this case, the project manager has to show confidence in each individual, offer regular encouragement, and understand that mistakes are opportunities for learning rather than occasions for criticism.

Figure 10.1 shows various degrees of delegation. The highest degree supports full empowerment of the project team. In most cases, the project manager should delegate to this degree. However, there may be some situations that require delegating to a lesser degree. For example, a lesser degree of delegation might be advisable if there was a critical problem in meeting the project objective, such as a potentially significant cost overrun or continuing test failures of a prototype. Similarly, a lesser degree of delegation might be appropriate if the person performing the work was in a stretch assignment.

FIGURE 10.1 **Degrees of Delegation**

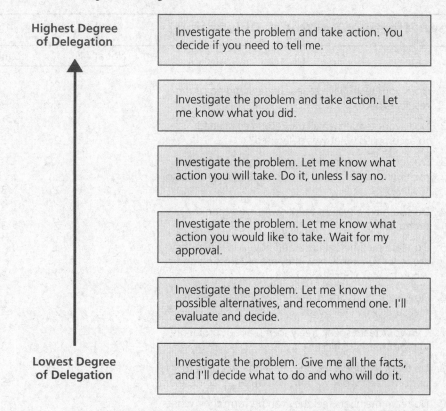

Highest Degree of Delegation

Investigate the problem and take action. You decide if you need to tell me.

Investigate the problem and take action. Let me know what you did.

Investigate the problem. Let me know what action you will take. Do it, unless I say no.

Investigate the problem. Let me know what action you would like to take. Wait for my approval.

Investigate the problem. Let me know the possible alternatives, and recommend one. I'll evaluate and decide.

Lowest Degree of Delegation

Investigate the problem. Give me all the facts, and I'll decide what to do and who will do it.

Figure 10.2 is a checklist for rating your effectiveness at delegation. It can be used by the project manager as a self-assessment instrument, or the project manager may choose to have the project team complete the checklist in order to get feedback on his or her effectiveness at delegation. In either case, the project manager should then focus on improving in areas that were rated low.

Managing Changes

The one thing that you can be sure will happen during a project is change. Despite the best-laid plans, changes will still occur. Changes may be

- Initiated by the customer or sponsor
- Initiated by the project team, including subcontractors, consultants, and vendors
- Caused by unanticipated occurrences during the performance of the project
- Required by the users of the project results

An important aspect of the project manager's job is to manage and control changes to minimize any negative impact on the successful accomplishment of the project objective. Some changes are trivial, but others may significantly affect the project work scope, budget, or schedule. Deciding to change the color of a room before it is painted is a trivial change. Deciding that you want a two-story house after the contractor has already put up the framing for a single-story house is a major change, which would certainly increase the cost and probably delay the completion date.

FIGURE 10.2 Delegation Checklist

How Effective Are You at Delegating?

	Not at All		Somewhat		Very Much
1. Does your team have a clear understanding of the results expected?	1	2	3	4	5
2. Does your team have all the resources needed to accomplish what was delegated?	1	2	3	4	5
3. Do you focus on the results you expect from team members, rather than on the details of how they do their work?	1	2	3	4	5
4. Do you have a system to follow up and monitor progress?	1	2	3	4	5
5. Do team members understand how and when they are to let you know how they are progressing and when to seek your advice?	1	2	3	4	5
6. Does your team understand how progress will be measured and evaluated?	1	2	3	4	5
7. Can your team speak freely to you about problems, without fear of criticism?	1	2	3	4	5
8. Do team members feel they have the freedom to perform their work without you over-managing them?	1	2	3	4	5
9. Do team members feel they can perform their work without fear of making a mistake?	1	2	3	4	5
10. Do you encourage team members to make decisions within the level of authority you delegated to them?	1	2	3	4	5
11. Do you provide coaching as needed?	1	2	3	4	5
12. Do you encourage and are you supportive of your team's suggestions?	1	2	3	4	5

Reinforce Your Learning

36. The project manager's job is to

and

changes to

any negative impact on the successful accomplishment of the project objective.

The impact a change has on accomplishing the project objective may be affected by when during the project the change is identified. Generally, *the later in the project that changes are identified, the greater their effect on accomplishing the project objective.* The aspects most likely to be affected are the project budget and the completion date. This is particularly true when work that has already been completed needs to be "undone" to accommodate the required change. For example, it would be very expensive to change the plumbing or wiring in a new office building after the walls and ceilings have been completed because some of them would need to be torn out and new ones installed. However, if such a change is made much earlier in the project—for instance, while the building is still being designed—the accommodation would be easier and less costly. The drawings could be changed so that the plumbing and wiring could be installed correctly the first time.

Reinforce Your Learning

37. At the start of the project, the project manager needs to establish a

that defines how changes will be

_____ ,

_____ ,

and

_____ .

At the start of the project, a **change control system** needs to be established for the process and procedures that define how changes will be documented, approved, and communicated. Agreement must be reached between the sponsor or customer and the project manager or contractor, as well as between the project manager and the project team regarding the way changes will be handled. Such a system must be communicated to all project participants. These procedures must address communication between the project manager and the sponsor or customer and between the project manager and the project team, including subcontractors, consultants, and vendors. If changes are agreed upon verbally rather than in writing and there is no indication of the impact the changes will have on the work scope, budget, or schedule, project costs can be greater than expected and schedules can run later than expected. Let us say, for example, that Mrs. Smith calls her contractor and tells him to add a fireplace to the house he is building for her. Based on her verbal authorization, the contractor installs the fireplace and chimney. Then, when he informs Mrs. Smith of the additional costs, she is shocked.

"You should have told me before you went ahead and did the work," she says.

"But you told me to go ahead and do it. It sounded like your mind was made up," he says.

"Well, I'm not going to pay this much; it is outrageous!" Mrs. Smith responds. And the hassle continues.

Whenever a customer requests changes, the project manager should have the appropriate project team members estimate the effects on the project cost and schedule. The project manager should then present these estimates to the customer and request the customer's approval before proceeding. *If the customer agrees to the changes, the project schedule and budget should be revised to incorporate the additional tasks and costs.* The change control system should include a log or status report of all pending, approved, and rejected changes.

Sometimes customers try to squeeze in changes for free by making them sound trivial or by circumventing the project manager and dealing with one of the individuals on the project team. The project manager needs to be sure that team members will not casually agree to changes that may require additional person-hours of work. Otherwise, if the customer does not agree to pay for the changes, the contractor will have to absorb the costs for the additional person-hours of effort and risk overrunning the budget for a particular work package or the entire project. This is often referred to as *scope creep*, which is a frequent cause of projects overspending their budget and/or not being completed on time.

Reinforce Your Learning

38. _____

is a frequent cause of projects

their

or not being

on

_____ .

· Sometimes changes are initiated by the project manager or project team. For example, suppose a member of the project team comes up with a new design approach that uses a different type of computer system than the customer originally wanted that will substantially reduce the project cost. In this case, the project manager would present a proposal for the change to the customer and get the customer's approval before making the change. The customer would probably give approval if the change reduced costs without any degradation to system performance. On the other hand, if the project manager asks the customer to extend the project completion date or to provide additional funding because the project team has run into difficulties that have caused schedule slippage or cost overruns, the customer might not agree. The contractor might have to absorb the cost overrun or spend additional money to add more resources temporarily to get the project back on schedule.

342 Part 3 *People: The Key to Project Success*

The project manager needs to make it clear to the project team that team members should not make any changes to their work that will increase costs beyond budgeted amounts, delay the schedule, or produce results that do not meet the customer's expectations. Such changes are another example of *scope creep*. For example, on a technical project a software engineer may think that she will please the customer by making slight enhancements to the software beyond what is required. However, she will not please the project manager if she overruns the budget for the software development task because of all the time she spends making a bunch of "slight enhancements" that are nice but are not necessary!

Some changes become necessary as a result of previously identified risks or unanticipated occurrences, such as an early snowstorm that slows down the construction of a building, failure of a new product to pass tests, or the untimely resignation of a key member of the project team. These occurrences will have an impact on the project schedule and/or budget and will require that the project plan be modified. In some cases, unanticipated events can cause the project to be terminated. For example, if early test results in a research project to develop an advanced ceramic material are not promising, the company may decide to terminate the project rather than spend more money with diminishing chances of success.

Perhaps the most difficult type of change to manage is that required of the users of the project result or end deliverable. In some situations, the project manager is responsible not only for managing the project to develop a new or improved system but also for implementing the resultant system among its users, who will have to change the way they perform their work. For example, in a project to design, develop, and implement a new ordering, billing, and collection system to replace the current system, the project manager might be responsible not only for managing the project to design and develop the new system but also for getting the users to accept the change from the old system to the new system.

There are some things a project manager can do to facilitate implementation and acceptance of such a change. *Open communication and a climate of trust are prerequisites for introducing change, reducing resistance to change, and gaining commitment to the change.* It is important to gain the users' support for and commitment to the new system, not merely their agreement that they need a better system. The project manager needs to share information about the change with the users. Such communication has to be carried out promptly, fully, honestly, and regularly. This means that the project manager must initiate discussions with the users before the new system is even designed, not wait until it is ready to be implemented. Discussing the system early will help squelch the rumor mill. The project manager needs to tell the users why the change is being made and how it will affect and benefit them. They need to believe that the change will benefit them; otherwise, the users will resent it rather than support it.

Discussions or meetings provide a good opportunity for people to express their concerns, fears, and anxieties. Anxiety and fear of the unknown can induce stress in people and build up resistance to change. During meetings to discuss the impending change, the project manager should not get into debates or be

defensive. She or he should empathize with people's concerns and fears, not discount or trivialize them. If possible, the project manager should have users participate up front in the decision to change, say, from a current system to a new system. Then she or he needs to involve them in planning and designing the new system; after all, they are the people who will be using it. The users also need to be involved in planning how to implement the new system—how to make the changeover from the current system to the new one. The project manager can provide support and rewards to help ensure successful implementation of the new system. A reward to the users might be that they receive computer skills training that will make them more knowledgeable and valuable. Finally, the project manager needs to be patient; only when the new system becomes fully utilized will the expected benefits be achieved.

Changes are going to occur on projects. The project manager has to manage and control the changes so that the project does not get out of control.

 REAL WORLD PROJECT MANAGEMENT

The Right Combination

Population growth, elimination of septic systems, and effluent water quality standards created a critical need for the development of a new Spokane County Regional Water Reclamation Facility in Spokane County, Washington, USA. The project team used a design, build, and operate approach with the goal to provide the greatest possible value while minimizing the short-term capital expenses and the long-term operating costs.

Having one team delivering all the phases of the project assured the county that one unit would be responsible and accountable, thus increasing the probability of meeting all the project deadlines, of reducing waste of public resources, and of protecting the environment. The traditional design, bid, and build approach was considered. Calculations indicated that the design, build, and operate approach could save up to 15 percent of the total project costs for design and construction compared to the design, bid, and build approach.

Initial adoption of a wastewater plan was made in 2002. Sites for developing the wastewater facility were evaluated over the following two years. The selected site was a brownfield site ideally located between the Spokane and North Valleys, near the Spokane River, and with room for expansion to serve the potential doubling of the population over the next 50 years of service. An aggressive timeline with a limited budget was developed for the request for proposals. The winning bid was required to have the facility operational in 3.5 years.

An Englewood, Colorado, USA, company, CH2M Hill, began design in January 2009 and started operations in 2012, seven months ahead of schedule and nearly $1 million under budget.

Partnering with a third-party facilitator at the start of the project ensured clearly defined goals and milestones. The project team accepted input from the project

owners, regulatory agencies, and other stakeholders for the project. The project manager collocated the key project team members with county personnel to facilitate expedient resolution of any problems and increase the sharing of creative ideas. Open communication and document sharing were implemented to provide information during meetings, reviews, and workshops.

The project team took advantage of local expertise and reduced expenses for labor by subcontracting companies located in the Spokane area. The project manager delegated authority for the construction of the educational facility, the main offices, a laboratory, and the control center. All the project teams were committed to technical innovation to meet the stringent requirements of the project related to effluent discharge requirements and public health and safety.

The project manager led a team committed to sustainable development. All areas are contained to manage odor control and the digester's biogas is used for cogeneration of energy to power electrical and heating equipment used by the facility. Project plans included almost a quarter of all building materials to be manufactured from recycled materials.

The facility received the 2012 National Design-Build Award in the water and wastewater category for the project team's approach for a single point of responsibility for the design and construction services. The project manager, the project team, and the stakeholders were the right combination to develop a state-of-the-art treatment facility in Spokane County.

Based on information from Nelson, D. and R. Smith (2013). "The Right Combination," *Civil Engineering (08857024), 83*(7/8), 58–63.

CRITICAL SUCCESS FACTORS

- Successful project managers accept responsibility for making sure the customer is satisfied and the work scope is completed in a quality manner, within budget, and on time.

- The project manager needs to be proactive in planning, communicating, and providing leadership to the project team to accomplish the project objective.

- The project manager needs to inspire the project team to succeed and to win the confidence of the customer.

- By involving the project team in developing the project plan, the project manager ensures a more comprehensive plan and gains the commitment of the team to achieve the plan.

- Successful project managers are proactive in addressing problems. They do not take a "let's wait and see how things work out" approach.

- The project manager needs to have a project management information system that distinguishes accomplishments from busyness.

- Effective project managers have strong leadership ability, the ability to develop people, excellent communication skills, good interpersonal skills, the ability to handle stress, problem-solving skills, negotiating skills, and time management skills.

- Successful project management requires a participative and consultative leadership style, in which the project manager provides guidance and coaching to the project team. The effective project manager does not tell people how to do their jobs.

- Project managers show they value the contributions of team members when they seek advice and suggestions from team members.

- Project managers can foster motivation through recognition. People want to feel they are making a contribution and need to be recognized. Positive reinforcement helps stimulate desired behavior; behavior that is recognized or rewarded gets repeated.

- The effective project manager does not monopolize, seek the spotlight, or try to take credit for the work of others.

- Capable project managers are optimistic and have high, yet realistic, expectations of themselves and each person on the project team.

- Projects should be fun. Project managers should enjoy their work and encourage the same positive attitude on the part of the project team members. The project manager should set a positive example for the team in terms of expected behavior.

- A good project manager provides opportunities for learning and development by encouraging team members to take the initiative, take risks, and make decisions. Rather than create a fear of failure, the project manager realizes that mistakes are part of the learning and growth experience.

- Good project managers spend more time listening than talking. They listen to the needs expressed by the customer and the ideas and concerns expressed by the project team and stakeholders.

- Communication by project managers needs to be timely, honest, and unambiguous.

- The project manager should create an atmosphere that fosters timely and open communication without fear of reprisal and must be open to differing viewpoints.

- When unforeseen events cause turmoil on a project, effective project managers remain composed and do not panic.

- Effective project managers recognize that the best solution often emerges from differences of ideas, viewpoints, experiences, and opinions.

- The project manager must maintain integrity and respect for the other party throughout the negotiating process.

- To make effective use of their time, project managers need to have self-discipline, be able to prioritize, and be willing to delegate.

- At the start of a project, the project manager needs to establish a change control system that defines how changes will be documented, approved, and communicated.

SUMMARY

It is the responsibility of the project manager to make sure that the customer is satisfied that the work scope is completed in a quality manner, within budget, and on time. The project manager has primary responsibility for providing leadership in planning, organizing, and controlling the work effort to accomplish the project objective. In terms of planning, the project manager has to clearly define the project objective and reach agreement with the customer on this objective. In terms of organizing, the project manager must secure the appropriate resources to perform the work. In terms of controlling, the project manager needs to monitor actual progress, compare it with planned progress, and take immediate corrective action if actual progress falls behind planned progress.

The project manager is a key ingredient in the success of a project and needs to possess a set of skills that will help the project team succeed. The project manager should be an effective leader who inspires the people assigned to the project to work as a team to implement the plan and achieve the project objective successfully; be committed to the training and development of the people working on the project; be an effective communicator who interacts regularly with the customer, project team, the project organization's upper management, and other stakeholders; and have good interpersonal skills. It is important that

the project manager develops a relationship with each person on the project team and effectively use interpersonal skills to try to influence the thinking and actions of others.

Effective project managers can handle stress and have a good sense of humor. In addition, they are good problem solvers who recognize that the best solution often emerges from differences of ideas, viewpoints, experiences, and opinions. Negotiating skills are also essential for project managers. Good project managers also manage their time well.

Project manager competence can be developed through experience, learning from others, interviewing effective project managers, conducting a self-evaluation and learning from one's own mistakes, getting a mentor, participating in education and training programs, joining organizations, reading, earning a credential, and becoming involved with volunteer organizations in which these skills can be applied.

Project managers need to be good delegators. Delegation involves empowering the project team to accomplish the project objective and empowering each team member to achieve the expected results for her or his area of responsibility. It is the act of allowing individuals to carry out assigned tasks successfully.

One other important component of the project manager's job is managing and controlling changes to minimize any negative impact on the successful accomplishment of the project objective. To do this successfully, the project manager needs to establish a change control system for the process and procedures that define how changes will be documented, approved, and communicated. The project manager must prevent scope creep, which can result in overspending the project budget and/or not completing the project on time.

QUESTIONS

1. Describe what the project manager should do to perform the planning, organizing, and controlling functions for a project. Give some specific examples.
2. What are some essential skills for an effective project manager? How can these skills be developed?
3. What leadership skills have project managers with whom you have worked possessed? How can you develop these leadership skills?
4. Describe how being rewarded or not being rewarded has changed how you worked on a project. Were there other rewards that would have been more appropriate for you or your team members?
5. Describe why a project manager needs good verbal and written communication skills.
6. What is meant by the term interpersonal skills? Give some examples of interpersonal skills, and explain why they are important.
7. What are some things a project manager can do to help create an environment in which a project team will feel motivated?

8. Describe a time when negotiation resulted in a win-lose outcome. What changes could have been made to make the result a win-win outcome?
9. What is meant by the term delegation? Why is delegation essential for project management? Give some examples.
10. What are some barriers to effective delegation?
11. Why is it important to manage changes during a project? How are changes initiated? Give some specific examples.
12. Describe some ways a project manager can make a project more fun and team members more committed.
13. Think of a project on which you have worked. Describe what made the project manager for that project effective or ineffective. How could the project manager have done a better job?
14. List 20 statements (of no more than six words) such as "Thank you" or "Good job" of what you might say to thank or compliment someone on your project team.

INTERNET EXERCISES

For the website addresses of the organizations mentioned in these exercises, go to "Internet Exercises" at the book's companion website at www.cengagebrain.com. It is suggested that you save this website in your "Favorites" list for easy access in the future.

1. The Project Management Institute sponsors a blog, Voices on Project Management, by a number of bloggers. The list of bloggers continues to grow and change. Globally dispersed, they represent a number of different industries and opinions. Review the blog entries by date or by a topic of your interest. Write the titles and the names of the authors of your favorite five blog entries.
2. On the Voices on Project Management blog from exercise 1, click on the category "Teams" link. Read and summarize one of the entries. What did the project manager do right or wrong in this entry?
3. Search the Web for "effective project leadership." Based on your search, briefly describe some of the suggestions you found.
4. Search the Web for "effective delegation." Describe what you found. How does it relate to the topics presented in this chapter?
5. Visit the home page of the Project Management Institute. Check out the "Professional Development" link and then the "PMI Career Headquarters" link. Describe at least three of the project management jobs that are posted.

CASE STUDY 1 Codeword

Codeword is a medium-size firm that designs and manufactures electronic systems for the mass transit industry. It competes with other firms to win contracts to provide such systems. When Codeword receives a contract, it

creates a project to complete the work. Most projects range from $10 million to $50 million in cost and from one to three years in duration. Codeword can have 6 to 12 projects going on at any one time, in various stages of completion—some just starting and others finishing.

Codeword has a handful of project managers who report to the general manager; other people report to their functional manager. For example, the electronics engineers all report to the manager of electrical engineering, who reports to the general manager. The functional manager assigns particular individuals to work on various projects. Some people work full time on a project, whereas others split their time among two or three projects. Although individuals are assigned to work for a project manager on a specific project, administratively they still report to their functional manager.

Jack Kowalski has been with the company for about 12 years, since graduating from college with a BS in electronic engineering. He has worked his way up to senior electronics engineer and reports to the manager of electrical engineering. He has worked on many projects and is well respected within the company. Jack has been asking for an opportunity to be a project manager. When Codeword is awarded a $15 million contract to design and manufacture an advanced electronics system for a new aircraft, the general manager promotes Jack to project manager and asks him to run this project.

Jack works with the functional managers to get the best people available assigned to the project. Most of the people are buddies who have worked with Jack on previous projects. However, with Jack's position as senior electronics engineer vacant, the manager of electrical engineering has no one with the appropriate level of expertise to assign to Jack's project. So the manager hires a new person, Alfreda Bryson. Lured away from a competitor, Alfreda has a Ph.D. in electronic engineering and eight years' experience. She was able to command a high salary—more than Jack is making. She is assigned to Jack's project full time as the senior electronics engineer.

Jack takes a special interest in Alfreda's work and asks to meet with her to discuss her design approaches. Most of these meetings turn into monologues, with Jack suggesting how Alfreda should do the design and paying little attention to what she says.

Finally, Alfreda asks Jack why he is spending so much more time reviewing her work than that of the other engineers on the project. He responds, "I don't have to check theirs. I know how they work. I've worked with them on other projects. You're the new kid on the block, and I want to be sure you understand the way we do things here, which may be different than at your previous employer."

On another occasion, Alfreda shows Jack what she thinks is a creative design approach that will result in a lower-cost system. Jack tells her, "I don't even have a Ph.D. and I can see that that won't work. Don't be so esoteric; just stick to basic sound engineering."

During a business trip with Dennis Freeman, another engineer assigned to the project who has known Jack for six years, Alfreda says that she is frustrated with the way Jack treats her. "Jack is acting more like the electronics engineer for the project than the project manager," she tells Dennis. "Besides, I have forgotten more about designing electronics than Jack ever knew! He really isn't up to date on electronic design methodologies." She also tells Dennis that she's

planning to discuss the matter with the manager of electrical engineering and that she would never have taken the job with Codeword if she had known it was going to be like this.

CASE QUESTIONS
1. Do you think Jack is ready to serve as a project manager? Why or why not? How could Jack have prepared for his new role?
2. What is the major problem with the way Jack interacts with Alfreda?
3. Why do you think Alfreda has not had an open discussion with Jack about the way he is treating her? If Alfreda approaches Jack directly, how do you think he will respond?
4. How do you think the manager of electrical engineering will respond to this situation? What should the manager do?

GROUP ACTIVITY
Course participants should split into groups of four or five students to discuss the following questions:

* What should be done to remedy the situation?
* What could have been done to prevent the situation?

Each group must then choose a spokesperson to present its conclusions to the entire class.

CASE STUDY 2 ICS, Inc.

Ivana is the owner of ICS, Inc. an information systems consulting firm of 20 employees. The company mostly designs and implements information technology projects for small and medium-size businesses in the metropolitan area. Although ICS has a sufficient level of business, the environment is becoming more competitive as more entrepreneurs are starting their own information technology consulting businesses. Ivana does all the marketing for ICS and is the primary contact between ICS and its customers.

ICS just received a contract from a Fortune 100 company to design and implement an e-business system for one of their distribution centers. ICS beat out several competitors, including some larger national consulting firms, to win this contract. This was due in part to ICS bidding a bare bones low price, and Ivana promising the customer that ICS would complete the project in six months, even though the customer specified that the project had to be completed in nine months or less. She knows that if ICS successfully completes this project and shows that it can beat the customer's expected schedule, it could lead to a larger contract to implement similar systems in the client's other distribution centers throughout the country.

As soon as Ivana heard that ICS won the contract, she called eight of her employees together whom she wanted to work on the project. "Some of you may not be aware of it, but I submitted a proposal to a very large client, our largest ever, to implement an e-business system for one of their distribution centers. This is a really important project for me because if we are successful, there

will be other future projects with this customer, and ICS can become a major consulting firm—my dream come true. I must tell you, this is a fixed-price contract, and I cut our price as low as I could to increase our chances of winning the contract. I also promised them that we could complete the project in six months, even though they would have been satisfied with nine months. So I want to be very clear with all of you, this project is very important to me and ICS, so I expect each of you to put in whatever time is necessary to get it done on time. You'll have to figure out how to get your other work done in the meantime. And, I want to emphasize, mistakes will not be tolerated. There is too much at stake. I need to leave for a business lunch now. But here are copies of the proposal I submitted. Look it over, and then get together and get to it."

As they left the conference room, Patrick, a systems designer, said, "Let's all read the proposal and get together about 9 o'clock tomorrow morning to figure out who needs to do what."

Ivana overheard Patrick's comment, and she piped in, "Tomorrow! Maybe you didn't hear me say how important this project is. I suggest you read the proposal now, and get together this afternoon or evening."

Ester, a programmer spoke up, "I have an appointment with my obstetrician this afternoon for my six-month checkup."

Ivana snapped, "Well, you'll just have to reschedule it. The baby's not due for three more months anyway. What's the big deal? My mother delivered five children with a midwife, no doctor, and we all survived."

After Ivana left, Ester, with tears in her eyes, told the others, "What a witch. If I didn't need the health insurance benefits, I'd quit today."

The group got together later that afternoon. Patrick took the lead in facilitating the discussions, only because he was the longest-term employee. Harvey, the other systems designer in the group, and one of the newer and younger people in the group, asked, "Patrick, are you, like, going to be, like, the leader on this project?"

"That's not the way things really work around here. We all know who the real project manager is, don't we?" responded Patrick. And most of the group answered in unison "Ivana!" and laughed.

As the group discussed the proposal, many questions came up. And there was a difference of opinion between Patrick and Harvey regarding the system design approach. Patrick's approach was less risky, but might be more time-consuming; Harvey's approach was more risky, but would take less time if it worked. Patrick said, "Let me try to meet with Ivana in the morning and get some answers, if that's possible."

"Maybe we should all meet with her," said Harvey.

"Ivana's not a big fan of long meetings with a lot of people. She thinks they're a waste of everyone's time," answered Patrick.

Patrick met with Ivana the next morning. "Well, does everybody have everything figured out?" asked Ivana.

"Actually, we stayed late last night discussing the proposal, and we have some questions. The proposal seemed ambiguous in some…."

Ivana interrupted, "Ambiguous! The customer didn't think it was ambiguous. I don't think it's ambiguous. So now you tell me why you think it's ambiguous."

"Well, for example, Harvey and I have come up with two different design schemes; one more risky but might take less time, the other less risky but could take longer," stated Patrick.

"One meeting and you guys are arguing with each other like little children," Ivana jumped in. "Didn't you ever hear of teamwork? Here is what I want—less risky and less time. No should's, could's, or might's. You two are just going to have to figure it out and not waste any time. Do I have to make all the decisions around here? What else? I don't have all day. And I'm glad to hear that everyone was willing to work late last night because that's the kind of commitment it's going to take to get this project done on time. You know, I pay top salaries, and I expect people to do whatever it takes to get the job done. And if anybody can't handle it, they can go find a job somewhere else. They'll see that the grass isn't always greener on the other side of the fence."

As Patrick turned and left Ivana's office, she said, "By the way, as a reward for winning the contract, I'm treating myself to a two-week vacation in Europe. And tell the others that when I get back, I hope to find the project is well on its way; and no fighting."

Later in the day, as Ivana was walking down the hallway, she saw Ester and said, "I assume you were able to reschedule your doctor appointment."

Ester replied, "Yes, but not for two more weeks. It's going to be tough trying to keep up with the work during these last three months."

"Tough?" responded Ivana. "Let me tell you what tough is. I helped raise my four younger brothers and sisters after my mother died giving birth to my youngest sister. Then I worked my way through college, going at night for almost 10 years while raising four children of my own. So the next time you think you have it tough, just think about how tough some other people have had it. I hope you can get most of your part of the work done on the project before your baby arrives. I'm counting on you."

At about 6 o'clock, Harvey stopped by Ivana's office. "Gotta minute?" asked Harvey.

"Only a minute," responded Ivana. "I'm meeting a friend for dinner, so make it quick."

"There is a computer conference in Las Vegas next month," Harvey said, "and I was wondering if I could have your approval to go? There are a lot of new things I could learn that may help us on this project."

"You've got to be kidding!" answered Ivana. "You want me to pay to send you to some conference to party while we have a deadline to make on this project? And everybody else is going to be back here working their butts off? Where is your sense of priorities? Don't you feel any responsibility to the rest of the project team? I swear, I am the only one around here who thinks about teamwork! Maybe when the project is over, you can find some conference that's closer and cheaper. I've got to go. By the way, tell whoever leaves last tonight to make sure the coffee pot is turned off. It was left on last night." As Ivana walked briskly by Harvey, she murmured, "Sometimes I feel like I have to be everybody's mommy around here."

CASE QUESTIONS

1. Considering Ivana's management style, how should the group of employees assigned to the project proceed?
2. How should the project members interact with Ivana throughout the project?
3. Why do you think Ivana behaves the way she does?
4. Should the project members approach Ivana about her management style? If so, how?

GROUP ACTIVITY

Select five course participants to perform a skit of this case in front of the class. One person will be the narrator describing the scene and the transitions between scenes. The other four participants will play the roles of Ivana, Patrick, Ester, and Harvey and read their lines.

At the conclusion of the skit, have the entire class discuss their responses to the case questions.

REFERENCES

A Guide to the Project Management Body of Knowledge (PMBOK® Guide) Fifth Edition. Newtown Square, PA: Project Management Institute, 2013.

AlSherif, J. and K. Jonsson (2013). "Women Working Upward," PM Network, 27(4), 24.

Gale, S. F. (2012b). "Ports Prep for Panama's Megaships," PM Network, 26(5), 8–11.

Bengtsson, L. and N. Ryzhkova (2013). "Managing Online Users in Open Innovation: The Case of a Nordic Telecom Company," Communications & Strategies, 89, 37–53.

Bredin, K. and J. Söderlund (2013). "Project Managers and Career Models: An Exploratory Comparative Study," International Journal of Project Management, 31(6), 889.

Brion, A., V. Chauvet, B. Chollet, and C. Mothe (2012). "Project Leaders as Boundary Spanners: Relational Antecedents and Performance Outcomes," International Journal of Project Management, 30, 708–722.

Chipulu, M., J. Neoh, U. Ojiako, and T. Williams (2013). "A Multidimensional Analysis of Project Manager Competences," IEEE Transactions on Engineering Management, 60(3), 506–517.

Crawford, L., E. French, and B. Lloyd-Walker (2013). "From Outpost to Outback: Project Career Paths in Australia," International Journal of Project Management, http://dx.doi.org.ezaccess.libraries.psu.edu/10.1016/j.ijproman.2013.03.003.

Fretty, P. (2012). "Mind Your Business," PM Network, 26(8), 50–54.

Gutiérrez, E. and M. Magnusson (2013). "Dealing with Legitimacy: A Key Challenge for Project Portfolio Management Decision Makers," International Journal of Project Management, http://dx.doi.org.ezaccess.libraries.psu.edu/10.1016/j.ijproman.2013.01.002.

Hadad, Y., B. Keren, and Z. Laslo (2013). "A Decision-making Support System Module for Project Manager Selection According to Past Performance," International Journal of Project Management, 31, 532–541.

Hwang, B. and W. J. Ng (2013). "Project Management Knowledge and Skills for Green Construction: Overcoming Challenges," International Journal of Project Management, 31, 272–284.

Nelson, D. and R. Smith (2013). "The Right Combination," Civil Engineering (08857024), 83(7/8), 58–63.

Omorede, A., S. Thorgren, and J. Wincent (2013). "Obsessive Passion, Competence, and Performance in a Project Management Context," International Journal of Project Management, 31(6), 877.

Verburg, R. M., P. Bosch-Sijtsema, and M. Virtiainen (2013). "Getting It Done: Critical Success Factors for Project Managers in Virtual Work Settings," *International Journal of Project Management, 31,* 68–79.

Zhang, F., J. Zuo, and G. Zillante (2013). "Identification and Evaluation of the Key Social Competencies for Chinese Construction Project Managers," *International Journal of Project Management, 31*(5), 748–759.

CHAPTER 11

The Project Team

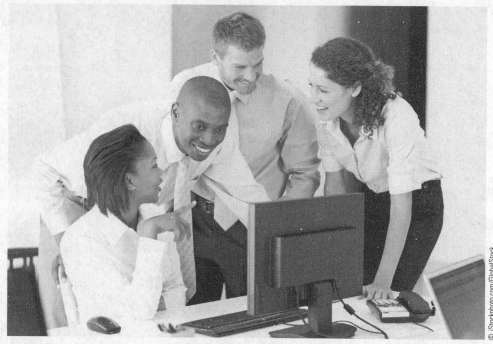

© iStockphoto.com/GlobalStock

Concepts in this chapter support the following Project Management Knowledge Areas of *A Guide to the Project Management Body of Knowledge (PMBOK® Guide)*:

Project Human Resource Management

 REAL WORLD PROJECT MANAGEMENT

Global Project Team Members have Common Ground

Project teams on global projects for global companies are multicultural and, more often than not, virtual. Understanding the cultural dimensions of team members

begins with an understanding of the cultural dimensions. Having cultural intelligence is one of today's most necessary project management skills.

Roberto Toledo, PMP (Project Management Professional), managing partner of Alpha PM Consulting, worked with a German company to complete a project with an international team this past year. Each of the members of his project team was assigned to multiple international projects. Toledo quickly realized that everyone on the team had a similar vision of work, problem solving, and decision making. It did not matter what nationality the team member was. All had a common company-specific shared vision.

Toledo also observed that team members from different nationalities had different points of view related to punctuality and commitments. These different perceptions caused the project manager to change focus from the tasks to be completed and the scheduled due dates to the people working on the project and their perceptions of their roles, responsibilities, and cultural beliefs.

The project manager had to develop his cultural intelligence by using cultural dimensions. These dimensions are abstract ideas about what is good, right, or desirable in a society. They are found when examining the social norms of the society. The cultural dimensions are evident in the practices and ways of thinking and the code of conduct for the individuals.

Having respect for the different cultures of the team members, the project manager helped the team to embrace the individual diversity and worked to have the team develop its own team identity. The members worked to create a set of values that aligned with the organization's culture that was respectful of the member's cultural dimensions yet established the team's own culture.

The project manager asked himself about each multicultural team he managed, "What is accepted, desired, and expected from my team?" He then included the team members in the process to develop each team's own set of norms and values. They developed their own common ground.

What Toledo observed about the team's shared vision was created through open, careful, and honest interactions with the team members and the project manager. Toledo recommends to project managers, "When leading a global team, the best way to work with multiple cultures is to create one of your own." The shared vision helps the team work more efficiently to attain the project's goals and create a productive work environment with a high functioning team.

Based on information from Toledo, R. (2013). "Common Ground," *PM Network, 27*(2), 66.

A **project team** is a group of individuals working interdependently to accomplish the project objective. **Teamwork** is the cooperative effort by members of a team to accomplish this common goal. The effectiveness, or lack thereof, of the project team can make the difference between project success and project failure. Although plans and project management techniques are necessary, it is the people—the project manager and the project team—who are the key to project success; project success requires an effective

project team. This chapter covers the development of an effective project team. You will become familiar with

- How teams are acquired and assigned
- The development and growth of teams
- The project kickoff meeting
- Characteristics of effective project teams and barriers to effectiveness
- Being an effective team member
- Team building
- Valuing team diversity
- Ethical behavior
- Sources of conflict during the project and approaches to handling conflict
- Problem solving and brainstorming
- Effective time management

LEARNING OUTCOMES

After studying this chapter, the learner should be able to:

- Explain how teams are assigned and formed
- Identify and describe the stages of team development
- Plan and conduct a project kickoff meeting
- Discuss characteristics of effective teams

- Identify and describe at least five barriers to team effectiveness
- Be an effective team member
- Take actions to support team building
- Identify at least five dimensions of diversity, and discuss the value of team diversity

- Behave ethically in a project environment
- Identify at least four sources of conflict on projects, and explain how to handle conflict
- Apply the problem-solving process and the brainstorming technique
- Manage time effectively

Acquiring the Project Team

When a project is initiated by a sponsor through a project charter or similar authorization or is outsourced to a contractor, one of the first things the sponsor or contractor needs to do is select the project manager. One of the first things that the project manager must do is to obtain and put together a project team. To do that, he or she must have a sense of the types of expertise, experience, or skills needed; how many of each type are required; and when they will be needed. For smaller projects, the project manager may identify or acquire the entire project team at the beginning of the planning phase of the project. For larger projects or projects that may have a longer time span (for example several years), the composition and size of the team will most likely change throughout the project. For such projects, the project manager may initially select or acquire a small team of key people or leaders for the planning phase of the project, and then also have them do or lead the work early in the performing phase. The small team of key members or leaders helps define the detailed human resource

Reinforce Your Learning

3. Project team members are assigned based not only on their

and

but also on who is

_____ .

requirements for the project and determine the composition and size of the project team, and how each may vary over the life span of the project.

Ideally, a project manager would like to have the option to hand-select specific people he or she wants on the project team. Realistically, very few project managers have that luxury. In most projects, the project team members are selected or assigned based not only on expertise and experience but also on availability.

In many project or contractor organizations, the quantities of the various types of expertise or skills are limited. Organizations that may be performing multiple projects concurrently may not have sufficient quantities of people with the needed skills to satisfy all the demands. Multiple projects may be competing for the same human resources, or specific individuals. So the project manager may be limited in which people or how many people may be available to be selected or assigned to his project. In other situations, a contractor may have submitted a proposal to a customer to do a project and anticipated that specific people in the contractor's organization would be available to work on the project. However, if the customer delays making a decision on selecting a contractor, or if in the meantime the contractor receives a contract from another customer to do a project, then some of the specific people who the contractor had expected to work on the project may no longer be available. So even with a human resource requirements plan that defines the expertise and skills required, at what quantities, and for what periods of time, perhaps the predominant constraining factor in selecting the project team is *availability* of the right people at the right time. In organizations that perform multiple projects at any given time, as some projects are completed, people are reassigned to project teams for new projects that are starting. Some people may be assigned full time to one project, while others may be assigned to work part time on several concurrent projects. Other people may only be required for a certain period of time on a project rather than for the entire project duration.

The project manager may need to use his or her negotiating skills to obtain specific people for the team from managers of organizational units who are responsible for the pools of various types of human resources (designers, videographers, crafts- and tradespeople, marketing specialists, engineers, trainers, and so forth). For example, the project manager may have to compromise and use two part-time people to perform certain activities rather than one full-time person because there are no people with the required expertise available full time when needed. See Chapter 13, Project Management Organizational Structures, for further related information.

If the required human resources are not available from within the project or contractor organization, the project manager may need to hire subcontractors or consultants to fill the gaps in skills or quantities. In other situations, the project organization may simply need to hire more people with certain experience, expertise, or skills if they have and foresee more projects and can continue to assign the new hires to other projects in the future. If there is a sustained demand, the organization can be more confident about hiring additional full-time people rather than outsourcing work to subcontractors or consultants, which builds the expertise internally rather than relying on external resources.

Project teams should be kept as small as feasible throughout the project. The more team members there are, the greater the chances for inefficiencies. For example, if there are more people than needed, some people may spend more time on tasks than is necessary and some work efforts may stretch out, expand,

or create scope creep, which will drive up actual costs and increase the likelihood of overspending the budget for a work package or the project. It is a good practice to minimize the number of full-time project team members and use part-time people or people for short periods of time, as needed.

Project Team Development

A personal relationship between two people takes time to develop. Initially, you may be curious about each other but apprehensive about letting your guard down and opening yourself up to the other person. As you get to know each other a little more, you may begin to notice differences in your attitudes and values, and disagreements may arise. You may be anxious about whether the relationship will or should continue. As you work through your differences, you may get to know each other better and become friends. As you spend more time together, you may develop a close relationship that helps you to be open with each other, accept each other's differences, and enjoy participating together in activities that are of mutual interest.

Likewise, teams evolve through various stages of development. In many projects, people who have never worked together are assigned to the same project team. This group of individuals must develop into an effective team to successfully achieve the project objective.

B. W. Tuckman has defined four stages of team development: forming, storming, norming, and performing (see Figure 11.1).

FIGURE 11.1 Stages of Team Development

First Stage — Forming

Second Stage — Storming

Third Stage — Norming

Fourth Stage — Performing

FORMING

Forming is the initial stage of the team development process. It involves the transition from individual to team member. Similar to the early phase of a relationship, it is when individuals on the team begin to get acquainted. During this stage, team members generally have positive expectations and are eager to get started on the work to be accomplished. The group begins to establish an identity and attempts to define and plan the tasks that need to be done. In this phase, however, little

actual work is accomplished because of the high level of anxiety that individuals have about the work itself and about their relationships with each other. Team members are unsure of their own roles and the roles of the other members of the project team. In the forming stage, the team needs direction. Members depend on the project manager to provide direction and structure.

Feelings characteristic of this stage include excitement, anticipation, suspicion, anxiety, and hesitancy. Individuals do a lot of questioning in the forming stage: What is our purpose? Who are the other team members? What are they like? Individuals are anxious about whether they will fit in with the other members and be accepted. They may be hesitant to participate because they are unsure how other members will react. Members wonder whether their input will be valued and whether their role in the project aligns with their personal and professional interests.

During the forming stage, the project manager needs to provide direction and structure. In giving orientation to the project team, the project manager must clearly communicate the project objective and create a vision of the successful result of the project and the benefits it will provide. Project constraints regarding the work scope, quality requirements, budget, and schedule must be stated. The project manager also needs to discuss the makeup of the project team: the reasons team members were selected, their complementary skills and expertise, and each person's role in helping to accomplish the project objective. Establishing structure is another task the project manager must perform in this phase. This includes defining initial processes and procedures for team operation and addressing such items as communication channels, approvals, and documentation. These processes and procedures may be improved by the team as it develops through its later stages. To reduce some of the team members' anxiety, the project manager should discuss his or her management style and expectations regarding the work and behavior of the people on the project team. The project manager should have a *project kickoff meeting* with the project team as early as possible during the forming stage (this is discussed later in this chapter). It is also important to get the team working on some initial tasks. In this stage, the project manager gets the team to participate in developing the project plans.

STORMING

The second stage of team development is known as *storming*. Like the teenage years, it is usually tough on everyone, but you have to go through it. You cannot get around it or avoid it.

The project objective and scope become clearer in this stage. Members start to apply their skills to work on their assigned tasks, and work begins to progress slowly. When reality sets in, though, it may not match individuals' initial expectations. For example, tasks may be more extensive or difficult than anticipated, or cost or schedule constraints may be tighter than expected. As team members begin to perform their tasks, they may feel increasing frustration with dependence on the direction or authority of the project manager. For example, they may have negative reactions to the project manager and to the operating processes and procedures that were established in the forming stage. Team members now begin to test the limits and flexibility of the project manager and the ground rules. During the storming stage, conflict emerges and tension increases. There is

a need for agreement on methods for handling and resolving conflict. Motivation and morale are low in this stage. Members may resist team formation—they want to express their individuality as opposed to team allegiance.

The storming stage is characterized by feelings of frustration, anger, and hostility. As individuals begin to perform their tasks, they have more questions about their roles and responsibilities with respect to other team members. As they begin to follow operating procedures, they question the viability and necessity of such procedures. Members wonder how much control and authority they have.

In the storming stage, the project manager still needs to be directive, but less directive than in the forming stage. She or he needs to provide clarification and better definition of individual responsibilities and of interfacing activities among team members. It is necessary to begin involving the team in problem-solving activities and to start sharing decision making in order to empower the team. The project manager should acknowledge and tolerate any frustration expressed by team members and not become defensive or take it personally. This is the time for the project manager to provide an understanding and supportive environment. It is important to give members an opportunity to express their concerns. The project manager has to provide guidance and foster conflict resolution and not try to suppress any frustration, hoping that it will go away by itself. If the discontent is not addressed, it will build up and could result in dysfunctional behavior later, putting the successful completion of the project at risk.

NORMING

After struggling through the storming stage, the project team moves into the *norming* stage of development. Relationships among team members and between the team and the project manager become settled in this stage. Interpersonal conflicts are resolved for the most part. In general, the level of conflict is lower than it was in the storming stage. Discontent, too, is reduced, as individuals' expectations align with the reality of the situation—the work to be done, the resources available, the constraints, and the other individuals involved. The project team has accepted its operating environment. Project procedures are improved and streamlined. Control and decision making are transferred from the project manager to the project team. Cohesion begins to develop. There is a sense of team. Individuals feel accepted as part of the team, and they accept others as part of the team. There is an appreciation of each member's contribution to accomplishing the project objective.

Trust begins to develop in this stage, as team members start to confide in one another. There is a greater sharing of information, ideas, and feelings; cooperation increases. Team members give and ask for feedback and feel that they can freely and constructively express their emotions and criticisms. A feeling of camaraderie emerges as the team goes through a socialization process. Personal friendships may develop that reach beyond the work environment.

During the norming stage, the project manager minimizes directiveness and takes on a more supportive role. Work performance accelerates, and productivity increases. The project manager should recognize the project team for the progress being made.

PERFORMING

The fourth stage of team development and growth is the *performing* stage. In this stage, the team is highly committed and eager to accomplish the project objective. The level of work performance is high. The team feels a sense of unity and

pride in its accomplishments. Confidence is high. Communication is open, frank, and timely. During this stage, members work individually or in temporary subteams, as needed. There is a great degree of interdependency—members frequently collaborate and willingly help each other with work beyond their own assigned tasks. The team feels fully empowered. As problems are identified, appropriate team members form subteams to solve the problems and decide how the solution should be implemented. There is a feeling of satisfaction as progress is made and recognized. Individual members realize that they are experiencing professional growth as a result of working on the project.

During the performing stage, the project manager fully delegates responsibility and authority, thereby empowering the project team. She or he focuses on helping the team execute the project plan and on giving recognition to team members for their progress and accomplishments. At this stage, the project manager concentrates on project performance with respect to the scope, budget, and schedule. The project manager's role is to facilitate and support the development and implementation of corrective actions if actual progress falls behind planned progress. It is also at this stage that the project manager acts as a mentor, supporting the professional growth and development of the people working on the project.

Figure 11.2 graphically illustrates the levels of work performance and sense of team during the four stages of team development and growth. The amount of time and effort it takes a team to move through each of the stages depends on several factors, including the number of people on the team, whether team members have worked together before, the complexity of the project, and the teamwork skills of the members.

FIGURE 11.2 **Level of Functioning at Various Stages of Team Development**

Project Kickoff Meeting

The project manager should schedule *a project kickoff meeting*, also referred to as a *project orientation meeting*, with the project team. It should be held as early as possible during the forming stage of team development. This is a very important

meeting to inform team members, reduce anxiety, manage expectations, and inspire the team. It sets the tone for the entire project. A sample agenda for such a meeting is shown in Figure 11.3. The following are some topics that might be discussed under each of the agenda items:

FIGURE 11.3 Project Kickoff Meeting Agenda

> ## Project Kickoff Meeting
> ### Agenda
> 1. Welcome and Introductions
> 2. Project Overview
> 3. Roles and Responsibilities
> 4. Processes and Procedures
> 5. Expectations
> 6. Closing Comments

1. *Welcome and introductions.* The project manager should provide a brief, warm, and enthusiastic welcome. An important first step in team development is to have the participants, including the project manager, introduce themselves and provide some information about their experience and expertise. This not only gets them involved in the meeting but also informs all the participants about other team members. This should *not* be done by quickly going around the room and asking each person to merely state their name. Such an approach discounts the person's value and potential contribution to the project. Sufficient time should be allocated for this agenda item because it is a building block for further team development and team building. However, to ensure that some participants do not use an inordinate amount of time, when the project manager sends out the agenda in advance of the meeting, he or she should indicate that each person will have a specified time limit to tell about his or her experience and expertise.

2. *Project overview.* The project manager should discuss the elements of the project charter, project proposal, or contract and other background documents or information. These documents should be distributed well in advance of the meeting to give participants sufficient time to review them and come prepared with any comments or questions. This agenda item should be allocated plenty of time so that all questions are addressed. The project manager will need to employ good facilitation skills to keep the discussions on track. See the section on effective meetings in Chapter 12 for further information. The project manager may want to invite the sponsor or customer to this part of the meeting to speak about the importance of the project.

3. *Roles and responsibilities.* The role and responsibilities of each participant should be discussed so that everyone knows each other's role. Clarification needs to be provided about any perceived or identified overlaps or gaps in responsibilities. If applicable, an initial project organization chart should be provided showing the project reporting relationships, as well as project job descriptions, if appropriate.

4. *Processes and procedures.* This topic should include a discussion of such items as documentation requirements, approval requirements and processes, communication protocols, and so forth. If the project organization has a change control system, it should be reviewed with an emphasis on avoiding scope creep. If there is a communication plan for the project, it should be distributed to all participants. A communication plan usually includes a list of documents that will be generated during the project, who the authors of each document are, to whom each document should be distributed, the frequency of the document distribution, and who may need to approve or take other action on the document. See the section on the project communication plan in Chapter 12 for further information. This agenda item could also include a discussion of problem-solving and conflict-resolution processes. Any documents related to the project processes and procedures should be made available to all project participants, usually through a shared electronic file. Also during this agenda item, to foster team building, the project manager can organize the participants into small groups to work on a process-oriented activity, such as creating ground rules or a code of conduct for behavior at future project team meetings, and then have each group share their list.

5. *Expectations.* The project manager should discuss the stages of team development to help manage expectations of what the team will go through (especially regarding the storming stage) as the members grow into a high-performing team. This is also the time on the agenda for the project manager to demonstrate his or her leadership and inspire the participants to work as a team; respect others; value each person's contribution; have high expectations of themselves and others; communicate openly, honestly, and in a timely fashion; maintain ethical behavior; and so forth.

6. *Closing comments.* The project manager should again ask if there are any comments or questions and make sure that everyone leaves the meeting with clear expectations of the work to be done and everyone's role. The meeting should end on a high note, with the team eager and enthusiastic to contribute to the success of the project and looking forward to an enjoyable experience during which they can develop and expand their skills and abilities. Another team-building activity that can be valuable is to have a team meal (lunch or dinner) at the end of the meeting so that team members can socialize and get to know each other better.

The project kickoff meeting can take several hours or several days, depending on the size and complexity of the project and the number of participants. It is important to allow enough time and not hurry through it. It is time well spent. If the project has a virtual team with members geographically dispersed, then electronic communication tools should be used to make sure everyone participates. See the section on collaborative communication tools in Chapter 12 for additional information.

For larger projects—for example, those that may span several years—the project manager may need to periodically have similar orientation meetings, or a modified version thereof, as new people are added to the project team. In some cases, the manager may choose to have one-on-one individual orientation meetings with people. Also as new people join the project team, the project manager should send out an announcement about them, as well as formally introduce them at the next project meeting.

Effective Project Teams

A project team is more than a group of individuals assigned to work on one project; it is a group of individuals working interdependently and cooperatively to accomplish the project objective. Helping these individuals develop and grow into a cohesive, effective team takes effort on the part of the project manager and each member of the project team. As was noted at the beginning of the chapter, the effectiveness, or lack thereof, of the project team can make the difference between project success and project failure. Although plans and project management techniques are necessary, it is the people—the project manager and project team—who are the key to project success; project success requires an effective project team.

CHARACTERISTICS OF EFFECTIVE TEAMS

The following five characteristics are associated with effective project teams.

CLEAR UNDERSTANDING OF THE PROJECT OBJECTIVE

The scope, quality requirements, budget, and schedule must be well defined for a project team to be effective. If the project objective is to be accomplished, each team member must have the same vision of the project result and the benefits it will provide.

CLEAR EXPECTATIONS OF ROLES AND RESPONSIBILITIES

Members of an effective team know how their work must fit together because they participated in developing the project plans. Team members appreciate each other's expertise, skills, and contributions to accomplishing the project objective. Each person accepts responsibility for carrying out her or his part of the project.

RESULTS ORIENTATION

Each person on an effective project team has a strong commitment to accomplishing the project objective. By setting a good example, the project manager sets the tone for the energy level. Team members are enthusiastic and willing to spend the time and energy necessary to succeed. For example, individuals are willing to work extra hours or weekends or skip lunches when necessary in order to keep the project on track.

HIGH DEGREE OF COOPERATION AND COLLABORATION

Open, frank, and timely communication is the norm on an effective project team. Members readily share information, ideas, and feelings. They are not shy about asking other members for help. Team members act as resources for each other, beyond just doing their assigned tasks. They want to see other members succeed in their tasks and are willing to help and support them if they are stuck or faltering.

Reinforce Your Learning

18. An effective project team has a clear understanding of the project

and clear expectations of

and

_____ .

Reinforce Your Learning

19. Effective project teams have a

orientation; each person has a strong commitment to accomplishing the

_____ .

There is a high degree of

and

_____ .

They give and accept feedback and constructive criticism. Because of this cooperation, the team is creative in problem solving and timely in decision making.

HIGH LEVEL OF TRUST

Members of an effective team understand interdependency and accept that everyone on the team is important to project success. Each member can count on the other members to do what they say they will do—and at the expected level of quality. There is a shared sense of trust. Team members care for and about one another. Because differences are accepted, members feel free to be themselves. Differences of opinion are encouraged, freely expressed, and respected. Individuals are able to raise issues that may result in disagreement or conflict without concern about retribution. Effective project teams resolve conflict through constructive and timely feedback and positive confrontation of the issues. Disagreement is not suppressed; rather, it is seen as normal and as an opportunity for growth and learning.

Figure 11.4 is a checklist for rating the effectiveness of a project team. It is recommended that team members complete this assessment instrument periodically during the project. After the scores of all team members have been summarized, the team, including the project manager, should discuss how to improve in any areas that were rated low.

BARRIERS TO TEAM EFFECTIVENESS

Although every project team has the potential to be highly effective, there are often barriers that impede a team's achievement of the level of effectiveness of which it is capable. Following are barriers that can hinder project team effectiveness and some suggestions for overcoming them.

UNCLEAR VISION AND OBJECTIVE

The project manager needs to articulate the project objective, as well as the project scope, quality requirements, budget, and schedule. She or he needs to create a vision of the project result and the benefits it will provide. This information needs to be communicated at the very first project kickoff meeting. At this meeting, the project manager needs to ask team members if they understand this information and answer any questions they may have. The information should then be provided in written form, along with any clarification given during the meeting, to all members of the project team.

Periodically, the project manager needs to discuss the project objective at project status review meetings. At these meetings, she or he should always ask whether anyone has any questions about what must be accomplished. Telling the team what the project objective is only once, at the beginning of the project, is not sufficient. The project manager must say it, write it, distribute it, and repeat it frequently.

UNCLEAR DEFINITION OF ROLES AND RESPONSIBILITIES

Individuals may feel that their roles and responsibilities are ambiguous or that there is overlap in the responsibilities of some individuals. At the beginning of the project, the project manager should meet individually with each member of the project team to explain why he or she was assigned to the project, describe his or her expected role and responsibilities, and discuss how they relate to the

FIGURE 11.4 **Team Effectiveness Checklist**

How Effective Is Your Project Team?

	Not at All		Somewhat		Very Much
1. Does your team have a clear understanding of its goal?	1	2	3	4	5
2. Are the project scope, level of quality, budget, and schedule well defined?	1	2	3	4	5
3. Does everyone have clear expectations of his or her own role and responsibilities?	1	2	3	4	5
4. Does everyone have clear expectations of other members' roles and responsibilities?	1	2	3	4	5
5. Does everyone know the expertise and skills that each person brings to the team?	1	2	3	4	5
6. Is your team results oriented?	1	2	3	4	5
7. Does everyone have a strong commitment to accomplishing the project objective?	1	2	3	4	5
8. Does your team have a high level of enthusiasm and energy?	1	2	3	4	5
9. Does your team have a high degree of cooperation and collaboration?	1	2	3	4	5
10. Are open, frank, and timely communications the norm?	1	2	3	4	5
11. Do members readily share information, ideas, and feelings?	1	2	3	4	5
12. Do members feel free to ask other members for help?	1	2	3	4	5
13. Do members willingly help one another?	1	2	3	4	5
14. Do team members give feedback and constructive criticism?	1	2	3	4	5
15. Do team members accept feedback and constructive criticism?	1	2	3	4	5
16. Is there a high level of trust among the project team members?	1	2	3	4	5
17. Do members follow through on what they say they will do?	1	2	3	4	5
18. Is there an openness to differing viewpoints?	1	2	3	4	5
19. Do team members accept one another and their differences?	1	2	3	4	5
20. Does your team constructively resolve conflicts?	1	2	3	4	5

other team members' roles and responsibilities. For some projects, job descriptions may be provided that outline team members' roles, areas of responsibility, levels of authority, and performance expectations. Project team members need to feel free to ask the project manager to clarify any areas of ambiguity or overlap whenever they become apparent. As the project team develops the project plan, each member's tasks should be identified using a tool such as a work breakdown structure, a responsibility assignment matrix, or a network diagram or bar chart. Copies of these documents should be given to everyone and be made readily available so that each team member can see not only her or his own assigned tasks but also other members' tasks and how they all fit together.

LACK OF PROJECT STRUCTURE

Individuals may feel that everyone is working in a different direction or that there are no established procedures for team operation. This, too, is a reason for the project manager to have the team participate in developing the project plan. A tool such as a network diagram shows how everyone's work fits together to accomplish the project objective. At the beginning of the project, the project manager should establish preliminary operating procedures that address such issues as communication channels, approvals, and documentation requirements. Each procedure, as well as the rationale for establishing it, needs to be explained to the team at a project meeting. The procedures should also be provided in written form to all team members. If some team members do not follow the procedures or circumvent them, the project manager needs to reinforce the importance of everyone consistently following established procedures. However, the project manager needs to be open to suggestions for eliminating or streamlining procedures when they no longer contribute to the effective and efficient performance of the project.

LACK OF COMMITMENT

Team members may not appear to be committed to their project work or the project objective. To counter such indifference, the project manager needs to explain to each individual the importance of his or her role on the team and how he or she can contribute to the success of the project. The project manager also needs to ask team members what their personal and professional interests are and look for ways that the project assignment might help satisfy these interests. She or he should try to determine what motivates each individual and then create a project environment where these motivators are available. The project manager also needs to recognize the accomplishments of each person and support and encourage his or her progress.

POOR COMMUNICATION

Poor communication occurs when team members lack knowledge about what is happening on the project and individuals do not share information. It is important for the project manager to have regular project status review meetings with a published agenda. Various project team members should be asked to give a briefing on the status of their work. Participation and questions should be encouraged. All project documents, such as plans, budgets, schedules, and reports, should be kept up to date and distributed in a timely manner to the entire project team. The project manager should encourage team members to get together

to share information, collaborate, and solve problems as needed, rather than wait for official project meetings. Also, physically locating all members of the project team in the same office area can enhance project communication.

POOR LEADERSHIP

To keep the project team from feeling that the project manager is not providing effective leadership for the team, the manager has to be willing to periodically solicit feedback from team members by asking questions like "How am I doing?" or "How can I improve my leadership?" However, he or she must first establish a project environment in which individuals feel free to provide feedback without fear of retribution. The project manager should state at an early project meeting that feedback will be requested periodically and that others' suggestions for improving his or her leadership skills are welcome. For example, a project manager might show interest in improving her leadership skills to enhance her own contribution to the success of the project. Of course, the project manager then must be willing to follow up on appropriate suggestions, whether they involve additional training, changing behaviors, or modifying project procedures.

TURNOVER OF PROJECT TEAM MEMBERS

When team composition changes often—that is, when new people are continually being assigned to a project and others are leaving—the flow of individuals may be too dynamic for the team to gel. A project team made up of a small number of individuals with long-term assignments will be more efficient than a project team composed of a large number of individuals with short-term assignments. The project manager should acquire individuals for the project team who are sufficiently versatile in expertise and skills that they can contribute to many areas of the project and thus be assigned to a project for a long period of time. Although the project manager should not try to execute the project with a multitude of individuals with narrow expertise who will be assigned to the project for only short intervals, in some cases it may be appropriate for individuals with specific expertise to be assigned to the project for only one task or for a limited time.

DYSFUNCTIONAL BEHAVIOR

Sometimes an individual exhibits inappropriate behavior, such as hostility, bullying, excessive clowning around, or making disparaging personal remarks, that is disruptive to the development of an effective team. The project manager needs to meet with this individual, point out the disruptive behavior, and explain that it is unacceptable because of the impact it is having on the rest of the project team. The individual might be offered coaching, a training seminar, or counseling, if appropriate. The project manager must make it clear, however, that if the dysfunctional behavior continues, the person will be released from the project team. Of course, the project manager needs to be prepared to follow through, if necessary.

EFFECTIVE TEAM MEMBERS

Being a member of a project team should be an enriching and satisfying growth experience for each individual. However, growth will not just happen by itself. It requires a sense of responsibility, hard work, open-mindedness, and a desire for further self-development. Although the project manager is ultimately responsible for the success of a project, each member of the project team shares in that

responsibility. What people who work on projects have in common is that they enjoy the challenge of accomplishing something and working as part of a team. Each member of the project team needs to help create and foster a positive and effective project environment.

Effective team members plan, control, and feel accountable for their individual work efforts. They have high expectations of themselves and strive to accomplish their assignments under budget and ahead of schedule. They manage their time well. They make things happen; they do not just let them happen. Effective team members do not simply work on a task until they are told to stop; rather they are self-directed and follow through on assignments and action items. They take pride in doing quality work instead of expecting other team members to finish, clean up, or redo any of their sloppy or incomplete work. Each team member can count on all the other team members to perform their respective tasks in a quality and timely manner so as not to delay or impede the work of other team members.

Effective team members participate and communicate. They do not sit back and wait to be asked; they speak up and participate in meetings. They take the initiative, communicating with other team members and the project manager in a clear, timely, and unambiguous manner. They provide constructive feedback to each other. In particular, effective team members feel responsible for identifying problems, or potential problems, as early as possible, without pointing the finger or blaming other individuals, the customer, or the project manager for causing the problems. Effective team members are not only problem identifiers but also problem solvers. When a problem has been identified, they suggest alternative solutions and are ready and willing to collaborate with other team members to solve the problem, even if it is outside of their assigned area of responsibility. Effective team members do not have a "that's not my problem" or "that's not my job" attitude; rather, they are willing to pitch in to help the team accomplish the project objective. They have a "**we**" attitude and tend to speak in terms of "we, us, and our" rather than "I, me, and my."

Effective team members help to create a positive, constructive project environment in which there is no room for gossip, whining, or divisiveness. They are sensitive to the diverse composition of the project team and show respect for all members of the team. They respect others' viewpoints. They do not let pride, stubbornness, or arrogance get in the way of collaboration, cooperation, and compromise. Effective team members put the success of the project above personal gain.

It has been said that *there is no I in TEAM*—there are no individual winners or losers. When a project is successful, everybody wins!

TEAM BUILDING

Legendary baseball manager Casey Stengel once said, "It's easy to get the players. Gettin' 'em to play together, that's the hard part." **Teamwork** is the cooperative effort by members of a team to accomplish a common goal. **Team building**— developing a group of individuals into a team to accomplish the project objective—is an ongoing process. It is the responsibility of both the project manager and the project team. Team building helps to create an atmosphere of openness and trust. Members feel a sense of unity and a strong commitment to accomplishing the project objective. Chapter 10 discussed various things that the project manager can do to foster and support team building. The following

Reinforce Your Learning

29. Effective team members plan, control, and feel _____ for their individual work efforts. They have high _____ of themselves.

Reinforce Your Learning

30. Effective team members _____ and _____. They are not only problem identifiers, but also _____.

Reinforce Your Learning

31. Think about projects in which you have been involved. What are some characteristics of individual team members that made them effective contributors?

Reinforce Your Learning

32. Team building is the responsibility of both the

and the

_____ .

discussion provides a few ways that the project team can help the team-building process.

Socializing among team members supports team building. The better team members get to know one another, the more team building is enhanced. To ensure that individual members communicate with one another frequently, situations need to be created that foster socializing among team members. Team members can initiate some of these situations.

The team can request that team members be physically located in one office area for the duration of the project. When team members are located near one another, there is a greater chance that they will go to each other's offices or work areas to talk. Also, they will pass each other more frequently in common areas such as hallways and have a chance to stop and talk. Such spontaneous informal discussions can be very informative and also help to build relationships. Discussions should not always be work related. It is important that team members get to know one another on a personal basis, without being intrusive. A certain number of personal friendships will develop during the project. Having the entire project team located in one area prevents that "us versus them" feeling that can arise when parts of the team are located in different parts of a building or plant. Such a situation can result in a project team that is really a set of several subgroups rather than a true team. Colocation is not possible with *virtual teams* that are geographically dispersed. Effective electronic communication tools and protocols need to be used to facilitate team building among members of a virtual team. See the section on collaborative communication tools in Chapter 12 for further discussion.

Reinforce Your Learning

33. _____ among team members supports

_____ .

Individual members need to

with one another frequently.

The project team can initiate social events to celebrate project events—for example, reaching a critical milestone, such as a successful design review meeting with the customer or customer acceptance of a major deliverable. The team can also schedule events just for stress relief. An after-work get-together for pizza, a team luncheon, an informal lunch in the conference room, a monthly birthday celebration, a weekend family picnic, and a trip to see a sports event or theater production are examples of events the team can organize to foster socializing and team building. It is important that such activities include everyone on the team. Although some individuals may not be able to participate, everyone should at least be invited and encouraged to participate. Team members should use these events to get to know as many other team members (and their families, if they participate) as possible. A good rule of thumb is to always try to sit next to someone you do not know too well and strike up a conversation—ask questions, listen to what the other person says, look for areas of common interest. It is important for individuals to avoid forming cliques composed of several people who always hang together at every event. Engaging in social events not only helps to develop a sense of camaraderie but also makes it easier for team members to engage in open and frank communication while working on the project.

In addition to organizing social activities, the team can periodically call team meetings, as opposed to project meetings. The purpose of team meetings is to discuss openly such questions as the following: How are we working as a team? What barriers (such as procedures, resources, priorities, or communications) are impeding teamwork? What can we do to overcome these barriers? What can we do to improve teamwork? If the project manager participates in team meetings, he or she should be treated as an equal—team members should not look to the manager for the answers, and the manager should not pull rank and override the

consensus of the team. It is a team meeting, not a project meeting. Only team-related issues, not project items, should be discussed.

Team members should foster team building in whatever ways they can. For example, as new people join the team during the project, the project team needs to make a special effort to make them feel welcome and integrate them into the team. For example, team members can organize an informal reception for new team members, or stop by their office to welcome them and introduce themselves. They should not expect the project manager alone to be responsible for team building.

VALUING TEAM DIVERSITY

Globalization, changes in demographics, and the need for individuals with unique skills are causing changes in the composition or diversity of project teams. *Diversity* is differences among people. Diversity is about acknowledging, understanding, and valuing differences and creating a work environment that recognizes, respects, and harnesses differences among team members for the benefits of accomplishing a shared goal, such as the project objective. However, differences can create barriers to team performance. Miscommunication and misunderstanding may be more likely to happen between people who are different. If the differences within the project team are not valued as a strength, they can lead to low morale, diminished trust, reduced productivity, greater tension, and suspicion and become a serious impediment to team performance. Team members should feel valued and have a sense of belonging. Diversity of the team brings unique ideas and perspectives to projects. Each team member has unique experiences, skills, and values to bring to the team. Such differences can lead to more creative, faster, and higher-quality problem solving and decision making.

Chances are that most project teams are diverse in more ways than you think. The following are some dimensions of diversity:

Reinforce Your Learning

34. Diversity of the team brings

ideas and

to projects.

- *Age or generation.* Many teams have a mix of members of various age groups—younger, older, and in-between. Three or four generations can be represented on a team. Each generation has different experiences that shape values and perspectives and thus responds to different motivational factors. Older team members may value security, a strong work ethic, and adherence to rules and may prefer face-to-face meetings, whereas younger members may value work/life balance and informality, dislike close supervision, and prefer electronic communications with others.
- *Appearance.* Team members are different in weight, height, facial features, hairstyle, clothing, jewelry, body piercing, and tattoos, just to name a few things. These characteristics can become a barrier to team effectiveness if some team members make assumptions about other members' competence or performance based on their appearance.
- *Ethnicity or ancestry.* Driven by globalization, projects have team members located around the globe as well as project work packages that may be outsourced to subcontractors on several continents. Moreover, descendants of immigrants are accessing higher education and attaining skilled positions. Therefore, more project teams include people in or from different countries or with various national ancestries. Team members may have not only different levels of language proficiency but different customs and norms as well. Behaviors and words or phrases that are not considered offensive in one

culture may be considered offensive in another culture. Team members may have different concepts of time (punctuality), communication styles (greetings, eye contact, hand gestures, personal space), and perceptions of appropriate protocol (formality, hierarchy), as well as different views on the role of women or elders. Team members need to exhibit patience when another person is struggling with the language or pronunciations.

- *Gender.* Project teams increasingly include a higher proportion of women, as more women enter and stay in the workforce, particularly in positions that require specific high-demand skills, such as in information and technology fields. Men and women may behave and communicate differently due to disparities in their socialization process. Different communication styles can lead to misinterpretation and misunderstanding.

- *Health.* Teams are diverse with respect to the health or wellness of their members. This includes physical and mental abilities, as well as behavioral disorders. Some of these differences are visible, such as prostheses or a cane, while other health matters are less visible, such as a heart condition or anxiety disorder. Team members need to accommodate each other with respect to health matters and not "label" people or discount their capabilities and contributions because of health-related limitations.

- *Job status.* Many project teams include members of different levels of experience and skills, as well as different levels of seniority and job titles. Team members should not make assumptions about the potential contribution of another member based on his or her job title or position. Excluding team members from meetings or problem-solving discussions because they may be considered to hold a lower-level position or do not have the specific expertise can be a missed opportunity for some new and creative ideas.

- *Marital and parental status.* With respect to conditions such as people getting married at a later age, getting divorced, having been married several times, becoming widowed, blending families, having both spouses working, or being single parents or childless couples or partners, the composition of project teams is more diverse. Team members should not make assumptions about the availability or effectiveness of other members based on their marital or parental status, such as assuming that a single person would have more time to work on a challenging assignment. Members need to accommodate the unique needs of team members, such as finishing a meeting on time so a member can pick up his or her child from child care by a certain time.

- *Race.* With globalization, migration between countries, and growing numbers of racial minorities who are gaining access to higher education and attaining skilled positions, project teams increasingly have a mix of people of traditionally underrepresented races. Team members should avoid stereotyping others in the team who are from different races. Individuals from various races can bring different and enriching perspectives to project team discussions and processes.

- *Religious affiliation.* Just as globalization affects the composition of project teams with respect to ethnic and racial diversity, it also impacts teams with respect to religious diversity. There are variety of religions worldwide, including Buddhism, Christianity, Hinduism, Islam, and Judaism. Each religion has particular practices such as daily prayer times, observance of holy days, dietary restrictions, and so forth. Individuals may have great devotion

to their religious beliefs and practices. Team members need to respect other members' religious practices and accommodate them in accomplishing the project schedule.

- *Other aspects.* Other aspects of diversity among the project team can include sexual orientation; political affiliation; personal habits, such as smoking; and personal interests, such as hunting, traveling, and so forth. Like the other dimensions of diversity mentioned above, these elements need to be respected, even if there may be personal disagreement, in order to create the environment of trust and support that is necessary for successful team performance.

Stereotyping is categorizing individuals into a group and then conferring on them the characteristics that we believe apply universally to all members of that group. Project team members should not stereotype or make assumptions about a team member's behavior or performance based on their diversity. Do not attribute a team member's performance to a particular diversity characteristic (gender, age, race, and so forth)—for example, "That activity was very tedious and required attention to detail. Kim did a good job on it because Asians and women are good at those kinds of tasks." Similarly, do not blame team members for something that went wrong and relate it to their diversity (e.g., physical disability, language skills)—for example, "His task did not get done on time because he could not keep up with the rest of the team due to his heart condition," or "We had to do everything over because her directions were not clear because of her poor language skills."

Team members should not exclude or have lower expectations of certain diverse groups, as seen by, for example, assigning them less challenging tasks or assuming that a female team member cannot handle additional responsibilities because of her family obligations. Differences do not imply inferiority or superiority. Do not discount a team member's comments or contribution just because of diverse characteristics—for example, not asking the opinion of a younger team member, a clerical worker, or a craftsperson.

Do not identify, label, or refer to team members by drawing attention to their diversity—for example, "He's the one in the wheelchair," or "the old guy," or "the Hispanic," or "the girl with the tattoos," and so forth. Nor should team members make derogatory or insensitive remarks or engage in behavior that demeans the dignity of others—for example, making fun of the spelling or pronunciation of a person's name rather than asking the person for the correct pronunciation; what someone is wearing, such as a turban or nose ring; or a person's religious practice, such as saying a prayer before he or she eats a meal.

It is inappropriate for team members to tell jokes, ridicule, or make fun of a diversity characteristic of a team member or a particular group. Such behavior often reinforces stereotypes. Innuendoes are also made by what is said or written (electronic messages), the words used ("those people," "them"), how it is said (in a disdainful tone), or body language used (smirking, raising eyebrows, shaking head). Even if unintentional, a person may use a phrase or term that confuses or embarrasses another team member. Although one team member may think a comment is funny, another person may consider it offensive or hurtful. Also, there is a chance that a person may be offended because they have an acquaintance or family member who may be in the group (for example, those with a physical disability) that is the brunt of the joke.

Reinforce Your Learning

35. What are some dimensions of diversity?

Reinforce Your Learning

36. Team members should not _____ or make _____ about a team member's behavior or _____ based on his or her _____.

Inappropriate behavior regarding diversity includes closed-mindedness, stereotyping, labeling, excluding, ridiculing, insulting, harassing, intimidating, and discriminating. An individual who is offended or a victim of such behavior may not react or speak up. The team member may develop resentment for certain team members, which could affect team cohesion, morale, and performance. If a team member feels something that was said or done is offensive, he or she should address it with the offender and perhaps take the opportunity to educate the person about why it was offensive. Any diversity issues or conflicts should be addressed immediately so that they can be resolved before they fester and "explode" at a later time. If a team member exhibits unacceptable behavior regarding the various aspects of diversity, or sees such behavior from other team members, the concern needs to be discussed with the project manager or the organization's management about how the issues should be addressed—on an individual basis, with the group of individuals involved, or with the entire team. Diversity-related issues that are not addressed can have serious impacts on the project team and work environment, resulting in frequent conflicts, a hostile climate, strained communication, or poor performance, as well as causing specific team members increased anxiety, nervousness, and stress. It could also lead to a formal complaint by an individual or group and could possibly result in lawsuits against the project contractor and/or specific team members. It could also lead to disciplinary action against individual team members, including dismissal from the team or termination of employment.

What can a project organization do to create and sustain a supportive and positive climate for diversity? There are things that can be done by the project organization, project manager, and individual team members in this regard.

Two actions the project organization can take are to have a written policy regarding diversity and to provide training about diversity in the workplace. The goals of the policy might be to create a work environment where (1) all team members flourish, (2) differences are respected and valued, (3) the right of all team members to participate and contribute is respected, (4) each team member is valued and respected for his or her unique contributions, and (5) there is zero tolerance for breach of respect or intolerant behavior.

Barriers to valuing diversity include lack of awareness and lack of understanding. Therefore, a training session on diversity should raise awareness, create understanding, and help diminish misunderstanding and conflict. Providing a training session on diversity to the project team at the beginning of the project to inform them of the organization's policy, and incorporating case studies and role plays, is a helpful approach. Mandating such training sends a message that the project organization places high importance on valuing diversity. One outcome of the training might be that team members become comfortable asking questions about differences and preferred interactions in the workplace. An example of how additional informal training can take place throughout the project might be to have team lunches where team members of different nationalities bring ethnic food to share and explain some of their customs.

The project manager must promote and foster a respectful and supportive work environment that removes barriers to valuing diversity, values differences, and encourages participation by all team members. She or he must establish and clearly communicate expectations and exemplify the expected behavior. The project manager should discuss the importance of respecting and valuing diversity at a project team meeting at the beginning of the project and periodically

throughout the project, as well as discuss those expectations with new members as part of their orientation when they join the team.

Team members can also do things to support valuing diversity and the contributions of all team members. Individual team members can make a personal commitment to understand and value diversity and respect the differences of other team members. Do not make assumptions about other team members' value or potential contributions. Be aware of and acknowledge your own stereotypes of diverse groups. Demonstrate respect by striving to learn from team members who are different from you. Look for occasions for "learning opportunities." Make an effort to enhance your awareness and understanding of the various dimensions of diversity through participation in training, reading, social activities, informal discussions, and so forth. For example, take the time to get to know other team members outside of the work environment in a more relaxed social setting. Be open-minded, exhibit professional behavior, act in a civilized manner, and have a considerate regard for others.

Diversity for the project team is about acknowledging, understanding and valuing differences, and creating a work environment that recognizes, respects, and harnesses differences for the benefits of accomplishing a shared goal. It should be seen and valued by the project team as a strength that can enrich communication, foster better relationships, create an enjoyable workplace, and enhance team performance. Diversity of the team brings unique ideas and perspectives to projects. Each team member has experiences, skills, and values to contribute to the team. Such differences can lead to more creative, faster, and higher-quality problem solving and decision making. Team members need to interact with each other based on each person's unique differences. Having a common goal such as the project objective can bring a diverse group together.

Key points to remember regarding valuing team diversity follow:

Reinforce Your Learning

39. What are some reasons why the project team should value diversity as a strength?

- Do not make assumptions or judgments about team members' value-added contributions just because of their diversity characteristics.
- Think before you speak. Once something is said, you cannot take it back, and you may lose the respect of other team members.

Ethical Behavior

Bill stopped by Pat's office and said, "Hey, Pat, what'dya say we skip out this afternoon and go golfing. The boss isn't around. If anybody asks, we can just say we're going to the construction site to check on some stuff. We've been working hard so we deserve it, and we shouldn't have to charge it to our vacation time. We're a lot more productive than some of the other people around here anyway. I told the boss the task we're working on would take us 10 days, and we should easily finish in about 6 days, just like I figured we would anyway. So hey, we've got some time coming to us."

Is Bill's behavior ethical? What should Pat do? As the owner of a small business, if some of your employees did this and you found out about it, what would you do?

There are situations when, rather than doing the right thing, individuals rationalize their actions, saying, "It's not hurting anyone," or "Everybody does it." Some people will try to get others to go along with them, or be party to the action, to validate their behavior. Their thinking is that it must be okay if another person also agrees to do it.

Reinforce Your Learning

40. Customers and suppliers want to do business with a project contractor they can _____.

Not only is ethical behavior necessary within a project organization but it is also crucial in project business relationships with customers, suppliers, and sub-contractors. Customers and suppliers want to do business with a contractor or project organization they can trust. Trust is especially important regarding the information that the project manager or team members communicate to the customer. Withholding or falsifying information is unacceptable, especially in situations where potential safety consequences are concerned. There certainly may be gray areas of reporting. For example, when do you tell a customer of a potential problem—immediately, when the problem is identified; after you have attempted to resolve the problem; or once you have developed an action plan to resolve the problem? Will the customer overreact too soon? It is important to communicate honestly about such situations in a timely manner that is objective and neither unnecessarily alarming nor misleading.

Throughout any project, situations may arise that can provide an opportunity for unethical behavior or misconduct. Some examples are:

- Intentionally submitting a low bid on a proposal with the intention of charging the customer for high-priced changes after you get the contract.
- Purchasing materials from suppliers who give you "kickbacks" or gifts for doing business with them, rather than using fair, open competition practices.
- Being dishonest in time-card reporting of hours worked, resulting in over-charges to the customer.
- Padding or falsifying travel expense reports.
- Plagiarizing the work of others and taking credit for it.
- Knowingly using marginal or unsafe materials or designs.
- Taking project supplies or using project equipment for personal use.
- Putting pressure on the project team to charge more or fewer hours than they actually worked to mislead management or the customer that the project expenditures are within budget.
- Knowingly approving test results that are inaccurate.
- Paying off inspectors to approve work that otherwise may not have passed inspection.

Many circumstances during a project can be debatable regarding ethical misbehavior. For example, if a project schedule slips, is it because the contractor or a project team member intentionally provided unrealistic time estimates originally, or was he or she genuinely optimistic that the work could get done in the estimated duration? It really points to "intention" or doing something knowingly—was the intent to knowingly mislead? Intentional distortion, deception, or misrepresentation is outright unethical.

What can a project organization do to promote ethical behavior and reduce the chances of any misconduct?

Certainly, the project manager must set the tone and expectations and must exemplify ethical behavior. If the project team sees the project manager taking actions or making decisions that are ethically questionable, they will think that it is okay for them to do the same thing. The project manager must be committed to always doing what is right and fair and communicate the same expectations to the project team.

Two actions a project organization can take to help prevent any wrongdoing are to have a written policy on ethical behavior and to provide training about ethics in the workplace. A policy on ethical behavior should include topics on expectations, a

Reinforce Your Learning

41. Two actions an organization can take to help prevent any wrongdoing are to have a

on ethical behavior and to provide

about ethics in the workplace.

process for reporting misconduct, and the consequences of engaging in unethical practices. The Project Management Institute developed a *Code of Ethics and Professional Conduct,* which is an excellent guide for people involved in projects. It can also provide a framework for a project organization's policy on ethical behavior.

Providing a training session on ethical behavior to inform the project team of the organization's policy, and incorporating case studies or role plays, is a helpful approach. Employees who participate in ethics training are less likely to engage in wrongdoing. Mandating such training sends a message that the project organization places high value on ethical behavior.

The project manager should discuss the importance of ethical behavior at a project team meeting at the beginning of the project and mention it regularly at meetings throughout the project. Also, when new members are brought into the project team, the project manager should discuss the importance of, and expectations for, ethical behavior as part of an orientation meeting. Ethical actions, such as a project team member raising an issue about an unsafe design, should be encouraged, acknowledged, and appreciated. Misconduct or conflict-of-interest activities must be addressed and appropriate disciplinary action taken to show that such behavior is unacceptable and will not be tolerated.

Project team members need to be informed that if they are not sure of or hesitant about a possible ethical or conflict-of-interest situation, they should bring it to the attention of the project manager before taking action. The project organization should also establish a nonthreatening process for individuals to report any actions by others that they consider unethical or misconduct. For example, this process might include a procedure for individuals to report such matters anonymously, or to be able to report them to or discuss them with an independent party, such as the human resources manager. If a case of wrongdoing is reported—for example, someone alleges that a person on the project team is falsifying travel expense reports—the organization must thoroughly investigate such allegations for facts versus hearsay before any disciplinary action is taken.

Ethical behavior is everyone's responsibility, not just the project manager's. Every member of the project team must be accountable for his or her actions. Personal integrity is the foundation for workplace ethics. Individuals who have a mindset of trying to "get away (from being caught) with things" will erode that foundation. Other members of the project team need to put peer pressure on such individuals to help modify the behavior by communicating that they do not agree with, condone, accept, or want to be party to such behavior.

A point to keep in mind when guiding ethical behavior on projects is to not do anything that you would not want your family, friends, neighbors, or coworkers to read about or see in the news or on a social networking site.

Reinforce Your Learning

42. _____

is the foundation for workplace ethics.

Conflict on Projects

Conflict on projects is inevitable. You might think that conflict is bad and should be avoided. Differences of opinion are natural, however, and must be expected. It would be a mistake to try to suppress conflict, as it can be beneficial. It provides an opportunity to gain new information, consider alternatives, develop better solutions to problems, enhance team building, and learn. As part of the team-building process, the project manager and project team need to openly acknowledge that disagreement is bound to occur during the performance of the project and reach a consensus on how it should be handled. Such a discussion needs to take place at

the beginning of the project, not when the first situation occurs or after there has been an emotional outburst. It should be addressed at the project kickoff meeting.

The following sections discuss the sources of conflict on a project and approaches to handling these conflicts.

SOURCES OF CONFLICT

During a project, conflict can emerge from a variety of situations. It can involve members of the project team, the project manager, the customer, and other stakeholders. Here are eight sources of potential conflict on projects.

WORK SCOPE

Conflict can arise from differences of opinion about how much work should be done, how the work should be done, or at what level of quality the work should be done. Take the following cases:

- In a project to develop an order-tracking system, one team member thinks that bar coding technology should be used, whereas another individual thinks that keypad data entry stations should be used. This is a conflict over the technical approach to the job.
- In a community festival project, one team member thinks that mailing an advertisement about the festival to each household in the town is sufficient, whereas another thinks that the mailing should be sent to all residents in the county, advertisements should be placed in newspapers, and a website established. This is a conflict over how much work should be included.
- As part of a project to build a home, a contractor has put on one coat of paint in each room in the house. Upon inspection, however, the customer is not satisfied that one coat is sufficient and demands that the contractor put on a second coat at no additional cost. This is a conflict over the level of quality of the work.

RESOURCE ASSIGNMENTS

Conflict can arise over the particular individuals assigned to work on certain tasks or over the quantity of resources assigned to certain tasks. In the project to develop an order-tracking system, the person assigned the task of developing the application software might want to be assigned to work on the database because it would give her an opportunity to expand her knowledge and skills. In the community festival project, the team members charged with painting the booths might think that they need more volunteers assigned to help them in order to finish the work in time.

SCHEDULE

Conflict can result from differences of opinion about the sequence in which the work should be done or about how long the work should take. During the planning stage at the beginning of the project, when a team member estimates that her tasks will take six weeks to complete, the project manager may respond, "That is too long. We will never get the project done on time. You have to do it in four weeks."

COST

Conflict often arises over how much the work should cost. For example, suppose a market research company provided a customer with an estimated cost for conducting a nationwide survey and then, when the project was about 75 percent

complete, told the customer that the project would probably cost 20 percent more than originally estimated. Or what if more people were assigned to a late project to bring it back on schedule, but now expenditures are way above budget. Who should pay for the cost overruns?

PRIORITIES

Conflict is likely to result when people are assigned to work on several different projects concurrently or when various people need to use a limited resource at the same time. For example, an individual has been assigned to work part of her time on a project team within her company to streamline some of the company's procedures. However, she has a sudden increase in her regular workload, and her failure to spend the anticipated amount of time on her project assignments is holding up the project. Which has priority—her project assignment or her regular work? Or suppose a company has one supercomputer capable of doing complicated scientific data analysis. Several project teams need access to the computer during the same time period in order to maintain their respective schedules. The team that cannot use the computer will be behind schedule. Which project team has priority?

ORGANIZATIONAL ISSUES

A variety of organizational issues can cause conflict, particularly during the storming stage of team development. There may be disagreement over the need for certain procedures established by the project manager with respect to documentation or approvals. Conflict can result from poor or ambiguous project communication, lack of information sharing, or failure to make timely decisions. For example, conflict is likely to arise if the project manager insists that all communications flow through him or her. Another case may be that there are not enough project status review meetings. When a meeting is finally held, information is unveiled that would have been helpful to others if it had been known several weeks earlier. As a result, some team members may have to redo some of their work. Finally, there could be conflict between some or all of the project team members and the project manager because of his or her leadership style.

STAKEHOLDER ISSUES

Conflict can arise from issues with certain stakeholders. For example, a group may object to the routing of a new highway or pipeline and take an adversarial position including the threat of public demonstrations and a media campaign. Or the staff of a medical practice may be upset because they feel there is a lack of funding and time for adequate training for a new electronic medical records system. Or some stakeholders may feel that the project manager is not providing timely or sufficient information about the status of a project.

PERSONAL DIFFERENCES

Reinforce Your Learning

43. What are common sources of conflict on projects?

Conflict can emerge among members of the project team because of differences in individuals' values, attitudes, or personalities. In the case of a project that is behind schedule, if one team member is working evening hours to try to get the work back on schedule, she may resent the fact that another member always leaves at the normal time to have dinner with his wife before she leaves for her evening job. Or two team members may have strong differing political viewpoints that are affecting their relationship and work performance and jeopardizing the success of the project.

There may be times during the project when there are no conflicts. On the other hand, there will be times when there are many conflicts from various sources that need to be handled. Conflict is inevitable on projects, but it can be beneficial if handled properly.

HANDLING CONFLICT

Conflict is not just for the project manager to resolve; conflict between team members should be handled by the individuals involved. Dealt with properly, conflict can be beneficial. It causes problems to surface and be addressed. It stimulates discussion and requires individuals to clarify their views. Conflict can force individuals to search for new approaches; it can foster creativity and enhance the problem-solving process. If it is handled properly, conflict helps team building. However, if it is not handled properly, conflict can have a negative impact on the project team. It can destroy communication—people stop talking and sharing information. It can diminish team members' willingness to listen to and respect others' viewpoints. It can break down team unity and reduce the level of trust and openness. Focus must be kept on the issue, not on the personalities of the people involved.

Reinforce Your Learning

44. Handled properly, conflict can be

_____.

Researchers Blake and Mouton and Kilmann and Thomas have identified five approaches that people use to handle conflict.

AVOIDING OR WITHDRAWING

In the avoiding or withdrawing approach, individuals in conflict retreat from the situation to avoid an actual or potential disagreement. For example, if one person disagrees with a second person, the second individual may simply remain silent. This approach can cause the conflict to fester and then escalate at a later time.

COMPETING OR FORCING

In the competing or forcing approach, conflict is viewed as a win-lose situation. The value placed on winning the conflict is higher than the value placed on the relationship between the individuals, and the individual who is in a position to do so handles the conflict by exerting power over the other individual. For example, in a conflict between the project manager and a member of the project team regarding which technical approach to use for designing a system, the project manager may simply pull rank and say, "Do it my way." This approach to handling conflict can result in resentment and deterioration of the work climate.

ACCOMMODATING OR SMOOTHING

The accommodating or smoothing approach emphasizes the search for areas of agreement within the conflict and minimizes the value of addressing differences. Topics that may cause hurt feelings are not discussed. In this approach, the value placed on the relationship between the individuals is greater than the value placed on resolution of the issue. Although this approach may make a conflict situation livable, it does not resolve the issue.

COMPROMISING

In the compromising approach, team members search for an intermediate position. They focus on splitting the difference. They search for a solution that will bring some degree of satisfaction to each individual. The solution, however, may not be the optimal one. Take the case where members of the project team are estimating durations for

various project tasks. One member says, "I think it will take 15 days." Another says, "No way; it should not take that long. Maybe 5 or 6 days." So they quickly split the difference and agree on 10 days, which may not be the best estimate.

COLLABORATING, CONFRONTING, OR PROBLEM SOLVING

In the collaborating, confronting, or problem-solving approach, team members confront the issue directly. They look for a win-win outcome. They place high value on both the outcome and the relationship between the individuals. Each person must approach the conflict with a constructive attitude and a willingness to work in good faith with the others to resolve the issue. There is an open exchange of information about the conflict as each sees it. Differences are explored and worked through to reach the best overall solution. Each individual is willing to abandon or redefine his or her position as new information is exchanged, in order to arrive at the optimal solution. For this approach to work, it is necessary to have a healthy project environment in which there is a high level of trust, relationships are genuine, and people do not fear retribution if they are honest with each other.

Reinforce Your Learning

45. What are five approaches to handling conflict?

Differences can escalate into emotional arguments. When individuals try to resolve a conflict, they cannot let themselves be drawn into an emotional state. They need to be able to manage, but not suppress, their emotions. They need to take the time to understand the other person's point of view. The following section provides a helpful approach to collaborative problem solving.

Unnecessary conflict can be avoided or minimized through early involvement of the project team in planning; clear articulation of each member's role and responsibilities; open, frank, and timely communication; clear operating procedures; and sincere team-building efforts by the project manager and project team.

Problem Solving

It is unusual for a team to complete a project without encountering some problems. Normally, various kinds of problems arise along the way, some more serious than others. For example, the project can fall a few weeks behind schedule, jeopardizing completion by the customer's required date. Or the project may be in budget trouble—maybe 50 percent of the money has been spent, but only 40 percent of the work has been accomplished. Some problems are of a technical nature—a new optical sensor system is not providing the required data accuracy, or a new piece of high-speed assembly equipment continues to jam up and ruin expensive components. How effectively the project team solves problems may make the difference between project success and project failure.

A NINE-STEP APPROACH TO PROBLEM SOLVING

To help project teams effectively solve problems, a disciplined, creative, and effective approach to problem solving is needed. Here is a nine-step approach to problem solving, followed by a discussion of brainstorming—a technique helpful in several steps of the problem-solving approach.

 1. *Develop a problem statement.* It is important to start with a written statement of the problem, which gives definition and boundaries to the problem. The problem statement provides a vehicle for the members of the problem-solving team to agree about the exact nature of the problem they are trying

to solve. The problem statement should be as specific as possible because it will help to focus the subsequent steps of the problem-solving process. It should also include quantitative measures of the extent of the problem because the measures can be used as criteria later on to help determine whether the problem has indeed been solved.

- An example of a poor problem statement is "We are behind schedule." An example of a better problem statement is "We are two weeks behind schedule. It looks as if we will miss our customer's required finish date, which is four weeks from now, by two weeks unless we do something. If we do not make the customer's required date, she will be entitled to a 10 percent price reduction according to the contract."
- Another example of a poor problem statement is "The sensor system doesn't work." A better statement is "The sensor system is giving erroneous data when it measures the rounded corners of parts."

2. *Identify potential causes of the problem.* There can be many reasons why a problem has occurred or is occurring. This is especially true of technical problems. Take a project involving the development of a multiple-user computer system, in which data are not being passed from the central computer server to all the user work stations. The cause could be a hardware or software problem, or it could be a problem with the server or with some of the work stations. A technique often used to identify potential causes of a problem is *brainstorming.* This technique will be discussed in the next section.

3. *Gather data and verify the most likely causes.* In the early stages of the problem-solving process, the team is often reacting to symptoms rather than dealing with what might be causing the problem. This is particularly likely to happen when the problem is described in terms of symptoms. Suppose a person goes to a doctor and says he has been getting headaches. The doctor realizes that there could be many causes, such as stress, a tumor, a change in diet, or a problem in the environment. So the doctor will attempt to gather additional data about some of the most likely causes by asking questions and possibly having the patient undergo some tests. The doctor will then use this information to narrow down the list of possible causes of the problem. It is important for the team to get beyond the symptoms and gather the facts before moving on to the next step: identifying possible solutions. Otherwise, much time may be wasted developing solutions to symptoms rather than to the cause of the problem. Gathering data, whether it is through asking questions, interviewing people, running tests, reading reports, or analyzing data, takes time. However, it must be done to focus the team's work in the rest of the problem-solving process.

4. *Identify possible solutions.* This is the fun and creative step in the problem-solving process. It is also a critical step in the process. Team members need to be careful not to jump to the first solution suggested or even the most obvious solution. They will be disappointed later on when that first or obvious solution does not work and it is back to the drawing board. For example, when a project is two weeks behind schedule, the obvious solution may be to just ask the customer if it is okay for the project to be delivered two weeks late. However, that solution could backfire. If the project manager approaches the customer and asks if it is okay for the project to be delivered late, the customer may react negatively, threaten not to do business with the

company ever again, and call the project manager's boss to complain about the project being late. The brainstorming technique, discussed later, is very useful in this step to help identify several possible solutions.

5. *Evaluate the alternative solutions.* Once various potential solutions have been identified in step 4, it is necessary to evaluate them. There may be many good, yet different, solutions to the problem. Each viable solution should be evaluated. The question then becomes, "Evaluated against what?" Criteria have to be established. So in this step, the problem-solving team has to first establish the criteria against which alternative solutions will be evaluated. Once the criteria have been established, the team may want to use an evaluation scorecard similar to the one in Figure 3.2. Each criterion can be weighted differently, depending on how important it is. For example, the cost of implementing the solution may be weighted more heavily than the estimated time it will take to implement. Like step 3, this step may take some time if you need to gather data to evaluate the alternative solutions intelligently. For example, it may take time to pull together information on the cost of parts or materials needed for some of the solutions, especially if you need to get price estimates from various vendors or suppliers. Each person on the problem-solving team should complete an evaluation scorecard for each of the possible solutions. These scorecards will be used in the next step.

6. *Determine the best solution.* In this step, the evaluation scorecards completed in step 5 by each member of the problem-solving team are used to help determine the best solution. They become a basis for discussion among the team members. The scorecards are not used as the sole mechanism for determining the best solution; they are used as input to the decision-making process. Here is where it becomes important to have a well-rounded team in terms of relevant expertise. The decision as to which is the best solution is based on the knowledge and expertise of the members of the problem-solving team, in conjunction with the evaluation scorecards.

7. *Revise the project plan.* Once the best solution has been selected, it is necessary to prepare a plan for implementing that solution. Specific activities need to be defined along with their estimated durations and costs. The persons and resources needed for each task must also be identified. The project team members who will be responsible for implementing the solution should develop this planning information. It must then be incorporated into the overall project plan to determine what impact the solution will have, if any, on other parts of the project. Of specific interest is whether the selected solution will cause other problems. For example, the best solution to the technical problem with the sensor system may be to order a new part from a vendor, but if it takes two months for the vendor to make and ship the part, this solution may cause the whole project to fall behind schedule and jeopardize meeting the required project completion date. If this risk was not taken into account in step 5, the problem-solving team may have to revisit the solution to determine whether it is still the best solution.

8. *Implement the solution.* Once a plan has been developed for implementing the best solution, the appropriate team members should go ahead and perform their respective tasks.

9. *Determine whether the problem has been solved.* Once the solution has been implemented, it is important to determine whether the problem has indeed been solved. Here is where the team goes back to the problem statement in

step 1 and compares the results of implementing the solution to the measure of the problem defined in the problem statement. The team has to ask, "Did the selected solution accomplish what we hoped it would? Is the problem solved?" The solution may have only partially solved the problem, or perhaps it did not solve the problem at all. For example, maybe after the new part ordered for the sensor system was installed, the system still gave erroneous data. If the problem has not been solved, the problem-solving team needs to go back to steps 2 and 3 to see what else could be causing the problem.

Depending on the magnitude and complexity of the problem, the above nine-step problem-solving process can take a few hours or several months. The problem-solving team should include those individuals most familiar with the problem as well as individuals with specific expertise that may be required. Sometimes the individual with the necessary expertise may be an outsider to the project team, such as a consultant who can provide a fresh perspective.

BRAINSTORMING

Brainstorming is a technique used in problem solving in which all members of a group contribute spontaneous ideas in a nonjudgmental environment. Before team members select a solution to a problem, they should make sure that they have explored as broad a range of options and ideas as possible. Brainstorming is a way to generate a lot of ideas and have fun doing it. Brainstorming generates excitement, creativity, better solutions, and greater commitment. It is particularly useful in two of the steps in the nine-step approach to problem solving: step 2, identify potential causes of the problem, and step 4, identify possible solutions.

In brainstorming, the *quantity* of ideas generated is more important than the *quality* of the ideas. The objective is for the group to produce as many ideas as possible, including novel and unorthodox ones.

The team sits around a table, with a facilitator at a flip chart, computer with projector, or whiteboard to record ideas. To start the process, one member states an idea. For example, during a brainstorming session to identify possible solutions for a project that is two weeks behind schedule, the first member might say, "Work overtime." It would then be the next member's turn to state an idea, such as "Bring in some temporary help." And so forth. The process continues around the table, with each person stating only one idea at a time. Anyone who cannot think of an idea when it is his or her turn can simply say, "Pass." Some people will come up with ideas that build on ideas previously mentioned by others. *Building* involves combining several ideas into one idea or improving on another person's idea. As the ideas are stated, the facilitator records them for everyone to see. This round-robin process continues until no one can come up with any more new ideas or the time limit is up.

Two important rules must be followed for brainstorming to work: *no discussion and no judgmental comments*. As soon as a participant has stated his or her idea, it is the next person's turn. Individuals should simply state an idea and not discuss, justify, or try to sell it. Other participants are not allowed to make any comments at all, supportive or judgmental, and no one may ask questions of the person who stated the idea. Obviously such "killer" comments as "That will never work," "That is a stupid idea," or "The boss will not go for that" are not allowed, but participants also must be cautioned not to use body language, such as raised eyebrows, a cough, a smirk, or a sigh, to send judgmental messages.

Brainstorming can be an effective and fun way of helping a problem-solving team come up with the best possible solution.

Time Management

People involved in projects are usually very busy working on their assigned tasks, communicating, preparing documents, attending meetings, and traveling. Therefore, good time management is essential for a high-performance project team. Following are some suggestions to help you manage your time effectively:

1. *At the end of each week, identify several (two to five) goals that you want to accomplish the following week.* List the goals in priority order, with the most important (not the most urgent) first. Take into consideration the time you will have available; look at your schedule for the week to see whether you have meetings or other commitments. Do not attempt to create a multiple-page, exhaustive list of all the things you would like to do. Keep this list of goals within sight so you will look at it frequently.

2. *At the end of each day, make a to-do list for the next day.* The items on the daily to-do list must support the achievement of the goals you set for the week. List items in priority order, again with the most important (not necessarily the easiest or the most urgent) first. Before you prepare the to-do list, look at your schedule for the day to see how much time you have available to devote to accomplishing the items on your list. You may have meetings or appointments that will reduce the amount of time available. You should also allow some flextime in your day's schedule to accommodate unexpected things that may come up. Do not make an exhaustive list of everything you would like to accomplish when there is no time to get it all done—that just causes frustration.

 List only what you can realistically accomplish. Do not get in the habit of feeling that whatever is not accomplished can just be rolled over to the next day. You will find more items rolled over than accomplished! It is important to write out the to-do list, not just keep it in your head. Writing it out builds commitment to doing it.

3. *Read the daily to-do list first thing in the morning, and keep it in sight all day.* Set everything else aside, and start working on the first item. Focus and self-discipline are extremely important. Do not divert your attention to less important items that may be less challenging, such as reading nonessential electronic messages, checking your social networking sites, or filing. As you complete an item, cross it off the list; this will provide a sense of accomplishment. Then start right in on the next item. Again, do not let yourself get sidetracked into working on less important items in between completing the items on your list.

4. *Control interruptions.* Do not let phone calls, electronic messages, or walk-in visitors divert you from working on the items on your to-do list. You may want to set aside a block of time each day to return and make phone calls and to reply to and send electronic messages rather than letting them interrupt your work throughout the day. There may be times when you want to close your door so that people will know not to interrupt you. When you are working on a particular item on your to-do list, clear away other paperwork to eliminate the temptation to reach over and start working on something else.

5. *Learn to say no.* Do not let yourself get drawn into activities that will consume your time but not contribute to accomplishing your goals. You might have to turn down invitations to participate in meetings or trips, serve on committees, or review documents. You may have to cut short hallway conversations. Learn to say no, or you will overcommit yourself and end up a very busy person without accomplishing your goals.

6. *Make effective use of waiting time.* For example, always carry your smartphone, electronic tablet, or reading material with you in case you get stuck in an airport, a traffic jam, or a dentist's office.

7. *Try to handle most paperwork and electronic messages only once.* Go through your incoming mail or electronic messages at the end of the day so that it will not divert you from working on your day's to-do list. There may be something in your mail or e-mail that will lead you to add an item to the to-do list you prepare for the next day. When going through your mail or e-mail, take action on each document while you are reading or holding it:

 • If it is junk mail, throw it out or delete it without reading it.
 • If you can throw it out or delete it after you read it, do so; file it only if you cannot get it somewhere else if you need it.
 • If a response is required, either send a brief electronic reply or hand-write a response on the document and return it to the originator.
 • If the document will require an extended period of time to read, either incorporate time to read it on one of your future to-do lists (if the item could make an important contribution to your weekly goals) or put it in your briefcase so that you can read it when you are stuck waiting somewhere (see item 6 above).

8. *Reward yourself at the end of the week if you accomplished all your goals.* Make sure you are honest with yourself. Reward yourself for accomplishing all your goals, not for working hard and being busy but not accomplishing your goals. In your mind, the reward must be an incentive and payoff tied directly to accomplishing your goals. If you do not accomplish your weekly goals, you should not reward yourself. Otherwise, the reward will be meaningless and will not constitute an incentive to accomplish the goals.

Reinforce Your Learning

48. What are some things you can do to manage your time effectively?

 REAL WORLD PROJECT MANAGEMENT

A Look at Meeting Impact on Postmeeting Productivity

Project meetings occur at a set schedule with two or more project team members in an effort to achieve a predefined work-related goal. Some project team members do not see a value in meeting. Other team members view meetings as an opportunity to meet the complex demands of a project's objectives.

To determine what role meetings play for one financial services company in the United States, project team members from a software development group collected and analyzed a year of meeting data. They examined the impact of diversity (tenure, staffing, functional role), meeting size, and meeting history on the amount of work completed after attending the meetings. The meeting history is related to the number of times the software development group met for project meetings.

The software development group met to discuss how individual team members' actions were part of the team-level objectives. Without the meetings, the achievement of the project goal would have been in question. Working in isolation limited the ability of team members to know where their part of the project fit with other members of the team.

After analyzing the year of meeting data, the team found that tenure diversity and meeting history can improve the likelihood of an increase in the amount of work completed after attending a project meeting. The other factors examined did not show any difference in the amount of work completed after the project meetings. Although the findings suggest an increase in productivity, the team wanted to know more about the influential nature of tenure diversity and meeting history.

The team observed that the greater the amount of time an employee spent within the organization increased the volume of organizational knowledge the employee possessed. Workers with less tenure at a company were observed to have novel ideas and more limited organizational knowledge. The research team found that the project team was more effective at solving problems if more senior members attended the meeting with the more junior members of the team. The interactions observed in the meetings indicated that the more junior members of the team encouraged innovation. The longer tenure employees provided critical organization-specific knowledge and drew on their past experiences to help solve problems and frame solutions. The more senior and the more junior members of the team provided a mix of attitudes, experiences, perspectives, and values to the team meeting discussions.

The meeting data analysis indicated that as the team matured together, they developed procedural routines within the group on how the meetings functioned and how the team interacted with each other. As the team members learned more about each other and the aspects of the projects each member was responsible to complete, the interactions of the team members demonstrated a coordination of thoughts and consistency in their perspectives. The declarative knowledge about the project deepened as the number of meetings increased. As this foundational knowledge increased, the team members found they could examine the details of the task requirements more easily. The complex actions that the team members needed to complete after the meeting were clearer allowing the project team members to accomplish more of the tasks following the meetings. With each meeting, the coordination increased as did the productivity following the meetings.

Meetings are necessary to coordinate activities for a project team. The research results indicate project team experienced the time necessary to develop the relationships between the team members necessary to form a team that needed little direction from management to perform at a high level of accomplishment. The understanding gained by the software development group could help management to leverage the findings to promote increased productivity of project teams by ensuring that senior and junior members of a project team meet and interact on a regular schedule and are given the time to develop the necessary relationships to solve problems and increase productivity.

Based on information from Crawford, J. and L. K. Leonard (2012). "Predicting Post-Meeting Work Activity in Software Development Projects," *Team Performance Management, 18*(1/2), 59–77.

CRITICAL SUCCESS FACTORS

- Project success requires an effective project team. Although plans and project management techniques are necessary, it is the people—the project manager and project team—who are the key to project success.

- Putting a group of people together to work on a project does not create a team. Helping these individuals develop and grow into a cohesive, effective team takes effort on the part of the project manager and each member of the project team.

- Project teams should be kept as small as feasible throughout the project.

- A project kickoff meeting should be held as early as possible to inform members, reduce anxiety, manage expectations, and inspire the team.

- Characteristics of effective project teams include a clear understanding of the project objective, clear expectations of each person's roles and responsibilities, a results orientation, a high degree of cooperation and collaboration, and a high level of trust.

- Each member of the project team needs to help create and foster a positive project environment.

- Effective team members have high expectations of themselves. They plan, control, and feel accountable for their individual work efforts.

- Members of effective teams have open, frank, and timely communication. They readily share information, ideas, and feelings. They provide constructive feedback to each other.

- Effective team members go beyond just doing their assigned tasks; they act as a resource for each other.

- Diversity of the team brings unique ideas and perspectives to projects.

- Individual team members make a personal commitment to understand and value diversity and respect the differences of other team members.

- Diversity is valued as a strength that will enrich communication, foster better relationships, create an enjoyable workplace, and enhance team performance.

- Ethical behavior is crucial in project business relationships with the customer, suppliers, and subcontractors.

- The project manager and the project team need to acknowledge openly that disagreement is bound to occur during the performance of the project and reach consensus on how it should be handled.

- Effective project teams resolve conflict through constructive and timely feedback and positive confrontation of the issues. Disagreement is not suppressed; rather, it is seen as normal and as an opportunity for growth.

- Handled properly, conflict can be beneficial. It causes problems to surface and be addressed. It stimulates discussion and requires individuals to clarify their views. It can foster creativity and enhance problem solving.

- Conflict is not just for the project manager to handle and resolve; conflict between team members should be handled by the individuals involved.

- Each person must approach the conflict with a constructive attitude and a willingness to work in good faith with others to resolve the issues.

- To effectively manage their time, team members should establish weekly goals and make daily to-do lists.

SUMMARY

A team is a group of individuals working interdependently to accomplish the project objective. Teamwork is the cooperative effort by members of a team to achieve this common goal. The effectiveness, or lack thereof, of the project team can make the difference between project success and project failure.

When a project is initiated, one of the first things the project manager must do is obtain and assemble a project team. Team members are assigned based not

only on their expertise and experience but also on availability. Project teams should be kept as small as feasible throughout the project.

Project teams evolve through various stages of development. Forming, the initial stage of the team development process, involves the transition from individual to team member. During this stage, individuals on the team begin to get acquainted. During the storming stage, conflict emerges and tension increases. Motivation and morale are low. Members may even resist team formation. However, after struggling through the storming stage, the team moves into the norming stage of development. Relationships among team members and between the team and the project manager have become settled, and interpersonal conflicts have been resolved for the most part. The fourth stage of team development and growth is the performing stage. In this stage, the team is highly committed and eager to achieve the project objective. The members feel a sense of unity.

The project manager should schedule a project kickoff meeting with the project team as early as possible during the forming stage of team development to inform the members, reduce anxiety, manage expectations, and inspire the team. It provides an opportunity for team members to get to know each other. The project manager should provide an overview of the project and discuss roles, responsibilities, processes, procedures, and expectations.

Characteristics often associated with effective project teams include a clear understanding of the project objective, clear expectations of each person's role and responsibilities, a results orientation, a high degree of cooperation and collaboration, and a high level of trust. Barriers to team effectiveness include unclear vision and objective, unclear definition of roles and responsibilities, lack of project structure, lack of commitment, poor communication, poor leadership, turnover of project team members, and dysfunctional behavior.

What people who work on projects have in common is that they enjoy the challenge of accomplishing something and working as part of a team. Each member of the project team needs to help create and foster a positive and effective project environment. Effective team members put the success of the project above personal gain.

Teamwork is the cooperative effort of a team to accomplish a common goal. Team building—developing a group of individuals into a team to accomplish the project objective—is an ongoing process. It is the responsibility of both the project manager and the project team. Socializing among team members supports team building. To facilitate socializing, team members can request that they be physically located in one office area for the duration of the project. They can also organize and participate in social events.

Diversity is about acknowledging, understanding, and valuing differences, and creating a work environment that recognizes, respects, and harnesses differences among team members for the benefits of accomplishing a shared goal, such as the project objective. Diversity of the team brings unique ideas and perspectives to projects. Each team member has unique experiences, skills, and values they bring to the team. Such differences can lead to more creative, faster, and higher-quality problem solving and decision making. Some dimensions of diversity include age or generation, appearance, ethnicity or ancestry, gender, health, job status, marital and parental status, race, and religious affiliation. Project team members should not stereotype or make assumptions about a team member's behavior or performance based on their diversity; nor should they identify, label, or refer to team members by drawing attention to their diversity. Barriers

to valuing diversity include lack of awareness and lack of understanding. Two actions a project organization can take to create and sustain a supportive and positive climate for diversity are to have a written policy regarding diversity and to provide training about diversity in the workplace. Individual team members can make a personal commitment to understand and value diversity and respect the differences of other team members. Diversity should be seen and valued by the project team as a strength that can enrich communication, foster better relationships, create an enjoyable workplace, and enhance team performance.

Ethical behavior is necessary within a project organization and is crucial in project business relationships with the customer, suppliers, and subcontractors. Customers and suppliers want to do business with a contractor or project organization that they can trust. Intentional distortion, deception, or misrepresentation is outright unethical. Two actions a project organization can take to help prevent any wrongdoing are to have a written policy on ethical behavior and to provide training about ethics in the workplace. A policy on ethical behavior should include topics on expectations, a process for reporting misconduct, and the consequences of engaging in unethical practices. Misconduct or conflict-of-interest activities must be addressed and appropriate disciplinary action taken to show that such behavior is unacceptable and will not be tolerated. Every member of the project team must feel accountable for his or her actions. Personal integrity is the foundation for workplace ethics.

Conflict on projects is inevitable. During a project, conflict can emerge from a variety of situations. It can involve members of the project team, the project manager, the customer, and other stakeholders. Sources of potential conflict on projects include differences of opinion on how much work should be done, how the work should be done, at what level of quality the work should be done, who should be assigned to work on which tasks, the sequence in which the work should be done, how long the work should take, and how much the work should cost. Conflict can also arise because of differences in individuals' values, attitudes, and personalities. Conflict is not just for the project manager to resolve; conflict among team members should be handled by the individuals involved. Dealt with properly, conflict can be beneficial because it causes problems to surface and be addressed.

It is unusual for a team to complete a project without encountering some problems along the way. A good nine-step problem-solving approach is to develop a problem statement, identify potential causes of the problem, gather data and verify the most likely causes, identify possible solutions, evaluate the alternative solutions, determine the best solution, revise the project plan, implement the solution, and determine whether the problem has been solved. Brainstorming is a technique used in problem solving in which all members of a group contribute spontaneous ideas in a nonjudgmental environment. In brainstorming, the quantity of ideas generated is more important than the quality of the ideas.

Good time management is essential for a high-performance project team. To manage their time effectively, team members should identify weekly goals, make a to-do list for each day, focus on accomplishing the daily to-do list, control interruptions, learn to say no to activities that do not move them closer to their goals, make effective use of waiting time, handle paperwork and electronic messages only once, and reward themselves for accomplishing their goals.

QUESTIONS

1. Discuss the stages of team development. Address the process, problems, and level of productivity of each.
2. What are the benefits of a project kickoff meeting? From your project experience, describe how the project kickoff meeting for one project could have been improved.
3. What are some characteristics associated with effective project teams? Can the same be said for an effective couple, orchestra, or professional sports team? Why or why not?
4. What are some common barriers to team effectiveness? Think of a team project on which you have worked. Discuss any barriers to success.
5. Why is it said that there is no I in TEAM? Do you agree or disagree? How can you be an effective team member?
6. Describe three activities that facilitate the process of team building. Must the project manager initiate all of these?
7. Describe some of the dimensions of diversity. List some ways you can capitalize on diversity in order to achieve your project objective.
8. What role does the project manager have related to ethical behavior on the team? What steps can be taken to help ensure a high level of ethical behavior? Describe a situation in which you were confronted with an ethical decision and the outcome of your decision.
9. Discuss some types of conflict that might arise during a project. Describe two situations in which you have experienced these types of conflict.
10. Describe the methods for handling conflict on a project. How was the conflict handled in the two situations you described in your answer to question 9?
11. The manager at a local bank noticed that after a new information system was installed at the bank, some of the customer transactions were not getting posted. The manager knew that this problem could lead to serious financial difficulties as well as unhappy customers. Describe how she could apply the nine-step problem-solving process described in the chapter to solve the problem.
12. With one or several friends, conduct a brainstorming session and list as many uses of a paperclip as you can.
13. How can people more effectively manage their time? Which of these suggestions do you currently practice? For the next week, attempt to manage your time better. Heed all the advice given in the book. At the end of the week, write a summary of your experience.

INTERNET EXERCISES

For the website addresses of the organizations mentioned in these exercises, go to "Internet Exercises" at the book's companion website at www.cengagebrain.com. It is suggested that you save this website in your "Favorites" list for easy access in the future.

1. *The Fish! Philosophy,* developed by Charthouse®, includes four simple, interconnected practices to help build stronger relationships within teams, with customers, or with others such as classmates, family, friends, or cow-orkers. Search the Web for resources related to *The Fish! Philosophy.* For

each of the four practices, list at least five ideas or actions that team members could do to build stronger relationships following that practice.
2. Search the Web for ideas on sources of conflict and strategies for conflict resolution. Summarize what you found and compare it to what was presented in this chapter.
3. Search the Web for ideas on time management. Print out the ideas listed on at least one site and discuss what you believe are the five most effective strategies for managing time.
4. Search the Web for a case study in project team building. Was the project manager successful in building his or her team? Why or why not? Describe at least one ethical dilemma that the project manager or team might have faced on the project.
5. Visit the home page for the Project Management Institute. Find the "Ethics in Project Management" page. Explore the ethics resources. Review and summarize the PMI Code of Ethics and Professional Conduct.

CASE STUDY 1 Team Effectiveness?

Colin and Raouf had been having one of their typical sidebar conversations during the meeting when an obviously irritated Henri looked at Colin. "In my 20 years of experience, I've never seen such a shabby hardware design. A first-year college student could do better," said Henri, raising his voice at Colin. "No wonder we're a month behind schedule. Now we're going to have to spend more time and money on redesign. If you were in over your head, Colin, you should have asked someone for help. I'll review the situation with Jack when he gets back on Friday. That's it—the meeting is over. We need to spend more time working than chitchatting at meetings." Everyone else on the project team was somewhat stunned by Henri's tirade, but it wasn't the first time. They all felt badly for Colin, but others had experienced the wrath of Henri in the past.

Henri is the hardware systems team leader, and Colin is a hardware system designer assigned to Henri's team. Jack, the project manager, was out of town several days for a meeting with the customer and had asked Henri to run the weekly project meeting in his absence.

After the meeting, Colin went to Raouf's office. Raouf is an application software designer. Colin and Raouf have developed a friendship during the past year. They discovered that they both graduated from the same university, a couple years apart. They are among the younger members of the project team, along with Fatima, the software system team leader. "I'm gonna get that jerk if it's the last thing I do," Colin told Raouf.

"Take it easy, Colin. You're right; he's a jerk. Everybody knows he doesn't know what he's doing, and he is in over his head. We all have his number," responded Raouf. "But notice that Henri never behaves like that in front of Jack. Only when Jack isn't around or in meetings when Jack isn't there."

"Well, I'm gonna see Jack first thing on Friday when he gets back and tell him about Henri. Nobody needs to take that kind of crap in front of everybody," Colin said.

"Maybe you should talk to Henri first, Colin," suggested Raouf.

"Yea, right!" chuckled Colin.

"What do you think Jack will do?" asked Raouf.

"Fire him, I hope," answered Colin.

"I doubt it," Raouf said, "Jack seems to always cut him a break, like he feels sorry for him or something."

"Maybe Jack should be concerned about all the good apples, and get rid of the one bad apple!" replied Colin.

Jack was back in the office Friday morning. He was just taking off his jacket when Colin appeared. "Jack, at one of the project meetings you said you had an open door policy, so I'm here to talk to you about a problem with Henri," Colin said. Jack began unpacking his briefcase and had a lot of things to catch up on after being out the whole week. He saw Colin was upset, so he said, "Sure, Colin, I have about 10 minutes before I need to meet with our contracts department to go over some amendments to the contract."

Colin blurted out, "This won't take long. I just want to say that while you were out, Henri accused me of being a lousy designer in front of the whole project team. He blamed me for the project being a month behind schedule. He always does this kind of stuff. Why do you let him get away with it? Nobody likes him. Can't you get rid of him or assigned to some other project?"

Jack was taken aback. He responded, "Colin, you really seem upset. Let's get together on Monday when I have more time, and you can have the weekend to cool off."

"There's nothing more to talk about. That's all there is to it. You can ask anybody if you don't believe me," replied Colin, as he left Jack's office.

Jack asked Rosemary, his administrative assistant, who had been intently eavesdropping on the conversation from outside of Jack's office, to schedule a meeting with Henri for later that afternoon. At that meeting, Jack told Henri about Colin's comments. Jack knew Henri had been under stress because his son had recently been arrested for selling drugs. Henri told Jack, "It sounds to me like Colin overreacted and blew things way out of proportion. At the meeting, I told Colin that there were some shortcomings in his design and suggested he get together with some folks and take another look at it. You know how these young people are; they have got to learn to be responsible for their actions."

"What about the project being behind schedule? That's news to me," asked Jack.

Henri replied, "Well, I didn't mean it was Colin's fault. To be honest with you, Fatima and her group of software whiz kids aren't the hardest workers. I mean, I always see them clowning around and yakking with each other and bothering my hardware team. No wonder the project is behind schedule. Anyway, don't worry about Colin. He's young and will have to learn to develop a thick skin. I'll talk to him. I'll tell him to stop hanging around with those software people so he doesn't develop any bad habits."

That same Friday afternoon, Colin went around asking most of the younger members of the project team to meet for a few drinks at a happy hour after work. They included most of the software people, and Rosemary, Jack's administrative assistant. She is attracted to Colin and has been hoping he'd ask her out. She told Colin that she overheard Henri tell Jack that Fatima and the software group were causing delays in the project because they spend too much time fooling around rather than working. Later in the evening, Colin went over to talk with Fatima and Raouf who had been sitting together. Colin told them, "I have firsthand information that Henri told Jack that the project is way behind

schedule because of your software team. I suggest you go and talk with Jack. Henri is poisoning this project. If Jack believes him, we'll all be fired before this project is over. Hey, I had the guts to go to Jack. Now you've got to do it, too. We have got to stand together against Henri. Jack has to be told that Henri is a big bag of wind and is disrupting the whole project team and causing dissension, and that's why the project is behind schedule. Simply put, the project will never be successful as long as Henri is working on it. And that is going to affect all of our careers—being associated with a failed project. Jack won't have any choice when he sees it's all of us against Henri."

CASE QUESTIONS

1. What are some things Colin could have done in or after the meeting when Henri verbally attacked him?
2. Is there anything more Raouf could have done during or after his meeting with Colin to prevent the situation from escalating?
3. Could Jack have handled his meeting with Colin in a better way? Was there anything Jack could have done after his meeting with Colin and before he met with Henri? What are some things Jack could have done in his meeting with Henri?
4. What should Fatima do?

GROUP ACTIVITY

Divide the class into four groups and assign one of the case questions to each group to discuss and develop responses. Each group must identify a spokesperson to present its responses to the entire class.

CASE STUDY 2 New Team Member

Straight Arrow Systems Corp. located in Los Angeles, develops and builds custom systems. Its major customer is the military market. One of its current projects is to develop a personnel identification and tracking system, referred to as the PITS.

Bob Slug is the team leader for the hardware development work package. There has been a higher than normal turnover of people on Bob's team. Today, Bob is just finishing up a brief orientation meeting with his newest team member, Brad. It is Brad's first day at Straight Arrow Systems. Brad recently graduated from a large university in southern California. His father is in the military, and prior to college, Brad lived in various countries where his father was stationed.

"Before I introduce you to the rest of the team at the weekly project team meeting this afternoon, I want to briefly give you some background on each of the people so you know what you're in for," Bob told Brad, as he rolled his eyes. He continued, "They certainly are a different group of characters. Sometimes I wonder how we get anything done. You'll probably eventually hear that we've had some turnover on the team, but I think it was for the best. There were people who just didn't fit in, if you know what I mean.

"First, there's the Asian lady: Yoko something or other. I can't pronounce it so I just call her 'Yoyo,'" Bob says with a chuckle. He continues, "Those people are good at detailed tasks so I pretty much assign her to double-check the work of some of the other people. By the way, whenever she brings in lunch, it smells up the whole place, as you can imagine. Who knows what kinds of food they eat.

"Then there's Autumn. Cute! She looks like she's still in high school. She's always got one of those iPods plugged into her ears so it's hard to take her seriously. When she talks, she uses all these 'techie' terms. These young people just don't know how to communicate; all they do is sit in front of their computer all day. And she is always asking me how she is doing. I mean, I'm not her mommy. Anyway, I kind of got my arm twisted into hiring her because management said I didn't have enough females on my team. Then they wonder why I have turnover. Next thing you know, she'll be pregnant and leave, too.

"And I have Jared, the kid with the tattoo. Need I say anything more?" said Bob, as he shook his head. "If he doesn't respect his own body, how can I expect him to respect my authority? He probably gave his parents a hard time, too.

"Tyrell is the black guy, obviously. He doesn't say much; probably doesn't feel like he fits in because he's the only black on the team, and you know how they like to always hang out with each other. I expect he'll probably leave so I don't give him any long-term tasks.

"Jay is the guy with the turban. Does he really have to wear that? I mean, come on, this is America. I also wonder about him. He is always looking down when he is around women and he never shakes hands with any of them. How could he not look at Autumn?

"There is Tanya. She's got a couple of small kids. I'm not sure if she's married. Anyway, I can't count on her because she's always out because her kids are sick; and she can't work late because she has to pick up the kids from the babysitter. A mother with young kids should be staying home with them, like my wife.

"And you'll see that Jose is always on the phone talking in Spanish so nobody else knows what he's saying. Obviously, he's not pulling his weight, and I think the rest of the team resents him. By the way, he has five kids; and before you ask, yes, he is Catholic." Bob said with a laugh. He went on, "He's another one I got pressured to hire.

"And there is Brenda 'the blimp.' You won't miss her," Bob said, with a big grin. "When we have meetings with the customer, I obviously make sure Brenda has other things to do. I don't want them to get any bad images of the team. On the other hand, I try to make sure Autumn comes to those meetings; she's a real 'looker' if you get my drift," Bob said, as he winked.

"Stan is the guy who looks like he's a hundred years old. He should have retired a long time ago. He's too old to have any good ideas; I never even bother asking him. He's just hanging on to collect a bigger pension, and everyone knows it.

"Fred is the guy in the wheelchair. He's okay, but takes forever to get things done and keep up. I have to make sure I don't give him any tasks that are too challenging, or he'll slow down the rest of the team.

"Finally, there is Sandy. Nobody likes her. She has a hard time building relationships with the rest of the team; seems like she doesn't trust anybody. No wonder she's divorced. Somebody told me she has a kid on drugs. I guess that's no surprise; she's not the greatest role model. She also never seems to hang around any of the guys on the team. What does that tell you?" Bob said, raising his eyebrows.

"How does management expect me to drive this bus, when I have so many flat tires?

"Thank goodness I have Bill on the team. I have known him for a long time. We went to the State University together, and both of our families go to the same Methodist church. We also both served in the military together; so he's a real task master who I know I can always count on."

Bob goes on, "I want you to know, Brad, that I'm not prejudiced or anything like that. I'm just a straight shooter and call things as I see them. Some of the people may not like that, but at least they know where I stand. These people are who they are. I don't know where they all come from; I certainly don't see them in my neighborhood or at my church on Sundays. They just don't have the work ethic they should have, like Bill and me. They just have some strange values. Most of them will never get ahead if they don't change their attitudes. I got to do my best to get the job done with who I got. But it's difficult to get anything done, let alone having to always worry about who might get offended by what you say and then they might go whining to management or threaten to sue you. It's not like the good old days, when everybody was the same. Frankly, I don't think some of them like working with each other because they can't see past their differences. Some of them even think I'm the one who is different; can you believe that?

"So you can see, with the team I am stuck with, that it is a real challenge to complete our hardware development tasks on time. Some days, I REALLY think this project is the PITS! If I had more people like Bill on the team, things would be a lot simpler.

"Brad, it looks like Bill, you, and I are going to have to carry the team. We are the only ones who are different. I hope I can count on you to pick up the slack and help get the hardware development back on schedule. And Brad, don't go telling anybody what I told you about these people, because if word got back to them it would probably get them all stirred up and they'd go running off to complain to management, and I'd lose my trust in you."

CASE QUESTIONS

1. Bob is demonstrating what behaviors with respect to valuing team diversity? What are some alternative choices for what Brad can do next? What should he do?
2. What should any of the team members do?
3. What could be done to improve the climate for diversity in this case?
4. What do you think Bob's direct supervisor would do if she were aware of Bob's actions?

GROUP ACTIVITY

Divide the course participants into teams of three or four to discuss this case and develop responses to the case questions. Have each team select a spokesperson to present its responses to the entire class.

REFERENCES

A Guide to the Project Management Body of Knowledge (PMBOK® Guide) Fifth Edition. Newtown Square, PA: Project Management Institute, 2013.

Beringer, C., D. Jonas, and A. Kock (2013). "Behavior of Internal Stakeholders in Project Portfolio Management and Its Impact on Success," *International Journal of Project Management*, 31(6), 830–846.

Blake, R. and J. Mouton (1978). *The New Managerial Grid.* Houston, Texas: Gulf Publishing Co.

Chang, K., H. Yen, C. Chiang, and N. Parolia (2013). "Knowledge Contribution in Information System Development Teams: An Empirical Research from a

Social Cognitive Perspective," *International Journal of Project Management*, *31*, 252–263.

Chow, P. T., S. O. Cheung, and K. Y. Chan (2012). "Trust Building in Construction Contracting: Mechanism and Expectation," *International Journal of Project Management*, *30*, 927–937.

Crawford, J. and L. K. Leonard (2012). "Predicting Post-Meeting Work Activity in Software Development Projects," *Team Performance Management*, *18*(1/2), 59–77.

da Silva, F. Q. B., A. C. C. França, M. Suassuna, L. M. R. de S. Mariz, I. Rossiley, R. C. G. de Miranda, T. B. Gouveia, C. V. F. Monteiro, E. Lucena, E. S. F. Cardoza, and E. Espindola. (2013). "Team Building Criteria in Software Projects: A Mix-Method Replicated Study," *Information and Software Technology*, *55*(7), 1316.

Han, J. and A. Hovav (2013). "To Bridge or to Bond? Diverse Social Connections in an IS Project Team," *International Journal of Project Management*, *31*(3), 378–390.

Heising, W. (2012). "The Integration of Ideation and Project Portfolio Management—A Key Factor for Sustainable Success," *International Journal of Project Management*, *30*, 582–595.

Hosseini, M. R. and N. Chileshe (2013). "Global Virtual Engineering Teams (GVETs): A Fertile Ground for Research in Australian Construction Projects Context," *International Journal of Project Management*, http://dx.doi.org.ezaccess.libraries.psu.edu/10.1016/j.ijproman.2013.01.001.

Karjalainen, H. and R. Soparnot (2012). "Interpersonal Cooperation in Multicultural Working Context," *International Business Research*, *5*(6), 73–82.

Liang, T., J. C. Wu, J. J. Jiang, and G. Klein (2012). "The Impact of Value Diversity on Information System Development Projects," *International Journal of Project Management*, *30*(6), 731–739.

Lundin, S. C., H. Paul, and J. Christensen (2011). *Fish: A Remarkable Way to Boost Morale and Improve Results*. London: Hodder & Stoughton.

Park, J. and J. Lee (2013). "Knowledge Sharing in Information Systems Development Projects: Explicating the Role of Dependence and Trust," *International Journal of Project Management*, http://dx.doi.org.ezaccess.libraries.psu.edu/10.1016/j.ijproman.2013.02.004.

Sivasubramaniam, N., S. Liebowitz, and C. L. Lackman (2012). "Determinants of New Product Development Team Performance: A Meta-analytic Review," *Journal of Product Innovation Management*, *29*(5), 803–820.

Slawek, J. J. (2013). "Face Your Fears," *Smart Business Chicago*, *10*(7), 5.

Thomas, K. and R. Kilmann (1975). "The Social Desirability Variable in Organizational Research: An Alternative Explanation for Reported Findings," *Academy of Management Journal*, *18*(4), 741–752.

Toledo, R. (2013). "Common Ground," *PM Network*, *27*(2), 66.

Tuckman, B. and M. Jensen (1977). "Stages of Small-group Development Revisited," *Group & Organization Studies*, *2*(4), 419–427.

CHAPTER 12

Project Communication and Documentation

Tim Graham/Alamy

Concepts in this chapter support the following Project Management Knowledge Areas of *A Guide to the Project Management Body of Knowledge (PMBOK® Guide)*:

Project Communications Management
Project Integration Management
Project Human Resource Management
Project Stakeholder Management

 REAL WORLD PROJECT MANAGEMENT

Knowledge Sharing Supports the Military's Mission

Knowledge sharing within the United States' military services used a number of tools including online knowledge portals and dashboards to provide a range of

sharing from training and professional development to communities of practice. The digital repositories of information and automated business processes were the result of a study on information and knowledge management.

The military services and the Department of Defense decided that knowledge management was needed in order to inform other units, especially those not yet deployed, about the lessons learned in the regions where fighting and missions were taking place. "We are using discussion forums to share information. The learning curve is shorter for new units when we have effective knowledge sharing to counter an enemy that is very agile, and changes operating tactics frequently. This saves lives," commented Joseph Oebbecke, Chief Knowledge Officer, U.S. Army Training and Doctrine command.

Social media, Internet video, and collaboration sites were accessible within the Army networks and served as a means of knowledge exchange between the Army's different operations. The goal was for Army operational commanders to lead discussions, to have engineers share expertise with war fighters to provide feedback to those carrying out the missions. This adoption of team communication was a change in culture and a step toward achieving the goal of modernizing the Army to be a knowledge organization.

Shared workspaces and virtual work environments had changed how daily activities for operational command were conducted within the divisions. By means of a collaborative environment, Microsoft SharePoint, soldiers updated an Excel spreadsheet that appeared as an actionable item on a general's dashboard. The speed of communication increased the agility, effectiveness, and success of the units. Oebbecke stated, "The goal is to provide the right knowledge to the right person at the right time and place."

As well as the sharing helped inform other war fighters and soldiers, not all aspects of the adoption were without obstacles. Acceptance and use by those not familiar with sharing knowledge and knowledge management systems lagged those who were more familiar. Convincing those new to the systems to use them presented significant difficulties.

At the conclusion of military projects, the shared information was evaluated. Best practices for information sharing between operations were identified by making comparisons of what was planned to what actually occurred within projects with similar levels of complexity. The identified best practices were labeled as knowledge nuggets and recorded to be used within the next projects.

Implementing the best practice nuggets in other projects helped increase the return on investment and helped the units perform more efficiently. Douglas Weidner, chairman, KM Institute, who has offered training in the U.S. military, concluded, "The best practice management process provides a proven process not only to bring the worst up to the best, but in doing so, to make the best even better."

Based on information from Lamont, J. (2011). "Knowledge Sharing Supports the Military's Mission," *KM World, 20*(8), 6–7.

This chapter discusses an element vital to the effective performance of a project: communication. Communication takes place between the project team and the customer or sponsor and other stakeholders, among the project team members, and between the project team and its organization's upper management. Communication may involve two people or a group of people. It can be verbal or written. It can be face-to-face or involve some medium, such as phones, voice mail, e-mail, text messages, letters, memos, videoconferencing, document development systems, or shared Web 2.0 tools. It can be formal, such as a report or a presentation at a meeting, or informal, such as a hallway conversation or a text message. This chapter covers various types of communication used during the project. You will become familiar with

- Suggestions for enhancing personal communication, such as face-to-face discussions and written communication
- Effective listening
- Various types of project meetings and suggestions for effective meetings
- Formal project presentations and suggestions for effective presentations
- Project reports and suggestions for preparing useful reports
- Controlling changes to project documents
- A project communication plan
- Communicating with stakeholders
- Collaborative communication tools

LEARNING OUTCOMES

After studying this chapter, the learner should be able to:

- Discuss and apply techniques to enhance personal verbal and written communications
- Describe four barriers to effective listening and apply techniques to improve listening and understanding
- Prepare for and facilitate effective project meetings

- Prepare for and make informative and interesting presentations
- Prepare useful, readable, and understandable reports
- Explain how to control changes to project documents

- Create a project communication plan
- Communicate effectively with project stakeholders
- Describe collaborative tools used to enhance communication on projects

Reinforce Your Learning

1. _____

and timely

are essential for

project management.

Personal Communication

Poor communication is often the root cause of failure to accomplish a project's scope, schedule, budget, or customer satisfaction objectives. Effective communication and timely information flow are essential and the lifeblood for successful project management.

Effective and frequent personal communication is crucial to keep the project moving, identify potential problems, solicit suggestions for improving project performance, keep abreast of whether the customer is satisfied, maintain

stakeholder engagement, and avoid surprises. Personal communication can occur through words or nonverbal behavior, such as body language. It can be face-to-face or through some medium, including phone, voice mail, e-mail, texting, letters, memos, videoconferencing, document development systems, or shared Web 2.0 tools. Personal communication can be verbal or written.

VERBAL COMMUNICATION

Reinforce Your Learning

2. Identify two types of personal verbal communication.

Personal verbal communication can be face-to-face or via phone or computer. It can be by means of voice mail or videoconferencing. Information can be communicated in a more accurate and timely manner through verbal communication. Such communication provides a forum for discussion, clarification, understanding, and immediate feedback. Face-to-face communication also provides an opportunity to observe the body language that accompanies the communication. Even phone conversations allow the listener to hear the tone, inflection, speed, volume, and emotion of the voice. Body language and tone are important elements that enrich verbal communication. Face-to-face situations provide an even greater opportunity for enriched communication than do phone conversations.

Reinforce Your Learning

3. Body language can be used not only by the person talking, but also by the

as a way of providing

to the person talking.

Body language can be used not only by the person talking but also by the listener, as a way of providing feedback to the person talking. Positive body language can include direct eye contact, a smile, hand gestures, leaning forward, and nodding in acknowledgment or agreement. Negative body language can be a frown, crossed arms, slouching, fidgeting, gazing or looking away, doodling, or yawning. In personal communication, people need to be sensitive to body language reflective of the cultural diversity of the participants, whether they are team members, the customer, or other stakeholders. When communicating with individuals from other cultures or countries, you need to be aware of their customs regarding greetings, gestures, eye contact, and protocol. For example, hand gestures, proximity to the person with whom you are communicating, and touching have different meanings in different cultures.

Reinforce Your Learning

4. In personal communication, people need to be sensitive to body language reflective of the

of the participants.

When communicating verbally, a person must be careful not to use remarks, words, or phrases that can be construed to be sexist, racist, prejudicial, or offensive. Comments do not have to be made directly to a particular person to be offensive. Remarks made in a group setting can be distasteful to some individuals in the group. They may find certain statements hurtful to themselves or to an acquaintance. Comments about ethnic customs, surnames, dialects, religious practices, physical characteristics or appearance, or mannerisms can be offensive, even if the offense is unintentional or the comment is said in jest.

A high degree of face-to-face communication is especially important early in a project to foster team building, develop good working relationships, establish mutual expectations, and build trust. Locating the project team in a common area facilitates communication. It is much easier to walk over to someone's office to ask something than to call the person on the phone and maybe wait several days for your call to be returned. However, voice mail allows individuals to communicate verbally in a timely manner when face-to-face communication is not possible. It is not always feasible to locate the project team in a common area, especially if it is a virtual team that includes members or subcontractors in different geographic locations. In such cases, videoconferencing can be helpful, if available.

Project team members need to be proactive in initiating timely communication with other team members and the project manager to get and give information, rather than waiting for an upcoming project team meeting that could be several weeks away. The project manager, in particular, should get out of the

Reinforce Your Learning

5. Project team members need to be _____ in initiating timely communication to _____ and _____ information.

office on a regular basis and drop in on individual team members. She or he should take the initiative to visit the customer or the project organization's upper management for face-to-face communication, rather than waiting to be summoned to a meeting. If a visit to the customer requires distant travel, the manager should initiate regular phone discussions between visits.

Verbal communication should be clear, concise, honest, and unambiguous. Sometimes attempting to be overly tactful, especially in communicating a problem or concern, can mislead and result in unclear expectations. You should check for understanding of what you wanted to communicate by asking for feedback. If you are not sure whether a point you made was understood by the other person, ask the other person to state her understanding of what you said. Similarly, if you are not clear on a point the other person was trying to communicate, paraphrase what you think the other person said to ensure mutual understanding.

Reinforce Your Learning

6. Identify two methods you can use to check for understanding during verbal communication.

Finally, the timing of verbal communication is important. For example, you should not barge into a colleague's office and interrupt him if he is in the middle of doing something important. Rather, in such a situation, ask him when would be a good time to get together. You should indicate about how long you need to talk with him and what you want to discuss. He will then know whether to expect a 10-minute discussion on a trivial matter or a 1-hour discussion on a critical subject. Similarly, when making a phone call to another person, you should state at the start what topics you want to discuss and how long it might take, then ask if now is a good time or if you should call back at a more convenient time.

WRITTEN COMMUNICATION

Reinforce Your Learning

7. What are two types of personal written communication?

Personal written communication is generally carried out through internal correspondence to or among the project team and external correspondence to the customer or others external to the firm, such as subcontractors or some stakeholders. Written correspondence is normally transmitted through e-mail or can be sent as hard copy. Formal project documents such as contracts and amendments, which require signatures, are usually sent as hard copy.

E-mail is a way to communicate efficiently with a group of people when it is impractical to have a meeting or when the information needs to be disseminated in a timely manner. Written communication should be used only when necessary. Project participants are usually very busy and do not have time to read trivial messages or irrelevant documents containing information that could have been communicated verbally at the next project meeting.

An e-mail may be appropriate as a follow-up to a face-to-face conversation or a phone call, confirming decisions or actions rather than relying on a person's memory. When an e-mail is used to confirm verbal communication, other people who were not involved in the verbal discussion but who may need to know the information should also be copied on the e-mail. Also, such written communication can be important if a member of the project team leaves the project—the replacement person will have a record of communications regarding previous actions and decisions.

Written communication should be used mostly to inform, confirm, and request—for example, to remind the project team that the customer will be visiting on a certain date or to ask team members to provide written input for a quarterly project progress report to the client.

Written communication should be clear and concise and should not include lengthy dissertations or voluminous extraneous attachments. Project participants are busy with their assigned work tasks and will perceive being flooded with e-mails or electronic messages as more of a hindrance than a help.

Your written communication is a reflection of you, so be professional. Spelling errors, poor grammar and punctuation, and inappropriate language give a poor impression of you. Work related e-mail should not include emoticons or text message abbreviations; it is considered unprofessional, and not all recipients may understand the abbreviations or may misinterpret them. KWIM :-) Refrain from sending an emotionally charged e-mail. Rather save a draft, review it the next day, and you will most likely revise it to tone down the emotions and be more professional.

EFFECTIVE LISTENING

The purpose of communicating should be *to reach understanding.* "I know that you believe that you understand what you thought you heard me say. But what you do not realize is that what you thought you heard is not what I meant." Communicating is more than talking and hearing. The heart of communication is not words, but understanding—not only to be understood, but also to understand. The person speaking often assumes that the listener(s) understands what she said. Half of making communication effective is listening. Failure to listen can cause a breakdown in communication.

Here are some common barriers to effective listening:

Reinforce Your Learning

8. Failure to

can cause a

in communication.

- *Pretending to listen.* You listen and think faster than the average person talks. This may lead to drifting, boredom, or thinking about what you want to say in response.
- *Distractions.* If you try to do something else, such as answer the phone or read or send a text message, while someone is talking to you, you will not be able to focus on the person talking. It is also easy to get distracted by people walking by or what is happening outside the window.
- *Bias and closed-mindedness.* Hearing what supports your views and turning off the things with which you disagree is known as selective listening. Bias in listening can also be attributed to feelings about the speaker's clothing style, looks, tone of voice, or mannerisms.
- *Impatience.* If you are anxious for the person talking to get to the point or having a hard time waiting for a chance to interrupt and speak, you may tune out what the speaker is saying.
- *Jumping to conclusions.* If you begin to draw conclusions about what is being said before the person talking has finished, you may not hear the whole story or all the facts.

Reinforce Your Learning

9. List some common barriers to effective listening.

Listening is more than just letting the other person talk. It must be an active, not a passive, process. Active listening increases understanding and reduces conflict. Here are some suggestions for improving listening skills:

- *Focus on the person talking.* Looking at the person who is speaking helps you concentrate and pay attention to the speaker's body language.
- *Engage in active listening.* Provide verbal and nonverbal feedback to the person talking. This can include body language, such as nodding in acknowledgment of something the person said, smiling, or simply leaning

forward attentively. It can be a verbal comment that does not require a response from the speaker, such as "That is interesting," "I see," or "Uh huh." It can be paraphrasing what the speaker said, as in "What you are saying is …" or "What you mean is …" Such paraphrasing will give the speaker an opportunity to clear up any misunderstandings.

- *Ask questions.* When you need clarification or more information about something the person said, ask a probing question, such as "Could you tell me more about that?"
- *Do not interrupt.* When a person is talking, listen to the whole thought or wait for an appropriate pause before breaking in with a question or comment. Do not interrupt and change the subject before the person talking has completed the message.

Reinforce Your Learning

10. What are some things you can do to improve your listening skills?

Good listening skills are important if project team members are to be effective in communicating with one another, the customer, and other stakeholders.

Meetings

A meeting can be a vehicle for fostering team building and reinforcing team members' expectations, roles, and commitment to the project objective. This section covers various types of meetings that may take place during a project and provides suggestions for ensuring that meetings are effective.

TYPES OF PROJECT MEETINGS

The most common types of project meetings are

- Project kickoff meeting
- Status review meetings
- Problem-solving meetings
- Design review meetings
- Postproject evaluation meeting

See Chapter 11 for more information about the project kickoff meeting and Chapter 9 for more information about the postproject evaluation meeting.

It is not unusual for a contract between a customer and a project contractor to include requirements for periodic status review meetings and specific design review meetings.

STATUS REVIEW MEETINGS

Reinforce Your Learning

11. What are the primary purposes of a status review meeting?

A project status review meeting is usually led or called by the project manager; it generally involves all or some of the project team and may also include the customer and/or the project team's upper management. The primary purposes of such a meeting are to inform, to identify problems, and to identify action items. Project status meetings should be held on a regularly scheduled basis so that problems and potential problems can be identified early and surprises that could jeopardize accomplishing the project objective can be prevented. For example, project status review meetings might be held weekly with the project team and less frequently with the customer—perhaps monthly or quarterly, depending on the overall duration of the project and the contractual requirements.

A sample agenda for a project status review meeting is shown in Figure 12.1. Here are some of the subjects that might be discussed under each of the agenda items:

- *Accomplishments since the last meeting.* Key project milestones that were reached should be identified, and actions on items from previous meetings should be reviewed.
- *Cost, schedule, and work scope—status.* Performance should be compared to the baseline plan. It is important that status be based on up-to-date information regarding completed activities and actual expenditures.
- *Cost, schedule, and work scope—trends.* Any positive or negative trends in project performance should be identified. Even if a project is ahead of schedule, the fact that the schedule has been slipping over the past several weeks might indicate that corrective action should be initiated now, before the project falls behind schedule.
- *Cost, schedule, and work scope—forecasts.* Based on current status, trends, and the project activities yet to be completed, the forecasted project completion date and forecasted cost at completion should be reviewed and compared to the project objective and the baseline plan.
- *Cost, schedule, and work scope—variances.* Any differences between actual progress and planned progress with respect to cost and schedule for project

FIGURE 12.1 **Project Status Review Meeting Agenda**

Project Status Review
Team Meeting

Agenda

8:00 AM	Accomplishments since last meeting	
	• Hardware	Steve
	• Software	Alex
	• Documentation	Wendy
8:30	Cost, schedule, and work scope	Jack
	• Status	
	• Trends	
	• Forecasts	
	• Variances	
8:50	Risk assessment update	Teresa
9:00	Stakeholder issues update	Jack
9:10	Corrective actions, if necessary	As appropriate
9:30	Opportunities for improvement	All
9:40	Open discussion	All
9:55	Action item assignments	Jack
10:00	Adjourn	

work packages and activities should be identified. These variances can be positive—for example, being ahead of schedule—or they can be negative—for example, overrunning the budget for the earned value of work that has been accomplished. Negative variances will help pinpoint both current problems and potential problems. Particular attention should be given to those parts of the project that have had negative variances that are continuing to get worse.

- *Risk assessment update.* Determine if there are any changes to the likelihood of occurrence or the potential impact of any of the previously identified risks. Particular attention should be given to reviewing the trigger points for each risk to determine if any risk response plans are on the verge of having to be implemented. Identify any new risks.

- *Stakeholder issues update.* Review the stakeholder issue log to make sure that any contentious issues are being addressed in a timely manner. Also identify issues which have been resolved as well as any new issues that have become known.

- *Corrective actions.* In some instances, corrective actions to address problems and potential problems might take place at the status review meeting—for example, receiving customer or management approval to proceed with the purchase of certain materials or authorization of overtime to get the project back on schedule. In other cases, separate problem-solving meetings may be required so that appropriate members of the project team can develop corrective actions—for example, to develop a response to a stakeholder issue to change the planned location of a chemical storage facility because of its proximity to an elementary school.

- *Opportunities for improvement.* Opportunities for improvement should also be identified. For example, a member of the project team might point out that the technical specifications could be met by using an alternative material or piece of equipment that is substantially less expensive than the one the team originally planned to use. Or a team member might suggest that substantial time could be saved by replicating and slightly modifying existing software rather than developing completely new software.

- *Action item assignment.* Specific action items should be identified and assigned to specific team members. For each action item, the person responsible and the estimated completion date should be noted. The completion date should be estimated by the person responsible for the action item. When people verbalize their commitment to a date at a meeting in front of other people, they will usually strive to meet that date.

It should be noted that listening to the information provided at a status review meeting is one way, but not the only way, for a project manager to get a true understanding of the project status. He or she needs to validate what was said at the status review meeting through personal communication with individual members of the project team. The project manager should also ask to see any tangible products, or deliverables, such as drawings, prototypes, or reports. This will both validate that the item is really complete (and not just almost or essentially complete) and show that the project manager is genuinely interested in the individual's work and acknowledges its importance to the successful accomplishment of the project objective.

PROBLEM-SOLVING MEETINGS

When a problem or potential problem is identified by an individual project team member, that person should promptly call a problem-solving meeting with other appropriate individuals, not wait for a future status review meeting. Identifying and resolving problems as early as possible is critical to project success.

The project manager and the project team need to establish guidelines at the beginning of the project regarding who should initiate problem-solving meetings and when, as well as the level of authorization required to implement corrective actions.

Problem-solving meetings should follow a good problem-solving approach, such as the following:

1. Develop a problem statement.
2. Identify potential causes of the problem.
3. Gather data and verify the most likely causes.
4. Identify possible solutions.
5. Evaluate the alternative solutions.
6. Determine the best solution.
7. Revise the project plan.
8. Implement the solution.
9. Determine whether the problem has been solved.

See the section on problem solving in Chapter 11 for further information about the nine-step problem-solving approach.

DESIGN REVIEW MEETINGS

Projects that involve a design phase, such as development of an information system, design of a website, or design of a floor plan for a hospital renovation, may require one or more design review meetings to ensure that the sponsor or customer agrees with or approves of the design approach developed by the project team or contractor.

Take the example of a company that hires a consultant to design, develop, and implement an information system to track customer orders from order entry through receipt of payment. The company may require that the consultant review the system design with appropriate company representatives before approval of the next phase of the project, which involves detailed development of the system and purchase of hardware and software. At a later stage in the project, the company may want a stakeholder group of certain employees to review and approve the user interface and screen formats developed by the consultant to ensure that they meet the needs and expectations of the people who will be using the system.

In many projects, there are two design review meetings:

1. *A preliminary design review meeting* occurs when the project team or contractor has completed the initial design, concept drawings, specifications, or flowcharts. The purpose of this preliminary design review meeting is to get the sponsor's or customer's agreement that the design approach meets the requirements and to gain approval from the customer before ordering materials that have a long delivery time so as not to delay the project schedule.
2. *A final design review meeting* occurs when the project team or contractor has completed the detailed specifications, drawings, screen and report formats,

Reinforce Your Learning

12. True or false: When members of the project team identify problems or potential problems, they should wait until the next scheduled status review meeting to bring them up for discussion.

Reinforce Your Learning

13. On many projects, there are often two design review meetings: a

design review meeting and a

design review meeting.

and the like. The purpose of this final design review meeting is to gain approval from the sponsor or customer before starting to build, assemble, and produce the project deliverables.

EFFECTIVE MEETINGS

Before, during, and after a meeting, the person organizing or leading the meeting can take various steps to ensure that the meeting is effective.

BEFORE THE MEETING

- *Determine whether a meeting is really necessary* or whether another mechanism, such as a conference call, is more appropriate.
- *Determine the purpose of the meeting.* For instance, is it to share information, plan, collect input or ideas, make a decision, persuade or sell, solve a problem, or evaluate status?
- *Determine who needs to participate in the meeting*, given its purpose. The number of participants should be the minimum number needed to achieve the purpose of the meeting. Project team members are usually busy on their work activities and do not want to participate in meetings to which they have nothing to contribute or from which they have nothing to gain. Individuals who are invited to attend the meeting should know why they are being asked to participate.
- *Distribute an agenda well in advance of the meeting* to those invited. The agenda should include:

 - Purpose of the meeting.
 - Topics to be covered. Items should be listed from most important to least important. If time runs out, the most important items will have been covered.
 - Time allocated for each topic and who will cover the topic, make the presentation, or lead the discussion.

 Figure 12.2 is a sample agenda for a project review meeting with a customer. Accompanying the agenda should be any documents or data the participants need to review *prior* to the meeting. Sufficient time should be given between distribution of the announcement and the date of the meeting to allow participants to adequately prepare for the meeting. Some participants may need to collect and analyze data or prepare presentation or handout materials.
- *Prepare visual aids or handouts.* PowerPoint slides, graphics, charts, tables, diagrams, pictures, and physical models are effective visual aids. Often, these materials focus the discussion and prevent a lot of rambling and misunderstanding. A picture is worth a thousand words!
- *Make meeting room arrangements.* The room should be large enough that people are not cramped and uncomfortable. Seats should be arranged so that all participants can see each other; this will foster participation. The appropriate visual aids and accessories (projector, screen, computer, flip charts) should be in the room and be tested before the meeting starts. If any presenters are going to use PowerPoint slides, it saves time to have the files loaded on the computer before the meeting starts. Refreshments should be ordered if the meeting is

Reinforce Your Learning

14. To ensure that a meeting is effective, what are some steps that the person organizing or leading the meeting should take before the meeting?

FIGURE 12.2 **Customer Project Review Meeting Agenda**

Project Review
Meeting with Customer

Agenda

8:00 AM	Opening comments	Jeff
8:15	Technical review	
	• System design	Joe
	• Training	Cathy
	• Installation plans	Jim
10:00	Break	
10:15	Project status	Jeff
	• Schedule	
	• Cost	
11:00	Risk assessment	Teresa
11:15	Stakeholder issues	Jeff
11:30	Proposed changes	Joe
12:00	Open discussion (box lunches)	
12:30	Decisions and action items	Jeff
1:00	Adjourn	

going to be long. For example, box lunches may be served in order to allow meeting discussions to continue over a working lunch.

In some cases, a conference room may be designated as the "project room," where all project meetings are held or where project team members can meet for problem-solving discussions. Sometimes, such project rooms have project plans, schedules, status charts, and system diagrams posted on the walls for easy reference by all project team members.

DURING THE MEETING

- *Start the meeting on time.* If the meeting leader waits for a few latecomers, people will get in the habit of showing up late, because they know the meeting will not start on time anyway. If the meeting starts on time, people will get in the habit of arriving on time rather than suffer the embarrassment of entering a meeting already in progress.
- *Designate a note taker.* Someone should be assigned (preferably before the meeting) to take notes. The notes should be concise, and they should cover decisions and action items, assignments, and estimated completion dates. Detailed meeting minutes can be a burden both to take and to read later and therefore should be avoided.

Reinforce Your Learning

15. True or false: It is always a good idea to wait for everyone to arrive before starting a meeting, even if it is beyond the scheduled start time.

- *Ask all participants to turn off their cell phones, iPods, and other electronic communication devices* so that everyone's full attention is focused on the meeting.
- *Review the purpose of the meeting and the agenda.* Be concise, and do not give a lengthy discourse.
- *Facilitate—do not dominate—the meeting.* The project manager should *not* lead all the discussions, but should get other participants to lead the discussions on their assigned topics. A good facilitator will:

 - Keep the meeting moving and within the scheduled time frame.
 - Encourage participation, especially from individuals who appear hesitant to participate.
 - Limit discussion by participants who have a tendency to talk too much, repeat themselves, or stray from the topic at hand.
 - Control interruptions and side conversations.
 - Clarify points that are made.
 - Summarize discussions and make transitions to the next topics on the agenda.

 It is helpful to have the project team participate in developing meeting guidelines at a project team meeting at the beginning of the project, such as at the project kickoff meeting, so that everyone understands and is committed to what behavior is expected during project meetings. An example of a code of conduct for team meetings is shown in Figure 12.3.

- *Summarize the meeting results* at the end of the meeting and make sure all participants have a clear understanding of all decisions and action items. The meeting leader should verbalize these items to help avoid any misunderstandings.
- *Do not overrun the scheduled meeting time.* Participants may have other commitments or subsequent meetings. If all agenda items are not covered, it is better to schedule another meeting for the people involved with those items. These should be the lower-priority items anyway, because the agenda topics should have been arranged in order of most to least important.
- *Evaluate the meeting process.* Periodically, at the end of a meeting, allocate time for the participants to openly discuss what took place and determine whether any changes should be made to improve the effectiveness of future meetings.

Figure 12.4 is a checklist for rating the effectiveness of a meeting. The project team members might complete this assessment instrument periodically during the project. After the scores of all team members have been summarized, the team, including the project manager, should discuss how to improve the areas that were rated low.

AFTER THE MEETING

Publish the meeting results within 24 hours after the meeting. The summary document should be concise and kept to one page if possible.

It should confirm decisions that were made and list the action items, including who is responsible, the estimated completion date, and expected deliverables. It may also list who attended and who was absent. The meeting results should be distributed to all individuals who were invited, whether or not they actually attended

FIGURE 12.3 Team Meeting Code of Conduct

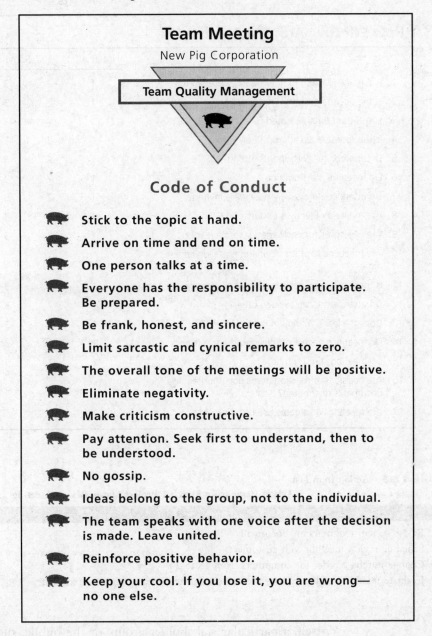

the meeting. The meeting notes should not include a detailed narrative of the meeting discussions. Figure 12.5 is a sample action item list from a meeting.

Effective meetings, like successful projects, require good planning and good performance.

Presentations

Often, the project manager or members of the project team are called on to give a formal presentation. The audience may be representatives of the customer's organization, the project organization's upper management, the project team

FIGURE 12.4 Meeting Effectiveness Checklist

How Effective Are Your Meetings?

	Not at All		Somewhat		Very Much
1. Is the agenda sent in time to allow preparation?	1	2	3	4	5
2. Is the agenda properly sequenced?	1	2	3	4	5
3. Is sufficient time allocated for each item?	1	2	3	4	5
4. Is the room set up appropriately?	1	2	3	4	5
5. Do appropriate participants attend?	1	2	3	4	5
6. Do meetings start on time?	1	2	3	4	5
7. Do attendees know why they were invited?	1	2	3	4	5
8. Are meeting objectives understood?	1	2	3	4	5
9. Are objectives for each agenda item clear?	1	2	3	4	5
10. Are meetings kept on track and not allowed to digress?	1	2	3	4	5
11. Is there balanced participation of all attendees?	1	2	3	4	5
12. Do attendees listen to each other?	1	2	3	4	5
13. Does the leader maintain control?	1	2	3	4	5
14. Do meetings have a positive, productive tone?	1	2	3	4	5
15. Do meetings finish on time?	1	2	3	4	5
16. Are decisions and action items documented and the documents distributed?	1	2	3	4	5
17. Are meetings a valuable use of time?	1	2	3	4	5

FIGURE 12.5 Action Item List:

Action Items from March 1 Project Status Review Meeting

ACTION	WHO	BY WHEN
1. Revise system requirements document	Tyler	March 10
2. Schedule review meeting with customer	Jim	March 11
3. Change purchase order for computers from 15 to 20	Maggie	March 19
4. Evaluate feasibility of bar coding and optical character recognition for data entry	Hannah	March 19

itself, a particular stakeholder group, or the public, such as at a conference. The audience may be one person (the customer) or several hundred attendees at a national conference. The presentation may last 10 minutes or an hour or more. The subject could be an overview of the project; the current status of the project; a serious problem that is jeopardizing accomplishment of the project objective, such as a forecasted schedule delay or cost overrun; an attempt to persuade the customer to expand or redirect the project work scope; or a response to a stakeholder group regarding their concern about a safety issue.

In such situations, you, the speaker, are in the spotlight. Following are some suggestions that may help you prepare and deliver your presentation.

PREPARE THE PRESENTATION

- *Determine the purpose of the presentation.* Is it to inform or to persuade? What do you want to accomplish? For example, do you want the audience to understand the project, or do you want the customer to agree to suggested changes in the project work scope?
- *Know the audience.* What is their level of knowledge or familiarity with the subject? What is their rank--are they senior managers and key decision makers, or are they your peers? What is their potential influence on the project?
- *Make an outline of the presentation.* Only after you have made an outline should you develop a script of the presentation. Read it over and over and over, but do not try to memorize it.
- *Use simple language that the audience will understand.* Do not use jargon, acronyms, or terminology that the audience may not understand. Do not try to impress the audience with your word power! Do not make remarks that can be construed to be sexist, racist, prejudicial, offensive, sarcastic, or profane.
- *Prepare notes or a final outline that you will use or refer to during your presentation.* Yes, it is all right to use notes.
- *Prepare visual aids and test them.* Visual aids, such as PowerPoint slides or videos, can enhance your presentation. Use a font size that is large enough for the slides to be readable from the most distant seat in the presentation room. Text slides, graphs, diagrams, and tables should be simple and not too busy; there should not be a lot of text, and diagrams should not be too complex. There should be one idea per chart or slide, and no more than four lines of text per slide and eight words per line. Otherwise, the audience will be more focused on reading your slides than listening to what you are saying. Multicolor graphics are more appealing than plain black and white text, but choose colors carefully, because you can overwhelm your audience with too many colors or poor contrasting color combinations that are difficult to read.

 If a video is used, it should be brief, usually less than 6 minutes. The audience is not coming to watch a video, they are coming to listen to you; do not rely on a video to be a substitute for you speaking.
- *Practice, practice, practice—more than you think you should.* You may want to do a trial run in front of your peers. Ask for their feedback; solicit suggestions on how you might improve the presentation. Some criteria that they can use to evaluate your presentation are:

 - Organization: Opening, introduction, outline, logical flow, transitions, conclusion, closing
 - Content: Comprehensive/complete, level of detail, clarity, length of presentation
 - Professional behavior: Eye contact, delivery mannerisms, gestures, professional presence and appearance
 - Language and voice: Correct use of grammar, enunciation, voice projection and tone, enthusiasm, pace of delivery, use of terminology or jargon
 - PowerPoint slides and visual aids: Readable, concise, understandable, use of graphics, videos, other exhibits

- *Make copies of handout materials.* If audience members do not have to take a lot of notes, they will be able to give their full attention to the presentation.
- *Request the audiovisual equipment well in advance.* Whether it is a computer, projector, microphone, lectern, or pointer, you do not want to find out at the last minute that it is not available. Make sure you have enough copies for everyone.
- *Go into the meeting room when it is empty or not in use and get a feel for the surroundings.* Stand in the place where the presentation will be made (in the front of the room, at the lectern, or on the stage). Test the projector and microphone.

Reinforce Your Learning

16. What are some important things to do in preparing a presentation?

DELIVER THE PRESENTATION

- *Expect a bit of nervousness; all speakers experience it.* Just remember that you know more about the subject you are talking about than most of the audience members do.
- *Turn off your cell phone* or other technologies that could cause a distraction to you or the audience.
- *Know your opening lines.* The opening lines are crucial; have them down pat. They must be delivered in a confident and relaxed manner. This is where credibility is established with the audience. You cannot afford to fumble over the opening lines or say something that may alienate the audience.
- *Use the 3-T approach in your presentation:*
 - First, tell them what you are going to tell them (your outline).
 - Then, tell them (the body of your presentation).
 - Finally, tell them what you told them (your summary).
- *Talk to the audience, not at it.* Maintain as much eye contact with the audience as possible, and refer to your notes as little as possible (you will be glad you practiced plenty of times beforehand).
- *Speak clearly and confidently.* Do not speak too quickly or too slowly. Speak in short, understandable sentences—not long, complex, rambling sentences. Pause appropriately after a key point or before moving on to a new item. Use appropriate inflection in your voice to help make a point. Do not present your speech in a monotone. Stand up straight and speak with confidence.
- *Use appropriate gestures to help make a point.* Use hand movements, facial expressions, and body language. Do not stand frozen to one spot; move around, if appropriate. In a large auditorium, it is better to have a portable microphone than to be locked to a lectern with a fixed microphone. If you do walk around, whether in a small meeting room or an auditorium, always face the audience when you speak; never speak with your back to the audience, such as facing the projector screen.
- *Do not read your slides to the audience.* Elaborate on the single idea illustrated by each visual aid and give examples, if appropriate. The audience is not coming to hear you read your slides; they are coming to listen to what you have to say (not read).
- *Do not stand in front of your visual aids.* Do not stand in a position where you block any of the audience's view of the projector screen, flip chart, or other visual aids.

- *Build interest in your presentation.* Develop your "story" with logic and reason. Gradually increase the tempo of your presentation.
- *Keep to the key points in your outline.* Do not digress or wander off the topic or your outline. You will waste time and confuse the audience.
- *When making key points, explain to the audience why they are important.*
- *Sum up your points on a particular item before moving on to the next item on your outline.*
- *Know your closing lines.* The closing is as important as the opening. Tie the closing to the purpose of the presentation. Finish with conviction and confidence.
- *Allow time for interaction with the audience, if appropriate.* Ask if there are any questions. You should state at the beginning of your presentation whether there will be time for questions at the end of the presentation or whether the audience can interrupt with questions during the presentation. The latter option can be risky if you have a fixed time slot or an agenda to complete. However, if it is a presentation to a customer conducted in a small meeting room, responding to questions on the fly may be more appropriate than expecting the customer to hold all questions until the end of the presentation. In fact, part of your presentation strategy may be to draw the customer into a discussion to elicit her or his reactions or opinions.
- *When responding to questions, be sincere, candid, and confident.* Do not overanswer questions; otherwise you will limit the number of questions that can be asked in the time available. If you do not know the answer or cannot divulge the answer, say so; that is a legitimate answer. Do not be defensive in responding.

Reports

Written reports are just as important as verbal reports in communicating information about a project. The required types, content, format, frequency, and distribution of reports that the project organization must prepare may be specified by the customer in the contract, or identified in the project communication plan.

Some reports may be distributed to a large number of recipients. It is important to know who will be receiving copies of reports. The audience could be very diverse and could include people who are very knowledgeable about the project, as well as individuals who know only what they read in the periodic reports they receive. Recipients of the reports may have different levels of technical sophistication, and some may not understand certain technical language or jargon.

It is important to keep in mind that *reports must be written to address what is of interest to the readers, not what is of interest to the person writing the report.*

The following sections discuss two common types of project reports and offer suggestions for ensuring that reports are useful.

TYPES OF PROJECT REPORTS

The two most common types of project reports are:

- Progress reports
- Final report

PROGRESS REPORTS

It is important to keep in mind that a progress report is not an activity report. *Do not confuse activity or busyness with progress and accomplishment.* The customer, in particular, is interested in project accomplishments—what progress has been made toward accomplishing the project objective—rather than on what activities were keeping the project team busy.

Reports on project progress can be prepared by project team members for the project manager or their functional manager (in a matrix organization), by the project manager for the customer, or by the project manager for the project organization's upper management.

Progress reports usually cover a specified period, called the **reporting period**. This period could be a week, a month, a quarter, or whatever best fits the project. Most progress reports cover only what happened during the reporting period rather than cumulative progress since the beginning of the project.

A sample outline for a project progress report is shown in Figure 12.6. Items that might be included in a project progress report include the following:

- *Accomplishments since the previous report.* This section should identify key project milestones that were reached. It could also include a report on achievement (or lack of achievement) of specific goals set for the reporting period, such as the completion of specific milestones or deliverables.
- *Current status of project performance.* Data on cost, schedule, and work scope are compared to the baseline plan.
- *Progress toward resolution of previously identified problems.* If little or no progress has been made on items brought up in previous progress reports, an explanation should be provided.

Reinforce Your Learning

19. The primary purpose of progress reports is to report on project _____

rather than on what _____

were keeping the project team busy.

FIGURE 12.6 **Project Progress Report Outline**

Progress Project Report
for the Period July 1 to September 30

Table of Contents

1. Accomplishments since prior report
2. Current status of project performance
 2.1 Cost
 2.2 Schedule
 2.3 Work scope
3. Progress toward resolution of previously identified problems
4. Problems or potential problems since prior report
5. Planned corrective actions
6. Milestones expected to be reached during next reporting period

- *Problems or potential problems since prior report.* Problems can include (1) technical problems such as prototypes that do not work or test results that are not what they were expected to be; (2) schedule problems such as delays encountered because some activities took longer than expected, materials were delivered late, or construction delays were caused by bad weather; and (3) cost problems such as cost overruns because materials cost more than originally estimated or more person-hours were expended on activities than had been planned.
- *Planned corrective actions.* This section should specify the corrective actions to be taken during the next reporting period to resolve each of the identified problems. It should include a statement explaining whether the project objective will be jeopardized, with respect to scope, quality, cost, or schedule, by any of these corrective actions.
- *Milestones expected to be reached during next reporting period.* These goals should be in accordance with the latest agreed-upon project plan.

None of the information in the progress report should be a surprise to the readers. For example, any identified problems should already have been discussed verbally prior to the preparation of the written progress report.

FINAL REPORT

The project final report is usually a summary of the project. It is not an accumulation of the progress reports, nor is it a chronological day-by-day story of what happened throughout the project. The final report might include the following:

- *Customer's original need*
- *Original project objective*
- *Customer's original requirements*
- *Description of the project*
- *Degree to which the original project objective was met* in terms of scope, quality requirements, budget, and schedule. If it was not met, an explanation should be included.
- *Actual versus anticipated benefits* to the customer as a result of the project.
- *Future considerations.* This section could include actions the customer might want to consider in the future to enhance or expand the project results. For example, if the project was constructing an office building, future considerations might be to add a parking deck, a fitness center, or a day care center adjacent to the building. If the project was organizing a community festival, future considerations might be to change the time of year, extend the duration of the festival, or to take action to improve the pedestrian traffic flow.
- *A list of all deliverables* (equipment, materials, software, documents such as drawings and reports, and so forth) provided to the customer.
- *Test data from the final acceptance testing* of a system or piece of equipment, which provided the basis on which the customer accepted the project results or deliverables.

USEFUL REPORTS

Taking into consideration the following guidelines when you are preparing project reports will help ensure their usefulness and value to the recipients:

- *Make reports concise.* Do not try to impress the recipients with volume. The volume of a report does not equate with project progress or accomplishment.

If reports are kept brief, there is a better chance that they will be read. Furthermore, report preparation can be a time-consuming activity; the project manager should therefore try to minimize the time needed by the project team to develop input to the project reports.

- *Make reports readable and understandable.* Use short, understandable sentences rather than compound, complex, paragraph-length sentences. Long paragraphs will tempt the reader to skip down the page and miss important points. Use simple language that the various recipients will understand. Do not use jargon, terminology, or acronyms that some readers may not understand. Read the report aloud for content and style. Is it easily readable and understandable, or does it sound stilted and confusing?
- *Put the most important points first*—in the report and in each paragraph. Some readers have a tendency to read the first sentence and then skim over the rest of the paragraph.
- *Use graphics where possible*—such as charts, diagrams, tables, or pictures. Remember, a picture is worth a thousand words. Do not make the graphics too busy. Have one concept or point per graphic. It is better to have several clean graphics than a single cluttered one.
- *Pay as much attention to the format of the report as to the content.* The report should be open, inviting, and organized in a manner that is understandable to the readers. It should not be cluttered or in a small size type font that is difficult to read. It should not contain material, graphics, or forms that are confusing or illegible.

Reinforce Your Learning

21. What are some important guidelines to keep in mind when preparing a report?

Written reports, like verbal communication, leave an impression—positive or negative—with the audience. Care and thought should be given to preparing reports. Report preparation should be looked on as an opportunity to make a positive impression, rather than as a burdensome, time-consuming activity. It may be worthwhile to ask periodically for feedback from the recipients of the reports regarding the reports' value and usefulness in meeting their needs and interests, and to solicit any suggestions they might have for enhancing the reports.

Control Document Changes

In addition to project reports, many other documents may be created by either the project team or the customer during the project. Some examples are design sketches, specifications, engineering drawings, material lists, maintenance instructions, training materials, floor plans, and software for controlling the movements of a robot. Project documents can be text, drawings, forms, lists, manuals, photographs, videos, or software. They can be on large paper, such as an engineering drawing, or in electronic format, such as a PowerPoint document or a simulation video.

Revisions to project documents can result from changes initiated by the customer or by the project team. Some changes are minor; others are major, affecting the project work scope, budget, and schedule. An example of a minor change is updating the drawings and assembly instructions for festival booths because a benefactor donated canopies for all the booths. An example of a major change is a change in the location, size, and type of some of the windows requested by the customer upon seeing the house being built. In this case, it is important that the

contractor stop work on those particular windows and inform the customer of any additional costs or schedule delays that might be caused by the requested changes. These changes should be documented in writing for the customer, and the customer should approve the changes before work proceeds and any new materials are ordered. When the changes are approved, the house plans and drawings need to be revised to incorporate the changes.

Throughout a project, various project documents will be revised to incorporate .changes. At the start of the project, a **document control system**, also referred to as a *configuration control system*, needs to be established for the process and procedures that define how changes to documents will be documented, approved, and communicated. Such a system must be communicated to all project participants. It is important for the project team to know which is the latest version of a document so that they can perform their work correctly based on the most current information and documentation. For example, the buyer would not want the builder to use outdated drawings if the architect had just made revisions that changed the locations of interior walls.

It is good practice to put on each page of each type of document: (1) the date of the latest revision, (2) a sequential revision number, and (3) the initials of the person who made the changes. For example, a notation in the lower right corner of a drawing of the floor plan for an office arrangement may indicate Rev. 4, 12/29/14, ES, which denotes that the latest version of the floor plan is revision number 4, which was made on December 29, 2014, by Elisabeth Smith (ES). For documents created using software such as Microsoft Word, the application has capabilities to track detailed changes to documents.

Just as important as keeping up to date with revision numbers and dates on documents is timely distribution of updated documents to appropriate people on the project. When changes are made to documents, the updated documents should immediately be distributed to any project team members whose work will be affected by the changes. Also, when revised documents are distributed, they should be accompanied by a cover memo explaining the changes that were made to the previous document. This will be helpful to people receiving the document so that they will not need to go back and compare the new document to the old one and try to find the changes. If only a few changes are made to a document, distribution of the particular pages that were changed may be all that is required. When changes are extensive, it may make sense to distribute the entire revised document rather than just the revised pages. See the section on managing changes in Chapter 10 for related information.

Project Communication Plan

Not all stakeholders or project team members want or need all project documents. A **project communication plan** defines the generation and distribution of project documents among project stakeholders throughout the project. It identifies the various documents, who is responsible for creating each document, by when or how frequently each document must be distributed, to whom each document is to be distributed, and what action each recipient is expected to take. The project charter or contract often includes sponsor or customer requirements for specific documents, including frequency, the need for customer approvals, and who in the customer organization should receive copies of which documents. For any external resources that are used on the project, such as

Reinforce Your Learning

22. At the _____ of the project, a document _____ system needs to be established that defines how _____ to documents will be _____, _____, and _____.

Reinforce Your Learning

23. When _____ are made to documents, they should immediately be _____ to project _____ whose _____ will be _____ by the changes.

Reinforce Your Learning

24. A project _____ plan defines the _____ and _____ of project _____ among project _____.

FIGURE 12.7 Project Communication Plan

DOCUMENT	AUTHOR OR ORIGINATOR	REQ'D DATE OR FREQUENCY	RECIPIENTS	ACTION REQUIRED (I, C, OR A)	COMMENTS

Key: **I**: For Information Only; **C**: For Review & Comments; **A**: For Review & Approval

subcontractors, consultants, or vendors, the project organization will define requirements regarding documentation, approvals required, and distribution and include such requirements in subcontracts or purchase orders.

Figure 12.7 is a generic template for a project communication plan; each row in the matrix would include information related to a specific project document. The following elements might be included in the plan:

- *Documents* include project charter, contract and amendments, project communication plan, requirements document, project scope document, quality plan, work breakdown structure, responsibility assignment matrix, network diagram, schedules, budgets, risk management plan, stakeholder issue log, project procedures, change orders, design documents, drawings, specifications, material lists, instruction manuals, training materials, test plans, test results, formal acceptance of deliverables, meeting agenda, minutes of meetings, applied time and percent complete reports, travel request and expense reports, progress reports, subcontracts and amendments, purchase orders, and invoices.
- *Author or originator* is the name or title of the person(s) responsible for creating or preparing the document.
- *Required date or frequency* can be the specific date by which the document must be completed and distributed to recipients. For example, some documents may be a required project deliverable, such as preliminary specifications, for which the customer has a required completion date and with which a progress payment may be associated. Other documents, such as progress reports, are to be completed and distributed at regular intervals, such as biweekly, monthly, or by the 15th of each month. Yet other documents such as contract amendments, purchase orders, revisions of drawings, or specifications may not have a specific required date or regular frequency, but instead they are generated on an "as needed" basis.
- *Recipients* include the name or title of each person to whom the document is to be distributed. This is referred to as the *distribution list* for a document.
- *Action required* indicates what action each recipient of a document is expected to take after receiving the document. For example, the document might be distributed to some stakeholders only for their information, it could be provided to some recipients to review and provide comments, or the recipient might be the customer or sponsor who is expected to review and approve a particular document, such as a design or report.

- *Comments* might include special notes or conditions related to a specific document, such as approval required within one week, document to be translated into Spanish, document contains proprietary or confidential information, and so forth.

The project communication plan needs to be updated as stakeholders or their information needs change, or if new people or new documents are identified.

Stakeholder Communication

The project team should welcome stakeholder input, involvement, discussions, and debate. It will build support for the project. Communicating with stakeholders requires the project team to employ effective verbal and written communications, and in particular effective listening to achieve understanding. Stakeholders' concerns should be addressed early, positively, and in a timely manner; and not confrontationally, put off, ignored, or dismissed. The project manager needs to provide opportunities for regular two-way communication with each stakeholder, not just when an issue or concern is identified. The project manager and team need to listen, be open-minded, thoughtful, and behave professionally; and not dominate the discussions, overreact, become defensive, or lose control of their emotions. In most situations each stakeholder should be dealt with separately because each has their unique interests and concerns, rather than dealing with all stakeholders as a group.

It is important to have regular communication with the various project stakeholders. The project team needs to keep stakeholders informed regularly of project status, updates, and changes; otherwise they may jump to the wrong conclusions about the status of issues that are important to them. Such information should be provided in writing or posted on the project website to minimize the chance of misinterpretation of verbal discussions and presentations, or rumors.

Rather than just providing information at meetings with stakeholders, the project team should provide opportunities for questions, discussions, and comments. During the meetings the project team members should make use of active listening techniques. After the meetings the project manager should follow up by providing a written copy of the responses to stakeholder questions and concerns or post such information on the project website. This will minimize any misunderstandings, misinformation, or reinterpretation of information that may be passed along verbally to any individuals who were not at the meetings.

Stakeholder engagement and support are important to the successful performance of a project and accomplishment of the project objective. Regular and open communication, trust, respect, open-mindedness, and a positive win-win attitude are keys to successful stakeholder engagement.

Collaborative Communication Tools

Meetings create a forum and opportunity for team collaboration. However, face-to-face meetings are not always feasible, timely, or practical, especially when many team members are involved and there are constraints such as travel. *Virtual project teams* may be geographically dispersed, with team members located in various buildings in an office complex, or in different offices in various cities within a state, across the country, or on several continents. Also with telecommuting, some team members may work from their domiciles.

There are various collaborative communication tools, such as teleconferencing, content management systems, extranets, collaborative project workspaces on the Web including Web 2.0 tools, and groupware that allow all or some of the members of the project team, including subcontractors and the customer, to communicate and collaborate with each other. Use of such collaborative communication tools can be important when team members are in different geographic locations, making it inconvenient or impractical for them to physically come together in a common location for a face-to-face meeting. These tools facilitate the sharing of project information and can enhance the communication, collaboration, teamwork, productivity, and performance of the project team. Collaborative communication tools range from e-mail, which relies on writing and reading, to audio-based tools such as conference calls, and videoconferencing, which is based on both audio and video. For project communications that are not face-to-face, e-mail is the most frequently used method for transmitting and distributing project information. Information can be distributed quickly and efficiently to the project team or various subgroups through an assortment of distribution lists.

Electronic communication devices such as smartphones and tablets may have features and apps that can provide team members with greater access and flexibility while using various interactive telecommunication technologies and collaboration tools such as e-mail, Internet access, videoconferencing, document management, and Web 2.0 collaboration tools. These devices allow for increased productivity, instant access to information, and enable users to manage their business hours more efficiently.

Teleconferencing allows the live exchange of information among members of the project team. It includes tools such as conference calls and videoconferencing. It can help facilitate the sharing of information in a more interactive way than e-mail. Teleconferencing eliminates travel costs and allows team members to be more productive by not having to travel to meetings. Conference calls allow people at different locations to interact using voice/audio, while videoconferencing enriches the interaction by using both audio and video. Videoconferencing can involve multiple locations where several team members gather in rooms equipped with cameras and displays. Web videoconferencing, where each participant is connected using their own personal computer, electronic tablet, or smartphone, is another tool used to conduct live meetings over the Internet. This technique may be particularly helpful to team members who are telecommuting and may not be able to travel to a common location where the videoconferencing equipment is set up. Web or desktop videoconferencing may allow participants to also share data, documents, or video, such as a spreadsheet, PowerPoint slides, or a webcast, for other participants to view from their personal computers or tablets during the session. Similar to preparing for a face-to-face meeting, it is good practice to prepare and distribute an agenda to participants before the session and provide copies of materials (project documents, presentation slides, etc.) that will be referenced during the session. When scheduling a teleconference, you need to be sensitive to differences in the time zones of the participants.

Document management systems can provide a central repository for project information and capture the efforts of team members into a managed content environment. A content management system is used to manage the content of a website, documents, or files. Such a system can be used by a group of contributors to share, develop, add to, and edit documents, such as a project report, technical specification, or an instruction manual. Such systems can also provide

Reinforce Your Learning

26. Teleconferencing includes tools such as

calls and

_____ .

document management information, such as a log sheet of who accessed which documents and when, and what changes they may have made. Some systems may also incorporate automatic routing of documents for approvals, including e-mail notification, for example.

A computer server may be dedicated to a specific project, or there can be reserved space on a server as a place to share project documents and files, such as requirements documents, proposals, specifications, contracts, drawings, forms, plans, schedules, budgets, a common project calendar, meeting agenda and action items, project reports, presentation materials, and so forth. An extranet is a "private" network that uses the Internet to securely share a repository of project information among the project team, subcontractors, and customer. It can be a restricted part of a website where registered users need to log in to access project information and documents. Project workspaces on the Web allow for complete Web access to all project information across multiple projects and provide numerous reporting and communication tools.

Groupware is another collaborative tool. It is software that helps people involved in a common task. Groupware can support team idea generation, brainstorming, problem solving, and decision making. An example of such groupware is a group decision support system, which is software that facilitates group decision making. It is particularly useful for idea generation and brainstorming. Session participants provide their own input simultaneously. The system allows participants to contribute anonymously, when appropriate. It also allows the group to categorize, rank, and vote on various statements or entries. Reports, including graphics, of the results can be produced automatically.

 REAL WORLD PROJECT MANAGEMENT

Communicate for Success: Research Studies Find Relationship

The Project Management Institute (PMI) recently released the 2013 Pulse of the Profession In-Depth Report: The Essential Role of Communications. Researchers concluded that more than half of the money at risk in a project is due to poor or substandard communications.

Ineffective communications were cited as the primary cause for one-third of the project failures reported and as having a negative impact on the success of more than half of the respondents' projects. To reinforce the importance of communications in projects, Mark A. Langley, PMI president and CEO, stated, "Without a considerable focus on communications, even the most thoroughly planned strategic initiatives are at risk of underperformance. At every level of the organization, stakeholders should understand how projects and programs connect to the overall organization strategy, and be speaking a common language that facilitates collaboration and clearly identifies evolving expectations for project outcomes. Companies that cut corners on communications are unnecessarily incurring extra risk."

The Pulse report researchers found a relationship between communications and company performance. High performance companies were compared to lower performing companies. Performance was measured on success rates of projects

completed on time, on budget, and within the goals stated for the project. High performance organizations experienced an average for more than four projects completed on time, on budget, and within the goals out of every five projects started (80 percent). Lower performance organizations reported project completion at rates less than 60 percent of the time (less than three projects completed on time, on budget, and within the goals out of every five projects started).

High performing organizations reported implementing a formal communication plan nearly twice as frequently as those companies identified as lower performing for project completion. Comparisons of the communication plans revealed that the high performing organizations experienced achievement of the projects' desired objectives three times more frequently than those without a project communication plan. Effectiveness of communication was measured and indicated that effective communication strategies resulted in companies being identified as a high performance organization, meaning completing greater than 80 percent of their projects on time, on budget, and within the goals, at more than five times the rate of companies without effective communication strategies and plans.

Another study, the FD | Forbes Insights 2010 Strategic Initiatives Study Adapting Corporate Strategy to the Changing Economy, reported the importance of communication to the strategic planning and execution process. Almost all CEOs (92 percent) and nearly half of the respondents (46 percent) reported on the critical and integral nature of communications to strategic initiatives. More than seven out of every ten (73 percent) of the responding companies reported plans to increase communications to improve workforce engagement. However, there seems to be a disconnection between upper management's perception and what actually is occurring in the organizations whose leaders responded to the study's survey. Two out of every three executive sponsors stated that the communications in their organizations were doing a good job communicating the connections between projects and the strategic initiatives of the company and less than half of the project managers agreed (46 percent).

Project communication is critical for successfully completing projects on time, on budget, and within the goals. Project managers and upper level management agree that effective communication strategies are important to project completion and for the company to achieve its strategic initiatives. As you take on project management roles in your organization, be sure to communicate the evolving project expectations through a formal communication plan to increase the likelihood of completing projects on time, on budget, and within the goals.

Based on information from Anonymous (2013). "PMI Finds That More Than Half of All Project Budget Risk is Due to Ineffective Communications," *Professional Services Close-Up.*

CRITICAL SUCCESS FACTORS

- Effective and frequent personal communication is crucial to successful project management.

- A high degree of face-to-face communication is important early in the project to foster team building, develop good working relationships, and establish mutual expectations.

- Body language and customs reflective of cultural diversity must be considered in communications.

- Be careful not to use remarks, words, or phrases that can be construed to be sexist, racist, prejudicial, or offensive.

- The heart of communication is understanding—not only to be understood, but to understand. Half of making communication effective is listening. Failure to listen can cause a breakdown in communication.
- Communication should be clear, concise, honest, unambiguous, free of jargon, and not offensive.
- Achieving customer satisfaction requires ongoing communication with the customer to keep the customer informed and to determine whether expectations have changed. Regularly ask the customer about the level of satisfaction with the progress of the project.
- Keep the customer and project team informed of the project status and potential problems in a timely manner.
- Project status meetings should be held on a regular basis. Have the team develop meeting guidelines at the project kickoff meeting at the beginning of the project so that everyone understands and is committed to what behavior is expected during project meetings.
- Do not confuse busyness and activity with accomplishment when communicating project progress.

- Reports must be written to address what is of interest to the readers, not what is of interest to the person writing the report.
- Make reports concise, readable, and understandable. Pay as much attention to format, organization, appearance, and readability as you do to the content.
- At the start of the project, a document control system needs to be established that defines how changes to documents will be documented, approved, and communicated.
- When documents are updated, they should immediately be distributed to all team members whose work will be affected.
- At the beginning of the project, prepare a project communication plan to ensure that all stakeholders will receive the information and documents they need.
- Regular and open communication, trust, respect, open-mindedness, and a positive win-win attitude are keys to successful stakeholder engagement.

SUMMARY

Project communication takes various forms, including personal communication, meetings, presentations, reports, and project documentation. Communication can be face-to-face or through some medium, including phones, voice mail, e-mail, text messages, videoconferencing, document development systems, or shared Web 2.0 tools. It can be formal or informal. Personal communication can be either verbal or written. Verbal communication can be face-to-face or via phone or computer. Information can be communicated in a more accurate and timely manner through verbal communication. Such communication provides a forum for discussion, clarification, understanding, and immediate feedback. Body language and tone are important elements in verbal communication. Body language and customs reflective of cultural diversity must be considered in communications. Verbal communication should be straightforward, unambiguous, free of technical jargon, and not offensive. Asking for or providing feedback enhances understanding.

Personal written communication is generally carried out through internal or external correspondence. Such means can be used to communicate effectively with a large group of people, but should not be used for trivial matters. Written communications should be clear and concise and should be used mostly to inform, confirm, or request.

Listening is an important part of making communication effective. Failure to listen can cause a breakdown in communication. Common barriers to effective

listening include pretending to listen, distractions, bias and closed-mindedness, impatience, and jumping to conclusions. Listening skills can be improved by focusing on the person talking, engaging in active listening, asking questions, and not interrupting.

Project meetings are another forum for project communication. The three most common types of project meetings are status review, problem-solving, and design review meetings. The purposes of a status review meeting are to inform, identify problems, and establish action items. Items often covered include accomplishments since the previous meeting; cost, schedule, and work scope—status, trends, forecasts, and variances; risk assessment update; stakeholder issues update; corrective actions; opportunities for improvement; and action item assignment. Problem-solving meetings are called when problems or potential problems arise. They should be used to develop a problem statement, identify potential causes, gather data, identify and evaluate possible solutions, determine the best solution, revise the plan, implement the solution, and evaluate it. Design review meetings are for projects that include a design phase. They often include a preliminary design review meeting, in which the customer reviews the initial conceptual design, and a final design review meeting, in which the customer reviews completed, detailed design documents. These meetings are a mechanism for gaining customer approval before proceeding with the remainder of the project effort.

Before any meeting, the purpose of the meeting and the people who need to participate should be determined, an agenda drawn up and distributed, materials prepared, and room arrangements made. The actual meeting should start on time, notes should be taken, and the agenda reviewed. The meeting leader should facilitate, not dominate, the meeting. After the meeting, decision and action items should be published and distributed.

Project managers and team members are often called on to give formal presentations. In preparing for the presentation, it is important to determine the purpose of the presentation, find out about the target audience, make an outline, develop notes and visual aids, make copies of handout materials, and practice. You should start by telling the audience what you are going to tell them, then tell it to them, then summarize the presentation by telling them what you told them. The presentation should be clear, simple, and interesting, and should conclude within the allotted time.

Written reports are often required during a project. The two most common types of project reports are progress reports and final reports. Progress reports often cover accomplishments since the prior report, the current project status, any potential problems that have been identified and corrective actions that are planned, and goals that should be accomplished during the next reporting period. Final reports provide a summary of the project and often include items such as the customer's original need, the original project objective and requirements, a description of the project, benefits resulting from the project, and a list of deliverables produced. All reports should be clear, concise, and readable. They should be written to address what is of interest to the readers, not the writer.

Throughout a project, many types of documents may be created, such as specifications, manuals, or drawings. They may need to be revised as a result of changes made by the customer or the project team. At the start of the project, a document control system needs to be established for the process and procedures that define how changes to documents will be documented, approved, and communicated.

A project communication plan defines the generation and distribution of project documents among stakeholders throughout the project. It identifies the

various documents, who is responsible for creating each document, by when or how frequently each document must be distributed, to whom each document is to be distributed, and what action each recipient is expected to take.

Communicating with stakeholders requires the project team to employ effective verbal and written communications, and in particular effective listening to achieve understanding. Stakeholders' concerns should be addressed early, positively, and in a timely manner; and not confrontationally, put off, ignored, or dismissed. The project manager needs to provide opportunities for regular two-way communication with each stakeholder, not just when an issue or concern is identified. The project manager and team need to listen, be open-minded, thoughtful, and behave professionally; and not dominate the discussions, overreact, become defensive, or lose control of their emotions. Stakeholder engagement and support are important to the successful performance of a project and accomplishment of the project objective.

Collaborative communication tools allow all or some of the members of the project team, including subcontractors and the customer to communicate and collaborate with each other. This can be important for a virtual project team with members in different geographic locations, as it is often not convenient or practical for them to physically come together in a common location for a face-to-face meeting. These tools facilitate the sharing of project information and can enhance the communication, collaboration, teamwork, productivity, and performance of the project team. They can also support and advance team idea generation, brainstorming, problem solving, decision making, and document development and management.

QUESTIONS

1. Discuss why verbal and written communication is important to project success, and describe several ways of enhancing such communication.
2. Why are listening skills important in effective communication? How can you improve your listening skills?
3. For the next few days, observe the body language of the people with whom you communicate. Describe some of the positive and negative things they do.
4. Discuss why it is important to be sensitive to the diverse composition of a project team, especially with regard to communication.
5. List 10 best practices (do's and don'ts) for electronic communication etiquette in a business environment.
6. What is the purpose of status review meetings? When should they be conducted? What should be covered at such meetings?
7. Why are problem-solving meetings conducted? Who should call such meetings? Describe the approach that should be followed.
8. What should be done before a meeting to properly prepare for the meeting? What should be done during a meeting to ensure that the meeting will be effective? Describe how personal computers, cell phones, tablets, and other technologies could help or hinder meeting effectiveness.
9. If you were asked to advise someone on how to prepare for and deliver an important presentation, what would you say? For each step listed, state why it is important.
10. Why are progress reports an integral part of project communications? What should they include? How are they different from a final report?
11. Why is it important to control changes made to project documents? How can you achieve effective control?

12. Describe what is meant by the terms collaborative communication tools and Web 2.0 tools and provide a list of some of these tools. How can these tools help improve project communications?

INTERNET EXERCISES

For the website addresses of the organizations mentioned in these exercises, go to "Internet Exercises" at the book's companion website at www.cengagebrain.com. It is suggested that you save this website in your "Favorites" list for easy access in the future.

1. Search the Web for "effective project communication." Summarize at least one website and compare it to what was presented in this chapter. What new insights did you gain from this website?
2. Search the Web for "effective listening skills." Identify several helpful techniques that were not presented in this chapter.
3. Search the Web for "effective meeting strategies." Identify several helpful techniques that were not presented in this chapter. In addition, identify at least one tool that allows you to run electronic or online meetings. Describe the features of this tool.
4. Search the Web for "project reports." Print out and describe at least one website that discusses methods for writing effective project reports or provide a one-page review of a software package that helps managers write project reports.
5. To improve communications, many projects today have their own website and promote sharing using Web 2.0 tools. Search the Web for at least one Web-based collaborative communications software tool. Describe what this tool does. Do you think this product can be used to improve project communications?

CASE STUDY 1 Office Communications

Cathy Buford is the design leader on a project team for a large, complex technical project for a very demanding customer. Joe Jackson is an engineer assigned to her design team.

It is about 9:30 A.M. when Joe walks into Cathy's office. Her head is down, and she is hard at work.

"Hey, Cathy," says Joe, "going to the Little League game tonight? Ya know, I volunteered to coach this year."

"Oh. Hi, Joe. I'm really busy," Cathy tells him.

Joe then proceeds to sit down in Cathy's office. "I hear your kid is a pretty good ball player."

Cathy shuffles some papers and tries to focus on her work. "Huh? I guess so. I am so swamped."

"Yeah, me too," Joe says. "I had to take a break to get away from it for a while."

"Since you're here," Cathy says, "I've been thinking that maybe you should evaluate using bar coding or optical character recognition technology for data entry. It might.... "

Joe interrupts. "Look at those dark clouds forming outside. I hope the game isn't rained out tonight."

Cathy continues, "Some of the advantages of these technologies are...." She goes on for a few minutes. "So what do you think?"

"Huh? No, they won't work" is Joe's response. "Trust me. Besides, the customer is a low-tech kind of guy, and it would increase the project costs."

"But if we can show the customer that it could save him money and reduce input errors," Cathy persists, "he probably would pay the extra needed to implement the technologies."

"Save him money!" Joe exclaims. "How? By laying off people? We already have too much downsizing in this country. And the government and politicians aren't doing anything about it. It doesn't matter who you vote for. They're all the same."

"By the way, I still need your input for the progress report," Cathy reminds him. "I need to e-mail it to the customer tomorrow. As you know, I'll need about 8 to 10 pages. We need a thick report to show the customer how busy we've been."

"What? Nobody told me," says Joe.

"I sent the design team an e-mail a couple of weeks ago, saying that I needed everyone's input by last Friday. You could probably use the material you've prepared for the project status review meeting tomorrow afternoon," Cathy responds.

"I have to make a presentation at the meeting tomorrow? That's news to me," Joe tells her.

"It was on the agenda distributed last week," says Cathy.

"I don't have time to keep up with all the e-mails in my inbox," Joe snorts. "Well, I'll just have to wing it. I'll use some of the slides from my pitch six months ago. Nobody will know the difference. Those meetings are a waste of time anyway. Nobody cares about them. Everybody thinks they are just a waste of two hours each week."

"Anyway, can you e-mail me your input for the progress report by the end of the day?" asks Cathy.

"I have to leave early for the game."

"What game?"

"Aren't you listening to anything I say? The Little League game."

"Maybe you should start working on it now," Cathy suggests.

"I just have to call Jim, my assistant coach, first about the game tonight," says Joe. "Then I'll write up a couple of paragraphs. Hey, hold on a minute, I'll call Jim right now!" Joe picks up Cathy's desk phone and calls Jim and proceeds to ask Jim several questions about the game. Cathy tries to focus on her work as Joe talks very loudly to Jim. After hanging up, Joe remarks, "Can't you just take notes at the meeting tomorrow when I give my pitch? That should give you what you need for the report."

"It can't wait until then. The report has to be e-mailed tomorrow, and I'll be working on it late into the night."

"So, you won't be at the game?"

"Just e-mail me your input."

"I'm not being paid to be a typist," Joe declares. "I can write it much faster. You can get somebody to type it. You'll probably want to edit it anyway. The last report to the customer looked completely different from the input I provided. It looked like you completely rewrote it."

Cathy looks back down at her desk and attempts to continue her work.

CASE QUESTIONS
1. What are some of the communication problems presented in this case?
2. What should Cathy do? What do you think Joe will do?
3. How could Cathy and Joe have handled this situation better?
4. What could have been done to prevent the communication problem between Cathy and Joe?

GROUP ACTIVITY
Have two participants in the class act out this scenario. Immediately afterward, have a class discussion that addresses the four questions above.

CASE STUDY 2 International Communications

"Samuel, this is Angelique calling again. It is Wednesday at 9 o'clock. I need to talk to you. I haven't heard from you in a while, and I need an update on the project. There are also some changes to the equipment placement in the building that I want to discuss with you. I tried to e-mail you several times over the past couple weeks, but I get a message back that my e-mails are undeliverable. Are you having a problem with your e-mail? Please call me today. I have to give a report to our board of directors on Monday, and I need to know the status of the project."

Angelique hung up the phone after leaving the voice message. She was not happy. She had been trying to get in touch with Samuel for several weeks. She thought to herself, "That's it! If he doesn't call back today, I'm calling his boss first thing in the morning."

Angelique was the newly appointed plant manager for ElectroTech Corporation's new manufacturing facility that Thomson Industries was designing and building for ElectroTech in Ireland. She was currently located at ElectroTech's headquarters in Boston, but would be relocating to Ireland as soon as the construction started.

Samuel was the project manager for Thomson Industries, the prime contractor for the design and construction of the new factory. His office was in Dallas. Although he had managed several projects in the past, they were smaller and were in the Dallas region. He had gotten to know most of the subcontractors from working with them on various projects. The ElectroTech project was by far the largest and most complex project ever assigned to him. For example, on this project, two of the major subcontractors who would be supplying equipment for the factory were located in Germany and Japan.

At the start of the project, Samuel called a brief team meeting and confidently told them, "Boston and Ireland are no different than Dallas. And as far as the German and Japanese subcontractors are concerned, my approach will be straightforward. Build the equipment according to our specifications and deliver it on time, or they don't get paid. It's as simple as that. No excuses, no negotiations. The ElectroTech contract has a bonus clause in it for early completion, and I intend to make it. So we've got to play hardball with all our subcontractors; we can't let any of their delays screw up our chances for the bonus. And another thing—we need to be very tough on entertaining any changes from the customer. That will give them a reason for delays and an excuse for not paying the bonus."

"We've got some pretty good senior people assigned to this project so we should be able to start fast. Everyone should pretty much know what needs to be done, so we shouldn't have to spend a lot of time in meetings discussing

and figuring things out. We can focus all our time on doing the job rather than talking about it. Don't bog me down with paperwork or e-mails. I'll have enough to do tracking our budgets and schedules, keeping on top of our subcontractors, keeping ElectroTech from making a bunch of changes, and keeping our own management off our backs."

When Samuel came back to his office after lunch, Penny, his administrative assistant, said, "I checked your voice messages, and Angelique left another one. She said she needs to talk to you—something about changes. She also said something about your e-mail not working."

Samuel responded, "Changes, I knew it! That's exactly why I don't want to talk to her. Just like a woman, changing her mind already about something or another. Thank god men don't do that, or we'd never get anything done. And as for my e-mails, I had Larry do something to my computer so whoever sends me an e-mail will get a message back that it's undeliverable. After a while they'll get the message that I'm not interested in getting copies of everybody's e-mails full of trivia and details."

Penny told Samuel, "You really should check your e-mails; some could be very important."

Samuel snapped back, "I've managed plenty of successful projects—all without e-mail. More work and less talk—that's the key to project success."

Penny said, "Maybe I can ask Larry to have your e-mails forwarded to me, so at least I can screen them."

"Go ahead if you want to," replied Samuel. "You're just going to make a whole lot of work for yourself. If something is really important, people will figure out how to get in touch with me. How do you think we managed before we had e-mail? Besides, with you screening my voice mail, I can control my time and decide who I need to talk to and when, and not get snagged by people calling me and telling me why they can't do something; they always figure a way to get it done anyway. They've just got to get in the habit of solving problems when they come up, and not running to the boss and whining about it."

Samuel didn't return Angelique's voice message. The next morning, she called Michael Jetson, vice president of projects for Thomson Industries and Samuel's boss. She blasted him about Samuel not returning her phone calls and e-mails. She threatened to put a hold on all future payments of Thomson's invoices if Samuel didn't get back to her.

Michael walked to Samuel's office. Samuel was reviewing the project cost reports. "Samuel, I got a call from Angelique at ElectoTech. She was pretty upset. She said you haven't returned her calls, and she needs to talk with you."

Samuel responded, "That's absolutely right. And you know why I'm not getting back to her? Because she wants to make a whole bunch of changes and that will delay this project big time and screw up our chances for that early completion bonus."

"I told her you'd call her back, Samuel, so please get back to her today. This is an important project for us, and I don't want an unhappy customer," said Michael.

"Michael, you know how women are. They get emotional over things. I'll get back to her and calm her down. It would have been nice if she would have told me that she was going to call you rather than just going around my back, but that's a woman for you!" replied Samuel.

After Michael left Samuel's office, Penny brought in a fax from the Japanese subcontractor. It stated, "We have reviewed the recently revised equipment specifications that you sent us. We found that they were changed without our

knowledge. Some of the performance requirements have changed significantly, and we regret that they cannot be met unless we do substantial engineering redesign. We would like to meet with you to discuss the additional costs required for such additional design efforts to meet your revised specifications."

Samuel said, "That's a joke. We're not paying them an extra dime. They got plenty of money in the subcontract to do as much design that is needed. I'm not about to negotiate with them for more money. They better realize that in America we don't do business that way, or at least I don't. Penny, draft a letter to them for my signature telling them that we do not see a basis to provide additional funds. They knew the initial specifications were marked preliminary and should have anticipated that further engineering design would be required once things got firmed up. Make the letter short and firm. I don't want to leave any opening for getting into any of those you-got-to-save-face negotiations."

"Two more things, Penny," said Samuel. "Schedule a project meeting tomorrow with whoever is around. I've got to get an update on some of this stuff that's going on. I need to find out if anyone has been talking with the Japanese or Angelique without me knowing about it. I tell you, if I find out that's been going on, some folks are going to have some sore butts after the meeting. Don't people know it's their job to keep me informed? And a second item. Call Angelique and see if she can fly to Dallas on Friday for a meeting. I don't have time to go there; I've got a tennis match with an old buddy Friday night. Besides she's the one who needs to talk to me, so let her come here. Maybe that will cool her down. Also make reservations for us at that new restaurant near the mall. After I sweet-talk her over a couple drinks at lunch, I'll suggest she go to the mall to shop before she heads back to Boston. Shopping—that's what women need to get rid of their stress, right, Penny?"

CASE QUESTIONS

1. What are the communication errors Samuel made?
2. What should Angelique do when she gets the phone call from Penny asking her to come to Dallas to meet with Samuel?
3. Is there anything more Michael could have said or done in his conversation with Samuel about Angelique's phone call? Should Penny do anything about Samuel's communication style and insensitive comments?
4. What would be the elements of a good communication plan for managing a multinational project such as this?

GROUP ACTIVITY

Divide the course participants into groups of three or four to develop responses to the case questions. Each group should identify a spokesperson to present its responses to the entire class.

REFERENCES

A Guide to the Project Management Body of Knowledge (PMBOK® Guide) Fifth Edition. Newtown Square, PA. Project Management Institute, 2013.

Allen, K. (2012). "Power to the People," *PM Network, 26*(1), 50–55.

Anonymous (2013). "Lessons from the London Olympic Build," *New Zealand Management, 60*(6), 41.

Anonymous (2013). "PMI Finds That More Than Half of All Project Budget Risk Is Due to Ineffective Communications," *Professional Services Close-Up.*

Badir, Y. F., B. Büchel, and C. L. Tucci (2012). "A Conceptual Framework of the Impact of NPD Project Team and Leader Empowerment on Communication and Performance: An Alliance Case Context," *International Journal of Project Management, 30,* 914–926.

Cheung, S., T. Yiu, and M. Lam (2013). "Interweaving Trust and Communication with Project Performance," *Journal of Construction Engineering & Management, 139*(8), 941–950.

Daim, T. U., A. Ha, S. Reutiman, B. Hughes, U. Pathak, W. Bynum, and A. Bhatla (2012). "Exploring the Communication Breakdown in Global Virtual Teams," *International Journal of Project Management, 30,* 199–212.

González-Ibáñez, R., M. Haseki, and C. Shah (2013). "Let's Search Together, but Not Too Close! An Analysis of Communication and Performance in Collaborative Information Seeking," *Information Processing & Management, 49*(5), 1165–1179.

Howell, I. (2013). "Digital Master Builder Q&A With Newforma Inc's CEO," *ENR: Engineering News-Record, 270*(20), 1.

Hsu, J. S., S. Shih, J. C. Chiang, and J. Y. Liu (2012). "The Impact of Transactive Memory Systems on IS Development Team's Coordination, Communication, and Performance," *International Journal of Project Management, 30,* 329–340.

Jackson, M. B. (2011). "Supply & Demand," *PM Network, 25*(11), 54–55.

Klarner, P., M. Sarstedt, M. Hoeck, and C. M. Ringle (2013). "Disentangling the Effects of Team Competences, Team Adaptability, and Client Communication on the Performance of Management Consulting Teams," *Long Range Planning, 46*(3), 258–286.

Lamont, J. (2011). "Knowledge Sharing Supports the Military's Mission," *KM World, 20*(8), 6–7.

Lee, N. and E. M. Rojas (2013). "Visual Representations for Monitoring Project Performance: Developing Novel Prototypes for Improved Communication," *Journal of Construction Engineering & Management, 139*(8), 994–1005.

O'Mara, D. L. (2012). "Rush University Medical Center: New Tower the Gem of Chicago," *Security Dealer & Integrator, 34*(1), 30–32, 34–37.

Tillson, J. (2011). "Not-So-Modest Proposal," *PM Network, 25*(9), 55.

Wardale, D. (2013). Towards a Model of Effective Group Facilitation. *Leadership & Organization Development Journal, 34*(2), 112–129.

Voss, M. and A. Kock (2012). "Impact of Relationship Value on Project Portfolio Success—Investigating the Moderating Effects of Portfolio Characteristics and External Turbulence," *International Journal of Project Management,* http://dx.doi.org.ezaccess.libraries.psu.edu/10.1016/j.ijproman.2012.11.005.

Zhang, L. (2012). "Managing Project Changes: Case Studies on Stage Iteration and Functional Interaction," *International Journal of Project Management,* http://dx.doi.org.ezaccess.libraries.psu.edu/10.1016/j.ijproman.2012.11.014.

© iStockphoto.com/urbancow/René Mansi

Concepts in this chapter support the following Project Management Knowledge Areas of *A Guide to the Project Management Body of Knowledge (PMBOK® Guide)*:

Project Integration Management
Project Human Resource Management

REAL WORLD PROJECT MANAGEMENT

Knowledge Flows in a Functional Organization Structure with a PMO

Researchers examined the relationships and communications of the members of a project management office (PMO) in a large development and manufacturing company of medical and health care products in China. Recently the company had changed to

project orientation from a process orientation. The nearly 90 project managers hold professional certifications in project management and are assigned to projects based upon the type of project, its scope, and priority by their PMO managers in the different functional units within the company. The PMO is a virtual project management office and is led by a central PMO manager and five virtual PMO managers in each of the functional unit lines of production.

The five virtual PMO managers work with the expert project managers for the lines of production to perform projects that are labeled A, B, or C based upon the project's scope, complexity, and importance for the organization. The central PMO manager serves as a director of all the projects to make sure the projects selected by the five PMO functional unit managers to be completed are aligned with the organization's strategic plans and goals and does not interact with any of the day-to-day project management of the projects. The hierarchical structure of the organization provides the organization centralized decision making and a central IT platform for knowledge collection and dissemination.

A social network analysis of the organization was conducted to investigate the formal and informal knowledge sharing between the central PMO manager, the five virtual PMO managers, and the project managers. Of the 90 project managers, 89 answered the questions about who they help and who helps them, about with whom they have collaborated, and about the value of the central PMO office to their projects' success.

Sixty of the project managers reported helping other project managers, 29 reported not helping anyone, and 6 did not report receiving any help from others. Of the 196 connections between the project managers reporting who they help, only 87 of the connections were confirmed that the project manager received help. This analysis revealed that project managers overestimate the importance of their communications and recipients do not acknowledge the new knowledge as help or give credit to the source of the help.

The hierarchical structure of the organization would suggest that the five virtual PMO managers would be central to the communications for the projects within the functional units and communicate with each other about projects to coordinate collaboration. Results indicated that these PMO managers had little communication between each other, shared knowledge with their expert project managers, and did not share as much information with the other project managers. Further analysis of the PMO manager communication exchange revealed that communication usually occurred during formal meetings and rarely on ad hoc informal conversations. The functional unit organization structure limits opportunities for project managers to work with others in the different production lines and for the PMO managers to work together.

The reported helping by regular project managers was confirmed by others at a much higher rate than the stated helping by the functional unit PMO managers or the expert project managers. To examine why the peer-to-peer knowledge transfers were confirmed in the analysis at this higher rate than the interactions with the PMO managers or expert project managers, the project managers were asked to identify those with whom they have collaborated on projects before. A comparison of the collaboration and who they help/who helps them responses indicated that the

project managers tend to seek information from those with whom they have collaborated in the past. These connections in the social network analysis confirmed that prior collaboration establishes trust and identification of expertise.

The nature of a functional unit organization does not always inhibit sharing of information across units. The analysis exposed the limitations the organization was imposing on its workers. Part of the lack of collaboration was residual from the process orientation. Management consciously has made changes to the organization to help increase communication across the functional units and have more collaboration and knowledge sharing by the PMO managers.

The PMO office is valued by the project managers throughout the organization. The results of the communication analysis imply that the PMO office is not central in communication; however, when asked if they could accomplish all that they do without the PMO, an overwhelming majority replied that they could not. The project managers responded they need help from the PMO office and their fellow project managers.

Based on information from Müller, R., J. Glückler, M. Aubry, and J. Shao (2013). "Project Management Knowledge Flows in Networks of Project Managers and Project Management Offices: A Case Study in the Pharmaceutical Industry," *Project Management Journal, 44*(2), 4–19.

Although there are various configurations in which people can be organized to work on projects, the most common types of organizational structures are functional, autonomous project, and matrix. The examples here relate to industrial companies; however, the concepts are applicable to other sectors, such as service businesses, government and public agencies, and not-for-profit organizations, including healthcare organizations, educational institutions, and charitable foundations. You will become familiar with

- The characteristics of the three types of organizational structures
- The advantages and disadvantages of each
- The role of a project management office

LEARNING OUTCOMES

After studying this chapter, the learner should be able to:

- Explain the three types of project management organizational structures
- Discuss the advantages and disadvantages of each type of project management organizational structure
- Describe the role of a project management office in a matrix organizational structure

Functional Organizational Structure

A **functional organizational structure** is one in which individuals are organized in groups that perform the same function or have the same expertise or skills.

Figure 13.1, on pages 438–439, represents such a structure for an industrial business that sells standard electronics products. Functional organizational structures are typically used in businesses that primarily sell and produce standard products. For example, a company that manufactures and sells electronic medical devices may have a functional organizational structure. In the functional organizational structure, groups consist of individuals who perform the same function, such as engineering or manufacturing, or have the same expertise or skills, such as graphics design or mechanical assembly. Each functional group, or component, concentrates on performing its own activities in support of the company's business mission. The focus is on the technical excellence and cost competitiveness of the company's products, as well as the importance of the contribution of each functional component's expertise to the company's products.

A company with a functional organizational structure may periodically form project teams to work on internal company projects, such as developing new products, implementing a new information system, redesigning the office floor plan, improving manufacturing processes, implementing an energy reduction project, or updating the company policy and procedures manual. For such projects, a multifunctional project team is formed, with members selected by company management from the appropriate subfunctions in marketing, engineering, manufacturing, and procurement. Team members may be assigned to the project either full time or part time, for a part of the project, or for the entire project duration. In most cases, however, individuals continue to perform their regular functional jobs while they serve part time on the project team. One of the team members, or possibly one of the functional managers or vice presidents, is designated as the project leader or manager.

In a functional organization, the project manager does not have complete authority over the project team, because administratively the members still work for their respective functional managers. The project manager may have project authority, but the functional manager retains administrative and technical authority over the people who are assigned to the team. Because team members view their contribution to the project in terms of their technical or functional expertise, their allegiance remains to their functional managers. If there is conflict among the team members, it usually works its way through the organization hierarchy to be resolved, slowing down the project effort. On the other hand, if the company president gives the project manager the authority to make decisions when there is disagreement among team members, decisions might reflect the interests of the project manager's own functional component rather than the best interests of the overall project. For example, take a situation in which there is disagreement about the design of a new product, and the project manager, who is from the engineering function, makes a decision that reduces the engineering design cost of the product but increases the manufacturing cost. In reporting project progress to the company president, the project manager then makes some biased comments regarding the viewpoints of team members from other functional components, such as "If manufacturing were more willing to consider other production methods, they could make the product for a lower cost. Engineering has already reduced its design costs." Such a situation could require the company president to get drawn into handling the conflict.

Because projects are not a part of the normal routine in a functional organizational structure, it is necessary to establish a clear understanding of the role and responsibilities of each person assigned to the project team. If the project

Reinforce Your Learning

1. The functional organization emphasizes the importance of the contribution of each functional component's

to the company's products.

Reinforce Your Learning

2. A company with a functional structure may periodically form project teams to work on

company projects.

Reinforce Your Learning

3. True or false: In a functional organization, individuals continue to perform their regular functional jobs while they serve part time on a project team.

FIGURE 13.1 **Functional Organizational Structure**

manager does not have full authority for project decisions, then he or she must rely on leadership and persuasion skills to build consensus, handle conflict, and unify the team members to accomplish the project objective. The project manager also needs to take the time to update the other functional managers in the company regularly on the status of the project and thank them for the support of their people assigned to the project.

There may be situations in which a team is assigned to work on a project that is strictly within one particular functional component. For example, the manager of technical documentation may form a project team of editors and documentation specialists to develop common standards for all technical documents. In such a case, the particular functional manager has full authority over the project, and conflict can be handled more quickly than when it arises within a multifunctional project team.

Companies with functional organizational structures may outsource a project, such as the development of an information system, or a specific work package, such as the creation of training videos, to external subcontractors or consultants.

Autonomous Project Organizational Structure

An **autonomous project organizational structure**, also referred to as a *projectized* organizational structure, is one in which each project operates as its own somewhat independent entity with dedicated resources assigned solely to each project. Figure 13.2, on page 440, illustrates such a structure for a business that sells rapid transit projects to cities and counties. An average customer order will be for a multimillion-dollar project that will require several years for engineering, manufacturing, and installation. This company is in the projects business; it does not produce standard products. It works on multiple projects at any one time, at various stages of completion. As projects wind down and are completed, the company hopes to get contracts for new projects. People are hired to work on a specific project; they may be reassigned from a project just completed if they have the appropriate expertise. Each project team is dedicated to only one project. When their project is completed, unless team members are assigned to another project, they might be laid off.

FIGURE 13.2 **Autonomous Project Organizational Structure**

In the autonomous project organization all the resources needed to accomplish each project are assigned full time to work on that project. A full-time project manager has complete project and administrative authority over the project team. The organization is well positioned to be highly responsive to the project objective and customer needs because each project team is strictly dedicated to only one project.

An autonomous project organization can be cost inefficient both for individual projects and for its parent company. Each project must pay the salaries of its dedicated project team, even during periods of the project when they are not fully utilized. For example, if a delay in one part of the project leaves some resources with no work to do for several weeks, project funds must cover these costs. If the amount of unapplied time becomes excessive, the project can

become unprofitable and drain the profits from other projects. From a company-wide viewpoint, a projectized organization can be cost inefficient because of the duplication of resources or tasks on several concurrent projects. Because resources are not shared among projects, they are usually not diverted to a similar concurrent project even when they are not fully utilized on the project to which they are dedicated. Also, there is little opportunity for members of different project teams to share knowledge or technical expertise, as each project team tends to be isolated and focused strictly on its own project. However, there may be some company-wide support functions that serve all the projects. Figure 13.2 shows, for example, that the human resources function serves all projects, because it would not make sense for each project to hire its own human resources staff. And, by having a common human resources functional component, the company is likely to have consistent human resources policies and procedures.

In an autonomous project organization, detailed and accurate planning and an effective control system are required to assure optimum utilization of the project resources in successfully completing the project within budget.

Autonomous project organizational structures are found primarily in companies that are involved in very large projects. Such projects can be of high-dollar value and long duration. Projectized organizational structures are prevalent in the construction and aerospace industries.

Matrix Organizational Structure

A **matrix organizational structure** is a hybrid of the functional and autonomous project organizational structures, in which resources from appropriate functional components are temporarily assigned to particular projects that have project managers from the project component of the organization. Figure 13.3, on pages 442–443, shows such a structure for a business that sells custom automation systems. Each customer order is for a unique system. Some systems sell for as little as $50,000 and take four to six months to design and produce, whereas others cost several million dollars and can take up to three years to complete. Like Ajax Rapid Transit Project, Inc., in Figure 13.2, Specialized Automation Systems, Inc., is in the projects business; however, its business involves a greater number of smaller-size projects. It is working on multiple projects at any one time, and these projects vary in size and complexity. Projects are continually being completed and started.

The matrix organization provides the project and customer focus of the autonomous project structure, but it retains the functional expertise of the functional structure. The project and functional components of the matrix structure each have specific responsibilities in contributing jointly to the success of each project and the company. The project manager is responsible for the project results, whereas the functional managers are responsible for providing the resources needed to achieve the results.

The matrix organization provides for effective utilization of company resources. The functional components, such as systems engineering, testing, and so forth, are home of the technical staff and provide a pool of expertise to support ongoing projects.

Project managers are part of the projects component of the organization. When the company receives an order for a new system, the vice president of projects assigns a project manager to the project. A small project may be

FIGURE 13.3 Matrix Organizational Structure

Reinforce Your Learning

8. In a matrix organization, the _____ components provide a pool of _____ to support ongoing projects.

assigned to a project manager who is already managing several other small projects. A large project may be assigned a full-time project manager.

The project manager then meets with the appropriate functional managers to negotiate the assignment of various individuals from the functional components to work on the project. These individuals are assigned to the project for the period of time they are needed. Some individuals may be assigned to the project full time, whereas others may be assigned only part time. Some people may be assigned to a project for its entire duration; others may work on only one part of the project or even off and on throughout the project, depending on when their expertise is needed and how many of their hours the project budget can support. In a matrix organization, it is not unusual for an individual from a functional

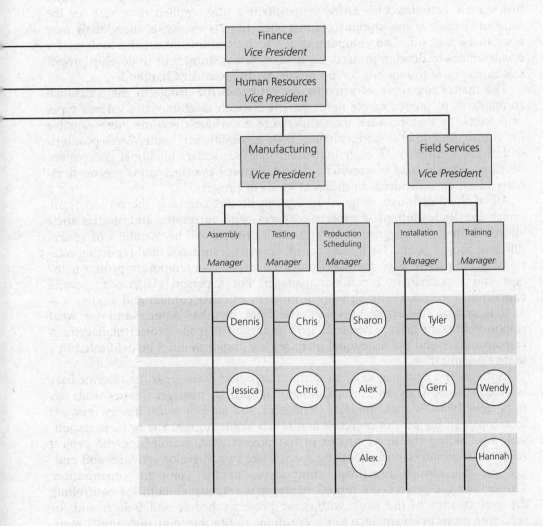

component to be assigned part time to several concurrent projects. Figure 13.3 shows, for example, that Jack, Cathy, Rose, Chris, and Alex are all working part time on two projects. Some projects do not require certain types of expertise. For example, projects A and C do not require any mechanical engineering expertise, and project A does not include any training.

Sharing of individuals' time among several projects results in effective utilization of resources and minimizes overall costs for each project and for the entire company.

As projects or particular assignments are completed, available individuals are assigned to new projects. The objective is to maximize the number of functional person-hours applied to work on projects within the constraints of individual project budgets, and to minimize the unapplied time because the salary costs for unapplied time have to be absorbed by the company, reducing overall company profitability. Of course, unapplied time must be provided for vacations, holidays, illness, training activities, and work on proposals for new projects.

Reinforce Your Learning

9. The matrix organizational structure results in effective utilization of

and minimizes overall

because it allows for the

of individuals' time among several

_____.

It is important to note that if the total amount of unapplied time of the functional staff is high, the company may be unprofitable even though each project is completed within its budgeted hours. This will happen if the company is not working on enough projects to utilize the people in some of the functional components. The company always needs to have new projects coming in as other projects are completed, in order to maintain a high applied time rate for the functional staff. If the amount of unapplied time is excessive, individuals may have to be laid off. The company needs to be continually on the lookout for opportunities to develop projects for new or past customers or to develop proposals in response to requests for proposals, as discussed in Chapter 3.

The matrix organization provides opportunities for people in the functional components to pursue career development through assignment to various types of projects. As they broaden their experience, individuals become more valuable for future assignments and enhance their eligibility for higher-level positions within the company. As each individual in a particular functional component develops a broad base of experience, the functional manager gains greater flexibility to assign individuals to different kinds of projects.

Reinforce Your Learning

10. In a matrix organization, each member of a

has a dual reporting relationship—to the temporary

manager and to a permanent

manager.

All of the individuals assigned to a given project comprise the project team, under the leadership of a project manager who integrates and unifies their efforts. Individuals assigned to several small projects will be members of several different project teams. Each member of a project team has a dual reporting relationship; in a sense, each member has two managers—a temporary project manager and a permanent functional manager. For a person assigned to several concurrent projects, changing work priorities can cause conflict and anxiety.

It is critical to specify to whom the team member reports and for what responsibilities or tasks. Therefore, it is important that the project management responsibilities and the functional management responsibilities be delineated in a matrix organization.

In the matrix organizational structure, the *project manager* is the intermediary between the company and the customer. The project manager defines *what has to be done* (work scope), *by when* (schedule), and *for how much money* (budget) to accomplish the project objective and satisfy the customer. She or he is responsible for leading the development of the project plan, establishing the project schedule and budget, and allocating specific work packages or activities and budgets to the various functional components of the company organization. Throughout the project, the project manager is responsible both for controlling the performance of the work within the project schedule and budget and for reporting project performance to the customer and to the company's upper management. A project administrator may be assigned to each project to support the project manager and project team in planning, controlling, and reporting.

Reinforce Your Learning

11. In a matrix organization, the project manager defines

has to be done, by

_____,

and for how much

to accomplish the project

and satisfy the customer.

Each *functional manager* in a matrix organizational structure is responsible for *how the assigned work activities will be accomplished* and *who* (which specific people) *will do each activity*. The functional manager of each organization component provides technical guidance and leadership to the individuals assigned to projects. He or she is also responsible for ensuring that all work packages or activities assigned to his or her functional component are completed in accordance with the project's technical and quality requirements, within the assigned budget, and on schedule.

In a multiple project environment, each functional manager can have many individuals assigned to parts of many concurrent projects, particularly if projects

Reinforce Your Learning

12. In a matrix organization, each functional manager is responsible for

the work will be accomplished and

will do each task.

are too small to require full-time people or if projects need certain expertise for only brief periods. The functional manager must continually monitor the assignments of the individuals within her or his functional component and make any needed reallocations in response to changing conditions on various projects, such as schedule delays or customer changes. For example, if a project is delayed because the customer is taking longer than anticipated to review and approve engineering drawings or because the shipment of a piece of equipment from a vendor is taking longer than estimated, individuals assigned to the project should be temporarily reassigned to other projects, if possible. In a situation in which a project is behind schedule and in jeopardy of not being completed by the customer's required due date, the functional manager might temporarily assign people from portions of other projects that have positive slack or are ahead of schedule.

The matrix organization provides a checks-and-balances environment. The fact that potential problems can be identified through both its project and its functional structure reduces the likelihood that problems will be suppressed beyond the point where they can be corrected without jeopardizing the success of the project. The matrix organizational structure allows for fast response to identified problems because it has both a horizontal (project) and a vertical (functional) path for the flow of information.

Reinforce Your Learning

13. The matrix organizational structure allows for fast response to identified problems because it has both a

and a

path for the flow of

_____.

Figure 13.3 shows an organizational component for the vice president of projects to whom the project managers report. Such a unit plays an important role in the matrix organizational structure. This organizational component is often referred to as the **project management office** (**PMO**). This office oversees and coordinates multiple projects. It can help to resolve priority conflicts between projects and can facilitate decisions regarding priority among projects in terms of least overall risk to the company and customer relationships, especially if the company has other current or proposed projects for a given customer. The PMO may also provide support, such as project management training for project teams, and provide administrative support staff for projects. The PMO can establish consistent procedures and develop best practices and templates for planning, monitoring, and controlling projects; data gathering; documentation; and project reporting, for example. It could be the repository for archived project documents and manage a knowledge base of lessons learned. Often the PMO provides central support for the company's project management information system.

Reinforce Your Learning

14. The

plays an important role in the

organizational structure. It

and

multiple

_____.

Advantages and Disadvantages of Organizational Structures

The previous sections discussed the characteristics of the functional, autonomous project, and matrix organizational structures. Table 13.1 lists some of the more significant advantages and disadvantages that are particular to each of the three organizational structures.

FUNCTIONAL ORGANIZATIONAL STRUCTURE

By bringing specialists from the same discipline together in one organizational unit, a functional organization reduces duplication and overlap of activities. It provides the benefits associated with specialization: an environment in which individuals can share and keep up with the knowledge and skills of their particular discipline. For example, all individuals in a computer engineering unit can share software and discuss approaches to developing computer systems.

TABLE 13.1 Advantages and Disadvantages of Organizational Structures

	ADVANTAGES	DISADVANTAGES
Functional Structure	• No duplication of activities • Functional excellence	• Insularity • Slow response time • Lack of customer focus
Autonomous Project Structure	• Control over resources • Responsiveness to customers	• Cost inefficiency • Low level of knowledge transfer among projects
Matrix Structure	• Efficient utilization of resources • Functional expertise available to all projects • Increased learning and knowledge transfer • Improved communication • Customer focus	• Dual reporting relationships • Need for balance of power

Functional organizations can be insular, though, with each functional component concerned about only its own performance. Teamwork with other functions is not emphasized, and there is little cross fertilization of ideas among functions. Project focus is not emphasized, and decisions may be parochial rather than in the best interests of the overall project. The hierarchical structure slows communication, problem resolution, and decision making.

Take the case in which there is a problem with product failures. Engineering thinks it is because manufacturing is not producing the product properly. Manufacturing claims it is because engineering did not design it properly or because there were errors in the engineering drawings provided to manufacturing. Such a problem could work its way up and down through the chain of command, and its resolution may rest with the company president. The functional organization lacks customer focus. There is a stronger allegiance to the function than to the project or the customer.

Reinforce Your Learning

15. What are some advantages and disadvantages of the functional organizational structure?

AUTONOMOUS PROJECT ORGANIZATIONAL STRUCTURE

In an autonomous project organization, all the individuals on the project team work for the project manager. Therefore, he or she has full control over the resources, including authority over how the work gets done and by whom. There is no conflict with other projects over priorities or resources, because all the resources for a project are totally dedicated to that project. The project organization is highly responsive to the customer. For example, if the customer makes changes to the project work scope, the project manager has the authority to reassign resources to accommodate the changes immediately.

The project organizational structure can be cost inefficient because of underutilization of resources. With individuals assigned full time to the project, there may be times when work activity slows down and team members are not working at a high level of productivity. When things are slow, individuals have a tendency to stretch out their work to fill up the time available. If there is nothing else to work on, a one-week activity can stretch out to two or three weeks, causing project costs to increase. Also, if some people do not have any tasks to do for temporary periods, their unapplied time is still a cost to the company

and erodes the company's profitability. Another factor affecting cost inefficiency in projectized organizations is the potential lack of opportunity for cost efficiencies from leveraging activities with other concurrent projects. For example, if project teams from several projects ordered their materials and supplies jointly instead of independently, they might be able to get better prices from vendors.

In the autonomous project organizational structure, there is a low level of knowledge transfer among projects. Individuals are dedicated to working on one project. They do not have a functional "home" to serve as a source of shared functional expertise and knowledge. Also, at the end of a project, people may be laid off if there is not a new project to which they can be assigned. In such cases, what they learned on the project is lost to the company. In a projectized organization, team members experience high anxiety about reassignment as their project nears completion, especially because they do not have a functional home to which they can return.

MATRIX ORGANIZATIONAL STRUCTURE

The matrix organizational structure tries to capitalize on the advantages of both the functional and the autonomous project structures while overcoming their disadvantages. The matrix structure allows efficient utilization of resources by having individuals from various functions assigned to work part time, if necessary, on specific projects or by having them assigned for only a limited duration to certain projects. Furthermore, it is not unusual for individuals in a specific function to be working on two or more projects concurrently. Because they have a functional home, individuals can be moved among projects as necessary to accommodate any project changes. For example, if one project is delayed, the functional manager can deploy some of its team members to other projects rather than have their unapplied time increase costs to the company.

The matrix structure provides a core of functional expertise that is available to all projects, and thus this expertise is better utilized. Individuals in a functional component have a common discipline and can collaborate with and learn from one another. This functional component provides a home for individuals at the end of a project while they are waiting to be assigned to other projects. Their knowledge stays with the company, ready to be used on future projects. As people work on more and various projects, they experience greater learning and growth, and their knowledge and skills are transferred from project to project.

The matrix structure also facilitates improved communication, allowing for more timely problem identification and conflict resolution.

Project team members have two channels through which to send warnings about a potential problem—the project manager and the functional manager. These dual communication paths increase the chances that problems will be identified rather than suppressed.

Finally, the matrix organization is customer focused. The project manager is the designated focal point for communication with the customer, and the functional units are set up to support projects.

Members of a project team in a matrix organizational structure have a dual reporting relationship: temporarily they report to a project manager while administratively they still report to their functional manager. If an individual is assigned to work on several projects, he or she can have multiple managers.

This can cause anxiety and conflict over work priorities. These individuals have a permanent allegiance to their functional home, which is strained by their required allegiance to the project team. A company that uses a matrix organizational structure must establish operating guidelines to assure a proper balance of power between project managers and functional managers. Conflicts will arise between project managers and functional managers regarding priorities, the assignment of specific individuals to projects, technical approaches to the work, and changes to projects. If there is an imbalance of power, such conflicts may not be resolved in a manner that will be in the best interests of either the customer or the company.

REAL WORLD PROJECT MANAGEMENT

Verizon Wireless Wins Project Management Office of the Year Award

The Verizon Wireless Marketing Program and Portfolio Office set a goal to have 90 percent of its top projects finish on time, to deliver its other projects at least 70 percent on time, reduce its cycle time by 50 percent, and have 100 percent alignment of the organizational resources to the top prioritized projects. The challenge required the Marketing Project Management Office (PMO) to examine its goals and processes.

Not only did Verizon Wireless' Marketing PMO meet their goals, they surpassed them. The independent panel of judges for the PM Solutions Project Management Office of the Year Award included in their comments, "They were challenged to deliver top projects on time 90 percent of the time. They now deliver 100 percent." The award is given to a PMO for the team's development and maturation to have an organizational structure that supports effective management and delivery of projects. The PMO has implemented new ideas, instituted processes that led to measureable improvements in project management, and realized business benefits.

In addition to exceeding their top project completion goal of 90 percent to have 100 percent of the top projects delivered on time, the PMO delivered the remaining projects 80 percent on time, reduced cycle time by 58 percent, and experienced 100 percent alignment of resources to the top projects. The panel of judges concluded from the review of the application, "Verizon Wireless' Marketing PMO is mature, thorough, innovative, and tightly woven into the fabric of the business."

Theo Bell, vice president, Verizon Wireless Marketing PMO, acknowledged, "We have worked very hard but it comes with rich rewards for our company and for our PMO team. PM Solutions' well-respected award not only recognizes our accomplishment but also celebrates the significant impact that a PMO—a highly supported PMO—can make on any organization's long-term business goals."

J. Kent Crawford, PMP, chief executive officer of PM Solutions, announced, "Verizon Wireless has wisely invested in the PMO to help drive the entire organization forward and operate more strategically. They have set the bar with best-in-class portfolio management and elite project manager talent that have reduced project

costs and guaranteed quality to customers. Their impressive business results deserve to be lauded."

PMOs oversee and coordinate multiple projects, provide support, establish consistent procedures, resolve priority conflicts, and centralize governance and document repositories including lessons learned. Verizon Wireless' Marketing PMO's mission is to be "the financial advisor and delivery arm for the strategies of the organization." The Marketing PMO was recognized as the Project Management Office of the Year in 2012 due to its corporate strategy for enterprise-wide project improvement and 100 percent project alignment in its efforts to achieve its mission.

Based on information from Anonymous (2012). "Verizon Wireless Wins Project Management Office of the Year Award," *Business Wire and PMO of the Year 2012*, http://www.pmsolutions.com/articles/PMO-of-the -Year-2012.pdf.

CRITICAL SUCCESS FACTORS

- In a matrix organization, it is important to delineate the project management responsibilities and the functional management responsibilities.
- When implementing a matrix organizational structure, operating guidelines should be established to assure proper balance of power between project managers and functional managers.
- Project teams should be kept as small as feasible throughout the project.

SUMMARY

The three most common structures used to organize people to work on projects are functional, autonomous project, and matrix organizational structures. These structures are applicable to a large majority of businesses, as well as public and not-for-profit organizations.

The functional organizational structure is one in which individuals are organized in groups that perform the same function or have the same expertise or skills. It is typically used in businesses that primarily sell and produce standard products. The focus is on the technical excellence and cost competitiveness of the company's products, as well as the importance of each functional component's contribution of expertise to the company's products. For projects, a multifunctional project team is formed, with members selected from the appropriate subfunctions. In this structure, the project manager does not have complete authority over the project team, because administratively the members still work for their respective functional managers. If there is conflict among the team members, it usually works its way through the organization hierarchy to be resolved. A company with a functional organizational structure may periodically form project teams to work on internal projects, or it may outsource a project or specific work packages to external resources, such as subcontractors or consultants.

The autonomous project organizational structure is one in which each project operates as its own somewhat independent entity with dedicated resources assigned solely to each project. It is used by companies that are working on multiple projects at any one time and do not produce standard products. People are hired to work on a specific project, and each project team is dedicated to only one project. When the project is completed, team members may be assigned to another project if they have the appropriate expertise. A full-time project manager has complete project and administrative authority over the project team. A projectized organization is well positioned to be highly responsive to the project objective and customer needs because each project team is strictly dedicated to only one project. From a company-wide viewpoint, an autonomous project organization can be cost inefficient because of the duplication of resources or tasks on several concurrent projects. Also, there is little opportunity for members of different project teams to share knowledge or technical expertise. Autonomous project organizational structures are found primarily in companies that are involved in very large projects with high dollar values and long durations.

The matrix organization is a hybrid of the functional and autonomous project organizational structures, in which resources from appropriate functional components are temporarily assigned to particular projects that have project managers from the project component of the organization. It is appropriate for companies that are working on multiple projects at any one time and projects that vary in size and complexity. It provides the project and customer focus of the project structure while retaining the functional expertise of the functional structure. The project and functional components of the matrix structure each have their responsibilities in contributing jointly to the success of each project and the company. In addition, the matrix organization provides for effective utilization of company resources. The sharing of individuals' time among several projects results in effective utilization of resources and minimizes overall costs for each project and for the entire company. All of the individuals assigned to a given project comprise the project team, under the leadership of a project manager who integrates and unifies their efforts.

In the matrix structure, the project manager is the intermediary between the company and the customer. The project manager defines what has to be done, by when, and for how much money to accomplish the project objective and satisfy the customer. The project manager is responsible for leading the development of the project plan, establishing the project schedule and budget, and allocating specific work packages or activities and budgets to various functional components of the company organization. Each functional manager is responsible for how the assigned work activities will be accomplished and who will do each activity.

The project management office plays an important role in the matrix organizational structure. It oversees and coordinates multiple projects. It can help to resolve priority conflicts between projects and can facilitate decisions regarding the priority among projects. The project management office may also provide project management training, provide administrative support staff for projects, establish consistent procedures, and develop best practices and templates for planning, monitoring, and controlling projects.

The advantages of a functional organizational structure are no duplication of activities and functional excellence. Disadvantages include insularity, slow response time, and lack of customer focus. The autonomous project organizational structure has control over resources and responsiveness to customers as

advantages. Cost inefficiency and low level of knowledge transfer among projects are its disadvantages. The advantages of a matrix organizational structure include efficient utilization of resources, functional expertise available to all projects, increased learning and knowledge transfer, improved communication, and customer focus. Its disadvantages are the dual reporting relationships and the need for a balance of power.

QUESTIONS

1. Describe what a functional organization is. Make sure you discuss the advantages and disadvantages of this structure.
2. Describe what an autonomous project organization is. Make sure you discuss the advantages and disadvantages of this structure.
3. Describe what a matrix organization is. Make sure you discuss the advantages and disadvantages of this structure.
4. Which type of organizational structure is often used by companies that produce standard products? Why?
5. Discuss some of the problems that might be encountered when a functional organization develops new products.
6. Why is an autonomous project organization considered to operate like its own somewhat independent entity?
7. Why is an autonomous project organization sometimes considered to be cost inefficient?
8. Which organizational structure is considered to be a hybrid? Explain.
9. How does a matrix organization provide for career development?
10. What are the responsibilities of the project manager in a matrix organization?
11. What are the responsibilities of the functional manager in a matrix organization?
12. What are the responsibilities of the vice president of projects in a matrix organization?
13. What is the role of a project management office? What organizational structure best supports having a project management office, and why?

INTERNET EXERCISES

For the website addresses of the organizations mentioned in these exercises, go to "Internet Exercises" at the book's companion website at www.cengagebrain.com. It is suggested that you save this website in your "Favorites" list for easy access in the future.

1. Search the Web for "functional organizational structures." Summarize at least one website and compare it to what was presented in this chapter. What new insights did you gain from this website?
2. Search the Web for "autonomous project organizational structures." Summarize at least one website and compare it to what was presented in this chapter. What new insights did you gain from this website?

3. Search the Web for "matrix organizational structures." Summarize at least one website and compare it to what was presented in this chapter. What new insights did you gain from this website?

4. Search the Web for "project management office." Summarize at least one website and compare it to what was presented in this chapter. What new insights did you gain from this website?

5. Search the Web for "project management successes and failures." Write a one-page review of a story or case study that you found and include your thoughts as to how the project organization might have affected the outcome.

CASE STUDY 1 Multi Projects

Multi Projects, Inc., is a well-established consulting firm with 400 employees. It has many projects going on at the same time for various clients. Multi Projects has a good reputation, and nearly 30 percent of its business is from previous clients. It targets growing companies for future business and has been successful in this area, too. Because of the growth, things have been quite hectic, with employees trying to keep up with the work, keep old clients satisfied, and bend over backward to accommodate new clients. Multi Projects has been hiring new employees—in fact, it has grown from 300 to 400 employees over the past two years.

Multi Projects has a matrix organizational structure. As new projects come in, a project manager is assigned. One project manager may be assigned to several projects at one time, depending on the sizes of the projects. Projects range in value from $20,000 to $1 million and can be from one month to two years in duration. Most projects are about six months in duration and worth about $60,000 to $80,000. The firm performs a range of consulting services, including market research, manufacturing system design, and executive recruiting. Its clients are medium to large corporations and include banks, manufacturers, and government agencies.

Multi Projects just got a call from Growin Corporation, which wants to go forward with a project that Multi Projects proposed nearly six months ago. Partners at Multi Projects are surprised by the good news. They had thought the project was dead. They are also very interested in carrying out a first project for Growin Corporation because it is a rapidly growing company. Multi Projects sees an opportunity to do several projects with Growin Corporation in the future.

Jeff Armstrong has been assigned as project manager for the Growin Corporation project. He has been with Multi Projects for about a year and has been anxious to get a challenging project to manage. He worked on the proposal for the Growin project.

Tyler Bonilla is a senior systems engineer. He has been with Multi Projects eight years. He has an excellent reputation, and previous clients with whom he has worked usually request that he be assigned to their projects. He enjoys his work, even though he is extremely busy. He is currently working full time on a project for Goodold Company, a previous client. Goodold said that one of the reasons it does business with Multi Projects, rather than with another consulting firm, is the great work Tyler does on their projects.

Jennifer Fernandez is the manager of systems engineering. She has been with Multi Projects about 15 years. Tyler reports to Jennifer, but because of his heavy workload and associated travel, he does not get to see Jennifer very often, other than at her monthly staff meetings.

Julie Capriolo is the project manager for the Goodold Company project. She has been with Multi Projects for about two years. Tyler is assigned to her project full time. The project has a tight schedule, and everyone is putting in extra hours. Julie feels a lot of pressure, but she has a good project team—she relies heavily on Tyler. She had heard from a friend who used to work with Jeff that Jeff is very ambitious and will do whatever it takes to make himself look good. This had not been of concern to Julie because she and Jeff have separate projects and do not run into each other very often.

The day Jeff is assigned to be project manager on the Growin Corporation project, he runs into Tyler in the hallway. "We got the Growin project," he tells Tyler.

"Great," responds Tyler.

Jeff continues, "You know, one of the big reasons they gave the project to us rather than another consulting firm is because we promised you'd be the lead systems engineer on the project, Tyler. They were impressed with you when we met with them to present our proposal. When do you think you can start work on the project?"

"Unfortunately, I can't. I'm tied up on the Goodold project, and things are really hectic. I'll be on that project for another four months," says Tyler.

"No way!" exclaims Jeff. "This Growin project is too important to me—I mean, to us. I'll take care of it."

"You'd better talk to Jennifer," Tyler tells him.

Jeff stops by Jennifer's office. She's busy, but he interrupts her. "I gotta have Tyler Bonilla on my Growin project. He wants to work on it, but he said I should talk to you."

"That's impossible," says Jennifer. "He's assigned to Julie Capriolo's Goodold project for the next four months."

"Julie? Who's she? Never mind. I'll find her and work it out. You probably have somebody else you can assign to her project," replies Jeff, as he quickly bolts out of her office in search of Julie.

"That's my decision, not yours or Julie's!" shouts Jennifer. But by that time Jeff is gone and does not hear what she says.

Julie is meeting with her project team in the conference room. Jeff knocks on the door and opens it. "Is there a Julie in here?" he asks.

"I'm Julie," she responds.

"I need to talk to you ASAP. It's important. Oh, by the way, sorry for interrupting." Looking toward Tyler, who's in the meeting, Jeff says, "Hey, Tyler, catch you later, buddy, after I talk with Julie." Jeff then shuts the door and goes back to his office. Julie is noticeably disturbed at the interruption.

After her meeting, Julie calls Jeff. "This is Julie. What did you want to talk to me about that was so urgent?"

"About reassigning Tyler to my project. He's interested, and I've already talked to Jennifer about it," answers Jeff.

"That's impossible," declares Julie. "He's critical to the Goodold project."

"Sorry," says Jeff, "but if the Growin project is successful, we'll get more business from them than we ever got from the Goodold Company."

"It's already after 6 o'clock and I have to be out of town for a week, but I'll discuss this with Jennifer as soon as I get back," snaps Julie.

"Yeah, sure, whatever," responds Jeff.

The next day Jeff calls a meeting with Jennifer and Tyler. He starts by telling them, "I called this meeting to figure how soon Tyler can begin working on the Growin project and how you [looking at Jennifer] can get somebody to take his place on what's-her-name's project."

"I think Julie should be here for this discussion," says Jennifer.

"She couldn't make it. Apparently she's out of town for a week, and we need to get going on the Growin project." Jeff tells her. "We need to prepare for a meeting with them next week. Besides, Tyler is the one we're talking about, and he'd rather work on the Growin project. Right, Tyler?"

"Ah, well, now that you've asked, I am getting tired of working on the Good-old projects," replies Tyler. "I'm not learning anything new. I mean, it's okay, but I'd like a change."

Jennifer is astonished. "You never mentioned that to me, Tyler."

Jeff breaks in, "Well, I guess it's settled. Jennifer, you assign somebody else to the Goodold project who'll feel a little more challenged and tell Julie when she gets back. In the meantime, me and my buddy Tyler have got a lot of work to do to look good for our meeting with the Growin people next week."

CASE QUESTIONS

1. Why is Jeff so anxious to get started on the Growin project?
2. What is wrong with Jeff's approach to handling this situation?
3. What should Jennifer do to resolve this situation?
4. What advantages and disadvantages of the matrix organization are apparent from this story?

GROUP ACTIVITY

Have an open discussion among course participants regarding the following questions:

- What should Jennifer do next?
- What should Tyler do?
- What could have been done to prevent this situation?
- How could each of the four individuals have handled the situation better?

CASE STUDY 2 Organize for Product Development

Stevens Corporation is a multidivision manufacturing company with diversified products serving the aerospace, automotive, and medical markets. Its medical instruments division is located in the Midwest and has a plant with over 1,000 employees. It sells various medical instruments, such as analyzers, monitoring equipment, and testing instruments to hospitals and medical laboratories. It is a market leader, and its business has been steady. It has a very good reputation and commands a premium price for its products. However, the business is not growing as fast as the rest of Stevens' divisions or as fast as the board of directors thinks it should. They feel that the division's management has become complacent. There are several new competitors entering the market with products that

have more features and lower prices. Last year, the chief executive officer told Kareem, general manager of the medical instruments division, that he had to start developing new and enhanced products in order not to lose market share to the emerging competitors.

Kareem has worked his entire 20-year career in the division and is an electronics engineer who worked on many of the current products. He thinks they are still quality products and that the marketing department needs to do a better job of convincing the customers that Stevens' products are still the best value compared to unproven competitors' products. He also thinks that the manufacturing department can reduce costs through tougher negotiations with suppliers and by making process improvements.

He believes that Stevens' reputation will eventually knock the new competitors' products out of the market. Therefore, he is hesitant to allocate any more resources to any product development efforts than are necessary to pacify the CEO and board of directors. He wants to maintain the division's profit margin, which is used to determine his year-end bonus.

Kareem's approach was to establish four product development teams. Each team was assigned a different product that was being threatened by competitor products, with the goal of developing enhancements that would match or beat the competing products. He simply assigned each of his four department managers to head the four product development teams. He thought this would create some friendly rivalry. The four department managers are:

- Tanya—Manager, Marketing
- Khalid—Manager, Electronic Engineering
- Lee—Manager, Computer Systems Engineering
- Tony—Manager, Manufacturing

Kareem has been getting more frequent questions from the CEO about the status of the product developments. Kareem knows that progress has been slow, and that he really has not put a priority on it because he believes Stevens will simply outlast its competitors, who, he thinks, are losing money on their lower-priced products.

Kareem had his annual performance review sessions with his department managers last week and asked them about the product development projects. Here is what each of them told him:

Tanya, manager of marketing, said that none of the managers, including Kareem, are giving priority to the product development projects because they are too busy with their regular work. She said the product development efforts should be market-driven, not engineering-driven. The other product development teams led by Khalid and Lee are not interested in any input from the Marketing Department; they just want to develop highly sophisticated, overengineered products that will be too complicated for customers to use. She also said that Tony is only interested in how to make any new products cheaper, not necessarily better, because he thinks that a lower manufacturing cost per unit is the ultimate goal. Tanya suggested to Kareem that he approve a new position of product development manager, who should report directly to her and would have full responsibility for all product development projects.

She told Kareem that several key people from each of the other departments should be permanently reassigned to the product development manager to work solely on product development projects. Tanya also expressed her belief that the

other three department managers seem to side with each other against her because she is a woman and has only been with the division a short time. She accused them of being a bunch of "good old boys" who have never gone outside the plant to talk with customers in the 20 plus years they have all been there. If Kareem does not approve hiring a product development manager who would report to her, Tanya said, she would seriously have to reconsider her interest in staying at Stevens Corporation. She has an excellent reputation in the industry; many other companies would welcome her. Kareem knows that it took him a while to fill the marketing manager position, and he had had to pay a higher salary than he had wanted to get Tanya to come to Stevens.

Khalid, manager of electronic engineering, told Kareem that the product development projects are not progressing because the computer systems engineering department is always fighting among themselves about whether product features should be done with hardware or software. He said that Lee has already announced that he intends to retire at the end of the year. Khalid told Kareem that when Lee retires, he should not be replaced; rather, the computer systems engineering department should be merged into Khalid's department. He said he would then have better control over the product development projects, which should be led by engineering anyway because all product enhancements require engineering and design expertise. He saw no need for marketing or manufacturing to be involved. He said marketing's job should be to sell the products engineering develops, and it's manufacturing's job to make the products the way engineering designs them. He also said that by not replacing Lee, Kareem can make up some of the money paid for the "overpriced" marketing manager.

Lee, manager of computer systems engineering, told Kareem that he had evaluated the competitors' products and the big difference is that their products are software based whereas Stevens' products are electronics based, as they have been for years. Lee reminded Kareem that it was years ago that both of them engineered those electronic products. But today it is a different environment, with new technologies and approaches, and Stevens has to redesign its products to be software based. He suggested that when he retires at the end of the year, Kareem should appoint Nicole as the new manager of the computer systems engineering department. Lee believes that Nicole is young, bright, knows software design better than anyone in his department, and could do a great job in leading the product development projects. She has a master's degree in computer engineering and an MBA. She is interested in having Stevens' products meet customers' needs. Nicole frequently has discussions with Tanya about marketing and customers and competitors. Lee told Kareem that if Nicole is not promoted, she will probably leave Stevens and go to another company, maybe even one of the competitors, where her talents might be better utilized.

Tony, manager of manufacturing, told Kareem that he (Kareem) needs to get more involved in the product development projects and "start knocking some heads together." He said marketing and Khalid and Lee are trying to make too many changes to the products, and that will just increase the price or reduce profit margins. Tony believes that the other managers have no concern for costs or any manufacturing process changes that would have to be made. Tony suggested that Kareem start having regular product development status meetings to find out what is "really" going on and see all the "politics." He said all the other department managers care only about their own department looking good, and they are not willing to share information or cooperate with the other

teams. As a result, all the product development teams were suffering, and it was getting worse each day. He told Kareem that what started out as a friendly rivalry among the teams has turned into outright nasty competition. He again warned Kareem to do something before it begins to drag down the corporation's overall profitability and the CEO has all their jobs or even recommends selling the division to a competitor.

Finally, the CEO calls Kareem to a meeting and tells him that the latest marketing report shows the medical instruments division has lost market share for the second consecutive quarter and wants to know why Kareem does not have any new product enhancements out in the market yet. Kareem admitted that he has not been on top of the product development efforts and has not given them the priority that he should. He thought the competitors would fold. Kareem discussed his approach to establishing the product development teams and the feedback he just got from his department managers. The CEO was not happy and told Kareem that he was relying too much on doing things in the same old ways and that he had better look for new ideas and approaches or his position would be in jeopardy.

The CEO told Kareem that the situation is critical, and the board of directors is losing their patience. When the board hired her as CEO last year, they expected her to move Stevens from a good national company to a great global one, and that all the other divisions are moving in that direction while the medical instruments division is staying flat in spite of an increasing global market for their products.

The CEO told Kareem that she is going to bring in a management consultant to evaluate what is going on in his division and make recommendations to her about how to get the product development effort organized and on an accelerated track.

CASE QUESTIONS
You are the management consultant hired by the CEO.
1. How would you initiate your assignment with Kareem and the department managers?
2. Develop a list of questions you would ask.
3. Assuming the department managers tell you the same things they told Kareem, what recommendations would you make to the CEO, including any changes to the organizational structure, to improve the management of product development projects?
4. What guidelines would you recommend for how the departments or new functions should work together on product development projects?

GROUP ACTIVITY
Divide the course participants into groups of three or four members to develop responses to the case questions. Each group should choose a spokesperson to present its responses to the entire class.

REFERENCES

A Guide to the Project Management Body of Knowledge (PMBOK® Guide) Fifth Edition. Newtown Square, PA: Project Management Institute, 2013.

Anonymous (2013). "BuilderMT Shares Market Share Leadership Position with Microsoft for Residential Construction Project Management Software," *Business Wire*.

Anonymous (2013). "Hill International Awarded Construction Management Contract by NJ TRANSIT," *NASDAQ OMX's News Release Distribution Channel.*

Anonymous (2013). "PBworks Releases Project Management Software," *Wireless News.*

Anonymous (2013). "PM *Alliance* Selected for Project Management Support of Caterpillar Diesel Generator Set Project," *PR Newswire.*

Anonymous (2012). "Project Management Offices Grow in Popularity," *Computer Economics Report*, *34*(5), 8–13.

Anonymous (2012). "Project Management Offices of the Year 2012," *Project Management Solutions*, http://www.pmsolutions.com/articles/PMO-of-the-Year-2012.pdf.

Anonymous (2012). "Verizon Wireless Wins Project Management Office of the Year Award," *Business Wire.*

Chellinsky, A. W. (2013). "A Strongly Matrixed Life," *Contract Management*, *53*(3), 46–53.

Isfahani, K. (2012). "Leveraging the Project Management Office as a Partner in Innovation," *PM World Today*, *14*(3), 1–4.

Jerbrant, A. (2013). "Organising Project-Based Companies: Management, Control and Execution of Project-Based Industrial Operations," *International Journal of Managing Projects in Business*, *6*(2), 365–378.

Laslo, Z. (2012). "The Adjustment of Locus of Influence and Organizational Forms Towards Better Project Portfolio's Performance," *Management (1820-0222)*, (65), 51–62.

Martinelli, R., T. Rahschulte, and J. Waddell (2012). "Systems Thinking and Program Management," *PM World Today*, *14*(3), 1–4.

Martinsuo, M. (2012). "Project Portfolio Management in Practice and in Context," *International Journal of Project Management*, http://dx.doi.org.ezaccess.libraries.psu.edu/10.1016/j.ijproman.2012.10.013.

Müller, R., J. Glückler, M. Aubry, and J. Shao (2013). "Project Management Knowledge Flows in Networks of Project Managers and Project Management Offices: A Case Study in the Pharmaceutical Industry," *Project Management Journal*, *44*(2), 4–19.

Mustafa, A. (2012). "The Failure of Management Consultants to Leave Behind Sustainable PMOs—a Better Model Is Needed," *PM World Today*, *14*(2), 1–3.

Pemsel, S. and A. Wiewiora (2013). "Project Management Office a Knowledge Broker in Project-Based Organisations," *International Journal of Project Management*, *31*(1), 31–42.

Schultze, U. (2011). "The SOX Compliance Journey at Trinity Industries," *Journal of Information Technology Teaching Cases*, *1*(2), 91–113.

Spalek, S. (2013). "Improving Industrial Engineering Performance through a Successful Project Management Office," *Engineering Economics*, *24*(2), 88–98.

Spalek, S. (2012). "The Role of Project Management Office in the Multi-Project Environment," *International Journal of Management & Enterprise Development*, *12*(2), 172–188.

Turner, N. and L. Lee-Kelley (2013). "Unpacking the Theory on Ambidexterity: An Illustrative Case on the Managerial Architectures, Mechanisms and Dynamics," *Management Learning*, *44*(2), 179–196.

Unger, B., H. Gemünden, and M. Aubry (2012). "The Three Roles of a Project Portfolio Management Office: Their Impact on Portfolio Management

Execution and Success," *International Journal of Project Management*, *30*(5), 608–620.

Ward, J. and E. M. Daniel (2013). "The Role of Project Management Offices (PMOs) in IS Project Success and Management Satisfaction," *Journal of Enterprise Information Management*, *26*(3), 316–336.

Young, M. and K. Conboy (2013). "Contemporary Project Portfolio Management: Reflections on the Development of an Australian Competency for Project Portfolio Management," *International Journal of Project Management*, http://dx.doi.org.ezaccess.libraries.psu.edu/10.1016/j.ijproman.2013.03.005.

APPENDIX A

Project Management Information Systems

Numerous project management information systems (PMISs) are available that help the user to plan, track, and manage their projects. In recent years, PMISs have become very easy to use and often can be customized to fit the needs of the user. A PMIS provides a powerful suite of Web-based tools to support many of the topics covered in this text. This appendix provides:

- A discussion of the common features available in most PMISs
- Criteria for selecting a PMIS
- A discussion of some advantages of using a PMIS
- A discussion of some concerns of using a PMIS
- A discussion of how to find vendors offering PMISs

Project Management Information Systems Features

The following list of features offered by most of today's PMISs, although by no means complete, gives a general overview of the types of features available. It should be noted, however, that different PMISs provide different features, and some of the features listed are not found in every project management package. In addition, some products do a much better job than others in providing software support for some of these features.

1. Budgeting & Cost Management

One of the most important features that PMISs provide is the ability to effectively plan and manage the costs of projects. Features often include:

- *Billing and billing methods*

As discussed in the text, projects can be charged to customers in a variety of ways. Most PMISs allow selection of fixed price, time and materials, milestone completion, and percent-to-completion billing methods. In addition, automated billing procedures can be defined.

- *Cost-to-completion tracking*

This feature permits the user to track the progress of each task and automatically calculate the expected remaining cost to complete each task and the expected cost to complete the entire project.

- *Earned value management*

As described in Chapter 7, it is important for the project manager to understand the value of work actually performed. Tools to support earned value calculations and management are common in PMISs.

- *Multiple currency*

With the global business environment of today, many projects have components that

span several countries. Some PMISs can handle the tracking and reporting of currency from multiple countries.

- *Payroll integration*

 Many of the PMISs comply with the direct integration of project data with the most common payroll systems that are available.

- *Percent-to-complete tracking*

 It is extremely important for the project manager to track each task as a project is being worked on. Percent-to-complete tracking lets the user report progress on a percentage basis as a means to help keep a project within its budget.

- *Project accounting and cost control*

 The ability to track projected versus actual expenses, track labor and nonlabor costs, track earned value, and forecast revenue and profitability are just a few features of project accounting software within PMISs. Numerous tools exist for helping the project manager track and control costs.

- *Project cost estimating*

 As discussed in Chapters 3 and 7 of the text, it is very important for the project manager and the project team to properly estimate the costs of individual tasks and the cost of the entire project. PMISs help do this and also provide features for capturing and using historical data to help better estimate future projects.

- *Time and expense reporting*

 All PMISs provide features for tracking time and expenses. Timesheet functions provide the ability to designate billable and nonbillable time, as well as various work schedules and holidays. Expense reporting features help the user to create customized expense reports, define expense categories, and track receipts and paid items.

2. Communications

The communication features of PMISs have come a long way. Most systems provide a suite of tools, such as those noted below:

- *Automatic e-mail notifications*

 These features can be used to automatically inform a team member when he or she has a task that is due in a few days. They can also be used to inform a team member if he or she has a task that is past due. Because of the interdependencies of many tasks, this feature can also automatically inform others who might be affected by a task that is behind schedule.

- *Collaboration management*

 Because PMISs are now Web-based, they have the capability to provide access to project data from virtually any computer in the world that has Internet connectivity. Therefore, each project team member and the client can have their own log-in access and receive real-time information about the project.

- *Customer collaboration*

 Customer collaboration features allow project managers to receive client's input and approval electronically. It also permits the client to view real-time progress reports on the project.

- *Discussion forums*

 To facilitate an open exchange of ideas, newer versions of PMISs often include Web-based discussion forums that allow the project team and the customer to have an open, electronic dialogue about any aspect of the project. Users can see previous comments and create a string of ideas and suggestions.

- *E-mail integration*

 The ability to send virtually all project information from the system directly to a team member or customer's e-mail account is a nice feature of modern software. E-mails can also be sent at predefined times and in predefined formats—for example, providing a daily morning update on the budget to the client.

- *File attachments*

 The ability to attach multiple files and multiple file formats to project information is now a common feature of PMISs.

- *International characters*

 With the globalization of projects, many PMISs allow the selection from multiple

international character sets when planning, tracking, or communicating information about the project.

- *Message center*

 This feature allows for a virtual location to be set up for the posting of critical information about a project. For example, if a shipment of materials was delayed, a message could be posted to the message center informing all team members and the client.

- *Mobile access*

 With the convergence of the latest technologies, many PMISs now allow for mobile access to project information from cell phones and PDAs, thereby allowing the users to access data virtually anytime and anywhere.

- *Multiple languages*

 In addition to working in English, many PMISs now allow users to work in several languages, such as Chinese, French, Spanish, and many others.

- *Online meetings*

 Several PMISs provide features that support online meetings, Web conferencing, webinars, screen sharing, and live collaboration tools. This can save time and reduce travel expenses for geographically dispersed users.

- *Information quality assessment*

 Applying a quality control methodology helps organizations effectively manage the information within the PMIS. Management of the quality of information reduces the potential of poor quality of information shared and increases the control of the optimum amount of information shared. Other ratings related to priority and audience help communicate essential information at the appropriate quality level.

3. Documentation Management

One of the most important features of a PMIS is the ability to document a project from beginning to end. The following is a list of some features that are available:

- *Approval process and routing*

 To streamline the workflow, process documents can be routed electronically via predefined paths and can include sections so that approvals can be noted before items are processed.

- *Change order management*

 This feature makes possible the tracking of billable and nonbillable change orders, and the estimating and tracking of their effect on project budgets and schedules. Change orders can often be billed and tracked via numerous methods.

- *Contract management and automation*

 Several PMISs have contract templates and allow implementation of some business rules and billing rates for specific projects. Many of the common contract provisions, such as those discussed in Chapter 3, are provided in the templates.

- *Meeting management and action items*

 As discussed earlier, many of the newer PMISs provide an environment for online meetings. However, from a documentation standpoint, the software allows the project team to track relevant discussion, decisions, and action items.

- *Project charter information*

 The project charter feature captures critical information about a project, for example, who the project sponsor is, what the project is supposed to accomplish, why the project is being done, and what the major assumptions and/or risks are.

- *Requirements management*

 This feature supports the documentation and tracking of the major deliverables for the project.

- *Time off requests*

 This feature tracks personal and vacation time of project members, and automates requests for time off and the approval or rejection of that request as well. Workload reports can be automatically updated to properly manage the human resources.

4. Integration and Customization

Most PMISs allow for the customization of the user interface and the reports to suit the particular needs of a project. In addition, they

provide linkages with many other popular information systems.

- *Customizable user interfaces*

 Users often have the ability to change the look and feel of the user interface. They can change colors, fonts, and backgrounds, as well as customize input screens and project reports.

- *Importing/exporting*

 Many PMISs allow the user to bring in information from other applications, such as word processing, spreadsheet, and database applications. The process of bringing information into a PMIS is called *importing*. Similarly, it is often possible to send information from the PMIS to those applications. The process of sending out information is called *exporting*.

- *Multimedia integration*

 Many PMISs allow for the full range of graphics, animation, voice, and video to be incorporated into the project. Videos or animation can be very useful, for example, to show the customer the latest design of a bridge or a building.

5. Online Tutorials

During the past few years, the online help tools for PMISs have come a long way. PMISs now often include very detailed demos, online help, in-depth tutorials, and even full video presentations.

6. Project Planning

All PMISs allow the user to define the activities and resources that are needed to perform a project. The list below provides an overview of some of the important project planning features.

- *Network diagrams and bar (Gantt) charts*

 One of the important features of a PMIS is the ability to easily and quickly generate network diagrams and bar (Gantt) charts based on current data. Once the baseline plan has been created, any modifications to the plan can easily be entered into the system, and the diagrams and charts will automatically reflect those changes. A PMIS lets

tasks in Gantt charts be linked together so that the precedence activities can be shown. Typically, the user can jump back and forth between Gantt chart and network diagram displays with a single command.

- *Project time estimating*

 During the planning phase, all activities can be defined along with their appropriate time estimates. Based on the interdependencies, and other factors such as vacation time and holidays, the PMIS will calculate an overall project time estimate.

- *Scheduling*

 PMISs provide extensive support for scheduling. Most systems will build Gantt charts and network diagrams based on the task and resource lists and all of their associated information. Any changes to those lists will automatically be reflected in the schedules. In addition, users can schedule recurring tasks, set priorities for scheduled tasks, perform reverse scheduling (from the end date backward to the beginning), define work shifts, schedule elapsed time, schedule tasks to start as late as possible or as soon as possible, and specify a must start by or must finish by date or a no earlier than or no later than date.

- *Task management and interdependencies*

 Just as the PMIS lets a resource list be maintained, it also permits an activity or task list be maintained. For each task, the user can provide a title, a start date, a finish date, comments, and estimated durations (including optimistic, most likely, and pessimistic estimates in various time scales) and can specify any precedent relationships with other tasks, as well as the person(s) responsible. Typically, a PMIS allows several thousand tasks to be associated with a project.

- *What-if analysis*

 One very helpful feature of PMISs is the ability to perform what-if analysis. This feature lets the user explore the effects of various scenarios. At some point in a project, the user might ask the system, What if— were delayed by a week? The effects of the delay on the entire project would

automatically be calculated, and the results would be presented. Almost any variable (people, pay rates, costs) in a project can be tested to see the effects of certain occurrences. This type of analysis enables the manager to better control any risks associated with the project.

- *Work breakdown structure*

 In addition to the features mentioned above, most PMISs allow you to create a work breakdown structure (WBS) similar to the one presented in Chapter 4. WBSs are very useful tools to aid in the planning process.

7. Project Portfolio Management

Many project managers today are running multiple projects and tracking significant issues related to those projects. The list below provides some features that can help:

- *Issue management*

 The issue management feature helps team members or the customer to electronically note any issues that they have with a project. The issues can cover a wide range of topics and can be tracked and responded to electronically.

- *Knowledge management*

 There are often certain business rules and/or historical data and/or experiences that can help provide insights and guidance into successfully completing your projects. A few of the newer PMISs have functions that allow you to build in some of this knowledge and expertise.

- *Lessons learned management*

 Opportunities to record lessons learned during the project provide a resource for reference by other project team members during and after the project. Access to the lessons learned in a combined file for multiple projects within the PMIS helps project team members to be more aware of lessons learned such as potential issues or efficient practices.

- *Multiple project management*

 Experienced project managers often oversee several projects simultaneously, and team members are assigned to more than one project simultaneously, with their time divided between the projects. Most PMISs provide support for these situations. They often can store multiple projects in separate files, with connecting links between the files; store multiple projects in the same file; handle several hundred or even several thousand projects at the same time; and create Gantt charts and network diagrams for multiple projects.

8. Project Tracking and Control

Tracking progress, actual costs, and actual resource use is a fundamental component of project management. PMISs allow the user to define a baseline plan and compare actual progress and costs with those in the baseline plan. Most PMISs can track tasks in progress, completed tasks, associated costs, time expended, start and finish dates, actual dollars committed or spent, and resources used, as well as remaining durations, resources, and expenses.

- *Critical path analysis*

 A PMIS will calculate the critical path for a project and often display it in red. In addition, for any activities not on the critical path, the PMIS will calculate the slack.

- *Milestone tracking*

 Milestones should be defined for each project, and a PMIS will support tracking progress toward those milestones. Any milestone that has been successfully completed can be displayed on a variety of reports, and team members can be informed electronically.

- *Subcontractor tracking*

 This feature allows the tracking of subcontractors who are assigned to projects. Time on task, fees, and numerous other items can be tracked.

- *Task priorities*

 When tracking the progress of a project, the level of priorities can often change. This feature permits setting and redefining the priority of any given task based on a particular situation. Task priorities are often defined as low, normal, high, or urgent, but they can also be defined on a numerical scale such as 1–10.

- *Task reminders*

 As noted above under point 2, Communications, automatic e-mail notifications can be sent. These can take many forms. One popular form is to remind the person responsible that a task is scheduled to start, a task is scheduled to finish, or certain levels of progress should have been achieved.

9. Report Generation

Most of today's PMISs have extensive reporting capabilities. Among the reports they can generate are (a) reports on the project as a whole; (b) reports on the major milestones; (c) reports that provide a variety of information with respect to a date range—such as tasks that have been completed within that range, tasks that are in progress, and tasks that will start within that range; (d) financial reports that show a full range of information, including budgets for all tasks as well as the entire project, tasks and resources that are over budget, cumulative budgeted costs, actual costs, and committed costs; (e) earned value analysis and management reports; (f) resource allocation reports for each resource or group of resources involved in a project; and (g) baseline to actual variance reports.

- *Customizable reporting*

 Almost all PMISs allow the user to customize reports, by selecting the data wanted along with the report format desired (that is, font, color, etc.).

- *Dashboard indicators*

 Dashboard indicators provide a visual report that the project manager can customize to get a quick snapshot of information that is most important to him or her. For example, the project manager's dashboard can provide a visual summary of what tasks are done, which are due, and which are overdue. Likewise, it could present a visual summary of which tasks are under or over budget.

- *Filtering*

 Filtering enables the user to select only certain data that meet some specified criteria. For example, if the user wants information on just the tasks that require a certain resource,

a simple request tells the PMIS to ignore tasks that do not use that resource and display only tasks that do use that resource.

- *Real-time reporting*

 All of the reports generated via PMIS can provide real-time, up-to-date information, assuming the project database has been properly updated.

- *Sorting*

 Sorting lets the user view information in a desired order, such as pay rates from highest to lowest, resource names in alphabetical order, or task names in alphabetical order. Most PMISs allow multiple levels of sorting (for example, by last name and then by first name).

10. Resource Management

PMISs can maintain a resource list consisting of resource names, the maximum amount of time that resources are available, standard and overtime rates for resources, accrual methods, and textual descriptions of the resources. Constraints can be assigned to each resource, such as the number of hours or times that it is available. The PMIS will highlight and help correct overallocations and perform resource leveling and resource smoothing.

- *Assignment tracking*

 Users can also assign resources to a task or a percentage of a task, set priority levels for resource assignments, assign more than one resource to the same task, and keep memos or notes on each resource.

- *Calendars*

 All resources can have their own individualized calendar, stating when they are and are not available.

- *Resource allocation and planning*

 A PMIS will track any resource assignments that are made and make sure they are not overallocated. Many PMISs can also perform some version of resource leveling or resource smoothing, as discussed in Chapter 6.

- *Resource utilization*

 Resource utilization charts can be created to provide an overview of the utilization rates for each resource. This can be very helpful as

project managers try to make the best use of available resources.

- *Skills tracking*

 This feature allows the assignment of resources by skill level. Resource profiles can include skill levels, certifications, experience levels, and training and educational levels.

11. Risk Management

Project risks are uncertain events or circumstances that could have an impact on a project. The degree to which a PMIS supports risk management varies greatly. Several tools allow the user to define possible risks, determine the probability that they will occur, and predict the impact on the schedule and budget if they occur. These risks can be directly associated with individual tasks within a project or with the project as a whole.

12. Sales and Business Development

Several of the PMISs include a feature related to business development. Some of the features include:

- *Automated lead generation*

 This feature automatically takes information directly from Web-based lead forms and informs the sales team so that they can follow up. Should a project be created, that information can then be imported into the project database.

- *Client management*

 Some PMISs provide an integrated view of sales and client information. Project managers, with approved access, can see any relevant notes, history, contacts, and ongoing communications with the client or potential client.

- *Sales dashboard*

 A sales dashboard provides a visual summary of pertinent sales information. This information might include sales pipeline information, sales metrics, sales quotas and expectation, geographical territory displays, and numerous actual versus projected reports.

13. Security & Access Controls

A critically important feature of PMISs is security and access rights features. Some PMISs provide password access to the project management program itself, password access to individual project files, and password access to specific data within a project file (such as pay rates). Different views can be given to the project manager, team members, and the client.

Criteria for Selecting Project Management Information Systems

Following is a list of factors to consider before purchasing a PMIS. Depending on your individual needs, and the needs of your organization, certain factors may be more or less important to you than they are to other people.

1. *Capacity.* Here, the main concern is whether the PMIS can handle the number of tasks you expect to perform, the number of resources you think you will need, and the number of projects you expect to be managing simultaneously. For most organizations, the software capacity is not an issue.

2. *Documentation and online help facilities.* The quality of documentation and online help facilities varies greatly among PMISs. Consideration should be given to the readability of the online user's manual, the logical presentation of ideas in the user's manual, the level of detail of the online help, the number and quality of examples provided, and the level of the discussion of advanced features.

3. *Ease of use.* This is often an important factor in the selection of any type of software package. Consideration should be given to the look and feel of the PMIS: the menu structures; available shortcut keys; color displays; the amount of information in each display; the ease with which data can be entered or modified; the ease with which reports can be generated; the quality of the reports that are produced; the consistency among screens; and the amount of learning required to become proficient with the PMIS.

4. *Features available.* Here, consideration must be given to whether the PMIS provides the features that are required for your organization. For example, does the package include

work breakdown structures and both Gantt charts and network diagrams? How good are the resource-leveling and smoothing algorithms? Can the PMIS sort and filter information, monitor the budget, produce customized calendars, and help with tracking and control? Does it have the capability to check for and help resolve overallocation of resources?

5. *Installation requirements.* The considerations here are the hardware and software required to run the PMIS: the memory required, the amount of hard disk space required, the processing speed and power required, the type of graphics display needed, and operating system requirements.

6. *Integration with other systems.* More and more in today's digital world there is a convergence of numerous electronic systems. If you are working in an environment where pertinent data are stored in various places, such as databases and spreadsheets, then special attention should be given to the integration capabilities of the PMIS. Some PMISs allow very basic integration with a few popular information systems, whereas others provide sophisticated integration with distributed databases and even object-oriented databases. In addition, the ability of the PMIS to export information to word processing programs, spreadsheets, human resources systems, and payroll systems may affect your decision.

7. *Internet features.* Although all modern PMISs allow project information to be posted and shared directly through the Internet, there is great variance in the Web-based tools they contain. For example, the online support for the communications features mentioned in the previous section should be evaluated.

8. *Reporting capabilities.* PMISs vary in the number and types of reports they can provide. Some support just the basic planning, scheduling, and cost reports, whereas others have extensive facilities for providing reports on individual tasks, resources, actual costs, committed costs, progress, and so on.
In addition, some PMISs are easier to customize than others. Reporting capabilities should be given a fairly high priority, because the ability to produce extensive and powerful reports is a feature that most users rate very highly.

9. *Security.* Some PMISs provide greater levels of security than others. If security is important, then special attention should be given to the methods of restricting access to the PMIS, to each project file, and to the data within each file.

10. *Vendor support.* Special attention should be given to whether the vendor or dealer provides technical support, the price of that support, and the reputation of the vendor.

Advantages of Using Project Management Information Systems

There are numerous advantages of using PMISs. Some of these advantages follow:

1. *Ability to handle complexity.* It is obvious that PMISs can handle certain aspects (especially numeric aspects) of large-scale projects more easily than a person can manually. For projects that have just a few activities and span a short period of time, a manual approach may be feasible. But for projects that involve thousands of activities and thousands of resources and span a few years' time, a PMIS provides indispensable assistance with the level of complexity.

2. *Accuracy.* Accuracy is greatly improved by using a PMIS. For large projects, manually drawing network diagrams, calculating start and finish times, and monitoring resource usage are very difficult. PMISs have accurate algorithms for calculating project information and contain numerous built-in routines that check for user errors.

3. *Affordability.* Excellent PC-based PMISs can be purchased for under $200.

4. *Ease of use.* Over the past few years, PMISs have become extremely easy to use. They can often be mastered with only a minimal amount of training.

5. *Maintainability and modifiability.* With manual systems, it is often difficult to maintain and modify project information. With a PMIS, any change in the data will automatically be reflected in all the project documents, such as

diagrams, cost tables, and resource allocation charts.

6. *Record keeping.* A major benefit of PMISs is their ability to keep excellent records. For instance, data can be kept on individual team members' schedules, each task, costs, and resources used. These data can be used to produce high-quality reports and can be helpful in planning future projects.

7. *Speed.* Once input data have been collected and entered, almost every imaginable calculation can be done very rapidly by the PMIS. Manually creating or revising plans, schedules, and budgets can take hours, days, or weeks.

8. *What-if analysis.* Another very beneficial feature of PMISs is the ability to perform what-if analysis. What-if analysis, as discussed earlier, allows the user to see the effects of various scenarios on a project. These different scenarios can be run on the PMIS, and their effects can be evaluated. This helps the project manager to prepare and plan for certain contingencies and to assess consequences.

Concerns about Using Project Management Information Systems

Although there are numerous benefits to using PMISs, there are also a few concerns to be considered and pitfalls to be avoided, if possible.

1. *Distraction.* For some project managers, a PMIS can be distracting. A manager can spend too much time playing with, and focusing on, the PMIS, with all of its reports and features, and forget about the most important part of a project: the people.

2. *False sense of security.* The PMIS can sometimes lull project managers into a false sense of security. First, project managers might believe that, because they have a powerful PMIS, they can manage and accomplish more than is actually feasible. Second, managers might think that, although a project is slipping, the PMIS will be able to figure out a way to get it back on track. Third, if the PMIS is not used properly, the reports might show that the project is doing fine, when in reality the project is not. Just because the PMIS says

everything is all right does not necessarily make it so.

3. *Information overload.* PMISs provide a great number of features and a huge amount of information. At times, the sheer quantity can be overwhelming. Only needed features of the PMIS should be used. Project managers have to resist the temptation to use features that produce more reports or more data without contributing to the successful completion of the project.

4. *Learning curve.* It does take a certain amount of time to become proficient in the use of a PMIS. The amount of time required varies, depending on the individual's background. For those not currently using computers and business software, there can be a significant learning curve. However, the amount of training typically required to master a PMIS has been decreasing over the past few years as PMISs have become easier and easier to use.

5. *Overreliance on software.* Because PMISs have become so easy to use and because they provide so many appealing features, project managers have started relying heavily on them. Individuals with little or no knowledge of the fundamentals of project management sometimes use a PMIS without really understanding what they are doing. If the basic concepts of project management have not been mastered, the PMIS will not make much of a difference. Stated simply, the PMIS is just a tool to help you do your job more effectively and efficiently—the PMIS cannot manage a project. You must manage the project, relying mainly on your skills and the skills of your team.

Project Management Information Systems Vendors

Numerous PMISs are available that provide support for the project management process. Almost all of the vendors provide online demos of their products or free trial software that can be downloaded.

A simple Internet search for project management information systems, project management software, or project management information

system directory will provide links for hundreds of vendors and consultants. Several of the websites provide a list of the top-selling PMISs, as well as a review of their features. Other sites actually compare popular PMISs and report which features they provide and give a summary of the strengths and weaknesses of each.

Summary

This appendix discusses several features that are typically found in project management information systems. Among the most common are budgeting and cost management, communications, documentation management, integration and customization, portfolio management, online tutorials, project planning, project tracking and control, report generation, resource management, risk management, sales and business development, and security and access controls.

Criteria are given for selecting a project management information system, including capacity, documentation and online help facilities, ease of use, features available, integration with other systems, installation requirements, reporting capabilities, Internet features, security, and vendor support.

Finally, a list is provided of the advantages of and concerns about using project management information systems. The benefits include accuracy, affordability, ease of use, ability to handle complexity, maintainability and modifiability, record keeping, speed, and what-if analysis. Concerns include becoming distracted by the PMIS, a false sense of security, information overload, the learning curve, and overreliance on the PMIS.

Questions

1. Discuss at least 10 common features of project management information systems. In your opinion, which of these are the most important?
2. Discuss how the Internet can facilitate project communications.
3. Discuss the criteria that should be considered when purchasing project management information systems. If you had to rank these in order of importance, how would you rank them?
4. What are some of the advantages of using project management information systems?
5. What are some of the concerns about using project management information systems? Do the advantages outweigh the concerns? Explain your answer.

Internet Exercises

1. Perform a search for project management information systems. Provide a summary of three different software systems.
2. Perform a search for project management information systems directory. Provide a list of the top-selling project management information systems.
3. Search the Internet for a website or a recent article that compares two or more popular project management information systems. Discuss the criteria that were used for evaluating the systems. What do you think were the three most important criteria and why? Are there other criteria you would have used and why?
4. Download a free trial version of a project management information system. What system did you choose and why? What do you think are the key features of the system you chose?

References

Anonymous (2012). "Automation Science; New Automation Science Data Have Been Reported by Investigators at Kwangwoon University," *Technology & Business Journal*, Aug 7, 624.

Anonymous (2012). "Bamboo Solutions Extends the Capabilities of Microsoft Project with Best-Selling Project Management Application for Microsoft SharePoint," *Business Wire, Mar 19*, n/a.

Anonymous (2012). "Hill International Receives $16 Million Program Management Contract from the Los Angeles Metro," *NASDAQ OMX's News Release Distribution Channel, May 12*, n/a.

Arnold, P. and A. Javernick-Will (2013). "Projectwide Access: Key to Effective Implementation of Construction Project Management Software Systems," *Journal of Construction Engineering & Management*, 139(5), 510–518.

Caniëls, M.C. J. and R. J. J. M. Bakens (2012). "The Effects of Project Management Information Systems on Decision Making in a Multi Project Environment," *International Journal of Project Management*, 30(2), 162.

Fitsilis, P., K. Kirytopoulos, and V. Leopoulos (2011). "Assuring the Managerial Capability of Public Organizations Implementing Projects," *International Journal of Managing Projects in Business*, 4(2), 329–344.

Fotoohi, H. (2012). "The Effects of a Multilevel Web-Based Daily Reporting System on Knowledge Management of a Multi Project Organization," Paper presented at the 331-XIX European Conference on Knowledge Management.

Heravi, G. and M. Ilbeigi (2012). "Development of a Comprehensive Model for Construction Project Success Evaluation by Contractors," *Engineering, Construction and Architectural Management*, 19(5), 526–542.

Hsu, J. S., Y. Hung, Y. Chen, and H. Huang (2013). "Antecedents and Consequences of User Coproduction in Information System Development Projects," *Project Management Journal*, 44(2), 67–87.

Liu, Z. and L. Chen (2011). "Research on MIS Design for Real Estate Company," *Research in World Economy*, 2(2), 50–54.

Miller, J. (2013). "Collaboration, Visibility Key to Successful Project Automation Plan," *Control Engineering, April 2013*, 44.

Narayanaswamy, R., V. Grover, and R. M. Henry (2013). "The Impact of Influence Tactics in Information System Development Projects: A Control-Loss Perspective," *Journal of Management Information Systems*, 30(1), 191–225.

Stare, A. (2011). "Reducing Negative Impact of Project Changes with Risk and Change Management," *Zagreb International Review of Economics & Business*, 14(2), 71–85.

Vaughan, J. L., M. L. Leming, M. Liu, and E. Jaselskis (2013). "Cost-Benefit Analysis of Construction Information Management System Implementation: Case Study," *Journal of Construction Engineering & Management*, 139(4), 445–455.

APPENDIX B

Project Management Websites

Appendix B is a list of organizations whose websites provide access to information and resources regarding project management. For the updated website addresses of the organizations in this appendix, make an Internet connection and go to www.cengagebrain.com. At the Cengagebrain.com home page, search for the ISBN of your title (from the back cover of your book) using the search box at the top of the page. This will take you to the product page where free companion resources can be found. Navigate to Appendix B. It is suggested that you save the book's companion website in your "Favorites" list for easy access in the future.

Agile Alliance

Agile Leadership Network

Alliance for Sustainability in Project Management

allPM

EQ Toolbox

International Association for Project and Program Management

International Centre for Complex Project Management

International Construction Project Management Association

International Project Management Association

Niwot Ridge websites for Project Management Resources

ProjectManagement.com

Project Management Benchmarking Network

Project Management Center

Project Management Discussion

Project Management Insight

Project Management Institute

Project Manager Community LinkedIn

Project Smart

Scrum Alliance

Software Program Managers Network

APPENDIX C

Project Management Associations around the Globe

Appendix C is a list of project management associations in countries around the world. For the updated website addresses of the associations in this appendix, make an Internet connection and go to www.cengagebrain.com. At the Cengagebrain.com home page, search for the ISBN of your title (from the back cover of your book) using the search box at the top of the page. This will take you to the product page where free companion resources can be found. Navigate to Appendix C. It is suggested that you save the book's companion website in your "Favorites" list for easy access in the future.

Global	International Project Management Association
	Project Management Institute
Armenia	Armenian Project Management Association
Asia Pacific	Asia Pacific Federation of Project Management
Australia	Australian Institute of Project Management
Austria	Projekt Management Austria
Azerbaijan	Azerbaijan Project Management Association
Bangladesh	Institute of Project Management Bangladesh
Bosnia-Herzegovina	Udruženje za Upravljanje Projektima u Bosni i Hercegovini
Brazil	Brasilian Association for Project Management
Bulgaria	Bulgarian Project Management Association
Canada	Project Management Association of Canada
Chile	Corporación Chilena de Dirección de Proyectos
China	Beijing Project Management Associates
	Project Management Research Committee China
	Project Manager Union
Columbia	Asociación Colombiana de Gestión de Proyectos
Costa Rica	Asociación de Dirección de Proyectos de Costa Rica
Croatia	Croatian Association for Project Management
Cyprus	Cyprus Project Management Society
Czech Republic	Project Management Association Czech Republic

Denmark	Danish Project Management Association	**Kenya**	Kenya Association of Project Managers
Egypt	Management Engineering Society	**Kosovo**	Kosava Project Management
Estonia	Estonian Project Managers Association	**Latvia**	Latvian National Project Management Association
European	European Community Project Managers' Association	**Lithuania**	Lithuanian Project Management Association
Finland	Project Management Association Finland	**Malaysia**	Malaysian Asset and Project Management Association
France	Association Francophone de Management de Projet	**Mexico**	Asociación Mexicana de Ingeniería de Proyectos
	Société Francaise pour l'avancement du Management de Projet	**Nepal**	Project Management Association of Nepal
Germany	Deutsche Gesellschaft für Projektmanagement e. V.	**Netherlands**	Project Management Association Netherlands
Greece	Network of Project Managers in Greece	**Nigeria**	Project Managers Development Association of Nigeria
Guatemala	Asociación de Project Management de Guatemala	**Nordic**	Network of Nordic Project Management Associations
Hong Kong	Hong Kong Institute of Project Management	**Norway**	Norwegian Association of Project Management
Hungary	Project Management Association Hungary	**Panama**	Asociación Panameña de Gestión de Proyectos
Iceland	Project Management Association of Iceland	**Peru**	Asociación Peruana de Dirección de Proyectos
India	Project and Technology Management Foundation	**Poland**	Project Management Association Poland
	Project Management Associates	**Portugal**	Associação Portuguesa de Gestão de Projectos
Indonesia	Indonesian Society of Project Management Professionals	**Romania**	Project Management Romania
Iran	Iran Project Management Association	**Russia**	Russian Project Management Association
Ireland	Institute of Project Management Ireland	**Serbia**	Serbian Project Management Association
Italy	Associazione Nazionale di Impiantistica Industriale	**Singapore**	Society of Project Managers
Japan	Project Management Association of Japan	**Slovakia**	Project Management Association of Slovakia
Kazakhstan	Kazakhstan Project Management Association	**Slovenia**	Slovenian Project Management Association

South Africa	Association for Project Management South Africa	**Tanzania**	Project Management Association of Tanzania
Spain	Asociación Española de Dirección Integrada de Proyecto	**Turkey**	Istanbul Project Management Association
	Asociación Española de Ingeniería de Proyectos		Turkish Project Management Association
Sweden	Swedish Project Management Association	**Ukraine**	Ukrainian Project Management Association
Switzerland	Swiss Project Management Association	**United Kingdom**	Association for Project Management
			Major Projects Association
Taiwan, China	Taiwan Project Management Association	**United States**	American Society for the Advancement of Project Management

Acronyms

ACWP	Actual Cost of Work Performed	LF	Latest Finish time
AF	Actual Finish time	LS	Latest Start time
ALAP	As Late As Possible	PDM	Precedence Diagramming Method
ASAP	As Soon As Possible	PERT	Program Evaluation and Review Technique
BAC	Budget At Completion		
BAFO	Best and Final Offer	PMBOK®	Project Management Body of Knowledge
BCWP	Budgeted Cost of Work Performed		
BCWS	Budgeted Cost of Work Scheduled	PMI	Project Management Institute
CAC	Cumulative Actual Cost	PMIS	Project Management Information System
CBC	Cumulative Budgeted Cost	PMO	Project Management Office
CEV	Cumulative Earned Value	PV	Planned Value
CPI	Cost Performance Index	RAM	Responsibility Assignment Matrix
CPM	Critical Path Method	RFP	Request for Proposal
CV	Cost Variance	SDLC	Systems Development Life Cycle
EAC	Estimated cost At Completion	SOW	Statement of Work
EF	Earliest Finish time	TBC	Total Budgeted Cost
ES	Earliest Start time	TCPI	To-Complete Performance Index
EV	Earned Value	TS	Total Slack
FCAC	Forecasted Cost At Completion	WBS	Work Breakdown Structure
FS	Free Slack		

ACWP	Actual Cost of Work Performed		LFT	Latest Finish time
AFT	Actual Finish time		LS	Latest Start time
ALAP	As Late As Possible		PDM	Precedence Diagramming Method
ASAP	As Soon As Possible		PERT	Program Evaluation and Review Technique
BAC	Budget At Completion			
BAFO	Best and Final Offer		PMBOK	Project Management Body of Knowledge
BCWP	Budgeted Cost of Work Performed		PMI	Project Management Institute
BCWS	Budgeted Cost of Work Scheduled		PMIS	Project Management Information System
CAC	Cumulative Actual Cost			
CBC	Cumulative Budgeted Cost		PMO	Project Management Office
CEV	Cumulative Earned Value		PV	Planned Value
CPI	Cost Performance Index		RAM	Responsibility Assignment Matrix
CPM	Critical Path Method		RFP	Request for Proposal
CV	Cost Variance		SDLC	Systems Development Life Cycle
EAC	Estimated cost At Completion		SOW	Statement of Work
EFT	Earliest Finish time		TBC	Total Budgeted Cost
ES	Earliest Start time		TCPI	To-Complete Performance Index
EV	Earned Value		TS	Total Slack
FCAC	Forecast Cost At Completion		WBS	Work Breakdown Structure
FS	Free Slack			

CHAPTER ONE

1. What are some attributes of a project?

 - A clear objective
 - Interdependent tasks
 - Use of various resources
 - A specific time frame
 - A unique or one-time endeavor
 - A customer
 - Degree of uncertainty

2. Identify three projects in which you have been involved during your lifetime.
 Answers will vary.

3. What are eight factors that constrain the achievement of a project objective?

 - Scope
 - Quality
 - Schedule
 - Budget
 - Resources
 - Risks
 - Customer satisfaction
 - Stakeholders

4. Match the phases of the project life cycle, listed first, with the descriptions, that follow:

C	First phase	A. Planning
A	Second phase	B. Performing
B	Third phase	C. Initiating
D	Fourth phase	D. Closing

5. A project is authorized using a document called a *project charter*.

6. The result of the planning phase is a *baseline plan*.

7. In the performing phase, the project plan is *executed* to produce all the *deliverables* and to accomplish the *project objective*.

8. Project management involves first *establishing* a *plan* and then *executing* that *plan*.

9. The project *objective* must be agreed upon by the *sponsor* and the individual or organization that will *perform* the project.

10. What are the keys to successful stakeholder engagement?

 - Regular and open communication
 - Trust
 - Respect
 - Open-mindedness
 - Positive win-win attitude

11. *Cultural awareness* and sensitivity are not only important, but *imperative* for successful *global* project management.

CHAPTER TWO

1. The initiating phase of the project life cycle starts with the recognition of a *need, problem*, or *opportunity*.

2. Project selection involves *evaluating* potential projects, and then *deciding* which of these should move forward to be *implemented*.

3. What are the four steps in the project selection process?

 - Develop a set of evaluation criteria
 - List assumptions for each project
 - Gather data and information for each project
 - Evaluate each project against the criteria

4. A *project charter* is used to formally *authorize* a project and summarize the key *conditions* and *parameters* for the project.

5. List at least eight elements that could be included in a project charter.

 - Project title
 - Purpose
 - Description
 - Objective
 - Success criteria or expected benefits
 - Funding
 - Major deliverables
 - Acceptance criteria
 - Milestone schedule
 - Key assumptions
 - Constraints
 - Major risks
 - Approval requirements
 - Project manager
 - Reporting requirements
 - Sponsor designee
 - Approval signature and date

6. What is the purpose of a request for proposal? To solicit proposals from potential contractors to do the project.

7. What are some elements that may be included in a request for proposal?

 - Project objective
 - Statement of work
 - Customer requirements
 - Deliverables
 - Acceptance criteria
 - Customer-supplied items
 - Approvals required
 - Type of contract
 - Payment terms
 - Required schedule
 - Instructions for the content and format of contractor proposals
 - Due date for proposals
 - Proposal evaluation criteria
 - Funds available

8. Care should be taken not to provide *information* to only some of the *contractors* that is not provided to all interested contractors because it would give some of them an *unfair competitive advantage*.

CHAPTER THREE

1. *Relationships* establish the foundation for successful funding and contract *opportunities*.

2. Relationship building requires being *proactive* and *engaged*.

3. Establishing and building *trust* is key to developing *effective* and successful *relationships*.

4. Building effective and successful relationships takes *time* and *work*.

5. Contractors need to *develop relationships* with potential customers long *before* customers prepare an RFP.

6. What is the outcome of a successful pre-RFP/proposal marketing effort? The outcome is eventually winning a contract from the customer to perform the project.

7. What are some factors that a contractor should consider when deciding whether to respond to an RFP?

 - Competition
 - Risk
 - Consistency with business mission
 - Opportunity to extend and enhance capabilities
 - Reputation with the customer
 - Availability of customer funds
 - Availability of resources to prepare a quality proposal
 - Availability of resources to perform the project

8. Contractors need to be *realistic* about their ability to prepare proposals and about the *probability* of winning the contract.

9. The proposal process is a *competitive* process. A proposal is a *selling* document.

10. In a proposal, the contractor must highlight the *unique* factors that *differentiate* it from *competitors'* proposals.

11. A proposal should address three topics or contain three sections. What are they?

 - Technical section
 - Management section
 - Cost section

12. What is the objective of the technical section of a proposal?
 The objective is to convince the customer that the contractor understands the need or problem and can provide the least risky and most beneficial solution.

13. What is the objective of the management section of a proposal?
 The objective is to convince the customer that the contractor can do the proposed work and achieve the intended results.

14. What is the objective of the cost section of a proposal?
 The objective is to convince the customer that the contractor's price for the proposed project is realistic and reasonable.

15. What elements might each of the three sections of a proposal contain?

 Technical section

 - Understanding of the need
 - Proposed approach or solution
 - Benefits to the customer

 Management section

 - Description of major tasks
 - Deliverables
 - Project schedule
 - Project organization
 - Related experience
 - Equipment and facilities

Cost section

 - Labor
 - Materials
 - Equipment
 - Facilities
 - Subcontractors and consultants
 - Travel
 - Documentation
 - Overhead or indirect costs
 - Escalation
 - Reserve
 - Profit

16. What are some items a contractor needs to consider when determining a price for a proposed project?

 - Reliability of the cost estimates
 - Risk
 - Value of the project to the contractor
 - Customer's budget
 - Competition

17. The focus of a proposal should be on *quality* of the *content*, rather than the *number* of pages.

18. Contractors must continue to be *proactive* even after the proposal is submitted.

19. A contractor bidding on a fixed-price contract must develop *accurate* and *complete* cost estimates and include sufficient *reserves*.

20. Write the word *low* or *high* in each box, depending on the degree of risk for the customer and contractor associated with each type of contract.

	Customer Risk	Contractor Risk
Fixed price	Low	High
Cost reimbursement	High	Low

21. A measure used to determine the success of proposal efforts is known as the *win ratio*.

CHAPTER FOUR

1. The project *objective* establishes *what* is to be *accomplished*.

2. The project objective is usually defined in terms of the *end product*, *schedule*, and *budget*.

3. The project scope defines *what* needs to be done.

4. What sections should the project scope document include?

 - Customer requirements
 - Statement of work
 - Deliverables
 - Acceptance criteria
 - Work breakdown structure

5. The project team must avoid scope *creep.*

6. To avoid quality problems, there needs to be a *quality plan.*

7. The key to quality control is to monitor the quality of the work *early* and *regularly.*

8. The work *breakdown* structure is a *deliverable-*oriented *hierarchical decomposition* of the project *work scope.*

9. The work *breakdown* structure establishes the *framework* for *how* the work will get done to produce the project *deliverables.*

10. The lowest-level work item for any given branch of the work breakdown structure is called a *work package.*

11. The responsibility *assignment* matrix designates *who* is responsible for accomplishing each *work item* in the work breakdown structure.

12. An activity is also called a *task.*

13. A *network diagram* defines the *sequence* of *how* the activities will get done.

14. A network diagram *arranges* activities in the appropriate sequence and defines their *dependent relationships.*

15. Refer to Figure 4.9.
 a. When "Prepare Mailing Labels" and "Print Questionnaire" are finished, what activity can be started?
 "Mail Questionnaire & Get Responses"

 b. In order to start "Input Response Data," which activities must have been finished immediately beforehand?
 "Mail Questionnaire & Get Responses" and "Test Software"

16. Refer to Figure 4.9.
 a. In order to start "Test Software," which activities must have been completed immediately beforehand?
 "Develop Data Analysis Software" and "Develop Software Test Data"

 b. True or false: Once "Print Questionnaire" is finished, "Mail Questionnaire & Get Responses" can start immediately.
 False; "Prepare Mailing Labels" must also be finished in order for "Mail Questionnaire" to start.

CHAPTER FIVE

1. The estimated *resources* for an activity will influence the *estimated duration* to perform the activity and the *estimated cost* of the activity.

2. When estimating resources for activities, the *availability* of each resource has to be taken into account.

3. It is necessary to estimate the *types* and *quantities* of resources required for each activity.

4. True or false: The duration estimate for an activity should include the time required to perform the work plus any associated waiting time.
 True

5. The estimated *duration* for an activity must be based on the *quantity* of *resources* required to perform the activity.

6. The overall window of time in which a project must be completed is defined by its *estimated start* time and *required completion* time.

7. What is the equation for calculating an activity's earliest finish time?
 EF = ES + Estimated Duration

8. The earliest start and earliest finish times for activities are determined by calculating *forward* through the network diagram.

9. Refer to Figure 5.4. What are the earliest start and earliest finish times for "Pilot-Test Questionnaire"?
 ES = Day 13, EF = Day 33

10. What determines a particular activity's earliest start time?
It is determined by the latest of all the earliest finish times of all the activities leading directly into that particular activity.

11. What is the equation for calculating an activity's latest start time?
LS = LF − Estimated Duration

12. The latest finish and latest start times are determined by calculating *backward* through the network diagram.

13. Refer to Figure 5.7. What are the latest finish and latest start times for "Input Response Data"?
LF = Day 112, LS = Day 105

14. What determines a particular activity's latest finish time?
It is determined by the earliest of all the latest start times of all the activities emerging directly from that particular activity.

15. When a project has a positive total slack, some activities can be *delayed* without jeopardizing completion of the project by its required completion time. When a project has negative total slack, some activities need to be *accelerated* to complete the project by its required completion time.

16. The total slack for a path of *activities* is common and *shared* among *all* the *activities* on the *path*.

17. The longest path of activities from the beginning to the end of a project is called the *critical* path.

18. Refer to Figures 5.9 and 5.10. Of the two activities entering into activity 11, "Input Response Data," which activity has free slack? What is its value?
Activity 10, "Test Software"; 50 − (−8) = 58 days

19. If actual *performance* is behind *planned* performance, *corrective action* should be taken *immediately*.

20. What are the two kinds of data or information that need to be collected during each reporting period?

- Data on actual performance
- Information on any changes to the project scope, schedule, or budget

21. True or false: In general, it is better to have a shorter reporting period during a project.
True

22. Project *management* is a *proactive* approach to *controlling* the project to accomplish the project *objective*.

23. What three schedule elements will be affected by the actual finish times of completed activities?

- The earliest start times of the remaining activities
- The earliest finish times of the remaining activities
- The total slack

24. Changes to the project can affect *scope*, *schedule*, and/or *budget*.

25. In analyzing a project schedule, it is important to identify all the paths of activities that have *negative* slack.

26. When analyzing a path of activities that has negative slack, what two kinds of activities should you look at carefully?

- Activities that are in progress or to be started in the immediate future
- Activities that have long estimated durations

27. List four approaches to reducing the estimated durations of activities.

- Apply more resources
- Assign a person with greater expertise or more experience
- Reduce the scope or requirements
- Increase productivity through improved methods or technology

28. Calculate the expected duration for an activity having the following time estimates: $t_o = 8$, $t_m = 12$, and $t_p = 22$.

$$t_e = \frac{8 + 4(12) + 22}{6} = 13$$

29. Compute the expected duration (t_e) and the variance (σ^2) for the following beta probability distribution.

$$t_e = \frac{5 + 4(8) + 23}{6} = 10$$

$$\sigma^2 = \left(\frac{23 - 5}{6}\right)^2 = 9$$

30. What percentage of the area under this normal curve is shaded?

 34 percent

31. If 95 percent of the area under the following normal curve is between the two labeled points, what is the standard deviation? What is the variance?

 Because there are a total of four standard deviations ($+2$ and -2) between 12 and 32, $4\sigma = 32 - 12 = 20$, and thus $1\sigma = 5$.
 Variance $= \sigma^2 - (5)^2 = 25$.

CHAPTER SIX

1. At a minimum, network diagrams illustrate the *technical* constraints among activities. However, when limited resources are available, the network diagram can also be drawn to reflect *resource* constraints.

2. A resource *requirements* plan illustrates the expected *utilization* of *resources* by time period during the time span of the project.

3. Resource leveling attempts to establish a schedule in which resource utilization is made as level as possible *without* extending the project beyond its *required completion* time.

4. Resource-limited scheduling develops the *shortest* schedule when the quantity of available resources is fixed. This method will *extend* the project completion time if necessary to keep within the resource limits.

CHAPTER SEVEN

1. The estimated cost of an activity is based on the *types* and *quantities* of the *resources* required to perform the activity.

2. List the elements that can be included in the estimated costs for an activity.

 - Labor
 - Materials
 - Equipment
 - Facilities
 - Subcontractors and consultants
 - Travel
 - Reserve

3. The estimated cost for an activity should be *reasonable* and *realistic*.

4. The first step in the project budgeting process is to *aggregate* the *estimated* costs for each *work package* in the work breakdown structure and establish a *total budgeted cost* for each work package.

5. Referring to Figures 7.1 and 4.5, what is the total budgeted cost for each work package?

1.1	$13,400
1.2	$11,100
2.1	$5,100
2.2	$10,000

6. Once a total budgeted cost has been established for each work package, the second step in the project budgeting process is to *distribute* each TBC over the *expected time span* of its work package.

7. The *cumulative budgeted cost* is the amount that is budgeted to accomplish all the *work* that is scheduled to be performed up to a specific point in time.

8. Look at Figures 7.5 and 7.7. How much did the "Design" work package and the "Build" work package each contribute to the $4,000 cost overrun at the end of week 8?

	Amount	Overrun or Underrun?
Design	$2,000	Underrun
Build	$6,000	Overrun

9. Cumulative earned value is calculated by first determining the *percent complete* for each work package and then multiplying it by the *total budgeted cost* for the work package.

10. List the four cost-related measures used to analyze project cost performance.

- TBC (total budgeted cost)
- CBC (cumulative budgeted cost)
- CAC (cumulative actual cost)
- CEV (cumulative earned value)

11. What is the cost performance index for the "Design" work package in the packaging machine project at the end of week 5?

$$CPI = \frac{\$24,000}{\$22,000} = 1.091$$

12. What is the cost variance for the "Build" work package in the packaging machine project at the end of week 8?
CV = $30,000 − $46,000 = −$16,000

13. Using the first forecasting method described, calculate the forecasted cost at completion for the "Build" work package in the packaging machine project.

$$FCAC = \frac{\$60,000}{0.65} = \$92,300$$

$$\left(\text{Note: } CPI = \frac{\$30,000}{\$46,000} = 0.65\right)$$

14. Using the second forecasting method described, calculate the forecasted cost at completion for the "Build" work package in the packaging machine project.
FCAC = $46,000 + ($60,000 − $30,000) = $76,000

15. In analyzing cost performance, it is important to identify all of the work packages that have a *negative* cost variance or a cost performance index of less than *1.0*.

16. When evaluating work packages that have a negative cost variance, you should focus on taking corrective actions to reduce the costs of activities that will be performed in the *near* term and those that have a *large* estimated cost.

17. The key to managing cash flow is to ensure that cash *comes in* faster than it *goes out*.

18. If sufficient funds are not available to meet expenses, a contractor may need to *borrow*

money. This adds to the cost of the project, because the contractor then has to pay *interest* also.

19. What are the normal and crash times and costs for activities B, C, and D in Figure 7.14?

	Normal Time	Normal Cost	Crash Time	Crash Cost
Activity B	9 weeks	$80,000	6 weeks	$110,000
Activity C	10 weeks	$40,000	9 weeks	$45,000
Activity D	8 weeks	$30,000	6 weeks	$42,000

20. What are the cost-per-week rates to accelerate activities B, C, and D in Figure 7.14?
B: $10,000 per week; C: $5,000 per week; D: $6,000 per week

21. If all the activities in Figure 7.14 were performed in their crash times, what would be the total project cost?
$259,000

CHAPTER EIGHT

1. A risk is an *uncertain* event that, if it *occurs*, can jeopardize the accomplishment of the *project objective*.

2. For each risk that is *identified*, the potential *impacts* must be *estimated*.

3. Risk assessment involves determining the *likelihood* that a risk will *occur* and the *degree* of *impact* it will have on the project *objective*.

4. A risk *response plan* is a defined set of *actions* to prevent or *reduce* the likelihood of *occurrence* or the *impact* of a risk, or to *implement* if the risk event occurs.

5. A risk *assessment matrix* is a tool for assessing and *managing risks*.

6. *Project meetings* are a good forum for *regularly* reviewing, *updating*, and *addressing* risks.

CHAPTER NINE

1. The fourth and final phase of the project *life cycle* is *closing* the project.

2. Successful projects should end with some type of *recognition* and *celebration*.

3. What are the two types of internal postproject evaluation meetings the project manager should have?

- An individual meeting with each team member
- A group meeting with the entire project team

4. The purpose of identifying and documenting *lessons learned* is to capitalize on the *knowledge* and *experience* gained on the project to *improve performance* on *future* projects.

5. The project team should *not* wait until the *end* of the project to capture and *document lessons learned*.

6. During project closing, copies of project *documentation* should be properly *organized*, *filed*, and *archived*.

7. List three reasons for having a postproject evaluation meeting with the customer.

- To determine whether the project provided the customer with the expected benefits
- To assess the level of customer satisfaction
- To obtain feedback

8. For a contractor, what are two potential consequences of having a project terminated early by a customer who is not satisfied?

- The contractor may suffer a financial loss.
- The contractor's reputation may be damaged.

CHAPTER TEN

1. What two benefits does the project manager realize by involving the team in developing the plan?

- A more comprehensive plan
- Commitment of the team to accomplish the plan

2. The project manager secures the *appropriate resources* to perform the work and then assigns *responsibility* and delegates *authority* to specific individuals for the various tasks.

3. The project manager implements a project management information system to serve what two functions?

- Track actual progress
- Compare actual progress with planned progress

4. The project manager has primary responsibility for providing leadership for what three management functions?

- Planning
- Organizing
- Controlling

5. Project leadership involves *inspiring* the people assigned to the project to work as a team to implement the *plan* and accomplish the *project objective* successfully.

6. Project leadership requires *involvement* and *empowerment* of the project team.

7. The capable project manager understands what *motivates* team members and creates a *supportive* environment in which individuals work as part of a high-performing team.

8. People want to feel that they are *contributing* to the project and need to be *recognized*.

9. Showing *appreciation* and *complimenting* individuals will *motivate* them to be more *engaged* in contributing to the *success* of the project.

10. A project manager sets the tone for the project team by establishing an environment of *trust*, high *expectations*, and *enjoyment*.

11. People working on projects look for *affiliation* and *socialization*; they do not want to work in *isolation*.

12. Leadership requires that the project manager be highly *motivated* and set a *positive example* for the project team.

13. A good project manager believes that all individuals are *valuable* to the organization and that they can make greater contributions through *continuous learning*.

14. Rather than create a fear of *failure*, the project manager acknowledges that mistakes are part of the *learning* and *growth* experience.

15. A good project manager values and expects continuous *self-improvement*.

16. List five reasons why it is important for the project manager to use frequent communication.

 - To keep the project moving
 - To identify potential problems
 - To solicit suggestions for improving project performance
 - To keep abreast of customer satisfaction and stakeholder issues
 - To avoid surprises

17. A high degree of communication is especially important early in the project to help build a good *working relationship* with the project team and to establish clear *expectations* with the customer.

18. What are three ways in which a project manager communicates?

 - Meetings
 - Informal conversations
 - Written reports

19. Good project managers spend more time *listening* than *talking*.

20. Give three reasons the project manager should establish ongoing communication with the customer.

 - To keep the customer informed
 - To determine whether there are any changes in expectations
 - To keep abreast of the degree of customer satisfaction

21. Why does communication by project managers need to be timely, honest, and unambiguous?
 Such communication establishes credibility, builds trust, and prevents rumors.

22. The project manager should have an informal *conversation* with each person on the project team and with each key individual in the *customer* organization.

23. The project manager should use *open-ended* questions and do a lot of *listening*.

24. The project manager needs to have a good sense of *humor* and needs to stay *physically* fit.

25. In solving problems, the project manager needs to be able to see the *big picture* and how potential solutions might affect other parts of the project.

26. Effective negotiations result in a *win-win* outcome for *both* parties. It requires the project manager to be *flexible* and willing to *compromise*.

27. The project manager must maintain *integrity* and *respect* for the other party throughout the *negotiating* process.

28. What skills and abilities do effective project managers have?

 - Leadership ability
 - Ability to develop people
 - Communication skills
 - Interpersonal skills
 - Ability to handle stress
 - Problem-solving skills
 - Negotiating skills
 - Time management skills

29. a. Identify one skill you want to develop.
 b. Identify three things you can do to develop that skill.
 c. Select one of the three things you listed above and pick a date by which you will have accomplished it.
 Answers will vary.

30. Delegation involves *empowering* the project team to accomplish the *project objective* and each team member to achieve the *expected results* for his or her area of responsibility.

31. Project managers should not tell individuals *how* to do the assigned tasks.

32. When assigning individuals to specific tasks, the project manager needs to take into consideration the person's *capabilities*, *potential*, and *workload*.

33. Effective delegation requires that the project manager have *confidence* in each member of the project team.

34. Delegation requires that individuals be *accountable* for achieving the expected results.

35. Changes may be initiated by the *customer* or by the *project team* or may be caused by *unanticipated occurrences* during the performance of the project.

36. The project manager's job is to *manage* and *control* changes to *minimize* any negative impact on the successful accomplishment of the project objective.

37. At the start of the project, the project manager needs to establish a *change control system* that defines how changes will be *documented*, *approved*, and *communicated*.

38. *Scope creep* is a frequent cause of projects *overspending* their *budget* or not being *completed* on *time*.

CHAPTER ELEVEN

1. A project team is a group of individuals working *interdependently* to accomplish the project *objective*.

2. Teamwork is the *cooperative* effort by members of a team to accomplish a *common* goal.

3. Project team members are assigned based not only on their *expertise* and *experience* but also on who is *available*.

4. Project teams should be kept as *small* as feasible *throughout* the project.

5. During the forming stage, *little* actual work is accomplished because of the high level of *anxiety* that individuals have.

6. In the forming stage, individuals do a lot of *questioning*.

7. During the forming stage, the project manager must provide *direction* and *structure* for the project team.

8. During the storming stage, *conflict* emerges and *tension* increases.

9. During the storming stage, team members wonder how much *control* and *authority* they have.

10. During the storming stage, the project manager needs to provide *guidance* and foster *conflict resolution*.

11. In the norming stage, *conflict* and *discontent* are reduced, *cohesion* begins to develop, and there is a sense of *team*.

12. During the norming stage, *trust* begins to develop. There is a greater sharing of *information*, *ideas*, and *feelings*; *cooperation* increases.

13. In the norming stage, *work performance* accelerates and *productivity* increases.

14. During the performing stage, there is a great degree of *interdependency*; members frequently *collaborate* and willingly *help* each other with work beyond their own assigned tasks.

15. During the performing stage, the project manager fully *delegates* responsibility and authority, thereby empowering the project team.

16. What are the four stages of team development and growth?

 - Forming
 - Storming
 - Norming
 - Performing

17. The project *kickoff* meeting should be held as *early* as possible during the *forming* stage of team development.

18. An effective project team has a clear understanding of the project *objective* and clear expectations of *roles* and *responsibilities*.

19. Effective project teams have a *results* orientation; each person has a strong commitment to accomplishing the *project objective*. There is a high degree of *cooperation* and *collaboration*.

20. Effective project teams have a high level of *trust*. They are able to resolve conflict through constructive and timely *feedback* and positive *confrontation* of the issues.

21. The project manager needs to articulate the project *objective* frequently. At periodic meetings, he or she should always ask whether anyone has any *questions* about what must be accomplished.

22. The project manager should meet individually with each team member, to tell the member why he or she was *assigned* to the project and describe his or her expected *role* and *responsibilities*.

23. The project manager needs to establish preliminary operating *procedures* at the beginning of the project, but be open to suggestions for *eliminating* or *streamlining* them when they no longer *contribute* to the effective and efficient performance of the project.

24. The project manager should try to determine what *motivates* each individual and then create a project *environment* where these motivators are available.

25. It is important for the project manager to have regular project *status review* meetings with a published agenda. *Participation* and questions should be encouraged during such meetings.

26. A project manager should periodically solicit others' suggestions for improving her or his *leadership* skills.

27. A project team made up of a *small* number of individuals with *long* term assignments will be more efficient than a project team composed of a *large* number of individuals with *short* term assignments.

28. What are some barriers to team effectiveness?

- Unclear vision and objective
- Unclear definition of roles and responsibilities
- Lack of project structure
- Lack of commitment
- Poor communication
- Poor leadership
- Turnover of project team members
- Dysfunctional behavior

29. Effective team members plan, control, and feel *accountable* for their individual work efforts. They have high *expectations* of themselves.

30. Effective team members *participate* and *communicate*. They are not only problem identifiers, but also *problem solvers*.

31. Think about projects in which you have been involved. What are some characteristics of individual team members that made them effective contributors?
Answers will vary.

32. Team building is the responsibility of both the *project manager* and the *project team*.

33. *Socializing* among team members supports *team building*. Individual members need to *communicate* with one another frequently.

34. Diversity of the team brings *unique* ideas and *perspectives* to projects.

35. What are some dimensions of diversity?

- Age or generation
- Appearance
- Ethnicity or ancestry
- Gender
- Health
- Job status
- Marital and parental status
- Race
- Religious affiliation

36. Team members should not *stereotype* or make *assumptions* about a team member's behavior or *performance* based on his or her *diversity*.

37. Two actions an organization can take to support a positive climate for diversity are to have a written *policy* regarding diversity and to provide *training* about diversity in the workplace.

38. Barriers to valuing diversity include lack of *awareness* and lack *of understanding*.

39. What are some reasons why the project team should value diversity as a strength?

- Enrich communication
- Foster better relationships
- Create an enjoyable workplace
- Enhance team performance

40. Customers and suppliers want to do business with a project contractor they can *trust*.

41. Two actions an organization can take to help prevent any wrongdoing are to have a *written policy* on ethical behavior and to provide *training* about ethics in the workplace.

42. *Personal integrity* is the foundation for workplace ethics.

43. What are common sources of conflict on projects?

- Work scope
- Resource assignments
- Schedule
- Cost
- Priorities
- Organizational issues
- Stakeholder issues
- Personal differences

44. Handled properly, conflict can be *beneficial*.

45. What are five approaches to handling conflict?

- Avoiding or withdrawing
- Competing or forcing
- Accommodating or smoothing
- Compromising
- Collaborating, confronting, or problem solving

46. What are the nine steps involved in problem solving?

- Develop a problem statement
- Identify potential causes of the problem
- Gather data and verify the most likely causes
- Identify possible solutions
- Evaluate the alternative solutions
- Determine the best solution
- Revise the project plan
- Implement the solution
- Determine whether the problem has been solved

47. In brainstorming, the *quantity* of ideas generated is more important than the *quality* of the ideas.

48. What are some things you can do to manage your time effectively?

- Identify weekly goals
- Make a to-do list each day
- Focus on accomplishing your daily to-do list
- Control interruptions
- Learn to say "no"
- Make effective use of waiting time
- Handle paperwork and e-messages only once
- Reward yourself

CHAPTER TWELVE

1. *Effective communication* and timely *information flow* are essential for *successful* project management.

2. Identify two types of personal verbal communication.

- Face-to-face communication
- Telephone conversations

3. Body language can be used not only by the person talking, but also by the *listener*, as a way of providing *feedback* to the person talking.

4. In personal communication, people need to be sensitive to body language reflective of the *cultural diversity* of the participants.

5. Project team members need to be *proactive* in initiating timely communication to *get* and *give* information.

6. Identify two methods you can use to check for understanding during verbal communication.

- Ask the other person to state their understanding of what you said
- Paraphrase what you think the other person said

7. What are two types of personal written communication?

- Internal correspondence among the project team
- External correspondence with the customer or some stakeholders

8. Failure to *listen* can cause a *breakdown* in communication.

9. List some common barriers to effective listening.

- Pretending to listen
- Distractions
- Bias and closed-mindedness
- Impatience
- Jumping to conclusions

10. What are some things you can do to improve your listening skills?

 - Focus on the person talking
 - Engage in active listening
 - Ask questions
 - Do not interrupt

11. What are the primary purposes of a status review meeting?

 - Inform
 - Identify problems
 - Identify action items

12. True or false: When members of the project team identify problems or potential problems, they should wait until the next scheduled status review meeting to bring them up for discussion.
 False; they should immediately initiate a problem-solving meeting with the appropriate team members.

13. On many projects, there are often two design review meetings: a *preliminary* design review meeting and a *final* design review meeting.

14. To ensure that a meeting is effective, what are some steps that the person organizing or leading the meeting should take before the meeting?

 - Determine whether a meeting is really necessary
 - Determine the purpose of the meeting
 - Determine who needs to participate
 - Distribute an agenda
 - Prepare visual aids or handouts
 - Make meeting room arrangements

15. True or false: It is always a good idea to wait for everyone to arrive before starting a meeting, even if it is beyond the scheduled start time.
 False; if the meeting leader waits for latecomers, people will get in the habit of showing up late because they know the meeting will not start on time anyway.

16. What are some important things to do in preparing a presentation?

 - Determine the purpose of the presentation
 - Know the audience
 - Make an outline
 - Use simple language
 - Prepare notes
 - Prepare visual aids
 - Practice
 - Make copies of handout materials
 - Request audiovisual equipment
 - Go into the meeting room and get a "feel" for the surroundings

17. What are some important things to keep in mind when delivering a presentation?

 - Expect a bit of nervousness
 - Turn off your cell phone or other technologies that could cause a distraction to you or the audience
 - Know your opening lines
 - Use the 3-T approach
 - Talk to audience members, not at them
 - Speak clearly and confidently
 - Use appropriate gestures
 - Do not read your slides
 - Do not stand in front of your visual aids
 - Build interest by developing your story
 - Do not digress
 - State why key points are important to the audience
 - Sum up each point before moving on
 - Know your closing lines
 - Allow time for questions from the audience
 - Be sincere, candid, and confident in responding to questions

18. Project reports should be written to address what is of interest to the *readers*, not what is of interest to the person *writing* the report.

19. The primary purpose of progress reports is to report on project *accomplishments* rather than what *activities* were keeping the project team busy.

20. True or false. A project final report is an accumulation of the progress reports prepared during the project.
 False. It is a summary of the project.

21. What are some important guidelines to keep in mind when preparing a report?

- Make it concise
- Make it readable and understandable
- Put the most important points first
- Use graphics
- Make the format open, inviting, and organized

22. At the *start* of the project, a document *control* system needs to be established that defines how *changes* to documents will be *documented*, *approved*, and *communicated*.

23. When *changes* are made to documents, they should immediately be *distributed* to project *team members* whose *work* will be *affected* by the changes.

24. A project *communication* plan defines the *generation* and *distribution* of project *documents* among project *stakeholders*.

25. It is important to have *regular communication* with the various project *stakeholders*.

26. Teleconferencing includes tools such as *conference* calls and *videoconferencing*.

CHAPTER THIRTEEN

1. The functional organization emphasizes the importance of the contribution of each functional component's *expertise* to the company's products.

2. A company with a functional structure may periodically form project teams to work on *internal* company projects.

3. True or false: In a functional organization, individuals continue to perform their regular functional jobs while they serve part time on a project team. True

4. In an autonomous project organization, all resources are assigned *full* time to work on a particular project. The project manager has complete *project* and *administrative* authority over the project team.

5. An autonomous project organization can be cost *inefficient*.

6. Autonomous project organizational structures are found primarily in companies that are involved in very *large* projects.

7. The matrix organizational structure provides the project and *customer* focus of the *autonomous project* structure, but it retains the functional *expertise* of the *functional* structure.

8. In a matrix organization, the *functional* components provide a pool of *expertise* to support ongoing projects.

9. The matrix organizational structure results in effective utilization of *resources* and minimizes overall *costs* because it allows for the *sharing* of individuals' time among several *projects*.

10. In a matrix organization, each member of a *project team* has a dual reporting relationship—to the temporary *project* manager and to a permanent *functional* manager.

11. In a matrix organization, the project manager defines *what* has to be done, by *when*, and for how much *money* to accomplish the project *objective* and satisfy the customer.

12. In a matrix organization, each functional manager is responsible for *how* the work will be accomplished and *who* will do each task.

13. The matrix organizational structure allows for fast response to identified problems because it has both a *horizontal* and a *vertical* path for the flow of *information*.

14. The *project management office* plays an important role in the *matrix* organizational structure. It *oversees* and *coordinates* multiple *projects*.

15. What are some advantages and disadvantages of the functional organizational structure?

Advantages:

- No duplication of activities
- Functional excellence

Disadvantages:

- Insularity
- Slow response time
- Lack of customer focus

16. What are some advantages and disadvantages
 of the autonomous project organizational
 structure?

 Advantages:

 - Control over resources
 - Responsiveness to customers

 Disadvantages:

 - Cost inefficiency
 - Low level of knowledge transfer among
 projects

17. What are some advantages and disadvantages
 of the matrix organizational structure?

 Advantages:

 - Efficient utilization of resources
 - Functional expertise available to all projects
 - Increased learning and knowledge transfer
 - Improved communication
 - Customer focus

 Disadvantages:

 - Dual reporting relationships
 - Need for balance of power

Glossary

A

acceptance criteria The quantitative criteria that the customer or sponsor uses to validate that a deliverable meets the customer's requirements or expectations and that serve as the basis for the customer's acceptance of the deliverable.

activity A defined piece of work that consumes time. Also referred to as a *task*.

activity cost estimate *See* activity estimated cost.

activity duration estimate *See* activity estimated duration.

activity estimated cost The estimated total cost of an activity based on the types and quantities of resources required to perform the activity. Also referred to as *activity cost estimate* or *estimated activity cost*.

activity estimated duration The estimated total elapsed time for how long an activity will take from start to finish, including associated waiting time. Also referred to as *activity duration estimate* or *estimated activity duration*.

activity estimated resources An estimate of the types and quantities of resources required to perform an activity. Also referred to as *activity resource estimate* or *estimated activity resources*.

activity list A consolidated list of specific activities that need to be performed to produce all the project deliverables and to accomplish the project objective.

activity resource estimate *See* activity estimated resources.

actual cost The amount of costs actually expended and committed to accomplish the work performed. Also referred to as *actual cost of work performed (ACWP)*.

actual cost of work performed (ACWP) *See* actual cost and cumulative actual cost (CAC).

actual finish time (AF) The time at which a specific activity is actually completed.

agile project management An approach to reduce product development time while minimizing risk through continuous interaction between the customer and small self-organized teams that produce increments of working product features in short time iterations while rapidly adapting to changes in requirements.

as-late-as-possible (ALAP) schedule A schedule based on the latest start time of each activity in the project.

as-soon-as-possible (ASAP) schedule A schedule based on the earliest start time of each activity in the project.

autonomous project organizational structure An organizational structure in which each project operates as its own somewhat independent entity with dedicated resources assigned solely to each project. Also referred to as *projectized organizational structure*.

average duration *See* expected duration.

B

bar chart A planning and scheduling tool that displays project activities along a time scale. Also referred to as a *Gantt chart*.

497

baseline plan A set of integrated project documents that shows how the project scope will be accomplished within budget and on schedule and is used as a benchmark to which actual performance can be compared.

best and final offer (BAFO) A final price for a project, submitted by a contractor at the request of a customer who is considering proposals from several contractors for the same project.

beta probability distribution A distribution that is frequently used to calculate the expected duration and variance for an activity based on the activity's optimistic, most likely, and pessimistic time estimates.

bid/no-bid decision An evaluation by a contractor of whether to go forward with the preparation of a proposal in response to a customer's request for proposal.

brainstorming A technique in which all members of a group contribute spontaneous ideas in a nonjudgmental environment.

budget at completion (BAC) *See* total budgeted cost (TBC).

budgeted cost of work performed (BCWP) *See* earned value (EV) and cumulative earned value (CEV).

budgeted cost of work scheduled (BCWS) *See* cumulative budgeted cost (CBC).

C

change control system The process and procedures that define how changes will be documented, approved, and communicated.

client *See* customer.

closing phase Fourth phase of the project life cycle, during which actions are taken to close the project including archiving project documents and documenting lessons learned.

committed cost Funds that have been obligated for an item that has been ordered or purchased but not yet paid for, and therefore are not available to be spent elsewhere on the project because they will be needed at some later time to pay for the item. Also referred to as *obligated cost* or *encumbered cost*.

configuration control system *See* document control system.

constraint A restriction or limitation that may affect the performance of the project.

contingency reserve *See* reserve.

contract An agreement between a contractor, who agrees to perform the project and to provide a product or service (deliverables), and a customer, who agrees to pay the contractor a certain amount of money in return.

contractor An individual or organization to whom a sponsor or customer outsources the project work.

control process *See* project control.

cost performance index (CPI) A measure of the cost efficiency with which the project is being performed; the cumulative earned value divided by the cumulative actual cost.

cost-reimbursement contract A contract in which a customer agrees to pay a contractor for all actual costs incurred during a project, plus some agreed-upon profit.

cost variance (CV) An indicator of cost performance; the cumulative earned value minus the cumulative actual cost.

crash cost The estimated cost of completing an activity in the shortest possible time (the crash time).

crash time The shortest estimated length of time in which an activity can be completed.

crashing *See* time–cost trade-off.

critical path In a network diagram, any path of activities with zero or negative total slack. The longest (most time-consuming) path. *Also see* most critical path.

critical path method (CPM) A type of network planning technique.

cumulative actual cost (CAC) The amount of costs actually expended and committed to accomplish all the work performed up to a specific point in time. Also referred to as *actual cost of work performed (ACWP)*.

cumulative budgeted cost (CBC) The amount budgeted to accomplish all the work scheduled to be performed up to a specific point in time. Also referred to as *planned value (PV)* or *budgeted cost of work scheduled (BCWS)*. *Also see* time-phased budget.

cumulative earned value (CEV) The value of the work actually performed up to a specific point in time; total budgeted cost multiplied by the percentage of the work estimated to be complete. Also referred to as *budgeted cost of work performed (BCWP)*.

customer The entity that provides the funds necessary to accomplish a project. It can be a person, an organization, or a partnership of people or organizations. Also referred to as a *sponsor* or *client*.

customer requirements Functional, operational, and performance specifications or capabilities defined by the customer that must be met.

D

deliverable A tangible item or product produced by the project team in accordance with customer requirements during and at the completion of the performance of the project.

dependent relationship The sequence in which activities must be finished before other activities can start. Also referred to as *precedence relationship*.

diversity Differences among people.

document control system The process and procedures that define how changes to project documents will be documented, approved, and communicated. Also referred to as *configuration control system*.

due date The date, specified in a request for proposal, by which a customer requires potential contractors to submit proposals.

E

earliest finish time (EF) The earliest time by which a specific activity can be completed; the activity's earliest start time plus the activity's estimated duration.

earliest start time (ES) The earliest time at which a specific activity can begin based on the project estimated start time and the estimated durations of preceding activities.

earned value (EV) The value of the work actually performed. Also referred to as *budgeted cost of work performed (BCWP)*.

encumbered cost *See* committed cost.

estimated activity cost *See* activity estimated cost.

estimated activity duration *See* activity estimated duration.

estimated activity resources *See* activity estimated resources.

estimated cost at completion (EAC) *See* forecasted cost at completion (FCAC).

evaluation criteria The criteria that an organization uses to evaluate potential projects and support project selection, or that a customer uses to evaluate proposals from competing contractors.

exception A variation from a customer's specified requirements, stated by a contractor in a proposal.

expected benefits *See* success criteria.

expected duration (t_e) The duration for an activity calculated from the activity's optimistic, most likely, and pessimistic time estimates, as follows:

$$t_e = \frac{t_o + 4(t_m) + t_p}{6}$$

Also referred to as the *mean* or *average duration*.

F

fixed-price contract A contract in which a customer and a contractor agree on a price that will not change regardless of how much the project actually costs the contractor. The price remains fixed unless the customer and contractor agree on changes.

forecasted cost at completion (FCAC) The projected total cost of all the work required to complete a project based on the actual cost expended, the earned value of work performed, and the remaining work to be done. Also referred to as *estimated cost at completion (EAC)*.

free float *See* free slack (FS).

free slack (FS) The amount of time that a specific activity can be delayed without delaying the earliest start time of its immediately succeeding activities; the relative difference between the amounts of total slack for activities entering into that same activity. It is always a positive value. Also referred to *as free float*.

functional organizational structure An organizational structure in which individuals are organized in groups that perform the same function or have the same expertise or skills.

funding *See* project funds.

G

Gantt chart A form of bar chart. *See* bar chart.

I

indirect costs *See* overhead cost.

information system (IS) A computer-based system that accepts data as input, processes the data, and produces information for users.

initiating phase First phase of the project life cycle, during which projects are identified, selected, and authorized.

issue log A document that lists specific issues, concerns, or questions that various stakeholders identify and the status of the response or resolution.

L

laddering A method of showing the dependent relationship of a set of activities that is repeated several consecutive times and allows the activities to be completed in the shortest possible time while making the best use of available resources.

latest finish time (LF) The latest time by which a specific activity must be completed for the entire project to be finished by its required completion time.

latest start time (LS) The latest time by which a specific activity must be started for the entire project to be finished by its required completion time; the activity's latest finish time minus the activity's estimated duration.

loop An illogical relationship among a path of activities that perpetually repeats itself.

M

management reserve *See* reserve.

matrix organizational structure A hybrid of the functional and autonomous project organizational structures, in which resources from appropriate functional components of an organization are temporarily assigned to particular projects that have project managers from the project component of the organization.

mean duration *See* expected duration.

milestone A key event in a project.

milestone date A target date for the occurrence of a key event in the project schedule.

milestone schedule A list of key project events and their target dates.

most critical path In a network diagram, the most time-consuming (longest) path of activities; the path of activities that has the lowest value—either least positive or most negative—for total slack.

most likely time estimate (t_m) The estimated duration in which an activity can most frequently be completed under normal conditions.

N

network diagram A tool for arranging and displaying specific activities in the appropriate sequence and defining their dependent relationships.

noncritical path In a network diagram, any path of activities with positive total slack.

normal cost The estimated cost of completing an activity under normal conditions, according to the plan.

normal probability distribution A bell-shaped distribution of values that is symmetrical around its mean value.

normal time The estimated length of time required to perform an activity under normal conditions, according to the plan.

O

objective What is to be accomplished; the tangible end product that the project team must produce and deliver. It is usually defined in terms of end product or deliverable, schedule, and budget. It may include a statement of the benefits that will be achieved from implementing the project. Also referred to as *project objective*.

obligated cost *See* committed cost.

optimistic time estimate (t_0) The estimated duration in which an activity can be completed if everything goes perfectly well and there are no complications.

overhead cost A percentage of the direct costs of a particular project, added to a contractor's proposal to cover costs of doing business, such as insurance, depreciation, general management, and human resources. Also referred to as *indirect costs*.

P

path A continuous sequence of activities in a network diagram.

payment terms The basis on which the customer will make payments to the contractor. Also referred to as *terms of payment.*

percent complete An estimate in percentage form of the proportion of the work involved in performing a specific activity or work package that has been completed.

performing phase Third phase of the project life cycle, during which the project baseline plan is executed to produce all the project deliverables and to accomplish the project objective. It includes performing the work, monitoring and controlling progress, and managing changes to accomplish the project scope on schedule and within budget.

pessimistic time estimate (t_p) The estimated duration in which an activity can be completed under adverse conditions, such as in the presence of unusual or unforeseen complications.

planned value (PV) *See* cumulative budgeted cost (CBC).

planning Determining what needs to be done, how it will get done, who will do it, how long it will take, how much it will cost, and what the risks are.

planning phase Second phase of the project life cycle, during which a baseline plan is developed. It includes defining the project scope, identifying resources, developing a schedule and budget, and identifying risks.

precedence diagramming method (PDM) A type of network planning technique.

precedence relationship *See* dependent relationship.

predecessor activity An activity that must be finished before a dependent successor activity can start.

price A contractor's total aggregated estimated costs plus its desired profit for project.

probabilistic activity duration The use of three estimated durations (optimistic, most likely, and pessimistic) to calculate an expected (average) estimated duration for an activity when there is a high degree of uncertainty.

program evaluation and review technique (PERT) A type of network planning technique.

progressive elaboration An approach to planning a project in greater detail as the project progresses and more information is known or becomes clear.

project An endeavor to accomplish a specific objective through a unique set of interrelated activities and the effective utilization of resources.

project authorization *See* project charter.

project charter A document issued by the project sponsor that authorizes the project and commits funds for the project. Also referred to as *project authorization* or *project initiation document.*

project communication plan A document that defines the generation and distribution of project documents among project stakeholders.

project control Regularly gathering data on actual project performance, comparing actual performance to planned performance, and taking corrective action immediately if actual performance is behind planned performance.

project estimated start time The time or date when a project is expected to begin.

project funds The amount of money a sponsor or customer authorizes or commits for the project. Also referred to as *funding.*

project initiation document *See* project charter.

project life cycle The four phases through which a project progresses: initiating, planning, performing, and closing.

project management Planning, organizing, coordinating, leading, and controlling resources to accomplish the project objective.

project management information system (PMIS) A computer-based system that can help and support project managers and project teams in planning, monitoring, and controlling projects.

project management office (PMO) An organizational component that oversees and coordinates multiple projects, provides project support resources and services, and establishes project processes and procedures.

project manager The individual who provides leadership to the project team to accomplish the project objective.

project objective *See* objective.

project quality plan A document that defines the specifications, standards, and codes that must be met during the performance of the project work, and the procedures for quality tools and techniques, to assure and control quality. Also referred to as *quality plan*.

project required completion time The time or date by which a project must be completed, usually established by the sponsor or customer.

project scope *See* scope.

project scope document A document that includes the customer requirements, statement of work, deliverables, and acceptance criteria.

project selection Evaluating potential projects and then deciding which of these should move forward to be implemented.

project team A group of individuals working interdependently to accomplish the project objective.

projectized organizational structure *See* autonomous project organizational structure.

proposal A document, prepared by a project organization or contractor, that includes a proposed approach, schedule, and budget for meeting the project requirements and accomplishing the project scope.

Q

Quality

quality control Monitoring the quality of the work early and regularly throughout the performance of the project, comparing results with quality standards, and making any necessary corrective actions immediately.

quality plan *See* project quality plan.

R

reporting period The time interval at which actual project performance will be compared to planned performance.

request for proposal (RFP) A document, prepared by the customer, which defines the project

requirements and is used to solicit proposals from potential contractors to do the project.

required schedule The dates or times by which the sponsor or customer wants the project and key milestones completed.

reserve An amount of cost a contractor may include in a proposal to cover unexpected situations that may arise during a project. Also referred to as *contingency reserve* or *management reserve*.

resources The people (including subcontractors and consultants), materials, equipment, and facilities required to perform the project and produce the project deliverables.

resource-constrained planning An approach to creating a network diagram and schedule in which the sequence and dependent relationships of activities are based on resource constraints that take into account the availability of a limited quantity of resources.

resource leveling A method for developing a schedule that attempts to minimize the fluctuations in requirements for resources without extending the project schedule beyond its required completion time. Also referred to as *resource smoothing*.

resource-limited scheduling A method for developing the shortest schedule when the quantity of available resources is fixed. This method will extend the project completion time, if necessary, to keep within the resource limits.

resource requirements plan A table that illustrates the expected utilization of resources by time period during the time span of the project.

resource smoothing *See* resource leveling.

responsibility assignment matrix (RAM) A table that designates the individuals or organizational units responsible for accomplishing each work item in a work breakdown structure.

risk An uncertain event that if it occurs can jeopardize accomplishing the project objective.

risk assessment Determining the likelihood that a risk event will occur and the degree of impact the event will have on the project objective.

risk assessment matrix A table that includes potential risks, their potential impact, likelihood of

occurrence, and response plan. Also referred to as *risk register*.

risk category A grouping of potential sources of risk by topic.

risk identification Determining which risks may adversely affect the project objective and what the impact of each risk might be if it occurs.

risk management The identification, assessment, control, and response to project risks to minimize the likelihood of occurrence and/or potential impact of adverse events on the accomplishment of the project objective.

risk register *See* risk assessment matrix.

risk response plan A defined set of actions to prevent or reduce the likelihood of occurrence or the potential impact of a risk, or to implement if the risk event occurs.

S

schedule A timetable for a project indicating when activities are planned or need to be started and finished.

scope All the work that must be done to produce all the project deliverables that meet the customer requirements and acceptance criteria and accomplish the project objective. Also referred to as *project scope* or *work scope*.

scope creep Expanding the scope of the project by making changes to the scope without appropriate approval.

scrum An agile project management methodology often used for software development projects.

sponsor *See* customer.

sprint A fixed time frame during which a team develops, delivers, and demonstrates a working increment, or portion, of the final end product.

stakeholder Individuals or entities involved in, or who may influence, or who may be affected by, a project, such as the customer/sponsor; project team, including the project manager, subcontractors, and consultants; end users or consumers; and advocacy groups.

stakeholder register A document that identifies stakeholders including their key contact information, role

or specific topics of interest, expectations, any known issues, and areas of potential influence.

standard deviation A measure of the dispersion, or spread, of a distribution from its expected value; the square root of the variance.

statement of work (SOW) A document that outlines the major tasks the customer wants the contractor or project team to perform to accomplish the project scope and produce all the deliverables.

subcontractor An individual or organization to whom a sponsor, customer, or contractor outsources a specific portion of the project scope.

subnetwork A portion of a network diagram that represents a specific work package or a somewhat standard or well-established set and sequence of activities.

success criteria The outcomes or expected quantitative benefits that will result from implementation of the project. Also referred to as *expected benefits*.

successor activity An activity that can be started after its immediate predecessor activities are finished.

summary network A network diagram that displays a small number of higher-level activities.

systems development life cycle (SDLC) A project management planning tool consisting of a set of phases or steps to be completed over the course of development of an information system.

T

task *See* activity.

team building Developing a group of individuals into a team to accomplish the project objective.

teamwork The cooperative effort by members of the project team to accomplish the project objective.

terms of payment *See* payment terms.

time–cost trade-off A methodology to reduce the project duration incrementally with the smallest associated increase in incremental cost. Also referred to as *crashing*.

time estimate *See* activity estimated duration.

time-phased budget The distribution by time period of the total budgeted cost for a work package

or project over its expected time span based on when specific activities are scheduled to be performed.

to-complete performance index (TCPI) The rate of performance required for the remaining work in order to complete the project or a work package within its total budgeted cost.

total budgeted cost (TBC) The aggregate amount of the estimated costs of all the specific activities to perform and complete a work package or the project. Also referred to as *budget at completion (BAC)*.

total float *See* total slack (TS).

total slack (TS) If it is a positive value, it is the amount of time that the activities on a particular path can be delayed without jeopardizing completion of the project by its required completion time. If it is a negative value, it is the amount of time that the activities on a particular path must be accelerated to complete the project by its required completion time. Also referred to as *total float*.

V

variance A measure of the dispersion, or spread, of a distribution from its expected value.

virtual team A project team whose members are geographically dispersed and have minimal in-person, face-to-face contact.

W

win ratio The percentage of the number or dollar value of a contractor's proposals that result in contractual agreements with customers.

work breakdown structure (WBS) A hierarchical decomposition of the project work scope into work packages to be executed by the project team to produce the project deliverables.

work item An individual piece or component of a project in a work breakdown structure.

work package A piece or component of the project work at the lowest level of any branch of a work breakdown structure.

work scope *See* scope.

Index